Contemporary Cultural
Anthropology

Little, Brown and Company

Boston   Toronto

Contemporary Cultural Anthropology

Michael C. Howard

The University of the South Pacific

Patrick C. McKim

California Polytechnic State University
San Luis Obispo

Library of Congress Cataloging in Publication Data

Howard, Michael C.
   Contemporary cultural anthropology.

   1. Ethnology.   I. McKim, Patrick C.   II. Title.
GN316.H68   1982   306   82-17991
ISBN 0-316-37454-7

Library of Congress Catalog Card Number: 82-17991

ISBN 0-316-37454-7

9   8   7   6   5   4   3

HAL

Published simultaneously in Canada
by Little, Brown & Company (Canada) Limited

Printed in the United States of America

Design by Susan Marsh
Photo research by Ann Rahimi-Assa
Illustrations drawn by Elisa Tanaka
Inside cover maps drawn by Mary Reilly

Acknowledgments

Page 80 (Figure 4.1): Keith H. Basso, "Ice and Travel
   among the Fort Norman Slave: Folk Taxonomies and
   Cultural Rules," in *Language and Society*, Vol. 1 (1972),
   p. 35.
Page 82 (Table 4.2): *The World Almanac & Book of Facts*,
   1982 edition, copyright © Newspaper Enterprise Association, 1981, New York, New York 10166.
Page 139: Waldemar R. Smith, *The Fiesta System and Economic Change* (New York: Columbia University Press,
   1977), pp. 74-75.

Acknowledgments continued on page 439.

Preface

Our goal in *Contemporary Cultural Anthropology* is to introduce students to the complexity of human life in a manner as comprehensible and concrete as possible, making sure that they understand what we as anthropologists feel are essential aspects of culture. Throughout the text, we stress the ways in which societies are interrelated, hoping to provide students with a framework for understanding a constantly evolving world system. With this emphasis, we guide students to a perception of how cultural anthropology can promote both the understanding of human behavior and the solution of contemporary world problems.

Exploring the rich complexities of human life and culture requires a focused treatment that effectively communicates a depth and breadth of information. Many of the textbooks we encountered were either too idiosyncratic, presenting a narrow view of an intrinsically expansive discipline, or too encyclopedic, offering no unifying principle. Many approached the material at a level above the comprehension of most introductory students; those with a more accessible style often offered an overly simplistic approach. Dissatisfied with these choices, we have written *Contemporary Cultural Anthropology* to provide a comprehensive, coherent, *and* readable introduction to cultural anthropology.

Throughout the text, we have examined cultures through an ecological perspective that views humans as creative beings who seek to adapt to a multi-faceted environment. We have presented a dynamic ecology that shows humans trying to overcome problems in the environment and to reconcile factors such as population growth and limited resources in a particular adaptational strategy.

In keeping with our perspective that human culture is constantly evolving, we have integrated change and acculturation throughout every chapter of the text, rather than treating these areas in a separate chapter. Though our emphasis is on the contemporary world, we have placed contemporary adaptations in a historical perspective. We emphasize that we must not take any aspect of culture or any pattern of behavior or belief for granted. We must question why activities or beliefs come into existence, why they change or disappear, why they persist. And while we may not be able to arrive at answers for why people believe and act as they do, we can hope to understand the complexity of those forces that influence behavior and belief—such as population, resources, technology, ideology, and social organization.

We have carefully chosen ethnographic examples from a wide range of cultures that effectively illustrate the points we raise. Too often in introductory texts, however, we have found that the liberal use of ethnographic examples from too many unfamiliar cultures often obscures significant issues and gives the impression that anthropologists are little more than collectors of exotica. To strike a balance, we have also covered a few peoples—such as the Australian Aborigines—in more depth throughout the text to provide students with a more holistic view of culture.

Understanding the culture of any people today requires attention to how they fit into the modern world system. We emphasize that all societies are part of an evolving world order and examine the different ways and degrees to which they are incorporated. We have shown how the nature of this integration influences various aspects of people's lives. For members of small-scale societies, the world order has been very difficult to adjust to and in which to exercise influence. We devote an entire final chapter to how applied anthropology addresses the problems of these and other contemporary societies as they try to find an equitable place in the world system.

Eight anthropologists have contributed original essays—under the general title "Focus on People"—that describe a wide variety of fieldwork experiences. In each "Focus on People" essay, students will read a vivid account both of the anthropologist's work and the lives and concerns of a particular people. Extensive direct quotations from the Nasioi of New Guinea, the Mandinka of West Africa, and the Mayan Indians of Southern Belize, among several others, enrich the anthropologists' commentaries and help students better relate to both the differences and similarities among peoples of diverse cultures. A list of "Focus on People" essays, with descriptive quotations from each piece, appears on page xiii.

Throughout the text, we have provided extensive learning aids. Each chapter is preceded by a brief outline of the major points to be covered, providing students with a clear overview of topics under discussion. Concise, end-of-chapter summaries help students review chapter material. A carefully selected group of readings, organized by topic, follows each chapter. At the end of the book, a bibliography of material used in writing *Contemporary Cultural Anthropology* will provide students with further sources. Key terms—italicized in the text—are clearly defined within each chapter and in a comprehensive glossary at the end of the book. Maps on the inside front and back covers should help students identify peoples and locales discussed in the text.

An *Instructor's Manual* has been prepared to accompany the text. It includes suggestions for using the text, annotated film suggestions, learning objectives, and individual and class projects for each chapter of the text. The test bank in the manual provides over 700 test items: 40-50 multiple-choice questions and 5-10 essay questions for each chapter.

Acknowledgments

Producing a textbook is a complex undertaking, and it involves the work of many people. We are grateful to the following people who reviewed portions of the manuscript and made valuable criticisms and suggestions: Ruth F. Almstedt, San Diego State University; Roger E. Basham, College of the Canyons; Peter J. Bertocci, Oakland University; Peter J. Chroman, College of San Mateo; John J. Curry, University of Massachusetts at Amherst; Risa Ellovich, North Carolina State University; Ralph H. Faulkingham, University of Massachusetts at Amherst; Frederick C. Gamst, University of Massachusetts, Boston; Sidney M. Greenfield, The University of Wisconsin, Milwaukee; George L. Hicks, Brown University; M. Barbara Leons, Towson State University; Pamela C. Magers, New Mexico State University; Anthony Mendonca, Community College of Allegheny County; Emilio F. Moran, Indiana University; Eugene Ogan, The University of Minnesota; Ronald Provencher, Northern Illinois University; and Daniel J. Yakes, Muskegon Community College. At Little, Brown we would especially like to thank Jane Aaron, Janet M. Beatty, and John Covell. We would also like to thank Mary Pat Fisher for her able editorial guidance. Gratitude is also due to a number of friends and colleagues for their assistance, encouragement, and tolerance: especially Barbara and Cirila Howard, Norris Lang, Margarita Melville, Robert Randall, Judy Holland, Monte Tidwell, and Russell Reid. Finally, Linda Searcy Howard deserves special thanks for her patience and encouragement with what sometimes seemed like an endless task.

Contents

"Focus on People" Essays

Contemporary Cultural Anthropology

Chapter One

Introducing Anthropology

W E HUMAN BEINGS have probably always thought of ourselves as extraordinary creatures who occupy a unique position in the universe. This attitude is expressed, in one way or another, in most of the world's religions. For example, according to the Judeo-Christian-Islamic tradition, all living things were specially and individually created by God. However, God made humans with a unique property—a soul—by which they were rendered fundamentally different from all other creatures. Another example of the idea of human uniqueness can be seen in Australian Aboriginal religions. While these religions emphasize natural bonds between humans and other animals, humans are assigned a special role—maintenance of the world order through ritual—which makes them superior to other animals.

Modern science, which deals with natural phenomena that are directly or indirectly observable, approaches humans from a different perspective than does religion, ignoring questions of the existence of souls or the role of ritual in sustaining the world order. Even so, until very recently scientists continued the tradition of stressing how the extraordinary and superior attributes of the human animal place it in a special category, apart from other animals. Scientists recognized humans to be animals, but possessing traits and talents that were thought to be fundamentally different from any qualities found among the "lower" forms of life. The lives of nonhuman animals were said to be ruled by *instincts*—inheritable and unalterable behavioral tendencies to make complex and specific responses to environmental stimuli. Human be-

havior, on the other hand, was seen as being based on ideas and concepts that are socially learned and transmitted, rather than genetically inherited.

Not long ago anthropologists and scientists believed that humans were the only tool-using animals, and that only humans possessed the capacity for complex forms of communication. The sophisticated technologies and elaborate systems of communication possessed by humans were made possible by a remarkably large and complex brain. The development of the intellectual capacity of humans, associated with increasingly larger brains, was said to release humans from instinctive behavior and to lay the basis for learned behavior. This capacity also gave humans the means of adapting to almost any environment without undergoing major physical changes. Rather than having to alter our physical characteristics to live in a new environment, we humans use our brains to figure out how to get by, through the use of clothing, shelter or other means.

While this view is fundamentally valid, today we are discovering that our special qualities are not really as special as we once thought. Many other animals do not behave in response to biologically derived instincts alone; much of their behavior is conditioned by learning. We now know that a number of animals use rudimentary tools and that some are even capable of complex forms of communication. We have also learned that we, too, are conditioned by biology in often subtle and complex ways; like the behavior of other animals, our behavior reflects our biological makeup and our adaptation to an environment. We remain a unique species, but what we once believed to be differences in kind between humans and other animals are in many cases turning out to be just differences in degree.

OVERLEAF

Photojournalist and filmmaker Philippe Sénéchal listens to a sound recording made of field experiences for a film about the Nyangatom. Inhabitants of the Lower Omo Valley in southwestern Ethiopia, the Nyangatom are primarily pastoralists whose herding is supplemented by sorghum agriculture.

Culture

Perhaps the most important defining characteristic of humans is *culture*. The term *culture* as used here is not limited to operas, symphonies, paintings, and other artistic endeavors. These are seen by anthropologists as examples of culture: Culture itself is *the customary manner in which human groups learn to organize their behavior and thought in relation to their environment*. Defined in this manner, culture has three principal aspects: *behavioral, perceptual,* and *material*. The behavioral component refers to how people act, especially how they interact with each other. In child rearing, for example, parents and children tend to interact in a relatively patterned fashion. Then there is the matter of perception, the views people have of the world. For example, parents have a limited range of ideas about how they should act, how their children should act, and what significance parenthood carries in the scheme of things. Finally, there is the material component of culture—the physical objects that we produce.

Learning

Most of what goes into making up culture is a result of *learning*—modifying behavior in response to experience within an environment. Learning is practically universal among organisms. But no other organism has a greater capacity for learning than a human, or depends as much on learned behavior for its survival.

While the survival of most other organisms is to some extent safeguarded by instincts, humans rely heavily upon culture for their survival. People must learn how to live in a particular social and physical setting, biology playing but a minimal role. Think of the chances for survival that most urban-dwelling Westerners would have if suddenly stranded in a tropical area or arid desert. Without the help of someone who had learned how to live in the particular setting, the urbanite would probably quickly perish. Culture, in essence, constitutes the shared survival strategies of a group of people transmitted over generations.

The ideas and modes of behavior that constitute culture are transmitted largely by a complex system of symbols: *language*. Again, while all organisms can communicate in at least rudimentary fashion, and some, such as porpoises and chimpanzees, have highly developed means of communicating, humans have evolved an extremely complex system of communication that is unique to our species. Without it the creation of human culture as we know it would be impossible.

Society

Culture is not created in a vacuum, nor by isolated individuals. It is the product of humans interacting in groups. From their parents and from others around them, humans learn how to act and how to think in ways that are shared by or comprehensible to people in their group. Humans are by nature social animals. From birth to death, humans are biologically conditioned to live not as separate individuals, but as members of groups. Since the beginning of human evolution, our survival has been a cooperative enterprise. Even hermits do not escape the rest of humanity, for everything they think, know, or believe has been conditioned by others. Culture is a group effort and is *socially shared*.

We sometimes speak of those who share the same cultural perceptions and modes of behavior as members of a society. A *society* is a collection of people who are linked to one another, either directly or indirectly, through social inter-

Human culture and behavior are products of learning in response to the social and physical environment. Here a San father from southwestern Africa begins teaching his son about hunting—a skill that will help him meet the demands of survival.

action. It is through their common experiences that members of a society evolve shared cultural attributes. Culture and society are complementary concepts: they are two sides of the same coin. Without culture, societies as we know them could not exist, for there would be no common basis for interpreting one another's behavior. Similarly, without a society there would be no culture, for there would be no interaction by which people could share their knowledge, values, and beliefs. The sharing of culture comes about through interaction, and predictable interaction is made possible through values and attitudes that people hold in common.

Variations exist within both culture and society, however. The term *society* can be applied to the total human community, encompassing all of humanity. Alternatively, we may speak of American or Canadian society, or we may restrict ourselves to even smaller geographical or social groupings. We could conceivably speak, for instance, of southern California society or Navajo society. Culture too is something of a Chinese box concept. Just as there are societies within societies, there are cultures within cultures, the smaller ones often referred to as *subcultures*.

Just as people interact with one another in varying degrees, they share culture to different degrees. For example, most Americans share certain attitudes that are common virtually to all, such as a belief that everyone should have an equal chance to "make good" in life. At the same time, there are certain cultural concepts and practices that are shared by some Americans but not by others. For instance, many black Americans share certain handshaking conventions that are generally not used by whites. Not all black Americans shake hands in the same way, and many nonblacks shake hands in imitation of black patterns. Nevertheless, since a large number of American blacks have shared common experiences and developed similar strategies for living, they have formed something that is recognizable as American black culture. The manner in which many black males shake hands reflects a pattern of male camaraderie that has developed within an environment of discrimination and impoverishment and represents a symbolic demonstration of unity and cultural distinctiveness.

Subcultural variations are not static, for people interact with others outside their subgroup, and they respond to change. In the case of black handshaking, whites adopted this system of gestures through their interaction with

A familiar example of a subculture in the United States is the country club. Members choose to spend their free time with others of similar social and financial standing and of like values and beliefs.

blacks. In turn some blacks have abandoned or altered these gestures since they no longer demonstrate cultural distinctiveness, and in time they may cease to be an element of black culture.

Although our initial definition of culture referred to customary behavior, implying continuity, we should not ignore the fact that change too is a major feature of human existence: Culture, too, is dynamic. True, continuity often exists—black handshake patterns have persisted for several decades—but things rarely remain the same for long. In our more secure moments we may prefer to emphasize the unchanging nature of our social and physical universe, but change is never very far away.

Environmental Adaptation

The lives of humans, like those of other animals, are influenced by their surroundings, by their *environment*: the *physical environment*, which involves things like climate, rainfall patterns, and terrain; the *biotic environment*—all of the plant and animal life in a given area; and the *social environment*—interaction with other members of our species. A coastal Californian's environment would include the beaches, the almost desertlike terrain and climate, the animals that have survived or thrived with human occupation, and the mixture of humanity that has been drawn to the region.

These different aspects of the environment

and humans are interrelated in complex and systematic ways. The study of the relationship between organisms and their physical, biotic, and social environments is called *ecology*. The study of ecology can be approached from a very general, all-encompassing perspective, or from a narrower focus, emphasizing one or a few aspects. The aspect that is of most relevance here is what is commonly termed *cultural ecology*, how human culture influences the relationships of humans to their environment.

One of the primary tasks of cultural ecology is the study of human adaptation. *Adaptation* is the process by which a population or an individual adjusts to environmental conditions in order to maintain itself and survive, if not prosper. How an organism, species, or society adapts to its environment is called an *adaptive strategy*: the conscious or unconscious plans of action carried out by a population in response to its environment (Moran 1979: 325). The adaptive strategy of the Arctic-dwelling Inuit,* for example, includes the technologies and techniques Inuit have devised for hunting caribou, seals, and other animals in their environment, the types of clothing and shelter they manufacture or acquire through trade to survive in the harsh climatic conditions, and the ways in which they space themselves across the landscape, distribute food, control sexual relations, and manage interpersonal aggression.

Biological Adaptation

For virtually any species there are both biological and nonbiological aspects of their adaptive strategy. The biological aspects are of three sorts. First, there are relatively short-term ad-

---

*The term "Inuit" is used instead of "Eskimo" throughout the text, the latter being a European term for the native peoples of the arctic, while the former is an indigenous term currently used for purposes of identification by the indigenous peoples of the arctic themselves.

justments to the environment; for instance, humans sweat as the temperature rises. Then there are nongenetic adaptations. For example, in sedentary American society, exercise—jogging, aerobic dance, lifting weights—can alter an individual's physical attributes and contribute to a greater immunity to diseases and a longer life expectancy—changes that will influence that individual's future adaptational capabilities. Finally, there are long-term biological changes that alter the physical characteristics of the population as a whole. These physical changes which occur over generations, comprise *organic evolution*, the continuous process by which populations adapt to the opportunities and limitations of ever-changing environments. It is through the process of organic evolution over the past few million years that humans have come to assume their present characteristics.

The central mechanism of organic evolution is natural selection, which serves to link biological change and the environment. Charles Darwin, the nineteenth-century pioneer in the study of organic evolution, defined *natural selection* as a process whereby the best-adapted members of a population assume genetic dominance, because they are better able to survive and multiply than other members of the same population. It is a key element in the adaptive strategy of most species, as they develop physical peculiarities that allow them to exploit their surroundings better.

Cultural Adaptation

Physical alterations are not necessary for comfortable living in an environment, however. In addition to our biological flexibility, we humans can adjust our activity patterns, clothing, shelter, diet, and so forth, and by so doing create a relatively comfortable microenvironment for ourselves. Through culture we are capable of adapting relatively quickly to almost any earthly environment. We may not always like

This Inuit dwelling place reflects technological adaptation to the cold climate of the Anuktuvuk Pass area in Alaska. The entire timber-supported structure, five or six feet of which is underground, is covered with sod and provides considerable insulation and protection from the elements. Reindeer antlers protruding from the roof serve as decorations and hunting trophies. Oil barrels outside indicate the current heating method, and the gas containers are a sign of the transition in mode of transportation from dog sleds to snowmobiles.

the setting within which we find ourselves, and some environments are much easier for us to prosper in than others, but we humans are capable of devising ways to survive almost anywhere.

Freed from many of the biological and environmental constraints facing other organisms, humans have created a great diversity of adaptational strategies. The most significant of these are reviewed in chapter 5. These strategies are ways that groups of humans have learned to exploit their particular environment to promote their survival or prosperity. *Exploitation* in its most basic sense means to turn to economic account, or to utilize. It is common to think of exploitation in terms of minerals, plants, and animals. But other human beings may serve as resources within the environment as well. The adaptive strategies we adopt in exploiting our surroundings rely primarily upon three aspects of culture: technology, social organization, and ideology. For the sake of clarity, it is useful to treat these aspects separately. They are, nonetheless, closely interrelated.

Because of its concrete results, the role of

technology—the skills and knowledge by which people make things or extract resources—is the most obvious part of an adaptive strategy. The indigenous peoples of the Arctic, the Inuit, devised an array of technical means for meeting their subsistence needs and for achieving a reasonable level of comfort. They used spears, harpoons, hooks, and traps to catch and kill animals. To move across the sea and land they built boats and sleds and made snowshoes. To protect themselves from the elements they produced an array of clothes made from animal skins and built dwellings of ice and skins. All these activities took knowledge of local resources and technical skills passed down until very recently as part of Inuit culture.

The ways people organize themselves socially are as important a part of their adaptation as is their technology. One important social dimension of an adaptive strategy is the way labor is divided. In procuring plant and animal resources, traditional Australian Aboriginal foragers divided their labor primarily according to sex: Males hunted larger animals and females gathered plants. We speak of this differentiation of activities within a society as the *division of labor*. In our own society, the division of labor is more complex than that of Aborigines, involving highly specialized activities unheard of in any foraging society. How labor is divided in a society reflects the nature of its adaptive strategy as well as environmental conditions, particularly the resources available.

The availability of resources also influences other social aspects of an adaptive strategy, such as the size of groups. In the dry Great Basin area, where Shoshone Indians lived as foragers until the nineteenth century, food resources were too scarce to support large populations on a permanent basis. Accordingly, during the winter months single families went off by themselves, gathering food independent of other families. During the summer, when food resources were a bit more plentiful, the Shoshone formed larger, multifamily groups.

The third cultural component of an adaptive strategy is *ideology*—a people's values and beliefs. To many hunters, being able to recite the correct prayers is as important in hunting as is knowing how to set a trap or stalk an animal. A person's views of how to go about living in the world are not based solely on observable facts. How individuals interact with the environment is conditioned by their society's beliefs concerning the nature of the universe. The religious beliefs of Australian Aborigines stress harmonious relations with the environment. Through myth and ritual, these beliefs link humans with their natural environment, space people across the landscape, and promote the well-being of plant and animal resources. By contrast, miners and industrialists approach the world aggressively; their allegiance is to the wider industrial society that spans the globe, rather than to an arid piece of desert.

With the advent of industrial production, the manufacture of clothing was taken out of the home and the labor involved became much more specialized. In this scene from the Melanson shoe factory in Lynn, Massachusetts (c. 1915), women are engaged solely in a single aspect of shoe production—stitching.

Studying Cultural Variations

We live in a very complex world inhabited by groups of people pursuing a multitude of different interests and holding very different views about the nature of things in the universe, how they are related, and how the whole thing works. Each of us is to some degree the product of a specific social setting and associated cultural tradition. Our views are shaped by these factors in such a way as to make any universally applicable perception of the world order unlikely. It is difficult for us to see the forests for the trees, for our vision is blocked or restricted by the limitations of our own circumstances.

It is to this complexity of personal viewpoints and to the tremendous variation present in the human experience that the discipline of anthropology addresses itself. Simply defined, *anthropology* is the scientific study of humanity. Anthropology is not unique in this regard, since historians, economists, philosophers, medical researchers, psychologists, and theologians—to name but a few—are also students of the human condition. What is different about anthropology is not so much *what* is studied as *how* it is studied. Anthropology is distinguishable from other branches of human studies in the emphasis it places on universalism, holism, integration, and cultural relativism.

Universalism

A fundamental principle of modern anthropology is that all peoples are fully and equally human: whether Bushman, Inuit, or Irish, we are all of one species. There are no races that are "closer to the ape," and none that is more highly evolved than the others. Since we are all equally human, anthropologists are as interested in the Bam Buti (or Pygmies) and Austral-

ian Aborigines as they are in people living in the industrial societies of North America and Western Europe. No human group is too small, too remote, too ancient, or too unusual to merit the anthropologist's attention. *All* human beings—the living and the dead, the familiar and the exotic—are the subject of anthropological studies. They all tell us something important about the human condition, about the potentialities and limitations of the human species.

Holism

Economists study systems of production, exchange, and consumption. Political scientists study the bases of social order and conflict and the distribution and dynamics of power and authority. Other scholars in human studies select other specific facets of human experience for intensive study. Anthropologists, on the other hand, seek to comprehend *all* aspects of the human condition. Anthropologists want to understand a society's economy and political organization, but they also want to know about its religion, its rules of marriage and etiquette, its language, its technology, and how its children are raised. Furthermore, they look at humans as a species of animals. Thus, the holistic orientation in anthropology includes recognition of both the biological and the cultural aspects of human existence.

Integration

Anthropologists are interested not only in all things human, but also in how the various facets of human existence are interrelated. To the anthropologist, it is not enough to study, say, Navajo politics, art, religion, kinship, economics, and so on. The anthropologist views these aspects of Navajo culture as integral and as integrated parts of the larger biological and social environment within which the Navajo live: the arid lands of Arizona and United States society. Full comprehension of any custom is possible only when we take into account the broader context within which the custom occurs. Anthropologists are constantly striving to achieve that more inclusive perspective.

Cultural Relativism

In addition to its scientific goals, anthropology also has the aim of promoting understanding among those of different cultural backgrounds. The most important factor inhibiting our understanding of other peoples is ethnocentrism. *Ethnocentrism* is the interpretation of the behavior of others in terms of one's own cultural values and traditions. In its extreme expressions, ethnocentrism is cultural chauvinism—the attitude that one's own customs and beliefs are automatically and unquestionably superior to those of others.

Anthropologist I. M. Lewis has remarked that "ethnocentrism is the natural condition of mankind." Every person who is raised in a society is taught from earliest childhood how to think and act. This thorough indoctrination in the values of one's own culture is a lifelong process. The basic values and standards of our culture are continuously reinforced in religion, in public ceremonies, on television, at sports events, and at cocktail parties. Wherever we go, we are tutored in what is considered to be true, real, just, desirable, and important. Furthermore, we are not mere recipients of this indoctrination. Each of us is a teacher of others as well as a student. Through the constant give and take of social interaction we come to share beliefs, customs, and behavior patterns with other people and hence create our own culture.

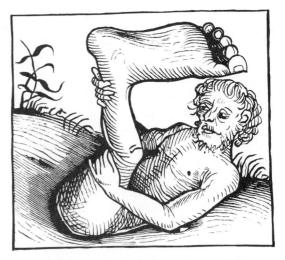

Ethnocentrism often not only entails attention to cultural differences, but also may involve viewing others as belonging to essentially different species. These drawings show a fifteenth-century French artist's conception of inhabitants of distant, unknown lands.

In some respects, the built-in ethnocentrism of all cultures serves as a positive force. It can give a people a sense of pride, well-being, and security. This is the aim of many consciousness-raising movements among ethnic minorities, such as Black Power, Red Power, and Brown Power. But ethnocentrism has a negative side as well. Extreme ethnocentrism is at the heart of all bigotry and discrimination. Oppressors have always justified their empires with an ideology that those they oppress and exploit are "backward," "primitive," or in some other way inferior. As was the case with eighteenth- and nineteenth-century European colonialists, oppressors often proclaim that by forcing their own systems and values on others, they are selflessly providing inferior peoples with the opportunity to improve their lot. But in fact they are often doing little more than destroying these peoples' way of life and seizing their lands.

Ethnocentrism does not promote understanding. In order to understand others, it is necessary to adopt a position of cultural relativism. *Cultural relativism* is judging and interpreting the behavior and beliefs of others in terms of *their* traditions and experiences. What is right in one culture is not necessarily right in, or for, another. In many cultures, the killing of infants is an accepted practice. Most Americans would judge infanticide to be morally wrong regardless of the circumstances. But in many societies, there are no safe and effective means of contraception or abortion, so birth control is sometimes carried out after the fact. This practice regulates a proper spacing of births and may, in addition, help to maintain a low density of population in regions where there is a scarcity of basic resources. In such a context, infanticide is a rational way of trying to avoid the problems associated with overpopulation or too rapid a rate of birth.

Cultural relativism does not mean that anything a particular people do or think must be approved or accepted without criticism. Rather, it means we should evaluate cultural patterns within the context of their occurrence.

The Fields of Anthropology

While the discipline of anthropology strives for a complete and systematic picture of humanity, no single individual possibly could command a detailed understanding of every aspect of the lives of all peoples. Consequently, specialization in anthropology is a practical necessity. Most anthropologists select one or two aspects of the human condition for intensive study, yet remain interested in relating their own specialized findings to what workers in other areas are doing. The major subdivisions of anthropology are physical (or biological) anthropology and sociocultural anthropology, each of which has many branches.

Physical Anthropology

Physical anthropology is the study of humanity as a biological phenomenon. Physical anthropologists study specimens both living and dead. Some study *fossils,* traces or remains of once-living organisms. By looking at the fossil remains of our now extinct forebears they can answer questions about when our ancestors began walking upright and at what stage of evolution humans achieved brain sizes of modern proportions. A complete picture of what life was like for our ancestors and how and why we evolved requires that the physical anthropologist enlist the aid of other specialists: paleoanthropologists, who specialize in the study of ancient human and prehuman society and provide data on ancient plant and animal life; geologists, who explain local physical and climatic conditions; and archaeologists, who provide information concerning our ancestors' tools, houses, and other material remains.

Other physical anthropologists specialize in investigating the biological diversity of modern populations. Since they are dealing with flesh-and-blood specimens, and not just bones and teeth, they have the opportunity to study such visible characteristics as skin color and hair texture. They can also look at traits that are all but invisible, such as blood types and genes. It is possible for them to study in detail the biological adjustments contemporary humans make to their surroundings as well.

Donald C. Johanson examining the fossil remains of "Lucy" found in Hadar in Ethiopia in 1974. The skeleton, about 40 percent complete, is between 2.9 and 3.8 million years old. The discovery of Lucy, together with the finding a year later of the remains of thirteen similar skeletons in the same area, raised a major challenge to previously accepted views of the origins of humankind and added a new species of hominid to the human's evolutionary line.

A major branch of physical anthropology that scarcely existed before the 1950s is *primatology,* the study of our nearest living relatives—apes, monkeys, and prosimians. Some primatologists focus on the study of primate biology, but more specialize in investigating the social behavior of primates such as chimpanzees, gorillas, and baboons. These studies contribute to our understanding of the behavior of our prehuman ancestors. For example, since primatologist Jane Goodall found that wild chimpanzees make and use crude tools on a fairly consistent basis, many paleoanthropologists have concluded that tool-using behavior among our ancestors is probably much more ancient than previously supposed.

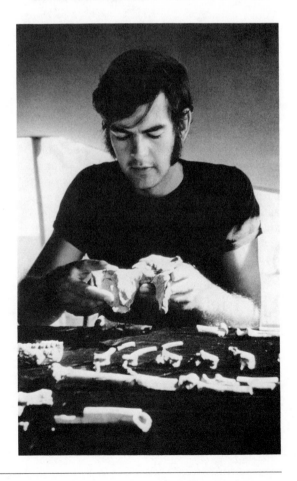

These archaeologists digging in Chan Chan, Peru carefully record the exact location of each finding and painstakingly clean, label, and catalog the collection. Excavation sites ranging from jungle forests to undersea locales to urban areas yield the findings from which archaeologists glean enormous amounts of information about past civilizations.

Sociocultural Anthropology

Sociocultural anthropology is the study of the social, symbolic, and material lives of humans. While physical anthropology concentrates on the study of the biological basis of the human condition, sociocultural anthropology is concerned with the social inheritance of humankind—all those aspects of human existence which are passed on through social and cultural experience rather than through genes. This endeavor takes three major forms—archaeology, anthropological linguistics, and ethnology, each of which contains numerous specialized branches.

Archaeology. *Archaeology* is the study of cultures of the past. While the physical anthropologist tries to reconstruct human evolution through the interpretation of fossils, the archaeologist attempts to reconstruct extinct societies and their cultures through the interpretation of *artifacts*, objects of human manufacture. For the most part, the archaeologist is limited to studying those expressions of human culture which are material and which may be preserved over long periods of time. This means that while the archaeologist is able to learn a fair amount about tools, weapons, pottery, diets, and house types of a long-extinct society, he or she will probably learn little about its nonmaterial culture, such as its kinship system and language. But physical evidence can suggest insights about nonmaterial aspects of extinct societies. For example, the discovery of Neanderthal burial sites containing bones laid out in a sleeping position and accompanied by tools and the remains of a meal suggests that these early humans must have believed in some kind of afterlife.

One of the major branches of archaeology is *prehistory*, the study of ancient preliterate cultures. In reconstructing the cultural lives of ancient peoples, prehistorians rely not only on material remains but also on the study of contemporary peoples whose life-styles are comparable with those of past societies. By studying present-day foragers, prehistorians can learn more about the ways in which our foraging ancestors lived: how they hunted, how they spaced themselves across the land, the nature of their religious beliefs, and so forth.

Another significant branch of archaeology is the field of *historical archaeology*. While many societies have left written records of their activities, these records are never a complete reflection of the people's lives. Archaeologists have become very good at extracting information from the incomplete material remains of these societies in order to catch every possible clue to what the daily lives of peoples of the past were like. Archaeological excavations at Pompeii and in the Nile Valley have provided detailed information on everything from people's religious practices to their eating habits. Likewise, recent excavations in California are yielding much new information about the daily operation of old Spanish missions and helping us to learn more about the early contacts between Native Americans and Europeans in the New World. These successes are partly due to the highly refined techniques of excavation and methods of analysis employed by archaeologists, but credit also goes to other specialists—such as historians, chemists, and biologists—who contribute their skills to the archaeological enterprise.

Anthropological Linguistics. The anthropological study of language, *anthropological linguistics*, is another major branch of sociocultural anthropology. Language is perhaps the most important single element of culture, because it is largely through language that we acquire and transmit culture to others. An entire chapter of this text is devoted to anthropological linguistics (chapter 4); for now, we will simply identify its main subfields.

Descriptive linguistics deals with how languages are constructed and how the various parts are interrelated to form coherent systems of communication. *Historical linguistics* concerns the evolution of languages, how languages grow and change. *Sociolinguistics* studies the relationship between language and social factors, such as class, ethnicity, age, and sex. Finally, a general field of study that is of interest to many anthropological linguists is *language and culture*, the examination of the ways language might affect how we think, or, conversely, how our beliefs and values might influence our linguistic behavior.

Ethnology. *Ethnology*, the systematic, comparative study of patterns and processes in living and recent cultures, is by far the largest branch of sociocultural anthropology, encompassing a vast array of subdisciplines. Historically, there have been two major ethnological traditions in the English-speaking world: *American cultural anthropology* and *British social anthropology*.

The American school of cultural anthropology has gained most of its inspiration from natural sciences, such as geology and biology, and from history. During the nineteenth and early twentieth centuries, ties with the natural sciences led American anthropologists to emphasize the study and classification of the material representations of culture—ceramics, baskets, clothing, and so forth. Less tangible aspects of culture such as kinship and religion were treated in much the same way as a biologist or geologist would treat butterfly or rock specimens: Kinship patterns were collected and classified as if they had the same characteristics as the material manifestations of culture, rather than as ideas and patterns of behavior. This approach to the nonmaterial side of culture has since fallen into disrepute, but the influence of natural science has continued under the label of *cultural materialism*. Cultural materialism no longer treats religious beliefs as if they belong to the same order of things as baskets; rather, it views them as different, but related, kinds of cultural phenomena. Placing an emphasis upon the physical environment and human technology—that is, culture processes related to population pressure, intensified use of resources, and depletion of the physical environment—cultural materialism seeks to analyze the ways in which ideas, practices, and the physical world are interrelated.

American ethnologists also have borrowed extensively from psychology and linguistics, placing an emphasis upon understanding the ideas and psyches of the people being studied. Those following this approach have come to be labeled *cognitive anthropologists*. According to this approach, culture is not something that can be observed directly, for in the final analysis, it exists only inside people's heads. From this perspective, culture consists essentially of ideas—values, standards, concepts, rules, and categories. Phenomena that can be observed directly—airplanes, plows, puberty rites—are not themselves culture, but merely expression of the basic ideas that comprise culture. Cognitive anthropologists study ideas instead of the social or material manifestations of culture.

Unlike the American school, British social anthropology has been influenced most by sociology. By and large, British ethnologists are less interested in the ways people think and the things they make than in how people *act* and organize themselves socially. For the most part, they have left the study of psychology, language, and history to specialists in those disciplines, and concentrated their own efforts on the analysis of social systems. Rather than seeking to get at the ideological or psychological mainsprings of culture, or to analyze how culture is linked to the physical environment, British social anthropologists have concentrated upon directly observable social behavior.

Ethnologists are divided not only by differing theoretical traditions, but also by other forms of specialization. Ethnology, which concerns understanding how and why cultures work, is built upon a body of descriptive material in which the vast array of human beliefs, practices, and achievements are laid out. This process of describing individual cultures—largely through fieldwork—is called *ethnography*. The amount of ethnographic information available on all human cultures is far too vast to be studied in depth by a single individual; most ethnologists specialize in the ethnography of one or two geographical areas, such as sub-Saharan Africa or the Amazonian Basin. Usually, an ethnologist will have done firsthand research among some group in the area, and for purposes of comparison and background will also be informed about other peoples in the region. In addition to geographic specialization, most ethnologists choose one or two *subject areas*, such as religion, politics, kinship or economics, for intensive study.

A Holistic View of Sociocultural Anthropology

American cultural materialism and cognitive anthropology and British social anthropology each represents only a partial picture of the human condition. For that reason, one of the primary aims of this text is to offer a synthesis of these approaches—to overcome the peculiarities of each of these traditions and to offer a holistic view of human culture that is more truly anthropological.

The coherence and direction for this task is achieved by building the synthesis upon a few central themes, and looking at how they are related to people's behaviors, perceptions, and material culture and to the physical world. These themes are *integration, adaptation, context,* and *dynamism.* All have been discussed to some degree, but let us look more closely at how they will be used in the chapters that follow.

With regard to integration, we will look at how specific beliefs and practices are related to other aspects of culture and to the encompassing environment. In trying to understand why people believe or act as they do, the anthropologist seeks to determine *causal relationships* among various phenomena. By looking at the various factors that produce a certain pattern of medical treatment, for example, we are trying to understand *why* that pattern exists and not some other. Methods of health care in Western industrial societies do not reflect an absolute medical standard for the treatment of illness; they are the product of a particular cultural tradition. To understand doctor-patient relations within this tradition requires looking beyond the physiological manifestations of the patient's illness and investigating such things as the ethnic and class backgrounds of the patient and doctor, the cultural rules for doctor-patient interaction, and the views of members of the culture toward the particular disease.

Direct causes are not always easy to determine. It is often more useful to think of *conditioning factors:* the range of interrelated factors that set the stage for something. This entails delving beyond the immediate to the less apparent motivating factors. For example, alcoholism among Native Americans is commonly explained as a result of unemployment, the availability of liquor, or the destruction of their traditional culture. No one would deny that these are contributing factors, but a full understanding of the causes of Native American alcoholism requires that we look beyond at the conditions in American society that deny these people a viable place in that society, and that destroyed their traditional way of life.

Our second theme is adaptation. As has already been noted, humans have devised a wide range of strategies for adapting to their environments. While recognizing this diversity, in this text we will pay special attention to two fundamental patterns of adaptation that are associated with social scale: small-scale and large-scale. *Small-scale* societies are characterized by localized social interaction and the exploitation of local resources. This localized orientation makes them relatively autonomous. For example, before their incorporation into Canadian society, the Inuit were largely independent of neighboring people. Although they did maintain relations with these neighbors, the Inuit preferred relations within their own fairly narrow social and spatial boundaries and relied almost exclusively upon local resources for their subsistence needs.

Large-scale societies, by contrast, are much less localized in orientation and much more dependent upon extensive and highly specialized interchange of goods, ideas, and people. Some large-scale societies, such as those of Canada or

India, encompass large and diverse populations and areas. Others, such as the island nations of Fiji or Tonga, are much smaller and more homogeneous. In these small nations, there is a high degree of social complexity and an orientation toward social and economic exchange beyond the local level that is not found in small-scale societies. While traditional Inuit moved about almost exclusively in the Arctic and manufactured most of the things that they needed from resources close at hand, Fijians maintain significant social and economic ties with others the world over.

There are few small-scale societies left in the world today, although there are some societies that exhibit vestiges of their more independent pasts. Why this is so relates to our third theme, context. Adaptational strategies exist in relation to an environmental context, and the context within which most people live is one of an increasingly integrated world. One of the givens of this text is that there are no known societies in the world today that are completely isolated. An analysis of any society, whether Fijian or Inuit, requires that we look at how that society fits within the context of this world system. This is not to say that local environmental conditions are not important; but the meanings they assume for those living there are strongly influenced by the international system. To most Pacific islanders their immediate physical surroundings are of considerable significance, but primarily in terms of their ability to attract tourists, international fishing fleets, or multinational mining companies and to produce wealth that is recognized in an international context.

The underpinnings of this worldwide social system are found in international trade. The manner in which societies are integrated into this system reflects their place in an international division of labor. As Immanuel Wallerstein (1979: 5) has noted, the defining characteristic of a social system is "the existence within it of a division of labor, such that various sectors

Pepsi Cola, one of the many multinational corporations that are a major component of the modern world system, is distributed in 147 countries and territories throughout the world. Here it is advertised on a beach in Nigeria.

or areas within it are dependent upon economic exchange with others for the smooth and continuous provisioning of the needs of the area." In small-scale societies this division of labor may occur within a single family or village. In large-scale societies like the United States there is a division of labor within national boundaries—there are factory workers, teachers, government bureaucrats, and so forth. But this division of labor and, in fact, almost all aspects of life in the United States are influenced by the place our nation has within the encompassing world system. The used-car salesman cannot be understood without reference to international considerations regarding the production and exchange of oil and automobiles. The *world system*, then, is a social system encompassing the entire world and entailing a single division of labor. Throughout the chapters that follow, we will refer to how people's beliefs and practices are related to this world order.

Our final theme is dynamism. By *dynamism* we mean that human culture is in a constant state of flux, always changing, always evolving. The present world system did not always exist; there is no assurance that it always will. The roots of this dynamism are in the very nature of human cultural adaptation. Our reliance upon culture has provided us with a valuable adaptive mechanism, allowing us tremendous flexibility, but it has left us vulnerable as well. Like other animals, we must reproduce ourselves biologically in order to ensure our continued survival; but, unlike most other animals, we must also seek to reproduce our culture. We must reproduce the knowledge and organizational patterns we have developed to acquire, produce, and distribute what we need or desire. People of the Fly River area of New Guinea traditionally have sought to ensure cultural reproduction by dramatic initiation rites in which youths are instilled with desired values and knowledge. In our society we use schools, television, and so on toward much the same end. However, people are not always able or even willing to reproduce things exactly as they were before. Conditions change, our goals, strategies, and knowledge change, and in the process human culture continues to evolve.

Summary

Like other animals, we humans are influenced both by our biological makeup and by our environment. But we differ greatly from other animals in the degree to which we have developed culture—learned and socially shared ways of behaving and thinking. We also differ from each other; cultural practices vary considerably from one society to the next and even among subgroups of the same society.

For humans, the environment to which our behaviors must be adapted includes social as well as biological factors. Cultural ecology is the study of interrelationships between humans and this multifaceted environment. Some adaptations are physiological changes—short-term, developmental, or passed down over long periods of time through evolutionary processes. Others are cultural strategies involving technology, social organization, and ideology.

Anthropology is the scientific study of humanity's varied behaviors. Anthropologists strive for a universal, holistic, integrated, and relativistic approach. Because their topic—all of humanity—is so broad and varied, individual anthropoligists explore only pieces of it. Physical anthropologists study biological data on living and ancient humans and primates. Sociocultural anthropologists focus on cultural aspects of human life. One branch, archaeology, studies artifacts and other clues to the lives of ancient peoples, both those who left written records and earlier peoples who did not. Another branch, anthropological linguistics, studies the structure and characteristics of languages for clues to understanding cultures and cultural processes. The third branch of sociocultural anthropology, ethnology, analyzes ethnographic descriptions of recent and living populations for general patterns and processes. American ethnologists have been heavily influenced by the natural sciences, history, psychology, and linguistics, whereas British ethnologists have been influenced by sociology.

To pull together the piecemeal insights of American ethnology's cultural materialism and cognitive anthropology and the British school's social anthropology, this book follows four themes to see how they are related to the three chief aspects of culture—behaviors, perceptions, and material productions. These themes—integration, adaptation, context, and dynamism—can be applied in varying degrees to all societies.

Suggested Readings

These are a few books that introduce the discipline and the people anthropologists study:

Bowen, Elenore Smith. 1964. *Return to laughter.* New York: Doubleday/Anchor. (Africa)

Duvignaud, Jean. 1977. *Change at Shebika.* Austin: University of Texas Press. (North Africa)

Fernea, Elizabeth. 1969. *Guests of the sheik.* New York: Doubleday/Anchor. (Middle East)

Liebow, Elliot. 1967. *Tally's corner.* Boston: Little, Brown. (United States)

Read, Kenneth. 1980. *The high valley.* New York: Columbia Univ. Press. (Papua New Guinea)

Ruesch, Hans. 1950. *Top of the world.* New York: Harper & Row. (Arctic North America)

Service, Elman. 1978. *Profiles in ethnology.* New York: Harper & Row. (brief descriptions of twenty-three different societies)

Siskind, Janet. 1973. *To hunt in the morning.* New York: Oxford. (South America)

Thomas, Elizabeth Marshall. 1959. *The harmless people.* New York: Vintage. (Southern Africa)

Turnbull, Colin. 1962. *The forest people.* New York: Doubleday/Anchor. (Central Africa)

Wilson, Carter. 1974. *Crazy February.* Berkeley: University of California Press. (Southern Mexico)

Chapter Two

The Growth of Cultural Anthropology

ANTHROPOLOGY IS NOT a static discipline with a fixed conception of what humans are and why they behave and think as they do. Like all other disciplines, it is constantly changing.

In many ways, anthropological ideas at any given time are reflections of the cultural environment of anthropologists; as this environment changes, so do anthropologists' views. For example, until quite recently, many anthropologists ignored or minimized the place of women. However, during the past few decades, recognition of the sexist bias within Western culture has led anthropologists to reevaluate the position of women in other societies and to reexamine older accounts of those societies. They now hope to present a more accurate view of women's roles and status.

But anthropology is not merely the product of the whims of a particular age; it is also the product of a gradual accumulation and testing of knowledge and ideas about people. Through the amassing of accurate ethnographic informa-

tion about people's behavior and beliefs and through the constant questioning and refining of theories of human culture, anthropology has grown into a more sophisticated discipline and profession concerned with the human condition.

In this chapter we will review the growth of anthropology as a profession and as a body of ideas. We will look at how anthropology changed from being the province of an odd assortment of amateurs concerned with exotic and often unimportant "native" customs to the profession of a group of highly trained specialists interested in all of humanity. And we will look at how the ideas of anthropologists grew from rather naive assumptions concerning the evolution of humankind to much more sophisticated attempts to explain how we go about living in the world around us. The story is not complete, of course; the science of humanity remains a continuously developing and ever-expanding process of discovery.

The Beginnings of Cultural Anthropology

While the roots of cultural anthropology can be traced through the history and intellectual traditions of Western culture as far back as ancient Greece, anthropology did not begin to take shape as a distinct field of study until the mid-nineteenth century. Largely on the basis of unscientific observation, Europeans had divided

OVERLEAF
Cross-cultural influences are dramatically illustrated by this comparison of a Babangi mask from the French Congo (wood, 35.5 cm high) with Pablo Picasso's *Demoiselles d' Avignon* (1907; oil on canvas, 243.9 x 233.7 cm). The two figures at right and one at left were repainted under influence of African sculpture.

humanity into a small number of physiologically based categories (see chapter 11). At this time there were no professional anthropologists, but a growing number of amateurs were interested in tracing relationships among the various "races" and in comparing the customs of exotic peoples. For these purposes, the first *ethnological societies* were established in Paris (1839), London (1844), and other major cities. The members of these associations shared the conviction that non-European peoples were worthy of study, but they differed about whether all peoples should be considered "truly human" (rather than some form of nonhuman primate) and why people looked and acted differently.

According to one popular theory of the day,

The English artist traveling with Captain James Cook during Cook's eighteenth-century Pacific explorations revealed much about his own values and customs in this distorted view of the Tahitians. Note the facial features, hair styles, and clothing that make them look more like Europeans than Polynesians.

humans had been created in a state of perfection, but had degenerated after the expulsion from Eden. Those who believed this theory claimed that some peoples (i.e., nonwhites) had "fallen" further than others from the original state of perfection. Another theory held that God had created the various "races" separately. In this view, it was considered no more a problem to explain the contrast between members of the Caucasoid and Mongoloid races than it was to show why tigers and ostriches are not alike. The major shortcoming of both theories was that they were based on theological, and not scientific, principles: they were based upon European religious traditions and not upon systematic observation. In addition, they tended to consider a people's way of life to be determined largely by biological factors.

Unilineal Evolution

A more scientific and humanistic approach to the study of humanity developed from another school of thought, which came to be known as *unilineal evolutionism*. The unilineal evolutionists drew inspiration from evolutionary theories gaining currency in biology and geology. Like animal species, they asserted, human cultures undergo changes over vast periods of time, with "primitive" stages of culture succeeded by more "advanced" stages. These first anthropologists are called unilineal evolutionists because they generally maintained that all cultures pass through essentially the same stages along a single line of development, moving from "savage" to "civilized." Contemporary "savages" (people whose life-style is in some ways similar to that believed to be associated with earlier periods of human cultural evolution) were seen as living cultural fossils. This theory was especially important at the time as a justification for the study of non-Western peoples, the idea being that by studying them we could learn something about our own past.

The concept of evolution made it possible to begin studying human nature systematically without resorting to theological dogma. But more important, the unilineal evolutionists made a clear distinction between biologically inherited characteristics and those acquired socially through learning. This distinction between race and culture offered a solution to a fundamental paradox in the study of humanity: the question of why we are all so alike, yet so different. The unilineal evolutionists recognized that there are racial differences in such traits as skin color, eye shape, and hair form. But they stoutly supported the principle of *psychic unity*, according to which all people have essentially the same mental capacities and potentials. Every person, they felt, is equal to everyone else at birth, and "the talents he may afterwards acquire...depend in great measure upon the state of society in which he is placed" (Robertson 1822:1: 218-19). In other words, the more important human differences are because of social environment, not biology.

Through their acceptance of the psychic unity of mankind, white unilineal evolutionists were willing to admit nonwhites as their peers in basic capabilities. But they could not accept the cultures of these people as the equals of their own. To European and North American unilineal evolutionists, it seemed obvious that some cultures were more advanced than others.

They saw *progress* as the most important feature of evolution, rather than simply change. To them, evolution was a sequence leading from the simple to the complex, or the primitive to the advanced. Grossly ethnocentric, they consistently viewed their own customs and beliefs as the most advanced.

Tylor: The Evolution of Reason. The most prominent of the unilineal evolutionists was an Englishman, Edward Tylor (1832-1917), an anthropologist at Oxford University. Tylor's most important contribution to anthropology was his concept of culture, which he defined as "that complex whole which includes knowledge, belief, art, law, morals, customs, and any other capabilities and habits acquired by man as a member of society." It was Tylor, more than anyone else, who established the distinction between biologically inherited characteristics and those we acquire through learning.

While Tylor considered all people to be equal in their capacity for "civilization," he felt that some cultures had progressed further than others. In Tylor's view, cultural evolution consisted of "the advance of reason." What distinguishes the "savage" from the "civilized man" is that the "higher" cultures have gone further in abandoning "superstition" (the Europeans' label for other peoples' unfamiliar religious beliefs) in favor of customs that have a supposedly rational basis and are based upon scientific principles. Recognizing that even Western cultures still maintain customs that do not make sense, Tylor explained these by his concept of *survivals*. These are customs originating in earlier evolutionary stages, and maintained through force of habit, despite the fact that they have lost their original meaning and function. For instance, Tylor explains the custom of saying "God bless you" after a sneeze as a survival of the ancient belief that the soul might leave the body during a sneeze, and that uttering the spell "God bless you" would counteract the danger (Tylor 1891:1: 98). Sur-

Saying "God bless you" after someone sneezes illustrates one type of a survival.

vivals were important to Tylor's approach, for he felt that they provided evidence of a culture's past history and could therefore be used to reconstruct cultural evolution.

Morgan: The Evolution of Technology. Another important proponent of unilineal evolution was a Syracuse, New York lawyer, Lewis Henry Morgan (1818–89). In *Ancient Society*, Morgan produced an elaborate developmental scheme of cultural evolution, dividing evolutionary progress into a series of stages based primarily upon technological innovation. For instance, cultures passed from "middle savagery" (characterized by foraging, with the capability of fishing and making fire) to "upper savagery" (with the introduction of the bow and arrow) and on into "lower barbarism" (with the ability to make pottery).

Morgan felt that such stages and technological innovations were associated with the evolution of other cultural patterns. For example, he proposed that the family had evolved through

six stages linked with the technologically based stages. While Morgan's linking of technology with other aspects of culture represented an important contribution, there were many problems with his actual schema. For one thing, although ethnographic knowledge had come a long way, it was still quite sketchy by today's standards, and Morgan had to rely on poorly collected data. Also, Morgan commonly relied upon supposition, distorting data by forcing them into his categories. In addition, his schema was ethnocentric, centering on Western technology and social organization.

Despite their ethnocentricity, the unilineal evolutionists' ideas were not without merit. In psychic unity, they could explain how it is that we are all alike; in progress, they could explain why we are so different. There were some fundamental problems with their approach, however. From the hindsight of more recent theories, we can see that in placing cultures in categories from most primitive to most advanced, they offered no adequate explanation of how cultures got from one stage to the next. Their overall view of the context that shaped people's lives was also very limited. In particular, they virtually ignored the influence of the physical environment. Furthermore, they tended to treat various aspects of culture, such as kinship and marriage patterns or religious practices, as isolated variables, rather than as part of an integrated cultural system.

In addition to their theoretical shortcomings,

unilineal evolutionists were hampered by poor data. Most were "armchair anthropologists" who had no firsthand experience with the non-Western cultures they were describing. The data on which they based their theories were collected largely by travelers, soldiers, explorers, missionaries, and traders. Information was often erroneous because it was not collected in an objective and systematic manner. The increasingly obvious need for more reliable data led to a new stage in the evolution of anthropology.

Professionalization

By the late 1870s anthropology was beginning to emerge as a profession. A major impetus for the growth of anthropology was the expansion of North American and European colonial powers—there was a need for more thorough research about the peoples under colonial domination. In the United States, especially in the Far West, the government desired information on Indians, who were being subdued and placed on reservations. Britain and other European nations had a similar interest in the peoples of their farflung empires. Anthropologists did not normally serve as agents of colonial administrations, however. Many were motivated primarily by a desire to record the customs of these people before they disappeared and were forgotten. For such researchers, theirs was principally a humanistic enterprise.

Museum Anthropology

Anthropology emerged as a profession primarily in museums. By the latter half of the nineteenth century growing collections of ethnographic materials in museums were starting to receive attention. Money from governments and wealthy individuals was made available in most industrial nations to support museum-

related work. During the 1870s and 1880s many museums devoted to the study of 'mankind' were founded in North and South America and Europe. Ethnographic collections came to play a larger role in natural history museums, until in some instances they became the primary focus of the museum.

Anthropology's link with museums influenced its development throughout the late nineteenth and early twentieth centuries. In the United States and continental Europe this link remains important to some extent even today. There were two particular ways in which museums affected cultural anthropology. One was an emphasis upon material culture, stemming from museums' concern for collecting displayable materials. Second, the museum orientation encouraged anthropologists to classify their data according to static natural history typologies (just like stones or butterflies) rather than focusing upon the dynamic aspects of culture. Human practices and ideas were treated as concrete static entities instead of as more ephemeral creations in a continual state of flux. Museum-related work also led to the treatment of culture as a collection of separate things, rather than a system of interrelated ideas and activities.

Academic Anthropology

The gradual introduction of anthropology to university curricula paralleled its growth in museums. Courses were offered on occasion at universities, often by self-taught anthropologists, during the latter part of the nineteenth-century. Joint appointments at museums and universities were fairly common and assured a continued link between museums and academic anthropology.

After 1900, the number of persons employed as full-time anthropologists in Europe and the United States grew, but very slowly. In the United States, for example, there were only a few dozen professional anthropologists by 1940. While only a handful of these were employed in universities, the university setting did serve to modify the museum influence on the discipline as anthropologists came into contact with other disciplines such as sociology and psychology.

In the 1920s and 1930s, anthropology departments were founded throughout the British Commonwealth, in Latin America, and elsewhere. The anthropologists in these countries were trained by Americans and Europeans, whose theories they tended to follow. At first, non-European and non-American anthropologists primarily provided systematically collected ethnographic data concerning the indigenous peoples of their own countries. Anthropology in these countries did not begin to develop on its own until after the Second World War.

Professionalization during the latter part of the nineteenth and early twentieth centuries allowed for great breakthroughs in the quality and quantity of ethnographic research. Ethnographic research with indigenous peoples had been conducted for many years, but on the whole its quality was uneven. Beginning in the 1870s, the quality of research began to improve markedly. And after the U.S. Bureau of American Ethnology employed a professional anthropologist in 1879 to conduct research among Indians in the Southwest, more and more professionals were sent by agencies and museums to conduct fieldwork. Franz Boas, who was to become a leading figure in American anthropology during the early twentieth century, conducted research with Inuit and Northwest Coast Indians in the 1880s and 1890s. A larger expedition from Cambridge University visited the Torres Straits between Australia and New Guinea in 1898 and 1899.

Although more information was being collected firsthand by anthropologists, the continuing museum bias in anthropology limited what information was recorded and how. The main emphasis remained upon collecting artifacts—weapons, tools, pottery. Only superficial attempts were made at studying culture as an integrated whole. Virtually no attempt was made to understand why things were as they were.

Diffusion

As more and more reliable information was amassed, the shortcomings of unilineal evolutionism became increasingly apparent. Scholars started to recognize that a simple, one-line scheme of universal progress was not adequate to explain the cultural diversity they were finding. They were discovering that all "savages" were not alike, and they felt it important to explain why.

Dissatisfaction with unilineal evolutionists' theories led to several new schools of thought. One was *diffusionism*, the view that the main process by which cultures grow, change, and develop is cultural borrowing. Morgan had assumed that each culture would progress through a series of stages marked by important inventions, such as the wheel, metallurgy, and the alphabet. Diffusionists, however, doubted that such important inventions occurred independently in each culture. They maintained that critical inventions are rare, and that most peoples who have, say, the wheel, did not invent it

Franz Boas poses as a Kwakiutl hamatsa dancer for a National Museum diorama, 1895.

themselves, but picked it up from a neighboring society. Since the process of diffusion (i.e., cultural borrowing) depends on "historical accidents" and not on some inevitable law of progress, the variations among peoples could be explained more convincingly.

The basic principles of diffusionism were first developed in Germany. Germany was in the forefront in establishing ethnographic museums, and hence German scholars were interested in studying specific culture "traits" (like fishhook styles or myths) and trying to explain their distribution. Prominent German diffusionists claimed that initially there were a limited number of cultural circles (*Kreise*), and that human culture had evolved through a process of diffusion from these points of origin. They proposed that "higher civilizations" like those of ancient Mesopotamia and Egypt had evolved in geographically favorable places. They felt that the basic inventions characteristic of civilization occurred in these regions, and that changes elsewhere resulted from the diffusion of these inventions through borrowing, migration, and conquest. This view of cultural evolution became known as the *Kulturkreis*, or "culture-circle," theory.

Many of the diffusionists' propositions represented little more than imaginative speculation, and cultures were still treated as accumulations of discrete traits rather than as integrated wholes. Nevertheless, diffusionism was a considerable improvement over unilineal evolutionism, primarily because of the significance it placed upon context.

Historical Particularism

Diffusionist ideas were brought to American anthropology by Franz Boas (1858–1942), a German-born ethnologist with museum training. He felt that the emphasis in ethnology should be on detailed study of the geographical distribution of culture traits. By analyzing these trait distributions, he argued, it might be possible to reconstruct the historical and psychological processes of cultural change. The American school of ethnology that Boas founded came to be known as *historical particularism,* because instead of seeking to discover universal laws governing the process of culture change, Boas called for investigation of the unique histories of individual cultures.

Many of Boas's followers turned to the study of *culture areas,* or regions where clusterings of shared cultural traits occur. The Great Plains of North America was one such culture area, for the Indians of this zone shared a number of customs and institutions. All hunted buffalo and placed a high value on warfare. Most of them had such institutions as the Sun Dance ceremony and military societies. When anthropologists mapped out such culture areas, they discovered that each tended to be closely correlated with a particular ecological zone, such as the Amazon River system or the Great Basin. Thus, the historical particularists were among the first anthropologists to recognize a relationship between culture and the physical environment.

Influenced by the museum emphasis of this period, diffusionists and historical particularists emphasized collecting specimens (cultural artifacts and traits), recording their distribution, and classifying them according to type. While this natural history approach surely has a place in anthropology, it is of little help in understanding cultures as integrated wholes, made up of interrelated parts.

Fieldwork methods of this period also limited understanding of cultures as systems. Ethnographers rarely spent very long with the peoples from whom they collected their data. As a result, while they were highly efficient at gathering baskets and proverbs, they did not learn much about the context of such specimens. A sense of cultural context can only be acquired through a relatively long-term acquaintance with a particular culture. Even Franz Boas, who so strongly emphasized the importance of fieldwork, rarely spent more than a week in a single Kwakiutl village or Inuit camp. Consequently, while he was able to amass large amounts of ethnographic details, Boas never had a clear picture of Kwakiutl or Inuit life, and he had little appreciation for the ways the various customs and institutions of these peoples were interconnected.

Toward an Integrated View of Culture

Throughout the first two decades of the twentieth century the museum tradition in ethnology prevailed over the academic tradition, but by 1920 changes were afoot. Some thinkers, influenced by European sociology, were beginning to develop the idea that culture was not a mixed bag of unconnected traits but an *integrated system,* made up of mutually interacting parts. As their contact and interaction with non-Western peoples increased, anthropologists began to realize that these other cultures were far more coherent and logical than had previously been recognized. For instance, they began to see that rituals can have an important connection with politics and that systems of kinship organization can play a vital role in economic spheres. Recognizing patterns of this kind is possible only if one has a fairly detailed and comprehensive familiarity with the culture in question.

Functionalism

One of the first attempts at an integrated systems approach developed as certain anthropologists departed from the natural history tradition in favor of a *functionalist* perspective. Instead of being interested in the origins or his-

Bronislaw Malinowski talks to a sorcerer during his fieldwork among the Trobriand Islanders (1915-1918).

tories of cultures and thinking of beliefs and customs as things, this new school asked new and different questions about how cultures work. Functionalists felt that what was most important about the Sun Dance ritual of the Dakota, for instance, was not where, how, and when it was invented and diffused, but how this religious ceremony functioned, how it fit in with the rest of Dakota culture.

To understand the complex interrelationships of elements in a total cultural system, anthropologists had to carry out intensive fieldwork over a period of months or even years. One of the first people to conduct research along these lines was Bronislaw Malinowski (1884-1942). Malinowski was born in Poland, but he studied anthropology in England. Between 1915 and 1918, he conducted research in the Trobriand Islands, near New Guinea. This

study became a model for future ethnographic research for it demonstrated that a long-term, in-depth acquaintance with an ongoing way of life could lead to far greater understanding of a people's culture than could a somewhat speculative reconstruction of their history based upon a random accumulation of traits.

According to Malinowski, all people have certain *basic needs*—requirements such as food, shelter, reproduction, and so forth—that are common to everyone. In addition, there exist *derived needs*—such as the need for art, or alcohol—that are not matters of life and death, but are ultimately traceable to more basic needs associated with the fundamental requirements for biological survival. Malinowski argued that culture functions do fulfill both kinds of needs. If this is so, then even some seemingly irrational customs might make sense after all. For example, Malinowski found that the Trobriand Islanders made extensive use of magic, in the form of spells, charms, and potions. Instead of explaining Trobriand magic by reference to their "savage" condition or to the process of diffusion, Malinowski reasoned that magic functions do reduce the tensions and anxieties that result from the uncertainties of life. He found, for instance, that the Trobrianders used magic when they were fishing in the dangerous open seas, but not when they were fishing in calm lagoons. Lagoon-fishing apparently involved no particular dangers, and hence provoked no feelings of anxiety. But the uncertainties of open-sea fishing created tensions that could to some extent be released through magic.

Malinowski deserves a great deal of credit for his advances in fieldwork, his literary ability in portraying the lives of Trobriand Islanders to European and North American readers, and his insights into certain adaptive dimensions of culture. Theory, however, was Malinowski's weak point. For example, if all people have the same basic needs that are met through the functions of culture, then why do all cultures not meet those needs in the same way? To this question, Malinowski had no effective answer. There was another problem as well. By emphasizing how culture functions to meet the needs of individuals, Malinowski failed to take adequately into account those sociocultural forces and factors which transcend the individual, such as revolutions, economic depressions, and social institutions like the family.

Structural-Functionalism

Malinowski's theoretical shortcomings were offset by his contemporary A. R. Radcliffe-Brown (1881-1955). Radcliffe-Brown was Malinowski's opposite in almost every way. Malinowski was an aristocrat, skilled in the social graces; Radcliffe-Brown was a product of the English lower-middle class. Malinowski was a great field-worker; Radcliffe-Brown's ethnographic research was, at best, ordinary. But Radcliffe-Brown had a remarkable gift for theory that enabled him to synthesize vast quantities of existing ethnographic data and reveal patterns previously unrecognized by other scholars.

Radcliffe-Brown was strongly influenced by the great French sociologist Emile Durkheim (1858-1917), who was one of the first to develop the idea of society as an integrated system of interrelated parts. Durkheim stressed that culture is the product of a community and not of single individuals. He argued that the ultimate reality of human life was sociological and not psychological: that it consisted of the social products of people interacting in groups over generations. This sociological reality (which Durkheim called the "collective consciousness") exists beyond the individual, and individual actions and beliefs are simply manifestations of this larger reality.

Similarly, Radcliffe-Brown likened society to an organism—an integrated whole whose existence depends on the proper functioning of its constituent parts. Moreover, he argued, society has a "life of its own," obeying laws that transcend the individual. His mission was to investigate the anatomy of society and document the dynamics of its components. Unlike the functionalism of Malinowski, which stressed how culture works to sustain individuals, Radcliffe-Brown's theory of *structural functionalism* focused on how various elements of social structure (such as a society's major groups and institutions) function to maintain social order and equilibrium.

If Malinowski and Radcliffe-Brown were observing a funeral ceremony, they would very likely look for different things and interpret differently what they saw. Malinowski would probably interpret the lamentations of the bereaved as a custom functioning to alleviate the tensions created in these individuals by the death. To Radcliffe-Brown, it would be more fruitful to look at the social groups and institutions involved and see how the behavior of the be-

Funeral rites for an infant in Nepal. According to
the structural functionalists, funeral rites are one of
the elements of social structure that help maintain
social order and equilibrium.

reaved serves to reaffirm the values of the society and promote the solidarity of group members. In other words, Radcliffe-Brown would stress how the funeral rites fulfill the "needs" of the social system, not of individuals. The two views are not mutually exclusive: culture clearly has functions for individuals as well as for societies. Nevertheless, since anthropology is primarily concerned with humans as sociocultural beings, Radcliffe-Brown's theories have been more productive in the long run than Malinowski's.

The functionalists and structural-functionalists were instrumental in establishing the concept of cultural integration and they refined fieldwork methods considerably. Their ideas were especially important for emphasizing the need to look at the social context within which customs and institutions occur if they are to be understood, rather than treating them as isolated traits. But the context they recognized was somewhat narrow. There was a tendency to draw the boundaries of the sociocultural system around local communities or groups and treat them like isolated units with no history. For instance, one study of the Tallensi of West Africa (Fortes, 1949) assigned almost no significance to the fact that the Tallensi had once been part of a large African empire and that at the time of the study were a subject people of the British, despite the fact that many of their social institutions could be understood adequately only by reference to this aspect of their history and current British colonial rule. Such studies by functionalists and structural functionalists also paid little attention to the influence of the physical and biotic environment upon culture.

One of the most important shortcomings of these schools, however, was their failure to deal adequately with sociocultural change. By looking at a social system as a set of mutually supporting elements, they made it hard to explain how change might occur. By definition, a perfectly integrated system is in a state of equilibrium. If this were the case, then change could only come from without, as in the case of European colonial expansion into Africa, rather than from within, as in internal competition for power or scarce resources. This theoretical limitation was not apparent to the scholars of this era, however, for they did not consider the explanation of change to be their main mission.

Culture and Personality

While English anthropologists were developing functionalism and structural functionalism in reaction against the treatment of culture as an accumulation of discrete traits, a number of anthropologists in the United States had become critical of this approach as well. In their search for the mechanisms of cultural integration these anthropologists chose to focus upon psychological rather than sociological factors—a development reflecting the close ties that had emerged in the United States by the mid-1930s between anthropologists and psychologists. Since it emphasized the relationship between culture and the individual, this new school of thought was labeled *culture and personality*. People were thought to assume certain personality characteristics in keeping with dominant themes present in their culture.

Ruth Benedict (1889–1948), a student of Franz Boas, was one of the foremost advocates of this approach during the 1930s and 1940s. She argued that there was a range of potential themes or types which would coordinate culture and individual psyche, and that it was possible to categorize whole cultures according to which of these strategies had been adopted. Over time, Benedict felt, aspects of a culture that contradicted this overriding theme were worked out, until the entire system became consistent with it. Her best-known work, *Patterns of Culture* (1934), discusses a few of these themes. The Apollonian type, which she felt was exemplified by the Zuni Indian culture, entailed a preference for compromise and avoidance of psychological and emotional excesses. Another type, the Dionysian, she assigned to the Kwakiutl, a warlike and competitive people of the northwest coast of North America. The Dionysian theme involved seeking out excitement, terror, and danger.

The culture and personality approach did not break totally with the museum-derived natural history tradition. What it represented was a blending of the typological emphasis of natural history with ideas current in psychology at the time. The natural history tendency to look for types was simply moved to a higher level of abstraction—to whole cultures instead of their parts.

The culture and personality approach was rife with problems. The categories proposed by Benedict and others were oversimplifications. These scholars viewed humans and their culture not as adaptive, but as existing almost in a vacuum, isolated from the physical world, other cultures, and history. And Benedict's discussion of cultural evolution consisted of little more than unsupported or unsupportable suppositions. As anthropology continued to develop, functionalists' views of cultural integration more often served as a point of departure for later theories than did those of the culture and personality school.

Specialization: World War II to the Present

By the end of World War II in 1945, the basic methods that characterize anthropology had been developed. Non-Western peoples had become fairly familiar to anthropologists, and these cultures were recognized as integrated and reasonable entities. At this time new trends in anthropological theory and areas of specialization began to emerge. These trends were accelerated by a marked increase in the number of professional anthropologists. In the earlier part of the twentieth century, there were so few anthropologists that they all knew each other. Today, there are thousands of anthropologists with diverse backgrounds, interests, and personalities creating a discipline of many and varied ideas, approaches, and specialties. The era of the ethnographic pioneer discovering unknown peoples is past. Today, some of the most stimulating discoveries are the insights anthropologists derive from asking old questions in new ways and from delving into uncharted areas.

The elements of contemporary anthropology are influenced by factors outside the discipline itself. After World War II, there was a very rapid acceleration in culture contact. People who previously were only marginally affected by the industrial world were rapidly drawn into the global economy and integrated into newly established nations. For many non-Western peoples, the past quarter-century has been a time of enormous upheaval and change. Western culture has suffered some turbulence during this period too. Inflation, the energy crisis, and pollution are forcing us to reexamine our values and institutions. Not surprisingly, the major emphasis in contemporary anthropology is on the study of change.

Neoevolutionism

The popularity of the idea that culture evolves had subsided early in the twentieth century. However, an American anthropologist, Leslie White (1900–75), played an instrumental role in keeping that notion alive. His revived version has been labeled *neoevolution*.

Like the unilineal evolutionists, White was interested in the general evolution of human culture, rather than the evolution of specific cultures. But instead of assuming cultural progress as a given, White attempted to explain what makes it occur.

To White, the primary force in cultural evolution was technological advancement. What distinguishes "advanced" from "primitive" cultures, he argued, is the amount of energy at their disposal. In a very "primitive" culture, people have only human muscle power as an energy source. Cultures evolve as humans find ways to harness new sources of power—domesticating draft animals and inventing means of capturing energy from wind, water, fossil fuels, and so forth. By increasing the amount of energy available, each technological advance makes possible greater social and cultural complexity and facilitates the growth of ever-larger sociocultural systems.

White's theory was an improvement over unilineal evolutionism in that it was based on a relatively objective concept of progress, but its shortcomings are apparent. His theory recognized few important relationships between culture and the wider environment; White's explanation of adaptation was relatively unsophisticated. Also, like his intellectual ancestors, Morgan and Tylor, White had no explanation for why some cultures progressed faster than others.

Cultural Ecology

Another important figure of the early postwar period was Julian Steward (1902–72). He focused on specific evolution—on the sequences of changes taking place within a particular culture or culture area. Steward recognized that the growth of culture is not exactly the same in the Amazon Basin as in the Valley of Mexico or the South Pacific. These are different environments, he argued, which place different demands on people. Evolution in one region will not be exactly like that in another.

Steward was the first anthropologist to stress the importance of the relationship between sociocultural systems and their environments, and he led the way in promoting the idea that culture is adaptive. Not only did he give the concept of cultural evolution an academic respectability it had not had since the end of the last century, he also laid the foundation for the study of *cultural ecology*. This approach stresses the investigation of how culture functions as a dynamic means of adapting to the conditions of local environments.

Theories of Conflict

A fundamental shortcoming of the anthropological perspectives discussed up to this point is their failure to deal with conflict. Pre-World War II anthropologists assumed a world that is very orderly, neglecting to include competition and conflict in their theoretical formulations. Motivations behind this omission probably included a desire to present cultures as integrated systems and to present the peoples being studied not as brutal savages, but as humans who lead orderly and sensible lives. Moreover, colonial conquest of the peoples studied had usually taken place before anthropologists arrived on the scene, leaving them to examine the lives of people existing under an externally imposed order. Some have argued that employment by colonial powers may have led anthropologists to ignore aspects of colonized peoples' social life that might reflect unfavorably upon the colonial government.

World War II and postwar struggles for liberation among colonial peoples in Africa, Asia, and elsewhere changed this situation dramatically. Conflict was present everywhere and anthropologists could no longer ignore it. While some anthropologists chose to view the competition and conflict they witnessed as arising

The demands of living are quite different in these vividly contrasting environments—the tropical rain forest of the lowlands of Brazil and the arid desert of Kenya.

out of unique postwar conditions, perceiving the period to be one of disequilibrium or perhaps a completely new situation, others argued that conflict was a normal part of human culture.

Neofunctionalism. One of the first to try to reform the functionalist perspective to fit postwar conditions was South African-born British anthropologist Max Gluckman (1911–75). Because of its reformist character, his approach can be labeled *neofunctionalism*. Gluckman (1949: 8) criticized Malinowski for his failure to treat conflict "as an inherent attribute of social organization." To Gluckman, feuds, estrangements within families, witchcraft accusations, challenges to authority, and the like were normal parts of social life. He argued that despite (or sometimes because of) conflict, social solidarity was maintained.

In *Custom and Conflict in Africa* (1956), Gluckman argued that the social order is main-tained through the checks and balances of overlapping allegiances. People may quarrel in terms of one set of traditional allegiances, such as those based upon kinship obligations, but they are also restrained by other allegiances imposed by custom. Thus, people who become enemies in one situation may become allies in another. Cousins who feud with each other in support of two quarreling brothers may join forces in a dispute with another kin group. Through the web of these crosscutting ties the social fabric is maintained. Gluckman even viewed rebellions as no threat to the social order. Rebels, following customary norms and procedures with rituallike precision, served to reaffirm rather than to undermine the traditional order. Their actions were "rituals of rebellion."

Gluckman succeeded in bringing conflict into the normal scheme of things, but he continued to emphasize the unchanging nature of the fundamental social order. He failed to deal ade-

quately with the question of structural change—how social orders are transformed or broken down. More important, social order itself was still treated as a given, and not as something to be explained.

Marxist Anthropology. Another group of anthropologists, drawing their inspiration from the writings of Karl Marx (1818–83), also view conflict as a normal part of human culture. Unlike Gluckman, *Marxist anthropologists* such as Stanley Diamond (1981), Claude Meillassoux (1981), and M. Godelier (1977) are concerned specifically with the relationship between conflict and cultural evolution, with the transformation of social orders.

In trying to explain the conditions that generated change, Marx emphasized the exploitative rather than harmonious nature of social relations. While functionalists assume that the maintenance of social order is of positive value, Marxists feel that most societies are character-

ized by an unequal distribution of resources and power. This imbalance creates a continual potential for conflict, with those who are better off constantly trying to maintain their position (the existing order) and those who are not so well off, disenchanted with the status quo, constantly threatening the existing order.

According to the Marxists, cultural evolution is characterized by a reordering of the means of production and distribution. This transformation is rarely smooth, since it involves one group's losing out to another. Although the old guard is not keen on losing its position, it is incapable of stopping this reorganization of society, because the traditional basis of its power is no longer applicable in the newly emerging order.

Marx did not view this evolution through conflict between the haves and the have-nots as a unilineal process. For example, he noted that the transition from a stage associated with various "tribal" economic systems may follow a number of different routes, depending upon local conditions. In addition, Marx viewed Western capitalist society not as the end of human cultural evolution, but rather as simply another stage—one that was to be followed by an end to monogamy, private property, and the state, and the rise of a more egalitarian communal society.

Studies of Cognitive Structure

While Marxists and neofunctionalists sought to explain the function of conflict in society, other schools of thought that began to emerge in the late 1950s and early 1960s focused on uncovering the cognitive structures providing order to culture. Two very different approaches to this effort are *structuralism* and *ethnoscience*. Despite their differences, both are heavily influenced by *structural linguistics*, the attempt to discover the structural principles underlying speech patterns.

Structuralism. The main proponent of the structural approach to the study of culture is French anthropologist Claude Lévi-Strauss (1908-). He has turned to the human mind as the point of origin for universal principles that order the ways in which we behave in and think about the world. According to Lévi-Strauss these universal principles are to be found in the structure of the processes of human thought. While his ideas have been influential in the study of kinship and mythology, their usefulness is limited because they are largely untestable and can be neither proved nor disproved. Furthermore, they do not explain variations among cultures.

Other structuralists have pursued the less ambitious task of trying to discover the structural operating principles of specific cultural systems. One of the leaders in this direction has been another French anthropologist, Louis Dumont (1911-). Dumont (1970) explained the caste system in India by reference to three structural

principles in that society: separation, hierarchy, and interaction. Although this approach is useful in pointing out some of the cognitive underpinnings of social behavior, it does not explain why such principles exist. This approach also treats cultural order as a given, and largely ignores the adaptive dimension of culture, by failing to link underlying structural principles with the physical and social environment.

Ethnoscience. Search for the structural principles in specific societies has been highly refined by the largely American school of *ethnoscience* (sometimes known as *cognitive anthropology*). Ethnoscientists seek to discover the structural principles of specific cultures by carefully analyzing ethnographic data. They collect information in minute detail and try to make sure that the structures they derive express the natives' point of view. Their main interest is in learning how people view their world: how the members of a society perceive and structure their environment through language categories and what rules or principles guide their decision making.

An early example of the ethnoscientists' approach was a study analyzing the color categories of a Filipino people, the Hanunóo, in an effort to understand how they divide the color spectrum (Conklin 1955). As we will see in chapter 4, this and later cross-cultural studies of color categorization have offered insight into the interrelationships among cultural, environmental, and physiological factors that determine color perception. Ethnoscientists' color perception studies also suggest that certain features of color classification systems are universal.

Symbolic Anthropology. Another approach that, like the studies of structures, emphasizes ideological rather than material aspects of culture is known as *symbolic anthropology*. In this perspective, culture is viewed as a system of shared symbols and meanings.

One of the principal advocates of the symbolic approach is American anthropologist

Clifford Geertz (1926–). Instead of relying solely upon people's statements about their culture, as ethnoscientists commonly do, Geertz argues that the cultural meanings of rituals, myths, kinship, and the like require examination of how they are actually used in the context of social life. In his analyses, Geertz focuses on significant cultural events and the cultural themes that he feels they exemplify. He analyzes Balinese cockfighting (1973), for example, as an embodiment of many of the fundamental themes of Balinese culture. He sees the etiquette of people attending the fights and the masculine symbolism of the roosters themselves as public enactments of Balinese cultural themes associated with poise, envy, brutality, status, pride, and chance. One particularly significant aspect of Geertz's view of culture is that he sees it as "disconnected." He does not view culture as a thoroughly integrated whole, but as a collection of often very contradictory emotions, beliefs, and rules.

Anthropology itself is not an integrated whole. Throughout the course of its history anthropology has been marked by a diversity of opinion and perspective. Given the scope of the undertaking—the study of the human condition—such differences are understandable, perhaps even inevitable. In the chapters that follow, we take a particular perspective in our study of the human condition that emphasizes cultural ecology, adaptation, integration, and change. This is clearly not the only approach possible. Perhaps one of the most important things to recognize is that no one approach has a monopoly on the truth. Yet in spite of anthropologists' differing viewpoints, there is one driving force behind all anthropological thought—a continual striving for objectivity, for a view of the human condition that transcends cultural bias.

Summary

From its beginnings in the mid-nineteenth century, anthropology has grown from the musings of a few ethnocentric armchair philosophers to the painstaking attempts of thousands of fieldworkers to understand how and why specific cultures work. This increasing scientific sophistication has been paralleled by continuing refinements and shifts in focus of anthropological theories.

The first important contribution to anthropological theory was *unilineal evolution*. Proponents of this theory saw human cultures as progressing along a single line, from more "primitive" to more "advanced" stages. Tylor felt that this progress was based on the advance of reason; Morgan attributed it to improvements in technology.

As museums and universities began to hire professional anthropologists, the quality of ethnographic research improved. Considering the old unilineal evolution model inadequate to explain the variations they were discovering among cultures, in the late nineteenth and early twentieth centuries anthropologists developed new ways of explaining cultural change. One was *diffusionism*—the idea that inventions and ideas are spread by borrowing, with changes perhaps radiating outward from a few advanced cultural centers. In contrast, Franz Boas's school of *historical particularism* studied the histories of individual cultures more carefully with an eye for possible patterns by which changes spread.

In contrast to the earlier museum-oriented

tendency to "collect" separate cultural specimens, be they pots or songs, by 1920 anthropologists were trying to see cultures as integrated wholes whose parts should be examined in relationship to each other, rather than separately. To the *functionalists*, such as Malinowski, cultural activities function to meet the needs of individuals. To the *structural functionalists*, such as Radcliffe-Brown, elements of a culture function to keep the social system itself working smoothly. The *culture and personality* school saw whole cultures developing certain personality themes that permeated all aspects of the system.

From World War II to the present, anthropology has spread into many specialized areas of inquiry. The *neoevolutionists* have looked again at cultural "progress," this time in an attempt to explain why changes occur. In Leslie White's view, cultures have evolved as they have harnessed more energy. The *cultural ecologists*, led by Julian Steward, see changes as attempts to adapt to a particular environment. Two other schools have looked at conflict as an explaining principle. To the *neofunctionalists*, conflict is simply a normal mechanism maintaining social order; to Marxist anthropologists, conflict between the haves and the have-nots will continually disrupt the existing order and lead to its alteration. Two more schools have tried to find the cognitive structures underlying culture: *structuralists* such as Lévi-Strauss have looked for universal patterns, while *ethnoscientists* have looked for culture-specific patterns. Finally, *symbolic anthropologists* have analyzed cultural events and institutions as symbols of a culture's beliefs, beliefs that are not necessarily integrated into a consistent whole.

Suggested Readings

There are a number of good general histories of anthropology, including:

Harris, Marvin. 1968. *The rise of anthropological theory.* New York: Crowell.

Hays, H. R. 1958. *From ape to angel: An informal history of social anthropology.* New York: Knopf.

Honigmann, John J. 1976. *The development of anthropological ideas.* Homewood, IL: Dorsey Press.

Kaplan, David, and Manners, Robert A. 1972. *Culture theory.* Englewood Cliffs, NJ: Prentice-Hall.

Malefijt, Annemarie deWaal. 1974. *Images of man.* New York: Knopf.

Voget, Fred W. 1975. *A history of ethnology.* New York: Holt, Rinehart & Winston.

There are also more detailed histories of particular periods or countries:

Hinsley, Curtis M., Jr. 1981. *Savages and scientists: The Smithsonian Institution and the development of American anthropology 1846-1910.* Washington, DC: Smithsonian Institution Press.

Kuper, Adam. 1975. *Anthropologists and anthropology: The British school, 1922-1972.* New York: Pica Press.

You may want to read original works by leading anthropologists, such as:

Malinowski, Bronislaw. 1922. *Argonauts of the Western Pacific.* New York: Dutton.

Mead, Margaret. 1928. *Coming of age in Samoa.* New York: Morrow.

Morgan, Lewis Henry. 1877. *Ancient society.* New York: Holt.

Steward, Julian. 1955. *Theory and culture change.* Urbana, IL: University of Illinois Press.

Stocking, George W., Jr., ed. 1974. *The shaping of American anthropology, 1883–1911: A Franz Boas Reader.* New York: Basic Books.

There are several biographies of well-known anthropologists:

Anshen, Ruth N., ed. 1979. *Letters from the field, 1925–1975: Letters of Margaret Mead.* New York: Harper & Row.

Douglas, Mary. 1980. *Edward Evans-Pritchard.* New York: Viking.

Mead, Margaret. 1972. *Blackberry winter: My early years.* New York: Morrow.

Resek, Carl. 1960. *Lewis Henry Morgan: American scholar.* Chicago: University of Chicago Press.

Steward, Julian H. 1973. *Alfred Kroeber.* New York: Columbia Univ. Press.

Chapter Three

Ethnographic Research

Preparing for Fieldwork
Choosing a Topic · Narrowing the Focus

Research Techniques
Participant Observation · Questioning
Probability Sampling

Conducting Fieldwork
Gaining Entry · Survival
Acquiring a Broader World View

The Field-worker's Social Responsibility

Summary

Suggested Readings

Focus on People
Living among the Nasioi of New Guinea

As anthropologists' theories have evolved, so have their methods of exploring the human condition around the world. Such research has always been hampered by a fundamental problem: When members of one culture come into contact with members of a very different culture, they have difficulty understanding one another.

This persistent difficulty has been more apparent when Europeans have come into contact with peoples whose life-styles are dissimilar to their own. Anthropology developed in large part out of the efforts of Europeans to understand, and govern, seemingly exotic peoples. But early nineteenth-century ethnographic descriptions and the information upon which generalizations and policies were formulated were often inadequate. Many of these early accounts reveal more about the observer than they do about the people being described. Charles Darwin, father of the idea of biological evolution, wrote a description of Australian Aborigines in the early 1800s that is typical of these early accounts:

A large tribe of natives, called the White Cockatoo men, happened to pay the settlement a visit while we were there. These men, as well as those of the tribe belonging to King George's Sound, being tempted by the offer of some tubs of rice and sugar, were pursuaded to hold a "corrobery," a great dancing-party. As soon as it grew dark, small fires were lighted, and the men commenced their toilet, which consisted in painting themselves in spots and lines. As soon as all was ready, large fires were kept blazing, round which the women and chil-

OVERLEAF
These drawings by a Yanomani Indian from the Amazon region of Brazil illustrate various animals and objects in the Yanomani myth about how the people got fire from the IYO ("ee-woe"), the large alligator-like creature in the center of this group.

dren were collected as spectators; the Cockatoo and King George's men formed two distinct parties, and generally danced in answer to each other. The dancing consisted in their running either sideways or in Indian file into an open space, and stamping the ground with great force as they marched together. Their heavy footsteps were accompanied by a kind of grunt, by beating their clubs and spears together, and by other gesticulations, such as extending their arms and wriggling their bodies. It was a most rude, barbarous scene, and, to our ideas, without any sort of meaning; but we observed the black women and children watched it with great pleasure. Perhaps these dances originally represented actions, such as wars and victories; there was one called the Emu dance, in which each man extended his arm in a bent manner, like the neck of that bird. In another dance, one man imitated the movement of a kangaroo grazing in the woods, whilst a second crawled up, and pretended to spear him. When both tribes mingled in the dance, the ground trembled with the heaviness of their steps, and the air resounded with their wild cries. Every one appeared in high spirits, and the group of nearly naked figures, viewed by the light of the blazing fires, all moving in hideous harmony, formed a perfect display of a festival amongst the lowest barbarians. [Darwin 1968: 450–51]

Undoubtedly, a foreign observer could have provided a similar description of dances in Darwin's Britain. Darwin does not provide much insight into the significance of the dances. However, the account does reveal Darwin's own prejudices, as indicated by his references to the people's primitiveness and his supposition that their dances had something to do with warfare.

Thanks to several decades of work by anthropologists, our understanding and appreciation of Australian Aboriginal culture has improved considerably. We now know that their body decorations have social and cultural significance

Anthropologist Francesca Merlan, a participant-observer in the highlands near Mt. Hagen, Papua, New Guinea.

and that the subject matter of such performances is related to complex beliefs about the nature of the world and their place in it. In the case of the dance Darwin witnessed, we know that only one group was involved, and that the performers were members of different subgroups known as the White Cockatoo and Crow. These names represent social divisions on the basis of which people are assigned complementary parts in dances and ceremonies.

We have a much clearer picture of the lives of other peoples today because of the research method of participant observation, developed by anthropologists over the past hundred years. In *participant observation*, a researcher lives with a people and observes their daily activities, learning how the group views the world and witnessing firsthand how they behave. This immersion in another culture ensures that groups other than our own are seen not only as sociological abstractions, but also as real people living within a complex setting.

To achieve an intimate understanding of a people, an anthropologist must spend more than a few days or weeks with them. Even after a year of systematic research among a people, communicating with them in their own language and sharing as much as possible in their lives, an anthropologist is only beginning to appreciate and understand their way of life. But only in this way can we start to understand what culture is all about and move away from static and stereotypic views of people.

Preparing for Fieldwork

While today's anthropologists may spend years living with the people they are studying, they may spend even longer preparing for their fieldwork. Their preparation includes the surprisingly complex matters of choosing a topic and narrowing its focus.

Choosing a Topic

Anthropologists' research interests are often triggered by their own life experiences. Anthropologist David Maybury-Lewis (1968: 13) describes the origins of his interest in South American Indians that eventually led him to live among the Shavante of Brazil:

As an undergraduate I once took a course in the discovery, conquest and settlement of Spanish America. I marvelled then at the skill of the early transatlantic navigators and at the audacity of the conquistadors; but what intrigued me the most were the first accounts of the American Indians. I conceived a romantic desire to know more about some of the people who had inspired such highly coloured narratives and who still, four hundred years later, seemed remote and exotic in a world jaded with travelogue.

Anthropologists who have been drawn to the discipline by their experiences with members of different cultures, such as service in the armed forces or Peace Corps, often choose to study those cultures. Decisions about specific research projects usually require more impersonal consideration, however. Projects may come about as a result of gaps in the ethnographic literature. In some areas of the world—the Amazon Basin, for example—the cultures of many peoples are practically unknown to us. In these places, the first priority for anthropologists is to fill out the "ethnographic map" of the area by doing holistic descriptions of these peoples, gathering information on such topics as their setting, history, technology, productive activities, food and drink, daily routines, sexual practices, social and political organization, medical beliefs, and religion.

Once a basic familiarity with the societies of a region has been established, in-depth research can follow. At this point, instead of addressing all aspects of a culture, the field-worker will focus upon a specific issue. Some examples: Waud Kracke (1978) chose political leadership as the topic of his study of the Kagwahiv of central Brazil, Stephen Hugh-Jones (1979) analyzed the religion of the Barasana by examining a men's secret cult, and Shelton Davis (1977) focused his work among Amazonian Indians on how economic development in the region is influencing their lives.

Studying Small, Isolated Societies. The choice of a research topic depends partly on what kind of society is being studied. The study of relatively isolated, nonindustrial societies has always been a major concern of anthropology. Studying these small-scale societies is important not only because we gain a more comprehensive view of the human condition in general, but also because these people are an important part of the contemporary world scene—a part that is often poorly understood. Many of these societies are undergoing rapid change and some of them have disappeared entirely in the face of the world's expanding industrial system. By drawing attention to nonindustrial peoples, anthropologists hope to increase Westerners' understanding of these groups, to alleviate their suffering, and to create conditions to allow for their survival.

Small-scale and large-scale societies are strikingly contrasted in these two scenes: an isolated Nuer village near the Ethiopian border and a busy street in Philadelphia.

Historically, small-scale societies were studied on a holistic basis, for their lack of specialization allowed anthropologists to see their cultural traits as parts of an integrated whole. Even today, with a greater emphasis on specific problem-oriented research, studies of small-scale societies continue to be general and holistic.

Studying Less Isolated Societies. Anthropologists also conduct fieldwork among less isolated people who are more integrated into the world system. Research among rural farmers or peasants began in the early part of this century. Studies of peasants became especially popular during the 1960s as a result of the Vietnam War, problems in India, and revolutionary movements in Latin America. Anthropologists have also carried out research in cities since the early days of the discipline; for example, the Women's Anthropological Society of Washington, D.C., conducted survey work in Washington's slums during the 1870s. The popularity of urban research surged after World War II, reflecting population shifts in many areas of traditional anthropological interest. In Africa, for example, the population of many cities more than doubled between 1950 and 1960—the people were moving to town and the anthropologists went with them.

To help fill in the ethnographic map of the contemporary world, anthropologists also study peoples who are incorporated into large-scale societies. These studies help us better understand specific countries and provide comparative general data about urban dwellers, peasants, factory workers, and other groups.

Until fairly recent times, studies of peasant villages or urban neighborhoods often treated such communities as if they existed in isolation, with little or no reference to social and economic relations beyond the local level. Contemporary anthropological studies, however, take into account the links between the community being studied and the wider society. Anthropologists see members of a particular community as actors in a local social setting and as participants in a much larger social system. Several large team projects have sought to look systematically at the different components of entire nations. One of these, led by Julian Steward (1956), was designed to analyze the major social components of Puerto Rican society. Members of the project selected a wide range of research settings, including coffee-growing and sugar-growing municipalities and privately and government-owned sugar plantations. Although individual researchers usually focus upon specific settings or problems in such projects, a sense of the larger whole is maintained by integration of the overall undertaking.

Narrowing the Focus

Once a topic is selected, an anthropologist must struggle with two theoretical problems: How might the information sought be explained? From whom should it be gathered?

Forming a Hypothesis. One of the primary aims of anthropology is to be able to explain why people act and think as they do. In pursuit of this goal anthropologists continually pose, test, and frequently reformulate hypotheses.

A *hypothesis* is a statement that something observed, such as a pattern of behavior, is associated with and caused by a particular set of factors. An anthropologist may observe, for example, that people are moving from rural areas to a city. A hypothetical explanation might be that two major factors are causing this shift: employment possibilities in the country are declining due to the mechanization of farming, and opportunities for employment are being created in the city because of an increasing demand for industrial and service workers.

To test the hypothesis, an anthropologist collects and analyzes ethnographic data. On the basis of these data a researcher rejects or accepts the validity of the hypothesis or recognizes the need to modify it. In trying to explain rural-urban migration, an anthropologist would probably find that other factors, such as improved transportation and the desire for better education, contribute to the process. He or she might also want to discover the reasons behind farm mechanization and urban industrialization. This would mean posing a new set of hypotheses. This process of posing, testing, and reformulating hypotheses provides a framework for anthropological research and also sharpens the discipline's theoretical perspective.

Anthropologists often pose hypotheses to test whether findings in a specific setting have wider applicability. David Aberle (1966), who conducted research among the Navajo, extended his specific research findings to a consideration of the wider consequences of people's responses to a religious movement. In the 1930s, the Bureau of Indian Affairs determined that many of the Navajo pasturelands were becoming eroded because of overgrazing. The bureau then ordered significant reduction in livestock, the mainstay of the Navajo economy. The measure was designed to protect the long-term interests of the Navajo, but in the short run, the policy nearly bankrupted some of the sheepherders. Aberle found that those most affected by reductions in herd size tended to join the Native American Church, which stressed the use of peyote as a means of gaining access to supernatural power. Moreover, Navajo who had become more integrated into mainstream American culture were less likely to join the Native American Church than those who were more traditional in outlook. These findings led Aberle to hypothesize that the type of religious movement to be found among oppressed peoples in general was dependent upon how they were incorporated into the wider social and economic system. He argued that "transformative" movements that preach withdrawal from the world will be found where people's traditional life-styles have been severely disrupted and where the disruption of traditional life and forced incorporation into a largely alien society are not accompanied by an acceptable new social status for the population. Testing such a hypothesis requires research in other settings and provides stimulus and direction for further fieldwork.

Determining Whom to Question. If, like David Aberle, a researcher decides to study the Navajo, he or she must ask some very fundamental questions. Who are the Navajo? Should only those living on the reservation be included, or should the study include Navajo who live in nearby towns or more distant cities? Should all individuals who consider themselves Navajo be included, even if they are not considered Navajo by a majority of those around them? Should persons be studied who do not consider themselves to be Navajo, but who by some standards such as kinship or cultural heritage are considered Navajo? Deciding whom to study is not as simple as it may seem.

The people a researcher decides to include in a study are called its *population*. A population may be determined by any of several criteria. One is the nature of the problem being addressed. If an anthropologist is interested in studying urban migration, for example, he or she would select persons who had migrated to cities, or those who had *not* migrated, or both. In narrowing the focus of the research the population might be determined on the basis of one or more other criteria: location or length of residence in the city, place of origin, ethnicity, social class, religious affiliation, or occupation. To study how people with strong ethnic traditions adapted to urban life, Edward Bruner (1973) looked at the members of a particular ethnic group, the Toba Batak, who had moved from the northern highlands of Sumatra to a particular coastal city, Medan. Selection of the population to be studied may also be influenced by social, residential, or environmental characteristics of the area being studied. A researcher may select as an appropriate population a village, valley dwellers, or a group of kin because these appear to be relevant units of analysis in the particular context.

A third basis for selection of a population might be local ways of classifying people. Bruner's decision to emphasize ethnicity in his study of urban migration was influenced by the fact that many urban-dwelling Indonesians consider ethnicity important. The use of locally inspired categories is an important means of deriving research populations, but we should be aware that they may not be the only appropriate ones. Bruner discovered that the importance of ethnicity in adaptation of Indonesian migrants to city life varies. For some Toba Batak, ethnicity significantly influences many aspects of their lives and most of their social relations are with other Toba Batak. For others ethnicity is not especially relevant and they build extensive social ties with non-Batak.

Thus, the concept of population must be a flexible one. Part of this flexibility involves recognition that the study of a particular group of people may require talking to others who influence or interact with them. An understanding of Toba Batak adaptation to life in Medan requires talking to more than just Toba Batak. The researcher must also know something of the non-Batak merchants and politicians who affect the adaptational process of the Batak.

Research Techniques

Precisely how anthropologists conduct their investigations depends upon a variety of factors. One is the setting of the fieldwork. Urban research poses problems that are quite distinct from those encountered on a small Pacific island. In the city the researcher is faced with problems associated with the greater number and variety of people, while on the Pacific island an important concern may be finding enough to eat, or trying to avoid tropical diseases. A second factor is the personal inclinations and theoretical biases of the researcher. Researchers with a psychological or cognitive perspective are likely to conduct their fieldwork differently from those who stress social behavior and interaction: the first emphasize people's statements and ideas, whereas the second focus on people's actual behavior. A third factor is the problem being studied. There is no single formula for anthropological fieldwork; each problem and research setting is distinct and anthropologists rely on different approaches in different projects. Nevertheless, some general characteristics are common to most anthropological research: observing, questioning, and probability sampling.

Participant Observation

An understanding of culture requires attention to both how people perceive the world and how they behave in it. But people's statements about their activities are not always accurate or sufficient explanations of their behavior. Whether consciously or subconsciously, an informant's reporting of events is likely to be selective and distorted; if at all possible, the researcher should also view people's behavior directly. Even direct observation does not ensure objectivity, however, for anthropologists

themselves are not without their own biases.

To appreciate the complexity of culture, an ethnographer must initially record events and conditions in as much detail as possible; selection and the search for patterns can come later. Recording people's behavior thoroughly and systematically requires certain skills. Learning to take notes quickly and unobtrusively under less than ideal conditions is useful. Anthropologists also often use cameras and tape recorders. Such aids may pose technical problems, such as trying to keep a tape recorder working in a tropical rain forest. They may pose social difficulties as well: people may not want their pictures taken or their statements recorded. In each setting the anthropologist must learn the most appropriate way to obtain accurate records of a people's actions and statements.

All people have restrictions about who may see many of their actions, and the field-worker must show respect for the privacy and wishes of the people being studied. Some activities may be closed not only to outsiders, but also to particular members within a society. While many rules may not apply to the anthropologist, he or she should take care to learn the cultural rules that will affect research. Overzealous attempts to view restricted behavior can easily ruin or terminate a research project, not to mention violating the right to privacy.

What anthropologists are allowed to observe in a society may change over time. Many Australian Aboriginal societies, for example, have strict limitations governing who may observe or participate in religious functions. In the past, after building up sufficient rapport with the people, anthropologists were usually allowed to attend and even photograph the most sacred of these. As long as they had little direct contact with members of any society besides their own, the Aborigines did not care what the anthropologists did with this material. In recent years, however, as Aborigines have become more integrated into Australian society, they have become upset to see pictures of secret rituals and sacred objects in print. Today, many Aborigines are much more cautious about allowing anthropologists to view their rites. Anthropologists have been responsive to their concerns and have tried to limit public access to the collected material that Aborigines deemed sensitive.

Questioning

Charles Darwin's misrepresentation of Australian Aboriginal dancing demonstrates how difficult it is to understand the meaning of an observed behavior without talking to the participants. Accordingly, much of anthropological research consists of asking people questions about their actions. The level of questioning depends upon the anthropologist's prior knowledge of a culture. Upon being introduced to a new and relatively unknown culture the anthropologist is likely to ask very basic questions, about where people live or how kin should behave toward one another. When he or she feels sufficiently at home in the culture to graduate to more sophisticated ideas, the researcher moves on to subtler questions, such as how the population deals with variations in expected behavior, why some behavior seems contradictory, and why people live where they do.

At the outset of fieldwork, it is not always possible to know the language or languages spoken, and it may be necessary to rely upon interpreters. Fortunately, anthropologists can often begin their language training before leaving for the field. Some universities have native speakers on their staffs who help train prospective researchers, and language tapes and written material are usually available. Learning the rudiments of a language in advance saves time and helps to avoid some of the initial difficulties associated with entering a foreign culture. When advance preparation of this kind is not possible, anthropologists spend the early period of their fieldwork striving to become fluent in a new language.

Asking questions takes more than simply learning basic grammar. The field-worker must also learn *how* to ask questions in a culture. Most cultures have prescribed ways of asking questions, often depending upon the nature of the question and the relative status of the person being addressed. The social setting within which the question is being asked may also be important. For example, it may be considered bad form to bring up a particular topic in the presence of children or females. Or the question, "Is sorcery practiced in your village?" may not be appropriate in a formal interview, especially if a sorcerer is among those present.

Formal Questioning. Although sensitive topics are best discussed in informal conversation, some questions can be dealt with systematically. Anthropologists use structured questionnaires to provide them with survey data on such topics as residential and landholding patterns, the distribution of wealth and income within a population, and people's attitudes or beliefs on topics ranging from religion to kinship. The questions asked may require a specific answer ("How old are you?") or they may be more open-ended ("How do you feel about Mexican-American employees?").

Before a questionnaire can be used in a meaningful way the anthropologist must have some experience with or knowledge of the culture. Dutch anthropologist Hans Dagmar describes the process that preceded his formal questioning of Aborigines living around the Australian community of Carnarvon (1978: 13–14):

During the first two months of fieldwork I collected material solely by means of participant observation including numerous informal

Anthropologist Margaret Kieffer questions a Mayan Indian weaver in Santiago Atitlán, a town on the south shore of Lake Atitlán, southwest Guatemala.

talks and unstructured interviews. After about two months I was able to draw up a list of almost all aboriginal households in the area. From this list I then made a selection of households the adult members (i.e., 18 years and older) of which I planned to interview with open-ended questions. In this I enquired into factual matters such as knowledge of Aboriginal culture, kinship relations, housing, education, employment, income and participation in voluntary associations and asked for opinions about Aboriginal traditional culture, internal relations within the Aboriginal community, the Aboriginal position in the institutions of the wider community and relationships with *Whites including such associations of Whites as government departments. . . .*

Since it was of great importance to conduct these interviews in a genial atmosphere I took extra care to be properly introduced to my respondents. Most of them I had become acquainted with during the first months of my stay in Carnarvon and to those I did not know well enough I asked to be introduced by a close relative or good friend.

Informal Questioning. Even when formal techniques are used, anthropologists usually derive a great deal of information in a less formal manner. Julia Crane and Michael Angrosino (1974: 56-57) point out that anthropologists' best interviews are often the result of chance encounters. One of them, while in the field, noticed an old man out in front of his house gathering stones and arranging them in patterns. His daughter-in-law was in labor, he told the anthropologist, and newborn babies were especially susceptible to wandering demons who might have been sent by family enemies. The stones would keep any such demons from entering. Through this chance encounter the anthropologist gained insight into the people's beliefs concerning the supernatural, social relationships within the family, and village factionalism.

Similarly, when Michael Howard began work in southern Belize with Mayan Indians he made little effort to gather information concerning their traditional religious beliefs, as the existing literature told him that these beliefs had largely disappeared. Initially this view was supported, as the people seemed rarely to discuss such things. One evening, however, while he was visiting one of the older members of the village, one of the younger persons present asked for a story. The "story" turned out to be a Mayan creation myth. This and similar events caused the researcher to pay more attention to traditional religious beliefs and practices. As a result of his informal questioning, a very different picture of the beliefs of these people slowly emerged, one in which many traditional aspects of their religion continued to play an important role.

Probability Sampling

The picture painted by formal and informal questioning is most valid when all or even a sizable proportion of the population is questioned. But when the population is large, interviewing everyone may be impossible. To avoid collecting data from a nonrepresentative segment of a large population, the anthropologist can use *probability sampling*, selecting a segment of the population whose responses will be taken as a miniature, relatively unbiased replica of the larger population.

One basic sampling technique is the *random sample*. This method involves selecting for questioning a significant number of persons from the entire population. To ensure that the sample is as random and unbiased as possible, all members of the population should have an equal chance of being selected. For example, all names could be placed in a hat and the desired number to be questioned drawn out. A random sample is best used when dealing with a relatively homogeneous population, such as a group of army recruits coming from similar areas and backgrounds. Ideally, a researcher will interview a wide enough spectrum of people to gain a general impression of how the population as a whole would have responded to the questions.

When a population contains a number of distinct subgroups, the researcher may wish to collect data separately from each one. This is called a *stratified sample*. In studying a small Pakistani village, John Honigmann (1970: 277) determined in an initial survey that the population was stratified into six levels: noncultivating landlords; cultivating landlords; tenant cultivators; craftsmen, tradesmen, and domestic servants; Marwari, a Hindu enclave in this otherwise Moslem community; and transient Brahui speakers living on the village outskirts. Consequently, Honigmann used a stratified sample of forty subjects from each of these categories.

In certain efforts, such as trying to reconstruct the history of a people from oral sources, anthropologists employ *judgment sampling*. Rather than talking to everyone or to some randomly selected population, they collect data from a limited number of *key informants* who have been selected on the basis of criteria deemed critical to the research; age, sex, education, experience, reputation for reliability, or length of residence in a particular locale. Michael Howard used a judgment sampling when he tried to piece together a history of Australian Aborigines living in and around the city of Perth (1981). After reviewing the limited amount of written material available (newspaper accounts, diaries, government reports), he surveyed the local Aboriginal population to discover as many likely informants as possible. Preliminary interviews with those who could be reached and were willing to be questioned allowed him to collect information on a range of basic topics and to narrow the sample to those who seemed most knowledgeable and reliable for further interviewing on specific topics.

Conducting Fieldwork

In addition to the scientific requirements of choosing a topic, observing, and questioning, anthropological fieldwork requires unusual personal adjustments. Participant observation is not carried out with the detachment typical of most academic research. The fieldwork setting is not a library or a laboratory; the objects of study are not on printed pages or under a microscope. They are other human beings with whom the anthropologist must live and interact. The intensity of social relations brought about by this type of research leads to emotional commitments and to unique ethical dilemmas. To leave the university and become immersed in a very different world, the anthropologist must learn new rules of behavior and new means of physical and psychological survival.

Gaining Entry

Rarely can anthropologists simply move into an area and start their research immediately. To begin with, the governments and institutions of many countries require some form of research permit. Obtaining one may be little more than a formality, or it may take months or years. On the positive side, this practice of prior clearance helps to ensure that research by outsiders reflects the perceived needs of the country or group being studied rather than exclusively those of the researcher. Anthropologists are also often required to deposit copies of their edited notes and papers in national archives or libraries, so that the results of their work will be available in the host area. On the other hand, such control may be used as a form of censorship to forestall research that may be critical of the interests of a particular segment of a society (such as its wealthy elite).

Gaining official permission to work with a people does not ensure successful research. Since anthropological research requires delving into the most intimate parts of a people's culture, the researcher must establish good rapport with his subjects. Successful fieldwork is rarely possible without the people's support. The anthropologist must convince the people that he or she does not represent a threat to their well-being, and be as honest as possible about their research aims. Given an honest opportunity to decide whether they want to be studied, people will not later feel they have been tricked into something. Honesty in this matter is also important for the sake of future research in the area.

Convincing people that the researcher is not a threat can be far from easy. Gerald Berreman (1972: xx) found that the Indian hill people, Pahari, were very suspicious of outsiders. Most of the outsiders who contact the Pahari are government agents, despised and feared for their extortions and interference with local affairs. Berreman notes, "As the variety of officials has proliferated, any stranger . . . may be a government agent, and as such he is potentially troublesome and even dangerous." Many people have only a limited number of categories for outsiders—government official, missionary, bandit. Such unflattering categories often limit interaction to superficial interchanges.

To escape negative stereotyping, the field-worker must get beyond the role of outsider and be brought more closely into local society. Complete incorporation is usually impossible, and from the standpoint of maintaining objectivity it is undesirable. But the anthropologist may be able to occupy a position somewhere between outsider and native. Berreman found that after he stayed four months in the Pahari village and made a speech about the need for Americans and Indians to know one another better, opposition to his presence began to wane. "Although I remained alien and was never made to feel that my presence in the village was actively desired by most of its members, I was thereafter tolerated with considerable indulgence" (Berreman 1972: xxvii). Many initial problems disappear over time as the field-worker's actions come to seem less exotic and as it becomes clear that no harm has come about as a result of his or her presence.

Survival

When fieldwork is carried out in poor and very isolated areas, mere physical survival can be a problem for the anthropologist. Even when conditions are not so severe, decisions about what to eat and where to live may have important effects on the research.

Isolation from markets may make procurement of food difficult. Maybury-Lewis (1968: 52) describes dining with his wife on gathered fruit and rice begrudgingly provided by a Sherente villager in Brazil:

Both of us ate ravenously, ignoring the children who gathered to watch the performance. I could feel my stomach distending as I forced more and more food into it. It was a habit we had learned since our arrival. When there is

food, eat as much as you can. You never know when you will eat again. A couple of lean days had persuaded us of the truth of this unspoken aphorism. Today we had the sensation which the Sherente cherish and which is much celebrated in their stories: the pleasure of feeling our bellies grow big with food.

Sometimes it is possible to bring large quantities of food into the field, but doing so creates other problems. It hinders rapport with the people by stressing the anthropologist's relative wealth. Also, one who has such a surplus is usually expected to share these goods with the people. Not to do so is considered bad manners. Stocks meant to last for months may therefore dwindle quickly. In some circumstances, the aims of a research project can interfere with food sharing. When Richard Lee (1969) studied foraging and food distribution among a group of Bushmen in the Kalahari Desert, the objectives of his study forced him into the role of miser, standing apart from the Bushman's customs of sharing. This made other aspects of his research more difficult to carry out. An alternative is to live off the land in a similar way as the people being studied. One difficulty with this option is that the field-worker may strain an already overexploited environment. Problems like these usually arise only in extreme circumstances, however; most field-workers are able to strike a balance between dependence on local and imported foods.

Deciding where to live and what to live in during fieldwork depends upon a number of factors. A primary one is the type of society being studied. Most desert-dwelling Australian Aborigines now live in relatively stable settlements; anthropologists who live with them frequently use trailers. With more mobile foragers, like those of the Amazonian region of South America who live in very temporary camps, anthropologists often live much as the people do, keeping their possessions to a minimum.

When an anthropologist is studying village or town dwellers, he must decide whether to live with a family or to establish a separate household. Living with a family may allow greater insight into a people's daily activities, but the field-worker's close ties with that family may inhibit other social relations. In the case of forest dwellers who all reside in a single longhouse or Inuit living in a communal icehouse there may be no choice. Even in a village with a large number of individual households, no one may be willing to take in an outsider. Surplus houses may also be in short supply. Berreman (1972: 3)

shared a three-room house that was "inferior to those inhabited by most villagers" with two to four water buffalo. A researcher may even have to construct a house.

Sometimes anthropologists must cope with health problems. A radical change in environment or diet frequently necessitates a period of adjustment accompanied by intestinal disorders. More severe diseases, such as malaria and yellow fever, abound in some research areas. While personal illness may be a way of gaining firsthand knowledge about a people's curing practices, or their sympathy, there are rarely any other benefits. In fact, by becoming ill the anthropologist may be perceived by the people as

Anthropologist Richard Lee setting up a field camp in the arid Kalahari Desert, South Africa.

a threat, as Charles Wagley (1977: 16) discovered while conducting research among the Tapirapé of Brazil. "The Tapirapé are not compassionate toward a visitor to their village when he is ill; they become nervous, fearing retaliation if he should die, and they fear that his disease will spread, as well it might." An anthropologist can minimize health problems by knowing what to expect and carrying a supply of preventive medicines and remedies. In preparing a fieldwork schedule, a wise researcher allows for time lost because of illness.

Field-workers often undergo mental strains as well. For many, the initial period of entry is a difficult and anxious time. Fear of failure and of not gaining rapport with the people are common. The researcher may not know the rules of behavior in the new culture, and may find it difficult to know how people are interpreting his or her actions and statements. In many ways the beginnng field-worker is a clumsy and not particularly knowledgeable child—a status that is hard for most university-educated adults to accept. The psychic distress caused by the strain of adjusting to a different culture is referred to as *culture shock.*

Although initial anxiety usually wears off as the field-worker's understanding of the people and their culture improves, psychological stress often persists. The intensity of social interaction required by participant observation in a small, closely knit society may be hard to handle for a person raised in an urban society where more individual autonomy and privacy is allowed. To escape the strain of being continually "on stage," researchers periodically get away from the fieldwork setting.

Not all anthropologists encounter all these problems. Some individuals adjust better to stressful situations than others, and some fieldwork conditions are simply easier than others. Even the most trying research, however, is not without personal and intellectual rewards. In time, anthropologists become accepted by most

of the peoples they study, and often develop true friendships with them. And learning about another society is a worthwhile endeavor that adds to our understanding of the diversity of human experience.

Acquiring a Broader World View

During the early part of this century, under the influence of Franz Boas and Bronislaw Malinowski, fieldwork became established as the "rite of passage" for aspiring anthropologists. It transformed the neophyte into a full-fledged practitioner. What the student of anthropology had learned from books and lectures was put to the test and given a grounding in the world beyond the university. Many anthropologists feel that their work is not simply a job; it is, "with music and mathematics, one of the few true vocations" (Lévi-Strauss 1961: 58). And it is ethnographic fieldwork that provides entry into this vocation.

In addition to promoting professionalism and producing ethnographic data, fieldwork may also play a role in consciousness raising. Ideally, participant observation forces the fieldworker to examine his or her assumptions about the world carefully. Participant observation extends people's view of the world, revealing the complexity of human existence and the variety of possible interpretations of situations. People who were strangers or mere abstractions become real in a way not possible through films, books, or television.

In a poor southern Tunisian village we'll call "Shebika," a number of young Tunisian researchers found their education and beliefs put to a rude test by the realities of the villagers' struggle for existence on the edge of the desert. Plans for development that had seemed logical and simple to put into practice in the capital city lost validity in Shebika. The group of researchers "lost the typically optimistic self-assurance which it had picked up from the rul-

An example of early fieldwork—W. J. McGee logging examples of Seri vocabulary at Encinas Ranch, Gulf of California, Sonora, Mexico (1895).

ing class in the capital city and realized what a gap there is between political programme and social reality" (Duvignaud 1970: 213). Their fieldwork taught them that plans for change had little chance for success if they were not based upon a thorough understanding of people through participant observation.

The harsh reality of life in Shebika also made more tangible the concept of the unity of humankind. Shebika's inhabitants were flesh-and-blood people. Along with this recognition came one of obligation—"We can't but feel responsible for these people who are part of ourselves" (Duvignaud 1970: 218). Fieldwork, then, may not only increase the researcher's awareness of the realities of poverty and the difficulties of bringing about change, but also can bring home more imperatively the desperate need for changes. Unlike the humanism of the distant intellectual, that of the anthropologist who has done fieldwork is grounded in practical experience and an awareness of concrete situations.

The anthropologist's probing and systematic questioning can lead people to look at and reflect on their culture more carefully. The process of consciousness raising among the researched is exemplified by Colombian anthropologist Gerardo Reichel-Dolmatoff's work with Antonio Guzmán, a Desana Indian from the isolated Vaupes region of Colombia. Guzmán was educated by missionaries and he attended high school. He served in the army and eventually moved to Bogota, the capital of Colombia. Unlike many persons of Indian origin, he never sought to hide his Indianness. He had sought "to find a balance, a way of life that would permit him to become a member of Colombia Creole culture without losing his identity as a native Indian" (Reichel-Dolmatoff 1971: xiv). As he sought with Reichel-Dolmatoff to make sense of the Desana belief system, Antonio Guzmán began to discover "for himself relationships in his own culture that he had not consciously established before" (1971: xix).

There can be no doubt that for the informant this work involved a profound self-analysis and a detailed reevaluation of his traditional culture and of the urban civilization to which he was becoming acculturated. Everything that was discussed during our interviews necessarily reaffirmed his traditional attitudes and put him, up to certain point, in conflict with his present way of life and his ambitions for urban education. Now, while describing and discussing his own culture, he discovered in it values and goals that, under the influence of his formal schooling, he had denied but whose permanent validity manifested itself with more and more insistence. [Reichel-Dolmatoff 1971: xx]

In this instance the informant not only gained insights into the nature of his Indian culture, but he also gained a greater appreciation of the value of this culture in the modern world, something his Western education had sought to undermine.

The Field-worker's Social Responsibility

By and large, anthropologists hope that the data they gather will benefit humanity. Anthropologists also generally feel obligated to help the people among whom they have lived and studied, the people who have befriended and assisted them in their work. It is not always easy, however, to tell whether anthropologists' actions are really helpful, and long-term consequences are often difficult to predict.

Cora DuBois conducted research in the village of Atimelang on the Indonesian island of Alor in 1938. While many of her findings were of interest to her professional colleagues, the fieldwork itself was not out of the ordinary. She had done no apparent harm to the people by the time she left and she had taught them a little about the outside world, providing the villagers with a bit of excitement. In 1942 the Japanese occupied the island of Alor.

Word reached the Japanese command in Kalabahi that the village leaders of Atimelang were claiming that America would win the war. This could have been nothing but the most innocent fantasy to my friends in Atimelang since they had never even heard of the United States prior to my arrival. But to the Japanese, suffering from all the nervous apprehensions of any oc-cupying power in a strange and therefore threatening environment, such talk could only mean rebellion ... so the Japanese sent troops to arrest five of my friends in Atimelang. ... In Kalabahi they were publicly decapitated as a warning to the populace.

There is no end to the intricate chain of responsibility and guilt that the pursuit of even the most arcane social research involves. [DuBois 1960: xiv–xv]

Anthropologists have to be sensitive to the potentially adverse effects of their work. By acting as informants for government administrators or corporate employees who want information about isolated regions of their country and its cultural minorities, anthropologists can benefit the people with whom they are working, correcting misinformation or acting as spokesmen on their behalf. But they may also unwittingly supply information that can be used against people. Anthropologists are privy to information about such illegal activities as smuggling, tax evasion, and the brewing of illegal beer. It is their duty to maintain confidentiality regarding the sources of such sensitive data and not to make public information that is likely to harm people.

Discretion is also required in publishing the results of fieldwork. While the majority of anthropological publications have not had harmful effects on people, this is not always the case. In publishing a comprehensive account of a society, anthropologists may include data that for the sake of the society would better have been left out. In a recent account of a poor African society displaced from its original homeland the author noted that a significant part of the economy is concerned with the smuggling of stolen cattle. The account is sufficiently detailed to allow government agents to move against the smugglers, an inexcusable blunder in an anthropological work.

A basic issue highlighted by the above example concerns the audience anthropologists address. While academics and some other citizens of industrial nations are the primary readers of anthropological writing, those we study may also read our accounts. Many people once labeled "illiterate primitives" now read, and most former colonies now boast institutions of higher education and even anthropology programs. It is important that anthropologists from industrial countries make their data available to these people. Anthropologists today are careful to see that their work gets back to the national archives of countries where they worked and if possible to the residents of the actual communities. Some have written books in the local language to be read and distributed among the people who were studied.

Field-workers must also be sensitive to the source of their funding. Most anthropological research is supported by universities, government agencies like the National Institute of Mental Health and the Atomic Energy Commission, or private organizations such as the Rockefeller Foundation. In most instances anthropologists are confronted with few ethical dilemmas by the sources of their financial support. But, as several anthropologists who worked in Thailand during the 1960s discovered, serious ethical problems can arise. These anthropologists were funded by a government agency to conduct fieldwork among isolated hill-dwelling peoples. The prospect was appealing because ethnographic data on these people was sparse. Eventually the anthropologists learned that the information they were collecting was being used for military purposes. Several anthropologists, feeling that their work was not in the best interests of anthropology or of the people with whom they had been working, quit the project (see Jones 1971).

One of the issues raised in the Thailand situation is the propriety of secrecy in anthropological fieldwork. Is it *ever* proper for anthropologists to hide from the people they are studying the sources of their support, the purpose of their research, and the uses to which it might be put? Most anthropologists consider it imperative that persons who are the object of anthropological research be provided with a clear understanding of these things from the outset. Secrecy about such matters is ethically questionable and harmful to the reputation of anthropology.

Summary

Cultural anthropologists' principal method of conducting research is participant observation, which requires that a researcher live with the people he or she is studying. The anthropologist begins by selecting a general area of interest. Anthropologists gather information on relatively isolated small-scale societies as well as different segments of large-scale societies. Then they focus upon specific topics and locales for fieldwork.

Preliminary research is usually very general. Once anthropologists have a fairly good idea of the nature of the area, they begin to focus upon more specific problems in their research. They formulate hypotheses to explain what they expect to find and define the population to be studied.

In actually conducting participant observation research anthropologists often face physical difficulties in recording information and social constraints regarding what they may view or record. A good deal of fieldwork consists of asking questions and anthropologists must learn the appropriate ways to question people in a society. Anthropologists ask questions formally through questionnaires as well as informally through conversations. Since it is not always possible or desirable to speak to everyone in a population, anthropologists frequently resort to probability sampling techniques—random sampling, stratified sampling, or judgment sampling.

Anthropologists must always get the permission of the people to be studied to conduct their fieldwork, and sometimes that of government or institutional officials as well. Since the anthropologist is to live among the people being studied it is essential that he or she build good relations with them.

There are a number of problems associated with living in the field, related to food, residence, health, and mental stress. But fieldwork turns people into full-fledged anthropologists, and it can also help broaden their view of the world in a very concrete way.

It is often difficult to assess the consequences of an anthropologist's work. To avoid possible ill effects for the people studied, anthropologists must be very careful about the disposition of the information they gather. Their responsibility also includes ensuring that the people they study have access to the results of the research.

Having reviewed the basics of anthropology, we now look at what anthropology has produced in terms of a picture and understanding of the human condition. Chapter 4 starts with that fundamental element of human culture, language.

Suggested Readings

Among the more general books of anthropological methods are:

Crane, Julia G., and Angrosino, Michael V. 1974. *Field projects in anthropology: A student handbook.* Morristown, NJ: General Learning Press.

Edgerton, Robert B., and Langness, L. L. 1974. *Methods and styles in the study of culture.* San Francisco: Chandler and Sharp.

Epstein, A. L., ed. 1967. *The craft of social anthropology.* London: Tavistock Publications.

Foster, George M., et al., eds. 1979. *Long-term field research in social anthropology.* New York: Academic Press.

Freilich, Morris, ed. 1970. *Marginal natives: Anthropologists at work.* New York: Harper & Row.

Jongmans, D. G., and Gutkind, P. C. W., eds. 1967. *Anthropologists in the field.* Assen: Van Gorcum.

Pelto, Perti J., and Gretal H. 1978. *Anthropological research: The structure of inquiry.* Cambridge: Cambridge Univ. Press.

Spradley, James P. 1980. *Participant observation.* New York: Holt, Rinehart & Winston.

There are a number of valuable personal accounts of fieldwork, including:

Alland, Alexander, Jr. 1976. *When the spider danced: Notes from an African village.* New York: Doubleday/Anchor.

Bowen, Elenore S. 1964. *Return to laughter: An anthropological novel.* New York: Doubleday/American Museum of Natural History. (set in West Africa)

Dumont, Jean-Paul. 1978. *The headman and I: Ambiguity and ambivalence in the fieldwork experience.* Austin: University of Texas Press. (set in Amazonian South America)

Fernea, Elizabeth W. 1969. *Guests of the Sheik: An ethnography of an Iraqi village.* New York: Doubleday/Anchor.

————. 1976. *A street in Marrakech.* New York: Doubleday/Anchor. (fieldwork among Moroccan women)

Huxley, Francis. 1957. *Affable savages: An anthropologist among the Urubu Indians of Brazil.* New York: Viking.

Malinowski, Bronislaw. 1967. *A diary in the strict sense of the term.* London: Routledge and Kegan Paul. (early fieldwork in Melanesia)

Maybury-Lewis, David. 1968. *The savage and the innocent.* Boston: Beacon Press. (fieldwork in Central Brazil)

Mead, Margaret. 1977. *Letters from the field: 1925-1975.* New York: Harper & Row. (fieldwork in the Pacific)

Mitchell, William E. 1978. *The bamboo fire: An anthropologist in New Guinea.* New York: Norton.

Powdermaker, Hortense. 1966. *Stranger and friend: The ways of an anthropologist.* New York: Norton.

Rabinow, Paul. 1977. *Reflections on fieldwork in Morocco.* Berkeley: University of California Press.

Read, Kenneth E. 1980. *The high valley.* New York: Columbia Univ. Press. (fieldwork in New Guinea)

Slater, Mariam K. 1976. *African odyssey: An anthropological adventure.* New York: Doubleday/Anchor. (fieldwork in East Africa)

For those interested in anthropologists' informants see:

Casagrande, Joseph B., ed. 1960. *In the company of man: Twenty portraits of anthropological informants.* New York: Harper & Row.

Among the books dealing specifically with ethical questions are:

Barnes, John A. 1980. *Who should know what? Social science, privacy and ethics.* Cambridge: Cambridge Univ. Press.

Cassell, Joan, and Wax, Murray L. 1980. *Ethical problems of fieldwork.* Special issue of *Social problems,* vol. 27, no. 3.

Horowitz, I. ed. 1967. *The rise and fall of Project Camelot: Studies in the relationship between social science and practical politics.* Cambridge, MA: M.I.T. Press.

Huizer, Gerrit, and Mannheim, Bruce, eds. 1979. *The politics of anthropology.* The Hague/Paris: Mouton.

Rynkiewich, Michael A., and Spradley, James K., eds. 1976. *Ethics and anthropology—Dilemmas in fieldwork.* New York: Wiley.

Wax, Rosalie, ed. 1971. *Doing fieldwork: Warnings and advice.* Chicago: University of Chicago Press.

Focus on People

Living among the Nasioi of New Guinea

Eugene Ogan

As a teenager, Eugene Ogan developed a deep interest in the Pacific Islands and in the people who live there. After graduating from the University of California, Berkeley, with a B.A. in anthropology, Ogan went on to graduate study in anthropology at Harvard University; as part of his doctoral work, Ogan went to Bougainville, an island off the eastern coast of New Guinea, in 1962 to study the customs of villagers who spoke the Nasioi language. The rapid pace of culture change, especially in connection with the development of a copper mine on Nasioi land, brought him back again and again; between 1962 and 1978, he lived for almost five years in Bougainville, New Guinea, and the Solomon Islands. He still writes to, and about, his Nasioi friends.

IN APRIL OF 1962, a United Nations team visited the island of Bougainville as part of its tour of the Trust Territory of New Guinea. During a public meeting at the administrative center in Kieta, a number of Nasioi men spoke out about their dissatisfaction with the Australians who administered the territory. They said that Australians treated them "like dogs," and asked that the UN turn Bougainville over to the United States, since American servicemen had made a favorable impression during World War II.

Unaware of this incident, I arrived in Kieta six months later, the first anthropologist ever to live among the Nasioi for an extended period. I was most concerned to make clear my purpose—to study "custom"—but was equally, if unthinkingly, clear about my American nationality. This caused Nasioi to perceive me as an agent of the American government, sent in response to their complaints. As a result, villagers offered to build me a house free of charge, so that I could move from the government rest house used by officers on patrol. I was grateful for this unexpected hospitality. Only after several months did I begin to understand Nasioi feelings about the situation in which they found themselves. As my understanding increased, so did my sympathy, but so too did my frustration that I could not help them as they expected.

Bougainville had been claimed by Germany as part of its New Guinea colony in 1886, and in 1902, missionaries, administrators, and planters began to settle on Nasioi land in the southeastern portion of the island. The Germans yielded in 1914 to the Australians, who were in turn driven out by the Japanese in World War II. The Allies took back the island, and Australian administration was restored under a UN trusteeship.

The version of this colonial history given repeatedly by Nasioi men was rather different:

When my grandfather was alive and my father

was a little boy, the Germans came. They gave us steel axes and cloth to cover our bodies. Then the Australians chased away the Germans and the Japanese chased away the Australians. The Americans chased away the Japanese so the Australians could come back. Now my grandfather is dead, my father is old, and I am a man. And what do we have? Still nothing more than steel axes and sarongs.

Nasioi struggled to understand how these aliens came to possess all the material wealth they enjoyed, but did not share with villagers. Nasioi had neither seen, nor been effectively taught about, the manufacture of such things as motor vehicles or cotton cloth. Because their traditional culture emphasized supernatural assistance in economic affairs, during the 1960s they worked out mission-influenced explanations for the differences between their lives and those of their colonizer "masters."

A middle-aged man: *You white people have so much and know so much. I think it's because your ancestors saw Jesus.*

A boy with some education: *You are like my father, and I know you will tell me the truth. Where does money really come from? It comes from God, doesn't it?*

A man trying to organize new forms of cooperative enterprise: *You say that LandRovers are made from a kind of stone [iron ore] found in the ground. Ah, but how did that stone come to be in the white man's ground? Didn't the ancestors put it there?*

During my first field trip in 1962–64, I was unable to provide villagers with a Western view of these issues. Questions and opinions like those above are often described in anthropological literature under the derogatory term "cargo cult." Actually they were perfectly reasonable, given traditional Nasioi beliefs and the distortions produced by the very nature of colonialism. The colonizers' domination was sup-

ported in part by the extent to which they could make Nasioi see themselves as inferior and the colonizer as possessing special gifts and powers. The struggles of the Nasioi to find a way out of their colonial dilemma did not stop with supernatural explanations, however, and each of my subsequent visits from 1966 to 1978 showed me new developments.

Ironically, it was the advent of a multi-billion-dollar copper project on Nasioi land—a much more exploitative form of colonialism than the plantations of 1962—that brought Nasioi to what outsiders would call political awareness. In that process I came to share the pain that they felt when the administration gave geologists and others free rein to roam over their land. Men living near the proposed mine site walked miles to beg me to intercede with the American government. When I finally convinced them I was powerless to help, they wept:

We are like women, we cannot drive these new people away. The police [at the mining camp] have guns but we do not. Perhaps we should attack them with spears so they will kill us.

Sporadic, nonfatal violence by Nasioi and other Bougainvilleans did not halt the progress of the mining development, but villagers' opinions did not change:

An older woman, 1971: *We weep for what is being done to our land [by the mine].*

An older man, 1972: *Our sons who are educated must help us against the copper company.*

I was finally able to relieve some of my frustrations in 1971 when a Bougainville priest, Father John Momis, and I presented a paper about the mine and the Nasioi at a public seminar at the University of Papua New Guinea. In this paper, which was widely quoted in the Australian press, we were able to put on record what Nasioi felt, in opposition to the public re-

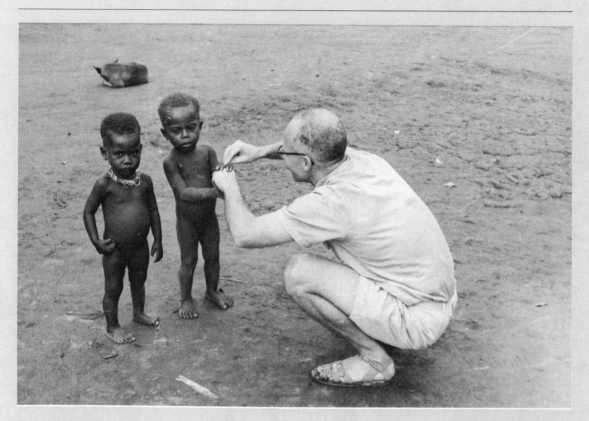

Eugene Ogan plays with two small Nasioi children during his fieldwork in New Guinea.

lations pronouncements by administration and mining company.

Many other changes took place in Bougainville during the 1970s. The copper mine was highly profitable to its alien owners, and islanders demanded more equitable distribution of its wealth. At the same time, Nasioi became increasingly enmeshed in the world market for cocoa and coconut products, while more and more young Nasioi men and women went on to secondary and tertiary education. When Papua New Guinea became independent in 1975, Nasioi were among the strongest supporters of a movement for Bougainville to secede and become independent. The central government yielded both a proportion of mining revenue and greater autonomy to a new provincial government which in turn developed local government institutions. Nasioi are still caught in a political economy over which they have little control, but a final quotation from a 1981 letter written by the educated boy, now a grown man, may illustrate the new approaches some Nasioi are taking toward their problems:

*The difficulties faced ... regarding the transport is now decreasing as the construction of road is going at a faster rate day by day....
Being a secretary for a youth group ... we made an amendment through Community Government to operate bus service and service station and also Cultural Centre in the region when the transport system is improved. In the group there are more than thirty members.*

危機

Chapter Four

Culture and Communication

The Communication Process
Sending and Receiving Messages · Redundancy

Communication and Sociability

Communication among Humans
Signs and Symbols · Language and Speech
Elements of Language
Other Modes of Human Communication

Language and Culture
Cultural Influence on Language
Linguistic Influence on Culture

Linguistic Variation
Distinct Languages · Dialects
Pidgins and Creoles

Linguistic Contact
Patterns of Contact
Diglossia and Multilingualism
Planned Linguistic Change

Historical Linguistics
Evolutionary Processes
Reconstructing Language History

Summary · Suggested Readings

Focus on People
Communication Problems in
the Southern Philippines

THE EXCHANGE OF information is one of the most universal features of life. Organisms are almost constantly transmitting and receiving information. Without effective means of communication, an eagle cannot locate its prey, a flower cannot attract a bee, a salmon cannot find its spawning site. Getting food, avoiding danger, and finding the right mate all hinge on sending out the appropriate signals at the right time and on picking up essential information from the environment. A failure in communication can result in loss of resources, injury, or even death.

Information exchange among humans has become a highly elaborated feature of our social lives. This chapter examines aspects of communication that anthropologists have studied for clues to understanding cultures and cultural processes: general characteristics of the communication process, relationships between complexity in communication and complexity in group structure, the structure of human verbal and nonverbal communications, links between language and culture, variations within a single language, use of more than one language tradition, and the reconstruction of processes by which languages evolve.

The Communication Process

Communication occurs whenever information is exchanged between a sender and a receiver. Information is transmitted by a sender via signals, such as a song, a sentence, a chest-thumping display, or a scent. At the other end, the information is received as a message.

Sending and Receiving Messages

As we all know from personal experience, what a signal means to the sender is not always what it means to the receiver. One person may smile at another to signal approval or friendship, for instance, but the message received may be quite different: "You are making fun of me," or "you think I am acting like a fool." The potential for misunderstanding exists in all communicative transactions.

OVERLEAF

The Japanese word for *crisis* consists of these two characters: the top character means *danger*; the bottom character means *opportunity*. To the Japanese, a crisis is not only a time of danger but also a time of opportunity.

Sending signals of one kind or another is inevitable. Simply by existing, any plant or animal betrays information as to its size, shape, and location. Even camouflaged, organisms continue to emit signals. The flatfish, or sole, can alter its skin color to match the color and texture of the ocean floor. But it cannot camouflage its odor and electrical field, signals that mean "dinner" to a shark that swims close enough to detect them.

Since it is impossible to avoid sending signals entirely, the trick is to transmit appropriate information to appropriate receivers at appropriate times. From the point of view of the sender, the key to success lies in effective *impression management*: if signals must be transmitted, let them be to the advantage of the sender. In many instances, good impression management requires that signals be true. In other cases, it may be to the advantage of the sender to transmit purposely misleading signals.

Through impression management, the sender of signals hopes to control, in some way, the response of the receiver. However, there are limits to this power. Like the sole, an organism may be

Gestures are often used to emphasize oral communication, as in this heated political discussion in Milan, Italy.

unable to control all the signals it emits. Another difficulty lies in the fact that a sender cannot always determine who the receivers will be. A prostitute needs to communicate the nature of his or her business to potential customers, but the signals used are also likely to attract the police. A third problem: the sender may intend one thing by a signal, but the receiver might get a message that means something else entirely.

Redundancy

For both senders and receivers, there is some uncertainty present in all communication. Nei-

ther senders nor receivers have complete control over the meaning of the information they exchange. However, uncertainty can be reduced by *redundancy*—the repetition or reinforcement of a signal or message. An angry man, for example, may reinforce his verbal signal—"I'm mad as hell at you"—with other signals, such as a forceful tone of voice and aggressive gestures.

A receiver of contradictory or misleading messages may also be helped through redundancy. If we are not certain of someone's sincerity, for instance, we will watch carefully for consistency in the signals he or she emits. If what a man says is not reinforced by how he says it, we are likely to suspect that he is just "playing a part." Even with overlapping cues, clear mutual understanding is rare.

Communication and Sociability

Effective communication is basic to the survival of all organisms, but some require more complex systems of information exchange than others. An octopus does not require a very sophisticated system of communicating: interactions with other octopi are rare, and not particularly complex. Octopi that meet either retreat, attempt to drive each other away, or mate. The signals required for these simple interactions need not be very complex.

Communication is far more complex among social animals. Ants, bees, penguins, baboons, and humans face their environments collectively, rather than simply as individuals. Survival depends not just on the adaptive abilities of the individual, but also on the ability of the members of a group to coordinate their behaviors and integrate their activities in the pursuit of common objectives. This teamwork would be impossible without efficient communication. Members of a group have to know what each is up to in order to work together effectively.

Communication complexity increases not only with the importance of interactions but also with the number of roles each actor plays. The repertory of roles that loners like octopi play in their simple, short-term encounters is very limited. The role relationships of social animals are considerably more complex. In a social setting, two individuals are likely to play a multitude of roles. At various times, they may be partners in sex, parenting, grooming, defense, and food gathering; the same two individuals may also be competitors over resources. As they work together or compete in a diversity of contexts, their behaviors must vary according to the situation. This complexity in role relationships requires a corresponding sophistication in communication.

While the communication systems of any social animals are always fairly developed, some have systems that are more highly elaborated than others'. Wolves, for example, have a more complex system of information exchange than

The role relationships of social animals like these two chimpanzees (here, a female greets a male) are quite complex and call for a corresponding sophistication in communication.

ants—most of the ant's behavior is biologically or genetically controlled, whereas wolves are much less the prisoners of their instincts. As noted in chapter 1, we humans are virtually devoid of genetically determined instincts, depending instead on culturally learned patterns of behavior.

The adaptive advantage in learned behavior is the flexibility that learning promotes. Because of our great capacity for learning, we humans can quickly alter our activities and procedures to meet diverse and unstable environmental conditions. But it is not enough for individuals to be able to change their behavior. Rather, successful adaptation requires the maintenance of maximum behavioral flexibility at the group level. In order to alter their activities in coordinated group fashion, social animals need to have flexible systems of communication. Among ants, much of the information exchanged is in the form of information-bearing chemicals, called *pheromones,* each of which probably has only one meaning. This one-for-one correspondence places a significant limitation on the flexibility of any communication. In contrast, humans communicate mainly through symbols. As we will see, symbols represent the ultimate in communicational flexibility, for their meaning is not fixed or automatic.

Communication among Humans

Humans rely more on learning, carry out a greater variety of activities, and play more diversified roles than any other animal, and their societies are the most complex in nature. It is no wonder, then, that human systems of communication are so flexible and highly developed. Humans exchange information through a wide variety of channels—sight, touch, sound, and smell—but the most important mode of communication among humans is verbal.

If anything can be said to be the most basic element of culture, it is language. Language allows us to exchange detailed information about both interior states or thoughts and exterior conditions. It is primarily through language that culture is transmitted from generation to generation, and a person's language greatly influences how he or she perceives the world. It is impossible to imagine what human life would be like without it.

Signs and Symbols

All communication is based upon signs. A *sign* is anything that can convey information, including physical objects, colors, sounds, movements, scents, and even silence. Among many animals, the meaning of a sign is *biologically determined.* A cricket does not need to learn how to chirp, nor does it need to learn what chirping by other crickets signifies: the meaning of chirping is part of its genetic makeup. In addition, the sign systems of most animals are *closed:* different signs cannot be combined to create new signs. Such animals cannot combine a sign meaning "I want to mate" with one meaning "danger," for example. For these animals, each sign functions independently. Such sign systems place considerable limitations on the flexibility and range of information exchanged.

Not all animals are limited to communicating through sign systems that are closed and determined. Some primates have communication systems that are based on *symbols;* human communication is based entirely upon symbols. A *symbol* is a sign whose meaning is *arbitrary.* Its significance is determined not by a genetic "program" but by social convention and learning. Words, whether written or spoken, are symbols, as is a crucifix, a coat of arms, or a flag.

Because the meaning of a symbol is arbitrary, different symbols may be used to mean the same thing. What English speakers call a *dog* is called a *Hund* by German speakers and *anjing* by speakers of Indonesian. Conversely, any particular symbol may have different meanings in different cultures. The swastika, for example, has highly negative connotations in Western cultures, due to its association with Nazis; but to Hindus it signifies good fortune. The meaning of any symbol is determined by culture, not by genes or biology.

The flexibility of human communication is further increased by another characteristic of symbols: they may be *multivocal*, that is, they often have multiple levels of meaning. A crucifix, for example, is a highly multivocal symbol. It may evoke hope in a life hereafter, or relief from suffering in this life, or the necessity for moral behavior—just to name a few of its connotations. By providing a single focal point to which a diversity of experiences may be related, such a symbol may help to integrate a variety of ideas.

A symbolic system of communication is also *open:* unlike other signs, symbols can be combined with one another to produce entirely new meanings. Rather than being restricted to a limited set of signs, humans can freely invent new terms and concepts, as when the words *smoke* and *fog* are merged to form "smog"—a new symbol with a new meaning.

Symbols are also *abstract*. The term *book* refers not only to the object you are now reading, but to all other like objects. This aspect of symbol use enables humans to generalize about things and events to a degree far beyond the capacity of other animals.

Because human society involves such complex relationships and because human adaptation requires responding collectively to rapidly changing conditions, it is essential that human

In Hindu culture, the swastika (at the center of this design) signifies good fortune. In contrast, the rise of the Nazi Party in Germany and its subsequent impact on world history ensured that the Nazi swastika became a well-known symbol of evil.

communication systems be equally complex and flexible. Symbols are the most complex and flexible devices for communication yet formed, allowing humans to adapt them to whatever purposes necessary.

Language and Speech

The terms *language* and *speech* are often used interchangeably, but there is a distinction between them. *Speech* consists of patterned verbal behavior, a concrete, observable phenomenon. *Language*, however, is an abstraction—a set of rules for generating speech—which exists only in people's minds and therefore is not observable. Just as the values, beliefs, and assumptions of culture guide and condition cultural behavior, so the code of a language generates speech behavior.

The capacity for language and speech is innate in all humans. All normal human beings are in fact "programmed" for linguistic interaction. Parents do not have to force their children to learn to talk in the same way that they enforce toilet training or table manners. Linguistic skills are something human children are naturally motivated to acquire.

The human brain is organized in such a way that humans are programmed for "symboling," for communicating through signs that have arbitrarily assigned meanings. The human talent for speech also has a biological basis. All normal human beings are endowed with a special kind of vocal apparatus that allows them to make the tremendously wide range of sounds required for speaking any language.

The anatomical complex upon which speech depends—the lips, teeth, palate, tongue, and larynx—occurs only in humans. We may not be the only animals with the capacity for language, however. A number of experimenters have attempted to teach language to chimpanzees. Early experiments failed, for as we now know, chimpanzees do not have the kind of vocal apparatus to produce the variety of sounds necessary for human speech. Researchers have switched to nonverbal languages (such as sign language, which is used by the deaf, and "Yerkish," an artificial language that makes use of geometric symbols), with considerably more success. Roger Fouts claims to have taught more than 240 signs to Washoe, a chimpanzee with which he has worked since 1965. He feels that Washoe, through her knowledge of American Sign Language, understands the equivalent of spoken English. More recently Fouts has been working with a younger chimp, which he claims is able to use two-sign combinations such as "come tickle" and "hot drink." In Fouts's view, chimpanzees have at least rudimentary talents for symboling, and therefore the capacity for language.

There are those who disagree. Herb Terrace (1979), working with another chimp, found that while Nim could learn signs, he was never able to use them in meaningful sequences. Terrace argues that reported cases of chimps combining symbols in a grammatical sense are the result of unconscious prompting by the investigator and not of the chimps' own ability to construct language. Although the debate is unresolved, it is obvious that chimps are a great deal more competent in their communicative abilities than was previously thought.

Elements of Language

Human languages have two main levels of structure: sounds and grammar. The analysis of a language's sounds is called *phonology*. Grammar has two dimensions: morphology and syntax. The *morphology* of a language determines how simple sounds are organized to form units of meaning, and the *syntax* determines how words are strung together to form statements.

Phonology. To describe a language, linguists must first determine what sounds it uses. Humans are capable of making a tremendous range

Nim Chimpsky uses the sign that asks Laura Pettito to "open" the container.

of vocal sounds, but no one language makes use of all of them. Some languages are based on a larger number of sounds than others. In English there are forty-five distinct sounds, while in most Polynesian languages there are only about fifteen. The sounds in one language are not exactly the same as those used in another. The German "ch" sound in the words *Ich* and *Buch* and the Spanish trilled "r" in *cerro* and *burro* do not occur in English.

The smallest linguistically significant units of sounds—units that alter the meanings of the words in which they occur—are called *phonemes.* In English, [p] and [b] are considered separate phonemes because one cannot be substituted for the other without changing meaning: *pat* and *bat* have distinctly different meanings.

A phoneme may consist of a single sound or a number of closely related sounds. For example, the [pʰ] sound in the English word *pike* and the [p] sound in *spike* are pronounced slighty differently: the [pʰ] sound in *pike* is *aspirated* (that is, it is accompanied by expelling air) while in *spike* it is *unaspirated.** But in English, the dif-

ference is not given any meaning, so speakers are largely unaware of it. Such variations of a single phoneme that do not affect meaning in a language are called *allophones.* Sounds that are allophones in one language may be distinct phonemes in other languages. In Hindi, for example, [p] and [pʰ] are not allophones, as they are in English, but separate phonemes. The difference between the two sounds is considered critical; it is as easily recognized by Hindi speakers as the difference between [p] and [b] is recognized by English speakers.

Morphology. Single sounds can be linguistically significant, but in most cases they do not have meaning in and of themselves. In order to create meaning, sounds are combined with one another to form morphemes. *Morphemes* are the smallest units of sound that convey meaning.

---

*Brackets around letters, as in the case of [p] and [b], are used to indicate minimal sound units. The small raised [ʰ] indicates an aspirated sound. If you place your hand in front of your mouth, you'll feel a puff of air when you say *pike,* but not when you say *spike.*

Leg, store, and *book,* all single morphemes in English, can each stand alone, so we call them *free morphemes.* Other morphemes, such as the suffix *-s,* which indicates plurality, cannot stand alone. Although *-s* adds new meaning and is thus considered a morpheme, it has no meaning except when attached to other morphemes, and is therefore called a *bound morpheme.* Morphemes are often combined to form new concepts, such as *bookstores,* a word consisting of three morphemes.

We have seen that not all sound contrasts are recognized as linguistically significant in a particular language. Some contrasts are considered separate phonemes, while others are allophones of a single phoneme. Similarly, at the level of morphology, variations that have the same meaning will be considered *allomorphs* of a single morpheme. For example, the prefixes *in-,* *un-,* and *non-* all indicate negation of what follows, and are therefore considered allomorphs and not distinct morphemes.

Syntax. All languages have standardized conventions for combining words to form statements that make sense to other speakers of the same language. These conventions are called the *rules of syntax.* The English sentence, "If you use the light meter properly, you'll get a good picture" can be translated into German by substituting German words for the English, but for a German speaker to make sense of the statement, the words have to be rearranged as well. In German, the statement would be, "Wenn Sie den Belichtungsmesser richtig gebrauchen, dann muss es ein gutes Bild geben." Translated back into English, but keeping the German syntax, the statement reads, "If you the light meter properly use, then must it a good picture give."

The rules of syntax are not learned in a fully conscious manner. All native speakers of English "know" the rules of syntax in that language; otherwise their speech would not make sense to others. Yet few could say exactly what these rules are. But the fact that a seven-year-old child can talk and be understood by others is proof that the child has, somewhat subconsciously, acquired a basic knowledge of syntax.

Syntax is a more important indicator of meaning in some languages than in others. In English, for example, there is a significant difference between *dog bites man* and *man bites dog.* But in Latin, *dog bites man* can be stated as either *canis mordet hominem* or *hominem mordet canis* without any change in meaning. In Latin, word endings (which are bound morphemes) play a special role in constructing sentences. For example, the object of a verb will always have an *-em* ending. A person understanding Latin will know who bit and who was bitten by noting the noun endings; the order in which the words occur is not important. One contrast that a linguist would therefore note between Latin and English is that English is more complex syntactically, while Latin is more complex morphologically.

Other Modes of Human Communication

Language is not the only means by which humans exchange information. In conversation, for example, humans communicate not only verbally, but also through facial expressions, voice tones, and gestures. Style of dress and grooming may also be iterpreted as messages by others, and even the ways in which people organize the space around themselves can have communicative significance. Anthropologists interested in studying communication have not restricted themselves to investigating only speech and writing systems.

Kinesics is the study of gestural communication—or "body language" (Birdwhistell 1960). Since all humans are essentially alike physically, much of our body language has universal meaning. For example, a smile probably conveys roughly the same range of messages in any part of the world. But kinesic commu-

From the body language expressed in this photograph, would you say a friendly conversation is going on or about to start?

nication is influenced by culture, so that some gestures or poses can mean one thing in one culture and something else in another (see Morris, et al., 1979). In the United States, it makes no difference whether an individual uses the left hand or the right when he or she gives someone a piece of candy. In Java, however, to offer anything with the left hand is considered an insult, or at least bad manners. Likewise, different gestures can convey the same meaning in different cultures. In northern Italy, as in the United States, a person shakes his or her head from side to side to mean "no," but in southern Italy and Greece the same meaning is communicated by an upword jerk of the chin.

While most of us are somewhat aware of how interaction is influenced by body language, we are probably less conscious of the ways in which information is exchanged through patterns of spacing. *Proxemics,* or the study of the cultural use of space, focuses on the "geometry of interaction" (Hall 1966). Spatial arrangements help to define the nature of interactions, such as the degree of formality or intimacy involved. In some interactions, such as a job interview, people will maintain a considerable distance from one another. In contrast, the conversational distance between two good friends discussing a personal matter will be very close.

The "appropriate" use of space and the meaning of spatial arrangements are defined differently from culture to culture. For example, in a London post office, stamp buyers are expected to stand in a queue without any physical contact with the others in line and patiently await their turn at the window. In Spain, however, queuing is virtually unknown. People crowd up to the window as best they can, and there is considerable body contact.

Another dimension of nonverbal communication involves *bodily adornment*. Everything about a person's appearance—such as clothing, hair style, jewelry, makeup—is likely to influence interaction with others. Conventions of dress and grooming serve as ready indicators of social status that affect behavior, especially interaction between relative strangers. A person wearing a police uniform will elicit different behavior than someone in a clown's suit. Bodily adornment thus helps to define particular situations within a cultural tradition.

Differences in dress and grooming are often quite important for cross-cultural interaction, for knowing the "language" of dress and grooming can be essential to communication among varied ethnic groups and cultures. In highland Guatemala, for instance, each Indian village traditionally had its own special customs of bodily adornment. Someone familiar with these local variations could immediately gather important information about a total stranger from his or her dress—marital, financial, or social status, for example. Scott Nind (1831), an early European resident of southwestern Australia, found that not knowing the language of bodily adornment can confuse cross-cultural understanding. In his discussion of initial contact between Europeans and Aborigines, he noted that the Europeans' preconceived notions about native adornment and social organization led them to misinterpretation:

we endeavoured to discover whether they had any chiefs, and for a long time believed they had; indeed we had fixed upon two or three individuals to whom we supposed that rank belonged. The natives whom we selected were fine, tall, active men, much painted and ornamented. . . . We subsequently discovered that they were all single men, which accounted for their constantly ornamented appearance [Nind 1831: 40-41].

Language and Culture

It is impossible to comprehend a culture without taking into account its language, probably its single most important element. It is also impossible to completely understand a language independent of its cultural context. As anthropologist John Beattie (1964: 31) puts it, "A people's categories of thought and the forms of their language are inextricably bound together." But despite the many ways in which culture and language influence each other, their integration is not absolute. Each has many properties uniquely its own that are not directly, or even indirectly, influenced by the other. People with cultures that are otherwise very similar may speak quite different languages, and similar languages may be spoken by people with very different cultures.

Cultural Influence on Language

There has been little research into whether culture might affect the grammatical structure of a language, but it is not particularly difficult to show that social and cultural factors can influence its vocabulary. To a Hawaiian, snow is snow, and there is no reason to have more than one word for it. Inuit, Lapps, and various Indian groups, whose livelihood and even lives may depend on their ability to distinguish between different types of snow conditions, have a large number of different words for snow (see table 4.1).

In any language, the elaboration of an area of vocabulary is related partly to the importance the area has in the society, partly to the actual diversity of phenomena encountered in the environment, and partly to the uses the vocabulary must be put to. The Samal of the southern Philippines, for example, have words for more than seventy kinds of fishing and for more than two hundred fifty kinds of fish. This is partly because fish are a main source of food and of cash income (Randall: n.d.). It is also owing to the general human ability to recognize essentially the same "natural" objects as scientists do.

Although all languages have both highly abstract and highly specific concepts, not all languages are the same in this respect. Languages such as Chinese and English, which have been associated with societies having an extensive division of labor over long periods, or which are spoken in many parts of the world, tend to elaborate general vocabularies. English words like *administrator, mammal, society,* and *rights* probably would not be found in a foraging society.

Also, research indicates that at least in some instances vocabulary is influenced by cultural, environmental, *and* physiological factors. This appears to be true, for example, of color terms. While all languages have highly specific words for color (such as *peach*), not all have the same number of general color words. Some languages have as few as two general color words, *warm-light* and *cool-dark*, while others, such as English and Hungarian, have as many as eleven or twelve. Berlin and Kay (1969) found that the number of color terms in a language increases in association with increases in economic and technological complexity. More recently, Kay and McDaniel (1977) have shown that the order in which general color terms are added as societies

tę ('ice')		
['solid ice']	*tędeibile* ('thin ice')	
	tędeiźile ('brittle ice')	
	tędeit`lé ('blue ice')	
	tędeitó ('thick ice')	
	tęta gòt`lé ('muddy ice')	
	tępiné ('slippery ice')	
	tęvú ('hollow ice')	
	tękʰapi̧ ('wet ice')	
['melting ice']	*tętsidènit'lé* ('black ice')	
	tęgá ('white ice')	
['cracking ice']	*tętseiyindlá* ('seamed ice')	
	tęč̌ęgóněčá ('cracked ice')	
	tęnetsile ('floating ice')	

Source: Basso, *Language in Society* (1972), p. 35.

TABLE 4.1
Words for *ice* used by the Slave Indians of Northern Canada.

develop reflects the physiology and neurology of the eye. "Orange," for example, is never found in a language without both "red" and "yellow," reflecting the neurological characteristics of the human eye. The appearance of "orange" is not merely a reflection of neurology, however, for it also tends to be associated with societies with standard dyes, pigments, and schools. The color vocabulary then, reflects not only the pan-human exposure to environmental color and the generally pan-human perception of color, but also the differential need of societies to talk about color.

Linguistic Influence on Culture

On the other side of the language/culture coin, language may determine or influence certain aspects of culture. There is at least one way in which language clearly helps shape our cultural practices: every language provides the basis upon which our perceptions of the world are organized. Language establishes categories by which things considered the same or similar can be distinguished from those which are considered different. The categories of one language will never be quite identical to those of another. In American culture, a person's mother is called by one kinship term (*mother*) and her sister by a different term (*aunt*). The Iroquois call both mothers and mothers' sisters by the same term. Such linguistic differences influence cultural behavior. Anglo-Americans relate to aunts differently than to mothers, but Iroquois are expected to relate to both in much the same way.

Some anthropologists have gone further and claimed that we are virtual prisoners of language. The classic expression of this position is known as the *Sapir-Whorf hypothesis*, named in honor of the anthropological linguists Edward Sapir (1884–1939) and Benjamin Whorf (1897–1941). According to the Sapir-Whorf hypothesis, the language a person speaks determines his or her world view:

Human beings do not live in the objective world alone, nor alone in the world of social activity as ordinarily understood, but are very much at the mercy of the particular language which has become the medium of expression for their society. . . . The fact of the matter is that the real world is to a large extent unconsciously built up on the language habits of the group. No two languages are ever sufficiently similar to be considered as representing the same social reality. The worlds in which different societies live are distinct worlds, not merely the same world with different labels attached. [Sapir 1929: 209–14]

The Sapir-Whorf hypothesis maintains that the tyranny of language goes beyond merely influencing the way people relate to their experiences, forcing them to perceive the world on terms that are built in to the language they speak. If this view is correct, speakers of different languages will have correspondingly different conceptualizations of how "reality" is constructed.

It is certainly true that a language places some limitations on how a person can express his or her thoughts. For example, since verb tenses are a basic structural feature of the English language, almost any statement made by an English speaker must specify whether the event in question is happening now, has already happened, or will happen in the future. But a speaker of Indonesian, which has no verb tenses, is not forced to make the same kind of time specifications that are required in English. In Indonesian, one cannot say "I went to the store." Instead, one says "I go to the store" whether that action occurs in the present or the past. According to the Sapir-Whorf hypothesis, the structural contrasts between the two languages give English speakers and Indonesian speakers very different views about the nature of time. The English language stresses periodicity by dividing time into distinct categories of past, present, and future, whereas in Indonesian time is seen as flowing and continuous. However, although statements might be easier to make in one language than in the other, there are probably no thoughts or ideas that cannot be expressed in both languages. Indonesians can add a qualifier such as "yesterday" or "this morning" to their tenseless statements.

Although language and culture influence each other in many ways, both obvious and subtle, difficulties arise whenever one tries to show that culture *determines* language, or vice versa. The Sapir-Whorf hypothesis has helped to generate interest in investigating connections between language and culture, but the hypothesis remains unproved.

Linguistic Variation

Comparisons between languages in an effort to discover cultural influences are complicated by the fact that the boundaries between languages are not clear-cut. Further, some languages are spoken in many different dialects, and some ways of speaking are combinations of other languages. Linguistic experts find it very difficult to determine how many distinct languages are now in use.

Distinct Languages

How many languages are spoken in the world today? Estimates range from three thousand to five thousand, but no one is really certain (see table 4.2 for a list of the number of speakers of the world's major languages). As many as three thousand different languages used by South American Indians alone have been named in the literature, but this high number is deceptive. Problems in identifying separate languages are many. In the South American studies, in many cases a single language has been identified by more than one name. Furthermore, many of the language studies that are available are of poor quality, making it difficult to tell whether the language described by one linguist is the same as that described by another. Some languages named are now extinct; other categories overlap or are inappropriate. Once such categories are eliminated, there appear to be only three hundred to four hundred Indian languages currently spoken in South America. Yet as Sorenson (1973: 312) has concluded, "the linguistic map of South America remains impressionistic at best," and similar problems exist elsewhere.

One of the primary problems confronting anyone who wishes to compile a list of world languages (for example, see Voegelin and Voegelin 1977, and Ruhlen 1976) is defining what constitutes a separate language. Hindi and Urdu, spoken in India and Pakistan respectively, are written with different alphabets, associated with very different religious traditions (Hinduism and Islam), and historically influenced by different languages (Sanskrit and Arabic). Yet in conversation many speakers of these "separate" languages can understand one another. Often the perception of linguistic difference is influenced less by anything inherent

Name	Speakers (in millions)
1. Mandarin (China)	713
2. English	391
3. Russian	270
4. Spanish	251
5. Hindi (India)	245
6. Arabic	151
7. Bengali (Bangladesh; India)	148
8. Portuguese	148
9. German	119
10. Japanese	118
11. Malay or Indonesian	112
12. French	105
13. Urdu (Pakistan; India)	70
14. Punjabi (India; Pakistan)	64
15. Italian	61
16. Korean	59
17. Telugu (India)	59
18. Tamil (India; Sri Lanka)	58
19. Marathi (India)	56
20. Cantonese (China)	54

Source: Sidney S. Culbert, *World Almanac* (1982), p. 164.

TABLE 4.2
Major Languages of the World (1981)

in the languages than by social and political factors: in this case, the creation of the separate states of India and Pakistan. In determining boundaries between languages, linguists recognize the importance of both social and linguistic factors (Greenberg 1968: 36).

Generally the primary criterion for a distinct language is *mutual intelligibility*. Within any population individual competency in a language will vary, but for the most part speakers of the same language should be able to understand one another. One common way of measuring the degree of difference or similarity between two speaking traditions is to compare their vocabularies. While vocabulary alone does not tell us all that we need to know about how languages are related, it is the major factor influencing mutual intelligibility. Vocabulary comparisons are frequently made through a carefully constructed list of *core terms* found in every language: words like *woman*, *head*, and *rain*. Words used for such core terms in each language tradition are then compared to find similarities. Even when such a systematic method is used, there is still the problem of determining where to draw the boundary. How similar must two language traditions be to constitute a single language? How different must they be to be considered two distinct languages? Morris Swadesh (1971: 18–20) has developed a scale for determining the boundaries of linguistic units based upon percentages of shared words. Despite such proposals, however, there continues to be considerable disagreement in deciding what constitutes a separate language.

Dialects

To complicate the problem of distinguishing distinct languages, individual languages are not spoken or used in a uniform fashion. Variations occur within any language tradition. A *dialect* is a patterned language variant that is associated with a geographically or socially distinct speech community or speech context. People who speak different dialects of the same language should be able to understand each other; the point beyond which they cannot communicate should mark the boundary between two separate languages. But these distinctions are not always clear. An English-speaking person from Alabama and an English-speaking person from Boston can usually understand each other, though each may find the other's pronunciation and grammar a bit peculiar. Their variations on a single language are known as *regional dialects* and are usually easily identifiable.

Distinctive conventions of language usage also may be associated with factors such as class, ethnicity, or situation. These are known as *social dialects*. The contrasting speech styles of English cockneys and Oxford and Cambridge graduates are social dialects. Classbound social dialects occur in all societies in which class or caste distinctions occur. In fact, speech differences of this nature often are cultivated for the very purpose of defining or maintaining a separation between classes or castes. Any person coming from a lower-class background who hopes to rise in society knows from experience that "nothing stigmatizes a class more indelibly than its language" (Bolinger 1968: 138). Being able to "talk right" is almost always a critical factor in social mobility.

Other social dialects may occur in connection with such factors as religion, occupation, age, or sex. The speech style of a minister will differ from that of a longshoreman. The unique speech conventions of American teenagers provide a familiar example of the age-related dialects found in most cultures. Men and women too can have different patterns of speaking. The Garifuna (black Carib) of the Caribbean coast of Central America possess very distinct male and female dialects. The original Garifuna came about from a mingling of runaway male slaves and Carib-speaking Indian women. Their

A classic contrast in English social dialects occurs in *My Fair Lady* when the cockney Eliza Doolittle is coached in speaking "proper" English by Professor Higgins.

different origins continue to influence the speech patterns of men and women. The women speak the same dialect as the men, plus one that is used only when interacting with one another. In some instances the difference between these two dialects was sufficient to lead investigators to conclude, erroneously, that they were separate languages.

Frequently, there are social dialects linked with particular social situations. In many cultures, the same people use one distinct dialect on formal, public occasions, and another in private conversation. Presumably the style of speech Abraham Lincoln used when he chatted with his family was not the same as that which he used in the Gettysburg Address. How a particular social situation is defined can have an important impact on patterns of speech.

Individual speakers of a language may use several dialects in different contexts. The number of dialects used by a person will to some extent reflect the number of groups he or she associates with that have different modes of speech. These dialects, combined with the individual's personal speech peculiarities, produce what is known as an *idiolect*, the speech system of each person within a language community. The range of variety in individual speech systems tends to be greater in large-scale societies, simply because there are more "kinds" of people—members of different ethnic groups, classes, and subcultures.

Pidgins and Creoles

In addition to dialect variations within languages, there are variations known as pidgins and creoles that reflect contact between language traditions. Until very recently the study of pidgins and creoles was assigned a relatively minor place in linguistic analysis. Linguists and nonlinguists alike viewed them as marginal or inferior forms of speech. Many laypeople saw them as crude attempts by mentally inferior people to mimic the speech of supposedly more advanced people. Few students of language hold such views today. Creoles are now recognized as the dominant languages of several countries and they have been afforded official status in Haiti, Papua New Guinea, and Sierra Leone. Hancock (1971) lists eighty creoles and pidgins in his world survey. Because of their social and political importance in the world today, and the recognition that they can tell us a good deal about the dynamics of linguistic contact and change, language experts have begun to devote considerable attention to their study.

A *pidgin* is a simplified hybrid language developed to fulfill the communication needs of peoples who have no common language. The use of pidgins tends to be limited to particular situations, such as intercultural commerce and migratory labor. Normally a pidgin is not the native language any of the speakers use in a domestic setting, although sometimes it may serve as the native tongue of persons who are socially marginal. The term *pidgin* was first applied in the mid-nineteenth century to a speech form that had evolved in China as a result of interaction between Chinese and Europeans. It is now recognized as a widespread phenomenon that may occur whenever there is sustained contact among members of societies speaking different languages.

A well-known example of a pidgin is the *lingoa gêral* used extensively throughout Amazonian Brazil. *Lingoa gêral* is an intertribal pidgin based mainly upon the Tupi language. Early European settlers in Brazil, whose first contact with indigenous peoples was with Tupi speakers along the coast, used it in their dealings with Indians and eventually among themselves as well. It also became the primary language of some *mamelucos* (offspring of Indian mothers and Portuguese fathers) and blacks along the frontier. Such persons were considered marginal by both European settler and Indian society. Although it is being replaced by Portuguese, *lingoa gêral* has had an important effect on the way Portuguese is spoken in Brazil, especially by supplying words for the vocabulary.

Despite considerable variation, there are features common to most pidgins. In all pidgins the emphasis is on efficient and unambiguous communication. Pidgins usually simplify such things as gender and plurality, and they tend to reduce redundancies. For example, "*the* two big newspapers" becomes "tupela bikpela pepa" (two big paper) in Neo-Melanesian. Pidgins, however, may also develop distinctions not normally found in the original language. The vocabulary of most pidgins is relatively limited, reflecting the needs of the specific culture contact situation. The vocabulary of *lingoa gêral* includes terms for indigenous myths and religious beliefs, items of material culture (such as the term *maloca*, which refers to the large communal house common to many Amazonian cultures), and names of Amazonian animals, plants, and places.

When a pidgin becomes the mother tongue of a people it is referred to as a *creole*. Pidgins become creoles for two primary reasons (Todd 1974: 3). In some instances people are cut off from their mother tongue, and the pidgin comes to assume linguistic primacy. Such a process occurred with African slaves in the Caribbean when they were cut off from large numbers of speakers of their native languages. Another possibility is for the pidgin to become identified with achievement of a higher social status, encouraging people to speak it instead of their native tongue. This is essentially what happened in the case of Neo-Melanesian (the English-based creole spoken throughout much of the western Pacific) in Papua New Guinea.

In the process of creolization the language is changed, since it now must be "large enough to encompass all the communication needs of its speakers" (Decamp 1971: 16). It must become sufficiently complex and sophisticated to be usefully applied in a full range of social situations.

This process typically involves expanding the vocabulary and evolving a more elaborate syntax.

Most, but not all, of the major creoles spoken in the world today are based upon European languages (French, English, Dutch, Spanish, and Portuguese: the languages of the former colonial powers). The major regions where creoles are found include the Caribbean, western and southern Africa, southern and southeast Asia, and the Pacific. A creole known as Gullah was traditionally spoken in parts of Georgia and South Carolina. It shares many features with English-derived pidgins and creoles of West Africa, and has influenced the development of black English in the United States. At one time there were around 125,000 Gullah speakers, but their number has declined considerably as the region has become integrated more thoroughly into the regional variant of mainstream American culture. In other parts of the world, especially where creoles have been tied to the process of nation building in former colonies, the number of creole speakers is increasing.

Although pidgins and creoles traditionally have been restricted primarily to oral communication, this is changing. Formerly, most creole speakers in Melanesia, the Caribbean, and elsewhere were illiterate. If they did learn to read and write, it was in the locally dominant European language. The writing that existed in creole was done by noncreole speakers for the purpose of transmitting religious ideas or adding a bit of local color. This situation has changed since the Second World War as a result of increased literacy and nationalism. In areas where creole speakers predominate, creole newspapers are now common. Even advertisers have adapted to the local language as creole speakers have become consumers of industrial goods, as in this Neo-Melanesian advertisement:

Olgeta harim gut! Dispela sop ol i kolim 'Cold Power' i nambawan tru. Em i wasim na rausim tru ol kainkain pipia long ol klos bilong yu. [*Everybody listen closely! This soap powder, called "Cold Power," is definitely the best. It washes and completely removes all kinds of stains from your clothes.*] [*quoted by Todd 1974: 9-10*]

Creole writing has also gained greater recognition as a form of literary expression as Third World poets, dramatists, and novelists have sought to express their own experiences more accurately. The works of Nigerian novelist Chinua Achebe (1960, 1967) and Jamaican Orlando Patterson (1971), to name but two, provide examples of such writing.

Linguistic Contact

In addition to the numerous variations within and combinations among languages, linguists' attempts to map the regions of the world where particular languages are spoken are frustrated by overlapping. Even within very small communities there may be speakers of more than one language or very distinct dialect living together, and individuals themselves may speak more than one language.

Patterns of Contact

Patterns of social interaction result in the creation of what may be identified as linguistic communities. According to John Gumperz (1962: 30-32), a *linguistic community* consists of any group within which communication occurs and which has a recognizable communicational boundary. In southern Belize, for example, the

The store signs in both English and Hindi on this street in Suva, Fiji illustrate languages in contact.

linguistic community consists of members of six major ethnic groups, each with its own distinct cultural traditions and languages: Spanish-speaking Hispanics from Guatemala and Honduras, Mopan-speaking Maya Indians, Kekchi-speaking Maya Indians, Creoles who speak Belizean Creole, Garifuna or Black Caribs who speak Garifuna, and a mixed group of mostly English-speaking white expatriots. Because linguistic ability, inclination, or economic necessity are sometimes lacking, not all members of each ethnic group communicate with members of the other groups. Yet by and large these groups do interact and communicate on a regular basis, a pattern that has increased as a result of greater educational opportunities and increased economic integration of the region.

Within this larger unit, the linguistic community, a number of subunits can be identified. In particular, there is the *speech community*, which Dell Hymes (1972: 54-55) has defined as a "community sharing rules for the conduct and interpretation of speech, and rules for the interpretation of at least one linguistic variety." Members of a single speech community share a common set of ideas about language and its use: ideas about forbidden topics of conversation, procedures for making requests, means of expressing humor or irony, standards for duration of silence and level of voice within conversations, and so forth. In southern Belize the residents of a number of small mixed Mopan- and Kekchi-speaking villages may be seen as a single speech community because of their shared perceptions of the social use of language. This was not always the case. Not too many years ago the Kekchi and Mopan formed distinct speech communities, but over the years, through intermarriage and migration, they have come to form a single speech community.

Links among speech communities are formed on the basis of interaction and social ties among people across community boundaries. Such linkages, referred to as *speech networks*, are often formed because of economic factors. Bilibili Island of the Vitiaz Strait of New Guinea, for instance, is inhabited by about two hundred and fifty traders and potmakers. Individual islanders have trading partners on other islands who speak different languages but with whom they are able to communicate. While the speech network of each islander is limited to a few trading partners, the islanders as a community have ties with a wide range of different speech communities.

Diglossia and Multilingualism

Frequent contact with people of other language traditions may lead individuals to speak more than one variant of a single language or more than one language. Charles Ferguson (1959) coined the term *diglossia* to describe situations where two varieties of one language ("standard" forms, dialects, pidgins, or creoles) are spoken by persons in a speech community under different conditions. Use of more than one variant may have important cultural meanings. In Haiti, for instance, the vast majority of people speak what is commonly referred to as Haitian creole (which is derived from French), but the middle class and elite speak both Haitian creole and standard French. Standard French is clearly assigned a higher status in Haiti than creole, and an ability to speak standard French is a requirement for upward social mobility. Even among the elite, use of these two speech forms depends upon the relative social positions of those speaking and the setting of the speech situation. For diglossic Haitian elites,

Creole is used exclusively in private informal situations such as among peer groups of children and adolescents and between parents at home; French is used exclusively in formal public situations, such as in administrative proceedings or in official speeches. Both Creole and French are used interchangeably in private formal situations (receptions, conversations with mere acquaintances) and public informal situations (in shops, in conversation with friends). [*Valdman* 1975: 66]

In situations where both French and creole are

used, patterns of usage signal subtle shifts of roles and attitudes among speakers.

Individuals who speak more than one language are relatively common in all societies, a fact that American students taking their first foreign-language class sometimes find amazing. Multilingualism develops for a variety of reasons: growing up in a home where more than one language is spoken, schooling, traveling for work or some other reason to an area where another language is used, or living in border areas or in mixed ethnic communities. Although an ability to speak more than one language may be little more than a convenience for the speaker, it may also have considerable social and psychological significance. In situations where use of one's mother tongue results in stigmatization or deprivation of economic opportunities and political rights, an ability to speak another language (that of the dominant culture) may greatly enhance a person's social status and well-being.

To examine how the use of different languages influences attitudes, Wallace Lambert (1960) conducted a series of tests among bilingual French and English Canadians in Montreal. He asked people to evaluate the personality characteristics of the French and English speakers that they heard on tapes, without telling them that the speakers were bilinguals who had made matching recordings in both languages. Lambert found that both English and French Canadians evaluated the speakers more favorably when they spoke English than when they spoke French. He interpreted this attitude on the part of the French Canadians as a reflection of their minority status. They apparently assumed that the English speakers would occupy higher social positions, and seemed to have adopted many of the stereotypes held by English Canadians concerning the two ethnic groups.

Lambert was careful to choose speakers for his experiment whose use of either language exhibited little interference from the other, so that the French of a native English speaker would not betray his or her English-Canadian ethnicity, and vice versa. *Linguistic interference* occurs when familiarity with multiple languages or dialects results in a speaker's deviating from speech norms—when a person "has a funny accent" when speaking one of the languages. It is often a major problem for persons learning a second language for purposes of social mobility or acceptability—for Lapps trying to become assimilated into Norwegian society, for example. The Lapps in Norway constitute a distinct ethnic group with cultural traditions and a language that are markedly different from those of Norwegians. Because of their minority status and unfavorable treatment by Norwegians, many Lapps seek to conceal their ethnic identity in public by avoiding Lappish dress, modes of behavior, and speech. But the Norwegian that they speak tends to be noticeably different from that spoken by native Norwegian speakers. This interference makes it impossible for them to disguise their ethnic identity entirely.

Usually social and cultural considerations determine when a multilingual speaker uses a given language. In a study of ethnicity in a mixed Lapp-Norwegian township in northern Norway, Harald Eidheim (1971) found three spheres of social interaction: the public sphere, the closed Lappish sphere, and the closed Norwegian sphere. Although Lapp was the domestic language in forty of the fifty households, Norwegian culture and language predominates in public. Even when all of the persons in a public setting are Lapp, the language used is generally Norwegian. In a Lapp-owned store the owner will respond in Norwegian to anyone speaking to him in Lapp. Lapp is, however, spoken in the closed Lappish sphere—interaction with kin and other Lapps at home, in one's neighborhood, or occasionally in more public locales. But when Norwegians enter a closed Lappish sphere, people usually switch from Lapp to Norwegian. Eidheim (1971: 60) explains: "The Norwegian not only regards Lapp as an inferior language in a general sense, but also judges it highly improper and challenging if it is used in his presence." When Lapps wish to speak Lapp in public places, they are careful to move away from others and to speak briefly in low voices, switching immediately to Norwegian when a person of unknown or Norwegian identity approaches.

Planned Linguistic Change

Since the populations of most countries exhibit considerable linguistic diversity (for example, some seven hundred languages are spoken in Papua New Guinea), governments frequently try to reduce linguistic differences or barriers. In countries where a single language is spoken by the majority, the government may attempt to reduce dialectal variation or promote the acquisition of the dominant language by speakers of other languages. In countries with greater linguistic heterogeneity, such as the many newer nations whose boundaries are more a reflection of European colonial policy than of cultural similarity, the government may promote a single national language to encourage a sense of commonality among culturally different peoples.

Because of costs and shortages of trained personnel, such policies are rarely easy to carry out. Achievement of the government's goals is hampered further by people's loyalty to their own dialect or language. Language planning must take such factors into account. Implementation of a program requires basic research into how languages are perceived and used in the existing situation, training of instructors, and provision of facilities for instruction. These efforts take time and money, both of which may be very scarce in countries trying to overcome severe economic underdevelopment and create national unity.

Peace Corps volunteers often act as agents of planned linguistic change. Here PCV Joan Mayer loans French books to school children in Bozoum in the Central African Republic, which achieved independence from France in 1960.

Establishment of an official language can have a profound and inequitable impact on the segments of an ethnically heterogeneous country. If a language is chosen that is already spoken by one ethnic group, its members will gain political and economic advantages over those who must learn the language. There may be other political considerations as well. In Kenya, the government's choice upon independence from Britain was between one of the languages spoken by major ethnic groups, the language of the previous colonial administration (English), or Swahili, which was the mother tongue of some non-African coastal people and was employed as a trade language throughout much of East Africa. The indigenous African languages were ruled out to avoid promoting the interests of any one group. As a newly independent nation Kenya was not in favor of adopting English, the language of the colonial government, since it was felt that identity as an independent African nation required adoption of an African language. Swahili proved to be the best choice: it was not directly associated with any of the major ethnic groups, it was not identified with the colonial past, and a number of people already spoke it.

Historical Linguistics

Another way of studying languages is to look at the patterns by which they change. Like human culture, language is inherently dynamic; no language remains fixed. Just as societies and cultural traditions can merge or diverge or become distinct, so can languages. In other words, languages do evolve: they undergo systematic changes partly in response to conditions in the environment (especially the social environment) and partly as a result of forces within the languages themselves.

Evolution is not an inevitable process leading from simple to complex. Any culture that exists today has aspects of simplicity and complexity at the same time, and the same is true of language. For example, Indonesian has no verb tenses. Standard English contains a fairly large number of verb tenses, but American black English exhibits even greater complexity in its verb tenses than standard English.

Except for pidgins, all languages in the world today are fully developed, fully able to meet the communicative needs of their speakers. Evolutionary trends can be identified, however. For example, as social scale increases, the complexity of a few features of language, such as vocabulary, tends to increase as well. Persons in small-scale societies are capable of communicating as wide a range of concepts as people in large-scale societies, but their normal communicative needs are usually met with a more re-stricted vocabulary. As social complexity increases and the need arises to express new ideas, existing words may take on different meanings or be joined to form new words, or entirely new words may be borrowed or invented.

The study of how languages change is known as *historical linguistics*. The fate of a language and the ways in which it changes are primarily a reflection of the history of its speakers, and especially of the nature of their contact with speakers of other languages.

Evolutionary Processes

One of the evolutionary processes that has been identified is *extinction*. As a result of sub-jugation through conquest or other forms of forced change, certain languages may no longer be spoken. In the British Isles, for example, Pict and Cornish fell into disuse as those who spoke them either died or were absorbed into the emerging English society. Linguistic extinction does not necessarily mean that the society or persons who originally spoke the language have ceased to exist, although this is often the case. With the introduction of writing, which allows for the preservation of languages in printed form, extinct languages can be revived if social factors favor such a development. Before a language disappears entirely there is frequently a period of bilingualism, and it may take several generations for it to become completely extinct.

An extinct language may be replaced by a newly created language (as in creolization) or an already existing one. The latter is an expression of linguistic *expansion*, the spread of a language among a new population. As languages expand, they pick up traces of neighboring languages. *Borrowing* of words and other aspects of speech from other languages is especially noticeable in languages that have undergone considerable expansion. When the English subjugated indigenous peoples in North America, for example,

they picked up a number of words of Native American origin—such as *tobacco, potato, chocolate, hammock, raccoon*—and incorporated them into their language.

Linguistic *multiplication* refers to the process of differentiation within a language, the development of variant forms. It is frequently a by-product of expansion. As the use of Latin spread with the expansion of the Roman Empire, dialectical variants evolved, partly as a result of contact with other languages. Subsequent isolation of variant-speaking populations as the empire disintegrated led to a deepening of these differences until distinct languages evolved—the Romance languages.

Reconstructing Language History

Modern English has reached its present configuration through a long process of evolution. Because it has been a written language since the fifteenth century, reconstructing the history of the language is relatively simple. But for languages that have not been written down over the years, the problems of historical reconstruction are considerably greater. Despite the lack of firm data, however, it is still sometimes possible to reconstruct the grammars and vocabularies of the ancestral forms, or *protolanguages*, and to reconstruct the process of linguistic evolution.

Hypothetical protolanguages (such as proto-German, which would be ancestral to modern languages like German, English, and Swedish) can be reconstructed by comparing the grammars and vocabularies of the contemporary descendants of the original tongue. These reconstructions are supported primarily by the recognition that languages are systematically structured; hence, the changes that occur over time must be correspondingly patterned and systematic. The *comparative method*, as this approach to linguistic reconstruction is called, makes considerable use of *cognates*—words that have evolved from a common ancestral word. The English word *hound* and the German *Hund* are cognates, as are *to* and *zu* and *mine* and *mein*. Regularities in the slight differences among cognates are carefully analyzed to deduce the major patterns of the protolanguage.

Just as it may be possible to reconstruct extinct languages, it may also be possible to estimate the dates at which two languages diverged. For this purpose, Morris Swadesh (1971) developed a method known as *glottochronology*, or sound dating. This approach is based on the assumption that linguistic changes are orderly, and that the rate of linguistic change is essentially uniform. If the core vocabularies of two related tongues are compared and the differences between them counted, a rough estimate of when the split occurred can be determined. The ability to arrive at such dates is of

particular use in trying to reconstruct the early histories of peoples in terms of such things as their migratory patterns and contacts with other peoples. In this regard, glottochronology is sometimes used in conjunction with archaeological work to confirm patterns indicated by the material remains or to offer possible explanations for archaeological findings.

Not all scholars agree with Swadesh's methods and assumptions, however. The main critics of glottochronology challenge the idea that rates of linguistic change are as constant as Swadesh supposes. Since it is known that culture change in general is not uniform, there is little reason to assume that language changes at uniform rates. Although Swadesh's work has been of value, it is necessary to reserve judgment at this time on its ultimate reliability.

Summary

Although communication is essential to social life, inaccuracies arise between the sending and receiving of messages. An organism trying to control the impression it makes may use redundant messages to get its point across.

While communication among loners can be quite simple, social animals require a much more complex system of communication. Humans possess the most complex and flexible system of communication, its flexibility being based upon the use of symbols. Human language and speech are unique, but other animals too may possess some capacity for language. Our language is a complex system of patterned sound and rules for combining sounds to convey meaning or grammar. Humans also communicate by means of gestures (kinesics), the use of space (proxemics), and bodily adornment.

Language and culture are closely interrelated, though neither totally determines the other.

Culture influences language in a number of ways; in general, those things which are of most cultural significance receive the most attention. Language in turn provides shape to a people's lives, although it is doubtful that it does so to the extent argued by the Sapir-Whorf hypothesis.

There are thousands of languages in the world today, although the precise number is difficult to determine because of poor data and ambiguity about what constitutes a separate language. In addition to different languages there are also regional and social dialects, pidgins, and creoles. Another problem in determining linguistic boundaries is related to linguistic contact. Individuals are often multilingual and in different situations may be called upon to use a range of distinct speech forms, as in the case of diglossia. Such contact sometimes interferes with an individual's use of certain speech forms. It also can produce changes in the nature of languages themselves. Through contact and other means, languages are continually changing. Some aspects of linguistic change are looked at through the study of historical linguistics, which is concerned with processes of linguistic extinction, expansion and borrowing, and multiplication as well as with the reconstruction of protolanguages and patterns of linguistic change.

Although communication is an essential element of human adaptation, it will not feed or clothe people. In the next chapter we will look at the major adaptive strategies humans have devised as means of providing for their physical needs.

Suggested Readings

Among the numerous general studies of language are:

Bauman, R., and Sherzer, J., eds. 1974. *Explorations in the ethnography of speaking.* New York: Cambridge Univ. Press.

Blount, B. ed., 1974. *Language, culture and society: A book of readings.* Cambridge, MA: Winthrop.

Bolinger, D. 1975. *Aspects of language,* 2d ed. New York: Harcourt Brace Jovanovich.

Burling, Robbins. 1970. *Man's many voices: Language in its cultural context.* New York: Holt, Rinehart & Winston.

Eastman, Carol M. 1975. *Aspects of language and culture.* San Francisco: Chandler and Sharp.

Giglioni, P. P., ed. 1972. *Language and social context.* London: Nicholls.

Hymes, Dell, ed. 1964. *Language in culture and society.* New York: Harper & Row.

Sapir, E. 1921. *Language.* New York: Harcourt Brace Jovanovich.

Schane, S. A. 1973. *Generative phonology.* Englewood Cliffs, NJ: Prentice-Hall.

More specialized studies of language include:

Basso, Keith H. 1979. *Portraits of "The Whiteman": Linguistic play and cultural symbols among Western Apache.* Cambridge: Cambridge Univ. Press.

Bloch, Maurice, ed. 1975. *Political language and oratory in traditional society.* New York: Academic Press.

Hall, Edward T. 1966. *The hidden dimension.* New York: Doubleday. (nonverbal communication)

Hoenigswald, H. M. 1960. *Language change and linguistic reconstruction.* Chicago: University of Chicago Press.

Hymes, Dell, ed. 1971. *Pidginization and creolization of languages.* Cambridge: Cambridge Univ. Press.

Lakoff, R. 1975. *Language and woman's place.* New York: Harper & Row.

Mazrui, Ali. 1975. *The political sociology of the English language.* The Hague: Mouton.

Todd, Loreto. 1974. *Pidgins & creoles.* London: Routledge and Kegan Paul.

Valdman, Albert, ed. 1978. *Pidgin and creole linguistics.* Bloomington: Indiana Univ. Press.

Focus on People

Communication Problems in the Southern Philippines

Robert Randall

After earning a college degree in mathematics and chemistry in 1964, Robert A. Randall joined the Peace Corps and taught high school for nearly three years in a rural part of northern Nigeria. When he returned to the United States, Randall entered the graduate program in linguistic anthropology at the University of California, Berkeley. Accompanied by his wife and fellow anthropologist Nancy, Randall spent fifteen months in 1971–72 on a small island in the southern Philippines studying the way villagers tried to solve their economic and dietary problems. Randall returned to the Philippines briefly in 1980.

THE PHILIPPINES IS currently the world's seventeenth most populous nation. Among its thirty-nine million inhabitants, an enormous number of languages are spoken. American control of the Philippines led to the widespread use of English, but neither English nor any other language is spoken by a majority of the people. Cebuano, Tagalog (also called Pilipino), Ilocano, and Ilongo are the most widely spoken, but there are between forty and eighty other Malayo-Polynesian languages, several distinct Chinese languages, a Spanish creole, and even some Arabic.

Amid such linguistic complexity, it is little wonder that Filipinos commonly find themselves unable to understand what the majority of their fellow citizens are saying, thinking, or planning. Consider, for example, the predicament of a thirty-year-old woman in the southern city of Zamboanga. Her mother is Cebuano and her father is Chinese. Her paternal grandfather is Cantonese and his wife Fukien. The woman was raised in a Tausug area of the Philippines and educated in English. She is married to a Sinama-speaking Samal who also speaks Tausug and English. She told me, "You know, I speak four languages and I still cannot understand either my [Samal] mother-in-law or my [Fukien] grandmother."

Because of such communication snarls, speakers of different Philippine languages usually avoid visiting each other, eating together, forming friendships, marrying, or forming political alliances. One result is that Filipinos frequently form ethnic stereotypes based on very minimal personal experience, and they frequently offer very crude explanations of behavior in other ethnic groups.

Government in the Philippines has been dominated by English and the northern languages of Tagalog and Ilocano. Individuals who speak the distantly related southern languages have "been neglected for decades," governmental authorities concede.

Poverty is, of course, by no means limited to speakers of minority languages, but speakers of

This photograph by Robert Randall shows the Zamboanga City fish market in the Southern Philippines early in the day when the fish catch is arriving.

Philippine minority languages certainly have a worse experience of poverty than do those closer to the languages of power. This is partly because most high government officers have little direct knowledge of the complaints of minority language speakers, and, since they select compatible subordinates, they receive little relevant information from their assistants. As an example, consider this statement from a Cebuano-speaking lieutenant colonel who is politically responsible for a Tausug and Sinama-speaking area the size of a county: "I cannot speak Sinama at all, but I used to think I understood Tausug until I studied some Tausug anthropol-

ogy in defense college and realized how little I knew about their language." Because he knew no Sinama, he usually spoke with village leaders in his excellent colloquial English. But since English is a school language and many of the village leaders have had very little schooling, they are unable to voice complaints, and are reluctant to admit they have not understood.

Language difficulties create still other problems for the Samal. When a storm is imminent, weather reports broadcast the dangers in English or Tagalog. The Samal, who understand neither English nor Tagalog, are unaware of an impending storm until the winds pick up and the clouds darken. As a result, many Samal fishers are faced with being stranded for days in a city where they've gone to sell their fish and buy supplies. Since they generally don't have the money to stay in the city, they frequently risk drowning by sailing home in dangerous seas.

Communication is probably never more important than when someone becomes ill and medical help (and the money to pay for it) must be sought. Consider what happens when Samal get sick and the family must find money to pay doctor's bills:

"God!", we say, "if this sickness continues perhaps it will be death." We worry about that. Those are our thoughts. Therefore, we find money—we go into debt if there isn't any money saved for our medicine. That's our thinking.

With luck, a local Sinama-speaking relative will help pay. More often than not, though, Samal must ask more distant, wealthier relatives. In the southern Philippines, land is the main source of rural wealth. Traditionally, Yakan and Tausug farmed the land and traded rice to Samal fishers for fish. As a result of these trading relationships, there were often marriages among the children of the different groups. When Samal need money, then, it is easiest to approach Yakan or Tausug relatives.

If a loan cannot be arranged, Samal pawn the gold jewelry they keep as savings. In Zamboanga City, pawnshops are usually run by Chinese men married to women who speak Chabacano (a Spanish creole). Deals are conducted in Chabacano. To secure the debt until payback, the pawnbroker loans perhaps half the worth of the gold at 5 percent interest *per month*. The pawn ticket, however, plainly states the Philippine Usury Law, which allows a maximum interest rate of 2.5 percent per month. The law, which is enforceable, is written in English—so the Samal do not know about it. Hence, they pay 71 percent per year rather than the 38 percent legally permitted; they often forfeit their life savings because they can't read the law.

Once the money is obtained, the sick person is brought to a clinic. But the doctors and nurses speak very little Sinama, so there is little communication. Samal with some knowledge of English may go along to help, but, typically, the doctor learns little about the symptoms and history of the patient. Nor do Samal typically understand the physician's treatment instructions or the consequences of not following them. One Samal remarked, "We Samal don't just do whatever the doctor says. If he tells us to buy 20 pesos worth of the medicine, and we don't have much money, we just buy ten." Although only half a prescribed dosage often prohibits a cure, Samal typically do not know this, and are unlikely to ask the doctor.

What, then, is a multilingual nation to do about its "language problem"? There are few options. Traditionally, English has been used as a national language. It is, however, no easier for the child of uneducated Samal parents to learn school subjects in English than it would be for a North American child to learn them in Arabic or Burmese. As in many countries, therefore, the government has promoted an indigenous national language. Spanish and American colonialism ruled the Philippines from the central Philippine, Tagalog-speaking city of Manila. It was understandable, therefore, that when a national language was selected in the 1930s it was Tagalog. Unfortunately, Tagalog is not very closely related to southern Philippine languages such as Sinama.

Samal children, therefore, get their schooling in languages which are alien. Their teachers, moreover, frequently speak neither English, Tagalog, nor Sinama very well; some speak Sinama hardly at all. One village leader said, "We like to have Cebuano primary-school teachers because they are trusted by the Cebuano military leaders. If necessary, the teacher will vouch for us." Although it is easy to appreciate the village leader's reasoning, it is not easy to see how such teaching will produce the Samal doctors, lawyers, teachers, and administrators that Samal want.

Accordingly, Samal and members of many southern linguistic minorities have become understandably discontented with the pace of progress. Some are pushing for greater political autonomy or even secession, and the past decade has seen a bloody war and much human tragedy. Partly as a result of opposition, the national government has made a number of concessions, and has provided some scholarships for the minorities. But until the Philippines has one universally understood national language, or until speakers of each language have control over what is important in their lives, chances are that the linguistic and ethnic tensions will persist.

Chapter Five

Patterns of Subsistence

To SURVIVE WE must eat. But unlike other animals, we humans are rarely satisfied with getting food by gathering or killing whatever we come upon by chance. We desire more security, more stability, and often simply more to eat. Accordingly, we spend a good deal of time learning how to acquire food, and exploring ways to increase the amount available. In some instances food procurement is done on an individual basis, but more often it involves group efforts. Closely related to the procurement process is the manufacture of implements to assist us in gathering, capturing, or producing food. While many animals have devised simple tools to help them in acquiring food, humans have developed much more intricate and sophisticated tools than those employed by any other species.

Human existence is more than a matter of trying to get enough to eat, of course. We expect to obtain a much wider range of things if we are to live as "humans" and not as "animals." To us, the "necessities" of life are not only those things which we need to survive; often they are amenities defined by cultural prescription—companionship, clothing, shelter, means of transportation. We also produce many things that are not necessities. Even people with relatively simple technologies and few material possessions produce an assortment of toys, trinkets, and other nonessentials.

The strategies employed by people to procure and produce the fundamental things that they need or want are called *subsistence activities*. The type of strategy adopted by a group of people is closely related to the ways members of the group interact and to how they perceive the world around them. In this chapter we will look at the major patterns of subsistence that humans have devised, paying primary attention to the patterns that exist in the world today.

Although strategies vary from society to society, it is possible to think in terms of a limited number of broad types: small-scale foraging societies, small-scale farming societies, pastoralists, and large-scale societies. Each can be further broken down into subgroups that have even more in common. These similarities transcend cultural boundaries to some extent. For instance, despite their cultural differences, foragers in the Australian deserts and foragers in the forests of Central Africa have a good deal in common: the scale of their societies, daily activities, division of labor, and political organization.

The basic subsistence strategies do not exist in a vacuum, however. Local variation often results from human inventiveness and responses to environmental conditions. Many of the differences between small-scale subsistence farmers in highland New Guinea and Amazonian Brazil, for instance, reflect differences in the physical environment: the fertile soils in highland New Guinea permit dense concentrations of people within valleys, while conditions in the Amazon favor dispersed and relatively small settlements. The social environment must also be taken into account. European diseases, technology, and economic goals have drastically transformed the situation in colonized lands once inhabited by foraging peoples, altering subsistence activities of the indigenous peoples as they become integrated into a broader, industrially based social system.

Subsistence patterns are continually changing. Sometimes alterations are attempts to adapt to changes in the physical environment; sometimes they are the result of technological or organizational innovations people have devised to better exploit their surroundings. Over the past few centuries a key factor influencing subsistence patterns has been contact among people pursuing different subsistence strategies, which can be seen in the spread of Western large-scale society and industrial technology and the creation of the contemporary world system.

Small-Scale Foraging Societies

Up to ten thousand years ago all humans lived in small-scale societies and subsisted on wild plants and animals. Since this *foraging* form of subsistence supported human society for some two million years before alternative modes of subsistence evolved, the study of foraging is extremely important in understanding the development of human society and culture.

Very few foraging societies exist in the world today (see Bicchieri 1972). Foragers have not done well in competition with nonforagers. European expansion over the past few centuries, in particular, has led to the destruction of many foraging societies. Sometimes the destruction of these societies has been the result of disease, or even misdirected humanitarian efforts, but often the means have been violent. Foragers have at times tried to resist (see Roberts 1978), but with little success. Peoples like the Patagonians, the Tasmanians, and the Beothiks of Newfoundland were systematically exterminated. Others, like the Bushmen of southern Africa, were forced into inhospitable environments. Certain Australian Aborigines continue to hunt and gather, but these activities are now only a small part of their subsistence activities. Most desert Aborigines have gathered in large, permanent settlements, which are controlled by the government or by various church groups. Part of their subsistence needs are now met by welfare handouts, because their traditional way of life has been destroyed and many of them are unable to find employment in Australian society.

Today foraging groups are found almost exclusively in the harshest and most remote areas of the world: in regions that no one else wants to occupy and where competition is at a minimum (for example, Arctic regions, deserts, southern Africa, central Australia). Contemporary foraging societies differ in many ways from earlier ones, for contemporary foragers have evolved for thousands of years, usually in contact with and under the influence of nonforagers. These modern-day foragers are not simply relics of the Stone Age; their life-style is influenced by the contemporary world and they are, like it or not, active participants in the modern world system.

The popular view of foragers is that of people barely surviving on the edge of extinction. The contemporary societies that have contributed to this image, however—the Inuit, Bushmen, and other groups living today in the world's most arid regions—are far from typical of foragers prior to contact with nonforaging societies. Most foragers traditionally lived in moderate environments. In the typical traditional foraging society people worked for relatively brief periods (only two to four hours a day), with ready access to abundant food sources; real scarcity and hardship were rare. Anthropologist Marshall Sahlins (1972: 1) has characterized such foragers as the "original affluent society." Many of the harshest areas (like the Kalahari desert) were occupied only recently as a result of pressures by expanding societies of nonforagers.

There are three basic types of foraging adaptation (Martin 1974: 10): pedestrian hunting and gathering, equestrian hunting and gathering, and aquatic foraging. Although all are associated with relatively small-scale societies, aspects of the groups' lives differ considerably.

Pedestrian Hunters and Gatherers

Most foragers are pedestrian hunters and gatherers, hunting wild animals and gathering wild edible plants on foot. Contemporary pedestrian hunters and gatherers include most of the for-

This engraving from G. C. Musters's 1897 book *At Home with the Patagonians* shows equestrian hunters and gatherers swinging bolas in pursuit of game in the valley of Rio Chico, Patagonia.

agers in Australia, the Bam Buti and Bushmen of central and southern Africa, and the Cree and similar groups of northern Canada.

In most of these societies men hunt and women forage. The relative importance of hunting and gathering for these societies varies, but gathering generally provides the bulk of what is eaten. This means that women contribute the largest share of the food consumed. Women are also commonly responsible for food preparation, although men may prepare game. Despite the very important role of women in subsistence activities, men frequently occupy a higher status. While prestige may be acquired by being a good hunter, often relatively little glory is attached to being a skilled gatherer.

Most pedestrian hunters and gatherers are or-

ganized into small nomadic groups known as *bands*. The optimum size of a band for efficient use of resources is between fifteen and twenty-five persons, depending on the environment. Kinship plays a prominent role in recruitment to band membership. In fact, kinship is often the principal medium for expressing social and economic relations. It is likely to be through kinship that a person acquires the right to use specific territories for foraging purposes.

The members of a foraging band may range over a territory of under one hundred up to a few thousand square miles, depending primarily upon environmental conditions. The territories occupied by hunting bands of the Mistassini Cree of northern Canada, for example, increase in size the further north a band is located, reflecting a general thinning of resources and a change in key resources and how they are exploited. To the south the Cree rely heavily upon moose and bear, which are found in fairly predictable areas; in the north caribou, which travel over much more extensive areas, assume greater importance. Beaver, also of considerable economic importance, are more plentiful in the south. In the north, people must therefore range over a larger area in search of game (Tanner 1979: 40–42).

On the whole, population densities for foragers are relatively low. It is estimated, for example, that when Europeans arrived in Australia in the late eighteenth century the entire continent was occupied by only three hundred thousand people, all of whom subsisted by foraging.

Although the band is the primary group for social interaction and economic production and exchange among foragers, larger social groupings are also important. Bands are usually allied to a number of other bands with which they share common cultural features, speaking similar dialects or languages and exchanging members through marriage. The bands within this larger group may meet periodically when available resources permit. These gatherings involve anywhere from a few dozen people to several hundred, and last from a few days to several months. During these meetings major religious ceremonies are performed, marriages arranged, goods exchanged, and disputes settled (or initiated).

The technology of pedestrian foragers is not complex. It usually provides adequately for their subsistence needs, as well as additional comforts and luxuries. But because their mobility depends on their ability to carry all their possessions themselves, they accumulate relatively few material goods. Such constraints keep wealth differences to a minimum, limiting the development of social inequality and de-emphasizing individual ownership.

Except for differences associated with sex and age, there is very little labor specialization among pedestrian foragers. All adults are capable of manufacturing the items used by their sex and of carrying out most economic activities. Foragers do recognize differences in individual skill, allowing for a limited degree of specialization. For instance, a man who is especially skilled at manufacturing hunting implements might be rewarded with a share of the game killed by others using implements which he had produced, relieving him of some of the need to hunt for himself. But in these small-scale societies he will rarely be able to become a full-time craftsman.

Equestrian Hunters and Gatherers

Hunting from horseback is nearly unknown today. But this subsistence pattern was widely used by societies in the Great Plains of the United States and Canada and the pampas of South America from the seventeenth until the nineteenth centuries, after Europeans introduced the horse to the New World.

Equestrian hunters and gatherers tend to differ from their pedestrian counterparts in such factors as the size of social units, the degree of social and economic inequality, and, of course, their mobility. Equestrian groups have usually been larger, more mobile, and more likely to develop a social and political hierarchy.

The nineteenth-century indigenous population of Patagonia, southern Argentina, provides a glimpse of these differences between pedestrian and equestrian hunting and gathering (Williams 1979). Prior to their adoption of the horse toward the end of the eighteenth century, the Patagonians had lived in small, localized groups along the coast. The horse allowed greater mobility and a shift from a reliance upon coastal resources to an emphasis upon hunting ostrich, rhea, and guanaco (a type of llama). Adapting to the annual migratory patterns of these animals, the Patagonians moved from the coastal plain across the Patagonian plateau and into the foothills of the Andes each year. Their society underwent a number of changes as they formed larger, highly structured groups. The size of these groups varied during the year. While moving across the plateau they formed bands of ten to fifteen men and their dependents, each group totaling about seventy people, for this size met the labor requirements of their hunting activities on the game-sparse plateau. At either extreme of their migratory route, game was more concentrated, and a number of these bands would gather, forming a group of around three hundred fifty people sharing a common identity.

Aquatic Foragers

Hunting and gathering peoples who rely heavily upon fishing tend to form even larger, less equal societies, with more elaborate material cultures, although these societies still have much in common with other foragers. For all foragers, access to wild food supplies is critical; aquatic foragers meet this requirement not by following game on foot or horseback but by settling near waters rich in marine life.

Today this strategy is still used by the Kwakiutl and Haida of the northwest coast of North America, though these people tend to supplement their foraging activities with wage labor. Historical accounts of the Haida provide a clearer picture of their aquatic adaptation and an extreme example of the social scale and degree of social inequality that can accompany this pattern. In 1840 there were some eight thousand Haida living on the Queen Charlotte Islands and Prince of Wales Island off the southern coast of Alaska. By 1900 their numbers had dropped to nine hundred people living in five permanent villages (Swanton 1902). The Haida traditionally subsisted by fishing (primarily for salmon and halibut), trapping bear and other game, and gathering berries and roots. They possessed an elaborate fishing technology, including canoes more than fifty feet long. With these boats they ranged over hundreds of miles, frequently to raid other peoples. Their society was divided into kin groups. It was also highly stratified, with chiefs, servants, and even slaves. This life-style was supported by an abundance of resources and a technology that allowed a relatively large number of people to live in villages of plank houses, some of which could accommodate more than one hundred people.

Small-Scale Farming Societies

Although rather elaborate technologies and social structures could thus be built on a foraging life-style, and although at its simplest foraging met food needs with minimal effort, most of the world's cultures have turned away from this subsistence pattern. Nine to ten thousand years ago many societies began to domesticate plants and animals, gradually reducing their dependence upon wild foods. Production of domesticated crops and animals often required more labor than foraging, but it also resulted in greater food-producing capabilities in many environments. Agricultural production, or the cultivation of domesticated plants for subsistence, usually could support higher population densities than was possible with foraging, and generally allowed people to lead more sedentary lives.

Food Production Practices

Subsistence farmers in small-scale societies rely upon human or animal labor and employ simple tools. This type of production is sometimes referred to as *horticulture*, a term for any kind of garden cultivation.

A common method of agricultural produc-

Slash and burn agriculture: two Lacandon men of Naha' cut a giant mahogany tree in the process of clearing a cornfield.

tion among small-scale farmers is *shifting cultivation* (also known as *slash-and-burn agriculture*). A few thousand years ago, this type of agriculture was practiced by peoples all over the world. Today, other agricultural techniques predominate throughout much of the world, although shifting cultivation does continue to support millions of people. Its range, however, has been reduced, and it is now primarily associated with equatorial tropical regions.

Shifting cultivation entails use of the slash-and-burn method of field preparation: cutting down the natural growth on a plot of land by hand, burning it, and then planting crops in the burned area. Most tropical soils are very poor and rapidly lose nutrients. Burning produces a layer of ash that provides needed nutrients for crops. The soil fertility is rapidly depleted, however, and after one or two plantings the plot is left alone for a number of years until natural growth has again become lush enough to be burned. This *fallow* period may last only a few years in some areas, several decades in others,

depending on the fertility of the environment. In the Mayan village of Chan Kom, in northern Yucatan, after using a field for two or three years, the land is then left fallow for seven years (Redfield and Villa Rojas 1962: 53-54). In the poorer environment of Indonesian Borneo (Kalimantan), the land is left fallow for twelve to twenty years after two to three years' use (Hudson 1972: 8-9).

After burning, it is common for a number of different crops to be sown together, a pattern known as *intercropping*. Often root crops, cereals, and shrubs are sown together in a manner that simulates the original forest cover and protects the soil from erosion (Grigg 1974: 58). In the lowland Mayan village of Chichipate, Guatemala, for example, fields may contain as many as twenty-one different plants, including squash, chili peppers, sweet potatoes, maize, pineapples, tobacco, beans, manioc, sugar cane, peanuts, and onions (Carter 1969: 61-67). Once the planting is completed, little is done to the field until it is time to harvest. Activities such as weeding and taking steps against pests are rare, as is the use of fertilizer. As long as the land is not overworked, shifting cultivation provides good return for relatively small input, particularly in tropical areas.

Not all small-scale farmers practice this method of shifting cultivation. In the higher altitudes of central Mexico, a modified system is practiced that involves tilling, weeding, and shorter fallow periods. In western Africa, fallow land continues to be planted, although less intensively, and the plot is not allowed to return fully to its natural state. Some small-scale farmers employ even more intensive methods, especially in more fertile environments, such as the banks of rivers and lakes in nontropical areas. Limited use of animal waste for fertilizer and crop rotation in many instances allow prolonged use of fields. It is important to recognize, however, that the "cost" of such inputs in terms of resources and labor is much higher than with less intensive methods. In some areas, because of local environmental and market conditions, these costs may be too high. In many areas, such as the Amazonian rain forest, the effort is simply not justified under existing conditions, and the less intensive pattern of shifting cultivation remains the soundest adaptation.

Many small-scale subsistence farmers augment their diet with wild game and plants. The Mundurucu of the Brazil interior, for example, grow carbohydrates in their gardens: sweet and bitter manioc, maize, beans, melons, rice, yams, sweet potatoes, squash, pineapples, bananas, sugar cane, and a variety of spices (Murphy 1974). Most of their protein needs are provided by hunting and fishing. The fruits and nuts that they gather add variety to their diet and provide an important supplement during the rainy season.

Small-scale farmers often possess a wide variety of domesticated animals for consumption and transportation. In many of these societies domesticated animals assume a very important place in the subsistence base and in the overall social system. Among the Tsembaga of highland New Guinea, pigs are eaten only on special occasions, such as major rituals and during illness (Rappaport 1967). Pigs help clean up garbage around Tsembaga settlements, and their rooting activities in fallow gardens hasten the reforestation process. They are also one of the primary items of exchange: feasts in which pig meat is distributed are of considerable importance in creating and maintaining social and political alliances.

Social Organization

People practicing shifting cultivation live in camps or villages of various sizes. In the Amazon Basin, before Europeans radically altered the situation, village size ranged from fewer than one hundred inhabitants in the western region near the Andes to more than one thousand toward the Atlantic coast. Both the size and stability of such settlements are influenced by the local ecology. People living in areas with poor potential for agriculture and relatively long fallow cycles often live in small villages, moving every few years to remain close to their fields. In some instances a series of sites will be occupied over several decades, and after the forest has had time to return to its natural state the people return to the same site. Shifting cultivators living in areas where more intensive use of the land is possible often have fairly stable villages, larger than those found in less favorable environments.

As with foragers, the societies of most small-scale farmers are organized around kinship, which plays a vital role in ordering social and economic relations. Land is usually owned by villages or kingroups, and a person's place of residence and access to land are commonly determined by ties of kinship. In many ways the family is the primary unit of production and consumption in these societies—to some extent paralleling the band among foragers—but a good deal of work is also carried out communally. Important tasks such as hunting, clearing fields, harvesting crops, and building houses are often done by large groups rather than by individual families.

The technologies of small-scale farmers are rarely much more complex than those of foragers, and all adults are generally able to perform those tasks common to members of their sex. People's age and sex are usually the most important factors determining the kinds of activities they will be involved in. Among the Mundurucu, as with many foraging societies, women are responsible for the more tedious types of work, which also provide most of the subsistence base—most agricultural labor, virtually all domestic chores, and the preparation and distribution of food. Men, on the other hand, hunt and fish, take care of occasional heavy agricultural work, and conduct the vil-

lage's external affairs. Their work is accorded higher status.

In part because of their more sedentary lifestyle, small-scale farmers are able to accumulate more things than foragers, but not much more. Shifting cultivators who live in humid tropical environments cannot accumulate many goods, since most are subject to rapid disintegration. In part because of this lack of durable goods, differences in wealth in these societies are minimal. A strong emphasis is often placed upon sharing of food and possessions. Mundurucu share wild game and food produced in their gardens with members of other families. Sharing ensures that every villager has enough to eat and serves to promote village solidarity. Despite the lack of wealth differences, members of these societies are not always social equals, for while accumulation of durable wealth may not be possible, status differences can come about through the exchange of goods and services.

Pastoralists

In areas of low and unpredictable rainfall, which are not well suited for agricultural production, animal herding is a useful adaptation. In some pastoral groups, only the herders move with the herds, while other members live in settled villages growing some crops; in other pastoral groups everyone moves with their migrating herds. We will consider these two pastoral variants separately, for they shape cultures in different ways.

Transhumance

Transhumance, which literally means "from one place to another on the earth," consists of limited crop production in the immediate vicinity of a village and migratory herding of animals. This pattern is found, for example, among

certain Mediterranean groups, the Navajo of the American Southwest, and the Hottentots in the drier areas of southern Africa.

Around the Mediterranean, with its pattern of long summer droughts and wet winters, a production system has evolved based upon cereals such as wheat and barley, tree and vine crops like olives and grapes, horticultural production of fruits and vegetables, and grazing sheep and goats. In the more impoverished Mediterranean environments the grazing of sheep and goats has assumed particular importance. The sheep and goats are grazed on coastal plains during the wet winter and spring and moved to the highlands when lowland vegetation dries up during the summer.

Among some groups, transhumance has rather disruptive social consequences. The six

Grazers in Crete—an example of transhumance.

hundred families of Sarakatsani, a Greek mountain community, for example, depend heavily upon the products and income derived from grazing sheep and goats (Campbell 1974). Their transhumant adaptation requires that male shepherds spend a good deal of time away from the village with their animals, grazing them on pastures leased from distant villages higher in the mountains. Grazing is conducted on a family basis; cooperation in the community beyond the family level is rare. This lack of social integration increases the potential for competition and antagonism among families, characteristics that are in fact quite noticeable among the Sarakatsani as they compete for scarce resources and attempt to defend family honor and well-being.

Pastoral Nomadism

In regions even less suited to horticulture or transhumance, many peoples build their subsistence patterns around nomadic movement with grazing herds. *Pastoral nomadism* is an eco-nomic adaptation and life-style characterized by lack of permanent habitation and primary dependence upon the herding of animals for subsistence, in contrast to the lives of pastoral transhumants, who are able to live in stable villages and who meet much of their subsistence requirements by agriculture.

Development of pastoral nomadism followed domestication of the horse in the Asian steppes and the camel in southwestern Arabia, both around 3000 B.C. The use of these animals for food and transportation allowed a more mobile pattern based on animal grazing than had previously been possible. From the steppes of Asia and southern Arabia, pastoral nomads spread into the drier areas of northern Africa and Asia. The areas they occupied—the high mountains and lowland deserts and the dry steppes—were sparsely settled by more sedentary populations. Pastoral nomadism developed in other parts of the world as well, such as among the Lapps of northern Europe, whose economy centers around reindeer herding.

Subsistence Activities. Movement is a central

feature of pastoral nomadism. Because of seasonal variation in the weather and its unpredictability in many of the regions occupied by pastoralists, they must move their herds to take maximal advantage of available pasture land. Many pastoral nomadic societies in the Middle East follow a traditional route, the *il-rah* ("tribal road"), over a widely diverse landscape. The pattern frequently entails gradual movement from a low-lying area, where they are in close proximity to sedentary peoples, to high and isolated mountain pastures. For example, the Shah Nawazi Baluch of southern Iran spend the winter months with their goats, sheep, and camels in stable herding camps of between five and twenty tents on a five-thousand-foot plateau. During the spring, the richest time of the year, camps move frequently, seeking the best grazing sites. During the early months of summer, movement slackens as the nomads become involved in harvesting grain. Late in the summer most of the group leave their herds under the care of shepherds and migrate down through the mountains to a drainage basin to take part in the date harvest. At this time they live in mud huts in the date groves. In midautumn they return to the plateau.

The kinds of animals pastoralists herd and the extent to which they are involved in agricultural production varies considerably. They also vary in self-sufficiency: pastoral nomads in Africa concentrate on meeting their own daily food needs whereas Middle Eastern pastoral nomads typically try to produce a marketable surplus that can be exchanged for other goods (Dyson-Hudson 1969: 76). But all pastoral nomads depend to some extent upon nonpastoral products, such as grains and fruits. Activities associated with acquiring these nonpastoral products significantly influence the way their society is organized and their annual cycle of activities. For example, before they were pacified by the Iranian government between 1928 and 1935, the Shah Nawazi Baluch supplemented their

yearly pastoral activities with raiding and slavery, as well as agriculture, hunting and gathering, and trade. Their animals provided milk products, meat, and raw materials for crafts. Their work in date palm groves yielded dates to eat and raw materials for ropes and mats. They supplemented these goods by occasional hunting and gathering of wild foods, and by predatory raiding of trade caravans and sedentary agriculturalists for food, slaves, and other valuables (Salzman 1971). Slaves and serfs were used in small-scale irrigated grain farming. The Shah Nawazi Baluch used most of what they raised or stole, but they exchanged some of their goods— especially items acquired from raiding—for products such as grain and cloth.

Social Organization. In part because of their reliance upon nonpastoral products, most pastoral nomads maintain important social and economic relations with farmers, merchants, and city dwellers. Within pastoral nomad societies, animals are usually owned by individuals or by family heads, and the primary group of production and consumption is the family. Families, however, must work with larger groups for efficient and coordinated use of resources, and often for protection as well. Accordingly, families are grouped into "individual herding groups" or *camps*. The size of the herding group will depend upon factors influencing optimum herd size and composition, and the distribution of age and sex differences within the human group. The composition of herding groups is constantly in flux. Among the Shah Nawazi Baluch, the average local group ranges from twenty persons to one hundred. As individuals mature and as herds grow, families and individuals leave to join other groups or to form new ones.

Above the camp level of organization, pastoral nomads are usually grouped into larger social alliances. The several thousand Nawazi Baluch consider themselves members of a single "tribe" because of their presumed descent from a com-

mon founding ancestor. For most pastoral nomads, kinship provides the primary medium of
social alliance. In some instances these tribes
may be quite large, numbering several hundred
thousand individuals. In the past, primarily because of the influence of central governments
and pressures to organize into larger groupings
for purposes of warfare, these tribes often joined
together to form larger confederacies. These
confederacies are rarely important today; even
in the past they tended to be highly unstable.

Within pastoral nomadic societies the division of labor is based primarily upon age and
sex. Almost all labor associated with herding
and agriculture is done by men, although there
are exceptions. Women generally are responsible for domestic activities and for producing
items associated with the home, such as hand-
woven rugs. Specialization within a group is
rare. But group members depend upon many
goods and services produced by the specialized
labor of persons who are not pastoral nomads—
itinerant traders and craftsmen, sedentary workers, and merchants.

Despite their mobility, pastoral nomads are
able to accumulate possessions, because they
can carry them on large pack animals such as
horses and camels. Also, since most pastoral nomads are integrated into national economies, especially in the Middle East, they are able to
accumulate wealth in a very mobile form: general-purpose money (see p. 144).

Unlike foragers, small-scale farmers, and
transhumants, pastoral nomads often exhibit
considerable differences in social status. These
differences reflect the ability of individuals to
accumulate wealth, and the need in many societies to coordinate the movement of large
numbers of people and animals. Status differences may also result from external influences,
raiding, or warfare. Traditions of warfare conducted on a large scale have encouraged the development of centralized authority, and the taking of slaves and use of serf labor by some
nomadic groups has led to the integration of
persons into their societies who are of a decidedly lower status.

On the whole, many of the differences between pastoral nomads and the societies discussed earlier are a result of the nomads' interaction with large-scale societies. Since the
nineteenth century the number of pastoral nomads has declined, because of pressure from national governments for the nomads to settle and
because of the expansion of more intensive systems of land use. There are still, however, over
15 million pastoral nomads, occupying an estimated 10 million square miles of the earth's surface (Allan 1965: 288). In countries like
Somalia, Saudi Arabia, Pakistan, Nigeria, Iran,
and Afghanistan, pastoral nomads remain a socially and economically important segment of
the population. It is highly unlikely that pastoral nomadism will disappear in the near future,
for in many arid regions it remains the optimum
method of production. Of particular importance is the fact that pastoralists have been able
to interact with larger political units without
suffering a total loss of autonomy. When they
come into contact with industrial societies, pastoralists are rarely reduced to the impoverished
status so common with foragers and indigenous
shifting cultivators.

Large-Scale Societies

The subsistence patterns we have looked at so
far involve relatively small-scale human groups.

The establishment of relatively dense populations dates from the rise of village farming

communities between 8000 and 6000 B.C. Agriculture is an intensive method of food production that supports larger and more sedentary populations than any other subsistence pattern. Since the advent of agriculture, intensification of production and population growth have greatly altered the nature of human society, leading to the development of larger social and political units (such as states, nations, and empires).

Development of Large-Scale Societies

Initially there were a limited number of centers where political units above the village level emerged. These were the "cradles of civilization" in the Middle East and southeast Asia. In these settings, previously autonomous villages were incorporated into larger units, cities often grew, and extravillage economic relations took on greater significance as the major crop plants and animals were domesticated, although their distribution was relatively limited. Between A.D. 1 and 1000 the "cradles" expanded: The population of Europe north of the Alps grew significantly, the Chinese expanded south of the Yangtse, the Bantu moved into southern Africa, and the New World civilizations of highland Mexico and South America expanded into surrounding areas.

Much of the growth of these centers was related to more systematic and intensive water management. Irrigation played a major role in agricultural change in the Middle East, China, Southeast Asia, central Mexico, and coastal Peru. In the Orient and the Indian subcontinent, the development of wet rice cultivation was of particular importance in supporting very dense populations.

Beginning in the fifteenth century, European exploration, expansion, and colonization further altered human society by creating a more integrated world system. Societies and populations were mixed and altered to an unprece-

dented extent. Crops and farming techniques that previously had been localized were spread over wider areas. In many parts of Europe, Africa, and Asia, a shift from existing crops to newly available New World crops such as maize and potatoes greatly improved the quantity and quality of the food supply (Crosby 1972: 165–202).

The formation of larger-scale societies was further encouraged by the growth of industrial methods of production. During the second half of the eighteenth century the economy of Britain, and to a lesser extent the economies of Western Europe and New England, were transformed by a series of mechanical inventions, especially the steam engine and a series of innovations in textile manufacturing. This "Industrial Revolution," a shift from slow hand methods of production to mechanized factory and agricultural production, resulted in major social changes whose impact was eventually felt throughout the world.

Differences Between Large- and Small-Scale Patterns

In general, as societies adopted machine technologies they shifted from traditional subsistence activities to newer methods that seemed to greatly increase the quantity of food and other goods that each worker could produce. Those people not needed in food production could specialize in other activities, move from rural areas to urban areas where jobs were concentrated, and use the money they earned to trade for their subsistence needs. Contemporary large-scale societies using this general strategy thus differ in degree from small-scale societies in a number of ways: use of machines rather than human or animal labor, intensity of resource use, specialization, trade, interdependency, and inequalities in wealth and social status. These features have both advantages and disadvantages.

An important productive innovation found in many large-scale societies is the use of machines driven by inorganic power sources to supplement or replace human and animal labor. By contrast, production among small-scale foragers and farmers and among pastoral nomads relies on human labor alone. Reliance on human labor is found in many large-scale societies as well, but in these settings its use represents one of several potential strategies. For instance, agricultural production in Mexico often involves the use of humans to hoe, dig, and plant by hand, and animals to pull carts and plows; few mechanical aids are used. There are areas of Mexico, however, where production depends heavily upon the use of tractors and other machines. But matters are rarely this simple. Which strategy is adopted in a particular setting can be influenced by international factors such as the availability of capital from international lending agencies or the desire of corporations to dump used machinery in underdeveloped nations, as well as by local political concerns like the strategies employed by national elites to retain a high concentration of wealth or union-management struggles.

The introduction of machinery has many social implications. It can be seen as a way of releasing workers from difficult and boring tasks. But all too often mechanization leads to considerable social disruption, especially where previous patterns of exploitation have been replaced by systems that make the original labor force largely irrelevant. When the workers on plantations or in cottage textile industries are replaced by machines, the result may be the displacement of a large number of workers who have little or no place in the new productive order. In some situations, however, it may take only a short time for individuals to find new ways to support themselves. For example, many Australian Aborigines who had worked part-time on farms moved to cities when agricultural production became heavily mechanized in the 1960s (Wilson 1965). In the cities Aborigines relied upon welfare payments and were able to find a variety of low-paying menial jobs. Mechanization can sometimes create new opportunities. In parts of India, the introduction of tractor mechanization along with tube-well irrigation has improved production and led to an increased demand for labor (Broehl 1978: 120).

A second difference in degree between subsistence patterns in small- and large-scale societies is the intensity with which resources are used. By greater intensity we mean that people produce more in terms of crops or other material goods out of the land on which they live. Thus, in food production, foraging and some forms of small-scale agriculture represent relatively unintensive adaptations to the land; relatively little is extracted from or produced out of the land. As social scale increases resources are used more intensively. By using locally available resources, wet rice farmers in East Asia, India, and Java can grow enough food to support four hundred to fifteen hundred people per square kilometer—far more than is possible employing less intensive slash-and-burn techniques. The intensive use of food-producing lands has increased dramatically in many parts of the world over the past two centuries with the introduction of machinery. During the twentieth century in particular, agricultural production has increased. Humans have been able to produce food for a rapidly growing population through more and more intensive use of the land. Land use and settlement is still relatively concentrated, however. Only about 11 percent of the earth's land is used for crop production and another 20 percent for grazing (Grigg 1974: 6). Today, some 80 percent of the world's people live on little more than 15 percent of the land. Many parts of the world remain sparsely populated, and in a number of these areas less intensive methods of production persist.

Such intensive land use exacts a price, how-

Intensive rice cultivation, Bali, Indonesia.

ever. The use of pesticides and artificial fertilizers, for example, while allowing us to produce more food, often endangers the health of those working the land as well as those eating what is produced, and even those living nearby (e.g., DDT contaminating mother's milk). Economic problems arise as well. Use of tractors allows for more intensive use of land, but requires substantial inputs like fuel, which may not be economically viable as fuel costs increase. Reliance upon technological supports has led to significant financial problems for many poor countries, burdened by foreign debts. Also, a problem may be created by putting people out of work in agriculture, sending them packing to the city, where they often become part of impoverished slum-dwelling populations. Power is a problem too—technology is often monopolized by those with power and wealth, what is produced and the profit from production going to help them and not the majority of people. We are often much better at coming up with technical solutions to problems than with dealing with the social consequences of our innovations.

Another difference between large- and small-scale societies is the degree of *specialization:* individuals repeatedly producing a single service or product for others rather than working at a variety of tasks to meet their own subsistence needs. There is relatively little specialization in most small-scale societies. Some individuals may perform special tasks, but they generally do so on a supplementary basis. In a band of a dozen persons or even a village of a few hundred inhabitants there simply is not enough work for a full-time butcher, barber, or priest. In the smaller Mayan villages of southern Belize, stores are run on a part-time basis; their operators rely primarily on agricultural production to meet their subsistence needs. Larger groupings, however, do allow for the emergence of full-time specialists. In Mayan villages of five hundred or more there is enough of a local market for individuals to devote all of their economic efforts to running a store. As social scale increases, an even greater degree of specialization can develop. In areas where Mayan villages are much larger, there are often not only a number of full-time specialists in the villages, but also the villages

A Guatemalan potter firing *comales*, which are used in the preparation of tortillas.

themselves may specialize, each producing particular goods that are exchanged through central markets.

With urbanization, industrialization, and the spread of the world system, the degree of specialization within a social unit takes a quantum jump. In a Mayan village, within each specialized process a single individual will generally be responsible for all of the work. A potter will collect his or her own materials, make the pots, and probably even sell them. In contrast, the production of a china place setting in a Sheffield industrial setting will involve the highly specialized labor of dozens or even hundreds of different individuals. A number of workers may be involved only in the application of glazes, for instance, month after month.

Such highly specialized industrial production is supposedly more efficient than more traditional means, but it has its drawbacks. Some social critics in large-scale societies, for example, feel that this extreme specialization gives workers a sense of meaninglessness, of detachment from the whole, as well as of boredom.

Another difference between large- and small-scale societies: in large-scale societies, the exchange of goods beyond the immediate social group is no longer a luxury; it is a necessity for survival. People living in cities, states, and empires depend upon the continual supply of goods from a wide range of sources for their day-to-day existence. Foragers and small-scale farmers are not so dependent, and for the most part they can exist as autonomous units.

The degree of specialization and the importance and extensiveness of exchange networks in large-scale societies result in a great *interdependency* between institutions, processes, and sociocultural units that are often very different. The subsistence patterns of foragers or shifting cultivators are complex, but not nearly so complex as the patterns found in most large-scale societies. There is a certain uniformity to the components of a foraging society, for most people are capable of manufacturing the material goods of their society. There are those who hunt and those who gather, but even this specialization is in a sense optional. For instance, men may consider it demeaning to dig for roots, but they can. The productive system of the United States, on the other hand, links industrial workers in New York and Detroit, farmers in South Carolina and Iowa, fishermen in Washington and Maine, and mine workers in West Virginia. They are interdependent because each of these individuals is incapable of producing most of the things that he or she consumes.

Differences of another sort become quite noticeable in large-scale societies: historically, *inequality* of social status and wealth has become much more marked as the scale of production and social organization increases. There is, simply, greater scope for the accumulation of wealth. The wealthiest and most influential person in a Mundurucu village is not really much more powerful than anyone else, nor does he or she own much more than fellow villagers. In many small-scale societies a great emphasis is in fact placed upon maintaining a semblance of social and economic equality, at least among those of similar age and the same sex. By contrast, significant socioeconomic inequalities are present in all large-scale societies. In fact, the accumulation and loss of wealth and power provides much of the dynamism of life in these societies.

Food Production Patterns

Although a great deal of production in large-scale societies is done by machine and by highly specialized workers, this is not the only means of production. In fact, a number of adaptive strategies are employed, some of them not unlike those employed by people in small-scale societies. Adaptive strategies for procuring or producing food range from large-scale versions of foraging and horticulture to large-scale plantations, grain farming, and ranching. Some large-scale cultures include a number of these adaptations.

Foraging. The collection of wild foods has not disappeared in large-scale societies, although the methods of collection and distribution tend to be quite different from those used in small-scale foraging groups. For example, Cree Indians today collect wild rice and trap

Contemporary "in-shore" fishing, St. Shotts, Newfoundland.

beavers, selling a portion of what they forage to enable them to purchase industrially produced goods such as chain saws and rifles. Hunting and collecting wild foods such as mushrooms or berries, though largely reduced to the status of "sport" or "hobby," remains an important subsidiary activity for many people.

One foraging activity in particular continues to be of considerable significance in large-scale societies: fishing. When fishing is carried out close to home, as among the northwest coast Indians, it may be characterized by relatively simple technology and labor-intensive production. Long-range fishing, on the other hand, as in the case of the tuna fleets which sail from the west coast of the United States to fish off South

America, are more likely to rely heavily upon large-scale technology, and upon mechanization rather than human labor.

Whether groups fish nearby or far away is closely related to their social organization. Among the fishing communities of coastal Newfoundland fishing is conducted nearby, using relatively small boats and nets. Fishing in these communities involves more personalistic social relationships than is the case with larger fisheries, in which relationships resemble those of many industrial settings. Thus, in St. Shotts on the southern shore of Newfoundland, crews are very small and usually kin based (Nemec 1972). Captain-crew relations tend to be egalitarian, reflecting the basic egalitarianism of this relatively poor community. The particular pattern of fishing in a place like St. Shotts has developed within a unique context, and any alterations in this environment will have repercussions throughout the society. Changes that promote the development of large-scale, highly technological fishing, such as government loan programs, may drastically alter the way people fish and in turn reduce the significance and nature of kin relations in the fishery and in the community as a whole.

Large-scale societies have also produced foraging adaptations that are unique to them, because of the presence of people who are excluded from the mainstream of social and economic life: beggars, and others who live off what others discard or give away. These people's social organization may be very fluid, with a highly transient population. On the other hand, sometimes they form groups, recruited perhaps on the basis of kinship or common place of origin. For example, Catholic activists working among ragpickers in Tokyo helped them form a cooperative which eventually became successful financially (Taira 1969).

Peasant Farming. Perhaps the majority of the people in the world today can be classified as peasants. The populations of most underdeveloped countries consist predominantly of peasants. In Africa, Asia, Europe, and Latin America there are hundreds of millions of peasants.

Peasants are farmers. The family farm is their basic unit of production and social organization. Although wage laborers are sometimes employed, the individual family provides most of the labor. The farm furnishes the bulk of the family's needs, as well as a surplus for sale. Throughout Asia, for instance, peasants grow rice on small family-operated farms, consuming about half of what they grow. They sell the rest to neighboring urban areas and in some cases foreign importers.

Peasant societies are characterized by a low level of specialization. They also tend to use relatively simple, labor-intensive production methods. In wet rice farming, for instance, humans use hand tools to continually repair the dikes and irrigation canals used to conduct water through the paddies. Water buffalo or oxen may help in preparation of the soil before planting; transplanting of seedlings by hand is usually carried out by women. Harvesting is also done by hand, with the aid of a knife or sickle. Both socially and technologically, wet rice cultivators therefore resemble small-scale farmers, but their incorporation into larger societies is more complete. Peasants are part of an encompassing stratified society, and they are strongly influenced by external social, political, and economic conditions. Their cultural traditions are derived both from metropolitan centers and from their immediate environment, creating what are sometimes referred to as "folk traditions."

One of the most significant features of peasants' lives is their underdog status, their domination by outsiders. They serve as primary producers for urban markets and rural elites, but have little control over the means of distribution and little political power. The result is often poverty. Turn-of-the-century Russian peasant households consisted of blood relatives of two or three generations growing grain on relatively small holdings (five to fifteen acres of sown land). Although the family owned the land they farmed, the high taxes on it took all or most of their surplus production, leaving no money for other necessities. Alternative sources of income were scarce. Little wage labor was available in the countryside, leading some peasants to move to the city to seek a better life. There was some craft production, but most of this was for household use, since there was little market for craft products (Shanin 1972).

Since peasants are often caught in such negative bonds with the larger society, their relations with nonpeasants are generally characterized by extreme defensiveness. They see themselves as continually having to defend against external

The largest sugar plantation in Ecuador, unusual because it is totally Ecuadorian owned. The plantation, located in Ingenio, San Carlos (coastal Ecuador), is heavily mechanized and employs from 11,000 to 13,000 workers with 35,000 migrant laborers.

pressures and exploitation. Their relative powerlessness and poverty are translated into suspicions of other villagers. One aspect of these suspicions has been labeled the "limited good" (Foster 1965; see Acheson 1972). This is the belief that because peasants have access to such limited resources, those individuals who have acquired wealth have done so at the expense of others. As a consequence, people who are wealthier than other villagers often try to conceal their wealth to avoid jealousy. There are also strong pressures for those who are wealthier to share with the community through such activities as sponsoring fiestas or purchasing items for churches or religious shrines. Such egalitarianism has much in common with situations among farmers in small-scale societies and reflects the personal nature of relationships in small farming communities. Peasants' relations with outsiders, however, are anything but egalitarian. Peasants frequently maintain patron-client ties with influential persons, motivated in part by their hope to limit exploitation by outsiders through those ties.

To a limited extent, peasants and the nature of their adaptation is influenced by their physical surroundings, but political and technological factors tend to be of greater importance. Their low socioeconomic status in most societies has limited their access to expensive technology and ensured that much of what they produce will be siphoned off. Where significant political changes have taken place in the societies at large, the lot of peasants has sometimes improved and their pattern of social organization altered. Since the Russian Revolution of 1917, taxes are less burdensome for Russian peasants and there is greater scope for the accumulation of wealth. The flow of goods between industrial centers and peasant villages has increased; the peasants can now sell more of what they produce and purchase more from others. Improved transportation, communication, and education have increased their ties with the outside.

Plantation Agriculture. Peasants are in a sense merely small-scale farmers who have been incorporated into large-scale societies. However, a great deal of the world's agricultural production is not the result of peasant labor but of farming enterprises on a much larger scale. One form of large-scale agricultural enterprise that developed with European expansion after the Middle Ages is *plantation agriculture*. Plantation agriculture developed primarily to provide the world's major industrial centers (which were located in the northern latitudes) with crops that can be produced solely, or more cheaply, in the tropics or subtropics, such as rubber, sugar cane, coconuts, sisal, or coffee. Most of these crops require years of maturation from planting to first yield; after several years production may fall off, requiring replanting. The optimum size of the production unit varies according to local climatic and soil conditions, the crop, and local political considerations. In parts of southeast Asia rubber plantations may be smaller than one hundred acres, while the Herbel rubber plantation (owned by Firestone Company) in Liberia is larger than one hundred and thirty-six thousand acres.

All of the products of a plantation are exported, in part to pay for the importation of machinery and food required to maintain the plantation system. Because a plantation's significant links are with its overseas markets, integration of the plantation into the immediate social environment is limited. In the case of new nations with long histories of plantation production, this situation has resulted in extreme dependence upon the market countries.

Plantation production is, to a large extent, labor intensive. Plantations require large, disciplined, but not especially skilled labor forces. In North and South America the labor was supplied initially by slaves imported from Africa. In other areas, and during the latter part of the nineteenth and twentieth centuries in the Americas, labor was supplied either by the existing local population or by persons brought in from such countries as China or India.

Initially, most plantations were family-owned enterprises. Ownership by large, multinational corporations is the norm in many parts of the world today. After the Second World War many plantations were taken over by the governments of newly independent nations. But even in these cases much of the operating capital for a plantation is likely to come from extranational sources such as foreign banks, and the plantations themselves continue to be closely integrated into the international market.

Owners are rarely present on the plantation, and they tend to influence its running only indirectly. Social organization among those living on the plantation is strictly hierarchical. The elite consists of the technical and managerial staff (see Lang 1977). Until recently staffs were almost entirely European or North American, but now citizens of the local country are much more common. Whether native or nonnative, staff members and their families tend to live in compounds on the plantation, remaining physically, socially, and culturally separate from the workers. The workers may reside in separate compounds on the plantation or in neighboring towns or villages. The workers themselves are often divided socially according to tribe, caste, ethnicity, or tasks they perform on the plantation. Today, workers on many plantations are also organized into unions, which frequently play an important role in all aspects of their lives.

Since the early part of the twentieth century, plantation agriculture has been declining in importance. With the abolition of slavery in the Americas, many plantations were broken up into smaller holdings and production was carried out by peasants. Since the Second World War, plantations throughout the world have increasingly been divided up among small-scale producers. Most of these smaller production units grow "plantation" crops for market in conjunction with other subsistence crops. For instance, many small-scale farmers in northern Belize grow sugar cane for sale on the international market along with maize and beans for local consumption. Impetus for breaking up large plantations in some instances came as pressure for land reform mounted in countries with large, landless rural populations. Often, however, the plantation owners themselves broke up their holdings. Rather than having to pay higher wages to laborers, they found it more profitable to retain control of processing and distribution while turning the labor-intensive production process over to small-scale farmers.

Large-Scale Mechanized Grain Farming. Large-scale agriculture does not always require a large labor force. The type of agricultural production that has come to dominate the nontropical regions of the world—and that recently has been spreading into the tropics as well—is exemplified in the large-scale, mechanized grain farm. Like plantations, grain farms focus upon growing only one or two crops, and the products are usually exported, or at least sold to relatively distant markets. Unlike plantations, however, these large grain farms are capital rather than labor intensive, depending upon a small work force and large inputs of money in the form of fertilizers and mechanical equipment. Grain farms are thus doubly dependent upon the industrial sector, which provides both the means of production and the markets for what is produced.

Although these operations are commonly owned by large corporations, they may be family or state owned. The social organization of these farming enterprises depends in part on whether the encompassing economic system is collectivist, as in the Soviet Union, or market oriented, as in the United States. In many parts of market-oriented North America and Australia the pattern is one of large, relatively independent adjacent farms, each with a small residential unit that may consist of no more than a single family and perhaps seasonal workers. Among a group of these farms will be a small town that provides services—including banks, government administrators, mechanics, and often a contingent of rather poor laborers who de-

pend upon periodic work on nearby farms. On collective farms residential patterns tend to be more villagelike, the village serving as both service center and place of residence for the farmers.

Ranching. A final subsistence pattern found in large-scale industrial societies is ranching. The origins of ranching are found in medieval European pastoralism, especially in the activities of Spanish sheepherders, the source of institutions like the rodeo and much of the equipment, attire, and vocabulary of ranching (Dusenberry 1963).

Today ranching is confined largely to regions where Europeans have migrated over the past few centuries: the drier areas of North and South America, Australia, New Zealand, and South Africa. As in plantation agriculture, the primary impetus behind the spread of ranching was the demand in the industrialized portions of the United States and Western Europe for goods that could be produced more cheaply elsewhere. As plantations transformed a great deal of the tropics into a source of cheap products for the industrialized world, so ranching did the same for the world's drier regions.

Ranching is highly specialized, most ranches raising a single type of animal, usually cattle or sheep. The precise nature of the adaptation will be influenced primarily by pasture and market conditions and by the technology available. Unlike the technologically unsophisticated ranches of the past, today's ranches usually employ and are highly dependent upon a wide array of industrial products. Ranches are also generally fairly large. Because of the poor quality of the land, to support one head of livestock per year takes from one or two acres in good areas to over one hundred in very dry regions. It has been estimated that over 60 percent of the livestock protein is produced on pasturage that is not suitable for agriculture (Pimentel, et al. 1975: 758).

The relationship between ranching and agri-

Mechanized wheat harvesting uses little labor, but requires considerable inputs of capital for energy (fuel) and equipment.

culture is a changing one. Much land that was once considered unsuitable for agriculture has become usable for at least limited agricultural production, as a result of technological innovations. In some areas agriculture has replaced ranching entirely, and in others a mix of stock raising and grain farming has evolved (Moran 1979: 236–41). This mixed adaptation allows the rancher to better weather the vagaries of climate and market than animal raising alone. Price variation still influences ranchers, however, for example, they tend to keep their cattle longer when prices are low, a situation that can lead to serious overgrazing (Moran 1979: 239).

The low carrying capacity of ranch lands results in low human population densities and considerable social isolation. Ranching cultures tend to reflect this situation with an emphasis upon individualism, isolationism, and hospitality. A good deal of visiting takes place among ranchers and with people in nearby towns, but as John Bennett points out, they are able to control the amount of contact they have with others (1969: 179). Ranching obviously is not the life for those who like the close and constant contact characteristic of village or urban life.

Industrial production, Whyalla steel mill, South Australia.

Ranches tend to have few permanent residents—family members or a hired managerial staff and a few assistants. The majority of laborers are commonly hired on a seasonal basis for roundups and shearing. There are a number of fairly specialized tasks to be done; those carrying out these tasks may occupy very unequal statuses, depending upon the size of the ranching operation and its ethnic composition. Small, not particularly affluent family-owned ranches usually have a limited division of labor and will be run on a fairly egalitarian basis. Large, corporate-owned ranching operations generally exhibit a great deal of specialization and social relations tend to be quite hierarchical. In the King Ranch Corporation, whose vast holdings stretch from Texas to Australia and Brazil, the upper personnel strata form a multinational managerial elite, while other laborers recruited locally occupy a lower status. On Australian sheep and cattle stations, managers and overseers form one distinct group, taking meals at the homestead or in their own cottages and interacting almost exclusively among themselves at public gatherings such as tennis parties. White station hands and stockmen eat "outside" in separate quarters and occupy a dominant position over Aboriginal laborers. Aborigines, in turn, occupy the lowest rung of station society, eating and interacting socially almost exclusively within their own group (Gruen 1965: 267).

Nonfood Production Patterns

The production of material goods other than food is a feature of all human societies. In small-scale societies the range of goods produced is relatively limited and the degree of specialization in producing and distributing them is minimal. In large-scale societies, a much wider range and a larger number of goods are produced, and production and distribution processes are more specialized. How nonagricultural goods are produced in large-scale societies varies a good deal, but there are two principal systems of manufacturing: craft production and industrial production.

The essential characteristic of *craft production* is the employment of hand labor in manufacturing an object, making it a labor-intensive form of production. In general, hand-crafted objects are produced by artisans (people skilled in the production of a narrow range of goods, such as cloth or pots), and the number of persons engaged in the production process is relatively small.

Despite the potential complexities of social interaction required of craft producers, craft production can be carried out within relatively small social units, such as a group of interconnected villages, with only a limited amount of external trade. By contrast, industrial production represents a considerable leap in terms of scale of production, degree of specialization, and reliance upon extensive exchange networks. *Industrial production* uses inanimate energy sources (sources other than human or animal) to operate machinery for the extraction and conversion of resources in a factory setting. It requires a relatively large and diverse labor force and relatively large amounts of capital. Industrial production has been employed on a limited basis in various societies for thousands of years. Only during the past two to three hundred years, however, since the beginning of the Industrial Revolution in eighteenth-century England, has it become a dominant feature of economic production. Since that time industrialism has been one of the driving forces behind creation of the present world system.

The nature of industrial production in any setting can be understood only in reference to the wider world system. Industry in Formosa, Canada, and Austalia is first of all a reflection of those countries' place within the international division of labor. The relative size of the country or social unit and its access to natural resources, transportation, technology, and labor will make a difference, too. In larger and more powerful nations, industrial production is more highly mechanized and skill intensive, and involves the manufacture of a much wider range of goods. Industrial production in most of the larger countries beyond Western Europe and North America is a relatively recent phenome-

non. During the Second World War, when countries like Brazil and Argentina were cut off from the industrial goods of Europe and the United States, they began to develop industries of their own. During the 1950s many of these nations, viewing industrialization as a way out of their relative poverty and powerlessness, pushed hard to industrialize. Strategies varied. Soon after India achieved its independence in the late 1940s, for example, the government launched a campaign to promote diversified industrial growth throughout India, such as bicycle factories in villages. Problems with this approach led the government in 1956 to shift toward a concentration of heavy industry in urban areas.

Throughout the Third World after the Second World War, the growth of industry in urban areas contributed to massive migration from rural areas, as the landless and poor sought work. This process continues at present in many parts of the world. Most of those coming to the factories have few skills to offer and are suitable workers only for labor-intensive industries that do not require highly skilled laborers. The resulting surplus of unskilled workers has eased somewhat in countries that have developed more comprehensive educational programs to train workers, such as Brazil and Indonesia. In these countries industries have become technologically more sophisticated and a larger percentage of the skilled workers are natives rather than foreigners. Although more people in these countries are now finding better-paying jobs, their economic advancement also contributes to more pronounced inequality and the formation of social classes, as we will see in Chapter 11.

When migrants from rural areas come to work in a factory, they have to make many adjustments. As Bruce Kapferer (1972: 1) has noted, "Industries and factories impose restrictions, regulations and an order on social activity previously unexperienced in the lives of many of the migrants." Industrial production entails a great deal of specialization, resulting in a labor force that is segmented according to task. This specialization limits universal interaction and tends to create social hierarchies. Although people who carry out similar tasks may interact a great deal, those whose tasks are more distinct tend to form separate social groupings. Welders and machinists and managers may interact within their group, but members of these respective groups are unlikely to interact with each other. In a capitalist system hierarchy, the upper stratum of industrial workers will be the owners, those in top management positions, and perhaps some of the most skilled technicians. In the middle will be those in lower managerial positions and a range of technicians such as chemists and engineers, with office workers and foremen occupying a slightly lower status. At the bottom in many industrial settings will be those who work on the shop floor, the actual laborers. They themselves may well be ranked according to seniority, skill, ethnicity, or place in their union. Most recent migrants, who are likely to be the least skilled workers, find themselves at the bottom of this order. Over time they may move up within the laboring sector, possibly even becoming foremen, but since they are likely to be lacking in education, they will probably be unable to occupy any higher positions.

The industrial setting has implications for those who work in it that are felt far beyond the factory itself. Kapferer (1972: 1) explains:

The work place is often the central locus for the expression and experience of major aspirations, disappointments, failures and frustrations of members of an urban industrial class. It is probably on the shop floor that workers most often experience the oppressive bite of the wider social and political systems in which they participate. Here also new forms of consciousness emerge which may override other loyalties not immediately relevant to their involvement in an urban industrial and political system.

This new consciousness can be expressed in terms of social class, an identity that replaces or subsumes other identities such as those of race or tribe. This pervasive influence can be seen in Africa. In Zambia, Zaire, Nigeria, and Zimbabwe the industrial sector now accounts for between 10 percent and 20 percent of the work force (World Bank 1979: 162). Although tribal identities and tribal associations remain of some importance in many African industrial settings, they are considerably less influential in people's lives than are trade unions. Their emergence was often rapid as workers sought ways to adjust to their new environment. A. L. Epstein (1958: xiv) noted that Tribal Representatives were "a flourishing institution" in all the Zambian mine workers' compounds he visited in 1951. But when he returned eighteen months later, all Tribal Representatives had been abolished in favor of the new African Mine Workers' Trade Union. In addition to new identities, industrialization drastically altered other aspects of Zambian mine workers' lives; marriage, the status of women, the significance and use of leisure time, and attitudes toward education (Powdermaker 1962).

While the number of persons employed in industry in these countries has increased, there remain many urban dwellers who are unable to find work in the factories, and unemployment and underemployment in Third World countries remain high. In fact, in recent years, increase of employment opportunities in factories has not kept pace with population growth.

While industrialization has been able to increase the potential for productivity, it has been a mixed blessing, particularly for those unable to share in its products and for those employed in boring or dangerous jobs. Many of the political and economic struggles in the world today center on problems related to industry—the distribution of the wealth created by industry, working conditions, and industrial pollution. In fact, recent increases in the productive capability, through the use of computers and highly sophisticated electronic technology, have in many ways only made matters worse: The production and use of this new technology allows for a greater concentration of wealth, eliminating jobs, and creating pollution problems through the use of dangerous toxic chemicals (see Siegel 1980).

Summary

Human groups have developed a great variety of ways to meet their subsistence needs. *Subsistence activities* are the strategies they employ to procure and produce the fundamental things that they want or need. Subsistence patterns are influenced by a range of environmental factors. Some are related to the physical environment—including natural resources like soils and minerals and climatic conditions—and some to the social environment. In looking at the social environment it has proven useful to examine subsistence activities in terms of social scale. With small-scale societies, at least in the past, the relevant social environment has tended to be rather restricted. In large-scale societies, and to a degree in the few remaining small-scale societies as well, the relevant social environment is quite extensive, ultimately encompassing the world system. Thus, whether we are examining industry, agriculture, or ranching, we must look not just at a society's local environment, but also at its place in the international division of labor.

Increasing social scale came about in conjunction first with the advent of agriculture and then with the increasing use of machinery for industrial production. These changes represented a progressively more intensive use of resources, with greater specialization, interdependence, and social inequality and a shift from human and animal labor to inorganic sources of power and machinery.

There are three major small-scale subsistence patterns. The first is foraging, or the collecting of wild foods, a basic strategy that can be divided into three main subtypes: pedestrian hunting and gathering, equestrian hunting and gathering, and aquatic foraging. The second pattern, small-scale farming, is characterized by the use of human and animal labor and a simple technology. Shifting cultivation is a method commonly employed by small-scale farmers, especially in the tropics. The third pattern, pastoralism, is practiced by peoples who subsist primarily by herding animals. There are two main forms of pastoralism: transhumance and pastoral nomadism.

In large-scale societies, foraging, especially fishing, continues to be a significant activity for some people. Other common forms of agriculture are peasant farming (labor-intensive methods on family farms), plantations (labor-intensive, large-scale production intended principally to provide a limited range of crops to industrial centers), large-scale grain farming (which employs mechanized means to produce grain on extensive holdings primarily for urban and industrial centers), and ranching (extensive commercial grazing that employs a small labor force with a variable degree of mechanization to produce animals).

Such agricultural patterns often free many people in large-scale societies to produce non-food items. Craft production is a labor-intensive means of production that employs hand labor, while industrial production uses inanimate energy sources to operate machinery. Like its food-producing patterns, a society's craft or industrial patterns will have strong effects on other aspects of people's lives.

Suggested Readings

Small-scale foraging societies:

Berndt, Ronald M., and Catherine H. 1970. *Man, land and myth in Northern Australia.* East Lansing: Michigan State Univ. Press.

Bicchieri, M. G., ed. 1972. *Hunters and gatherers today.* New York: Holt, Rinehart & Winston.

Lee, Richard B. 1979. *The !Kung San: Men, women, and work in a foraging society.* Cambridge: Cambridge Univ. Press.

Lee, Richard B., and DeVore, Irven, eds. 1968. *Man the hunter.* Chicago: Aldine.

————. 1976. *Kalahari hunter-gatherers.* Cambridge, MA: Harvard Univ. Press.

Marks, Stuart A. 1976. *Large mammals and brave people: Subsistence hunters in Zambia.* Seattle: University of Washington Press.

Nelson, Richard K. 1980. *Shadow of the hunter: Stories of Eskimo life.* Chicago: University of Chicago Press.

Service, Elman R. 1979. *The hunters,* 2d ed. Englewood Cliffs, NJ: Prentice-Hall.

Tonkinson, Robert. 1974. *The Jigalong mob: Aboriginal victors of the desert crusade.* Menlo Park, CA: Cummings.

VanStone, James. 1974. *Athapaskan adaptation: Hunters and fishermen of the Subarctic forests.* Chicago: Aldine.

Small-scale farmers:

Brookfield, Harold C., and Brown, Paula. 1963. *Struggle for land.* Melbourne: Oxford Univ. Press. (New Guinea)

Firth, Raymond. 1965. *Primitive Polynesian economy,* 2d ed. London: Routledge and Kegan Paul.

Harner, Michael J. 1972. *The Jivaro: People of the sacred waterfalls.* New York: Natural History Press.

Hogbin, Ian, and Lawrence, Peter. 1967. *Studies in New Guinea land tenure.* Sydney: University of Sydney Press.

Hudson, A. B. 1972. *Padju Epat.* New York: Holt, Rinehart & Winston.

Murphy, Yolanda, and Murphy, Robert. 1974. *Women of the forest.* New York: Columbia Univ. Press. (Amazonian Brazil)

Sutlive, Vinson H., Jr. 1978. *The Iban of Sarawak.* Arlington Heights: AHM.

Wagley, Charles. 1977. *Welcome of tears: The Tapirape Indians of central Brazil.* New York: Oxford Univ. Press.

Pastoralists:

Asad, Talal. 1970. *The Kababish Arabs.* London: Hurst. (North Africa)

Barth, Frederick. 1961. *The Nomads of South Persia: The Basseri tribe of the Khamseh confederacy.* Boston: Little, Brown.

Behnke, Ray H., Jr. 1980. *The herders of Cyrenaica.* Urbana: University of Illinois Press. (Lybia)

Campbell, J. K. 1974. *Honour, family, and patronage.* Oxford: Oxford Univ. Press. (Greece)

Cole, Donald P. 1975. *Nomads of the nomads: The Al Murrah Bedouin of the empty quarter.* Arlington Heights, IL: AHM.

Ingold, Tim. 1976. *The Skolt Lapps today.* Cambridge: Cambridge Univ. Press.

Irons, W., and Dyson-Hudson, N., eds. 1972. *Perspective on nomadism.* Leiden: E. J. Brill.

Leeds, Anthony, and Vayda, Andrew P., eds. 1965. *Man, culture and animals: The role of animals in human ecological adjustments.* Washington, DC: American Association for the Advancement of Science.

Salzman, Philip C., ed. 1971. *Comparative stud-*

ies of nomadism and pastoralism. *Anthropological Quarterly*, Special Issue, vol. 44, no. 3.

Spooner, Brian. 1973. *The cultural ecology of pastoral nomads*. Reading, MA: Addison-Wesley.

Stenning, Derek J. 1959. *Savannah nomads: A study of the Wodaabe pastoral Fulnni of Western Bornu Province, Northern Region, Nigeria*. London: Oxford Univ. Press.

Peasants:

Brintnall, Douglas E. 1979. *Revolt against the dead: The modernization of a Mayan community in the highlands of Guatemala*. London: Gordon and Breach.

Bundy, Colin. 1979. *The rise and fall of the South African peasantry*. Berkeley/Los Angeles: University of California Press.

Gamst, Frederick C. 1974. *Peasants in complex society*. New York: Holt, Rinehart & Winston.

Hinton, William. 1966. *Fanshen: A documentary of revolution in a Chinese village*. New York: Vintage.

Kahn, Joel S. 1980. *Minangkabau social formations: Indonesian peasants and the world-economy*. Cambridge: Cambridge Univ. Press.

Pearse, Andrew. 1975. *The Latin American peasant*. London: Frank Cass.

Pitt-Rivers, Julian A. 1961. *The people of the Sierra*. Chicago: University of Chicago Press. (Spain)

Potter, Jack M., Diaz, May N., and Foster, George M., eds. 1967. *Peasant society: A reader*. Boston: Little, Brown.

Shanin, Teodor, ed. 1971. *Peasants and peasant society*. Harmondsworth: Penguin.

Wylie, Laurence. 1964. *Village in the Vaucluse: An account of life in a French village*. New York: Harper & Row.

Industry:

Applebaum, Herbert A. 1981. *Royal blue: The culture of construction workers*. New York: Holt, Rinehart & Winston.

Beynon, H. 1973. *Working for Ford*. Harmondsworth: Penguin.

Clark, Rodney. 1981. *The Japanese factory*. New Haven: Yale Univ. Press.

Gamst, Frederick C. 1980. *The hoghead*. New York: Holt, Rinehart & Winston.

Kapferer, Bruce. 1972. *Strategy and transaction in an African factory*. Manchester: Manchester Univ. Press.

Kriegler, Roy J. 1980. *Working for the company: Work and control in the Whyalla shipyard*. Melbourne: Oxford Univ. Press. (Australia)

LeMasters, E. E. 1975. *Blue-collar aristocrats*. Madison, WI: University of Wisconsin Press.

Leyton, Elliott. 1975. *Dying hard: The ravages of industrial carnage*. Toronto: McClelland and Stewart. (Canada)

Nash, Manning. 1967. *Machine age Maya: The industrialization of a Guatemalan community*. Chicago: University of Chicago Press.

Pfeffer, Richard M. 1979. *Working for capitalism*. New York: Columbia Univ. Press.

Pilcher, William W. 1972. *The Portland longshoremen*. New York: Holt, Rinehart & Winston.

General works on cultural ecology:

Hardesty, D. L. 1977. *Ecological anthropology*. New York: Wiley.

Moran, Emilio. 1979. *Human adaptability*. North Scituate, MA: Duxbury.

Netting, Robert McC. 1977. *Cultural ecology*. Menlo Park, CA: Cummings.

Vayda, Andrew P., ed. 1976. *Environment and cultural behavior*. Austin: University of Texas Press.

Chapter Six

Economic Systems

I N A D D I T I O N T O their more obvious features reviewed in the last chapter, subsistence patterns are based on more abstract principles of production, ownership, and exchange. In this chapter we will look at the basic elements of *economic systems*, the organizational and institutional structure of systems people have developed to supply themselves with the necessities and niceties of life.

Systems of Production

When our early ancestors picked up a stone, chipped it, and put it on the end of a stick to turn it into an implement for hunting and fighting, they produced a weapon. *Production* involves significant transformation of an object for cultural purposes. An act of production often entails physically altering an object, as in chipping a stone to make a spearpoint, but it may simply be a matter of rearranging things to alter their nature or function, such as piling stones to make a wall. It also commonly involves combining objects to produce something that is at least functionally different. But production is more than an act of transformation; it is a systematically ordered series of acts set in a particular social and environmental context. Anthropologists are not so much concerned with the productive act itself as they are with the *system of production* of which the act is but a part.

Production processes can vary considerably from one society to another. In our own society, the production of weapons usually involves several successive transformations of a number of objects to produce an implement that is much more complicated than a chipped stone on a stick. The difference reflects a more complex technology than was possessed by our spearmaking ancestors. It also reflects our great interest in weaponry, generated in part by the sociocultural environment within which we live. It is this interest that leads us to put so much effort into the production of weapons.

Even the same product can be made in a variety of ways. A tortilla, made from maize flour, can be formed by hand after the maize has been ground on a stone metate or after it has been processed through a metal corn mill, which may be powered by hand or mechanically driven. A tortilla may also be produced from maize entirely by machine.

None of these processes is inherently better than the others. Each has its own costs and benefits. Making a tortilla by hand, for example, does not require investment in a machine or use of nonrenewable energy resources, and it does not produce polluting by-products. Each production process is a reflection of the requirements, interests, beliefs, and capabilities of the members of a particular society and of the ways in which labor is organized and energy harnessed in that society.

Those engaged in the production of a missile will be trained and organized in a very different manner than those involved in spearmaking. They are also likely to have dissimilar views of work, the world, and their place in it. The same is true of peoples who have different methods of food production, such as foragers and small-scale farmers. Australian Aboriginal foragers depend on the natural productive capabilities of

An example of a relatively uncomplicated production process. This Aborigine is peeling bark off a sapling to make a spear, Jigalong, Western Australia.

their environment, for example; the things that they procure from their surroundings require little effort by way of preparation or distribution. Acquiring food in such a manner requires primarily a good knowledge of the landscape and of the plant and animal life to be found on it. Labor is not highly specialized and most activities are carried out by relatively small, highly mobile groups with considerable economic self-sufficiency. The manner in which Aborigines organize their labor, space themselves across the landscape, and maintain an intimate relationship with the things to be found on the land has its ideological basis in, and is supported by, their religion, myths, and rites.

The Mundurucu of Amazonian South America have a somewhat different relationship to the productivity of the land. Although they rely to some extent upon what they can forage from

their natural surroundings, they depend to a greater degree upon slash-and-burn cultivation. This requires a different technology than hunting; they need implements to cut the bush and assist in planting. This pattern also means that people are organized in a different fashion. As with the Aborigines, there is relatively little specialization of labor, but the productive unit itself tends to be somewhat larger and more sedentary, consisting of a number of families linked in various ways within a village. The Mundurucu have an ideological basis for their system of production in their religion, which serves as a charter for the division and organization of labor. Mundurucu religion is less concerned with things of interest to foragers, such as the lay of the land and the procreation of animal species, than with things of social and ecological relevance to farmers, such as the weather.

The Environmental Context of Production

Systems of production are influenced by the local ecology, as well as by the social, political, and economic environment. Since no two settings are precisely alike, no two systems of production will be exactly alike. Therefore, while the productive systems of Aborigines, Inuit, and the Bam Buti of central Africa are similar, local conditions result in significant variation. It is impossible to thoroughly understand any system of production outside of its environmental context.

Many systems of production can exist only under very limited conditions. For example, camel nomadism is a system of production which requires a physical environment suitable for camels and the social space to move. The production systems of many small-scale foraging and agricultural societies are so finely attuned to specific physical and social settings that they cannot be transferred to different environments and cannot survive radical changes within their environments.

Systems of production associated with large-scale societies generally exhibit considerable flexibility, a fact that enhances their ability to adapt to very different environments. The productive systems characteristic of industrial North American society are adaptable to the interior prairies, the Pacific and Atlantic coasts, and even the Arctic tundra. In all of these settings, there will be adjustments for factors such as local resources, weather, and the proximity of particular markets, but in each of these settings the basic system of production will be much the same.

In some settings, however, the North American industrial pattern is highly vulnerable, because of its heavy reliance upon outside support. An industrial-based adaptation in the Arctic depends upon outside sources for most necessities: heating fuel, clothing, building materials, food, mechanical devices like snowmobiles, and parts to maintain them. This ability to gain access to products from very diverse sources is one of the distinguishing features of such large-scale production processes. However, should the system begin to collapse for internal reasons, such as class conflict, or a change in the external environment, such as the inability to acquire inexpensive fossil fuels, then it may no longer be possible to maintain an industrial system of production.

Social or political conditions are often more important than the physical setting in shaping the nature of systems associated with large-scale industrial production. For instance, in recent years industries in the United States have had to pay attention to problems of industrial pollution. This is rarely the case in industrial production in poorer nations with illiterate populations and governments willing to grant major incentives to multinational corporations. Such countries tend to place few restraints on industrial destruction of the environment.

Maintaining Production

Keeping a system of production going is not always easy. Disruptions such as wars and environmental crises must be dealt with, a steady supply of workers must be maintained, and labor and rewards must be distributed in satisfactory ways.

A sandstorm at Lamesa, in north-western Texas, 1953. This region can become a desert area—a dust bowl—when eroded topsoil is blown away by wind during drought.

Dealing with Disruptions

City dwellers often take for granted the wide range of products available, complaining if a certain brand of bread or toilet paper is no longer available. The comfort in which so many of us live is based upon the smooth functioning of systems of production and distribution that support these cities—systems that encompass most of the globe. But what happens when those systems break down? Immediately after the Second World War, when production throughout most of Europe was at a standstill because of the destruction and disruption of people, animals, factories, and farms, life in cities like Vienna or Prague was precarious. People found it almost impossible to acquire many essentials. It is difficult to maintain any system of production in the face of catastrophic environmental changes and human upheavals, and cities are especially vulnerable. While not

all crises are as great as the Second World War, human productive efforts are almost constantly beset by problems.

When a production process is disrupted, adjustments are needed to ensure the survival of the society. Production systems often have mechanisms for dealing with temporary or regular disruptions, such as brief droughts or other natural disasters. Foragers often maintain alliances with other foraging groups so that they may use the resources of the other's territory if their own is depleted. In our own society we adjust to drought in agricultural areas by ensuring that alternate sources of the products are available and by storing reserves. We provide for the primary producers themselves through disaster relief loans, welfare, and other means.

While many of the forces disrupting production may result from natural causes—cyclones, locusts, earthquakes, floods—ecology problems are often the result of human action. Overuse of land for agriculture or grazing may destroy the land's fertility, as occurred in the American Midwest in the 1920s and 1930s. While technological innovation may halt or reverse such destruction, the effects of such innovations are often difficult to predict in advance.

Because of the complex interrelatedness of many diverse variables within a system of production, even supposedly simple innovations may have far-reaching, and perhaps unforeseen, ecological and social consequences. For example, during the 1950s and 1960s the government of Guatemala encouraged Indians living in the highlands to begin growing wheat instead of crops like maize, largely for economic reasons. Traditionally, Indian families grew their crops in the highlands; during the slack period between the harvest and the next planting, they worked in the coastal lowlands on coffee plantations. The Indians became increasingly dependent upon the sale of wheat to meet their subsistence needs, for they had to purchase such staples as maize with their earnings. They discovered, however, that wheat production did not provide them with a dependable income. To meet their income requirements (which were becoming greater with inflation), the men began spending more of their time working as laborers on the lowland coffee plantations, leaving their families in the highlands to look after the wheat crop. They also began growing maize on available land in the lowlands. In addition to drastically altering the Indians' system of production, this innovation encouraged the breakdown of family relations as the men spent more time away from their wives and children. And the Indians more often contract diseases such as malaria now since they spend more time in the lowlands.

Replacing Workers

Like the things they produce, people grow old and eventually lose their utility. Another funda-mental requirement of any productive system is the replacement of people. All systems of production have mechanisms to try to maintain a steady flow of productive humans. This entails ensuring that people are produced in the first place, then making sure that they will be productive, usually through socialization processes whereby younger members of a society are tutored in the appropriate values and knowledge. Not only must people be produced, but they must be produced in appropriate numbers. The likelihood of stability for a system is enhanced if the population can be held relatively constant. Both rapid population growth and rapid decline place great strains on productive systems.

Many small-scale societies seek to limit population growth through infanticide, abortion, and various means of birth control. These practices, along with relatively high mortality rates, kept population growth for the world as a whole at a very slow rate for thousands of years, minimizing population-related stresses on people's economic adaptations. This situation began to change dramatically several hundred years ago; particularly since the Second World War, rapid population growth has been one of the major problems confronting many societies.

Loss of population through disease, warfare, or some other cause also places considerable stress on a system of production. If a population becomes too small, the members of a society may no longer be able to meet the labor requirements of their system of production. One path to survival is to switch to a different system. The rapid decline of the indigenous population of Central and South America during the sixteenth century, caused primarily by the introduction of European diseases, destroyed the early Spanish colonial production system, which required large numbers of laborers to operate mines and commercial agricultural enterprises. This system was replaced by one based upon self-sufficient farming and pastoral enterprises and the importation of slaves from Africa.

Systems threatened with population problems can also be maintained through migration out of overpopulated areas into underpopulated ones. Innovations may make new regions accessible. The introduction of the sweet potato into the New Guinea highlands a few hundred years ago took pressure off already settled areas by allowing people to grow crops at higher altitudes. The governments of many countries (such as Peru, Mexico, Indonesia, and Vietnam) have initiated programs aimed at shifting people out of crowded areas where populations are too dense to be supported by the existing system of production, into low-density areas.

Emigrants from crowded areas frequently seek opportunities in other societies. Many Turks, Italians, and other southern Europeans migrate to northern Europe to work at much higher wages than are available in their home countries. Leaving their crowded and economically troubled homelands takes pressure off those economies, while helping to support the economies of northern Europe, which often suffer from a shortage of laborers in low-paying, low-prestige positions. In these instances the migrants themselves may undergo radical changes, but the respective production systems are subject to less alteration.

Dividing Labor and Rewards

There is little that is natural about the ways in which societies assign tasks to particular types of people, or about the values that are placed upon types of work. Both the *division of labor* and its rewards are essentially products of a particular sociocultural setting. Maintenance of a system of production requires that people either accept or at least acquiesce in these practices. But people rarely simply accept the division of labor or the distribution of rewards. In

Migrants in the slums of Lima, Peru.

our own society, the women's rights and labor union movements bear witness to dissatisfaction. Even among so-called primitives compliance is rarely automatic. Like their American counterparts, Mundurucu and Mardudjara women complain about being given the most boring and least prestigious tasks.

In most instances little comes of people's complaints. Rather than seeing their problem as an aspect of the system, people frequently focus upon individuals—the bad or unfair headman, foreman, king, or president. When this is the case, if any changes at all are made, it is usually simply the replacement of a particular person— the people revolt against a cruel and despotic monarch only to replace him with another king. The structure of the system of production itself is not significantly affected. In fact such periodic cleansings, or "rituals of rebellion," to use Max Gluckman's terminology, often serve to strengthen a system rather than to undermine it. Sometimes the unfairness of the system comes under attack, but only minor adjustments are made. Under pressure Mundurucu males may occasionally help the women with the tedious task of preparing manioc flour, or union members may be awarded salary increases. Again, such token actions serve to take pressure off the system without altering it.

Sometimes, of course, significant changes do occur. One cause may be alterations in the environment of the system of production. Because of changes in external market conditions, for example, a task that was of little importance may come to assume greater importance and thereby alter the nature of the productive system. In many of the highland communities of Guate-

mala, males produce the bulk of the economically significant products through agriculture; women tend to domestic chores and market produce, and they make ceramic pottery, a craft that is afforded little prestige or tangible reward. If a major external market for their ceramic wares emerges, however, because of improved lines of communication or an influx of tourists, women's activities may assume more importance. In some cases, the increased significance of ceramic production has resulted in groups of mothers and daughters replacing groups of farm-working males as the primary unit of economic production, with men assuming the marketing role. Such changes have tended to reduce the significance of male bonds beyond the family, while strengthening those among women engaged in ceramic production, and in some cases have resulted in women's achieving a higher status in the society in relation to men.

Changes in systems of production may also result from interplay between internal problems within the system, such as class conflict and environmental changes. During the Second World War, a labor shortage in the United States temporarily created a large number of openings for women in areas of traditional male employment. This change played an important part in altering the sexual division of labor in the United States, and helped to serve as a catalyst for the women's movement. All systems of production have inherent problems that can lead to basic changes in the system under circumstances that produce an unusual strain on the productive system itself.

Distribution and Exchange

It is not enough simply to produce things. People must also decide how to distribute

them, for individuals have different needs, tastes, and desires, and often there is either not enough of something to go around, or a surplus. How to distribute products and resources is one of the fundamental questions facing all societies, and it is one for which the human mind has come up with myriad answers.

Ownership

Central to an understanding of distribution and exchange in any society is the concept of *ownership:* acknowledged supremacy, authority, or power over a physical object or process. Ownership within any society is rarely a simple concept. In our society we say that people own their homes. Yet through various ordinances and social constraints the state and a man's neighbors and kin have a good deal to say about what he does with or in his house. Under many circumstances police and other public employees can enter the premises regardless of the owner's wishes. The bank that holds a mortgage on a house also has rights over it. Oil companies may be able to drill holes on the site, mining companies can burrow under it, and city and state governments can tear it down to build a road, park, or civic building.

Among the Pintubi, a group of foragers in the Australian desert, ownership is denoted by the term *kanyininpa*, which may be translated as "having," "holding," or "looking after" (Myers 1982). The term is used to refer to possession of physical objects ("I have two spears"), to the relationship of parent to child ("my father looked after me and grew me up"), and to the rights individuals or groups may hold over sacred sites, religious ceremonies, songs, and designs. Ownership among the Pintubi entails both control and responsibility. A person controls or "owns" a child or sacred site, but he or she also has responsibilities toward these possessions. The idea of ownership is tied into an encompassing moral order, known as the "Law," which dictates what these responsibilities are. Ownership of land for the Pintubi comes about

Pintubi near Lake Mackay, Australia. Most of the Pintubi left their traditional country in the Gibson Desert between 1948 and 1966 for settled life. Thus until recently they lived as foragers in small bands. Today most Pintubi live in partly independent settlements (such as Yayayi, where Myers did his work), which are supported largely through funding from the Australian government.

through the inheritance of sacred sites and the territory associated with them, and entails obligations to perform rituals linked to the sites. Failure to carry out such obligations does not merely affect a person's status in relation to the land and society; it is seen as threatening to the entire moral and social order of the Pintubi.

This concept of land ownership conflicted with those of Europeans who colonized Australia in the eighteenth and nineteenth centuries and exerted control over Aborigines and imposed their own law. To Aborigines, non-Aboriginal Australians who did not inherit the land or perform the necessary rituals had no rights to it. To the European colonialists, the Aborigines did not own the land, since they had done nothing to it in terms of fencing or planting crops—they did not even have deeds. Clearly, Europeans and Aborigines had very different ideas about ownership. But more important, the Europeans wanted the land and they had the power to take it, which they did. The Aborigines were left in possession of those areas of no value at the time to Europeans, primarily isolated arid stretches of desert.

As the above examples illustrate, ownership is rarely absolute. There are almost always others who have some claims to whatever is possessed. Such rights may simply be based upon the different uses to which people may put the same resources, or they may be based on hierarchical claims of authority over a resource. The latter is especially prevalent in large-scale societies, where the state reserves considerable authority over the use and disposition of most things. The reality of limited ownership is not always readily felt, however, allowing persons in our own society to overemphasize the extent to which they own their homes or automobiles, and allowing Australian Aborigines or Native Americans to believe that they own the land on their reservations.

Distribution of Wealth

No matter how ownership is defined, some people seem to own more than others in all societies. Unequal distribution of *wealth* (objects or resources that are useful or that have exchange value) is a universal characteristic of human society. The extent and significance of this inequality, however, vary a good deal from one social setting to another.

Even in small-scale societies with few material possessions there will be differences in wealth. Among traditional Australian Aboriginal foragers like the desert-living Mardudjara (Tonkinson 1978), the distribution of utilitarian material goods was relatively equal. But males (and especially older males) monopolized ownership of the most valuable resources such as land and sacred paraphernalia. Wealth differences were traditionally even greater among those Aborigines living in areas where resources were more abundant. Among the Tiwi of northern Australian islands (Hart and Pilling 1979), older males were often much wealthier than other members of the society. For instance, the most influential elder males had a large number of wives, providing them with a great deal more food than was available to those with fewer wives. However, despite such recurring wealth differences, in societies with few material goods wealth could not effectively be passed on to the next generation and thus built up.

The relative inequality found in Australian Aboriginal societies pales in comparison with that found in most large-scale societies. The contrast in Western industrial societies between the wealth of economic elites and urban slum dwellers, rural sharecroppers, and migrant farm laborers is far greater. There is more wealth potentially available to accumulate in large-scale societies, and large-scale societies have mechanisms of social control (police and military) that support unequal accumulation.

Such inequality on a worldwide scale has led to the division of countries into those which are perceived to be "developed" and those which are called "underdeveloped." Developed nations include those countries commonly referred to as the *First World* (Western industrial capitalist nations) and *Second World* (industrialized socialist countries), as well as the wealthier oil-producing nations. The underdeveloped group, usually referred to as the *Third World*, is a loose category of about one hundred twenty countries characterized by low standards of living, high rates of population growth, and general economic and technological dependence upon wealthier industrial nations.

In addition to assessing relative differences in wealth between countries, it is important to look at the distribution of wealth within them. Considerable inequalities exist in all First and Second World countries, as well as in Third World countries. In Third World countries like Guatemala and Ecuador, small elites own most of the land and other material resources, and have annual incomes thousands of times greater than those of most of the population.

Almost half of the world's population earns less than seventy-five dollars per year (Chenery, et al., 1974), a figure that is generally equated with extreme poverty. A disproportionally large number of these people—about two-thirds—live in rural areas of poorer nations and are engaged principally in agriculture. The majority of anthropological research has been conducted in these settings among the rural poor, and it is through the writings of anthropologists that much of our present understanding of world poverty has emerged.

The Guatemalan village of San Miguel Ixtahuacan is typical of many of the villages studied by anthropologists:

The poverty here is extreme even by rural Guatemalan standards. There are signs of soil destruction everywhere—hillsides scarred with ugly red gashes where even weeds do not grow. Houses are small and crowded, and people dress in old, patched clothes. In late August and September Indians fill truck after truck; whole families—men, women, schoolchildren, and infants—embark on the long trip to coastal coffee fincas [plantations]. At the height of the coffee harvest, the municipio is virtually vacant, its citizens off sweating for others' profit.

Most houses are one-room huts . . . averaging

about 400 feet of floor space. Into these small dwellings are packed one and sometimes two or three families. A separate, windowless hut serves as a kitchen. Women spend much of their lives in these kitchens, squatting around the open fire or grinding corn for the monotonous Indian diet. Corn tortillas or tamalitos and beans, spiced with chile sauce, are the staples. Most families have meat about once a week, some much less frequently.

Except for seasonal agricultural labor, San Miguel has little to sell in the national market. . . . Family incomes and domestic budgets are consequently small. Families rarely spend more than Q200 ($200) to maintain themselves and their households over the year. . . . Although Miguelenses value the consumer goods now available in the shops of San Pedro, they can afford few of them. Surveying 24 . . . households, I found only six radios, three clocks, one treadle sewing machine, and one typewriter. The sewing machine, typewriter, and one radio all belonged to a finca labor recruiter. Most families have no luxury goods. [Smith 1977: 74-75]

The relative wealth of the labor recruiter alluded to in this description points to an important factor influencing unequal distribution of wealth: the place of the village in the national system of production. San Miguel and hundreds of villages like it serve as sources of cheap labor for the large commercial enterprises owned by the Guatemalan elite or foreign nationals. It is an arrangement that provides relative wealth to a few villagers, but for most serves only to meet the barest of subsistence needs.

Although the existence of economic inequality within rural villages has been noted by anthropologists for years (see Goldkind 1966), only recently have anthropologists tried to understand its causes and consequences. Anthropologists no longer simply record the situation in villages like San Miguel. Now they seek to understand it, by looking at the broader context within which villagers live: national politics, the international structure of trade in commodities like coffee, and so on. The need for comprehending how such inequality is produced has become even more pressing in recent years as the relative impoverishment of the majority of the world's population has increased.

Patterns of Exchange

The distribution of wealth within a society is the result of processes of *exchange,* the pattern of trade that exists in resources, goods, ideas, and services. Economic exchange is a universal aspect of human society. Individuals in all social settings are dependent upon others for satisfying some of their needs or wants, and human maturation (e.g., the differing requirements and perceptions of infants, adolescents, adults, and the elderly) requires that resources or ideas continually be transferred to meet changing needs.

Three basic patterns of exchange have been distinguished: reciprocity, redistribution, and market exchange. Each has different rules and effects on the people involved.

Reciprocity. Within small-scale societies most of the physical necessities of life are produced by and exchanged within minute social units, often families. Most material goods (spears, digging sticks, string bags) are produced by the individuals who will use them or by their spouses and kin. Most food is procured and processed within domestic groups or at most within a limited network of kin. Kinship is therefore an essential element affecting economic exchange within small-scale societies.

Exchange in such societies is often based upon *reciprocity:* the mutual exchange of goods and services. Although this direct exchange is most characteristic of small-scale societies, it is also found in larger-scale societies, as in transactions among friends and neighbors.

Marshall Sahlins (1965: 145-49) has delineated three forms of reciprocity: generalized,

balanced, and negative reciprocity. *Generalized reciprocity* refers to gift giving without any immediate expectation of return. Food, manufactured implements, and labor are simply given to another with no direct form of repayment. In a very general sense, it is expected that others will be equally generous. Social sanctions may be brought to bear against those who fail to live up to at least minimal expectations of sharing. *Balanced reciprocity* involves a more explicit expectation of immediate return, as when a Bushman trades a Tswana an animal hide for a negotiated quantity of tobacco (Marshall 1961: 242) or a Mayan Indian trades a day's work with another. Such transactions are usually based upon the exchange of surplus goods or labor and tend to be mutually beneficial. *Negative reciprocity* is an attempt to take advantage of another by forcing that person to exchange something which he or she may prefer to keep, or trying to ensure that what one receives is of greater value than what one gives in return.

Even these direct exchanges may create inequalities in distribution of wealth. Negative reciprocity is clearly an unequal transaction, and even in generalized reciprocity some people my end up with more than others. In societies where no one has much, inequalities are subtle, but they exist nonetheless. For example, when males of Australian foraging groups such as the Mardudjara return from large-game-hunting trips, most of the meat is shared among those present in the camp—kin and nonkin. The male who actually killed the game is usually expected to receive one of the least choice cuts. This system of generalized reciprocity reflects the people's inability to store large quantities of perishable meat, and it ensures that people will be fed regardless of their abilities or social standing. However, men can gain prestige as a result of their hunting prowess and translate this prestige into political influence and access to greater resources. Women who are skilled at gathering can help to enhance their husbands' reputations, but little glory falls to them except indirectly. Although women are the primary producers, it is the men who profit most from the system. The Mardudjara exchange system can thus be seen as an exploitative one, in which men monopolize surpluses that are largely the result of female labor. Yet Mardudjara women do not appear to feel particularly oppressed, partly because they are socialized to see existing differences as natural. This situation is unique neither to the Mardudjara nor to reciprocity, for most economic systems contain a degree of inequality and exploitation, and most have ideologies that obscure their exploitative nature.

Redistribution. Certain systems of exchange that are potentially nonexploitative can be called *redistributive.* In general, this term means distributing wealth in a way that differs from the existing pattern. Redistribution can take many forms. Among them are taxation, gift giving, and the potlatch.

All societies large enough to support a government have experimented with methods of collecting wealth from the people and then redistributing it—supposedly more equably and efficiently—in the form of goods and services. In our society, the method is *taxation.* Workers surrender part of their wealth to the government, which then returns it to the people through various programs—road building, public education, health care, food supplements for those with low incomes, agencies designed to protect citizens from abuses by business, and so on. Though people may elect representatives who will determine how the wealth turned over to the government will be redistributed, those who are taxed have relatively little control over what is done with their wealth.

Gift giving is a form of reciprocity that often serves as a direct means of redistributing wealth. Gift giving takes place when one person presents a gift to another who, at least for the moment, simply receives. Presenting goods to another as gifts is a very personal form of exchange that introduces certain emotional qualities into the relationship between giver and recipient. For instance, the recipient may feel indebted to the giver. Also, the question of relative status between those involved is immediately at issue, and the recipient must decide upon the appropriate manner of behavior and perhaps of reciprocating.

In our own society, gift giving generally is reserved for a limited number of special occasions (Christmas, birthdays, etc.) and it tends to follow particular patterns of behavior. Upon moving into any new society it is necessary to learn the appropriate rules of gift giving: when and how to give gifts, and how to receive them. The rules are not always explicit, or universally shared. The giving of gifts outside of clearly legitimate contexts may be seen as an illicit act—as a bribe—but there is often a fine line between gift giving and bribery.

The *potlatch,* a rather extreme form of gift giving in which large-scale distribution of surpluses is used to enhance one's own status, is an elaborate, at times quite dramatic, feast and gift-giving ceremony performed among northwest coast Indians. Such forms of competitive feasting and gift giving are quite common among small-scale agricultural and fishing societies and serve as a focal point of economic exchange among members of different social groups within these societies.

Our best descriptions of potlatching come from the Kwakiutl, who live on the northern end of Vancouver Island. The gifts presented in a potlatch might include slaves (at least until the mid-nineteenth century), canoes, Hudson Bay Company blankets, various manufactured articles, and perhaps a highly valued shieldlike sheet of copper. Hudson Bay Company blankets were the most common gift—several thousand blankets might be presented at a single potlatch (Codere 1950: 90–91)—and they served as the basic unit of account, the value of all

Kwakiutl potlatch, Alert Bay, British Columbia
(photograph taken c. 1910).

other goods being expressed in blankets. The feast itself was sponsored by a single individual on such occasions as a marriage, the birth of a first child, or the initiation of one's sister's son into a secret society, and served to validate the sponsor's receiving a high-status title.

The basic unit of Kwakiutl society was a kin-based group known as a *numaym*. The titles acquired by the potlatchers generally were associated with their position and prerogatives within the *numaym*. A person would prepare for a potlatch by accumulating the needed items largely through loans (on which interest was paid) from relatives. At the potlatch goods would be distributed not only to members of one's own *numaym*, but also to members of related kin groups who would be invited, often from other communities. This meant that goods were re-distributed not only within one's own group, but outside the community as well. Inter-community distribution of food through the potlatch served to ensure that surplus perishables were dispersed to a larger group of people.

While the potlatch served as a redistribution of goods, it was primarily a competitive event. There was keen competition among members of the elite to outdo each other in their largesse, and it was principally through the potlatch that a person could advance in social standing. The potlatch also highlighted competition among kin. The invited kin were not simply given a lot of goodies: they were placed in the potlatcher's debt. The potlatch demonstrated the allegiance that existed between related *numaym* through their joint participation, but it also allowed one group to attempt to demonstrate superiority.

Market Exchange. The third basic pattern of economic exchange, *market exchange*, involves

An Indian market in Pujilí, Ecuador, a town of about 3,000 people.

buying and selling of goods. The dominant feature of these transactions—price setting—is based on impersonal economic factors such as supply and demand rather than personal factors such as kinship and relative social status.

Market exchanges are further depersonalized by the use of money as a medium of exchange. In societies with a specialized division of labor, emphasis upon surplus production, and, most important, the necessity of carrying out economic transactions with relative strangers, direct gifts or exchanges of goods tend to be replaced with the use of money. The term *money* is rather imprecise and often used ambiguously. In essence, the term refers not so much to a physical thing as to a number of functions such as durability, transferability, and acceptability over a wide range of functions. As Belshaw (1965: 9) notes, all of these functions are dependent upon the characteristic of *liquidity,* "the relative ease with which a commodity . . . can be exchanged."

There are two basic types of money: special-purpose and general-purpose. The term *special-purpose money* refers to objects that serve as a medium of exchange in only limited contexts and that are interchangeable for only a particular range of goods and services. In many parts of Africa, cattle are used as money in the payment of bride price, in payment of compensation of a feud, and generally in evaluating the wealth of an individual or kin group. Pigs serve a similar purpose in many parts of Melanesia. Pigs and cows have certain advantages as media of exchange—for instance, they can be eaten and bred as well as traded. But using livestock as money also presents some problems. Animals lack the durability of many commodities, they must be fed and protected from disease and theft, and they may be a bother to transfer. Especially where durability and transportability are important criteria, inanimate objects have an advantage.

The Lele of the Kasai region of Zaire (formerly the Belgian Congo) use as special-purpose money a cloth which the males produce from combed palm fibers (Douglas 1958). The cloth is also used as clothing, but its primary importance is as a store of value and a means of payment. The Lele use the cloth in trade with neighboring people to pay for such items as hoes, knives, bells, pottery, baskets, and fish. Within Lele society the cloth is used as a means of payment for particular kinds of transactions— it is presented to wives when they bear children or report would-be seducers, to in-laws upon marriage, to newly admitted members of cult groups, and to specialists who perform healing rites and divinations. Pieces of cloth are used as a means of paying compensation for adultery and in assessing fines for fighting in the village. Cloth is also given as a gift in payment for products made by craftsmen who are not close relatives.

General-purpose money differs from the more limited versions in its comprehensiveness. In a society using general-purpose money, most material things and services can be bought or paid for with this one medium of exchange. One's wealth, work value, and even thoughts can be assessed in monetary terms.

The impact of introducing general-purpose money into societies where it was not previously used is often considerable. It may have very beneficial effects by expanding individual freedom, but it can also disrupt existing social relationships, increase people's dependency, and lead to their impoverishment. For example, the substitution of general-purpose money for cattle in marriage transactions in east Africa allowed young men greater freedom. But at the same time it destroyed existing patterns of paternal

authority within the family, undermined the political system based upon clan alliances, and encouraged the breakdown of herd management by kin groups. It also served to blur distinctions between marriage, liaisons, and prostitution (see Bohannan 1959).

Even though general-purpose money has become the dominant medium of exchange in most economic systems, reciprocal exchange and special-purpose monies often continue to be employed to a limited extent. This is true even in large-scale industrial societies, as in the exchange of Harley-Davidson parts among groups of bikers in the United States. Although the bikers' economic survival depends upon occasional jobs and often on the income of their "old ladies," within the group the exchange of Harley-Davidson parts plays a significant social and economic role. Maintenance of the bikes— the primary symbols of group identity—is dependent primarily upon a barter system, a system which minimizes the bikers' dependence upon the encompassing market economy. In one Texas group studied, the Bandidos, to overhaul a member's bike, friends

visit other bikers, even several who are not Bandidos. The parts come in, almost all of them from trades with other Harley riders. A few items, like piston rings, they buy from the dealership, though neither of them enjoys giving the dealer their trade. In their eyes, Harley dealers are little more than profiteering pirates. [*Reaves 1978: 214*]

The elevation of the Harley-Davidson to such an exalted status is partly a consequence of the extent to which it, unlike most other bikes, can easily be maintained independently of the market. There are only three different Harley-Davidson motors and it is relatively easy for groups to maintain stocks of all parts among their members.

Complete autonomy from "the rule of

money" is never entirely possible in Western society. Even for small-scale societies such as those of highland New Guinea or the Kalahari desert, where many aspects of the traditional nonmonetized exchange system remain, general-purpose money now influences the relative value of goods and services, as well as affecting social relations. The pig feasts in the New Guinea highlands may resemble those of the past in form, but their magnitude, the value of the items, and the status of individuals involved are all influenced by international market conditions and by the use of general-purpose money.

The introduction of market exchange via general-purpose money into economies throughout the world has been an integral part of the spread of the modern world system. General-purpose money is one of the most tangible forces integrating societies into the world economic system, because the flow of money produces both direct and indirect effects on almost all aspects of people's lives. Furthermore, it is both a symptom of and an important factor leading to greater dependency and impersonalization in economic systems: gift giving, moral obligations, and paternalism come to be replaced or overshadowed by impersonal market conditions, wages, legally binding contracts, and the decisions of the International Monetary Fund or World Bank.

Commerce

Another economic pattern that has drawn societies into the modern world system is *commerce*, the exchange of goods among different countries or regions.

Commerce is an important aspect of virtually all economic systems, whether small scale and localized or worldwide in scope.

The quest for resources and markets beyond the confines of one's own society is certainly not new. Over two million years ago the inhabitants of Olduvai Gorge traveled a few miles in search of suitable materials for their stone implements. But the scope of world commerce today is unprecedented, as is the extent to which people's lives are influenced by world commerce. In many small-scale societies, major changes have occurred within recent memory.

For example, forty years ago most of the things used and consumed by the people of Pueblo Viejo, a Mayan village in southern Belize, were produced by the villagers themselves. They grew their own food, employing only digging sticks, machetes, and axes. Their homes were made entirely from local resources, as were most of the furnishings—furniture, hammocks, clay bowls, and gourd utensils. They even made their own clothing, although some of the material and thread was purchased. The few things that they bought—machetes, axes, salt, and grinding stones—were paid for with money from the sale of a sack or two of maize or beans and perhaps a few blocks of *chicle* (the chief ingredient of chewing gum) extracted from nearby trees. The goods were purchased either in the coastal town of Punta Gorda, some thirty miles away, or from traders who came on foot from Guatemala. The point of origin of most of these goods was rarely farther away than Guatemala.

Today the situation is rather different. Many of the people continue to live in houses made of local resources, but some now live in houses made of milled lumber with wood or cement floors and galvanized, corrugated metal roofs. They produce most of the food that they eat, but not all of it; most of what they grow is sold in Punta Gorda to the government marketing board. Stores in the village stock such items as Carnation milk, Vick's Vaporub, Coca-Cola, Nescafé, Nestea, Lactogen, Milo, and even canned black beans. Metal grinders have replaced stone ones, and tin or plastic cups and bowls from Taiwan have taken the place of gourds and clay pots in most households. The

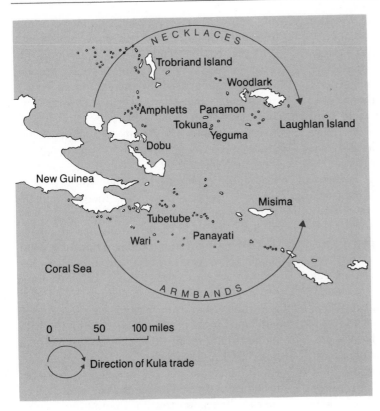

FIGURE 6.1

villagers now purchase hammocks made in Mexico, and much of their clothing is bought ready made or sewn on treadle sewing machines from material imported from the Orient. A radio, cassette tape recorder, or battery-operated record player is also a common feature in many homes. The economy of Pueblo Viejo is no longer as independent or as integrated into a localized commercial trade network as it once was. Today it is much more thoroughly incorporated into the commercial system of Belize, and that of the world at large.

Commercial relations among small-scale foragers or agriculturists can be quite involved. The *Kula*, for example, is an elaborate exchange system among certain Melanesian islanders involving expeditions of sailing canoes, trading partners, large-scale feasts, ceremonial exchanges of prized shell ornaments, and bartering over other goods to be exchanged (see figure 6.1). Though shorter on ceremony, commerce between larger-scale societies is characterized by a flow of greater quantities and varieties of goods and more extensive commercial networks than exchange among small-scale societies. The growth of early empires was accompanied by such networks. For example, the Phoenecians became masters of an extensive trade throughout the Mediterranean after 1200 B.C. This trade involved objects manufactured by the Phoenecians themselves, such as enameled jewelry and weapons and a purple dye extracted from mollusks; exportable surpluses from India and the Near East of wines, cereals, textiles, and precious stones; lead, gold, and iron from the south shores of the Black Sea; copper, cypress, and corn from Cyprus; ivory from Africa; silver from Spain; tin from Britain; and slaves from everywhere, all carried on the backs of camels and in the holds of ships. The early empires of the New World, the Inca, Aztec, and Maya, also engaged in extensive trade. In 1502, Columbus seized a large trading canoe along the coast of Central America carrying cotton goods from Yucatan, obsidian tools from central Mexico, and copper items originating in Michoacan.

European colonialism was essentially concerned with commerce. Columbus sailed to the Indies not simply out of curiosity, but in search of trade. The Europeans' search for raw materials and new markets for their products eventually transformed the world. They moved millions of Africans halfway around the world to work as laborers in the mines and plantations of the New World. Those who were left behind, and subsistence farmers the world over, were enticed or forced into the European market economy by the introduction of taxes or less subtle means. They were encouraged or forced to produce goods primarily of value to Europeans, to employ production techniques requiring the importation of European technology, and to buy a wide range of European products. Accordingly, the societies of non-European peoples everywhere were transformed to suit the needs of a colonial economy. The colonial period was one in which Europeans and North Americans sought to create a world suited to their needs, and the postcolonial societies studied by anthropologists today are both a reflection of and a reaction to this colonial transformation.

Relationships among Production Systems

As the world system has become more inclusive over the past few hundred years, systems of production have become more interdependent. Cree hunters of northern Canada continue to produce many of the things that they use from local resources, but they also purchase rifles, chain saws, traps, and clothing produced in distant industrial centers. They hunt bear and moose to meet their own subsistence requirements, but they also trap beavers to sell to Hudson Bay Company buyers. Furthermore, their very system of production has run into competition with the desires of industrialists, who have begun to construct dams on the Cree's hunting territory to provide electric power for homes and industries elsewhere in Canada. Just as it is impossible to study the productive systems of foragers today without also looking at their relationships with pastoralists, fishermen, miners, farmers, and industrialists, it is impossible to examine the industrial systems of Europe and North America without taking into account their relationships with production systems around the world that influence their supply of raw materials and provide markets for the goods they manufacture.

Relationships between systems of production fall into three basic types: symbiotic complementarity, hierarchical complementarity, and open competition. These categories are not mutually exclusive. All relationships between systems of production will include aspects of each. But these categories are useful because they represent fundamental differences of emphasis; they also tend to be linked with certain social and political relationships between groups.

Symbiotic Complementarity

When different systems of production complement each other—each providing goods and services needed by the other, without one

The Bedouin sheep and camel market in Beersheba, Israel. Middle Eastern pastoralists often come to the cities to sell animals and animal products so that they may buy the numerous agricultural products and other goods they need.

dominating the other—the pattern is labeled *symbiotic complementarity*. The groups or individuals involved in this mutual economic interdependence are usually relatively equal socially and independent of each other politically. To a large degree, symbiotic complementarity is relevant only to small-scale systems of production. Increasing scale and indirect interdependence tend to create more unequal relationships.

Symbiotic complementarity can take many forms. Sometimes two groups use the same land at different seasons for different yet complementary purposes. For example, some pastoral nomads who summer with their herds in the mountains of the Middle East bring their animals down from the mountains in winter into areas occupied by sedentary farmers to graze their herds on the stubble left after the fall harvest. The pastoralists' animals are fed, and they fertilize the farmers' fields in the process. Additional complementarity is provided by the nomads' provision of animal-derived products such as wool and cheese to the farmers in exchange for agricultural products. Occasionally pastoralists dominate farmers by gaining ownership of their land, and relationships between farmers and nomads tend to be less than harmonious at best, but there is little conflict inherent in the production activities of the two groups.

People may also occupy completely different areas and provide items to people in neighboring environments that are not available there. This pattern is also symbiotic complementarity, for the exchange of goods helps to maintain each of the respective systems of production. Forest-dwelling foragers like the Macu of South America and the Bam Buti of central Africa provide forest goods such as medicinal and edible plants and game to agriculturists who live beyond the forest, in return for agricultural and industrial products. Here again, inequality may emerge, and the Bam Buti and Macu are not well treated by their "more civilized" neighbors, but the groups nonetheless maintain a good deal of social and political autonomy. Such relationships are not static, however. The habitat of the Bam Buti is being destroyed by commercial loggers and land-hungry farmers, and the Macu find it increasingly difficult to maintain their independence from other Indians, settlers, government officials, and missionaries.

Within a single society, groups of people or even the same individuals may be involved in very different but complementary systems of production. Prior to the 1950s, Mayan agriculturists in southern Belize lived in very small and isolated hamlets, devoting part of the year to growing crops for subsistence needs. Between the harvest and the next planting, they would go into the forest to gather chicle and cut trees for sale to commercial buyers. The money they earned was used to buy a few consumer goods, including machetes and steel axes for their agricultural work. Two different production activities—subsistence agriculture and commercial forestry work—thus complemented each other within the same society, neither dominating the other. In more recent years, however, both forestry work and subsistence agriculture have given way to the production of crops for sale in markets (Howard 1977).

Hierarchical Complementarity

When systems complement one another but relationships are clearly unequal, often characterized by domination and exploitation, the relationship is one of *hierarchical complementarity*. A common pattern here is a large-scale industrial nation dominating the productive systems of other nations which provide it with resources, products, or markets. Such domination may be direct, as in the case of colonialism, or indirect through the control of strategic markets, credit, and local politics.

The slave trade in West Africa, by which Europeans obtained laborers for the economies of North and South America, provides a good example of indirect domination. Before the advent of the slave trade, West Africa was made up of a number of small empires and city states, which engaged in long-distance trade, and numerous independent villages of subsistence farmers. Beginning in the sixteenth century, Europeans established themselves along the African coast and initiated trade with the local African states, exchanging European manufactured goods (especially weapons) for slaves captured in the interior. The states involved in this trade became organized along military lines, several expanding their spheres of influence over other states and over the agricultural villages which supplied most of the slaves. Even when the slave trade was abolished in the nineteenth century, the hierarchical complementarity pattern was maintained, as the West African states shifted to producing agricultural products for European markets. This system of production was in turn altered during the latter part of the nineteenth century with the advent of direct European colonial domination.

Open Competition

When two systems of production come into conflict over access to the same desired resources, *open competition* emerges. In large-scale capitalistic societies, rival production systems often compete openly for the same consumer monies. The status of most small-scale societies reflects the extent to which they block large-scale societies' access to resources, and their relative powerlessness to resist the agents of such large-scale societies.

Amazonian Indians like the Mundurucu and Yanomamo have lived until fairly recently as nearly autonomous foragers and slash-and-burn agriculturists. During the past couple of decades, however, their habitat has attracted attention as a source of timber, mineral resources, and good farmland. Some groups of Indians have sought to resist this incursion, only to be killed, forced to retreat into the few areas left where they can hide, or placed on reservations. On the reservations the Indians are able to maintain something of their traditional way of life, but the continual loss of reservation land to non-Indians has made retention of their foraging and farming way of life increasingly difficult (Davis 1977). In the areas hardest hit by commercial interests, those Indians who have not died of disease or been killed have found new ways to subsist, working as servants, menial laborers, beggars, and prostitutes while their traditional culture has passed into history. Rather than complementing other production systems,

Yanomamo being relocated, on the back of a truck, to a mission station. There has been severe pressure on the Yanomamo and their environment from mining interests, cattle ranching, hydroelectric plants proposed on the Amazon and its tributaries, and gas and oil companies. Some hope for protecting the Yanomamo, as well as their territory, lies in a dedicated international human rights movement organized in 1979 with the creation of the Commission for the Creation of a Yanomamo Park (CCPY).

those engaged in open competition may ultimately destroy or be destroyed by those with whom they are in competition.

Summary

Economic systems consist of patterns of production, ownership, and exchange. What is produced depends upon environmental resources, though some industrial groups have built rather vulnerable production systems in areas where they are not fully supported by the local environment.

No matter where they are set up, production systems may face disruptions such as wars and environmental crises. To survive, the systems must make provision to cope with such crises, arrange for regular replacement of workers, and divide labor and distribute rewards in ways acceptable to the workers. Systems of production are often unstable; forces for change rather than maintenance of a system as it is may come from without or within.

Ownership tends never to be absolute; ideas of ownership can be quite complex. Considerable differences in how much is owned exist between societies and within them. Differences in the distribution of wealth within a society tend to be much greater in large-scale societies.

Wealth is distributed within and among societies by patterns of exchange. There are three basic patterns: reciprocity, redistribution, and market exchange. In reciprocal exchange, people trade one kind of good or service for another. Sometimes the trade is immediate, sometimes there is merely a generalized expectation of eventual repayment, and sometimes the exchange is forced. Redistribution of wealth may take many forms, such as taxation, gift giving, and potlatches. Market exchange is characterized by buying and selling of goods through the use of special-purpose or general-purpose money.

Today few societies are isolated from the world economic system. Groups are often drawn into contact with others through commerce. Relationships between systems of production, from individuals to whole societies, may reflect symbiotic complementarity, hierarchical complementarity, or open competition.

Suggested Readings

Among the general works on economic anthropology are:

Belshaw, Cyril S. 1965. *Traditional exchange and modern markets.* Englewood Cliffs, NJ: Prentice-Hall.

Clammer, John, ed. 1978. *The new economic anthropology.* London: Macmillan.

Dalton, George, ed. 1967. *Tribal and peasant economies: Readings in economic anthropology.* New York: Natural History Press.

Firth, Raymond, ed. 1967. *Themes in economic anthropology.* London: Tavistock.

Halperin, Rhoda, and Dow, James, eds. 1977. *Peasant livelihood: Studies in economic anthropology and cultural ecology.* New York: St. Martin's.

LeClair, Edward E., Jr., and Schneider, Harold K., eds. 1968. *Economic anthropology: Readings in theory and analysis.* New York: Holt, Rinehart & Winston.

Sahlins, Marshall. 1972. *Stone Age economics.* Chicago: Aldine.

Schneider, Harold K. 1974. *Economic man: The anthropology of economics.* New York: Free Press.

Seddon, David, ed. 1978. *Relations of production.* London: Frank Cass.

There are a large number of studies of particular economic systems, including:

Beals, Ralph. 1975. *The peasant marketing system of Oaxaca, Mexico.* Berkeley: University of California Press.

Cooper, Eugene. 1980. *The wood-carvers of Hong Kong: Craft production in the world capitalist periphery.* Cambridge: Cambridge Univ. Press.

Dewey, Alice G. 1962. *Peasant marketing in Java.* New York: Free Press.

Durham, William. 1979. *Scarcity and survival.* Stanford: Stanford Univ. Press.

Epstein, T. Scarlett. 1962. *Economic development and social change in South India.* Manchester: Manchester Univ. Press.

Gudeman, Stephen. 1978. *The demise of a rural economy: From subsistence to capitalism in a Latin American village.* London: Routledge and Kegan Paul.

Lockwood, Brian. 1971. *Samoan village economy.* Melbourne: Oxford Univ. Press.

Long, Norman, and Roberts, Bryan R., eds. 1978. *Peasant cooperation and peasant expansion in central Peru.* Austin: University of Texas Press.

Moran, Emilio. 1981. *Developing the Amazon.* Bloomington, IN: Indiana Univ. Press.

Richards, Audrey I. 1939. *Land, labour, and diet in northern Rhodesia.* London: Oxford Univ. Press.

Salisbury, Richard F. 1970. *Vunamami: Economic transformation in a traditional society.* Melbourne: Melbourne Univ. Press. (Papua, New Guinea)

Smith, Waldemar R. 1977. *The fiesta system and economic change.* New York: Columbia Univ. Press. (Guatemala)

Focus on People

Economic Aspirations and Means among the Mandinka

Peter M. Weil

Peter M. Weil spent one year (1975-76) living with the Mandinka in The Gambia (now Senegambia), West Africa; his fieldwork focused on the relationship between changes in economic and ecological processes since 1800 and changes in social organization. Since 1977, Weil has acted as a consultant on social factors in development for USAID, a United Nations Development Program, and other public agencies and private companies designing development projects for the Gambia River Basin and the Casamance River Basin (Senegal).

We have elected these people to replace you, the whites. These people are our sons. They have gone to Banjul [the capital] and forgotten us. They climb in high buildings and have forgotten we exist. [high-status elder man in a village community in The Gambia, 1975]

This statement from an interview about economic aspirations and the means to attain them demonstrates one of the two major ways in which Mandinka people see development—as a political endeavor. The other way is in terms of individual or group action at the local level, as the following remarks by a low-status young man in the same locale show:

I don't want and I don't need food or a house
[as] charity from the government or from people in other countries. I want to grow more food and more peanuts [the cash crop]. I want [to earn] more money. I want to build a new brick house for myself and my brothers. If a person loans me seed or the money to get it, if a person loans me the money for better tools to farm and build houses, I will have much more food and will build the houses. If there are no loans, with the blessings of Allah I will get what I am seeking [anyway]. I work hard. It will take longer, but I will get it. If you see that here in the compound [extended family household] we already have plows and carts, it is not because any person helped us. Hard work brought those things to us. But if someone helps us, it would be good.

These comments also show that assistance from the government or international development agencies is an acceptable supplement to the hard work needed to attain one's aspirations.

These two men live in a small country in West Africa, a poor country with one of the smallest rural per capita annual incomes in the world—about seventy-seven dollars. Since the sixteenth century, their society has been deeply involved in different types of hierarchical complementary relationships with the world market. Their society's initial involvement was

A Mandinka farmer bundling sorghum.

through the export slave trade, which lasted until the early part of the nineteenth century. Since that time, the society has increasingly committed its labor, land, and other resources to producing peanuts for sale to the industrializing states of Europe. During the colonial period (1894-1965), the central government established itself as the sole controller of the price to be paid to rural producers of peanuts, and the post independence central government continues to control that price. Thus, from the farmers' perspective, the means to meet their aspirations is inevitably political: if their elected representatives would only "remember" them (by raising producer prices), they would have the means to "get what [they are] seeking." Government administrators could also "remember" them by providing credit for the tools or seed that the farmers need to be more productive.

The farmers' sense of being remote from the government and abandoned by its personnel is often combined with a deep distrust.

As one Mandinka farmer says:

We are only farmers here. You know, we have only received one-half bag of rice [from international aid agencies through the national government] for each compound. Is that of any real value? All these things come from somewhere else, not really from them [the national government]. You know, a leader can be like a lion. He can eat all of his followers. We are sheep and goats behind the lions who are in the government. We vote for them. We pay our taxes. But they take from us. They do not give to us. They benefit from the [international agency] gifts of rice and powdered milk. More was given. We got little. They took it!

These feelings are strongly reinforced by a sense of being used by politicians. As an elderly low-status Mandinka man said in 1975:

When the PPP [the original rural political party and the party that still controls the national government] first started, when the leader of the party stayed here, he came and said that it was time for the white people [the British colonial government] to leave here . . . it was time for the black people to rule through the PPP. We said that if Allah allows it, he would. He said that if this village agrees to support him, things will change. He said that outside this village, everyone else in our area was a stranger. We said that we would tell all others in the area to support him and the party. You know, when the white people ruled, they had no friends [here]. Their only friend was the [law] book. When the black people came to power, they obtained many friends everywhere. Many friends gave money [to support candidates and the party]. Now [we] friends go to see [elected officials] to tell them of our needs. They do not help us. They tell us they will help us but they do not. The president does not know of our needs; they do not tell him and they do not allow us to see him in order that we may tell him.

Thus many Mandinka farmers are forced to rely on their individual or group local resources. But most do not attain a new, higher standard of living as a result of local resources. Many instead turn to the urban area of the capital as a source of the cash they see as the key to a better future. Young people, especially, are migrating for much or all of the year to urban areas in the hope of finding jobs. At best, though, most obtain only enough cash to feed and house themselves. With their migration, the rural area loses social resources vital to community and family life as well as a major source of the labor pool for the farmers who have chosen to stay. Given these current conditions, the aspirations of the large poor majority of Mandinka—both urban migrant and rural farmer—seem to go unmet.

Chapter Seven

Society

W OLF CHILDREN, A few hermits, prisoners in solitary confinement, and those stranded on desert isles aside, most of us spend a great deal of time in the company of other humans. It is generally as a group that we adapt to our surroundings and seek to ensure that our subsistence requirements are met. Even when we are alone, the demands and effects of social interaction are important influences.

How we perceive the world and how we behave in it are largely reflections of our interaction with others. Furthermore, our behavior and the behavior of others is relatively patterned and predictable. Perhaps too often for our liking, our own activities tend to follow a pattern that we sometimes refer to as a rut. *Society* is an abstraction of the ways in which interaction among humans is patterned.

In the last chapter we looked at how people produce, distribute, and exchange things. This chapter focuses on the social dimension of adaptation—the ways in which people order their interaction with their human environment.

Looking at Society

To figure out how society works, anthropologists can study either the structure or the function of social events or processes. Such analyses can be applied at every level of interaction, from whole societies linked by the world system down to the interactions of two individuals.

Analyzing Social Structure

Structure is the interrelationship of parts in a complex whole. When we look at the structures of whole societies, we see that groups that pursue similar subsistence strategies tend to have similar social structures. Their similarities will be modified somewhat by local conditions and historical circumstances. For example, Mayan communities in the Guatemala highlands and the southern Belize lowlands have similar administrative, kinship, economic, and religious structures. But since land is more abundant and

OVERLEAF
This pictograph made by Sioux Indians in the late nineteenth century documents their daily life— buffalo hunting, rituals, fighting—in a type of calendar for the past year (vegetable dyes on muslin, c. 1 × 3 meters).

political freedom greater in southern Belize, these structures tend to be more flexible than in Guatemala. Nevertheless, both sets of communities share with each other and with other small-scale societies a characteristic way of organizing people into social units that tends to be different from that found in larger-scale societies.

Small-scale societies, and smaller social units in general, tend to exhibit a high degree of internal cohesiveness. Emile Durkheim (1933) referred to the kind of social integration found in small-scale societies as *mechanical solidarity*. Societies so characterized possess very little division of labor, and people interact largely on a face-to-face basis. Everyone is familiar with everyone else. Everyone is also similar to everyone else, for they do much the same thing and share similar experiences. In addition to this *homogeneity*, or similarity, among the people, there is also a great deal of overlap in the units of their social structure. Among the Shoshone, the family and the foraging groups are virtually one and the same.

As the scale of society increases, its composition tends to become more varied and it begins to lose its homogeneous nature. As societies be-

Food production is quite different in large-scale versus small-scale societies. These Fijian villagers work together to catch fish, which they will either consume or market themselves. In contrast, food production in industrial countries is characterized by a highly specialized division of labor, as illustrated here in the production of hot dogs.

come larger, mechanical solidarity is replaced by what Durkheim referred to as *organic solidarity*: the social structure of societies assume many of the characteristics of an organism. Like the organs of the human body (heart, lungs, brain, and so on), the parts of such a society function in specialized ways, each contributing in a different way to the functioning of the society as a whole. As specialization within a society increases, Durkheim observed, so does the interdependency of its parts. In small-scale societies each social segment fulfills a wide range of functions, and is fairly independent. But in large-scale societies the parts fulfill much more distinct functions and therefore cannot function so independently of one another. In our own society, the farms or ranches or laboratories where food is produced are dependent upon a wide range of factories for fertilizers, machinery, and so forth. Transportation and the exchange of food are handled by yet other specialized institutions and groups, which are in turn dependent upon other kinds of factories and specialized services. Contrast this with an Amazonian

Indian village before its incorporation into Brazilian society: the entire process of food production and exchange could be carried out within a single family.

There are some pitfalls involved in adhering too literally to Durkheim's organic analogy. For one thing, unlike the human body, human society has no physical existence. Society is an abstraction of our actions and thoughts, and should not be assumed to function like a tangible organism. If we try to convert a mental construct or abstraction into a thing, to treat families or religious institutions as if they possessed the same properties as trees or dogs, we may begin to assume a degree of permanence in our abstraction that distorts understanding of social processes. From an organic perspective, Germany's Nazis of the 1930s can be viewed as a natural part of the social order rather than as a phenomenon that needs to be explained by attention to historical developments and socioeconomic processes. The organic analogy also suggests that there is relative harmony among the parts of a society; that everything functions to promote the well-being of the society and its members. If we make this assumption, we lose sight of power, control, domination, and competition—factors that are essential to an understanding of the dynamics of social life. Nevertheless, the idea of organic solidarity is useful for emphasizing the degree of interdependence that characterizes so much of social life in large-scale societies, even if it fails to provide a basis for understanding how and why the various components work.

Examining Functions

One way to get at the how and why of social life is to examine its *functions*—the purpose and effects, the intended and actual consequences of particular beliefs and actions. This is a complicated procedure, however.

While one function may be of primary im-

These Aboriginal children at Wiluna, Western Australia, are washing clothes. The manifest function of doing the laundry is to clean the clothes; a latent function is to prepare the children to become adults.

portance in any situation, most social activities serve a variety of functions. In addition, the function of any belief or practice depends upon one's point of reference. Marriage may perform one function for an individual, and quite another for a group of people or for an entire society. For an individual, marriage may serve as a means of acquiring a sexual partner, a socially legitimate companion of the opposite sex, a tax break, or a provider of social or economic security. For members of the couple's respective families, the new marriage may function as a political alliance, a new place to spend holidays, one less mouth to feed, or a new drain on resources. For the society as a whole, marriage may serve to regularize relations among people, to help order the ownership and transfer of various kinds of resources, and to ensure that children and old people are cared for. Marriage will not perform all of these functions in every social context, and it will also perform many others besides these. Furthermore, its functions may change over time as the environment changes.

Robert Merton (1968) has noted that there are two categories of social function: manifest and latent. *Manifest functions* are the results or purposes that are most obvious and that are explicitly stated. If you ask people why they are doing something, this is the reason they will give. People will say that they wash clothes to get them clean; welfare departments will say that they function to help the poor and needy. *Latent functions* are the less apparent effects.

They are inferences that can be made after careful study. Clothes washing by women may perform a latent function as a means of assessing their social standing in relation to their peers in terms of skill and diligence; it may also symbolize the inferiority of women in relation to men. And on the basis of research conducted primarily in New York, social scientists Frances Piven and Richard Cloward (1971) have concluded that welfare bureaus often perform a latent function as a means of regulating the poor by inducing people to behave in certain ways in exchange for needed services and funds. Often there are chains of these latent functions. By regulating the poor, welfare bureaus maintain the status quo, thereby enabling those who are better off to maintain their position in relation to those who might otherwise seek to undermine it. Latent functions often contradict popular conceptions of manifest functions.

The Individual and Society

In looking at the parts of society, we can start with the individual. The individual is the building block of society, for in one sense society is the product of the actions of its members. The members of a society do not act alone, however. Individuals are social actors whose behaviors are influenced by the social environment. It would be more accurate, then, to view society as the representation of the collective behavior of its members. Much of this collective behavior is highly patterned, conditioned by social forces that both spring from and transcend the individual.

In this section we'll examine the continual interplay of individual choice and social shaping: factors that influence an individual's choices of social behaviors, and the patterned relationships and more informal social networks that individuals both shape and are shaped by.

Influences on Individual Choices

Because society has no tangible existence, any permanence or regularity that it does exhibit will depend upon the repetition of people's actions. Society is therefore subject to the need for continual re-creation by individuals. The pattern that we associate with the Inuit family does not exist except insofar as individual Inuit continue to group themselves and to behave in the ways that have come to be associated with a particular family structure.

Society is the product of decisions people make concerning when, how, and with whom they are going to interact. Such individual decisions are influenced by a number of factors, some of which may be based on existing social patterns. One of these factors is individual perception: how people view their environment

Despite many changes in the wake of the industrial revolution, the church remains an important social institution in much of the industrialized world.

and the particular situation within which they must act, and what they perceive their options to be. Another factor is historical precedent, for what people do is almost always influenced by what was done in the past. The weight they give to this continuity depends on the extent to which they consider past actions to be relevant given their current circumstances, and the degree to which they interact continually with the same people and the same physical surroundings. A third factor is the nature of a person's or group's goals, since social interaction is goal oriented: we interact with others to achieve some end. Should our goals or those of the group change, so will the pattern of our social behaviors. For example, reciprocal labor exchange patterns among many small-scale farmers have been replaced by more impersonal patterns of market exchanges as the farmers have been integrated into larger social units. This change is related to a shift in people's goals from seeking prestige and egalitarian contact to seeking the maximum individual profits from the sale of their products.

Changes in individual behaviors may originate from without, as new opportunities or pressures favor reorientation of individual goals. But pressures from within for maintenance of existing patterns may also be strong. These pressures often come from established social *institutions*—practices based upon similar principles that display some degree of regularity. While there are many principles around which institutions may be organized, anthropologists have found that there are four primary ones (Beattie 1964). Some institutions are based upon principles of *kinship*, relations created by descent and marriage, such as the family. There are institutions concerned with *social control*, with politics and law. Government, courts, and the police fall within this category. Other institutions deal with *economic and property relations*, with the ways people produce and distribute things. Among these institutions are the farm, banks, and markets. A fourth category is institutions concerned with the *supernatural*—magic and religion. These include the church, monastaries, and religious brotherhoods.

Any institution is likely to be concerned to some degree with more than one of these primary organizing principles. Thus, the family is also concerned with social control, economic and property relations, and in many societies with the supernatural. The precise nature of these secondary concerns reflects conditions in specific environments and the suitability of particular institutions for assuming these roles. In colonial Mexico, churches often served as banks because of their power, characteristics of the legal system, inheritance patterns that allowed religious organizations to accumulate capital and property, the greater security that they offered over other institutions, and a range of other factors.

The process by which regularized patterns are created is sometimes referred to as *institutionalization*, or the standardization of modes of joint activity (Smith 1974: 208). When a religious prophet succeeds in regularizing people's beliefs and practices according to his or her preaching, this brand of religious belief and the social groups that form can be said to have undergone institutionalization. To understand such a process, we must look at the setting within which it took place, with special reference to the factors that allowed or encouraged regularization and the strategies of the prophet and his or her followers. For example, the Islamic Sanusiya Order of Libya, which is discussed in more detail in chapter 11, became a powerful religious institution because its founder used the relative neutrality of the order to fill the role of intermediary between rival groups of Bedouin, and later between the Bedouin and succeeding colonial administrations.

An important aspect of institutionalization is that it reduces options; it diminishes the range of choices a people can make, or are likely to. The degree to which this is true will vary. In a small community in which the Methodists have become socially dominant, there is likely to be informal pressure upon local businessmen, for example, to join that church rather than become Buddhists. The presence of a powerful state religion, as in the case of Spanish Catholicism in the fifteenth and sixteenth centuries, is likely to reduce people's options to an even greater degree. During the Inquisition, the leaders of the Spanish Church ensured religious conformity through imprisonment, torture, and execution.

Social Relationships

Processes like institutionalization tend to regularize our choices of how we interact and with whom. We use the term *relationship* for any regularized pattern of action between individuals. By placing such patterns in a social context we arrive at the concept of a *social relationship*.

The interaction of a woman and her female offspring may be viewed as a mother-daughter relationship, which can be expected to exhibit certain regularities, depending in large part upon the environment within which it is set. A Mexican-American mother and daughter in southern Texas will interact somewhat differently from an Inuit mother and daughter in Alaska since they are products of and actors within different sociocultural and physical environments. In trying to analyze these relationships we would look at the relevant environmental variables—economic activities and organization, religious beliefs and practices, residential patterns, family size and composition, the weather, government welfare programs, and so on.

While we can anticipate finding many common patterns of interaction among Inuit mothers and daughters there will also be individual differences, for each individual and each *dyad* (mother and daughter) occupies a unique place in the environment. Rather than thinking in terms of *the* mother-daughter relationship in a given society, we should recognize that there is likely to be a range of mother-daughter relationships, with varying characteristics. Three factors likely to influence the nature of a relationship within a particular society will be the ages and status of the people involved and the degree to which their kind of relationship has been institutionalized in that society.

Status and Role. Two primary questions need to be asked about social relationships: Who are they between? What are they about? (Beattie 1964: 36). Answers to these questions are often expressed in terms of status and role.

Status concerns social position—what people are in relation to one another. Status may be hierarchical in nature, as with rulers and subjects or prison guards and inmates, or it may be more egalitarian. Another distinction is often made between an ascribed status and one that is achieved (Linton 1936). An *ascribed status* is assigned, usually on the basis of birth: a girl born in Scotland automatically becomes a Scot. An *achieved status* is attained through the efforts of the individual: one becomes a teacher, carpenter, or lawyer as a result of schooling or vocational training. In some cases, status is both ascribed and achieved. To be born the heir to a throne does not automatically mean that a prince will become king, or that once he has he will be able to retain his crown. On the other hand, a student has an easier time becoming a lawyer if his or her father is wealthy, a graduate of a prestigious Law School, and influential in the legal profession.

Role is the part our society expects us to play in a given relationship, a set of activities that are thought to have some purpose and function in a particular context. A king is expected to govern; a subject is expected to submit to the king's authority. Such expectations cannot be understood in isolation, however. Precisely how a king or a subject is expected to behave will be defined by historical tradition and environmental conditions. A king may be expected not only to govern but also to intercede with the deities on behalf of his subjects or to give his blessing to certain products (cookies, tea, etc). Such expectations are not static. The role of Queen Elizabeth II is a far cry from that of Henry VIII, reflecting alterations in the English economy, the emergence of new forms of social stratification, and the transformation of the nature of the English state.

Although roles can only be understood in relationship to each other—mother to daughter, king to subject—roles cannot be viewed as taking place only in pairs. Kings have relationships with foreign ambassadors and the like who are not their subjects, and these relationships may influence how the roles of king and subject interrelate. Furthermore, individuals usually occupy a number of different statuses and perform a range of roles, any one of which may influence the others. The king may also be a father, a member of a cricket team, a husband, and an airplane pilot. Subjects who have royal or noble status themselves will be expected to have different kinds of relationships with a king than those who do not.

Social scale is frequently an important factor affecting statuses and roles. In small-scale societies with relatively little specialization, the range of distinct statuses and roles available to an individual tends to be much more limited than in large-scale societies with a greater degree of specialization. Among desert-dwelling foragers like the Shoshone different statuses and roles are available only on the basis of age, sex, and kinship. Few additional distinctions are made, with the exception of curer or religious specialist. Furthermore, statuses and roles tend to overlap greatly, forming a few clusters that are ascribed to individuals on the basis of their age and sex. Thus, all middle-aged Shoshone males can be expected to occupy more or less the same status and to perform roughly the same roles. In sharp contrast, a middle-aged male in a large-scale industrial society can be anything from an army general to a prison inmate, from a powerful politician to a powerless, unemployed wino. It is important not to confuse status and role with personality, for while

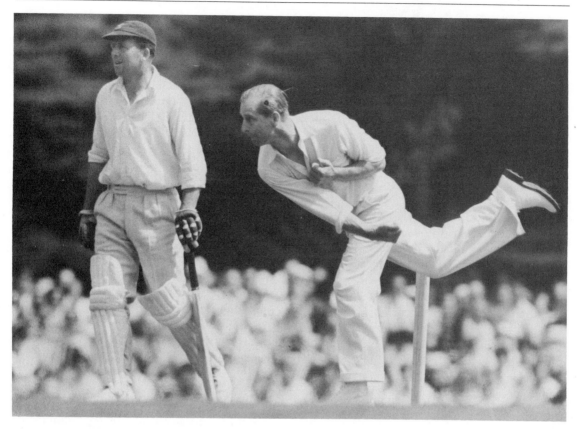

Prince Philip—the Duke of Edinburgh, husband of Queen Elizabeth II—as bowler, gives his all in this 1953 cricket match in aid of the National Playing Fields Association.

Shoshone may be homogeneous in terms of the statuses they occupy and the roles they perform, individual personalities vary a great deal.

Degree of Institutionalization. An additional question to be addressed when looking at regularity in social relationships concerns their degree of institutionalization: To what extent is a relationship supposed to prescribe behavior, and to what extent does it do so in practice? Among the more institutionalized relationships in most societies are those among kin. The members of a society recognize particular ways in which parents and their children, children

and their grandparents, siblings, and cousins act and are supposed to act with each other. Among the Mardujara Aborigines, behavior considered appropriate among kin varies from complete avoidance in some relationships to uninhibited joking in others. Avoidance relationships, such as that between a man and his mother-in-law, require "rapid evasive action" should either party come within twenty or thirty yards of the other. Such a pattern, sometimes known as *mother-in-law avoidance*, is common to many societies. At the other extreme are joking relationships; among the Mardudjara these exist among a wide range of relatives of the same sex and "involve rowdy exchanges of sexually explicit epithets and mock abuse" (Tonkinson 1978: 47). An important characteristic of such relationships is the ritualized or expected nature of behavior. Those involved in joking relationships are *expected* to engage in rowdy exchanges.

Like statuses, relationships vary in the degree to which they are freely chosen or automatically ascribed. In most instances, there is much less choice involved in being someone's sibling than in being someone's spouse. Perhaps the least ascriptive relationship in the majority of societies is that between friends. *Friendship* has been characterized as a voluntary, equal, and informal relationship that places mutual dimensions of intimacy and confidence on the persons involved. The personal nature of friendship results in relationships that are covert, autonomous, and unpredictable (Paine 1967). Friendship is covert in that much of its content is hidden from public view. It is autonomous to the extent that it is independent of kinship or other institutional arrangements. It is unpredictable, in part because of its autonomy and its highly personal rather than broadly social nature. As with all social behavior, friendship is also usually to some extent instrumental, in that friends interact with one another in pursuit of personal goals—such as a sense of worth or of being understood.

The personal nature of friendship should not lead us to discount the extent to which friendship patterns or behavior are conditioned by social and cultural factors. In any setting friendship will be somewhat institutionalized, but the degree of institutionalization can vary a great deal. In many societies, relatively institutionalized forms of friendship serve to augment or extend individual social networks beyond the realm of kinship. Among the Tapirapé of Amazonian Brazil, a formal form of friendship known as *anchiwawa* serves to extend personal alliances (Wagley 1977: 73–75). *Anchiwawa* are expected to engage in the mutual exchange of goods, often including their most valuable pos-

sessions (hammocks, macaws, clay cooking vessels, rifles). The *anchiwawa* relationship is not supposed to be among close relatives, and in the past, when the Tapirapé lived in a number of villages, *anchiwawa* relationships were often developed among residents of different villages, creating ties between individuals who normally would not exchange goods. The relationship was characterized by respect and formality; traditionally it was established by an intermediary and even involved avoidance in many settings. For instance, *anchiwawa* were supposed to turn aside to avoid passing each other on trails. Sometimes parents initiate these institutionalized relationships on the part of their children, carrying on exchanges until their children are old enough to do so. This aspect of the *anchiwawa* relationship points to the fact that friendships are not always altogether optional. The same point can be made in our own society, for parents and other friends influence our choice of friends.

Social Networks

Despite the social shaping of relationships, individuals do not act entirely in a patterned, stereotypical fashion. The weight of society in producing conformity is heavy in any setting, but it never entirely stifles creativity, and individuals are never mere passive actors playing out social roles. People can act creatively and part of their creativity involves the use of their social environment. To better understand how people both use and are influenced by their social environment, anthropologists turn to *social networks*—the bonds and links that form the social web within which we act.

Anyone who has tried to have a telephone installed in a country where services are limited and telephone company employees are not well paid knows something of the personal dimension of bureaucracy. Without paying the proper bribes or knowing the right people, one may have to wait years for a telephone. Whether trying to get a telephone or a new job, we continually mobilize potential links that exist within our personal social network. Analysis of this dimension of social life—the interpersonal links among people—is an important complement to the study of the nature of institutionalized relationships. It allows us to look at bureaucracies or kin-based groups in a less formal manner, to look beyond their public structures and see more clearly how such groups or institutions actually function.

The usefulness of such an approach can be illustrated by looking at academic departments in universities, for patterning of outside social networks often influences intradepartmental decision making. When the social networks of department members are highly interrelated or overlapping, there may be considerable homogeneity within a department. This may create a situation in which new faculty must either conform their theoretical perspectives and personal behaviors to a rather rigid or narrow set of expectations or else be given marginal status or forced to leave. In departments where the outside social networks of faculty members overlap little or not at all, chances are good that accept-

ability within the department will be more broadly defined—perhaps as not causing trouble or having an adequate publishing record. How such patterns evolve will be related to a number of considerations, such as the size of the department, its hierarchical structure, the potential for "empire building" on the part of individual faculty members, and the nature of the surrounding community. For example, in enclave universities in underdeveloped countries or regions where most of the faculty are recruited from societies with substantially different cultures from the surrounding populace, one can expect a very high degree of overlap in the social networks of department members because of their alienation from the local community. This is less likely to be the case in a cosmopolitan urban setting, where the faculty members are more likely to fit in with the culture of the community.

The Formation of Networks. Patterns of recruitment to social networks can differ from one society to another. In the small Mayan villages of southern Belize, a person's social network is built up primarily on the basis of kinship and *compadrazgo* (social links created by sponsorship of children in rites like baptism or con-

To most Guatemalan Indians, Catholic rites of passage are of great social significance. Here girls in San Lorenzo al Cubo prepare for the ceremony of First Communion, a rite that also serves as a pattern of recruitment to the social network in Guatemalan society.

firmation) to a more limited extent on the basis of less formal friendship. Many of the links created in village settings such as these are *multiplex*—they are formed on the basis of more than one criterion (Gluckman 1955: 18-19). For example, a person may be linked to another by three criteria: kinship, *compadrazgo*, and friendship. This multiplication of criteria tends to have the effect of intensifying links between persons, enhancing the extent to which individuals are willing or can be expected to honor obligations, or feel free to exercise rights implied in the links (Mitchell 1969: 27). The Maya of southern Belize feel much more secure in asking individuals with whom they have multiplex ties to help with farm-related work than individuals with whom they have fewer ties.

Even in small, tightly knit villages, not all social links will be multiplex. Those formed on the basis of a single criterion are termed *simplex*. For the Maya villagers, links across ethnic boundaries are frequently of this nature, being based upon friendship or some common interest, and often assuming a patron-client nature. An attempt to strengthen these links may lead to the creation of a *compadrazgo* bond. Villagers may seek a non-Indian patron in the form of a merchant or government employee, for instance. Likewise, non-Indian village teachers generally try to secure their position in the village—and their ability to obtain food—through the creation of *compadrazgo* links.

Which segment of a network will be employed at a given time will depend upon the context and the content of the various links. In recruiting people to assist in clearing a field or harvesting a crop a Mayan villager may call upon kin, compadres, or friends who are Indians. They can ask such people for help because this sort of thing is an important element in the content of links with other Indians. They will not attempt to recruit the non-Indians who are a part of their network, however. The links with non-Indians are formed for other purposes

and their content does not include an expectation of assistance in agricultural work.

Another important consideration in analyzing the formation of social networks is the durability of the links. Links that have a kinship component, for example, tend to be fairly durable. But even these are subject to destruction or activation by politics and factionalism. In one Mayan village studied, many links were no longer used for such things as recruitment to agricultural labor groups—even though they were based upon kinship and *compadrazgo*—because of factional strife. Their potential for reactivation remained, though. When a new village leader emerged who was able to overcome factional differences, many of these dormant links began to be used again (Howard 1977).

The Effectiveness of Networks. Like all elements of society, social networks both impinge upon personal behavior and offer individuals a vehicle to achieve desired goals (Boissevain 1973). As an example of the ways social networks influence individuals' behavior, studies in England (Bott 1957) and Zambia (Kapferer 1973) indicate that the structures of married couples' social networks influence how husbands and wives interact with each other. Roles that can be assigned to either sex are most likely to be found where the networks of the husband and wife overlap a great deal, while their roles tend to be more segregated as their networks become more distinct.

Emphasis upon the manipulative or utilitarian nature of social networks is prominent among studies of political contests such as elections, where success depends upon one individual's gaining the support of others. Mayer (1963: 120-22) mentions four potential sources of support for candidates in an Indian election studied: social relationships resulting from kinship, friendship, or common residence; patron-client or broker links; issues or principles; and opposition to someone or something else. The social network of the candidate plays a very important role in such a situation as he or she tries to use existing or potential social links to gain support.

The nature of networks and how they are used in a political context is often determined by external features in the environment. In the election of a delegate for the National Aboriginal Consultative Committee among Australian Aborigines in the city of Perth, personal social networks were found to play a decisive role (Howard 1978). Kinship ties were a major factor in the voting, as was the extent to which a can-

didate was perceived by other Aborigines to have useful links with non-Aboriginal patrons in government. This importance of kinship and of non-Aboriginal patronage reflects the disadvantageous way in which Aborigines have been incorporated into Australian society, particularly their lack of political power, and consequent dependence upon non-Aborigines. They have had to rely on kin for support in the harsh realities of their lives, and non-Aboriginal patronage has been the only possible link to those in power.

Social Groupings

Beyond our personal social networks, we tend to interact fairly often with various groups that we either choose voluntarily or are cast in with by the larger society. As individuals involved in political contests search for support or as religious leaders seek to assemble a following, for instance, their efforts may result in the formation of collections of people who interact on a fairly regular basis. Should the process continue with some success, the political party or church will assume a greater degree of internal organization and the people themselves will come to assume an identity as members of the Republican or Labor party, as Catholics or Mormons. The social process in such instances is one of *group formation*.

When anthropologists refer to a fully developed formal group organization, formed on whatever basis, they call it *corporate*. A *corporate group* is theoretically permanent; its members are recruited on the basis of recognized principles, they have common interests or property, and they have norms or rules fixing their rights and duties in relation to one another and to their property or interests. A *patrilineage* is a corporate group to which members are recruited on the basis of kinship, the principle being de-

scent through male lines from a common ancestor. A business corporation may recruit members—accountants, lawyers, managers, on the basis of their possession of desired skills, their acceptance of particular modes of behavior, and their sharing of roughly similar views of the world. But although both are corporate groups, membership in a patrilineage is more or less nonvoluntary, whereas membership in a business corporation is likely to be voluntary.

Nonvoluntary Groups

In nonvoluntary groups, membership is acquired at birth. We are born into a certain family or of a particular gender; our age group is likewise fixed. Lumping of people into multipurpose groups on the basis of these ascribed categories is the chief principle of group formation in small-scale societies. As social scale increases, many groupings tend to become more voluntary and specialized in nature. The most common types of ascriptive multipurpose groupings are based upon kinship, including lineages, clans, and moieties, (see chapter 8). Age and gender are also commonly employed to form such groups.

Younger Xavante boys being initiated by older boys into an older age set (central Brazil).

Age-based Groups. Age is a universally important factor determining social behavior. All societies possess a series of recognized age-based categories or *grades*. In many societies those who have not yet achieved adult status are denied the right to engage in a number of activities, from participation in rituals to driving vehicles or drinking alcoholic beverages. Movement into a new age grade usually means new expectations as well as new possibilities. Historical, demographic, and environmental factors may play a role in determining the function and significance of a particular age grade within a society. Those born during the post-World War II "baby boom" in the United States are a lump in the demographic profile that, because of its disproportionate size, moves through the years profoundly influencing all aspects of American life, from education and employment to housing and music.

In many small-scale societies, especially in Africa, those belonging to the same age grade are formed into corporate groups. The groups are called *age sets*. An age set is a group of individuals of similar age and of the same gender who share a common identity, maintain close ties throughout their lives, and together pass through a series of age-related statuses. As Colin Turnbull (1976: 51–52) has noted, the age-set system serves a number of important purposes:

it creates through dramatic and periodic rituals of initiation the strongest bonds of sentiment, binding large groups of men (particularly) throughout the land, regardless of kinship, in common cause. It provides a second major and distinct set of loyalties. It provides a means not only for distributing labor, but also for distributing authority. It provides young and old alike with clearly defined roles suited to the general capabilities of their age level. . . . It causes young men to act together, in defense of their land, their cattle, or their crops. It leaves most of the vital decisions to the elders who may no longer be agile enough to take part in the active life of the youth but who have the advantage of an accumulated store of wisdom. It enlarges social horizons, providing a new dimension in which a man or a woman may move to find friends as dependable as kin in times of need. It creates an almost spiritual community.

In essence, age sets function to support the creation of social order. They help to hold societies together by ordering relations among those of different ages and by creating links that cut across the boundaries of kin groups, providing the individual with an even greater range of people to call on for assistance.

The structure and significance of age sets vary considerably from one society to the next. Some follow a *linear* progression, in which those born during a specified period belong to a single set that moves up through a series of grades as the members grow older. Others adhere to a *cyclic* pattern, whereby sets accept new members on a periodic basis. In some societies age sets may perform a limited range of functions and have little influence on the overall structure and functioning of society; in other societies they are of tremendous importance.

The Nyakyusa of southeastern Africa have what may be characterized as an extreme example of age-set organization (Wilson 1963). At age twelve boys who have grown up working closely together leave their parental homes and move to a village of their own; they continue to return to their parents for meals and to work in their fathers' fields until they marry and set up their own households, at about age twenty-five. Younger brothers of the village founders join the community until it becomes large enough for the members to decide to close admittance. After a decade or so there will be a number of new age villages in the area and the fathers will hold a ceremony to hand over full political authority to their sons.

Sex-based Groups. All societies tend to group people by gender as well as age. In small-scale societies, people are automatically divided into sex groups that serve many purposes, such as carrying out the subsistence activities delegated to their sex. Large-scale industrial societies also commonly possess a range of sex-based groups (such as the League of Women Voters, the Boy Scouts, fraternities, and sororities), but membership in these is usually of a more voluntary nature and the groups tend to serve a much narrower range of purposes.

Even within a single small-scale society, the cohesiveness of sex-based groups may vary. In Amazonian Brazil, the Mundurucu household contains a sex-based group consisting of several closely related women of two or three generations. Usually the women are from the same village and have grown up together. They carry out most of their productive tasks as a group, gardening, preparing manioc, and cooking together. It is a secure group that is to a very large extent self-sufficient.

The males in the village have moved there from other villages upon marriage. When not engaged in subsistence activities, they spend much of their time in a single central men's house, a common feature in small-scale farming societies. While in a sense they form a group, it is not as well integrated as the women's. Since most of the men come from different villages and from different kin groups, they are relative strangers who share only their current place of residence and their maleness. Even male economic tasks are performed alone or in small groups, further diminishing their unity.

The formation of sex-based groups is tied to a range of environmental features such as kinship, residence, and subsistence patterns. As these change, patterns of group formation may change as well. Thus, the Mundurucu's sex group patterns are changing because of alterations in their economic adaptation. The Mundurucu have become increasingly dependent on working in relative isolation collecting rubber from sparsely distributed trees along the river to purchase consumer goods from traders. Many Mundurucu now live as isolated nuclear families, and others have moved to a mission settlement to be nearer rubber-collecting areas and the source of consumer goods.

Voluntary Associations

Special-purpose groups whose members are recruited on a nonascriptive basis—*voluntary associations*—are a common feature of life in large-scale industrial societies. They are found less often in small-scale societies, where most groupings tend to be ascriptive (such as kin-based groups). Nevertheless, several types of voluntary association may be found in small-scale societies.

Voluntary Groupings in Small-Scale Societies. Military associations develop in some small-scale societies that are engaged in warfare on a regular basis, although kinship groups and age sets are more likely to be the primary military units. The Cheyenne traditionally had five such societies: the Fox, the Dog, the Shield, the Elk (or Hoof Rattle), and the Bowstring (or Contrary), each with its own leaders, costumes, songs, and dances (Hoebel 1960).

Secret societies also occur in some small-scale societies, such as the Poro of Liberia and Sierra Leone (Little 1965/66). Members of the Poro society are said to have close contact with the supernatural and to possess magical powers. Its leadership tends to comprise those who hold public power, the secret society serving to support their public statuses. Young men who are initiated into the society attend "bush school" in an isolated part of the forest for several years, at which they learn secret rituals, the history of their people, and a variety of useful skills.

There are also religious cults, like those of the Tupi-Guarani of Brazil, reported by early European explorers and settlers (Lanternari 1963: 171–81). Tupi-Guarani prophets would gather large numbers of followers and then set off in search of some paradisal promised land.

The organization and significance of these voluntary associations in small-scale societies have changed considerably as a result of colonial expansion and domination. Military societies and secret societies came to function as a means of resisting conquest, either openly or covertly. Religious cults sometimes became a way of seeking escape from oppression through the promise of supernaturally inspired salvation. Not all religious movements that arise as a response to external domination are completely escapist in nature, however. As Peter Worsley (1957) has pointed out in regard to such movements in the Pacific, they may represent prerevolutionary attempts by indigenous peoples to resist domination.

Voluntary Groupings in Large-Scale Societies. Voluntary associations have developed in large-scale societies in response to two processes: urbanization and industrialization. Louis Wirth (1938), one of the early commentators on the subject, considered that the impersonality of the city and the sense of alienation that he assumed to be a feature of urban life resulted in the emergence of a "multiplicity of voluntary organizations directed towards as great a variety of objectives as there are human needs and interests." Such associations were seen by Wirth as replacing multipurpose groupings, such as those based upon kinship, that existed in rural and less industrialized settings. Multipurpose groups have not disappeared with the onslaught of civilization, nor have voluntary associations always assumed the importance suggested by Wirth, but there has been a general trend in this direction.

While anthropologists have studied a wide range of voluntary associations in many different settings, they have been especially interested in looking at associations formed by ethnic minorities and migrants to cities. These associations may be formed on the basis of re-

A voluntary association: the Cheyenne Lance Society (photograph taken in the late 1880s). A social and military group, the Lance Society (also known as the Coyote) were part of a ruling group along with chiefs. They also served a police function on buffalo hunts.

gional loyalties, ethnicity, or employment. Regional associations, for example, are common among poorer migrants to Lima, Peru, where they lobby the government on behalf of their members and assist new migrants in adjusting to city life (Mangin 1959). Likewise, ethnic or tribal associations abound in West African cities, where they serve many of the same functions as their Peruvian counterparts (see Little 1965; Meillassoux 1968). These associations sometimes play an important role in securing employment for their members, and their activities may overlap with more generalized voluntary associations such as labor unions or political parties.

Many anthropologists have sought to explain why voluntary associations develop in some urban settings but not in others. For example, although there are numerous regional associations among migrants to Lima, similar associations are rare in many other Latin American cities. Likewise, ethnic or tribal associations are distributed unequally in African cities. David Parkin (1969: 150–79) has suggested that important variables include numbers of the ethnic group in the town, their socioeconomic status, and the type of rural social structure that the migrants come from. Thus, Parkin (1974: 146; see Banton 1957: 195) hypothesizes that migrants from societies where political authority is vested in kin groups rather than in some specialized administrative structure will be more likely to form voluntary associations to assist them in dealing with external pressures or competition encountered in the city than are migrants coming from more centralized societies governed by chiefs. The latter are more likely to use readily available institutions of a less specialized nature, such as government bureaus or trade unions. Moreover, where migrants come from areas near the city ethnic associations generally are not found. In such cases the migrants can rely upon their home community or kin group for support or services rather than upon a voluntary association (Southall 1961: 38).

Another important question: How important are voluntary associations for the members? Attention to their manifest functions often provides only a very superficial understanding of the functions they actually serve. For example, many of the voluntary associations that have been formed by or for Australian Aborigines in cities, ostensibly to assist them in improving their political and economic lot, are quite ineffective. In fact, they often serve as a hindrance to Aboriginal attempts to improve their status.

The existence of these associations is easier to understand if attention is shifted to a more important latent function: they serve the government as part of a system of indirect rule or control (Howard 1978). Thus, although their stated purpose is to improve things for Aborigines, their primary purpose for those who actually control them (government administrators) is to make sure that things do not change.

The question of manifest and latent functions aside, ethnic associations are often not only ineffective, but also of only minor importance in the lives of urban migrants. Cohen (1969: 195) finds that memberships in West African ethnic associations tend to include only a small fraction of the total number of migrants who might join; even for those who do join, activities related to the association are of little relevance to the member on a day-to-day basis. Cohen points out that many of these associations meet quite irregularly and that much of their elaborate organizational structure is mere facade: "Nearly all of these associations have elaborate constitutions, but these are often the composition of public letter writers who charge a small fee for such a service" (195). Anyone studying a social aggregate such as these voluntary associations must recognize the importance of placing that aggregate in a broad context—the lives of individuals and their surrounding environment—to understand its meaning and significance.

Summary

As social creatures, we humans constantly shape and are shaped by our social environment. These interactions can be analyzed by looking at their structure or functions. Small-scale societies tend to be tightly integrated units consisting of a few multipurpose groups; large-scale societies tend to be composed of varied, interdependent elements. Within a society, beliefs and activities may serve certain obvious, or manifest, functions as well as less obvious latent functions.

The individual is the basic building block of society. The individual choices that add up to social patterns reflect both pressures for change and pressures for continuity. The latter is often expressed through established institutions; when any aspect of social life becomes institutionalized it tends to reduce the range of choices people are likely to make. Social relationships are often institutionalized according to the status and role given to those involved. But certain relationships—such as friendships in some societies—are characterized by fewer social expectations and greater freedom of individual choice. In some societies, however, even friendships are highly institutionalized.

Despite pressures toward conformity, individuals often act creatively to shape their own social environment. Anthropologists study this creative use of the social environment by means of the concept of social networks: the web of social links within which people act. Networks formed on the basis of many criteria are called multiplex; those formed on the basis of a single criterion are called simplex. The structure of

these networks may both influence individual behavior, as in interactions between husband and wife, and be used by individuals to further their own goals, as when politicians seek election.

On a more formal level, individuals organize or are organized into various kinds of groups. They are born into nonvoluntary groups on the basis of sex, age, and kinship. Such groupings tend to be rather strictly adhered to and multipurpose in small-scale societies. Voluntary associations are more common in large-scale societies, where they may serve a variety of manifest and latent functions.

Having looked at some of the general features of human society in this chapter, we now turn to a closer examination of certain aspects of society. In the next chapter we will look at kinship, and in the chapter following at sex, marriage, and the family.

Suggested Readings

Worth looking at concerning social organization and social structure are:

Banton, Michael, ed. 1965. *The relevance of models for social anthropology.* London: Tavistock Publications.

Beattie, John. 1964. *Other cultures: Aims, methods and achievements in social anthropology.* New York: Free Press.

Blau, Peter M. 1975. *Approaches to the study of social structure.* New York: Free Press.

Burnham, P. C., and Ellen, R. F., eds. 1979. *Social and ecological systems.* London/New York: Academic Press.

Firth, Raymond. 1964. *Essays on social organization and values.* London: Athlone Press.

Nadel, S. F. 1957. *The theory of social structure.* Melbourne: Melbourne Univ. Press.

Park, George. 1974. *The idea of social structure.* New York: Doubleday/Anchor.

There are two major collections that deal with social networks:

Boissevain, Jeremy, and Mitchell, J. Clyde, eds. 1973. *Network Analysis: Studies in human interaction.* The Hague/Paris: Mouton.

Mitchell, J. Clyde, ed. 1969. *Social networks in urban situations: Analyses of personal relationships in central African towns.* Manchester: Manchester Univ. Press.

Chapter Eight

Kinship

WHEN ANTHROPOLOGIST Laura Bohannon (1966) lived with the Tiv in West Africa, she tried one rainy day over three pots of beer to tell the story of *Hamlet* to the local chief and the men of his homestead. One of her biggest problems lay in trying to explain Shakespeare's story in ways that made sense within the Tiv's concepts of kinship and the behaviors expected of kin. She tried to explain why Hamlet was unhappy because his mother remarried soon after his father's death: "It is our custom for a widow not to go to her next husband until she has mourned for two years." Her listeners objected, "Two years is too long. . . . Who will hoe your farms for you while you have no husband?" And when Bohannon explained that Hamlet stabbed his would-be father-in-law Polonius through a curtain on the mistaken assumption that it was his mother's new husband, his father's younger brother, her listeners were outraged:

For a man to raise his hand against his father's brother and the one who has become his father—that is a terrible thing. . . . If your father's brother has killed your father, you must appeal to your father's age mates: they may avenge him. No man may use violence against his senior relatives. [1966, pp. 207, 212–13]

Despite their inability to interpret *Hamlet* in identical ways, Bohannon and the Tiv both recognized the importance of kin relationships in the story, for kinship is a feature of all human societies.

The reasons for this universality are to some extent biological: human infants are helpless and dependent on the care of others for a prolonged period, and bonds arise among people in relation to these conditions. But while biology may provide the basis for kinship, the ways in which people define and use kinship are determined by sociocultural, not biological, considerations. When anthropologists study kinship, they are concerned with social relations and cultural definitions. Rather than being universal, these vary widely. In different societies, people with the same biological—or marital—relationship may be defined differently, labeled differently, and classified variously as kin or nonkin.

Kinship Diagrams and Abbreviations

Before we start to unravel the complexities of differing interpretations of kinship, we need to cover a few preliminaries: the fundamental elements of kinship diagrams and the abbreviations anthropologists use when writing about kinship. They do not use drawings of family trees. These often artistic reconstructions show graphically how family members are related over generations. But they are not particularly useful for showing all of the intricacies of a kinship system. The branches can become quite muddled after a few divorces and remarriages. Moreover, many family trees are hard to understand until we can figure out the creator's particular logic in diagramming things.

Faced with the need to understand and compare a wide variety of kinship systems, anthropologists have developed a standardized notational system (see figure 8.1). At the heart of this system are six basic symbols:

1. A triangle to indicate a male
2. A circle to indicate a female
3. A square to indicate when the person's sex is unspecified

OVERLEAF

Family tree of the Ames family of North Easton, Massachusetts (1560–1937).

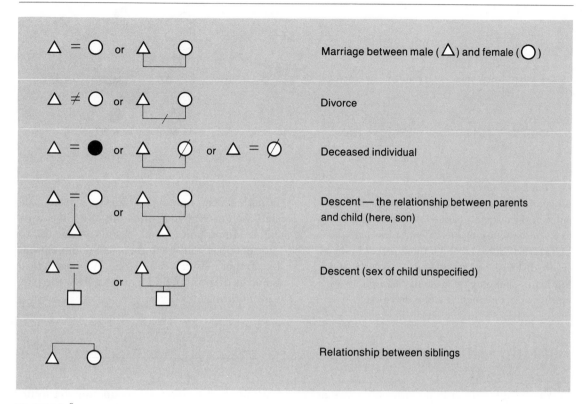

FIGURE 8.1

Standardized notations for diagramming kinship relations.

4. A vertical line to indicate descent, as from parent to child
5. A horizontal line with descending vertical lines to indicate codescent, as in the case of siblings
6. An equals sign or a horizontal line with ascending vertical lines to indicate marriage

It is often necessary to use other symbols as well. For deceased persons the symbol may be darkened or a line drawn through it. Divorce is represented by drawing a slash (/) across the horizontal bar of the diagram.

Anthropologists often center their kinship diagrams on a particular person. This person we refer to as *ego*, the individual from whose point of view we are tracing relationships. It is also of-

ten necessary to be aware of generational levels in relation to ego—whether they are ego's ancestors or descendants—for these distinctions can be important in determining how kin are classified.

Anthropologists also have devised shorthand notations to indicate many of the relational statuses of persons:

F for father	M for mother	S for son
D for daughter	B for brother	Z for sister
H for husband	W for wife	C for child

Because many other relationships are labeled ambiguously in our culture, most other kinship statuses are indicated by combinations of these abbreviations. Thus, what we call uncles would include mother's brothers (MB), father's brothers (FB), mother's sisters' husbands (MZH), and

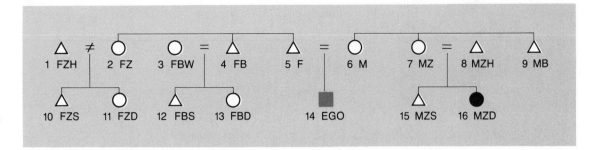

FIGURE 8.2
A hypothetical family diagram. Ego (14—the center point of the diagram) has no brothers or sisters. Ego's father (5) has a sister (2) and a brother (4). Ego's father's sister (2) and father's sister's husband (1) are divorced. Ego's mother has a sister (7) and a brother (9), but only the sister has married. Ego's mother's sister's daughter (16) is deceased.

father's sisters' husbands (FZH). In many kinship systems these distinctions are of considerable importance, and it helps to use a shortened version of cumbersome combinations like father's sister's son (FZS). A hypothetical family is diagrammed in figure 8.2 with the relevant notation.

Kinship Categories

In their study of kinship anthropologists are concerned with two separate, but interrelated, types of relationship: consanguinity and affinity. *Consanguinity* refers to biological relationship, that of "blood"; those so linked we call *consanguines*. Relationship "by blood" is what the term "kinship," strictly speaking, refers to. *Affinity* concerns relationships formed through marriage; people linked in this fashion are *affines*.

Basically, affines are the people married to our consanguines. Affinity is therefore determined by how a society defines consanguinity. Not all societies view blood relatedness in quite the same way. In some societies a child is considered to be related by blood to its mother only; in other societies just the opposite is true. The child's mother, for example, can be seen to function solely as a host while it matures, the father alone being responsible for having produced it.

If we find differences of opinion regarding the very basic question of who are to be categorized as blood relations, it should come as no surprise to discover that even more disagreement exists when we turn to more distant relatives. Take our father's brother, our uncle, for example. Some societies make no categorical distinction between him and our father; others use the same term for them and for one of our cousins (FZS). There is a great deal of variation in the ways people categorize kin. This variation is far from unlimited, however. There tend to be a few general principles around which categorical systems are built.

Defining Parents, Siblings, and Cousins

Two of the most fundamental relationships in any system of kinship are those between parents and children, and those between siblings. After all, these are the most immediate biological links that we possess. However, biology only provides the basis for these relationships. Definitions of these relationships are culturally constructed.

In our society a distinction is made between the actual biological father, the socially and legally recognized father, and the mother's husband. The same person may occupy all three statuses, but this is not necessary. When we talk about someone's father we usually mean his or her social father, who may or may not be the biological father. When divorced couples remarry, for the sake of clarity we sometimes use terms like *stepfather* and *real father*. In other societies things can become even more complex. The Nuer allow women and even ghosts to assume the status of social father, and in some Indian societies a group of brothers may be viewed collectively as social fathers of a single individual.

Definitions of siblings may be equally complex. In our society siblings are often all related by blood, but this is not necessarily the case. It is relatively common to make no distinction between siblings who are a couple's natural off-

spring and those who are adopted. And often no distinctions are made between children of a couple from previous marriages and those of the present one. The situation can become a great deal more complex in societies that allow individuals to have more than one spouse at the same time, for many half-sibling relationships occur between people who have the same mother or father, but not both.

Some societies further distinguish siblings according to relative age. One might use a different term for older brothers and younger brothers, or there might simply be a special term for the oldest brother. In still other societies siblings and cousins are categorized together. In some societies, for example, the same terms are used for sisters and all female cousins, and for brothers and all male cousins.

Cousins—the children of a sibling and his or her spouse—are also basic to any kinship system. In our society virtually the only distinction made is between those cousins considered too close for sexual or marriage purposes and those who are felt to be sufficiently distant. Although the reasons for making such a distinction are often couched in biological terms, the distinction in fact represents a strictly cultural pattern. In other societies, paternal cousins may be considered different than maternal cousins. And the relationship between *cross-cousins*—the children

FIGURE 8.3

Cross-cousins and parallel-cousins. Ego's cross-cousins are the offspring of ego's father's sister (1) and ego's mother's brother (4). Ego's parallel-cousins are the children of ego's father's brother (2) and ego's mother's sister (3).

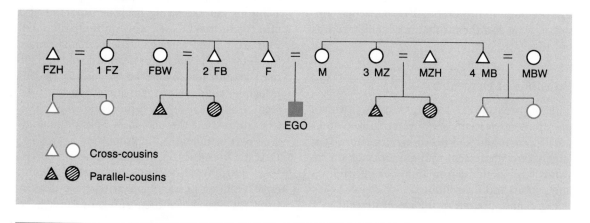

FIGURE 8.4
Patrilineal descent. The symbols outlined in color in this diagram are all
related through the male line to a
common ancestor.

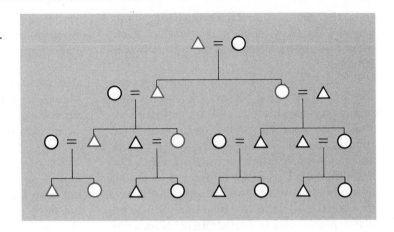

of two siblings—may be considered different than the relationship between *parallel-cousins*—children of two siblings of the same sex (see figure 8.3).

These distinctions are not random—they are deeply rooted in people's cultural traditions and social structures. The Kekchi distinction between older and younger siblings is related to their hierarchical view of family relations and to a system of inheritance favoring the oldest male sibling. Our own society's emphasis on physiological paternity is a peculiarity of our culture, linked to our religious and scientific heritage. Likewise, the distinction that many societies make between kinds of cousins is related to inheritance patterns and strategies. Many of these distinctions are also products of particular kinship systems and the manner in which descent is traced.

Principles of Descent

The organization of kinship systems involves questions of *descent*, socially recognized links between a person and his or her ancestors. It is largely through descent that our range of kin expands beyond the narrow limits of our siblings and parents and their siblings.

We cannot use our own ideas of descent as a model for understanding this area, for societies vary considerably in how they define descendants. To get a handle on the framework each society takes for granted as "the" way of tracing descent, anthropologists have categorized a number of principles by which different societies reckon descent. They are not just abstract constructs, however; they play a major part in shaping social life, from who inherits from whom to who participates in special ceremonies.

Many societies limit the range of persons through whom descent can be traced. The most restrictive way of tracing descent is *unilineal descent*—through a single line, male or female. Unilineal rules of descent affiliate a person with a line of kin extending back in time and also into the future, but selecting out only those kin who are related through male or female lines. We refer to the tracing of descent through male lines as *patrilineal descent*. According to this principle, children in each generation trace descent from their social father, and only those who are related through male lines are considered part of the same kin group (see figure 8.4). Descent traced through female lines is referred to as *matrilineal descent*. According to this principle, children in each generation trace descent from their social mother, and only those who

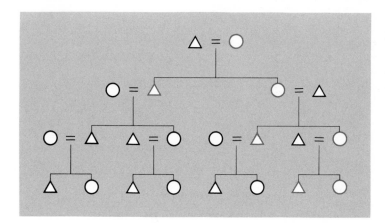

FIGURE 8.5
Matrilineal descent. The symbols outlined in color in this diagram are all related through the female line to a common ancestor.

are related through female lines are considered part of the same kin group (see figure 8.5).

Unilineal descent patterns tend to be found among affluent or stable foragers, small-scale farmers, and pastoral nomads. Which form of descent is adopted depends in part on environmental factors. For example, farming societies adhering to the principle of matrilineal descent are generally located bordering or outside of forested areas (Aberle 1961), and in areas where large domestic animals are absent. Population pressure and competition for scarce resources is usually absent among these peoples. As a result, warfare is infrequent or totally absent, as are its psychological and social results—aggression, competition, strong differentiation between public and private spheres, devaluation of women, and female infanticide. These environmental conditions that allow for matrilineal systems have decreased over the past few centuries. In a survey of slash-and-burn farmers, Martin and Voorhies (1975) found that only 24 percent were matrilineal. They suggest that the frequency was much higher in the past under more stable conditions, arguing that matrilineal descent tends to disappear when people are confronted with problems of expansion, competition, or intensification of production.

Some small-scale societies define kinship on less restrictive terms than patrilineal or matrilineal principles. Some trace descent separately through both male and female lines. According to this principle of *bilineal descent* (sometimes known as double descent) an individual often traces descent patrilineally for some purposes, matrilineally for others. Other societies recognize both matrilineal and patrilineal descent, but it is up to the individual to choose between them. In this *ambilineal descent* pattern, a person must usually adhere to his or her choice. Because of the elective element, ambilineal kinship groups can vary a great deal in each generation. Lastly, in some societies women trace descent through female lines only and males trace descent through male lines only, a principle referred to as *parallel descent.*

Another form of descent predominates in large-scale industrial societies, foraging societies occupying harsh environments or experiencing pressure from nonforaging peoples, and family-oriented transhumants and farmers living in fairly poor environments. This pattern, often called *cognatic descent*, allows a person to trace descent through all ancestors, male and female. All relatives on both sides are considered kin.

No matter what principle of tracing descent is employed, people in all societies promote or play down relationships according to circum-

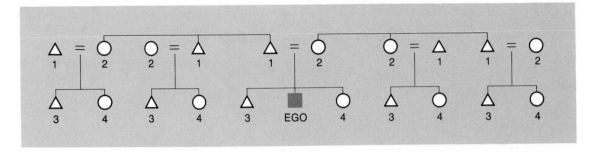

FIGURE 8.6
Hawaiian kinship system. Symbols with the same
number are referred to in the same way by ego.

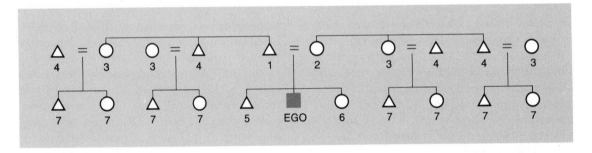

FIGURE 8.7
Eskimo kinship system.

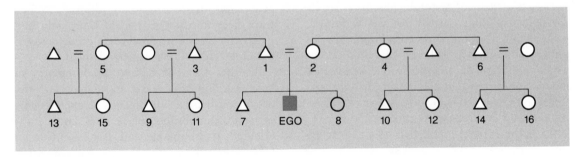

FIGURE 8.8
Sudanese kinship system.

stances. If the chance of an inheritance exists through a particular line, the relevant links become important. If potential embarrassment lies in ties to a certain line, those links will more than likely be ignored. In his discussion of Tunisian villagers and nomads, Jean Duvignaud notes that the people use and manipulate genealogies "like a game of chess" (1970: 72). They seek association with an unproven ancestor because of the prestige it brings, linking them with sacred genealogies and the pillaging tribes that came out of Egypt in the twelfth century. The people recite genealogies at great length, seeking to create a reality "by dint of rationalization, by the apparent coherence of a chain of marriages and connections and inheritances" (1970: 145), and yet these claims often have no basis in fact and they change with some frequency. In some instances family trees are bought or negotiated for. Young men sometimes wander from family to family, laying claim to a series of genealogies in the process.

The situation is not so fluid in all societies as it is in Tunisia. Some societies are very careful to maintain genealogical integrity. In most instances, however, it is best to see the way people trace descent as a reflection of current circumstances, rather than as historically accurate accounts of the past.

Systems of Labeling Kin

Not only do societies figure descent differently; they also apply different labels to their relatives. Although a vast array of kinship terminologies are to be found around the world, anthropologists have been able to isolate a limited number of general patterns in the ways people label kin. These we refer to as the Hawaiian, Eskimo, Sudanese, Omaha, Crow, and Iroquois systems, named after particular societies where they are employed.

Hawaiian System. See figure 8.6. This is the least complex system, using the smallest number of terms. All relatives of the same sex in the same generation are referred to by the same term. Thus, all female cousins are referred to by the same term as ego's sisters and all male cousins by the same term as ego's brothers. Likewise, all known male relatives of ego's parents' generation are called by the same term as are all female relatives of this generation. This system is often associated with ambilineal descent, which allows for a person to be affiliated with the kin group of either father or mother.

Eskimo System. See figure 8.7. This system, which is used by some Inuit societies, is also the one found in the United States. In this system cousins are distinguished from brothers and sisters, but all cousins are placed in the same category. Aunts and uncles are distinguished from parents and labeled separately according to sex. Unlike most other systems, in the Eskimo system no other relatives are referred to by the same terms used for members of the nuclear family—mother, father, brother, sister. This restrictiveness may be related to the fact that societies using this system usually lack large kin-based groups, emphasizing small family groups instead. Also, in these societies both the mother's and the father's sides are likely to be of equal social relevance, so no distinction needs to be made between, for instance, the mother's brother and the father's brother. Both are called simply "uncle."

Sudanese System. See figure 8.8. The Sudanese system makes the most distinctions possible. It uses distinct terms for all cousins on the basis of their relationship with ego, for example. The Sudanese system is associated with groups organized on the basis of patrilineal descent *and* with societies possessing a complex division of labor and marked social stratification. It may be that this terminological complexity mirrors complexity in social roles.

Omaha System. See figure 8.9. This system is usually associated with patrilineal descent. It uses the same term for a number of kin of the

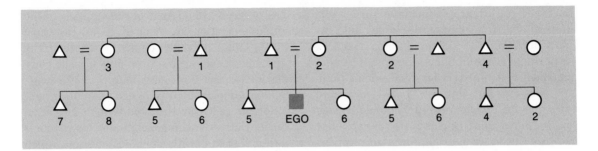

FIGURE 8.9
Omaha kinship system.

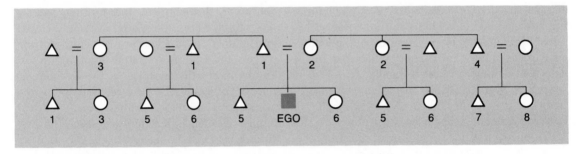

FIGURE 8.10
Crow kinship system.

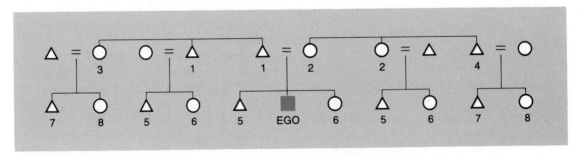

FIGURE 8.11
Iroquois kinship system.

same generation—for instance, ego's father and father's brothers are all given the same label. Generational distinctions are also made in ego's own generation. Male siblings and male parallel cousins (FBS, MZS) are all given the same title, and ego's female siblings and female parallel cousins (FBD, MZD) are lumped together under another label. Generational distinctions are not made in regard to most matrilineal relations, however. Ego's mother, mother's sister, and mother's brother's daughter are all assigned the same title, as are the mother's brother and mother's brother's son.

Crow System. See figure 8.10. The Crow system is to a degree the matrilineal equivalent of the Omaha system. The primary difference between the two is that in the Crow system relatives in the father's matrilineage (F, FB, and FZS; and on the one hand FZ and FZD on the other hand) are labeled as one respectively, while generational distinctions are made on the mother's side. Accordingly, ego's mother and

mother's sister are given the same name, ego's female siblings and female parallel cousins are given one name, and ego's male siblings and male parallel cousins are called by the same name.

Iroquois System. See figure 8.11. The Iroquois system is similar to the Crow and Omaha systems in the way persons of ego's parents' generation are treated: Ego's father and father's brother are assigned the same name, and ego's mother and mother's sister are likewise merged. The primary difference between the Crow and Omaha systems and the Iroquois system is in the way cross-cousins are treated. In the former systems they are given separate terms or merged with the previous generation. In the Iroquois system male cross-cousins are categorized together (FZS, MBS), as are female cross-cousins (FZD, MBD). This pattern may be linked with societal preferences for cross-cousin marriage, since cross-cousin marriage and Iroquois terminology are often found together (Goody 1970).

Kin-based Groups _____

Kinship is not an abstract system of classification anthropologists have devised to confuse students. It is a society's means of classifying people for real purposes. People use kinship for two primary social functions. First, kinship serves as a medium for transmitting status and property from one generation to the next. We refer to this process as inheritance. In virtually all societies people leave something that is coveted and needs to be distributed upon their death. To avoid chaos, the members of a society almost invariably devise rules for the inheritance of social and material property; quite often these rules are stated in terms of kinship. Second, kinship serves as a principle by which to establish and maintain social groups. In small-scale societies kinship is frequently the primary

or sole means through which groups can be formed. In large-scale societies, kinship's role in group formation tends to be much more limited.

Kin-based groups can be formed for a variety of purposes. They are often property-owning bodies, with the ownership of land, animals, ceremonial objects, or other forms of property vested in the collective membership. They may provide a basis for mutual aid, with their members helping one another in anything ranging from agricultural labor to burying the dead. They may serve aggressive or defensive ends, functioning as military units, or raiding or vengeance parties. They may serve ceremonial purposes, with the members joining to perform particular religious or civic ceremonies. They may also function as political bodies, as lobbying groups, or even as the primary administrative unit of a society.

Unilineal Descent Groups

Unilineal descent is one of the most common principles used in the formation of kin-based social groups. Membership in unilineal kinship groups is generally ascriptive: a person becomes a member at birth. Its ascriptive and unambiguous nature allows for the formation of discrete social groups, dividing everyone in a person's society into kin and nonkin. There are four basic types of groups that are based upon unilineal principles: lineages, clans, phratries, and moieties (see figure 8.12).

Lineages. A *lineage* is a group of kin who trace descent from a common ancestor or ancestress through known links. When descent is

traced through male lines the group is known as a *patrilineage*. When descent is traced through female lines the term *matrilineage* is used. Lineages are generally corporate groups that can serve a primary role in the distribution of wealth and political power. Among the Nuer, inheritance of cattle—their most important form of wealth—takes place exclusively within the lineage, from father to son or brother to brother. In many societies land is held jointly by lineage members. Lineage members often cooperate economically. It is often the responsibility of lineage members who are better off to ensure that others who are poor, infirm, or elderly are cared for. Religious life in lineage-based societies frequently emphasizes the worship of lineage ancestors.

Lineages can be divided and subdivided into smaller segments. This process of division, known as *segmentation*, takes place as the generational distance from the founding ancestor increases. Segmentation commonly occurs when lineages get too large or when antagonisms arise among members. The nearly one million Tiv, who live in northern Nigeria, believe that they are descended from a single male ancestor who lived some fourteen to seventeen generations ago (Bohannon 1953). The sons of this ancestor and male descendants in succeeding generations

FIGURE 8.12
Unilineal descent groups. Lineages, clans, phratries, and moieties are groups that can form an organizational hierarchy. A lineage is a subdivision of a clan, a clan is a subdivision of a phratry, and a phratry is a subdivision of a moiety. Societies are not always subdivided into four groups, however; some societies may have only one or two of these groups.

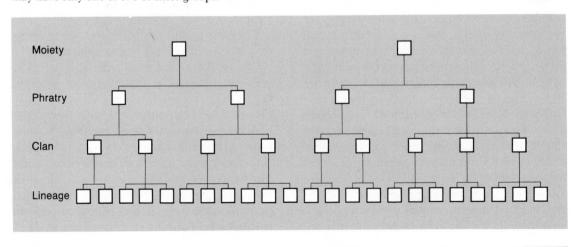

Members of Nuer patrilineage with some of their cattle at the junction of the Sobat and Pibor rivers, southeastern Sudan.

are viewed as the founding members of a series of sublineages. The process of lineage segmentation continues up to about three or four generations from the present living elders, at which point segmentation is supposed to cease. This final subdivision forms *minimal lineage segments,* which serve as the primary political and residential unit among the Tiv.

Alliance and competition among sublineages is based upon their degree of relatedness. Using figure 8.13 as an example, each minimal lineage (*H–O*) is an autonomous unit. Members of *H* and *I* will normally have little to do with one another. Should a member of either minimal lineage come under attack from, say, a member of *J,* however, members of both *H* and *I* would be expected to act in concert against a common enemy because of their common ancestor *D.* Likewise, all of those who are descended from *B* would be expected to be allied against those who are members of groups tracing descent from *C.*

When members of a lineage split into distinct segments they do not always continue to view themselves as being part of an encompass-

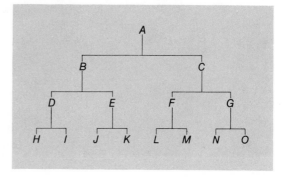

FIGURE 8.13
A model of segmentation. *A* represents the founding member of a series of sublineages (*B–O*). *H–O* are minimal lineage segments—the products of the final subdivision of the lineage. Among the Tiv, a minimal lineage segment serves as the primary political and residential unit. In segmentation, all sublineages consider themselves part of a single lineage.

ing lineage, however. They may form separate lineages. In some societies this process of *lineage fission* takes place with some regularity, as siblings in each generation split off and found new lineages. In societies where lineage fission is

Skidegate–Skittagetan totemic emblems of the Haida Indians, British Columbia (photograph taken c. 1900).

common, descent often is not traced more than a few generations—perhaps only as far back as there are living representatives of a generation.

Whether segmentation or fission is the predominant pattern is in part related to environmental considerations (Onwuejeogwu 1975: 124). In West Africa, for example, both patterns are found, but usually in very different settings. Where population growth and expansion occur, but resistance is met from outsiders, segmentation is likely to develop. The threat of external opposition makes it disadvantageous for groups to become too autonomous. With the segmentary model each sublineage can pursue

its own interests during peaceful periods, while being able to form readily into larger units when threatened by others. Where expansion and external threats are minimal, lineage fission is more likely to predominate.

Clans. Another major type of kin grouping is the *clan*—a group of kin who believe themselves to be descended from a common ancestor, but who cannot specify the actual links back to that ancestor. In some societies clan members form close-knit groups not unlike lineages. Often, however, as in most Scottish clans today, clan members are widely dispersed, rarely interacting on a clan-wide basis. Clan members may identify with a *totemic emblem,* an animal or plant.

Those recognizing membership in a clan can be expected to acknowledge certain mutual obligations, but these may be very limited. The Western Apache, for example, trace descent matrilineally and live in small farming settlements. In the past, those who worked in the early settlements took the name of the particular site. As the population grew, people moved away from these farms but continued to be known by the name of their original home. Clans formed among people who identified their common ancestry through the settlement names. The clan members sometimes have rights to clan lands, but the primary function of the clan is to serve as a basis for mutual aid (Kaut 1957).

Clans often encompass a number of localized, corporate lineages. The Yakö of Eastern Nigeria, for example, have small, landowning patrilineages. A group of these patrilineages usually live together as a clan in a section of a village. Each clan has a ritual leader who is in charge of the clan shrine and presides over informal meetings of lineage elders and notables. Under normal conditions clan members recognize their common descent. When disputes arise over household sites or agricultural land, however, lineage members tend to emphasize their distinctness (Forde 1964).

Phratries. A *phratry* is a descent group comprised of a number of supposedly related clans, the actual links usually being unrecognized. The Haida of the northwest coast of North America, for example, have two main phratries that are subdivided into a large number of clans (Sapir 1915). Each has its own identifying totemic emblem: the Raven phratry has the killer whale as its emblem, and the Eagle phratry the eagle. Phratry members have the right to exclusive use of their emblems on material belongings—their houses, boats, utensils, hats, and so forth. Members of both phratries may live within any settlement—Sapir notes that at one

time there were three distinct Eagle clans and three distinct Raven clans in a single settlement.

Phratries rarely serve an important social function. The common bond recognized among clans usually forms the basis for a rather weak alliance. This is not always true; Aztec phratries, for example, were significant political and religious groups which served as a basis for common ceremonial activity. But strong phratries are exceptions.

Moieties. Often whole societies are divided into two *moieties,* distinct unilineal descent groups that perform reciprocal functions for each other. In many societies persons must marry outside of their moiety, each moiety thereby providing the other with spouses. Moiety affiliation is often an important consideration in religious or ceremonial activities. The Mardudjara Aborigines have moieties based on patrilineal descent and at large ceremonial gatherings they group their camps into two "sides" by moieties. They also use this division in seating for certain men's rituals. Among the Seneca, a North American Indian society, each moiety performs mourning rituals on behalf of the other. Moieties may serve other purposes as well. Mardudjara moieties play an important role in intergroup gift exchange. In some North American Indian societies moieties compete against one another in games of lacrosse.

Many peoples associate the existence of moieties with dualities in the universe: land and water, night and day, sky and earth, war and peace, and so forth. Accordingly, moieties are commonly assigned names that identify them with these dualities.

Bilineal Descent Groups

In societies with bilineal systems, which trace descent both matrilineally and patrilineally, an individual is a member of both his or her mother's and father's lineage. This could con-

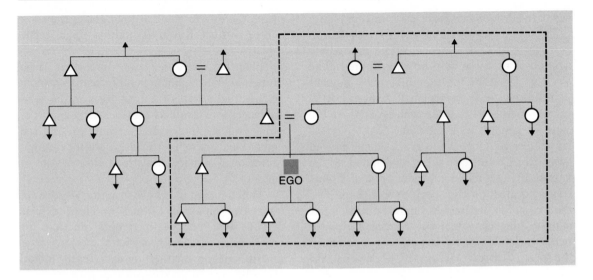

FIGURE 8.14

A kindred. A kindred is a group that is formed using ego-focused cognatic descent principles: people are related to a living person (ego) through both male and female lines. This diagram shows ego's kindred; ego's mother's kindred, however, is comprised only of those within the dashed line. (Arrows indicate continuation of the lines.)

ceivably cause confusion, but these lineages in most instances perform separate functions. Among the Lodagaba of West Africa, for example, a person inherits immovable property, such as land, from his father's side and portable property like money or grain from his mother's side (Goody 1959). Despite this separation of functions it is often difficult for these societies to form descent groups of much depth.

Cognatic Descent Groups

Among groups formed on the basis of kinship, unilineal and bilineal descent principles provide certain advantages. People are assigned to discrete, nonoverlapping groups, forming a ready basis for collective action. In contrast, the memberships of groups are bound to overlap in cog-

natic descent systems. Individuals will be members of several similar-purpose groups at the same time (Fox 1967: 147). Everyone is potentially the founder of a group, and the kin groups formed are not mutually exclusive. Thus, all of ego's grandparents might be the founders of coexisting kin groups, and ego could be a member of all of them. From the perspective of the individual, such a system offers adaptational advantages because of its flexibility: ego has a much wider range of kinship options than in unilineal descent. But there are problems as well, for if the cognatic principle is allowed to go unchecked it becomes very difficult to form unified groups, property and loyalties being widely and almost randomly dispersed.

There are two fundamentally different ways to approach the formation of groups on the basis of cognatic descent. In the *ancestor-focused* approach, groups can be formed by tracing descent from ancestors. The other approach is to form groups around a shared relative who is not an ancestor. This is an *ego-focused* approach. The network of persons linked to ego through ego-focused cognatic principles is called a *kindred* (see figure 8.14). One of the distinguishing features of a kindred is that no two individuals except siblings (and double first cousins) will have the same kindred. Furthermore, a kindred cannot persist beyond the life of the person upon whom it is centered.

Kindreds are rarely able to function as a group, though they may get together for certain rituals—such as birthdays, holidays, weddings, and funerals, in our society. The members of a kindred will have divided loyalties and their allegiance to ego's kindred will largely depend upon the strength of ego's personality and what ego is asking them to do. Kindreds tend to be loose collections of people who come together at ego's urging on occasion for some particular purpose. Among the Iban, one of the main activities of kindreds in the past were head-hunting raids. When an individual decided to stage a raid he would go around recruiting the members of his kindred. Each time the composition of the raiding party might be somewhat different. Among the Kalinga of northern Luzon in the Philippines, members of a kindred come together only to form vengeance parties when someone is killed, to share meat, and occasionally to help each other in small ways. The kindred is not a landholding group, and has little to do with inheritance or the ownership or distribution of most forms of property.

Ancestor-focused groups can function more like unilineal descent groups than is possible with kindreds, but for them to do so usually requires the imposition of some kind of restriction. This may be a rule or simply a matter of practicality. The most common type of restriction has to do with residence: a person may have the right to membership in a number of groups, but only be able to exercise that right if he or she chooses to live in the ancestor's territory. In New Zealand, for example, each Maori individual may have a great number of cognatically recognized ancestors and belong to a number of different descent groups, for the Maori keep genealogies tracing descent back to the mythical ancestors who first settled New Zealand. A man can claim membership to any number of *hapu*—landowning, territorial, ancestor-focused groups—as long as he is able to establish ancestoral connections to each of them. In practice, however, he can only reside with one *hapu* at a time, and he usually comes to identify and reside with his father's. The other groups to which he can claim a tie remain options.

The Significance of Kinship

The importance attached to kinship varies from one society to the next. Even within a single society it may vary.

In American society, the importance of kinship varies a great deal from one family or individual to the next depending upon circumstances and outlooks. For many of us, kin are an assortment of grandparents, aunts, uncles, and cousins, some of whom we have never met, and the rest of whom we encounter only on rare occasions. A few of our relatives may be important to us, or they may have been at some time in the past—our grandparents whom we visited on holidays, a cousin who was a childhood friend, an uncle who gave us a summer job—but for the most part they are fairly marginal to our lives. This is, of course, not true for everyone. Those of us who reside in the same town or neighborhood as our great-grandparents or even great-great-grandparents are likely to have a large number of relatives around whom we encounter frequently and who assume a large role in our lives. If our family is wealthy, or if a distant cousin dies leaving us a fortune, kinship can become quite significant. Among elite families, kinship networks are very important channels influencing the flow of wealth and power in America.

The importance of kinship in American society is not to be understood simply by reference to wealth or power, or even friendship, although these certainly are considerations. For a great many people what makes kinship important is its durability. Like other social institutions, kinship has a permanent quality that allows it to transcend individuals and their actions. It helps to provide us with a sense of security, with roots, in a world that is otherwise always changing and in which we may often feel alienated. We may enjoy the feeling that we are related to hundreds, even thousands, of people in other parts of the country, even if we know nothing about them as individuals. Some of us delight in going through telephone books when stranded in strange towns or airports, looking for persons with whom we share surnames—and perhaps calling them to see if we are related. All these potential relatives can have practical value. If our car breaks down outside of Gila Bend, we might try to find a cousin to ask for assistance. Chances are that he or she would help us.

Kinship also provides us with a sense of security by providing links to the past, through a variety of ancestors. Almost every family claims to be related to at least one national hero, although it is rarely clear exactly what the connection is. Many families have purchased from mail order firms coats of arms with an accompanying booklet telling of a few famous ancestors. Such coats of arms and claims of relationship to the once rich and famous have little practical importance, but they make people feel a little more significant. A person's ancestors can be of practical importance, however. Being a descendant of an early settler in many parts of the country, even though the ancestor in question might have been a rather unsavory sort, can

often be used to social advantage. The Daughters of the American Revolution and members of many similar organizations consider their ancestry of considerable significance. Ancestry is also of relevance in land claims throughout the Southwest associated with early Spanish land grants.

Important as kinship can be in our society, it pales in comparison with the significance it is afforded in many other parts of the world. In many societies in Africa, Latin America, Asia, and elsewhere kinship is a fundamental factor in all social interaction. For millions of people around the world kinship is perhaps the most important social factor influencing their lives, for in many ways it determines their role and status in society. In many societies to be without kin reduces a person to the status of outcast, with no hope of having a normal life, of marrying, of adequately meeting subsistence needs, or of being taken care of in old age. For all of these things one must depend upon kin. In many small-scale societies everyone in a person's social universe is either kin or a stranger. For many peoples kinship forms the basis of political, economic, and even religious organization. A society itself may be built of groups recruited on the basis of kinship. In many of these societies, especially in Africa and the Orient, ancestors are central to the social order. Ancestors are often the subject of worship, for they are seen as taking an active part in the lives of their descendants, bringing them good luck if respected and ill fortune if mistreated or ignored.

The differences between the role of kinship in American society, where kinship is a sometimes useful but rarely crucial part of social life, and in societies where it is a fundamental feature of social life reflect basic differences in the adaptive strategies of these societies. In what are sometimes referred to as kin-based societies, for example, kinship serves as a primary organizing feature for the production of goods and services. People work together and exchange what

Ancestry is still important to the elite of many industrial countries. Here members of the Continental Congress of the Daughters of the American Revolution (DAR) arrive for the opening of their 73rd congress in Washington, D.C. in 1964.

they produce because they are kin, and they do so largely in accordance with behavioral expectations linked to kinship. There is little segregation of kinship and economic roles.

In the essentially urban-industrial society of the United States, kinship plays but a small part in production and exchange. Productive activities and exchange are organized and governed according to principles that are not closely tied to kinship. People are recruited to work on the basis of the skills or knowledge they possess, for example. There is a feeling that family and economic roles should be kept separate—workers are expected to avoid bringing personal problems into the office or showing favoritism to a relative. Roles often overlap, of course, and kinship commonly influences how we behave at work.

As those societies where kinship serves as a key element in their adaptive strategy have been incorporated into the modern world system, the role of kinship generally has been reduced. Before the advent of colonial rule, for example, much of rural Africa was comprised of small agricultural and pastoral societies consisting of collections of kin-based groups. Members of these groups worked largely on a collective basis. Land and other forms of property were owned by the groups and administered by senior members of the group. Under colonial rule, this system was replaced in many parts of Africa by one dominated by wage labor and production for market instead of group consumption. The solidarity of the groups broke down as people sought to own property and accumulate wealth on an individual basis, a process which reduced the significance of kinship in their lives.

Incorporation into the world system does not demolish kinship's significance, but it begins to assume the optional nature characteristic in our society. In fact, for many peoples who have been impoverished by incorporation into the world system, kinship continues to be of considerable significance by providing one of the few sources of security available. Relatives share what little they possess to promote the welfare of the group instead of trying to survive as individuals.

Summary

While biology provides the basis for kinship, the ways in which kinship is used and defined are determined by sociocultural considerations. Even consanguinal, or blood relationships, with parents, siblings, and cousins are defined differently in different societies.

One of the ways anthropologists have tried to understand varying kinship patterns is to study how descent is perceived. While some societies figure descent unilineally—through either male or female ancestors and descendants—other societies use bilineal, ambilineal, parallel, or cognatic descent principles.

The "same" relatives are also given different labels in different societies. The many relatives we call "cousins," for example, are given more explicit labels in some other naming systems. The major kin-naming systems are Hawaiian, Eskimo, Sudanese, Omaha, Crow, and Iroquois.

Kinship has two primary social functions: inheritance and group formation. Some kin-based groups are formed on principles of unilineal descent. In order of increasing inclusiveness, these are lineages, clans, phratries, and moieties. In societies with bilineal descent, different lineages may be invoked for different purposes. Societies using cognatic descent principles may form ancestor-focused cognatic descent groups or ego-focused kindreds.

The general significance of kinship also varies from society to society. In the United States, kinship ties are often valued but they are kept separate from other roles. In kin-based societies, by contrast, kinship is of fundamental significance to the social order and to the lives of individuals. Differences in the significance of kinship reflect societies' differing adaptational strategies.

Suggested Readings

General works:

Bohannon, Paul, and Middleton, John, eds. 1968. *Kinship and social organization.* Garden City, NY: Natural History Press.

Buchler, I. R., and Selby, H. A. 1968. *Kinship and social organization.* New York: Macmillan.

Fox, Robin. 1967. *Kinship and marriage.* Harmondsworth: Penguin.

Graburn, Nelson, ed. 1971. *Readings in kinship and social structure.* New York: Harper & Row.

Keesing, Roger M. 1975. *Kinship and social structure.* New York: Holt, Rinehart & Winston.

Pasternak, B. 1976. *Introduction to kinship and social organization.* Englewood Cliffs, NJ: Prentice-Hall.

Schusky, E. L. 1965. *Manual for kinship analysis.* New York: Holt, Rinehart & Winston.

Specific studies:

Aschenbrenner, J. 1975. *Lifelines: Black families in Chicago.* New York: Holt, Rinehart & Winston.

Evans-Pritchard, E. E. 1940. *The Nuer.* Oxford: Clarendon.

Firth, Raymond. 1936. *We, the Tikopia: Kinship in primitive Polynesia.* London: Allen & Unwin.

Hiatt, Les R. 1965. *Kinship and conflict: A study of an Aboriginal community in northern Arnhem Land.* Canberra: Australian National Univ. Press.

Kelly, R. C. 1977. *Etoro social structure.* Ann Arbor, MI: University of Michigan Press. (Papua New Guinea)

Mayer, Adrian C. 1970. *Caste and kinship in central India.* Berkeley/Los Angeles: University of California Press.

Radcliffe-Brown, A. R., and Forde, D., eds. 1950. *African systems of kinship and marriage.* Oxford: Oxford Univ. Press.

Rigby, Peter. 1969. *Cattle and kinship among the Gogo.* Ithaca, NY: Cornell Univ. Press. (Tanzania)

Schneider, David M. 1968. *American kinship.* Englewood Cliffs, NJ: Prentice-Hall.

Stack, Carol B. 1975. *All our kin: Strategies for survival in a black community.* New York: Harper & Row.

van Velsen, J. 1964. *The politics of kinship: A study in social manipulation among the lakeside Tonga.* Manchester: Manchester Univ. Press. (southern Africa)

Chapter Nine

Sex, Marriage, and the Family

The Bounty's welcome off Point Venus was characteristically Polynesian. The Tahitian men and girls swarmed by the hundred from their canoes up the sides of the Bounty, cluttering the upper deck, climbing the rigging, scuttling down the ladders, chattering, laughing, shrieking. . . . Soon they were busily trading, and the minor chieftains exchanged gifts of live hogs and fruit for hatchets and mirrors. The coconut harvest was at its peak and the crew all drank deeply of the restorative milk as they bartered and made their choice of the girls who showed off their bodies with uninhibited enthusiasm. . . . As the sun went down over Point Venus the native men were ordered ashore. Only the lucky chosen girls, sometimes two to a man, were allowed to remain, sharing hammocks or lying linked with their lovers on deck through the hot night. [Hough 1972: 106-7]

Much to the delight of the sailors who accompanied Captain Bligh to Tahiti in 1788, Tahitian attitudes about sex were different from those in Europe. The way the sexual favors of local women were bestowed upon these sailors would have been unthinkable in Europe. No wonder many of the men on the *Bounty*, especially after ten months at sea, felt that they had arrived in paradise. For their part, the Tahitians found the arrival of the *Bounty* exciting, but their behavior toward the Europeans was not particularly extraordinary. In fact, it was quite in keeping with their traditional views of hospitality.

The views and actions of Europeans and Tahitians alike in this situation illustrate the social and cultural nature of sexual relations. Sex may be a basic biological drive, but it is also one that humans have manipulated and conditioned. To some extent sexual relations are influenced by personal preferences, but these preferences are rarely a matter of personal taste alone. Who we have sex with, what the act means, and even how it is performed will be influenced by social and cultural considerations. The same is true of marrying and forming family groups, for the patterns our society has devised for these important social behaviors cover only a few of a great variety of locally dictated possibilities.

Cultural Attitudes about Sex

The sexual drive and the attachments formed as a result of this drive are fundamental to the existence of human society: They are the basis of biological reproduction and part of the glue that holds society together. Our sexual drives function in a rather contradictory fashion, though, for while they promote bonds between persons, they can also result in competition, frustration, and ill feelings. Fearing chaos, we have managed to create from these tensions and contradictions a degree of order. We seem to rebel at the thought of sexual anarchy—even our orgies tend to be structured. Although some nineteenth-century writers searching for the origins of human behavior postulated a state of nature in which there was random mating, no evidence supports the presence of this "primitive promiscuity" in any society. In all societies that we know of, humans have sought to control this biological drive, and to create a sexual order that is socially and not biologically determined.

In the process, sex has come to be treated as a scarce resource that is employed in a strategic manner in accordance with the goals and condi-

OVERLEAF

Henry Moore's *Family Group* (1948–49). Bronze (cast 1950), 59¼ × 46½" at base, 45 × 29⅞".

South Sea maidens perform for modern travelers in Hawaii.

tions created by the social environment. For Inuit males, the sexuality of their wives can be used to strengthen important social ties with other males. For Mundurucu females their sexuality is a means of acquiring and holding a husband; in extramarital relations their sexuality can be used to seek revenge with the hope of improving existing relations or of destroying them and creating new ones. The relations and strategies of those engaged in sexual intercourse cannot be viewed in isolation from the society within which the individuals live, for the patterns and norms governing sexual exchanges vary in each social setting.

Sexual Restrictions

Societies differ in the degree to which they restrict sexual activities, which activities are restricted, and which people are defined as acceptable partners. But most groups have institutionalized ways of getting around these restrictions.

Degrees of Restrictiveness. At one extreme of the restrictions placed upon sex, we find groups such as monastic orders in which sexual relations are prohibited entirely. One of the fundamental characteristics of such a "sexless" society is that its members must be recruited from without. It is therefore dependent upon societies that do not prohibit sexual intercourse.

The head-to-toe, all-black dress of these women on Crete is a striking indicator of their society's limits on outward sexual expression.

Slightly less extreme are those societies that restrict relations between males and females to the minimum necessary for survival. Many societies in highland New Guinea, such as the Maring, are noted for marked hostility between the sexes. Their religious beliefs, economic activities, and even living arrangements emphasize this antagonism, as do their attitudes toward sex. Maring men feel that sex leads to physical dissolution and that sexual intercourse except on rare occasions

will cause a man's skin to become loose, wrinkled, and ulcerated, his flesh to waste away, his thought to become fuzzy, and his belly bloated. Some men say that it also causes coughing and the spitting up of phlegm. Youths worry that it will stunt their growth or even cause them to shrivel, loosen their hair, blemish their skin, and leave them generally weak and unattractive." [Buchbinder and Rappaport 1976: 21]

At a somewhat less restrictive level, some societies attempt to strictly limit sexual intercourse to married couples and to limit the number of potential spouses available to a person during the course of his or her life. Female virginity is often a highly esteemed value in these societies. Among Greek pastoralists like the

Sarakatsani, women are expected to remain virgins until marriage, "and even married women must remain virginal in thought and expression" (Campbell 1974: 270). A Sarakatsani girl who has a premarital love affair is supposed to be killed by her father or brother, although in practice she usually is spared. Divorce is virtually unheard of, and can only occur if the marriage has not been consummated. The Sarakatsani place considerable emphasis upon family solidarity, and "the sexual, reproductive, and working capacities of women belong exclusively to their families." To the Sarakatsani, female sexuality represents a threat to family honor; there are few better ways to shame a family than to seduce one of its women.

Where virginity is so highly prized, tests are often devised as proof of a woman's premarital chastity. In many Moslem countries and in parts of the European Mediterranean the blood-stained sheets of the nuptial bed are displayed the day after the wedding as "proof" of the bride's virginity.

Not all societies are so restrictive. In fact, there appears to be some correlation between social scale and restrictiveness: In small-scale foraging and farming societies sexual relations are often much more open, especially prior to marriage, than in large-scale societies.

Among the Trobriand Islanders of Melanesia sexual relations are relatively free and easy, within certain bounds (Malinowski 1929). Trobriand sexual behavior follows a general pattern according to age. Parents take no special precautions to prevent their children from witnessing their sexual activities, and from a very early age children engage in genital manipulation and oral stimulation of the sex organs. Once they are old enough boys and girls begin to have intercourse: "It is their play to *kayta* [to have intercourse]. They give each other a coconut, a small piece of betelnut, a few beads or some fruit from the bush, and then they go and hide, and *kayta.*" (Malinowski 1929: 48).

Upon reaching adolescence, Trobriand boys and girls assume a more serious part in village life and are treated more like adults. In recognition of their emerging sexuality, brothers and sisters are separated from each other and from their parents. The boys move into a house with bachelors or widowed male relatives or friends and the girls go to live with older female relatives. Adolescence marks a transition from the playful sexuality of childhood to the more serious relations that will precede marriage. The setting of lovemaking also changes, from the bush to some prepared "cozy corner" in a bachelors' or yam storage house. These liaisons eventually become more permanent, and marriage is usually preceded by a period in which a couple becomes publicly recognized as lovers. Even at this stage, however, sexual relations are not exclusive, and either partner will in all likelihood have occasional relations with others: only now a certain degree of decorum must be observed. The couple will share a bed on a regular basis, but they will not have their meals together, nor are there any services to be mutually rendered. This relationship is seen as a nonbinding preliminary test of compatibility before a decision is made concerning marriage.

Even people as relaxed in their sexual practices as the Trobriand Islanders may take a very unfavorable view of extramarital sexual relations. Adultery is a serious matter, and killings and suicides commonly result from marital infidelity. To them the bond of marriage implies a more exclusive relationship than "sweetheart" relationships; it is also seen to involve the couple's kin, who may take a hand in disputes arising over cases of adultery. Among the Trobriand Islanders as well as the Sarakatsani, adultery is seen as an affront to individual and family reputation. To the less restrictive Trobriand Islanders, marriage changes things; marriage changes very little for the uniformly restrictive Sarakatsani view of sexuality.

Not all societies take such a dim view of adultery, however. Among the Mundurucu of Amazonian Brazil, a woman is expected to acquiesce to her husband's advances, but a Mundurucu husband's control of his wife's sexuality is limited. Divorce among the Mundurucu is relatively common and marital fidelity is seen as an exception rather than the norm (Murphy and Murphy 1974: 153). This situation is in part a reflection of the fact that although males in Mundurucu society are dominant in certain spheres, females retain a great deal of personal autonomy. Other societies take an even more relaxed view of extramarital sex, emphasizing its role in expanding or strengthening social relations. The Toda of southern India consider a husband who would restrict his wife's sexual relations with men to whom she is not married immoral. Somewhat more restrictive in character is the practice among many Arctic-dwelling peoples, such as the Chuckchee of Siberia: husbands offer their wives as sexual partners to friends on a reciprocal basis.

Defining Acceptable Partners. Even with societies that do not restrict sex to marriage, certain considerations pattern relations by placing restrictions on sexual exchanges or channeling the personnel involved. Concepts of physical beauty can be quite influential. There are a few negative concepts that are nearly universal. Trobriand Islanders are not unique in their notion that "no one would sleep with" anyone who is diseased or deformed. In highly stratified societies, however, considerations such as wealth or social status can modify even these views. And most ideals of attractiveness are not universal. While the Trobriand classify obesity as a disease, placing those who are obese in the category of someone with whom no one would sleep, Rumanika, the nineteenth-century king of Karagwe (near Lake Victoria in central Africa), "kept an extraordinary harem of wives who were so fat they could not stand upright, and instead grovelled like seals about the floors of their huts" (Moorehead 1960: 47). In this brief account, the chronicler clearly shows his own bias about the attractiveness of obese women.

There are often more precise social constraints placed upon choice of sexual partners as well. Included here are *incest taboos,* or rules prohibiting sexual intercourse between specific categories of kin. There are usually sanctions involved, such as the threat of social ostracism, castration, imprisonment, or death. Such prohibitions are usually bolstered by myths or beliefs, like the idea commonly held in our society that the offspring of incestuous matings will be mentally retarded or physically deformed. It is important to note that there are no universally tabooed categories. The choice is made in most instances on the basis of social and cultural reasons rather than biological ones. Even prohibitions against mating within the nuclear family (mother-son, father-daughter, brother-sister) are not found in all societies. Various forms of intrafamilial sexual relations occurred and were seen as legitimate at least for the aristocracy in ancient Persia, Egypt, Hawaii, and Peru, in Athens before the time of Solon, and among pre-Mosaic Hebrews (Vivelo 1978: 217–18). Before 1892, the Mormons in Utah allowed the marriage of men to their daughters and sisters. In all of these instances there appear to be social rather than biological reasons for the demise of these practices—such as an increase in the Mormon population, or pressures from those holding other views.

Although sexual relationships between certain kin are prohibited in many societies, some peoples encourage sex between specific kin. This is particularly true in small-scale societies. Ronald Berndt (1978: 14) notes that among the Aborigines of Arnhem Land in northern Australia, "Pre- and extra-marital liaisons . . . usually brought together persons who were formally related to each other in acceptable ways—so that their union would not normally contravene the preferred patterns of betrothal and marriage."

This was as true of brief encounters as it was of more durable "sweetheart" relationships. In large-scale societies the role of kinship in choice of sexual partners may be slight, but other social factors such as ethnicity, religious affiliation, or social class may affect individual choices of partners.

Sidestepping the Restrictions. An interesting feature of all of these restrictions is that the members of most societies have devised legitimate means of getting around them. This can be seen as an attempt to acknowledge and order the effects of human frailty and the desire to taste forbidden fruit, although more prosaic functional explanations usually apply as well.

Many societies have highly structured ways of sidestepping their own sexual restrictions. An example of this is ritual sexual license, known as *gurangara*, which was an integral part of one of the major Aboriginal rituals of northern Australia, the Kunapipi or Gunabibi (Berndt 1951). Sexual partners in the *gurangara* included persons who are normally taboo to one another, such as those who called each other mother-in-law and son-in-law. According to the participants in the *gurangara*, its functions were to cement bonds of friendship, especially between members of different groups, and to draw women further into the sacred scheme of the ritual.

In some societies, gang rape is seen as a legitimate punishment for female transgressions, creating a situation in which normal sexual prohibitions are suspended. Such a punishment functions to symbolize male dominance; it also legitimizes a number of normally deviant activities. This form of punishment is meted out by Mundurucu males, for example, to women who have seen their sacred flutes (which are kept hidden from public view in the men's house) and to women who are openly aggressive sexually (since these women are perceived as a threat to male dominance). The rape may involve twenty or more men, including those who normally would be prohibited from having sexual intercourse with the woman, such as her parallel cousins.

Sex as Power

An important aspect of sexual behavior and ideology is their relationship to sacred and secular power. The link between sex and religious belief and ritual is manifest in many societies. Precisely what the relationship is can vary between viewing sex as a negative, threatening force and seeing it as a positive force promoting well-being and fertility. Australian Aborigines tend to fall into the second camp—as exemplified in Kunapipi fertility rituals. By contrast, some peoples view sex as pollution. Sarakatsani shepherds are careful to wash their hands after sexual intercourse to avoid contaminating the milk of the sheep to be milked (Campbell 1974: 26). And the people of Wogeo, New Guinea, feel that they must be periodically disinfected of the negative effects of sexual intercourse. Menstruation is thought to purify the women; the men "menstruate" by cutting their penises until they bleed (Hogbin 1970: 88–89).

Attitudes regarding the religious nature of sex are not always consistent. Many of the Kekchi and Mopan of southern Belize avoid sexual intercourse before and for some time after clearing their fields and planting crops, to avoid contamination and to ensure the well-being of the young plants. Some individuals, however, take a different approach: a husband and wife may simulate or actually have intercourse at each corner of their house the night before planting, to promote fertility. Such mixtures of attitudes may be a result of historical mixing of peoples. Thompson (1930: 50) argues that the use of intercourse by some Kekchi and Mopan as a fertility rite may be a surviving practice of the Chol, a group assimilated several centuries earlier. Attitudes within a single belief system may also vary according to the context: Roman Catholics emphasize chastity for priests and nuns but promote fertility among the lay population.

In the secular realm, sexual relations often reflect the distribution and nature of power in a society. Sex provides a stage for those wishing to demonstrate or compete for power. Thus, the relative status of males and females in a society is commonly expressed through the sex act itself. Mundurucu male ideology and public behavior express male superiority and this theme carries over into sexual intercourse:

Orgasm is sometimes reached by women, but it is our impression that in most cases climax is experienced only by the male. . . . Women are subservient to men in sex, the wife has no choice but to accept her husband's advances, and male satisfaction is the goal. There is little foreplay, and sexual encounters are brief in consummation. . . . The woman, then, usually derives far less satisfaction from the sex act than does the man, but she also understands that sex is the means by which one gets a husband and then holds him. [Murphy and Murphy 1974: 153]

Sex among the Mundurucu can be seen as a rather unequal exchange by which women gain or hold onto husbands or lovers in return for their acceptance of male superiority. Similar patterns of sexual behavior can be found in societies like the Sarakatsani and to some extent in our own where women occupy a subordinate status.

Women, of course, do not always occupy a lower status in sexual encounters. Sexual relations among lovers on the Micronesian island of Truk, for example, are quite competitive in nature. Males occupy a superior status in Trukese society, but Trukese women are far from subservient. Trukese males strive to attain a macho image through a reputation for sexual prowess. Prowess, however, is not measured simply by the number of conquests or children that a man

can boast. A Trukese male is expected to bring his lover to orgasm, often under very difficult conditions. Failure to satisfy one's lover can lead to ridicule and loss of reputation. Ward Goodenough has characterized sexual intercourse among Trukese lovers as "a contest in which the partner who first achieves orgasm is said to lose to the other" (1949: 619).

Power is also a factor in determining who people have sex with, especially in societies with marked differences in status and wealth. The chances that a poor black male in Nova Scotia or Alabama will have sexual relations with an upper-class white woman are fairly remote because they move in different circles and because their society's values discourage such relations. However, sexual relations between social classes can be used strategically to exploit or overcome inequality. Males of more powerful segments of a society are often able to use their status to sexual advantage. This use of sexual power was institutionalized in the medieval European custom of droit de seigneur, granting the lord of the manor the right to have sex with newly married women of lower status prior to their husbands.

From the perspective of those on the bottom, sex may provide a means of gaining status or wealth. Until slavery was abolished in the nineteenth century, for slave women in Brazil and elsewhere in the Americas becoming the mistress of a slaveowner was virtually the only way to escape from the extreme rigors of life as a slave. In less extreme circumstances, members of many minority groups in Western industrialized nations like our own seek out sexual partners and mates from higher status groups to escape the hardships associated with their minority status.

Sexual relations with those who are wealthier and more powerful can have mixed effects on the adaptive prospects of less powerful groups. While sexual relations with those of higher status may improve things for the individuals directly involved, they may have only a slight or

A group of Trukese males and females.

even an adverse effect on the lower-status group as a whole. It can be argued that those who seek wealth or improvement of social status by sexual means actually undermine the status of the group they are identified with by further exposing it to humiliation at the hands of those who are more powerful. Situations are rarely clear-cut, however. Faced with a dramatic loss of population and of the traditional basis of their livelihood, many groups of indigenous peoples in the Amazonian Basin have had to decide whether to retain their standards and probably doom their societies to eventual extinction, or to make an effort to survive by prostituting themselves to those who have taken their lands and brought diseases.

Sex is not simply a matter of love or recreation or producing offspring. It is an inextricable part of the totality of human society, and is above everything else a social and cultural phenomenon. A similar point will be made in the next section, which is concerned with marriage. Marriage too is not just a couple of people getting together out of love or necessity; it is very much a part and a product of human society and culture.

Marriage

In most societies the interaction of males and females involves more than occasional sexual encounters and exchange of food. Male-female relations are in fact an integral part of almost all aspects of social life. Given the significance of male-female relations and our proclivity for creating or imposing order, every society has developed institutions to regulate these relations. All fall into the category of *marriage:* a socially sanctioned sexual and economic union between men and women. In some societies this definition is expanded to include unions between members of the same sex.

Marriage as an Adaptive Measure

The near universality of marriage appears to be related to our mastering of several problems universal to the human species. One of these is the prolonged period of dependency of the human infant. Human babies require nearly full-time care for several years, longer than any other primate. Especially in labor-intensive foraging and agricultural societies, this dependency places a severe burden on the person responsible for child care (usually a female), since it interferes significantly with subsistence activities. During this period, the person tending the child in turn becomes dependent upon others. Marriage is the most common way of ensuring that the child and its caretaker are supported. This does not mean that the married couple alone assumes total responsibility for the child's upbringing. Others, including specialists and relatives, assist or may even assume a dominant role in caring for the infant, but only rarely do they entirely take over the married couple's role.

The second problem marriage seeks to solve is sexual competition. Unlike females of other species, women are more or less continuously receptive to sexual activity, leading to a greater likelihood of disruptive rivalry among males and females. Some scholars (mostly male) have argued that sexual competition is a threat to the survival of society in reproductive and economic terms and that the relative stability provided by marriage is the best way of coming to terms with this threat.

A third adaptational factor encouraging marriage is the sexual division of labor. Among foragers—the primary economic adaptation of humans for millions of years—males are responsible for hunting large game while women are responsible for gathering edible plants and killing smaller animals. Numerous authors argue that such a pattern best meets the adaptational needs of a foraging society. Among the Mardudjara of Australia, women gather food in groups if possible, allowing them to share child-care responsibilities. Mardudjara men, on the other hand, usually hunt alone or in pairs without

children to care for, for hunting requires far greater mobility than the slow-paced foraging activities of women. Marriage ensures that those of each sex gain access to the fruits of the other's labor: marital partners share with each other the food they find.

Some authors also suggest that marriage was traditionally, and in some instances still is, a means for males to gain dominance over females. Thus, although female foragers could meet most of their own needs, marriage ensured that the males gained access to the substantial products of female labor and thereby reduced their own workload. In our own society there is considerable debate over the labor performed by housewives and their dependency upon male wage earners. Many feminists argue that the housewife is an exploited laborer who performs necessary and often very tedious services for which she is compensated only to the extent to which her husband sees fit.

The adaptive advantages of marriage may diminish as social scale increases, for as social scale increases marriage becomes increasingly optional. Members of many small-scale societies assume that all adults will marry and that the only unmarried adults are either looking for a spouse or are widowed and too old to remarry. The Mundurucu have no social roles for bachelors or spinsters, and those who are unmarried are viewed with distrust as potential spouse-stealers or adulterers (Murphy and Murphy 1974: 145). In large-scale societies such as our own, parents, relatives and peers usually place pressure on individuals to marry, but it is also quite possible to occupy an acceptable place in society without ever having been married, as in the instance of lifelong bachelorhood in Britain. This liberalization reflects the increasing degree of specialization in these societies and the diminishing importance of kinship, and might lead one to speculate that marriage will eventually disappear. Such a development is not likely to occur in the near future, however, for sufficient pressures and adaptational advantages remain to ensure that most people will continue to marry.

Marriage as Formation of Alliances

Marriage is rarely just a matter of uniting brides and grooms. Those joined in wedlock have kin and friends who are affected by the creation of the relationship, and the act has other broad social implications as well. More often than not marriage serves to unite a wide network of people, providing a relatively durable bond or series of bonds of widespread social importance.

In rural Newfoundland the network of people united by marriage may include most of the community's inhabitants and those of the surrounding communities. Furthermore, these people may make up the most important element of the newlyweds' social environment. In large-scale, urbanized societies like the United States such networks can be quite small, especially when kin ties are limited and family members are widely scattered; interaction may consist of no more than an exchange of cards at birthdays and Christmas. But in all societies, the social links created by marriage may potentially serve a variety of purposes: to form economic units (such as fishing crews in Newfoundland), to establish political alliances (as in the Kennedy clan), and to expand the number of persons to go to for money, a job, or a place to stay while traveling.

Marriage as Exchange. Viewed from a group perspective, marriage becomes an exchange of personnel and resources that creates alliances based upon reciprocal rights and privileges. Not only is there an initial exchange of people and wedding gifts, but also there are usually expectations of future transactions among members of the respective groups. These expectations may be little more than the promise of help should the need arise, or they may entail a firm commitment to assist in warfare or political struggles. They may also involve a pledge to reciprocate at some future date with the exchange of yet another male or female in marriage.

Lévi-Strauss (1969) has analyzed marriage, primarily in small-scale societies, as generalized exchange systems. He focuses upon the exchange of women between groups. Lévi-Strauss begins by making a distinction between what he calls elementary and complex systems. *Elementary systems* are those in which the rules specify into which category or group of persons one should or should not marry. For example, the prescribed form of marriage among the Mardudjara is between cross-cousins. For a male, cross-cousins include mother's-brother's-daughters (MBD) and father's-sister's-daughters (FZD), and for a female they include mother's-brother's-sons (MBS) and father's-sister's-sons (FZS). Marriage to any other category of persons is considered wrong and possibly incestuous (Tonkinson 1978: 48–49). In *complex systems* the rules state whom one cannot marry, but they do not specify whom one should or must marry. A complex system might prohibit one from marrying certain categories of kin, or even members of a particular ethnic group, while leaving one's choice of spouse otherwise open.

Lévi-Strauss makes a further distinction between systems in which the exchange is direct and those in which exchange is more indirect. The simplest system of exchange is *direct* (or *symmetrical*) *exchange*. In direct exchange group A gives its women to group B, and group B gives its women to group A. When the entire exchange takes place in the same generation, it is called *immediate direct exchange* or *sister exchange*. When the preference is for long-term reciprocity, with an expectation that the sons or sons' sons of a family that gives one of its females in marriage will eventually be given a wife by the recipients, this pattern is termed *delayed direct exchange*: Group A gives group B wives in one generation and group B reciprocates in the next.

Indirect (or *asymmetrical*) *exchange* occurs when women move in one direction only. Group A gives wives to group B, group B provides wives for group C, and group C provides wives to group A, forming something of a circle of marriage exchanges. This pattern prevails in many Kachin villages in highland Burma (Leach 1954), two or three lineages of roughly equal status exchanging wives with one another.

Endogamy and Exogamy. *Endogamy* requires that one must or should marry within one's own group or category; *exogamy* requires or prefers marriage outside of a social group or category. Basically, exogamy serves to link groups together, while endogamy isolates groups and maintains them as distinct units.

The distinction between endogamy and exogamy depends on how one's own group is defined. In our society, we tend to marry people outside our own kin group but within our own socioeconomic stratum. No one would be imprisoned for marrying someone of a decidedly different social rank, but there are pressures and social practices that help to maintain strata endogamy. We socialize primarily with members of our own stratum, attend schools which are segregated along lines of social stratification, and are pressured by parents to choose friends and mates from our own stratum. Such practices help to maintain the unity and identity of the different strata and promote the sharing or monopolization of particular values, occupations, degrees and forms of wealth, and sometimes even linguistic characteristics within the boundary of each social stratum.

The family (nuclear or extended) is the primary exogamous unit in our society, and it is primarily between families, usually of the same social stratum, that marital exchanges take place. Something of the nature of this system is illustrated in marriage patterns among the wealthy elite of the United States and European nobility during the latter part of the nineteenth and early twentieth centuries (Galbraith 1977: 67–69). The newly affluent Americans of this period, as they saw it, lacked "class"; they were seen as rather crude by the more established, and usually much poorer, aristocrats of their own country and of Europe. In Europe such Americans found aristocrats all too willing to trade their family name for a share of American wealth. The principal marketplace was the Riviera:

Daughters of the American rich could here be traded for the esteem that went with older landed wealth and title, or sometimes merely the title. By this single simple step the new wealth achieved the respectability of age. And the anciently respectable got money, something they could always use. So inevitable was this bargain that they were negotiated by the scores, and brokers—often impoverished women of imagined social rank—appeared to make the deals. . . . By 1909, by one estimate, 500 American heiresses had been exported for the improvement of the family name, along with $220 million. [Galbraith 1977: 68]

Perhaps the most notable of these exchanges was between the Vanderbilts and the Churchills. Cornelius Vanderbilt was able to arrange to have his daughter marry into the Churchill family, one of the most honored in British history, for an initial payment of $2.5 million. With this (and eventually another $7.5 million) he was able to rid his family of its robber-baron identity, transforming them into people of the highest repute.

Australian Aborigines follow similar exogamous strategies on a smaller scale. They seek marriage partners outside their own immediate group to create alliances that will give them access to a wider hunting and gathering range. Such a strategy makes sense in Australia's interior desert, where the ever-present threat of scarcity and drought becomes even more acute for a group occupying too narrow a territory. So-

Anna Gould, the youngest daughter of American financier Jay Gould, became a countess when she married Count Marie Ernest Paul Boniface de Castellane in 1895. Upon marrying, the Count acquired access to Anna's yearly income of about $650,000 from her trust fund. In spite of this income, by the time this picture was taken in 1900, the couple had run up debts totalling $4.5 million. Anna left the Count shortly after this, went to France, and married the Count's cousin, the Duc de Talleyrand-Perigord.

ciological and ecological constraints place limitations on how far-ranging these alliances can become.

Families or small social groups do not always favor a strategy of seeking alliances through marriage with other groups. They may instead assume a defensive endogamous attitude, in an effort to maintain the group's identity and wealth. Often such societies prescribe marriage to particular categories of cousin. In nineteenth-century rural Brazil, for example, marriage between first cousins was common among plantation-owning families (Kottak 1979: 132). Inheritance law in Brazil granted estate rights to all sons and daughters and their descendants, and the practice of marrying cousins was an attempt to limit the potential dissipation of the estate. Similarly, among patrilineal Moslem peoples in the Near East and North Africa the preferential marriage for a male is to his father's-brother's-daughter (FBD), his patrilateral parallel cousin. This marriage practice ensures that property is kept within relatively narrow bounds, overcoming the threat to maintenance of family wealth posed by Islamic law, which calls for inheritance by sons and daughters. It also creates a strong social group of allied brothers and their children, particularly useful in the hostile and faction-ridden social environment that has traditionally existed in the areas occupied by Arabs. The ever-present hostility that surrounds this group, however, is to some extent a reflection of the isolationist principles by which the group formed and separated itself from other such groups in the first place. The result is a cyclic process in which the practice of parallel-cousin marriage encourages factionalism, which in turn promotes a continuation of this form of marriage.

Numbers of Spouses

Societies typically prescribe not only whom one should marry, but also how many people one may marry. In our own society a person who takes more than one spouse at the same time is known as a *bigamist*, and if caught he or she can be imprisoned. There is no natural reason for this custom. Many societies not only allow men to have more than one wife, but expect them to. The harems of Near Eastern potentates are not cultural rarities. Actually, *plural marriages,* in which a person has more than one spouse, are accepted in the vast majority of societies. Again, there is no natural reason for the custom. Whether a society tries to restrict marriage to a single spouse or encourages persons to have more than one spouse reflects the particular way that society has evolved and its current socioeconomic environment. Some societies that formerly allowed plural marriages no longer do because of economic reasons or the adoption of a religion that forbids them.

Monogamy. The form of marriage found in the United States and in most Western industrial nations is *monogamy*, marriage of one man to one woman at a time. Monogamy is not simply a norm in these societies; it is prescribed. Plural marriages are illegal. In societies where divorce is fairly common, individuals may enter in a series of marriages, marrying, divorcing, and marrying again, but still maintain only one spouse at a time. We refer to this pattern as *serial monogamy.*

Polygamy. Most societies prefer not to limit the number of spouses available to a person to one. The practice of having more than one spouse at the same time we call *polygamy*. There are two principal types of polygamy: polygyny and polyandry.

The term *polygyny* refers to marriage between one man and two or more women simultaneously. Worldwide, polygyny is permitted in a majority of societies. The possibility of polygynous marriage in a society, however, does not mean that all adult males in that society will have more than one wife. For them to do so in most cases would be a demographic impossibility. In a survey of Aboriginal inhabitants of Jigalong, Tonkinson (1974: 46–47) found that despite the preference of most married men for two wives, only 26.8 percent of the forty married men in the sample had polygynous marriages, with an average of 1.4 wives per husband. Among the Tiwi of northern Australia (Hart and Pilling 1979; Goodale 1971), older males who have been successful in accumulating wives may end up married to a dozen or two dozen women, but younger males may have no wives until their late thirties. Tiwi males do not necessarily remain celibate during the years before marriage, but their sexual relations with women remain illegitimate and their overall status in the community low.

Jealousy and interpersonal rivalry among cowives is recognized as a potential problem in most societies with polygynous marriage. Maintaining separate households for each wife is one way of trying to avoid conflict. Plateau Tonga husbands not only place their wives in separate dwellings, but also divide their property among them. Sharing of attention in such an arrangement can cause problems should the husband have noticeable preferences. The Tanala of Madagascar have dealt with this by ruling that a husband must spend a day with each of his wives in succession or be accused of adultery; a slighted wife is entitled to sue for divorce and receive considerable alimony. As this case indicates, the wives of polygynous unions are not always totally subservient to their husbands.

Another common attempt to soften jealousies among wives is to assign the wives hierarchical statuses. Senior wives are often given special privileges. The senior wife among the Lacandon of southern Mexico is the only female allowed to enter the family shrine when she brings in specially prepared ritual offerings (Tozzer 1907). In other societies, the older wife can dictate to the younger. Such practices may help to compensate an older wife who feels threatened by a younger and more attractive new wife by providing her with prestige and power.

The potential for tension is especially acute when the co-wives share no social bonds except the one with their husband. Elizabeth Colson (1971: 116) notes that Gwembe Tonga wives are unwilling to help each other except by cooking for each other in emergencies. The Gwembe Tonga custom of prohibiting marriage to women who are closely related has created a situation in which "their interests converged only in their husband, and this fact divided them." For support they turn to their own kin and children, rather than to the other wife or to the husband whose loyalties are compromised.

One way of getting around this problem is for a man to marry sisters, who presumably will get along well since they are accustomed to cooperating and living together in the same household. This practice is known as *sororal polygyny:*

a man marries one woman and thereby acquires the right to claim her younger sister in marriage, sometimes without additional ceremony or payment. This does not always work, for sisters do not always get along well, and being a wife is in many ways quite different from living with one's parents. However, sororal polygyny is found most often in societies with patrilineal descent groups; within such a context it is most likely to function as an effective deterrent to disharmony among co-wives, for the sisters are bound not only by sibling ties but also by duties imposed upon them by lineage affiliation. As Radcliffe-Brown has pointed out, for a woman "to quarrel with her sister or neglect her sister's children is not simply a neglect of her marital duties, it is contrary to her obligations to her closest kin" (1950: 65). There is no independent group that one of the wives can go to for support, for her kin are her co-wife's kin as well and even her children have ties constraining them.

Polyandry, marriage of one woman to two or more men at the same time, is a rare form of marriage. Most societies where polyandry is practiced on a regular basis are in South Asia: Tibet, India, Nepal, and Sri Lanka. One of the more common forms of polyandry is *fraternal polyandry,* where the husbands sharing the wife are all brothers. This is the dominant form of polyandry found among the Pahari of Jaunsar Bawar in northern India, described by Gerald Berreman (1962, 1975). Among these people the oldest brother customarily arranges the wedding. The brothers may marry other women as well; all share sexual access and the children call all the brothers "father," disregarding biological paternity. Berreman felt that the practice of polyandry in Jaunsar Bawar was related to a shortage of females. In other cases polyandry seems to be an adaptation to geographical mobility among males caused by military or commercial considerations, for polyandry ensures that a male will always be at home. Fraternal polyandry may be an adaptive strategy where brothers have inherited a limited amount of wealth or property and desire to pool their resources. By restricting the number of wives, the brothers also may limit the number of heirs competing for the estate in the future.

The Marriage Process

Marriage cannot be treated as a single event; it is a process that occurs over time. The process has essentially three parts: finding a potential spouse (or spouses), securing the marriage, and maintaining it. In our own society, a young couple meets, falls in love, and then, barring significant problems such as parental disapproval or being too closely related, marries. The wedding ceremony will vary according to social class, ethnicity and religious affiliation, and the pair's relations with their kin and others around them.

Once married they will establish their own household, if they have not already done so, and then become subject to the pressures that threaten to lead to a divorce. Should the marriage end in divorce, chances are that the individuals will remarry. This time the ceremony probably will not be as elaborate, and a whole new set of tensions may be created by parents, children from former marriages, and so forth. Not everyone does things in this manner in our society, especially the latter part of the process, but it does represent a relatively common series of events. Such a pattern is not at all common for many other societies, however. In fact, in a great many societies many of these events would be impossible or unthinkable.

Choosing a Spouse. In many societies personal choice in selecting a spouse is fairly limited. In small-scale or village-level societies,

Polyandrous Toda family, Octamund, India—one woman married to two brothers.

there are unlikely to be many potential spouses around when one is ready to marry. In a village of two hundred people, no more than one or two dozen possible choices are likely at best. If the village population is relatively stable and families have been intermarrying for generations, the number of possible marriage partners will be reduced further, since many who are an acceptable age will be considered too closely related. Those unable to find a spouse will be forced to look elsewhere; many will visit other villages, where they will find similar shortages, but fewer close relatives. Young Kekchi men from the highlands of Guatemala sometimes spend a couple of years traveling about northern Guatemala and southern Belize as itinerant merchants; they look not only for a little adventure and a way to earn money, but also for a mate.

One way of overcoming local shortages of potential spouses (although not very common) is to seize mates from elsewhere. This is known as *marriage by capture,* and typically involves the capture of women by men. Capturing wives was once fairly common among small-scale farmers in Melanesia and Amazonian South America, where the practice was closely related to warfare, and it is still practiced by some of these peoples. In some cases simply capturing a woman does not make her a man's wife. Among the South Fore of New Guinea, for example, for the marriage to be recognized the man has to pay the female's kin the appropriate bridewealth as in any other form of marriage (Glasse 1969: 22).

It is common practice in many societies for marriages to be arranged by the family or kin of the couple to be wed. Among the Bena Bena of highland New Guinea, for example, marriage is seen as the responsibility of the subclan. A man decides after consulting with other members of his subclan that it is time for his son to be married and a search is begun. The arrangements may be made by the father, but they are just as likely to be made by the father's brother or some other member of the subclan, or in some instances by even more distant relatives (Langness 1969: 40–41).

Australian Aborigines have essentially two means of arranging marriages: wife bestowal and mother-in-law bestowal (Maddock 1972: 46–54). In *wife bestowal,* a man is given a wife (often a widow). In *mother-in-law bestowal,* a woman becomes a man's mother-in-law with the promise that he will be able to marry a potential or existing daughter when she is old enough. Meanwhile, the man waits, often for years, currying favor with his "in-laws" until the time for the marriage arrives. During this long wait things can go amiss. The mother-in-law may die before having a daughter, the daughter may die, or one of the parties may try to back out. In general, the bestower gains a great deal from the arrangement because of the dependent relationship it establishes; the young man must endure it because of the relative shortage of potential spouses in these small societies. The right to bestow a daughter or mother-in-law may be assigned to the father or brother of the girl, the girl's mother's brother, or the husband of the mother-in-law. However, bestowal is never decided upon by a single individual, although there may be one person who has the final say. Other interested parties, including women and especially mothers, may take part in choosing the future husband, and the girl herself is unlikely to remain entirely silent in the matter.

Meeting the Terms. Once a man has obtained the right to marry someone he may be expected to perform tasks, called *bride service,* for his bride-to-be's parents. This service may be little more than bringing his future wife and her parents corn and firewood for a few months, as is expected among the Kekchi of southern Belize; he may be required to live with his future in-laws and work for them for several years, the traditional practice among Kekchi in high-

Modern Mayan marriage in Pueblo Viejo, southern Belize.

land Guatemala. Bride service may continue for some time after the couple is married, or in some instances it may begin after they are married. The most common reason given for the practice of bride service is that it compensates the family for losing one of its members.

In most societies it is customary to exchange more than just people through marriage. Money, labor, animals, and land may be exchanged by individuals or groups. This exchange may take the form of *bridewealth*, or *brideprice*, in which wealth of some sort is passed from the husband's group to the wife's. Like bride service, it is sometimes considered payment for the loss of the bride's companionship and labor. Since the practice is usually found among patrilineal descent groups, it is sometimes seen as an exchange of wealth for transferring the woman's potential offspring to her husband's group. Bridewealth is rarely paid in societies with matrilineal descent groups, where the children automatically become members of their mother's group.

Among the Nuer, young men use their family's cattle for bridewealth. The family itself may not have enough cows and may have to borrow cows from other relatives, widening the network of those involved in the exchange. The cows are then distributed to relatives of the bride's father and relatives of the bride's mother. The exchange of cows serves to reinforce the alliance between patriclans resulting from the marriage and also promotes redistribution of cows throughout Nuer society.

The introduction of a monetary economy has had severe repercussions on brideprice customs in many areas of the world. The introduction of money often breaks the hold that kin, and especially parents, have over the exchange, since money, unlike traditional forms of wealth, is more likely to be individually instead of family or group owned. Also, the introduction of money often creates inflationary cycles whereby ever greater amounts are paid, usually as a result of competition for prestige. Throughout much of Papua-New Guinea payment of bridewealth in cash has supplemented and often replaced exchanges involving more traditional forms of wealth, such as shell-money. But some peoples have reacted against this trend. The Tolai of New Britain (east of New Guinea), for example, "look on such practices with contempt, and see in them the reduction of marriage to a purely commercial transaction" (Epstein 1969: 216). The only time that they will use cash instead of shell-money is when outsiders marry Tolai women, and they have set upper limits on bridewealth payments according to the religious affiliation of those being married. The Tolai are very much a part of the modern world system, but they have not allowed market pressures to destroy an important part of their culture.

Many Indo-European societies have a somewhat different exchange custom called *dowry*. The dowry is usually seen as the woman's share of her inheritance from the group of her birth, which is taken with her upon marriage. For ex-

A Lese groom substitute and his helper display money to be paid to the bride's family (Ituri Forest, Zaire).

ample, among the Sarakatsani of Greece parents are expected to contribute to the establishment by their children of new households (Campbell 1974: 44–45). Family wealth—animals, money, and goods—is held in common, with the idea that it will eventually be distributed among the family members as an inheritance. Upon marriage a son usually continues to reside near his parents in an extended family group, and wealth is still held in common. A daughter, however, leaves to live with her husband and his family. The dowry that she takes with her upon marriage is seen as her portion of the family estate. As a result, both the husband's and the wife's family provide roughly equal amounts toward establishing the new household.

The Marriage Ceremony. Marriage is formalized by different means in different societies, but in all cases there will be some publicly recognized act or rite. The act may be a very simple one. After coming to an understanding with a woman, a young Tapirapé male will carry a load of firewood across the village plaza and deposit it at her family dwelling to make a public announcement of their marriage (Wagley

1977: 157). He then moves his hammock next to hers and becomes part of her household.

Village-level agricultural societies sometimes have more involved ceremonies. The Kgatla of Bechuanaland, in southern Africa (Schapera 1940), begin the marriage process with an engagement that may last two to three years, during which time a couple is referred to as "husband" and "wife" and gifts are exchanged. The husband-to-be is allowed to sleep with the woman to whom he was betrothed. (Before Christianization this was done openly; now it must be done in secret.) Before the wedding the bride spends a period of time in seclusion in her hut. Only her "supporter," generally a daughter of a maternal aunt or uncle, is allowed to see her. During this time she is supposed to get fat by eating porridge, milk, and meat. Before the wedding the bride and groom are doctored to protect them from witchcraft and other evils. The bride and her companions go to the dressmaker's house, where she puts on her wedding costume. Her parents then summon their future son-in-law and his companions to the dressmaker's house by sending him a pot of beer. If it is not a church wedding, a senior male relative tells the couple to link arms, and the procession returns to her home. At Christian weddings, the party goes from the dressmaker's to the church, where the couple are married; after the ceremony they return to the bride's home. After an elaborate and lengthy feast there, the couple goes to the groom's residence or village where another celebration is held. Before the couple is considered to be legitimately married, the brideprice transactions must also be completed.

Establishing a Residence. Once a couple is married, where will they reside? In our own society, the ideal residence is a separate dwelling, which may or may not be near either set of parents. We refer to such a practice as *neolocal* residence. The pattern fits in with our overall economic system and pattern of kin relationships: we sell our labor and move where jobs are available. Neolocal residence is associated not only with geographical mobility, but also with financial independence. A newly married couple who are poor or unemployed and who lack the capital to support themselves on an independent basis in our society often reside with one set of parents until their situation improves. The location of postmarital residence thus depends not simply upon what is ideal or preferred, but also upon a couple's specific needs and situations.

Neolocality is not the only residential preference; in many societies newly married couples do not aspire to owning their own homes and living independently of their parents. In societies where the most important bonds holding the group together are between men, the couple usually resides with the husband's group. After a woman is married she is to some extent cut off from her natal group and may become a permanent member of her husband's group instead. We refer to such a choice of residence as *patrilocal*.

Among peoples with matrilineal kin groups a woman usually lives with her own group after marriage, and her husband comes to live with her. This type of residence we call *matrilocal*. Unlike patrilocal residence in patrilineal societies, in this case the male does not give up membership in his natal group. He retains importance in the group of his birth as a person who is able to exercise authority over his sisters and their children, for he is the mother's brother. The importance of the mother's brother role sometimes allows an especially powerful man to establish residence with his natal group, taking his wife to live with him.

There are other types of residence as well. In *ambilocal* residence, the couple has a choice of living with or near the parents or kin of either bride or groom. *Bilocal* residence is somewhat different: the couple is expected to live for a period with or near the bride's parents and for another period with or near the groom's. A final main type of residential pattern is *avunculocal*: The couple lives with or near the groom's mother's brother.

Residential patterns are not always rigidly prescribed or uniform. In the Kekchi village of Pueblo Viejo, during the first few years of marriage it is not uncommon for a couple to shift from patrilocal to matrilocal residence a few times before settling fairly permanently. A man who decides to live near his parents sometimes finds that his wife returns home frequently to visit her mother or her sisters, and he may decide to move to her village or to her part of the village. Such a move is sometimes motivated by a desire to keep an eye on her activities, although other factors, such as disputes with his own kin, may also be critical. The village is divided into several factional groupings and choice of residence is often related to alliances within these groupings. If the factional leader is sufficiently skillful and able to attract followers he may be able to convince his daughters' husbands and even more distant relatives to live nearby. There are also physical considerations determining where one lives in Pueblo Viejo. Because of the frequent rainfall houses must be built on high ground, which in parts of the village is at a premium. There is a patrilocal bias in village residency, but the situation is very mixed and fluid.

Remarrying. After the marriage is legitimated much of married life centers on the family (discussed in the next section). The final part of the marriage process concerns events after a person's first marriage ends, either through divorce or death. While in a large-scale society like our own there is considerable variation in what people do once they are no longer married, in many societies patterns are more institutionalized, especially for widows and widowers.

In some societies, it is customary for a man's brother or some other member of his lineage to marry his widow after he dies. The rationale for this custom, which is called *levirate*, is that since the marriage involved the dead man's group a member of that group should replace him. The levirate is often found in conjunction with polygyny, patrilineal descent groups, and patrilocal residence. This practice ensures that the widow's children will continue to belong to the patrilineage.

Ghost marriage is a related practice found in many African societies. Among the Nuer, the brother of a deceased man may marry an unmarried woman "to the name of" the deceased. The children of this marriage are considered children of the dead man, and thus his heirs (Evans-Pritchard 1940). The Zulu of South Africa have two forms of ghost marriage (Gluckman 1950: 184). In one, when a man who is betrothed dies his fiancée is married to one of his kinsmen and she then bears children for the dead man. In the second form a man "wakens" a dead kinsman who had not been betrothed by marrying a wife to his name.

A complementary practice to the levirate is the *sororate*, in which a man marries the sister of his deceased wife. It too is associated with polygyny, patrilineal descent groups, and patrilocal residence, and may be a natural extension of sororal polygyny.

Another remarriage custom is *wife inheritance*. In this case, when a man dies his heir is expected to marry the widow. This practice is found in association with both patrilineal descent and matrilineal descent. In a matrilineal system a man inherits from his mother's brother, and one of the things he may inherit is the obligation to care for the deceased's wives.

All these institutions reflect a belief that people should remain married until they are clearly too old to function properly in a society. Like all institutions they limit personal freedom, and to some extent they emphasize the low status of women, but they also provide security for those who are widowed, ensuring that they will not be left to fend for themselves.

In other societies there may be norms to ensure that someone is responsible for taking care of widows without dictating who they remarry. A Kekchi widow may be taken care of by her own kin, her husband's, or her own children, depending upon the particular circumstances. If she is not extremely old it is expected that she will remarry, but there are no more restraints on her selection than if she were marrying for the first time.

Some societies actually discourage widow remarriage. Because the family into which a Sarakatsani woman has married does not want to lose her labor, her children, or their honor (since she would be having sexual relations with someone from another family), and because they forbid polygynous marriage, the Sarakatsani make it very difficult for widows to remarry.

All of these practices reflect certain patterns of social organization—the existence of kin groups with vested interests in what happens to a widow of one of its members. We can expect the practices to be retained only as long as the social conditions that generated them remain. In many parts of Africa, the destruction of corporate kin groups has been followed or accompanied by the destruction of related institutionalized means of remarrying widows.

Divorce too is a reflection of social and economic processes in the society at large. In our own society an increasing divorce rate can be linked to ideological and economic changes in the role of women as well as to changes in how families interact and are perceived. We can see this in other societies as well. The near impossibility of divorce among the Sarakatsani fits their overall social organization and their attitudes toward the family and toward females. In contrast, the ease with which Mundurucu women can divorce their husbands is related to the social and economic autonomy of Mundurucu women and to their matrilineality and matrilocal residence pattern.

Family Groups

One of the functions of marriage is the creation of the family. Families may exist independent of marriage, although this is not often the case; it is through marriage that families usually come into being as socially recognized, legitimate entities. In its most basic sense the term *family* refers to an intimate kin-based group, consisting of at least a parent and his or her children, that forms the minimal social unit that cooperates economically and is responsible for the rearing of children. Various people may be added to the parent-child nucleus, forming an economically cooperating, child-rearing family group that may or may not share the same dwelling.

Types of Family Groups

The typical American family so thoroughly incorporated into our ideology consists of a husband, a wife, and one or more children, all of whom live together in a single household. Many families in our society do not adhere to this norm, however. There are single parents with children, and there may be other relatives living with the family. If we look at other societies we discover that an arrangement like our American ideal is not even typical. In fact the nuclear family, as such a unit is called, is rather rare worldwide.

The *nuclear family group* is composed of a man, a woman, and their children. This group, as would be expected, is not the ideal in societies that practice polygyny or polyandry, nor is it considered normal in most societies with unilineal kin groups. The nuclear family group is fairly rare among small-scale agriculturists, and in fact does not occur frequently among any rural peoples. The nuclear family group is found primarily in two situations: in societies like the United States where social mobility, the hunt for jobs and improved social status, and the existence of specialized support systems (such as schools) tend to reduce the dependency of nuclear families upon others; and among more marginal foragers like the Inuit, whose precarious economic adaptation favors organizing into small, very mobile units for most of the year.

Since few environments encourage the existence of small, independent social groups, more common types of family organization are those referred to as complex or compound. Polygynous marriage leads to the creation of *polygynous family groups*, consisting of a man, his wives, and their children. The members of this family group sometimes live in the same household, each wife perhaps having her own territory centering on her fire hearth, but this living arrangement often causes problems. Co-wives often have separate dwellings to avoid conflict.

This results in matricentric households, where each wife lives in her own dwelling with her children.

Polyandry leads to the creation of *polyandrous family groups*. All of the members of a polyandrous family group—wife, husbands, and children—may live under a single roof, or the husbands may jointly occupy a separate men's hut.

There are also various forms of *extended family groups*, in which two or more families of at least two generations live together. A patrilocal extended family group consists of a man and his sons and their wives and children. A matrilocal extended family group consists of a woman, her daughter or daughters, and their husbands and children. An avunculocal extended family group consists of a man, his sister's son or sons, and their wives and children.

Finally, there are *joint family groups*, in which two or more relatives of the same generation and their spouses and children live together. The fraternal joint family group is a common example of this type; it consists of at least two brothers and their wives and children.

While only one or two of these family groups may represent the normative ideal of a society, in practice many of these forms may coexist in the same social setting. In Kekchi villages it is not uncommon to find nuclear families, various extended and joint family groups, and even an occasional polygynous family group (usually curers who have inherited wives from deceased patients). In each case, the pattern present reflects the strategies of people in relation to a broader social environment—the size of the village, factionalism, the network of the married couple, and how long they have lived in the village.

The Development Cycle

The cycle of birth, maturation, and death is a continuous one, and family groups are formed and evolve in accordance with this ongoing cycle. There are three main phases or stages in this development cycle (Fortes 1958). First is the phase of *expansion*. It begins with marriage and lasts until all children in the family are born and raised to reproductive age. The duration of this phase is limited primarily by the length of time a woman is fertile. During this period the offspring are highly dependent upon their parents. Second there is the phase of *dispersion and fission*. This may overlap with the first phase, for it begins with the marriage of the oldest child and continues until all the children are married. Where it is customary for the youngest child to remain to take over what is left of the family estate, this commonly marks the beginning of the final phase. The third phase—*replacement*—includes the death of the parents and their replacement in the social structure by families of their children.

At any given time, the phase a family group is going through may influence its residential patterns. Among the Iban (Freeman 1958) a couple may choose to live with the wife's or husband's family group, depending on where they are in the cycle. If one of the spouses is the last child remaining in the family after the others have married and left, for instance, he or she stays on as prospective heir.

Precisely what happens in the final stage as well as residential decisions throughout the cycle may depend upon inheritance customs. In some societies, the oldest child inherits most or all of the property. This is referred to as *primogeniture*. Younger siblings are either dependent on the oldest or are left to seek their fortunes on their own. In other societies, the youngest (usually male) child remains in the household of his birth and inherits the property of the parents. This is referred to as *ultimogeniture*, and usually leads to that child's taking over directly from his parents when the cycle begins anew. Such a child is also usually expected to care for the aged parents.

Acquiring Children

Children are an important element determining the form and evolution of family groups. How many children there are in a family depends partly on environmental factors. In earlier times, when old age was even more precarious than it is now, when the cost of having a child was insignificant, and when more Americans lived in the country, American families tended to be rather large by today's standards. As more of us moved to the city, as children became more a financial burden than an asset, and as social security took the place of family support of elderly members (to name a few contributing factors), families began to get smaller. In general, urbanization and industrialization tend to create conditions favoring smaller families.

The way people acquire children may be a matter of chance, but often it is not. Family planning, as we call it in our culture, is actually a rather widespread practice. The Tapirapé traditionally limited the number to three living children, and even stipulated that no more than two could be of the same sex (Wagley 1977: 135). This policy was maintained by a prohibition on sexual relations between a couple during the first year after they had a child, and by the practice of infanticide. It was not that the Tapirapé disliked children; rather, they did not "want to see hunger in their eyes" (Wagley 1977). They recognized that feeding more than three children is difficult and sought to ensure that those children they had were well provided for. Postpartum sex taboos (prescribed restraint from sexual intercourse after the birth of a child), infanticide, and abortion are relatively common means of limiting the number of children people have, or at least of spacing births.

Family groups do not always obtain children naturally from the female members. Adoption is another way of obtaining children through socially prescribed methods. In the United States adoption is handled by an *adoption agency*.

Children are brought to the agency for a variety of reasons by their parents or agents of the state. Great efforts are made to keep the natural parents and the adoptive parents from knowing each other, lest the former try at some future date to claim their child. There are, however, many cases of adoption in the United States by persons who are not strangers to the adoptees and who do not go through adoption agencies. About half of the adoptions in the United States are by relatives—the adoption of illegitimate children by their grandparents, the adoption of stepchildren, and the adoption of children of divorced or deceased relatives.

In many Pacific island societies adoption is a transaction between close relatives. There are no formal legal procedures. Futhermore, the natural parents are not stigmatized; on the contrary, they are usually considered generous. Whereas the natural parents of adopted children in the United States are usually unwilling or unable to assume parental responsibility, in these Pacific island societies the natural parents of adopted children are generally quite capable of caring for their children. They give their children up to be adopted either out of obligation or out of desire to help someone out. In Nukuoro in western Polynesia (Carroll 1970: 121) the act of adoption reflects the interdependency of relatives. Relatives are expected to be willing to share all of their resources, including children, especially when one of the relatives is in need.

There is another way of obtaining children: stealing or capturing them. This practice is found primarily among small-scale agriculturists such as those in Amazonian South America and New Guinea, where relations between groups are often tense and warfare is endemic. Sometimes the need to steal children is related primarily to practices that limit population growth. Relations between the sexes among peoples of the Trans-Fly region of New Guinea are so limited and hostile that in some of these societies homosexuality is the norm instead of heterosexuality (van Baal 1966). The birth rate among these people is so low that they are forced to raid their neighbors in order to perpetuate their population.

In many societies one of the most important factors influencing the number of children a family has is not the number of children produced, adopted, or stolen, but the number who live through early childhood. For many small-scale indigenous societies, newly introduced diseases have had devastating effects, killing large numbers of children as well as their parents. Throughout the world disease and malnutrition result in the deaths of millions of children every year and adversely affect the maturation of many more. Where there is high infant mortality, parents may seek to have a large number of children so that at least some will survive. Improvement in health conditions after the Second World War in areas where such practice was common often resulted in dramatic increases in population. Family planning is difficult under such unstable conditions and many strategies that worked in the past may no longer be appropriate. Where new patterns have emerged and family sizes have been altered significantly, the new patterns are usually interrelated with changes in other aspects of the people's lives as well, from sexual behavior to treatment of the elderly. No single aspect of human behavior, such as having children, can be separated from the web of interrelated environmental factors.

Summary

Male-female relations are conditioned by their social and cultural environment. The most basic element of male-female relations is sex. Our culture has a profound influence on how we perceive sex and with whom we have it. Societies vary in the degree to which they restrict sex and in their definitions of which people are acceptable sexual partners. In most societies, there are some socially acceptable means of getting around the usual restrictions. There is also a link in most cultures between sex and power.

Marriage is a socially sanctioned sexual and economic union between two persons. It is an adaptive measure, related to such factors as the prolonged period of dependency of human infants, sexual competition, the sexual division of labor, and, perhaps, male domination. It is also a means to the formation of alliances. Systems of marital exchange between groups may be elementary or complex, direct or indirect, endogamous or exogamous.

Although one spouse at a time is the only form of marriage allowed in our society, monogamy is not universal. Two forms of plural marriage, or polygamy, are found in many societies: polygyny and polyandry. Our version of the marriage process is not universal either. Societies place varying restrictions on the choice of a spouse. The terms of the marriage may involve bride service, brideprice, or dowry. The actual ceremony can vary a great deal in elaborateness. After the ceremony, housing possibilities include neolocal, patrilocal, matrilocal, ambilocal, bilocal, and avunculocal residence. Lastly there is the question of what happens when a spouse dies or a divorce takes place. Many societies have institutionalized remarriage through practices such as the levirate, ghost marriage, sororate, and wife inheritance.

In our society, the traditional family includes not only husband and wife but also some children. This nuclear family is not the only way of grouping close kin, however. In addition to the nuclear family group, there are four principal types of complex or compound family groups: polygynous, polyandrous, extended, and joint. The family group is not static; it follows a rhythmic cycle of expansion, dispersion, and replacement. Expressions of this pattern are influenced by a number of things, including inheritance customs such as primogeniture and ultimogeniture. Expansion involves the acquisition of children, either through natural procreation, adoption, or capture. How many children a family has and how they are obtained are influenced, like all of culture, by environmental factors.

Suggested Readings

General:

Bohannon, Paul, and Middleton, John, eds. 1968. *Marriage, family and residence.* New York: Natural History Press.

Goody, Jack R. 1977. *Production and reproduction: A comparative study of the domestic domain.* Cambridge: Cambridge University Press.

Goody, Jack R., ed. 1958. *The developmental cycle in domestic groups.* Cambridge: Cambridge University Press.

Goody, Jack R., and Tambiah, S. J., eds. 1973. *Bridewealth and dowry.* Cambridge: Cambridge University Press.

Specific:

Blesdoe, Caroline H. 1980. *Women and marriage in Kpelle society.* Stanford: Stanford University Press. (Africa)

Croll, Elisabeth. 1981. *The politics of marriage in contemporary China.* Cambridge: Cambridge University Press.

Glasse, R. M., and Meggitt, M. J., eds. 1969. *Pigs, pearlshells and women: Marriage in the New Guinea highlands.* Englewood Cliffs, NJ: Prentice-Hall.

Goodale, Jane C. 1971. *Tiwi wives: A study of the women of Melville Island, North Australia.* Seattle: University of Washington Press.

Kennedy, Theodore R. 1979. *You gotta deal with it: Black family relations in a southern community.* New York: Oxford University Press.

Martinez-Alier, Verena. 1974. *Marriage, class and colour in nineteenth-century Cuba.* Cambridge: Cambridge University Press.

Peristiany, J. G., ed. 1976. *Mediterranean family structure.* Cambridge: Cambridge University Press.

Potter, Sulamith H. 1980. *Family life in a northern Thai Village: A study in the structural significance of women.* Berkeley/Los Angeles: University of California Press.

Schapera, I. 1940. *Married life in an African tribe.* London: Faber and Faber.

Slater, Miriam K. 1977. *The Caribbean family: Legitimacy in Martinique.* New York: St. Martin's.

Tufte, Virginia, and Myerhoff, Barbara, eds. 1979. *Changing images of the family.* New Haven, CT: Yale University Press. (United States)

Focus on People

Mapuche Marriage Customs

Margarita B. Melville

Margarita B. Melville and Thomas R. Melville did fieldwork in south central Chile from June 1973 to August 1975. They spent their first year living in an Indian community on the island of Huapi, studying how modern education affected the value system of the community. During their second year, they taught at the Catholic University of Chile and continued to visit the community on Huapi. Most recently, Margarita Melville has been studying the acculturation of undocumented Mexican immigrants in Texas.

IN EARLY SEPTEMBER of 1973, Tom Melville and I arrived on the island of Huapi, in the lake region of south-central Chile, to begin an ethnographic study of the Mapuche Indian residents of the island.

We had heard that the Mapuche were an independent and aggressive people who had managed to resist colonization longer than most Indian groups in South America. After repulsing the invasion of Spanish explorers and colonizers in the 1500s, they continued their resistance to foreign domination and were not overcome until the early 1880s. At that time, through the combined efforts of Italian missionaries, European colonists, and the Chilean army, they were finally subdued.

After being granted hospitality in the home of a Mapuche family, Tom and I began to walk the many paths of the island, talking to and getting to know the people who lived there. In response to our many questions, they invariably had many of their own: What does an anthropologist do? What are you looking for? Why are you here? Where do you get your money? The political climate on the island contributed to an increased suspicion of us. A military coup had occurred only a few days after our arrival, and the inhabitants of the island were not sure what to make of us. Were we spies for the new government or refugees of the old? In either case, we presented a serious danger. As the weeks passed, we calmed their fears and explained that we hoped to write a book about them. This only helped to raise a new series of doubts and questions: Why can't we write about our own lives? What do ours matter to you? Why do strangers have to come here to write about us and perhaps make fun of us? Wouldn't it be good to leave our children our own record of how we lived our lives so that they will know in the future what our struggles have been?

This generated the idea of helping these Mapuche peasants to write their own book. They were determined to produce a written record they could leave their children. But the task was not without many difficulties. It is not easy to describe what it means for a man used to holding a plow to take up a thin little pencil; what is involved when someone with a fourth-grade education attempts once again to form letters and to write sentences expressing ideas and feel-

Anthropologist Margarita Melville tries out a Mapuche dugout.

them to school. We collected the manuscripts, did some superficial editing for grammar and spelling, and had them typed. We paid for a mimeographed version, had the copies bound, and gave these books to the authors to distribute themselves.

The following account was written by Pascual Pichuman Huircaman to explain their marriage customs:

Marriage customs in years gone by were very different from our customs today. Today, when a young man begins relating to girls and decides he wants to marry a particular young woman, he has a meeting with his father and his family, and then they decide to name two representatives to go and speak to the girl's father or "owner." They go and speak to him and come to some agreement. At that time, they call the girl in and they ask her if she agrees; if she doesn't, they just might oblige her to accept anyway. Thus, the families of the young man and girl come to some agreement. After a few months, they set a date for the wedding.

The day of the wedding, a big feast is held. Animals are killed; a cow, sheep and more. The girl's "owner" receives a horse or other animals. In other words, the girl is bought with several animals. People bring meat to eat at the feast. The trutruca *and* pufilka [Mapuche wooden wind instruments] *are played and there is a big dance to celebrate a Mapuche marriage.*

When an older man wants to marry a young girl or a widow, the same procedure is followed, except that there isn't such a big feast as when young people are marrying.

In times gone by, the custom was to steal the bride. It is different today, although young brides are still stolen sometimes. On the day of the "theft," the young man bides his time while some of his relatives, like uncles, cousins, brothers and brothers-in-law, plan how they will speak to the girl's parents so that there won't be too much trouble. Then the girl sneaks out to

ings; what it takes for someone whose eyes are accustomed to surveying fields in the bright sunlight to discipline them to concentrate on a piece of paper by the flickering light of a candle; what it means for someone whose body aches with the fatigue of strenuous labor to subject it to the confining attitude of bending over a ragged piece of paper. This is precisely what twelve men and women underwent to write their *Memorias de la Isla Huapi* (Memories of Huapi Island). As anthropologists, we provided encouragement, some coordination of subject matter, new notebooks when the field rats ate the old ones, and new pencils when their children took *where the young man is waiting for her. Later on, they have a wedding feast after the problems between the families have been settled. When the wedding is more according to Chilean style, they play other musical instruments like the guitar and the accordion.*

Bartolo Huenten adds:

In order to perform a Mapuche marriage correctly, the feast is held at the bride's home. The parents of the groom present the bride's mother with a shawl and the father with a horse or a cow. It is common for the groom to steal his bride in the night. Then three days later, he'll send word to the bride's parents by means of some relatives.

Our own research indicated that bride theft was preferred to avoid an expensive brideprice. The girl would sleep close to the door—indicating that some agreement had previously been achieved between the bride and groom. The groom would come on horseback, take the bride, and gallop away furiously. His brothers and cousins would stand ready to impede the pursuit of the bride's father, uncles, brothers, and cousins. The young man's skill at riding and his relatives' bravery and fighting ability would be attributes likely to win a father-in-law's grudging respect. These attributes were highly valued among the Mapuche and were the source of their ability to resist conquest and colonization for more than three and a half centuries.

Today, some young people continue to elope—having adapted an ancient custom to a modern setting. Eloping is designed to avoid an expensive bridal arrangement and wedding celebration when economic times are hard, without jeopardizing the legitimacy of the marriage. The evident change is that girls are now recognized as having a more active part in the decision.

Chapter Ten

Socialization

To THE SEMAI, a small group of relatively isolated forestdwellers in Malaysia, the thought of becoming angry is absurd. "We do not get angry," they explain (Dentan 1968: 55). Of course the Semai *do* get angry on occasion, but they deny the existence of such an emotion within their culture, and social pressures and cultural values minimize the likelihood of their becoming angry. They see themselves as nonviolent people. Almost from birth they are taught to avoid aggression and to feel shame should they behave aggressively. Should an individual hurt someone physically or emotionally, the injured party has the right to ask compensation and more than likely the aggressor will endeavor to make up for the ill-feeling he or she has caused.

The Semai attitude toward aggression seems peculiar to someone from Britain or the United States, because in Western culture denying the existence of anger or trying always to avoid hostility is considered not quite normal. To many brought up in a Western cultural tradition the Semai may seem weak and cowardly, or perhaps carefree and naive. A utopian desire for a world without conflict makes their attitude toward anger appealing to some. These perceptions of Semai culture reflect a distinctly Western view of the human condition, one that emphasizes conflict and aggression. Like Semai attitudes toward anger and violence, Western views of aggression are part of a cultural tradition that has been shaped by a unique set of historical and environmental conditions.

An Overview of Socialization

The general process by which we acquire our views and values from others is known as *socialization*. More specifically, we learn to behave as members of a particular society, learning its cultural rules and values, through the process known as *enculturation*.

We acquire an image of the world that is highly conditioned by the practices and beliefs of those around us. We are taught how to categorize the physical and social world and what these categories mean. The Semai categorize animals according to their habitat; fish, whales, and turtles are all in the same category. Likewise, the categories into which they divide their social and physical world differ from our own in many ways and carry with them many attitudes that are very different from those of West-

OVERLEAF

A classic American rite of passage, the graduation prom, as painted by Norman Rockwell for the *Saturday Evening Post*'s May 25, 1957 cover.

erners. Thunder squalls, for instance, they consider unnatural and caused by human action (Dentan 1968: 21–22), rather than natural phenomena over which humans have little control. While part of what is learned is a result of formal instruction, much of socialization occurs simply through interacting with others in a particular society.

The socialization process results in a degree of uniformity among the members of a society as they come to share values and attitudes. But there will always be considerable variation in the behavior and attitudes of the members of a society. Such variation is in part a reflection of the particular status and roles individuals occupy within a society. Beyond this, there is always some room for individual choice and individual peculiarities, particularly in large-scale societies. Pressures toward conformity and homogeneity are often greater in small-scale societies than in large-scale ones. Not all Semai are alike, but close and continuous interaction and the fear of disapproval lead to a high degree of uniformity. More options are usually available to those living in large-scale societies like our own, where there is a wider range of potential statuses and roles to occupy and greater opportunity for social mobility. The presence of options does not mean that they will be used, however. Within segments of large-scale societies—such as those associated with class, community, or ethnicity—people will often exhibit as much uniformity as do members of small-scale societies. This is as true of elite society in Philadelphia as it is of Mexican-Americans in East Los Angeles; in both cases, the pressures toward conformity to group expectations are considerable.

Socialization begins at birth. Although the early years of life are especially important in shaping an individual's views, the process continues until death. As people grow older their place in society changes and they must learn new modes of behavior. Expectations of children differ from those of adults, and as people achieve adult status they must learn how to behave in accordance with new expectations. What these differences are, and how great, will vary from one society to another; but there are always differences.

The process of socialization is also influenced by changes within the environment. Societies and the settings within which they exist are constantly changing, and people must adapt to these changes. What kinds of adjustment people make will depend partly upon the nature of the changes taking place and partly on the society's members' prior behavioral patterns and views of the world. The introduction of television in the United States in the 1940s altered socialization patterns as it came to function as a source of information, a mediator between members of a household or between individuals and the world beyond, and a baby sitter for millions of children. But it did not require any immediate or drastic reorientation in how Americans viewed the world. The total destruction of the social or economic bases of a society through conquest, disease, natural disaster, or revolution is a different matter. Such drastic changes often require fundamental alterations in how people view the world and in how they are socialized to live in it, for there is less room for continuity.

Reprinted under license from Morriseau Syndications, Burlington, VT

In a very broad sense our biological characteristics set limitations on what we can do and see and on how we can view the world. We cannot fly unaided, we can eat only certain foods, and we can see in only a specific range of the light spectrum. Within these limitations, however, a tremendous potential remains for innovation and imagination. There are also individual biological differences, for each person is born with a unique configuration of inherited tendencies and physical characteristics that will influence how he or she behaves. How important individual biological differences are will vary according to their nature and the social context. To be blind in an urbanized society that has ways of accommodating blind persons is far different from being blind among a group of desert foragers who have no means of looking after a blind person.

Cultural Orientations

What we learn within a particular society is part of its adaptational strategy. Each culture has its own way of looking at life and its own ideas about "right" and "wrong."

The Adaptive Nature of Cultural Orientations

The basic perceptions and behavioral patterns encouraged within a cultural tradition reflect the overall adaptational strategy of a society's collective membership. In dividing up game, Semai are careful to divide portions equally and to distribute them widely. The man who kills an animal gives portions to the heads of a number of households. In return, he can expect to receive game from all of these people. Central to the Semai exchange system are the ideas that one should not calculate what one receives and that one should share whatever one can afford (Dentan 1968: 49). Such values ensure that food is distributed to all members of their society, and thus provides a sense of security for those unable to support themselves because of ill health or injury.

Since perceptions, values, and attitudes represent strategies for dealing with specific environmental conditions, they will be affected by changes within the environment. For example, the introduction of money among the less isolated eastern Semai has greatly altered their exchange system and their views about the nature of exchange. Money requires that people calculate exchanges. And unlike food, it does not spoil and is easy to hide, making it easier for people to be selfish (Dentan 1968: 50).

Many of the environmental changes faced by the members of small-scale societies today are related to the expansion of the world system. Integration into the world system does not always mean the loss of traditional values for members of small-scale societies. At least in the short run, peoples sometimes are able to maintain important attitudes in the face of radical changes. When drawn into the British campaign against Communist rebels in Malaysia in the 1950s, the Semai were able to maintain their ideal of nonviolence by labeling their killing of rebels as temporary insanity. The maintenance of such values is often not possible, however, and one can speculate that should the integration of the Semai into Malaysian society become more thorough, they too will be caught up in the competitive and aggressive world of their neighbors.

World View

The basic cultural orientation of the members of a society—the way the people perceive their environment—may be referred to as their *world view*. As Robert Redfield has noted, our world view is the organization of ideas that answer the questions: Where am I? Among what do I move? What are my relations to things? (1952: 30). World view concerns the fundamental assumptions of a people about the nature of the world, as expressed somewhat systematically in their philosophy, ethics, ritual, and scientific belief (Wallace 1970: 142–43). Not all members of a society adhere to the same perceptions or beliefs, but these views are thought to represent the dominant themes of that society's culture as a whole.

The Desana, a small group of foraging and farming Tukano Indians in southern Colombia (Reichel-Dolmatoff 1971), provide an example of a world view and how it is expressed. The central theme of the Desana world view is the biological and cultural continuity of their society. This desire for continuity, common to many peoples, permeates all their activities and attitudes. As the Desana see it, this goal can be achieved only by minimizing competition through a system of strict reciprocity in all relationships with members of their society and with the animals. In their division of labor—men hunt and women are responsible for agricultural production—more prestige falls to the men, for the Desana view themselves as hunters, not farmers. But this contradiction with their goal of reciprocity is mediated through religion. During ceremonial gatherings, to emphasize their mutual interdependence, those of each sex place themselves "under the reflection" of the light (red or yellow) symbolic of the opposite sex. Reciprocity is emphasized in craft production, too. Although individuals specialize in producing canoes, manioc graters, baskets, and pottery, the Desana emphasize the mutual and equal exchange of goods, rather than competition, profit, or exploitation.

While in a sense there are almost as many world views as there are societies, similar types of society do tend to share similar views of the world. Foragers in the deserts of Australia apparently see the world in much the same way as foragers roaming Africa's Kalahari desert. In contemporary industrial nations, the world views of members of the elite are probably similar from one society to the next, as are the views of middle-class wage earners and of the poor. Oscar Lewis (1966) developed the concept of the "culture of poverty," common cultural attitudes and conceptions that he perceived among poor people in Western industrial nations: a feeling of helplessness, a withdrawal from political activity, and an orientation toward immediate consumption. The idea of culture of poverty has been much abused by writers and planners and as developed by Lewis has many shortcomings, but it does point out that living in impoverished circumstances with little real chance of improvement may lead to certain shared perceptions of the world. Not all poor people or foragers or farmers are alike, but like economic circumstances tend to produce like perceptions of the world.

The "Primitive" World View. A more general categorization used by many writers is the division of world views into "primitive" and "civilized." The so-called primitive world view is commonly associated with small-scale societies in which face-to-face social relationships predominate. The civilized world view, on the other hand, is associated with large-scale societies, where social relationships are commonly of a less personal nature.

The *primitive world view* is essentially a personal view of the universe in which humans are seen as united with nature rather than separate from it. The physical world within which humans find themselves is seen as animate and human relations with animals, trees, bodies of water, and other nonhuman things are seen as being like those between humans. As a part of nature, humans must take part in maintaining the natural order of things, rather than trying to dominate or change nature (Wallace 1970: 142). Ritual expresses such participation.

This primitive world view reflects the close social relationships that the members of small-scale societies maintain with each other and the close relationship with nature that their technology and adaptive strategies entail. Australian Aborigines, for example, assign religious significance to the entire physical landscape, and see themselves as united with animals and with particular territories through kinship and ritual. Their religion emphasizes the unchanging nature of the universe. Furthermore, it not only makes them a part of nature, but it also requires that they perform rituals to maintain the natural order. Through their rituals they reaffirm existing social relationships, support the procreation of animal species, and act out the creative activities of the mythical beings who laid down the social order of the universe. In these rites they do not simply assume the roles of mythical beings or of animals; they view themselves as *becoming* these beings and animals, and by so doing become one with the natural order.

Warwick Dix (1978: 86) mentions two Aboriginal men from a remote settlement in Western Australia who visited the state museum in Perth. Seeing a group of limestone boulders laid out decoratively beside a parking area, they decided that it must be a sacred site, the locale of some mythologically significant event, and began to negotiate for its purchase so that it might be protected. To the urban-dwelling Westerner this is an absurd idea, but within the view that all things in nature are part of an ordered moral universe which humans have responsibility to protect, and more specifically that all unusual geographical features are likely to be associated with the activities of mythic culture heroes, the idea is not ridiculous. Westerners often pay lip service to the animate nature of the physical universe and to their moral relationship with it (as exemplified in the writings of Tolkien), but

Life in an urban environment (this scene is of lower Manhattan) creates a world view that is in many ways different from that of persons living in smaller and more isolated villages.

they rarely really believe in these things. To most Westerners a rock is a rock. It may be worthy of value because of its beauty, marketability, or historical associations; but it is not a feeling entity, a living manifestation of godly acts, or an integral part of the moral universe.

The "Civilized" World View. The *civilized world view*, by contrast, reflects the impersonal nature of social relationships in large-scale societies—as exemplified in our relationships with the government or the military—and a technology that allows people to become distant from nature. In many ways, it is the exact opposite of the primitive world view. Instead of emphasizing the unchanging nature of the universe and placing humanity within this natural order, the civilized world view stresses our separation from nature and our role as conqueror of nature. Instead of living in harmony with the desert or the forest, we seek to dominate it, to transform it to suit our perceived needs. The non-Aborigines living in Australia's deserts build towns with roads, lawns, air-conditioning, and the like, seeking to make their desert habitat resemble a European suburb; the Aborigines of the desert seek to know and respect their habitat as it is.

Use of the terms "primitive" and "civilized" does not mean that one view is better than the other. They are simply different views of the universe that result in large part from the different social experiences of people living in large-scale and small-scale societies. Also, the terms are oversimplifications. People living in small-scale societies are not "children of nature," living in perfect harmony with their surroundings. The members of such societies do change many things in their environment through burning, hunting, or farming. Likewise, as exemplified by the environmental movement, members of large-scale societies do to some extent try to maintain harmonious relations with their surroundings. What these two views represent are differences in emphasis.

Values

A second major ingredient of a culture's orientation is its values. *Values* are emotionally charged beliefs about what is desirable or offensive, right or wrong, appropriate or inappropriate. Within any society there will be great variation in the values held by individuals. Even within our own families we are unlikely to have precisely the same values as our parents or siblings, and our differences with work associates or people who live in the same community or neighborhood may be even greater. But we

also have many values in common with these people. Not everyone in a small Ohio town will place a high value upon hard work, disdaining idleness, but the vast majority will have this value.

Common values are often associated with regions, social classes, or ethnic groups. In our own society we often speak of American values, middle-class values, or city values, recognizing that different life-styles can be associated with different value orientations. In each of these cases the values will be related to the particular setting, history, and adaptive strategy of the people. Peoples with long histories of warfare or military conquest will probably possess a range of values associated with militarism and aggression: a willingness to sacrifice, blind obedience to those in command, a low esteem for females.

In most cultures it is possible to identify a set of core values that are systematically related. *Core values* are the fundamental values that provide the basis for social behavior and the goals pursued by the members of a society. The Japanese emphasis upon duty, respect, and filial piety provides an example of such core values. They are values which, for example, help to give Japanese industry its particular character. Japanese companies function almost as patriarchal families, with the security, and the lack of freedom, that such a situation entails.

Many of the core values of a culture do not apply equally to all members of the society. Traits valued by the Trukese, inhabitants of a Micronesian atoll, are applicable primarily to men. Males are supposed to be public, assertive, strong, and willing to take risks and confront danger. While these are the most valued traits in Trukese society, the ideals for female behavior emphasize privateness, acquiescence, and an avoidance of danger and risk. These ideas have their counterparts in Hispanic culture with the contrasting values of *machismo* (manliness, bravery) and *vergüenza* (modesty, bashfulness, shame). Age also may make a difference. In Trukese and our own society young males are expected to be a bit wild, becoming more settled as they mature and marry.

Although core values are for the most part rather resistant to radical change, they are rarely absolutely static. Under certain circumstances they may change quite drastically in a very short time. For some members of a society (such as those who are older or who have a deep-seated interest in maintaining the old views) drastic changes may be difficult or even impossible to accept. During the past few decades, for example, many older people in our society had great difficulty in adjusting to changes in men's hair length. Most people, however, are relatively flexible, especially if there are strong incentives for them to change their values.

Changes in values are generally associated with alterations in the social or environmental context. The New England emphasis upon hard work and disdain for leisure in colonial times developed within a strong religious tradition and an economic system that favored such values. Social and cultural processes since the Second World War have weakened these values through the creation of a more secure and secularized middle class that is less inclined to renounce worldly pleasures. The old values have not entirely disappeared, however. Even though comfort and a leisurely existence are now quite acceptable among members of the middle class, the feeling remains that such a "privilege" should be afforded only to those who have worked hard in the past, thereby earning the right to a life of ease.

Personality

World view and values manifest themselves in the individual in what is called personality. More precisely, the term *personality* refers to "an inner system of beliefs, expectations, desires and values" (Stagner 1961: 8). Anthropologists approach the study of personality by looking at its various components and trying to discern their meanings in their social context. One of the components which receives a good deal of attention is emotion. In her study of Inuit life in northern Canada, for example, Jean Briggs (1970) found that in trying to adapt to life in a harsh environment the Inuit have promoted sociality by avoiding the expression of anger.

Such studies may be rather subtle, for an individual's personality has unconscious as well as conscious components. The unconscious part of our personality consists of a core of values, attitudes, and orientations that we are for the most part unaware of. This core serves as the "blueprint" for the conscious side of our personality.

The conscious part of our personality includes the overall view that we have of ourself, our *self-concept*. The Semai self-concept includes an image of nonaggressiveness, while that of Trukese males is almost the opposite. Self-concept includes a person's perception of how others view him or her, a perception whose accuracy varies a great deal from one person to the next. In forming a self-concept individuals usually choose to emphasize certain aspects of their personality over others. What the individual comes to emphasize usually coincides with more general cultural values.

Personality Types

We all like to think we are unique individuals, and to a degree we are individualistic. Nevertheless, no one is unique, and it is possible to generalize about personality tendencies in a population. It is possible, for example, to speak of personality types. In so doing, however, we must be careful to base our types upon careful analysis and not upon unfounded stereotypes, as in ethnic slurs. In compiling personality types, anthropologists usually focus upon what they find to be the dominant themes present in the personalities they study, while recognizing that individual personalities will be more complex and varied.

David Riesman (1953) distinguished three general personality types in the United States: tradition oriented, inner directed, and other directed. The *tradition-oriented* personality is found in small-scale societies, in which most activities are of a very routine nature. Values and actions in these societies are oriented toward and legitimated on the basis of tradition—thus a son behaves in a certain manner toward his mother because it is the traditional way of behaving.

In large-scale societies where life is much more varied, Riesman maintains, tradition alone does not suffice to give direction to life. In large-scale societies like the United States his other two personality types are more common. The *inner-directed* personality is characterized by a strong conscience and a sense of righteousness, as exemplified by the Puritans of colonial New England. A person with such a personality is compulsively driven and is the ideal type to expand a frontier, to conquer other peoples, and to exploit resources with a fervent single-mindedness. It is a type of personality that was presumably common in the early years of American history when the nation was in its expansive phase. In contrast, the *other-directed* personality has ambiguous feelings about what is right and wrong, is more adaptable, and is more responsive to the actions and expectations of others. To Riesman, this type of personality is more suited to the United States of the mid-twentieth century than to 'colonial New England.

Riesman's personality types do not coincide with the personalities of any particular individuals; they indicate tendencies or themes present in personalities. Also, they point to the important relationship between personality and the environment, for Riesman's types are closely interrelated with a society's environment and adaptive strategies.

The Modal Personality

There is a range of personalities and of personality types within any society. The *modal personality* of a group is the central tendencies of those personality characteristics found within the population. It is, in a sense, the average personality type found within a group, an average that should be based upon careful sampling of the population. The modal personality of a group will not be identical to the personality of any of its members; it represents merely a general tendency or pattern that is particularly useful for comparative purposes.

Attention to modal personality can be very useful in trying to understand social relations between groups. In his study of a highland Guatemalan community, John Gillen found that Indians and non-Indians had very different modal personalities. The Indian orientation was passive; they brought a high degree of fatalism to situations facing them. By contrast, the non-Indian attitude toward their surroundings, and especially toward others was aggressive, as they sought to overcome what they perceived to be obstacles or problems (Gillen 1951: 122). These differences are a result of radically different historical and social circumstances. The Indians are a powerless and impoverished people who were conquered by the non-Indians' ancestors, while the socially dominant non-Indians descended from those who conquered Guatemala in the sixteenth century. Their differing modal personalities not only reflect different social and historical situations, but also perpetuate differences between Indian and non-Indian, especially their different political and economic statuses.

The fatalism of Guatemalan Indians or the nonaggressiveness of the Inuit are not determined by biology; they are attitudes learned through interaction with others. To look at how values, attitudes, and beliefs are transmitted and at how personalities are formed, we will turn in the next section to the dynamic side of socialization.

Socialization Through the Life Cycle

Socialization is a continuous process. It lasts from birth to death, and according to some cultural traditions, continues even after death. Within any society this process tends to follow a general pattern associated with what may be referred to as the *life cycle*: birth, maturation, old age, and death. Precisely how these periods are divided and interpreted, however, varies from one society to another.

Childhood in some societies is seen as a single continuous phase, lasting until the onset of puberty. In other societies it is divided into a series of clearly defined phases. The Mardudjara Aborigines, for example, divide early childhood into distinct stages, with a particular label for each: newborn, able to sit up, able to crawl, walking but only just, walking properly, no longer breast fed, and no longer carried. After this, a person is simply referred to as a child until the onset of adulthood. The precise age at which childhood ends also varies among societies. In different societies the beginning of adult life may be variously defined as the onset of puberty, the time of marriage, or an age determined almost at random, as in our own society.

Even death is not treated the same in all societies. The Judeo-Christian tradition, for example, views the period after death from a linear perspective; death is considered to lead to a permanent existence in a noncorporeal or spiritual state. To Hindus, on the other hand, death is part of a cyclical process, and the spirit of the deceased will eventually be reborn.

However life's phases are defined, the socialization process will not be the same at different periods in the life cycle. Our experiences and requirements change with age. In any society the

As this !Kung father plays with his child he is informally socializing the child to the ways of !Kung society.

experience of a one-year-old child will be rather limited and its needs fairly basic—affection, feeding, and a bit of looking after. This situation contrasts sharply with that of a middle-aged male or female, whose responses to socializing influences will be influenced by decades of prior experience and whose social and psychological needs will be greater and more complex than those of a child. From society's point of view, its members' statuses and roles vary throughout the life cycle and each individual must become socialized to changes in his or her social position. For example, in our own society we say that adolescents need to learn to behave like adults, and we refer to the adjustments people must make upon retirement.

Child Rearing and Family Influence

Early childhood experiences are the most critical in forming an individual's personality and in socializing the individual to the ways of his or her society. These early experiences are for the most part unstructured and unplanned. Much of early childhood socialization is not the result of acts explicitly aimed at shaping the child's view of the world, although some acts will be. Rather, most of what goes on in the socialization process during this period is of an informal nature as people feed, care for, and play with the child.

The range of people influencing a child can vary a great deal from one society to the next and among different groups within the same society. To free the mother and father "from the burden of child rearing," elites in North American and European societies often leave their children with nurses or nannies during these early years. In such a situation the child's personality is given shape by the constant attention received from the nanny and by the distant and fleeting relationship with its mother and father. Among other members of these societies child rearing tends to take place within the con-

fines of the nuclear family, with most responsibility falling upon the mother. Contrast these two examples with many small-scale societies in which virtually everyone in the community assumes some responsibility for looking after each child. Unlike most Western children, Australian Aboriginal children are not separated from the rest of the community. The life of the camp goes on all around the child, and whether they are the child's parents or not, all adults take an active role in his or her rearing.

How those rearing a child interact with it can also vary considerably. Among Australian Aborigines, temper tantrums and other forms of misbehavior are treated with great indulgence by adults, and children usually get their way. Semai infants also are indulged by members of the community; physical punishment, which is rare, consists of a pinch on the cheek or a pat on the hands. Although overt coercion and physical violence are not a part of childhood socialization among the Semai and Australian Aborigines, children do receive direction. While the Semai do not resort to physical violence in trying to control their children, they commonly scare children. Semai children are taught to fear strangers, evil spirits, and violence in nature.

Whatever they are, the child's experiences are internalized and organized unconsciously, gradually shaping the individual's personality. Despite growing independence from those who raised us, these early childhood relationships provide shape to our personality for the remainder of our lives.

The continuing influence of early childhood social experiences can be seen in our identity as males and females. As Chodorow (1974: 43) has noted, differences in "male and female development arise out of the fact that women, universally, are largely responsible for early child care and . . . later female socialization." Both male and female begin life by developing a close bond with the female(s) responsible for their rearing. For the female this mother-daughter relationship becomes internalized as a core element within her personality. The male's personality, on the other hand, is shaped by a rejection of this bond, by a desire to establish a separate identity and to escape from the dependency of early childhood. He comes to define himself largely in negative terms—that which is not female. In industrial societies like our own where the father is absent a good deal of the time, the male comes to identify with a fantasized masculine role rather than with his father as a person. The male therefore becomes a fairly isolated individual, interacting with others largely on the basis of role stereotypes. In contrast, the female, whose identity does not require that she reject her bonds with her mother, lives in a social world of more concrete relationships. She is less concerned with individuality and identifies readily with her mother and other females.

Rites of Passage

Although much of our socialization takes place gradually, during certain periods defined as times of transition the social shaping of our lives is accelerated. Some of these may be closely associated with biological developments like first menstruation; others are influenced by sociocultural factors, such as school graduation, marriage, or retirement. For both the individuals involved and the society as a whole these transitions are important, and often rather stressful. Among peoples where the bride goes to live among the groom's kin, for example, marriage involves the loss of the bride and her labor to her natal kin group and her incorporation into a new group. The other females of the groom's kin group have to adjust to having a stranger in their midst; the bride is subjected to the trauma of being a stranger and being away from her mother and siblings for the first time in her life. And, of course, the bride and groom must adjust to being married to each other. Marriage is

The pendant worn by this Aboriginal youth from Jigalong, Western Australia, is a mark of his stage in the initiation process; he has been circumcised and subincised, but he is not yet eligible for marriage.

thus a period in which individuals must adjust to a new set of relationships and roles.

Transitional periods are frequently occasions for ceremonies that focus upon the importance of the person's change in status and affirm his or her new place in society. The rituals associated wih these transitions are called *rites of passage*. These rites commonly are comprised of three stages (Van Gennep 1960): separation, transition, and incorporation. The individual is first symbolically and often physically separated from society and his or her normal place in it. Separation is followed by a transitional stage in which the person is suspended between the old and the new. Finally, the individual is incorporated ritually into his or her new social position and reenters society. The graduation ceremony in our own society provides a good example of the stages of a rite of passage. We begin by having the graduates wear distinctive costumes and separating them from the others present. During the transitional stage there is a period of ritualized speechmaking in which the graduates are provided with words of wisdom intended to help them as they leave the ivory tower and enter the world beyond. The speeches are followed by the handing out of diplomas, after which the graduates and parents mingle and the graduates once again become part of the normal social order.

In addition to affirming an individual's movement through stages in the life cycle, rites of passage may serve another important socializing function: they are usually occasions to reinforce through ceremony and speech some of the dominant values of a society. A marriage ceremony, for example, can emphasize values associated with male-female, civil-religious, and other social, economic, or political relationships. Likewise, the graduation ceremony serves to instill in the graduates a sense of belonging to a community—a community from which they have become estranged during their years of study—and reminds the graduates of their responsibilities toward that community.

To examine in greater detail the function of rites of passage as value reinforcers, consider the Mardudjara Aborigines of western Australia (Tonkinson 1978). Mardudjara males must pass through a series of rites in order to achieve adult status and to become acquainted with the major teachings of the religion that permeates their lives. The first male initiation occurs when boys are young adolescents; it involves the piercing of the nasal septum. Several years later the most significant and elaborate, that of circumcision, takes place. Over a period of six to eight weeks the initiate is kept in seclusion from females and from noninitiated males, is not allowed to speak, and is considered symbolically dead. During his silent "death," the initiate is exposed to dances, myths, and sites of religious significance. After the circumcision ceremony, ideally performed by two mother's brothers, the initiate remains in seclusion until his penis has healed, at which time he is reborn and resumes his life among the living.

A year after circumcision, young men undergo another ritual: subincision, which entails cutting the penis lengthwise. The initiates are again secluded and taught more of the intricacies of Mardudjara religion. With completion of this rite, a youth achieves full manhood, the right to participate in sacred affairs, and the right to marry. Over the next decade young men progress through a series of additional initiation stages associated with religion. Their progress through these stages is dependent upon their reputation among older men, who expect younger men to provide them with meat, to participate willingly in activities, and to avoid causing trouble.

In addition to their functions as a means of religious instruction and as markers of a person's movement through the life cycle, these rites emphasize and reinforce the respect the Mardudjara give to males. The rites link the status of older males with religion, ensuring that disrespect shown to one's elders will also be interpreted as disrespect for the people's religious beliefs. Throughout the rites older men expect and are usually afforded absolute obedience and this attitude carries over into daily life. The rites also define and enforce the distinctions that exist in male-female relationships. Since females are excluded from participation in most aspects of these rites, the rites emphasize the separation of male and female roles, statuses, and labor characteristic of Mardudjara society. The rituals in effect function to convince males of their superior place in the scheme of things.

Education

Another important mode of socialization in most societies is *education*—systematic instruction or training. Through education individuals are given formal instruction concerning beliefs, ways of behaving, and the means of producing things according to the cultural traditions of their society. People are not simply taught history, reading, or weaving—they are given a distinct view about these things or a specific way to perform tasks. As Jules Henry has noted (1963: 32): "The function of education has never been to free the mind and the spirit of man, but to bind them." The history taught in American schools represents a distinctly if subtly American view of things, rather than providing the student with a completely unbiased account of past events. In describing the westward expansion of the United States, emphasis is typically placed upon the heroic deeds of explorers and pioneers, rather than upon Native American attempts to resist the seizure of their land or upon the acts of politicians and capitalists who promoted such expansion for personal gain and profit, regardless of human suffering.

Informal and Formal Education. In nonindustrial societies most educational instruction is given by example; learning results from observation and imitation of relatives, peers, and neighbors. Children see how adults perform tasks and how they behave. At first, children's imitation is in the form of play—making toy bows and arrows and shooting at insects or making mud pies. Play slowly disappears as children begin to take a more substantial role in community work. From an early age children accompany their parents on their daily round of activities, watching and then assisting until eventually they are able to perform required adult tasks on their own. Some education in small-scale societies is more formalized. This is especially true of more esoteric subjects such as magic, curing, and playing a musical instrument. Sometimes formal education is also of a more universal nature, as when all Mardudjara male children are isolated for weeks and given instruction about religious and legal traditions in preparation for initiation.

In large-scale societies formal education tends to be more pervasive. Individuals are instructed formally in a wider range of topics and they spend more time in specialized institutional settings, or schools. This is not necessarily because there is more to learn; rather, it reflects a shift of emphasis in the way people are taught and who is responsible for their instruction. In most large-scale societies some governmental authority or large institution such as the church assumes a primary role in education, resulting in a loss of instructional autonomy at the family and community level. In such situations education functions not simply to provide instruction, but also to promote homogeneity and a sense of identification with the state that supersedes more local and personal loyalties. The aim is to promote a common national culture.

Since the Second World War, the governments of many newly independent states have also placed considerable stress upon formal education. Such education is used to provide technical skills perceived to be necessary to lessen dependence on foreign technicians and to promote a basis for economic development. Since many of these states contain peoples from very different cultural backgrounds, schools are also used to promote a sense of nationalism and to reduce cultural differences.

Education for Economic Advancement. For individuals in underdeveloped countries and for poorer citizens of wealthier industrial states, education may be an avenue to desired economic rewards and higher social status. Even in very poor countries the potential social and economic rewards available to the educated can be substantial, the alternative being extreme poverty. In Nigeria, as in many Third World countries, those in administrative or "white collar" positions are affluent in contrast to the impoverished majority, and they lead lives similar to those of their counterparts in Western industrial nations. Education is a key to this affluence. As the principal character in Nigerian Chinua Achebe's novel *No Longer at Ease* notes:

A university degree was the philosopher's stone. It transformed a third-class clerk on one hundred and fifty a year into a senior civil servant on five hundred and seventy, with car and luxuriously furnished quarters at nominal rent. And the disparity in salary and amenities did not tell even half the story. To occupy a "European post" was second only to actually being a European. It raised a man from the masses to the elite whose small talk at cocktail parties was: "How's the car behaving?" [Achebe 1960: 91]

Desirable administrative posts in countries like Nigeria are scarce, however, and available only to those with substantial education. The cost of this education is considerable (see Lloyd 1974: 92–98). Tuition and board for a year at grammar school can easily amount to more than the yearly earnings of most Nigerians. Nevertheless, the potential rewards of education prompt many parents to devote all their available resources to their children's education. Education beyond the primary level is even more expensive, and scholarships are hard to come by. In some instances entire communities will pool their incomes to support a student, hoping they will be rewarded when their native son or daughter lands an influential position.

Education's Effect on Traditional Values. Western-style education frequently conflicts with the traditional values of non-Western peoples, and the benefits of such education in some instances may not be sufficient to override the costs. At the university level, education patterned on Western models often maintains a subtle dependency of emerging nations on industrial powers by creating an elite whose values are oriented toward those of Europeans and North Americans and who share more culturally with these peoples than with their native people. Such education often leads people to view the indigenous segments of their society with disdain as uncivilized barbarians, rather than as people with whom they share a common bond. Western-style education may also have undesirable effects at the primary level. In a study of education in the Cook Islands, Nancy and Theodore Graves (1978) found that Western-style teaching designed to promote individualism and competitiveness resulted in a loss of group commitment and cooperation among islanders. This situation has undermined the ability of the people to withstand the detrimental effects of their relative poverty and isolation through cooperation and a sense of communalism.

Western education in societies with non-Western cultural traditions often promotes sociocultural marginality—that is, it leads students to become disenchanted with their traditional culture while not fully integrating them into the new, leaving them marginal to both the old and the new way of life. Until recently, it was common practice in many parts of Western Australia for missionaries or government authorities to take Aboriginal children away from their parents and place them in schools run by Christian missionaries. The children were encouraged to reject their cultural heritage and to adopt the views of the missionaries. Almost no attempt was made to adapt the curriculum to the cultural needs of the Aboriginal children, and formal education, with its emphasis on memorization, began relatively late, after an early childhood spent in a different pattern of teaching. As a result the children performed poorly and learned little that was of use to them in either a white or Aboriginal context. Because of their education, many children lost their attachment to their traditional Aboriginal culture. Since they did not fit into white culture either, the result was a group of people with little commitment to any cultural tradition— they became people "in between" (Sackett 1978: 39–40).

The shortcomings of Western-style education in non-Western settings has become apparent in recent years, and the model itself has come under attack even within the countries where it originated. Educational reformers have sought to develop alternative approaches that better fulfill the needs of particular populations. We now know that promoting aggressiveness and competition is not a necessary part of learning even in our own society, much less on relatively isolated Pacific islands. Reform requires an understanding of traditional local educational systems. It also requires a thorough knowledge of the people being educated, and of their needs. Anthropologists, with their holistic perspective and their focus upon the integration of sociocultural factors, are seeking to provide analyses of this sort.

Socialization in Later Life

The period up to adulthood is by far the most important time for the enculturation of values and the formation of an individual's personality. But socialization does not stop at this point. Three patterns of socialization are of particular significance in later life: the reinforcement of values associated with one's society, learning how to adjust to new phases in the life cycle, and learning how to adapt to changes in one's environment.

Reinforcement of Values. During our early, formative years we are socialized to accept the core values and views of our society; pressure to do so continues throughout the remainder of our lives. To a degree, ordered social life requires that this be the case. The values and attitudes that predominate in any society represent only a small selection of the choices possible.

Therefore, the possibility of people's changing their minds and adopting different values and attitudes is always present. To reduce the chances that this will happen, a person's adherence to these views and values is reinforced in a number of ways.

One means of reinforcing core values and views is through public gatherings in which the members of a society are subjected to the desired messages as a group. Group sharing of the experience makes the individual concretely aware of being a part of society. Among Australian Aborigines periodic gatherings for religious ceremonies are the most important means of reminding individuals of the dominant values of their society. In these dramatic representations of mythical events, the members of the society as a group are made to feel as if they are a part of the mythical events through which the world was created. Public gatherings in our own society serve similar purposes. In Fourth of July celebrations or presidential inaugurations, hundreds of thousands of people join in a celebration of American patriotism.

People's adherence to prescribed values and views is reinforced in many ways. In our daily interaction with those around us, public values and attitudes are constantly brought up through gossip, debate, and friendly banter. In most societies today, continual reinforcement comes from without as well, through newspapers, magazines, radio, and television. The news reports that we receive, the fashion articles that we read, the music that we listen to all channel our perceptions and, not infrequently, reinforce the dominant values of our society. Through the media in our society we are pressured to consume, compete, and get ahead, and encouraged to view our own behavior as the most rational possible. The media in our country do allow room for individual interpretation and selection, but there are also pressures toward conformity.

Adjusting to Life-Cycle Changes. As we ma-

A pilgrimage is a traditional way to reinforce dominant religious values. Here men and women, segregated into separate groups during the long San Juan pilgrimage, carry their banners past a school in San Miguel de Allende in central Mexico.

ture we must adjust to new phases in the life cycle, coming to terms with new roles and physical changes. Sometimes these changes are small ones, as in the case of a person receiving a minor promotion in a company. In other instances the changes may be considerable, as when a person retires from a job that has been the focal point of his or her life for forty years. The greater the change the more one will have to adjust and the more one will have to learn.

Adjusting to new statuses and learning new roles are characteristically different in small- and large-scale societies. In most small-scale societies the range of roles and statuses available are relatively limited and fairly well known. There is room for individual choice, but the basic guidelines are pretty well established by tradition. Among the Mardudjara Aborigines, for example, everyone is expected to marry and have children. There are fairly rigid rules for determining potential spouses, and the prospective bride and groom probably have known each other for years by the time they actually marry. Learning how to behave in their new role is rela-

tively simple, for they have been able to observe in considerable detail the interaction of married couples in the camp as they grew up. Family and other kin are also likely to give them a great deal of advice about how to behave. And because of the public nature of life in the camp, their behavior will be subject to continual scrutiny and comment by other members of the community.

In almost all small-scale societies the range of *role models* (fictional or actual persons whose activities provide an ideal for role performance) that influences a person's behavior is limited: one's own parents, perhaps a good hunter or warrior, and maybe a few mythical figures. In large-scale societies, the range of statuses and roles is much greater. True, chances are that the life of a Bolivian tin miner's son will be little different than his father's. But particularly for those of the middle and upper classes, there is more potential for variation than in small-scale societies. In our own society a substantial minority do not get married, and many of those who do marry do not have children. The posi-

Advertisers have been quick to recognize Joe Namath's potential as a role model; if the former football star endorses a product, then it should be good, shouldn't it?

tion of parents is a poor indicator of what their children's lives will be like except for very general features. That a person is an accountant who married his childhood sweetheart and lives in a well-appointed suburb where he plays golf or tennis on the weekend tells us little about the lives of his children once they leave home. Chances are that his children will lead lives roughly similar to his own or that of his wife, but they are likely to pursue other occupations and some of them may lead very different lives.

Although some of the socialization for new statuses and roles in large-scale societies is carried out by parents or kin, much of it is not. Specialists like teachers and professional counselors assume an active role in socialization because labor is highly specialized and because there is considerable variation between generations. If one's father was a welder or chef, there is not much advice he can give his son or daughter about adjusting to life as a lawyer. Literacy also changes things, for one can turn to written sources for assistance. Furthermore, role models include not only those with whom one is acquainted, but also a wide assortment of celebrities and public figures, to say nothing of

fictional characters. For these reasons, socialization to changing roles in large-scale societies tends to be much less personal than in small-scale societies.

Adjusting to Environmental Changes. In addition to trying to adjust to the more predictable changes that accompany growing older, we must also come to terms with changes in our world. For those born in relatively isolated, small-scale societies, integration into the world beyond can be quite traumatic. Sometimes the trauma is so great that people cannot adjust. Many of those who have perished as a result of contact with Western civilization did not die from disease or murder, but from loss of the will to live in a world that is too different from the one they have known and that provides them little scope for a meaningful life. Under such circumstances age is often an important consideration, for the younger members of a society are usually better able to adjust to drastic changes.

Adapting to changes in the world around us can be hard even for those brought up in a Western cultural tradition, especially for older people who have formed fairly rigid ideas about what the future holds. Most people in a society like ours do adjust, however, albeit grudgingly, partly because we are socialized to expect and to some extent even to desire change. Our flexibility is also made possible by our reliance upon a relatively wide range of impersonal socializing devices. Socialization based upon the personal experiences of parents and a few other individuals is restrictive and not very useful to dealing with completely new circumstances. By being able to draw upon the experiences of a much greater range of people through books, counselors, or media-inspired role models, people in large-scale societies are often able to rely upon sources of assistance that are more relevant to their changing needs.

Deviants

The members of all societies have standards for judging appropriate behavior. They possess views about what constitutes an ideal person—an ideal expressed in their role models—and a normal person. The normal person usually is not expected to live up to the ideal. In fact, to do so can lead to censure—"Who does she think she is, acting so prim and proper?" Those who are judged to be normal are simply expected to behave in ways generally deemed acceptable and to hold views that are not considered too strange or threatening. Normal people are allowed a few peculiarities and occasional slips, but there are limits. Behavior or thought that goes beyond these limits is considered deviant and those who think or act in ways that are too far from the norm, especially if they do so with some consistency, are considered *deviants*.

Identifying Deviants

Anthropologists are primarily concerned with how the members of a society as a group reach and maintain a consensus about deviance. Definitions of deviance vary a great deal from one society to the next. A person labeled crazy in our society might be considered gifted or normal in another. In our society if you catch someone trying to cheat you and become angry, you are behaving normally, provided your anger does not lead you to act in too violent a manner. To Semai or Inuit, such a response would be a deviant one.

Which acts or statements are considered highly deviant can vary a lot from one society to the next. In our own society, proclaiming yourself a witch may be considered a bit odd, but so long as you otherwise live in accordance with social norms and do not engage in recognized illegal acts you will not be considered a deviant. In a society where belief in witchcraft is more widespread and witches are held responsible for many social ills, such a proclamation is virtually the same as admitting to mass murder.

All cultural traditions contain room for rationalizing occasional improprieties. For example, although the Semai consider violence abnormal, many took an active part in the British campaign against Communist insurgents in the 1950s. The Semai justified their action by attributing it to temporary insanity, to "blood drunkenness." In this way they avoided labeling themselves as deviants and upheld the Semai view that violence is wrong. Acts or beliefs that are felt to be extreme violations of what is considered normal (in our society, a brutal and calculated murder) may automatically cause one to be labeled a deviant.

How members of a society define deviance reflects their collective experience over generations and their adaptational strategy. Semai or Inuit consider violent individuals to be deviant because they are threats to an adaptational strategy that stresses harmonious social relations. Early childhood socialization fosters the transmission of these perceptions of deviance over generations. These learned attitudes toward deviance are reinforced in later life by the actions and statements of others with similar views. Experiences that result in frustration and insecurity may also shape attitudes toward deviance, for the deviant acts of others are often seen as related to one's own problems. To a Mayan Indian, frustration in hunting or in courting a member of the opposite sex is likely to be related to the work of a sorcerer. In our own society we are likely to blame bums, hoodlums, anarchists, and drug pushers for our problems.

Because of their relative homogeneity, members of small-scale societies tend to exhibit a high degree of consensus in regard to deviance. Most Mardudjara have the same view regarding which acts and individuals are deviant. There is usually a good deal less consensus in large-scale societies because of the greater diversity of socialization patterns, individual experiences, and goals. For instance, while some members of American society consider it deviant to drink anything alcoholic, the majority do not.

Groups too can be singled out as deviant. With small-scale societies such a designation is usually reserved for communities or groups other than one's own. The members of a certain kin group or community may be seen as "a gang of cutthroats and cheats" or "a den of thieves." More heterogeneous large-scale societies commonly contain groups that are designated as deviant. Throughout much of Europe gypsies are seen as such a group, as are motorcycle gangs like the Hell's Angels in the United States.

Definitions of deviance and attitudes toward deviants are not static. Social changes can have an important influence. During the Cold War hysteria of the 1950s many people in the United States considered anyone who might be labeled a Communist a deviant who threatened the social order. Interest in Communists waned in the 1960s and Americans turned their attention to other deviants who were more relevant to problems people considered foremost in their lives—rapists, robbers, welfare cheats. Changes in defining deviance can also result from attempts by particular members of a society to gain wider acceptance for their views, as in the efforts of homosexuals to liberate themselves from deviant stereotyping.

The Deviant's View

So far we have been discussing how people identify others as deviant. But what about the deviants themselves? Do they see themselves as deviants, as normal people, or as unjustly censured members of society? While there are people who consider themselves to be witches, often those accused of witchcraft do not agree with their accusers. The same is true of many people designated crazy in our own society.

That a person does not believe himself or herself to be a witch or to be crazy does not imply that he or she does not believe that such people exist. People may agree with a society's general view of deviants, but be unwilling to identify themselves as deviant. Many middle-class persons in our own society who engage in acts that are generally held to be deviant, such as stealing or smuggling, do not consider themselves criminals. This is in part because they have a stereotyped vision of the "criminal type" who is a very different sort of person than they are. A similar situation exists with groups considered to be deviant. Members of the Ku Klux Klan certainly do not consider the group to be deviant. In fact, they feel that it functions to uphold the fundamental values of American society.

Many deviants accept the general consensus regarding their status, however. This is not surprising, since deviants take their cues about how to identify deviants from the same cultural tra-

In their efforts to liberate themselves from the stereotype of deviants, lesbians march in a gay rights parade. A more open attitude toward homosexuality has marked several films of the 1980s, such as *Personal Best*, which portrayed two women who became friends, lovers, and competitors for the Olympics.

clined to act on a group basis in accordance with their cultural values, which emphasize group behavior and group loyalty. Even the characteristics that make people seem so deviant are largely products of the wider cultural tradition. Deviants may exaggerate certain values, as in the case of the patriotism of the Ku Klux Klan, or they may seek to demonstrate their rejection of values, as with the studied gross dress and behavior of the Hell's Angels. In either case, such deviance only makes sense within the broader social and cultural context. The Hell's Angels are reacting against and the Minutemen are exaggerating the values of a particular society.

Within the wider society, deviants often form distinct groups or subcommunities with their own adaptational strategies, values, and methods of organization. In a study of delinquency among lower-class boys in the United States, Albert Cohen (1955) looked at delinquents as members of peer groups. He found that much of the delinquents' behavior could be explained by reference to their striving for success in terms of group values. These values included doing malicious damage to persons and property, harassing police and neighborhoods, and circumventing school authorities. Cohen argued that these values were an expression of resentment against a society in which it was impossible for the youths to achieve success according to normal standards. The subcommunities of which deviants are a part are not always made up entirely of recognized deviants. To study prison society, for example, we must look at the prison staff and at numerous judicial authorities in addition to the prisoners themselves.

As individuals become members of deviant groups or subcommunities they become socialized to a new set of values and expectations. Those sent to prison for the first time must undergo a process of socialization as they adjust to prison life. This can involve a considerable

dition as do others; should their acts justify their being seen as deviants they are likely to agree with the label. Billy the Kid was quite aware of his deviant status, just as the Hell's Angels are of theirs. In fact, some people may gain some satisfaction from being labeled deviant.

In many ways, deviants are products and still members of the wider society and are influenced by its cultural traditions. In California jails, the black prisoners exhibit a high degree of individuality in keeping with the hustler image prevalent in lower-class ghetto culture, while the Mexican-American prisoners are more in-change, especially if the prisoner comes from a segment of society in which imprisonment is uncommon. Such an adjustment may only be a temporary one, as with "white-collar" criminals who can be expected to resume their normal life upon release from prison. On the other hand, it may result in a more fundamental transition. Some inmates of prisons and psychiatric hospitals become so thoroughly socialized to the ways of the institution that they subsequently find it impossible to adapt to life on the outside. Those who undergo such thorough transformations are likely to remain deviants unless some other drastic change in their circumstances forces or encourages them to move in another direction.

Summary

Members of different societies learn to view themselves and their world in different ways. The basic cultural orientation of the members of a society is called their world view. A society's world view is linked with its adaptational strategy and its environment. Similar economic circumstances produce roughly similar world views, as exemplified in Lewis's culture of poverty. In very general terms, it is possible to divide world views into primitive and civilized: the former view things in largely personal terms, the latter in a more impersonal fashion. In addition to general world views, within any cultural tradition it is possible to isolate core values that are fundamental in providing shape and meaning to people's lives.

On the individual's level, culturally learned attitudes are expressed in the personality. Its unconscious part includes a set of core values; its conscious part includes one's self-concept. Although each personality is unique, it is possible to generalize about the general trend of personalities in particular societies. Some anthropologists have therefore described personality types, such as those that are tradition oriented, inner oriented, and other oriented. In seeking to describe the average personality of the members of a society anthropologists use the concept of the modal personality, the central tendencies of the personality characteristics of members of a society.

World view, values, and personality develop throughout the life cycle by way of the socialization process. Socialization differs considerably from one society to the next; even the life cycle is divided and defined differently in societies. However childhood is defined, socialization during this early period is critical in forming an individual's personality. Transitional periods in the life cycle are often marked by rites of passage, which may ease a person's move into the next stage of life and may be used to reinforce cultural values.

Education is another significant mode of socialization in most societies. In small-scale, nonindustrial societies education is largely a matter of observation and imitation, with little specialized instruction being given. In large-scale societies education is conducted on a more formal basis in specialized institutional settings. Since the Second World War in particular, Western-style education has spread throughout the world. This has had important consequences for the nations concerned—some good and some not so good. Even after formal education ends, socialization continues in later life. The culture's values are reinforced and the person continually learns how to adjust to life-cycle and environmental changes.

Although these processes tend to shape people who conform to the group world view, values, and personality, there is always some deviance from these patterns. How members of a society define deviance is largely a product of their collective experience over generations and of their adaptational strategy. Those identified as deviants may or may not define themselves as deviant, but they are clearly still members and products of their society.

In chapters 7 through 9 we looked at the primary components of society and in this chapter we have examined how individuals become a part of society. These chapters were essentially concerned with showing how a society is put together. In the following three chapters we will shift our attention toward the forces which threaten to pull society apart and look at how these threats are dealt with. We begin in chapter 11 with ethnicity and social stratification.

Suggested Readings

General:

Barnouw, Victor. 1973. *Culture and personality.* Homewood, IL: Dorsey Press.

Berry, John W. 1976. *Human ecology and cognitive style.* New York: Wiley.

Honigmann, John J. 1967. *Personality and culture.* New York: Harper & Row.

Hsu, Francis L. K., ed. 1972. *Psychological anthropology.* Cambridge, MA: Schenkman.

Hunt, Robert, ed. 1976. *Personalities and cultures.* Austin: University of Texas Press.

LeVine, Robert A., ed. 1974. *Culture and personality.* Chicago: Aldine.

Mayer, Philip, ed. 1970. *Socialization: The approach from social anthropology.* London: Tavistock Publications.

Wallace, Anthony F. C. 1970. *Culture and personality.* New York: Random House.

Williams, Thomas R., ed. 1975. *Psychological anthropology.* The Hague/Paris: Mouton.

Case studies:

Briggs, Jean L. 1970. *Never in anger: Portrait of an Eskimo family.* Cambridge, MA: Harvard University Press.

Dentan, Robert N. 1968. *The Semai: A non-violent people of Malaya.* New York: Holt, Rinehart and Winston.

DuBois, Cora. 1944. *The people of Alor: A social-psychological study of an East Indian island.* Minneapolis: University of Minnesota Press.

Gillin, John. 1951. *The culture of security in San Carlos: A study of a Guatemalan community of Indians and Ladinos.* New Orleans: Middle American Research Institute.

Howard, Alan. 1970. *Learning to be a Rotuman: Enculturation in the South Pacific.* New York: Teachers College Press.

Kearney, Michael. 1972. *The winds of Ixtepeji: World view and society in a Zapotec town.* New York: Holt, Rinehart and Winston.

Levy, Robert I. 1973. *Tahitians: Mind and experience in the Society Islands.* Chicago: University of Chicago Press.

Mead, Margaret. 1928. *Coming of age in Samoa.* New York: Morrow.

Modiano, Nancy. 1973. *Indian education in the Chiapas highlands.* New York: Holt, Rinehart and Winston.

Whiting, B. B., and J. W. 1974. *Children of six cultures: A psycho-cultural analysis.* Cambridge, MA: Harvard University Press.

Focus on People

Formal Education in Southern Belize

Monte Tidwell

In the spring of 1981, Monte Tidwell traveled to southern Belize to study rural education in a small Central American country. He lived with the villagers of Pueblo Viejo gathering data to assess whether national educational policies took into account the needs of the Kekchi- and Mopan-speaking Mayan Indians of the village. Tidwell currently works with Pueblo to People, an organization devoted to increasing the informational and economic links between base-level groups in Central America and the United States.

THE SMALL COUNTRY of Belize, which only recently became fully independent from Great Britain, is on the Caribbean shores of the Central American mainland. It is a union of several diverse ethnic groups: the Creole, persons of largely African and some white extraction; the Garifuna or Black Caribs, who have settled along the southern coast; Spanish-speaking Mestizos; the Mayan Indians, of which there are three main groupings; and small but significant enclaves of Chinese, East Indians, Syrians, and Lebanese. One of the overriding concerns of government planners has been the integration of Belize's ethnically diverse groups into national institutional structures. They also see mobilization of the population in support of national goals as necessary for social and economic advancement. A large part of the task of promoting the ideals and values of nationalism and modernity rests with the educational system.

In the spring of 1981, I set out to assess the effectiveness of formal education as an agent for sociocultural change among the Kekchi- and Mopan-speaking Mayan Indians of southern Belize. For most of my time in the field, I resided in the relatively isolated village of Pueblo Viejo where a study of political change had been carried out by another anthropologist in 1972. My reasons for choosing this village were simple: (1) I could benefit from the previously gathered ethnographic material and focus more closely on the role of education in the village; and (2) I could more easily determine the types and degrees of changes that had occurred since the earlier study. I spent time in other Indian villages as well to gather comparative data.

Primary schools are now found in almost all the villages and are often the only visible link between a village and the rest of the nation. Primary education is compulsory for children between the ages of six and fourteen. Although it has become an accepted part of childhood, formal schooling is still treated as an essentially alien cultural institution in most villages. The teachers themselves are almost all from different cultural backgrounds, the vast majority of them being Garifuna.

Different perceptions of formal education are held by the various actors in the educational process. For the administrators, in general, education is seen as a means to help integrate the Indian population into the wider society and to modernize their view of the world. Numerous

Reading in front of the one-room school in Santa Elena, southern Belize. These children had come across books they had not seen before, and, after school had been let out, they eagerly looked through them.

times, however, administrators and teachers told me that the Indians have no desire to learn and that they do not really value education. They often lamented that the Indian children do not seem to care whether or not they pass their annual advancement exams but rather seem to just be "doing time" until they can leave school and start their own *milpa* (farm plot). As one teacher said:

Attitudes in the home hinder them because most of them are not looking into the future. They don't want to change. The most important thing to them is learning to earn a living in the milpa. *Many boys miss school regularly. They know they can reap rice and get some money in their pockets. That's all they want.*

Thus, the Indians are blamed for their lack of interest in school and progress, reinforcing the stereotype of them as uncivilized and backward people. They are seldom perceived as people who rationally assess the usefulness of education in terms of their own culture and the economic opportunities of the region.

The perceptions of formal education held by Indian parents reflect their evaluations of the utility and relevance of such education. Attitudes, of course, vary within and among villages. One parent who obviously has a strongly negative evaluation of education stated:

School can't put you nowhere. . . . What school

could give you if you go every day in school? It don't give you no kind of things like if you could buy your pants, if you could buy your shoes, if you could buy this in school. You don't get that. You have to work in the milpa. Then you could make your little money.

Another younger Indian man, also a parent, holds a more positive view of education:

When I notice myself, I don't know anything. I don't know how to write, I don't know how to read good, I don't know how to spell good. . . . Right now sometimes I worry because I want to be like some of the men [who] are educated men. Like in P. G. [Punta Gorda, the district capital] I see them and they have a good time. Whatever they do, I can't do it. . . . Up to now I realize that schooling is so much better.

Most Kekchi/Mopan parents *do* value a primary education, but not for the reasons that most Belizeans do. They believe it is essential for their children to learn a little English and a little math, usually relating both these skills to the increasing necessity of dealing with non-Indians. A primary education is often perceived of in this sense, almost as a defense against the outside world. It is not viewed by most as a means to modernize or alter their life style, but more as a means to protect it. In this context, passing an advancement exam loses its importance. The Kekchi/Mopan, for the most part, see their land and their traditional farming skills—not education—as their ultimate security. When asked whether a primary education was more important than what children learned at home, one man replied:

To me, it's the both. Both. The school and the farming I want them to learn in school, but suppose he did good in school and by the time he quit school he doesn't want to work in the bush. All what he have in his mind is education.

. . . That's all he have in his mind because by the time he is in school you don't show him how to farm in your farm. He don't know how to plant rice, he don't know how to plant beans, he don't know how to reap corn, and all what he know only education. So to me it's the both—both sides. Education and the farming.

Too much emphasis on education is sometimes perceived as being potentially detrimental to making a living. While a primary education is seen as being somewhat useful by the Kekchi/Mopan, high school or college is generally seen as being almost useless. A Kekchi man comments on those few Indians who have attended high school in the district capital:

Most of them don't want to do anything. That's all they have—education in their mind. But sometimes they can't get their job, like working in an office, and they have to stay without—without a job. And there is many jobs to do in the farming which they could do. But the only thing they have in their mind—they only don't want to work on the farm. . . . When they don't find no job to do they usually go and look for job like with the company that work with the banana, like in the Coke factory, like the factory in Belize [City] the flour mill. That's all they do for their living. Some of them they can't build their own house like we build the house on Saturday. They don't know how to start the house. . . . Only what they really want is a job like sitting down every day just waiting for their pay without working hard.

Whereas in most contexts, education confers status on an individual, in a Kekchi/Mopan village, a person with a high-school education is often given a negative appraisal. A complaint that came up regularly in one village involved the actions of a villager who had been to high school and his relationship with the *alcalde*, the leading village official:

It's only how he act in the village. Like when the alcalde *tells him such a thing he take it like nothing to him. He take care of himself but the only thing what he have is just a wicked mind. He don't pay no attention to what the* alcalde *tries to do in the village. He want to come over the* alcalde. *He doesn't respect the* alcalde. *Only because he is educated. He want to show that he know better than other. That's all he have in his mind. . . . He will try to humbug the* alcalde. *Maybe he will try to write a letter to the D.O. [District Officer] which is bad news for the* alcalde. *. . . He doesn't want to help the village. He wants everything for himself.*

The number of Indian children attending high school has grown over the years, and about 90 percent of them become teachers in the villages for a while. It would seem that Indian teachers would function better in the village schools, and they sometimes do, but there are problems. The main problem is that Indian teachers are much more approachable than Garifuna, Creole, or East Indian teachers, and are thus much more vulnerable to community pressure. Added to this is the opinion of some community members that it is not a good thing for an Indian to behave in nontraditional ways, i.e., not to be a farmer:

According to how I see, if we have an Indian teacher here, the people don't put good for the teacher because he's an Indian teacher. Because the Indian teacher have different ways than the black people. They [the parents] think hard to go and disturb the black people. But the Indians like me now, if they have a chance they can go and do what they like to an Indian teacher because they are just like them. And

they could go and talk all kinds of badness to the Indian teacher because they know he's an Indian just like them. So they take too much chance on their own people. But the black man, like the teacher here now, they don't take that chance.

The first thing they will start to do if we get an Indian teacher here . . . is say that that teacher is no good, he doesn't have no children so why is it he has to go and punish our children in school. It's the same thing with an [Indian] woman teacher. They might say, "Why is this woman lashing our children?"

Another complaint about Indian teachers is that the children will not learn English from them:

Some of our parents they don't like the teacher like that [being Indian] because when they are teaching in school they want to use that language [Kekchi or Mopan] and this is bad. Because the children already know that. It is their own language. They are sending them there to learn how to talk English good.

Even though Indian teachers may face these problems, there are an increasing number who seem to be able to cope with them. Teaching in the villages is one of the few occupational alternatives to farming that is open to Indians; and it seems inevitable that the number of Indian teachers will grow. Although many of them eventually go back into traditional roles, they will most certainly have an impact on the educational process. Whether or not this effect will be beneficial to the inevitable integration of the Indian population into the wider society remains to be seen.

Chapter Eleven

Ethnicity and Social Stratification

The Ballardong say that some remote tribes to the eastward are cannibals, and that they mark children at their birth who are eventually to be eaten. . . . I am convinced, however, that little dependence can be placed on stories of this sort respecting cannibalism; what we positively know being that most tribes practised it more or less, and that nearly all stoutly deny the fact, and accuse their neighbours of it.

So reported police constable David E. Hackett about the Aborigines in York, in Western Australia, in the late nineteenth century (in Curr 1886–87:1:342–43). None of the Ballardong had ever actually seen anyone eaten, but they were prepared to believe anything about their eastern neighbors that cast them in a bad light. The Ballardong had no empirical evidence that their neighbors were cannibals, basing their beliefs instead on misinterpretation of the purpose of circumcision (for the York people did not circumcise, a practice which of course has nothing to do with cannibalism). But the Ballardong's unfounded beliefs served to reinforce cultural differences between themselves and Aborigines living to the east and supported a feeling of group identity among the Ballardong by helping them to define themselves as distinct from others. Such beliefs in a we-they distinction are central

to *ethnicity:* people's behavior and beliefs which are related to perceived cultural differences.

Hackett's statement reveals not only the Ballardong's prejudices, but also the prejudices of white Australians toward Aborigines. His remark about Aboriginal cannibalism is based no more on observation than was that of the Ballardong. Most white Australians during the nineteenth century were certain that Aborigines did eat each other. European settlers simply assumed that the practice of cannibalism was a feature of most savage societies; the claims fit with their commonly held stereotypes and proof was by and large not thought necessary. Such beliefs helped white settlers to justify their maltreatment and displacement of Aborigines.

In this chapter we will look at two closely related dimensions of sociocultural differentiation: ethnicity and social stratification. A wide range of factors is involved in these ways of differentiating people, for ethnicity and social stratification influence and are influenced by almost all aspects of our lives. Like other aspects of the human condition, ethnicity and social stratification are dynamic processes that continually adapt to ever-changing environmental conditions.

Ethnicity

One of the major ways of drawing we-they distinctions is the concept of *ethnicity:* lumping people into groups on the basis of selected cultural or physical characteristics. Ideas about ethnic groupings involve concepts of race, perceived ethnic identity, ethnic symbols, and relations among ethnic groups.

The Concept of Race

Categorization of humans according to physical or racial characteristics appears among very early human societies. Prehistoric cave paintings in various parts of the world and decorations on

OVERLEAF

A rambling estate home, Osterville, Cape Cod. The same number of acres covered by this single New England estate often serves to house hundreds of people in one urban apartment building.

ancient Egyptian tombs refer to people of different racial origin. Anthropologists have discovered that peoples often make distinctions between groups according to presumed biological differences. Usually one's own type is considered normal—the Yanomamo call themselves "true men," the Aboriginal inhabitants of southwestern Australia refer to themselves as "the people"—in distinction to all others. The concept of *race*, or categorization according to physical traits, is virtually universal, as is the belief that the features chosen for purposes of categorization parallel differences in behavior.

As European civilization spread across the globe, race became the subject of systematic, scientific enquiry. It became an important issue as Europeans encountered people who differed so markedly from themselves as to raise doubts about their humanness. From the great variety of observable physical differences, Europeans developed universal classifications. Karl von Linné (1758-59) divided all humanity into four races: white, yellow, Negro, and Indian. In colonized areas where there was concern over the products of miscegenation, or mixing of these presumed races, racial categorizations became more complex. The Spanish carried such racial classification to an extreme in their American colonies. Magnus Mörner (1967: 58) provides a list of categories from eighteenth-century Mexico:

1. Spaniard and Indian beget mestizo
2. Mestizo and Spanish woman beget castizo
3. Castizo woman and Spaniard beget Spaniard
4. Spanish woman and Negro beget mulatto
5. Spaniard and mulatto woman beget morisco
6. Morisco woman and Spaniard beget albino
7. Spaniard and albino woman beget torna atrás
8. Indian and torna atrás woman beget lobo
9. Lobo and Indian woman beget zambaigo

10. Zambaigo and Indian woman beget cambujo
11. Cambujo and mulatto woman beget albarazado
12. Albarazado and mulatto woman beget barcino
13. Barcino and mulatto woman beget coyote
14. Coyote woman and Indian beget chamiso
15. Chamiso woman and mestizo beget coyote mestizo
16. Coyote mestizo and mulatto woman beget ahí te estás

Such classifications were often used to determine the political and economic statuses of peoples. David Hume (1748) stated that since Negroes were the only race not to have developed a major civilization (an idea since proven false), they were probably "naturally inferior to Whites." Even today many people think that humanity is divided into a small number of distinct races and that their differences reflect social and intellectual as well as physiological differences. When this attitude includes the belief that one's own "race" is superior to the others, it is known as *racism*.

Race as a biological concept has come under considerable attack in recent years. Today, few scholars can be found who will agree on any general racial classification. For many the concept has proven to be too vague to be of any use. No basic biological differences have been found among contemporary races, and race appears to be equally insignificant as a determinant of behavior in a biological sense. This is not to say that race is not important—as a sociocultural phenomenon it continues to be significant. But rather than trying to discover how people's race, in the biological sense, guides their behavior, anthropologists now focus upon how ideas about racial differences influence behavior and seek to explain why people continue to attach so much significance to such things as skin color and hair texture.

"No,no, me not honky...me Tarzan!"

What anthropologists have found is that race stands as a symbol for nonbiological differences—a reflection of cultural differences, different religious beliefs, and economic inequality and exploitation. As Brazilian anthropologist Verena Martinez-Alier (1974:6) has noted, "Strains and tensions in society that may be the result of a variety of factors are often justified and rationalized in terms of racial distinctions."

Ethnic Identity

Not too many years ago social scientists commonly believed that racism and ethnicity were rapidly disappearing throughout the world. They felt that race and ethnicity were ceasing to be significant issues in Western industrial nations and that they would soon be irrelevant in other nations as they became more urbanized and industrialized. In both industrial and industrializing nations, predictions of the demise of racism and ethnicity have been incorrect. If anything, ethnicity has undergone a period of revitalization. Even groups that were once thought to have lost their sense of ethnic identity are once again proclaiming their pride in

being members of distinct ethnic groups with their own cultural traditions.

The persistence of ethnicity is in many ways tied to the process of identity formation. From the earliest period of our socialization humans learn to value certain aspects of the cultural traditions of their society. We acquire what may be called *primordial*, or original, *attachments* to a particular way of life, and in the process learn to value that way of life more than other ways. In other words, we become ethnocentric.

Although our original ethnic identity rarely ceases to be significant, changes in our social situations may alter the nature and meaning of our ethnicity. While our ethnic identity may be rooted in early childhood socialization and in the perceived cultural traditions of our society, the significance of this identity at any given time will for the most part reflect current situations. The resurgence of Welsh and Scotts ethnicity in Great Britain, as exemplified in the formation of regional political movements, is not simply a reflection of primordial attachments to cultural traditions. Such attachments are important, of course, but the current ethnic militancy in these areas primarily reflects a reaction to socioeconomic conditions, perceived exploitation, and the requisites of political mobilization. Wales and Scotland have served as virtual colonies of England, particularly as sources of raw materials such as coal and oil. By emphasizing their cultural distinctiveness from the English, Welsh and Scotts activists have sought to mobilize political support in their bid to end the English exploitation they perceive.

Ethnic identification arises through experiences with other people—and often these are people of a different "group" who impose their own ideas about ethnic categories. Some of this

imposition of ethnic labels occurs in informal interaction; sometimes more formal processes are at work. Australian Aborigines did not see themselves as Aborigines until they were treated as a single ethnic group by their European conquerors. In Toronto, the government and most non-Italians lump persons of Italian heritage under the label of Italian. The Italians themselves do not recognize such a designation—"they see each other as Venetians, Sicilians, Calabrese, and so on" (Giuliano 1976: 4). One Indian tribe on the northwest coast, the Makah, was created about 1870 by the United States government from an aggregation of formerly autonomous villages (Colson 1953). In such situations it may take time before the

Ethnic identity remains important even in modern industrial societies. Here Scottish-Americans, suitably attired, arrive in Edinburgh for an international clan gathering.

people begin to apply these imposed categories to themselves; if there is no pressure to do so, they may never adopt them.

Ethnic Symbols

To lump others into ethnic groups—or to see oneself as part of an ethnic group—usually involves selection of particular aspects of a culture as characteristics defining ethnic identity (Mitchell 1956: 22). How people speak, what they eat, how they build their houses, what they wear—such traits, or presumed knowledge of such traits, are seen as markers identifying members of a "distinct" ethnic group. Often there will be a cluster of symbols, only some of which may be seen as absolutely essential for defining identity. Thus, while whites in the rural South of the United States may have some idea of the range of sociocultural patterns associated with being black, even if a black does not express these he or she will still be considered a black because of skin color—the essential definitional criterion selected.

The nature of these symbols may vary a great deal from one group to another and even among members of a single ethnic group. Not all southern whites have the same views about black ethnic identity, and their ideas will not correspond with the blacks' own views. Also, while poorer blacks may see some aspects of diet or behavior toward kin as part of being black, upwardly mobile blacks may not, wishing to identify more with the dominant white culture or to disassociate themselves with behavior they now consider beneath them. On the other hand, aspiring politicians seeking the black vote may consciously use some of these symbols, eating soul food or hiring black musicians to perform at public gatherings. Use of ethnic symbols depends upon a person's strategy in a particular situation.

The evolution of ethnic symbolism is related to the need to define ethnic groups in relation to one another. The process often becomes quite important as a result of progressive national integration: the incorporation of groups of people who at one time were relatively autonomous into an encompassing state structure. When the Kekchi and Mopan-speaking Maya Indians who today occupy the southern part of Belize (Howard 1980) moved into the area from Guatemala during the latter part of the nineteenth and the early twentieth centuries, they had little contact with members of other ethnic groups in Belize—Garifuna, Creoles, whites, Chinese, and others. Since World War II this situation has changed markedly, as the Kekchi and Mopan have been progressively integrated into the multiethnic Belizean society. As a result they have had to consciously define their ethnic identity—to develop a general, idealized picture of what it means to be a Mopan or Kekchi Indian. They have also developed conscious ideas about what it means to be a member of one of the other ethnic groups. These images, known as "basic value orientations" (Barth 1969:14), include the Indians' view of themselves as hard-working and honest in contrast with "lazy" Creoles and Garifuna and "crafty and dishonest" East Indians and Chinese. The idea also evolved among the Kekchi and Mopan that they should emphasize sociocultural homogeneity among themselves, playing down internal social and cultural differences.

Out of this general picture of what it is to be an Indian the Mopan and Kekchi have chosen specific symbols to characterize their identity. The symbols chosen are items, institutions, or practices that they perceive as central to their life-style and to the social fabric of their communities. Some of these are growing maize and black beans, practicing reciprocal labor exchange, wearing certain kinds of clothes, and eating certain foods. The thatched hut has emerged as a particularly important symbol of Indian identity, in contrast to the corrugated-metal-roofed houses of board or brick common among non-Indians. Construction of a thatched house involves reciprocal labor exchange and the use of local forest products. Corrugated-metal-roofed houses are built by paid (usually non-Indian) laborers and require the purchase of externally produced building materials. They are seen by many Indians as a means of flaunting one's wealth and social superiority. Indians who do build corrugated-metal-roofed houses are subject to adverse social pressures and stigmatized by other Indians.

Given the rapid changes that have occurred in southern Belize in recent years, it can be expected that the symbols employed by the Indians will change. Dress now almost never serves as an ethnic marker, for the men no longer wear distinctive clothing and fewer and fewer women can afford the traditional wardrobe. This process of developing symbols to fit with contemporary conditions is a feature of ethnicity in most settings—in searching for symbols of their distinctiveness, people pick from their past what suits them best today.

Ethnic Relations

Ethnic identity is primarily a product of interaction among members of social groups that perceive themselves to be different. While it may be of little importance on a day-to-day basis for members of small-scale societies who rarely interact with members of other societies, for those living in large-scale societies it is often much more significant. Especially in urban areas, a person is likely to encounter people of different ethnic identities while traveling to and from work, working, shopping, and watching television. Whether we-they distinctions arise depends on factors which promote either *boundary maintenance* (the process by which ethnic distinctiveness is maintained) or *assimilation* (the process by which distinctions between ethnic groups are eliminated). These include marriage patterns, patterns of occupational spe-

cialization, demographic characteristics, and politics.

Marriage Patterns. Marriage within an ethnic group tends to be an important factor in maintaining ethnic boundaries because it enhances group homogeneity (and hence indirectly group distinctiveness). In contrast, marriage across ethnic boundaries *may* promote assimilation. Faced with a shortage of women in the 1960s, the Tapirapé of central Brazil began to intermarry with the neighboring Carajá. This situation has been a major factor in speeding up the loss of a distinctive culture by the Tapirapé (Shapiro 1968:26). Young Tapirapé males who marry Carajá women form important social bonds with their Carajá in-laws by joining them as commercial fishermen and ceasing to live as Tapirapé agriculturists. Both Tapirapé and Carajá nevertheless remain part of an encompassing ethnic category—Indian—which distinguishes them from non-Indians. And rather than assimilating one group into the ethnic patterns of another, marriage between members of different ethnic groups may lead to the creation of new ethnic groups. The list of ethnic categories in colonial Mexico (see p. 259) indicates the range of identities that can be generated from only a few initial groups, in that case Spanish, Indians, and Africans (categories themselves representing a synthesis of an earlier plethora of ethnic divisions).

Occupational Specialization or Competition. Within multiethnic settings occupational specialization is often a common feature of ethnic groups, playing a significant role in the maintenance of ethnic distinctiveness. Although this specialization may promote interdependency between ethnic groups, relations between the groups are not necessarily harmonious or egalitarian. The nomadic Baluchi pastoralists of southern Iran and Pakistan tend to dominate social and economic relationships with other ethnic groups who share the same territory. For instance, many non-Baluchi who specialize in farming do so as share-croppers on land owned by the Baluchi. Others are forced by the Baluchi to pay tribute for protection.

Different ethnic groups may compete for jobs. Especially when people from rural areas move to the city, they often seek assistance from members of their ethnic group rather than competing on their own. The central figure in Nigerian novelist Chinua Achebe's *No Longer at Ease* is supported while in school in England and assisted in getting a job upon his return home by members of a voluntary association of fellow tribesmen who have emigrated to the capital city. In studying Monrovia, Liberia, Fraenkel (1964) notes how voluntary "tribal" associations function to exploit and maintain a monopoly over particular occupations.

Demography. *Demography,* or population characteristics, may also be an important factor influencing the nature of ethnic relations. Rapid population growth among members of a particular group may put pressure on them to expand their place in a society at the expense of another group. Conversely, a group's rapid loss of population may invite others to exploit a perceived advantage. Greater numbers do not always mean greater power, however. Very tense situations may be created when small ethnic minorities are able to dominate the politics and economics of an area at the expense of much larger groups, as in South Africa. On the other hand, when larger groups do gain economic and political ascendancy they may feel little compunction about oppressing ethnic minorities when their interests and those of the smaller groups are in conflict. Ethnic minorities that lack political power often have little recourse other than to seek external support or play upon the moral conscience of those in power.

Politics. Ethnic relations are both affected by, and affect, political activities. To the extent that people's use of ethnicity is related to their desire to gain or to maximize their position, eth-

nicity may be seen as an inherently political phenomenon. Lapps selecting which language to employ in multiethnic settings and ethnic associations in Monrovia seeking to monopolize occupations are at least indirectly acting politically. The political role of ethnicity is often even more direct; in many settings ethnicity is central to political dialogue. As Robert Norton (1973–74: 313) has noted in relation to ethnic aspects of politics in Fiji, ethnicity provides a general focal point for political solidarity, transcending individual differences. While other factors such as class may replace ethnicity as a focal point of political competition in some settings, ethnicity assumes prime political importance in many countries.

In South Africa, for example, during the early part of this century the Afrikaaner minority (descendants of early Dutch settlers) found themselves becoming progressively poorer in relation to members of other ethnic groups. They sought to reverse this trend by implementing racist policies aimed at curtailing the rights of nonwhites. In particular they sought to restrict land ownership and to relegate nonwhites to the role of inexpensive servile laborers. By 1948, through an alliance with other white South Africans, the Afrikaaners assumed control of the government. Through the 1950 Suppression of Communism Act, supported by a wide spectrum of the population during a wave of anticommunist hysteria, they suppressed any organization or individual opposed to them or their policies. They also began to enforce their apartheid policies of ethnic separation and domination. Their political success was translated into greater economic prosperity for them. The nonwhite South Africans who suffered from these changes were unable to successfully oppose them because of the relative unity and power of the white minority and because of their own internal divisions.

Social Stratification

As the South African example illustrates, ethnicity can be closely linked to economic and political inequality. The Afrikaaners used ethnicity as a means of attaining power and of defining the relative socioeconomic statuses of groups of people, assigning nonwhites lower statuses then whites. Ethnicity is not the only basis for inequality in South Africa, however, and even among whites there is a great deal of inequality in terms of wealth and power. Virtually all societies have developed some degree of inequality among their people through the process of *social stratification*—the division of members of a society into *strata* (or levels) with unequal wealth, prestige, and power.

Stratification and Adaptive Strategy

The pattern of stratification found in a society is related to its prevailing economic system, for stratification is based upon relative control of production and the ability to appropriate surplus. For example, during the early part of this century people in an area of southern Morocco were divided into three primary strata: the pastoral Ait 'Atta, various specialists (tinkers, merchants, priests, etc.), and farmers or serfs. The Ait 'Atta were the politically and economically dominant stratum because they owned herds of sheep and goats, and often extracted rent from the serfs, the poorest and least powerful group, to the extent of four-fifths of the crop. The specialists occupied a middle position because they were able to sell their services in exchange for a portion of the surplus wealth of the pastoralists and serfs (Coon 1958: 211–14).

Increasing social scale, productive capacity, and specialization of labor tend to increase the potential for stratification. In small-scale foraging and farming societies there is little specialization and a relatively small surplus to appropriate. Accordingly, differences in wealth and power in these societies are minimal. On the other hand, more intensive forms of agriculture and industrial production, and attendant increases in social scale and division of labor, result in far more potential for inequality.

Beliefs Supporting Stratification

Systems of social stratification are accompanied by beliefs that obscure or legitimate inequality. These beliefs maintain the existing system of stratification by drawing attention away from threatening areas and emphasizing common bonds, at least among those members of a society whose support is required. Widespread adherence to democratic and egalitarian myths in the United States and the Soviet Union, for example, helps to obscure the existence and allow for the survival of a ruling class—a small, integrated group of people who wield enormous power over the actions and even the thoughts of the other members of their society. In other societies, differences may be declared legitimate by the will of God, innate ability, or some other rationale. Louis XIV of France said he ruled by the will of God; the Nazis sought to rule on the basis of their proclaimed innate superiority. In feudal societies, those above view the world as hierarchically ordered and may consider themselves part of a "natural" aristocracy; peasants tend to accept their extreme inequality and exploitation as part of the natural order of things.

Ideologies supporting systems of stratification are also linked to notions of exchange. In all societies those who have less wealth and power are taught to think that they are getting something in return that justifies existing differences. Aboriginal women give up the surplus food they gather to men, who in turn perform rituals to ensure the survival of the world. The serf in medieval Europe gave a large part of his crop to his lord for protection. Citizens of the United States pay taxes in return for a wide range of services.

Conflict vs. Stability

The potential for conflict exists in all stratified systems. So long as there is a feeling among the different groups that the exchange is fair and so long as belief in the prevailing supportive ideology is maintained, however, a degree of stability is possible. If a particular group becomes dissatisfied with the arrangement, it may seek to change things. The likelihood of this happening in small-scale societies is minimal; inequalities are not so glaring as in large-scale societies, pressures to conform are strong, and few alternative views are available. The differences between strata in large-scale societies are much greater and tensions are more pronounced. Also, increased heterogeneity in experience, socialization patterns, and the range of views available to those in large-scale societies increases the likelihood of conflict. While fundamental changes in systems of stratification in large-scale societies are rare, existing tensions are often expressed in the form of riots, protests, and rebellions.

Adherence to an existing system of stratification is linked to the stability of a people's overall adaptation. Should the fundamental features of their adaptation begin to change, the traditional system of stratification will be undermined in all likelihood. The rise of the world system, the industrial revolution, increased population, and a number of other factors combined in the late eighteenth and early nineteenth centuries to create pressures that led to the destruction of the aristocratic hierarchy in Europe, replacing it with a system of stratification linked to capitalist production. Thus, as adaptational and economic patterns evolve, so do the ways in which the members of a society are stratified.

Systems of Stratification

Although stratification is found in all societies, its manifestations differ not only in degree but also in kind. In egalitarian societies, stratification is minimal. In nonegalitarian societies, people differ in wealth, prestige, and power according to a system of hierarchical ranking, caste, feudalism, or class.

Egalitarian Societies. The least stratified of societies are known as *egalitarian*, for people tend to treat each other as equals. Many foraging and small-scale agricultural societies are relatively egalitarian. Wealth differences are few, as is the amount of power available to any individual or group. The people possess norms that emphasize sharing and ideals of interpersonal equality. This is not to say that social stratification is nonexistent in these societies. Although the pre-twentieth century Copper Eskimo of northwestern Canada emphasized equality, they were not blind to the existence of differences. There were those who were respected on the basis of personal qualities, there were the *ataniq* who organized hunts, and there were shamans, who were sometimes feared because of their ties to the gods (Damas 1972). The Mardudjara-speaking Aborigines of Australia are stratified according to sex and age, and individuals can attain high status as curers or "lawmen." In comparison with nonegalitarian societies, however, stratification in these societies is relatively insignificant.

The egalitarian nature of small-scale societies is frequently undermined by contact with more hierarchically inclined societies. As a result of contact with Indian society, the Bihors (foragers of the Chota Nagpur plateau of central India) have come to possess an array of officials—headmen, priests, curers, conveners of meetings, and so forth—all of whom occupy higher positions than other members of their society (Sinha 1972). Often this transformation from egalitarian to nonegalitarian reflects the needs of

Eskimo shaman in Point Hope, Alaska, chants a song
for good luck in hunting whales. The bones in the
background are whale rib bones; the drum is made
from seal skin. Though part of an egalitarian society,
shamans are accorded more respect than others
because of their connections with the gods.

colonial authorities. In southwestern Australia white settlers created offices among the Aborigines to ease administration of these conquered people: they created "kings" and gave them brass plaques to wear around their necks. But even when these new statuses are created the majority of people may adhere to their egalitarian ideal and consider the newly created elite lacking in legitimacy.

The egalitarian ideal does not necessarily disappear with the appearance of large-scale societies. A degree of social and economic equality may be maintained within segments of the larger society. The egalitarian norm tends to be most pronounced among those occupying the lower socioeconomic strata of large-scale societies—peasants, factory workers, and pastoral laborers. Among peasants, egalitarian beliefs manifest themselves in what has been termed the "image of the limited good" (Foster 1965). Proponents of this view hold that a limited amount of wealth is available; by gaining more than one's share of this wealth one is depriving someone else. Peasant villagers stress that public behavior and appearance should not highlight differences among themselves: people should live in houses that look roughly alike, they should wear similar clothing, they should not own or purchase items that emphasize their wealth. This is not to say that all peasants within a village will in fact have equal resources or be of the same social status. Those who do have more, however, are expected to share their surplus with others, for which they will gain the acclaim of their neighbors.

Since the eighteenth century ideological traditions have developed in a number of industrial societies proclaiming as their goal the creation of social equality: various forms of communist, socialist, anarchist, and utopian thought. These ideas have naturally gained greatest support among those who have not done well in the existing economic order. Wherever these ideas have been put into practice—in communes, cities, or nations—inequality has continued to exist, although usually not in the same form or to the same degree as before. This gap between practice and theory has failed to dissuade many who still see the theories or ideologies as goals and not as statements about current conditions.

Rank Societies. In contrast to egalitarian societies, many societies divide people into hierarchically ordered groups that differ in status, and perhaps occupation and wealth. Often this hierarchy is fatalistically accepted by the lower as well as the upper groups, as being part of the natural order of things.

One such system is *ranking*: people differ in prestige according to a series of graded ranks. In ancient Panama (Helms 1976), for instance, there were high chiefs who ruled a number of villages. The high chiefs were shown a great deal of respect, traveled by litter, had the sole right to wear many fine ornaments, possessed large and well-provisioned households, and were given elaborate funerals that included the sacrifice of servants. Below the high chief were other members of the elite, or highest rank: aristocrats born to high status who served as administrators, warriors who served under the aristocrats controlling villages, and a lesser group of commoners who achieved social advancement for their own lifetime only on the basis of prowess in battle. Under the elite stratum was another stratum of commoners, primarily farmers who provided services for those above them—fishing for the elite, planting their crops, fighting for them, and building their houses. The lowest stratum was comprised of slaves, captives of war who served the elite.

In a rank society, those of higher rank tend to be wealthier, to live in better houses, and generally to lead a more comfortable life than those of lower status who provide them with goods and services. In exchange for this support members of the higher stratum provide public services, and sometimes are expected to redistribute some of their wealth through feasts and religious ceremonies.

Kinship tends to be an important criterion in determining status in rank societies. Individuals generally are born into a particular stratum, and there are often ranked kin groups. Upward mobility is sometimes possible, however, for individuals who show exceptional aptitude in warfare or religion. Religion, too, often plays an important role in rank societies: priests become members of the elite and those having elite status justify their special positions on the basis of religion.

Historically the formation of rank societies was associated with intensification of productivity by farming communities and exceptionally affluent foragers, such as the Kwakiutl of western Canada. This increased productive capability allowed for greater specialization and increased organizational complexity. These societies were also characterized by relatively dense populations. Rank societies consisted of confederations or a number of centrally administered villages and, accordingly, can be associated with the transition from small-scale societies to large-scale ones. The development of rank societies was often stimulated by contact and trade with larger societies. The Minangkabau of northern Sumatra, for example, came under the influence of a large trading empire centered in southern Sumatra, resulting in the creation of a nobility whose power and wealth was based on control of extensive regional and overseas trade in gold, spices, cloth, and forest produce (Kahn 1980).

European colonial expansion destroyed many rank societies. During the sixteenth-century the Spanish conquerors dislodged the members of many rank societies in Latin America from their native habitats and pushed them into marginal lands where it was impossible to support large populations or specialized artisans, priests, warriors, and nobles (Steward 1947). In western Panama inhabitants who were not killed by the Spaniards or by introduced diseases fled into the mountains. Eastern Panama was out of the way of the main thrust of Spanish conquest and colonization and the indigenous people, the San Blas Cuna, were able to remain and adjust more gradually. What remained in most cases were societies of simple farmers whose production was primarily for home consumption, and who exhibited little in the way of political and economic inequality or labor specialization.

The creation of the modern world system has not destroyed all systems of stratification based upon rank. In some parts of the world traditional systems of rank remain a significant part of contemporary patterns of stratification. The survival of rank systems generally has depended initially upon the degree to which they were deemed useful or nonthreatening to colonial administrators and subsequently upon the ability of the ranking system to perform useful functions for the people of newly independent nations.

Before the arrival of Europeans Pacific island societies possessed a variety of ranking systems. Ponape, for example, was divided into several independent states, each with its own supreme head and lesser grades of aristocrats with royal and local titles. Today, despite extensive social, political, and economic changes, the traditional hierarchical system remains a vital part of Ponapean life (Hughes 1982). Although the traditional ranking system has no formal place within the political system introduced by the American colonial administration after World War II, holders of traditional titles exercise a great deal of influence. Many of the rights and responsibilities associated with traditional titles continue to be recognized, such as the obligation by certain title holders to give yearly feasts. There remains among Ponapeans a strong and explicit appreciation of the Ponapean "way of life," and the ideas and activities associated with titles are intimately linked with this way of life. The system has also survived because of its

This photograph of a Ponapé chief and commoner was taken during an expedition in 1899–1900. Many of the rights and responsibilities that accompanied the traditional hierarchical system of Ponapé Island continue to be significant today.

flexibility. Leading Ponapean title holders have awarded new, lesser titles to prominent businessmen, church leaders, and politicians, ensuring that these people too have a stake in maintaining the system.

Caste Societies. Whereas strata in a rank society are differentiated by prestige—which may be earned during one's lifetime—in some large-scale, nonindustrial societies individuals are divided at birth into one of a number of occupationally specific hierarchically ordered statuses, or *castes*. Historically, caste systems can be viewed as elaborations of rank systems.

Perhaps the most comprehensive and striking example of a caste system is the one found in India. In fact, some anthropologists claim that India has the only true caste system (Dumont 1970). The Indian caste system appears to have evolved first in northern India more than two thousand years ago out of a blending of the indigenous Harappan civilization of chiefdoms unified by a priesthood and the nomadic Aryan tribes that invaded northwestern India around

1500 B.C. Hindu religion and culture and the related caste system developed out of the mixing of these two peoples.

Hindu religious belief provides a basis for the ordering and ranking of castes. It divides society into four categories of caste, called *varna*, on the basis of occupation. The *varna* are ranked according to their relative ritual purity—the extent to which their members are considered in a sacred sense to be clean or unclean. The highest *varna* is occupied by Brahmins, priests, and scholars, who are held to be the purest. Below the Brahmins in descending order of status and purity are the Kshatriyas, or warrior castes; the Vaisha, or merchant castes; and the Shudras, or menial workers and artisans. There is a fifth group occupying a position below the four *varna*, the untouchable caste, whose members perform work held to be polluting, such as cleaning toilets. According to Hindu belief, the *varna* into which a person is born reflects the quality of his or her actions in a previous life.

Hindu beliefs also provide a specific guide for

This Brahmin woman, a teacher of dance in
Bombay, specializes in Bharat Natyam, the temple
dance of South India. Though her family's apartment is small, her musicians stay with her; they have
to sleep on the balcony, where she usually discusses
dance matters with them.

the behavior of caste members. Higher-caste persons will not accept many foods or drinks from the polluted hands of those belonging to lower castes. Likewise, traditionally there were proscriptions against their having sexual relations with or marrying members of lower castes. Higher-caste members are also expected to avoid consuming polluting substances like meat and alcohol. While members of all castes are expected to try to live up to many of the Hindu ideals of behavior, those belonging to higher castes are expected to come closest to ideal behavior.

Traditionally castes have functioned within rather narrow localities—a village or at most a few linked villages (Kolenda 1978:40). Within this setting the population will be divided into a series of a few exclusive castes to twenty or more, ranked according to their place within the *varna* hierarchy. Each local caste forms a closed exogamous descent group with an occupational specialization that it offers in exchange for the products or services of other castes. Each caste group usually lives in its own quarter; untouchables live either on the fringes of a village or in a separate hamlet altogether. Usually a dominant family or caste controls the arable land and monopolizes the use of physical force.

In North India relations between higher and lower castes often take the form of *jajmani* relationships—patron-client relationships between families of different castes. The *jajmani* system serves as a primary means of economic exchange within village settings, both reflecting and helping to maintain the relative inequality of castes. In a major form of exchange, members of the dominant castes give grain in exchange for services from families with whom they have established a *jajmani* relationship.

The caste system is often presented as highly static, as an unchanging structure in which a person's status and occupation are determined at birth. This picture is not entirely valid. During the past few decades in particular the caste

system has undergone a great deal of change. Urbanization, industrialization, and political reforms have undermined the ascriptive nature of Indian society. Since 1948 the Indian government has sought to destroy inequalities resulting from the caste system, seeking especially to end discriminatory practices toward lower castes. New employment opportunities in the industrial and service sectors and increased education have served to undermine caste-imposed limits on economic advancement. As members of localized castes have come into contact with one another in cities and towns and in new occupations new castes have emerged—supercastes that fuse or incorporate the more specialized, local castes. The cooperative nature of inter-caste relations is also breaking down as those belonging to the lower castes have become less willing to accept their unequal status and wealth. As a result of these processes, while caste remains an important feature of Indian life, it has come to occupy a less central place as a determinant of social inequality.

Feudal Societies. Various agrarian societies have evolved systems of social stratification which can loosely be termed *feudal*. There are two primary strata of people within feudal societies—those who work the land, and those who support themselves by appropriating some of the produce and labor of the agricultural laborers. In medieval Europe members of these strata were often referred to as serfs and lords respectively. The lord provided military protection and in general served as a patron for the serf, or vassal. In return the vassal was expected to provide the lord with a variety of services and a substantial amount of his agricultural product. There is some degree of reciprocity involved in the lord-vassal relationship, in that each had specified rights and duties regarding the other. But the relationship is clearly not balanced—the lord got the better of the arrangement.

Feudalism develops out of particular circum-

Feudal society in Europe. Knights and their ladies hunt and cavort while their serfs till the fields (fifteenth-century drawing).

stances: the breakdown or lack of centralized authority within larger sociopolitical units. In western Europe the feudal system developed out of the chaos that ensued after the death of the emperor Charlemagne (768–814). In Latin America it took hold where Spanish colonial authority or postindependent governments proved unable to exert strong influence. Feudal societies are prone to petty warfare, and it is partly out of a desire to secure protection that relations between lord and vassal arose, for lords provided military protection to the farming population and assumed the rights of government.

The *hacienda* exemplifies feudalism in Latin America. In highland Peru, where this feudal system continues to be significant, there are three classes of persons: the landlord, or *hacendado*; the tenant-workers, called *colonos*; and the administrators or foremen hired by the *hacendado* (Long 1975: 268). While the *hacendado* has legal control of the land, it is the *colono* who works most of it. The *colono* pays for the use of the land in labor—working on the *hacendado*'s land, working as a servant in his house, and periodically clearing roads and water channels and carrying out repairs around the hacienda. These services usually leave the *colono* only enough time to satisfy his basic subsistence requirements. In addition to providing the colono with a small plot of land the *hacendado* is expected to give small amounts of money for the work done on the hacienda, provide alcohol and cigarettes for those involved in collective work parties, provide pasturage for the workers' animals and firewood for cooking, and feed people working on the hacienda.

Peruvian feudalism, and feudalism in general in the contemporary world, differs in a number of ways from feudalism as it existed in Europe. Rather than existing as a relatively isolated entity, a feudal system today is very much a part of the world system. As André Gunder Frank (1972) has pointed out, feudal societies today provide a larger part of their product to external markets than was the case in the past. This has meant that what is produced by these societies and the value that is placed upon products has come to depend more on external market conditions than upon local needs.

This integration of feudal systems into the modern world system has provided for the potential undoing of feudalism by presenting both lord and vassal with options. For the lord, for example, there is the option of mechanized agriculture, of relying upon machines and a few wage laborers rather than a large number of subservient vassals. For the vassal there is the chance to move to the city, or there are revolts and land seizures to break the hierarchical system. The role of state governments has also been a factor, as most governments in recent years have taken a more active role in affairs influencing areas under feudal structures. In the past when the state in Peru, for example, exercised any influence over feudal areas, it was to support the *hacendado* (for instance, by sending troops to quell periodic revolts). In recent years the Peruvian government has at times supported the workers through land reform, or it has sought to exert greater government control over the productive structure by replacing the *hacendados* with an administrative elite loyal to the central government (see Zaldívar 1974).

Modern Class-based Societies. The devel-

opment and spread of Western industrial capitalism has given rise to a fourth system of social stratification, a hierarchy of distinct social groups known as *social classes*. Classes can be associated with life-style or income, but primarily they are defined in relation to the means of production, by their role in the organization of industrial labor.

Modern classes developed in response to the growth of industrial production as a result of distinctions between those who owned the factories and machines and those who provided the labor to operate them. The spread of modern social classes as a basis for stratification has accompanied the diffusion of industrial production from western Europe and North America to the rest of the world during the past two centuries. As it has been diffused, social class has gradually replaced or encompassed other forms of stratification.

Rather than wealth per se membership in a class is determined by the means by which people acquire wealth. In a capitalist industrial society there are two *primary* classes: those who sell their productive labor in return for a wage, and those who own the means of production. Included in the first class are workers engaged in the production of agricultural and industrial goods, the *proletariat*—factory workers, farm laborers, and the like. Also included are those whose labor is concerned with the movement or distribution of what is produced. This group includes such occupations as clerical worker, truck driver, and stevedore. The second primary class, the *capitalist*, is made up of those who are concerned with the appropriation of what is produced and control of the circulation of what is appropriated.

While in general terms members of the capitalist class are wealthier than those of the wage-earning class, this is not always the case, and wealth differences within classes can be considerable. The wealth of wage earners is determined in part by how much they are paid for their labor. Their pay is influenced by a number of factors: how much their work is considered to be worth by members of the capitalist class, the relative demand for their particular type of work, and the political power of the workers as a result of unionization, lobbying, and such. Highly skilled laborers are usually paid much more than semiskilled or unskilled laborers. Workers in countries where labor is abundant and political rights of workers are few tend to be paid much less than workers in comparable jobs in countries where labor is not so abundant or where workers have more political power.

Striking coal miners confront Jay Rockefeller, Governor of West Virginia.

Textile workers in many parts of Asia and Latin America, for example, may be paid as little as twenty dollars a week, while in the United States their weekly pay may be more than two hundred dollars.

The wealth of capitalists comes principally from the profit they are able to derive, the difference between what goods cost to produce and what they can be sold for. For this reason many capitalists find it preferable to operate factories in countries where wages are low and where other costs such as taxes can be minimized. The actual wealth of individual capitalists depends on the success they have in finding and controlling sources of profit. Some capital-

ists may be completely unsuccessful in their search for profit and others may be able to find only small sources. In contrast, the wealthiest capitalists control enormous sources of profit. The Rockefeller family, for example, controls probably the largest corporate empire in the world. With wealth based upon ownership of a large percentage of the oil industry (through the $59 billion Standard Oil Trust), they have gained control of over $280 billion worth of corporations, employing more than four million people (see Collier and Horowitz 1976; Andreas 1974).

In a class-based society, class consciousness tends to be limited to the awareness of class membership and of the structure of class relations. Many class-based societies are imbued with egalitarian ideals that draw attention away from the structure of stratification. Persons belonging to one of the two primary classes do not always see themselves as members of a distinct class. They may view themselves as individual actors competing with those around them to "make it": as being rugged individualists or entrepreneurs. Or they may view themselves as belonging to a specialized segment of society having few common interests with other segments. Those holding the latter view see society as a collection of numerous discrete groupings—doctors, lawyers, electricians, bankers, etc. While there is an element of truth in such views, they ignore the fundamental principle of class stratification: control of the means of production.

Ambiguity is especially pronounced among wage earners who are not engaged in primary production: secretaries, factory foremen, teachers, policemen, and so forth. Members of this group commonly see themselves as part of a middle class. This separation into a class apart from those engaged in primary production is often based upon an assumption that those of the middle class earn more than other wage earners. While this is sometimes the case, quite commonly it is not. In the United States, for ex-

ample, many factory workers earn as much (or as little) as secretaries or teachers. Expectations or rules regarding appropriate dress can be another contributing factor—office workers are expected to dress more formally than those on the shop floor and therefore see themselves as being somewhat above factory workers. Perceived or actual cultural or ethnic differences among members of the same class also minimize unity.

Consciousness of class membership evolves through the perception of common interests. In labor union movements, those engaged in primary production have come to see themselves as having a wide range of common interests or problems. But those not engaged in primary production, such as foremen and secretaries, tend to have different interests and different allegiances. They may view themselves as being better off allied to those with the greatest power. In the United States these are the capitalists.

Both capitalists and wage earners may seem to benefit from these cross-class alliances. In many societies the power of wealthy capitalists is enhanced through alliances with wage earners in government. In Florida, for example, the state government actively supports the interests of the large corporations that control the citrus industry, providing them with legal, administrative, and technical assistance to increase their profitability. For the wage earners, the basis for such alliances is primarily economic: rewards go to those who best serve the interests of the capitalist class. In many Third World countries the most significant alliance is between the capitalist class and the military. In return for creating optimal conditions for corporate profit (for instance, by stifling labor unrest), the military in such countries as Brazil, Paraguay, and El Salvador has been rewarded in the form of wages, better living conditions, and military equipment.

Relations between the two primary classes are by their very nature competitive, however. The competitive nature of class relations establishes much of the dynamic of social relations in large-scale societies as various segments within the class structure seek to gain or maintain power. An early manifestation of this antagonism was the Russian Revolution of 1917—a revolt of peasants, laborers, and others against the aristocracy and capitalist class. One of the outcomes of such a revolution is that the state assumes control of the means of production. Rather than being owned by individuals, facto-ries come to be owned by the government. In countries where such a transformation has occurred, a new elite has tended to emerge. It is comprised of technicians and administrators who are able to wield the most influence in government on the basis of public service, political savvy, or technical expertise. Boundaries of strata in a class-based society are not only ambiguous; they are also in constant flux as a reflection of changes in the society's political and economic structure.

Summary

Ethnicity and social stratification are two major ways in which humans divide themselves into we-they groupings. Ethnicity is a complex of ideas about race, perceptions of ethnic identity, ethnic symbols, and relations between ethnic groups. Although the idea that observed physical differences such as skin color are biologically related to different ways of behaving is now largely discounted by scientists, it is still an important influence on people's perceptions of racial "groups." Consciousness of ethnic identity—of belonging to some physically and/or culturally distinct group—has not disappeared either, and is in fact resurging in some areas. Often this sense of ethnic identity is expressed through selected symbols.

Ethnic awareness arises through interaction of groups that perceive themselves to be different, a situation most common in large-scale societies. Factors that determine whether boundaries will be maintained or distinctions eliminated include marriage patterns, occupational competition or specialization by ethnic groups, demographic features, and politics.

Social stratification, though sometimes linked to ethnic distinctions, is a somewhat different way of classifying people. In stratification, people are divided into broad categories with unequal wealth, prestige, and power. Such divisions are legitimized by a society's beliefs, but may change if the society's fundamental adaptation changes.

Stratification differs in degree and kind from one society to another. The least stratified of societies are called egalitarian. In ranked societies, people are divided into strata that differ in prestige. In societies with caste systems, people are born into occupationally specific, hierarchically ordered statuses. Feudal societies divide people into two primary strata—those who work the land and those who appropriate their labor but provide certain services. Class-based societies have evolved industrial distinctions between wage earners and those who own the means of production.

Suggested Readings ———————————————

General studies of ethnicity:

Banton, Michael. 1967. *Race relations.* London: Tavistock Publications.

Barth, Frederick, ed. 1969. *Ethnic groups and boundaries.* Bergen/Oslo: Universtetsforlaget.

Bennett, John W., ed. 1975. *The new ethnicity.* St. Paul/New York: West Publishing Company.

Cohen, Abner, ed. 1974. *Urban ethnicity.* London: Tavistock Publications.

Despres, Leo, ed. 1975. *Ethnicity and resource competition in plural societies.* The Hague/Paris: Mouton.

Epstein, A. L. 1978. *Ethos and identity: Three studies in ethnicity.* London: Tavistock Publications.

Fried, Morton H. 1975. *The notion of tribe.* Menlo Park, CA: Cummings.

Holloman, Regina E., and Arutiunov, Serghi A., eds. 1978. *Perspectives on ethnicity.* The Hague/Paris: Mouton.

Sanbacka, C., ed. 1977. *Cultural imperialism and cultural identity.* Helsinki: Finnish Anthropological Society.

Case studies on ethnicity:

Blu, Karen I. 1980. *The Lumbee problem: The Making of an American Indian people.* Cambridge: Cambridge University Press.

Eidheim, Harald. 1971. *Aspects of the Lappish minority situation.* Bergen/Oslo: Universtetsforlaget.

Henry, Frances, ed. 1976. *Ethnicity in the Americas.* The Hague/Paris: Mouton.

Madsen, William. 1973. *The Mexican-Americans of south Texas* 2d ed. New York: Holt, Rinehart and Winston.

McFee, Malcolm. 1972. *Modern Blackfeet: Montanans on a reservation.* New York: Holt, Rinehart and Winston.

van den Berghe, Pierre L., and Primov, George P. 1977. *Inequality in the Peruvian Andes: Class and ethnicity in Cuzco.* Columbia, MO: University of Missouri Press.

Warren, Kay B. 1978. *The symbolism of subordination: Indian identity in a Guatemalan town.* Austin: University of Texas Press.

General studies on social stratification:

Berreman, Gerald D., and Zaretsky, Kathleen M., eds. 1981. *Social Inequality: Comparative and developmental approaches.* New York: Academic Press.

Beteille, Andre. 1977. *Inequality among men.* Oxford: Blackwell.

Sanday, Peggy R. 1981. *Female power and male dominance: On the origins of sexual inequality.* Cambridge: Cambridge University Press.

Stavenhagen, Rodolfo. 1975. *Social classes in agrarian societies.* New York: Doubleday/Anchor.

Case studies on social stratification:

Finney, Ben R. 1973. *Polynesian peasants and proletarians.* Cambridge, MA: Schenkman.

Gilmore, David D. 1980. *The people of the plain: Class and community in lower Andalusia.* New York: Columbia University Press. (Spain)

Goldman, Irving, 1970. *Ancient Polynesian society.* Chicago: University of Chicago Press.

Helms, Mary. 1979. *Ancient Panama: Chiefs in search of power.* Austin: University of Texas Press.

Kolenda, Pauline. 1978. *Caste in contemporary*

India: Beyond organic solidarity. Menlo Park, CA: Cummings.

Kuper, Hilda. 1963. *The Swazi: A South African kingdom.* New York: Holt, Rinehart and Winston.

Lloyd, P. C. 1974. *Power and independence: Urban Africans' perception of social inequality.* London: Routledge and Kegan Paul.

Middleton, John, and Tait, David, eds. 1958. *Tribes without rulers: Studies in African segmentary systems.* London: Routledge and Kegan Paul.

Moore, Sally Falk. 1958. *Power and property in Inca Peru.* New York: Columbia University Press.

Nash, June. 1979. *We eat the mines and the mines eat us: Dependency and Exploitation in Bolivian tin mines.* New York: Columbia University Press.

Chapter Twelve

Politics

I N ALL SOCIETIES there will be some competition for resources and some competition over ideas about how resources are to be acquired and used. In adapting to harsh environments, foragers like the Inuit or Mardudjara Aborigines emphasize cooperation in social relations and in the acquisition and distribution of goods. Despite their emphasis on noncompetitiveness, rivalries exist among these peoples, and competition for prestige, spouses, and the like does take place. At the other extreme, in a large-scale society like the United States competitiveness and aggressive social relations are a fundamental part of the adaptive strategy.

Competition is not limited to gaining actual possession of resources. It also involves striving to hold sway over the ideas of others concerning the manner in which things are distributed and the ways in which competition takes place. While there is relatively little disagreement over such matters among the members of most small-scale societies, in large-scale societies there are often many competing ideas and many groups or individuals seeking to assert their particular view. The ability to influence or control how people perceive things, how they behave, and how things are distributed involves having *power*, or the ability to act effectively over people or things. The competition for power is called *politics*.

Almost any action or statement may be political or may have political implications. Shaking hands with constituents or kissing a baby may signify nothing more than a wish to demonstrate friendship or affection, but when these actions are intended to influence power relations, they become political acts. Viewed from such a perspective, politics is a universal of social existence. But politics is not the same in all settings. Despite some underlying similarities, politics among Amazonian Indians, urban-dwelling Canadians, and Mexican farmers are very different. Different environments and cultural traditions produce dissimilar political goals and means of achieving these goals.

The Bases of Political Power

The struggle for power and the ability to wield power are central to politics. We say that parents have power over their children, that people have power over their pets, or that a government has power over people. What we mean is that they can influence what others do, that they can cause others to behave according to their own designs. The wishes and interests of those in power may coincide with those over whom they have power, creating an air of benevolence or irrelevancy. If a child acts in accordance with the will of his parents, it is largely irrelevant to him that they have the power to spank him. When a government places persons considered threatening to one's well-being in prison, one is likely to view this use of power in a good light. The ultimately coercive nature of power is thus often masked. The ability of those in power to coerce is not always hidden, however. When people contravene the wishes of those in power, force is often resorted to. The use of force will be considered in the next chapter. Here we will examine more subtle expressions of the struggle for power: authority, ideology, and political contests.

OVERLEAF

Dramatic political posters—like this one by Ben Shahn—have long been key vehicles for transmitting ideas in the struggle for power (1946; 73.4 × 98.5 cm, The Museum of Modern Art, New York, NY).

Authority

Power is often closely related to *authority*, the right to make a particular decision and to command obedience (Smith 1960: 18). The United States government has the right to pass a wide range of laws that control the lives of American citizens: it can tax them, it can even force them to fight others in the name of national interest. The United States government has the right to exercise power only in certain spheres and in certain ways, however. When its agents attempt to exercise power in areas where people feel they do not have the right or where they abuse their power, they are likely to encounter resentment and resistance. In this regard authority reflects the acceptable or tolerable bounds and content of power. What is acceptable or tolerable, though, is not simply a matter of voluntary consent on the part of the people of the United States, for the government controls sufficient resources in terms of personnel and wealth to allow it to actively influence what people perceive to be the scope of its authority. Any powerful group or institution will be restrained by the need to seek authority, while also being in a position to manipulate notions of authority.

Within any society there are likely to be distinct realms of authority. Talal Asad (1970) distinguishes two major realms among the Kababish Arabs of Sudan: the household and the

Political decision-making in Western industrial society: the Kansas State Legislature in session.

tribal. Power within the household sphere is held largely by the male household head on the basis of his role as husband, father, and manager of the family enterprise and his ability to control and use the household's animal property in a moral and effective manner. Power within the wider, tribal sphere is held by a *shaikh* and the lineage of which he is a member. The shaikh and his lineage gained authority by cultivating ties with the colonial and later national authorities who rewarded them with administrative posts. These posts allowed them to control access to and allocation of significant resources like water. The majority of Kababish feel that members of the shaikh's elite lineage are entitled to their authority to speak for the Kababish, to collect taxes, and to make other political decisions because they have the power to enforce their will. The elite themselves base their authority on historical precedent—in the past members of other kin groups pledged their allegiance to the shaikh in return for his protection—and on the legal rights associated with the offices they hold, preferring a more genteel rationalization for their place in Kababish society.

Realms of authority may be quite distinct, but often there are points of overlap. This is especially true in small-scale societies with a minimal division of labor where social roles and activities tend to overlap a great deal anyway. While Australian Aboriginal curers or medicine men are concerned primarily with healing and dealing with the supernatural, the status they derive from their activities carry over into many other aspects of life; they often possess an overall high status and an ability to influence people in many ways. Greater distinctiveness may be found in large-scale societies. Nonetheless, there may be significant points of overlap even between what are perceived to be relatively distinct realms. For example, in the United States, even though church and state are held to be distinct, each with its own particular realm of authority, the two are interrelated in many ways.

The state can interfere with religious practices considered inappropriate, as in peyote use among members of the Native American Church; likewise, religious leaders commonly take an active stand on political issues.

Ideas and Symbols

Politics are based not only on the wielding of authority but also on *political norms*—ideas about appropriate political goals and behavior. Through a process of political socialization people develop goals within a specific environment while also learning preferred means of achieving them. People may not actually adhere to these ideas in practice. For Aborigines living in the western Australian settlement of Wiluna,

one aspect of the traditional belief system is the notion that there should be no bosses. Ultimately, it is thought, all humans are equal in that they are all less than the Dreamtime-beings whose edicts they have to follow. Humans cannot make or change the law—it was established and laid down for all time in the creative epoch—so there is supposedly no need for leaders. Each person is aware of what must be done and also what should not be done. [Sackett 1978: 42]

Nevertheless, the people recognize that there are bosses and that inequality does exist, and they even change the law. Their belief about bosses nonetheless serves to condition political behavior. As an idealized view of the existing society, it becomes a political tool that can be used in political strategies (for instance, publicly accusing someone of being bossy).

When ideas are consciously and systematically organized into some form of program, they can be said to constitute an *ideology*. Ideologies are political to the extent that they are concerned with the distribution of power: the maintenance, reform, or overthrow of the

Political decision-making in Aboriginal society: a meeting at Wiluna Reserve, Western Australia.

existing structure. Australian Aboriginal law serves as political ideology by providing justifications for existing power relations between men and women, initiates and noninitiates, elders and others. Communist ideology, as expressed by Karl Marx and others, is concerned with altering the distribution of power, focusing upon the working class's wresting of power from the capitalists.

Organic vs. Rationalistic Ideologies. There are two forms of ideology: organic and rationalistic (see Hoare and Smith 1971; Rudé 1980). An *organic ideology* consists of ideas about how the world is or should be ordered held by the members of a society or a segment of a society, based upon their historical experience. A *rationalistic ideology* consists of a program of action based upon observation and/or introspection by philosophers, social scientists, and others seeking ordered sets of laws of social behavior. Individuals' beliefs concerning either organic or rationalistic ideologies will vary in any society, although there tends to be greater homogeneity of belief in small-scale than in large-scale societies. Not all Marxists or Communists agree even on some of the most basic elements of their ideology.

Each form of ideology may contain elements of the other. Ideas from rationalistic ideologies creep into the popular belief through sermons, political speeches, the printed word, radio, and television. Rationalistic ideologies in turn contain distilled elements of organic ideologies. For instance, modern capitalist ideology as expressed by conservative economists like Milton Friedman contains large doses of folk wisdom based upon the ideals and dreams of American capitalists.

Attempts to incorporate rationalistic ideologies into organic ideologies are political acts aimed at influencing the distribution of wealth and power. During the nineteenth century wealthy American capitalists promoted as organic ideology the dissemination of ideas contained within rationalistic ideologies that were supportive of their way of life: laissez-faire, the sacred right of property, social Darwinism. In contrast, those wishing to alter power relations promoted the rationalistic ideologies of socialism, anarchism, communism, and the like.

As small-scale societies have been incorporated into the modern world system their members have been subjected to the rationalist ideologies of large-scale industrial societies. People's receptivity to these ideologies has varied according to circumstance. Many native

VILLA EN LA SILLA PRESIDENCIAL.

Mexican revolutionary leaders Pancho Villa (seated in the chair of the ousted president) and Emiliano Zapata (at Villa's left) meet in Mexico City in 1915. After their deaths (Zapata died in 1919; Villa was assassinated in 1923), they became martyrs, symbols of the struggle for land and political rights for the common people of Mexico.

agricultural and foraging peoples have been unreceptive to the individualism and competitiveness of capitalist ideology. Others, such as people with long histories of entrepreneurship and trade, have had little trouble accepting these ideas. Acceptance of these ideologies is not always a matter of free choice, for there are often pressures, subtle or not so subtle, to accept the ideologies of politically and economically dominant societies. For example, indigenous peoples in the Soviet Union and the United States have been pressured to accept the dominant ideologies in these states through coercion, education, and the offering of political and economic incentives.

Political Symbols. Political ideologies and politics in general rely heavily upon symbolic imagery. Most of us are familiar with the time-honored symbols of American politics: Uncle Sam, the United States flag and other red, white, and blue trappings, and catch-phrases dealing with patriotism, equality, and the like.

Similarly, Mexican politics rely upon the eagle and serpent, portraits of heroes of the 1910 revolution against dictatorship and feudal oppression, and public affirmations of continuing adherence to the spirit of the revolution.

Symbols are useful politically for a number of reasons. They possess an intrinsic power to focus upon and conjure up strong basic emotions—feelings of hatred, of well-being, of happiness or despair. To become identified with such power is quite beneficial for someone with political ambitions. This is why politicians like to be surrounded with patriotic paraphernalia when they appear in public and why their speeches are rife with words or phrases that possess high symbolic impact, such as "honor," "honesty," and "courage." Politicians often compete for identification with relevant symbols. For instance, political parties in newly independent nations scramble for identification with the symbols of the national struggle for independence. Symbols also promote a sense of continuity and legitimacy, an advantage so long as most people are reasonably happy with the way things are going. If things begin to go badly, then it may be wise to identify with a symbol of the good old days: the flag of a former colonial ruler or a picture of the queen of England.

A politician's choice of symbols will be based upon the cultural experiences and traditions of the people and the politician's perception of their appropriateness under current political circumstances. Traditional Islam is categorically opposed to the use of painting and carving in construction of its ritual symbols, for example. In nations where Islam is the dominant religion, politicians seeking identification with this significant cultural influence will therefore avoid these means of expression.

Contests

Symbols are most visible during actual competitions for power. Political contests are the processes through which power is sought and challenged, and through which ideologies can be ultimately translated into practice.

Since an individual's or a group's power is never absolutely secure or free from challenge, political contests are a constant feature of any society. Politicians in our own society never seem to stop running for office, even after the election is over and long before the next one is due, for they are engaged in a continual struggle to survive, whether they recognize it or not. The Melanesian Big-Man, who builds his reputation and amasses wealth in pigs and other valuables by strategic manipulation of gift-giving ceremonies, is continually maneuvering to maintain or enhance his position and never really reaches a plateau from which he can rest. If a Big-Man stopped playing the game, stopped holding pig feasts, he would in essence stop being a Big-Man. To a certain degree, the same principle applies to anyone who has political power.

Competition is especially keen in most political communities during certain periods. The death of someone with power, leaving an unoccupied position of power for others to fight over, is one such time. Communities whose politics is structured through kinship usually designate a range of suitable heirs to bring some order to the potentially disruptive situation created by a powerful person's death. An eldest son or senior brother may be the preferred successor, for instance. Whatever the preference, there is almost always allowance made for an alternative; this flexibility avoids the risk of being stuck with an incompetent. Despite these provisions, even when there are only a few potential heirs disputes often erupt. Such rivalries usually do minimal damage to the overall political structure, however. For example, when succession disputes occur among potential lineage heads in African villages (see Turner 1957), the worst that generally happens is that one of the contenders and his followers leave to found a new village.

Political rallies, such as this one in Florence, Italy, have become a manifest feature of the process of seeking (or challenging) power in modern societies.

Today, heredity is less relevant in most political contexts than it has been in the past. This is not to say that it is no longer important—in American society it still helps politically to be a Rockefeller—but heredity is rarely viewed as the primary or legitimate means for assuming power. It has become a resource that is used only in combination with others, such as wealth. Towns, cities, and even nations may be ruled by oligarchies of elite families. Although these families may present a united front to other members of society, succession struggles like those in African villages commonly occur among family members. The basic difference is that in African villages kinship cuts across status differences, uniting members of the entire political community. Such bonds rarely exist between members of the oligarchy and the rest of the community, and power must be legitimized through some other means (such as coercion).

During the past few centuries, elections emerged as the focal point of political activity in many European and North American nations. Since the Second World War, electoral systems have been exported to countries throughout the world under the aegis of countries like the United States and Great Britain. Despite superficial similarities, elections have assumed many different roles in these often very dissimilar political environments and have commonly assumed characteristics quite unlike those of their countries of origin. For instance, democratic assumptions about elections—such as the belief that elections allow a greater dispersal of power among the population—have proven rather naïve. This is most obvious in those countries where elected bodies are given virtually no power, such as legislative bodies in Latin American dictatorships.

The People in Politics

Whether electoral, hereditary, or seized by force, political power ultimately resides in people. Within most societies there are three categories of people involved in politics: the political community, the political elite, and political teams (Bailey 1969: 23).

The Political Community

The political community consists of those people who adhere to roughly similar political norms and goals, and for the most part follow the same political procedures. Political communities may be as small as a nuclear family or as large as the British Empire. Each political community is unique to some degree, for it has evolved particular modes of political behavior and specific potential avenues for the acquisition of power. Some degree of generalization is possible, however. We find similar patterns of political behavior among people with similar socioeconomic adaptations; for example, we would probably find common patterns among people with similar foraging adaptations. And a political community is not isolated. Families, foraging bands, and pastoral tribes all interact with other, often very different, political communities.

Individuals often belong to several political communities at the same time. These may be interrelated to some extent, as are family, state, and national communities. Membership in a community is not always rigidly defined, nor do people always consider themselves members of communities with which others choose to associate them. During the Second World War, many people in the United States felt that Japanese-Americans had mixed loyalties because of their ancestry, even though the Japanese Americans considered themselves to be loyal Americans.

The Political Elite

Successful acquisition of political power within a community is a skill that requires learning and practice, and some people are simply better at it than others. Just as someone who ably fixes cars may not want to become a mechanic, however, many of those with political aspirations or skills may not care to take an active role in politics. People can never opt out entirely since politics so thoroughly permeates social life, but they may try to limit their political endeavors. In all societies there will be variation not only in terms of political belief and skill, but also in terms of active involvement. To become governor of Texas or a Big-Man in New Guinea requires an understanding of how to become one and the ability to carry out the process. It also requires the desire, and it may require hereditary qualifications. The *political elite* are those within a community who are entitled to or able to compete for power and leadership. Sometimes the political elite consists of a rigidly bounded group, but often its membership is diverse.

Leaders. Among those included in the political elite are *leaders*. A political leader is an individual who has the power to make decisions within and for a group. Although the scope of this power and how it is attained and maintained varies in different settings, the political power of all leaders is personal in nature. Such things as administrative office or the status of one's parents may give a person potential resources (or set political limits), but the actual dimension of power a leader achieves within a given setting is a matter of the leader's personal manipulation of available resources—connections, money, charisma, speaking ability, or strength.

Within any social setting there are numerous potential situations and statuses for leaders to attempt to exploit. Among traditional Australian Aborigines, potential niches are available within the spheres of ritual and curing. Individuals use their expertise in these areas, along with their political skills, to attempt to attain the status of leader. The eligibility requirements are minimal: Age and sex may be important, but skill, and desire and ability to lead without seeming to do so, are the main criteria. In other societies such as ours, there are more rigid criteria—wealth and/or education, plus sex and age—that must be met by those wishing to compete for significant political positions.

The status of leader tends to be rather insecure in most societies. The person who has attained it is rarely able to sit back and take leadership status for granted. Threats come from those who would like to usurp the leader's position and also from those who are jealous or resentful of anyone exercising power over them. To ensure the security of their status, leaders often try to develop a complex network of supports, recognizing that too heavy a reliance on one or a few will leave them vulnerable. The person who succeeds in gaining the status of leader through an office will generally then try to make that status as secure as possible and perhaps find alternative sources of support should that one fail. Members of Congress in the United States use resources available through their office to build ties with their constituents and also with influential people in Washington. They can turn to these people for support at election time and perhaps for assistance should they lose their bid for reelection (by being given an administrative position in government or a high-level position in industry, for instance).

The social functions of leaders vary according to the context and nature of their activities. In small-scale societies leaders usually help to maintain the status quo. While the personnel in power may change, their strategies and goals remain much the same. This is also true of many political leaders in large-scale industrial societies: rather than trying to change things, individuals try to gain power within existing parameters by appealing to customary beliefs and practices. The function of leaders is not always a strictly conservative one, however. Even in small-scale societies like those of the Australian Aborigines, leaders often bring about at least minor changes in their search for new sources of power and in their competition with each other.

New opportunities for leadership arise as a result of contact between groups, especially when such contact significantly influences power relations. European colonialism created new opportunities for many individuals. In some instances people joined to resist their new common enemy, as in the case of many Native American societies. New technologies and weapons introduced by Europeans often allowed greater concentrations of power among certain segments of the indigenous elite, such as those engaged in the slave trade in West Africa and in certain Polynesian societies. This power was often short-lived, however, as the Europeans began to assert their own power. The various kinds of leaders who arise under these circumstances are significant agents of change, whether by promoting resistance to or acceptance of a new order.

Middlemen. Those who seek positions of leadership by using conditions created by contact with other groups fall within the broad category of *middlemen*, or *brokers*—individuals who strive to benefit from the sociocultural gaps between groups. Not all middlemen are political leaders; but even when they are not they often assume political significance. Such is the case with *ladino* (hispanic non-Indians) middlemen in the Tzeltal (Maya) village of Oxchuc, located in southern Mexico. Henning Siverts (1971: 390–93) describes how these middlemen have exploited the office of secretary for political ends:

We find that [this position] is characterized by the requirement of a certain technical or professional skill which belongs to Ladino culture and is not shared by the Indian majority. It is just this cultural barrier that favors political activity on the part of the secretary. His status is administratively defined, but the limits are not set by the body of officials to which he is attached. The secretary is the strategic link between two cultures as well as between two different kinds of governments. The Indians have—in their governmental tradition—no ready means by which to control the incumbent, and, what is really important, the State administration, which the secretary represents, is too remotely situated to be able to control him effectively through su-pervision by superiors and checking by peers with a similar technical skill. The secretary stands as an isolated outpost and low paid employee of one administration and acts in status next to top in another. His de facto power derives from the potential backing he can call upon in case of need. Even if it were not true that he could appeal to his superiors in order to get, e.g., military assistance, Indians would be uncertain about the sanctions available to him; and this insecurity on their part is in itself a source of power for the secretary. What authors have stated as the fear of the Ladino secretary on the part of the Indians, is not so much the fright for his pistol as for the possible terrors that might be called upon from the outside world. Indian informants can tell you all kinds of dramatic stories about soldiers razing hamlets and neighborhoods.

One aspect of the middleman's power that this passage points to is its use of the unknown and the uncertain for political advantage. While such positions may serve integrative functions by providing links between different groups or cultures, in the middleman's search for power they may serve just the opposite purpose. The ladino secretary in Oxchuc helps to maintain distance between ethnic groups by promoting hostile relations between Indians and ladinos. Such a consideration is of particular importance for those concerned with promoting socioeconomic change, for they often rely upon local middlemen as change agents. Since the middleman gains his power from gaps, from differences, it is rarely in his interest to promote changes (such as socioeconomic development) that might undermine his own political position.

Political Teams

Political teams are the organized groups of people actively involved in politics. These include coalitions, factions, political parties, and multipurpose organizations.

Coalitions. Within all societies there are various sorts of loosely structured political groups that can be designated *coalitions*, temporary alliances for a limited political purpose (Boissevain 1974: 171). The least institutionalized form of coalition is what may be referred to as an action set. *Action sets* come into being when individuals call upon people within their personal social networks to act for some specific purpose. For instance, politicians in Indian elections utilize action sets in their electioneering, calling upon people for support on the basis of caste, residence, kinship, union membership, political party membership, religion, and economic bonds (Mayer 1966).

A more institutionalized form of coalition is *factions*, groups that act together within, and in opposition to some element of, a larger unit. Anthropologists studying factions in India have stressed their personal and temporary nature (Bailey 1969: 52; Nicolas 1968: 45–46), and especially the importance, if not the necessity, of leaders as the point of unity of the factions. Other anthropologists, working in other parts of the world, however, have found rather different situations. Kuper (1971: 15–16) notes that in African villages factions are fairly stable, the role of the leader being much less significant than in India. He feels that this situation may be related to the segmentary patterns of the kinship-oriented politics of these societies (see chapter 8).

Any analysis of factions must be dynamic, viewing their evolution over time and trying to isolate those factors bringing them into being and influencing their subsequent development. In the case of Pueblo Viejo, a Kekchi-speaking village in southern Belize (Howard 1977: 133), factions slowly evolved as the village grew in size, as land pressure increased, and as social and economic differences among villagers became greater. Initially, the factions were recruited pri-

marily on the basis of kinship and compadrazgo by individuals. They eventually became relatively permanent features of the village and as they did the role of the leaders who were responsible for their formation in the first place tended to wane.

Political Parties. The most institutionalized form of political grouping is *political parties*. Parties are a product of modern, large-scale societies and reflect the high degree of specialization present in such societies. The closest thing to a party in smaller, nonindustrial societies is a multipurpose group such as a patrilineage or a clan, which functions as a political organization in some contexts. Political parties, however, are formed primarily with one purpose in mind: to direct the policies of a government. In addition, they are characterized by a degree of internal organization that surpasses and is quite different from that of other political groups. They are usually organized around particular political beliefs and interests, and are usually more impersonal than other forms of political grouping. Another important feature of most political parties is that they are organized on a national level and frequently have a strong urban bias in their orientation and organization.

Before the Second World War political parties were not always of direct relevance to many peoples living in small-scale societies or in the more isolated parts of large-scale societies, but they were not entirely irrelevant either. If only indirectly, it did matter to even the most isolated members of the British Empire which party was in power in England, as the different parties pursued somewhat dissimilar colonial policies. Since the Second World War, party politics has come to be of even more direct relevance as parties have evolved within newly independent nations, and as these parties' activities have penetrated into even remote villages. Politicians from the capitol of Belize periodically visit the isolated Mayan villages in the south, making promises and at least seeming to listen to the villagers' views. The villagers have become aware that roads, schools, and the like are political commodities, and that their own political behavior will influence the flow of such spoils from without.

Political parties affect indigenous and ethnic minorities in other ways as well, especially in situations where two or more parties are in competition. For one thing, political parties in their search for support may increase tensions between groups. In Guyana, for instance, interethnic tension heightened as different political parties came to be identified with particular ethnic groups (Despres 1967). The different policies of political parties may also be of relevance to minority groups. Attitudes of Australian political parties toward multinational mining companies and Aboriginal land rights have had profound repercussions for Aboriginal people. If everything is potentially political, then everything is also of potential interest to political parties.

Multipurpose Organizations. Multipurpose organizations that serve significant political roles do not disappear with the advent of the nation-state and political parties. They continue to exist alongside, within or even in opposition to such specialized bodies.

The Freemasonic lodges in Sierra Leone provide an example (Cohen 1971). The Masonic lodges are concentrated in the capitol city of Freetown. Most of the members are Creoles, descendants of African slaves who were settled in the area by the British in the nineteenth century. Although the Creoles constitute less than 2 percent of the national population, they have traditionally dominated the civil service, the judiciary, and professions such as medicine, engineering, and teaching. They are in essence a highly privileged elite. With Sierra Leone's independence in 1961, the Creoles' political status was usurped by members of larger ethnic groups and their privileged position came under pressure. Initially the Creoles considered forming a separate political party to support their interests in government, but most realized that such a move would be foolish because of their insignificant number. Instead political activities and discussion were concentrated in Masonic lodges. The lodges themselves were not specifically political, but they came to serve political functions by providing the Creoles with a unified organization and a forum for political discussion. As Cohen (1974: 109) notes, such "secret" organizations commonly serve political purposes.

The Political Organization of Societies

In addition to the strategies of individuals and groups seeking political power, entire societies are characterized by particular ways of distributing power. The distribution of power in a society is related to the society's mode of adaptation. In small-scale societies, features such as a lack of durable foods and manufactured possessions, low population densities, and frequent moves tend to dissipate power. It is only once societies become more stable and able to produce more durable forms and greater quantities

of wealth that the potential for the concentration of power comes into being.

Anthropologists commonly divide systems of political organization into two broad categories: those associated with *states* and those associated with *stateless societies*. The first category includes those structures with centralized authority and highly administrative machinery and judicial institutions. Within this category are political organizations as diverse as those of the United States, the Kingdom of Tonga, and

the former Zulu empire. The second category is comprised of those systems of organization which lack the scale and degree of specialization of state governments.

Stateless Societies

There are two general types of stateless societies: *acephalous* (or headless) *societies* and *chiefdoms.* Among those societies which are designated acephalous are a range of small-scale polities associated with foraging, small-scale farming, and pastoral activities—such as those of the Mardudjara Aborigines, the Cree of northern Canada, and the Nuer of eastern Africa. Chiefdoms, such as those found in precolonial Polynesia, are generally associated with relatively intensive, small-scale agriculture. Today, both acephalous societies and chiefdoms are under the jurisdiction of encompassing state organizations, although in some instances they are able to retain a fair degree of autonomy.

Acephalous Societies. The primary unit of political organization among acephalous societies consists of those people who reside and work together in bands, camps or villages. The members of these primary units commonly are organized into loose alliances, known as tribes. A *tribe* consists of a group of people who share patterns of speech, some cultural characteristics, and a common territory, and who in general feel that they have more in common with each other than with their neighbors. It is an alliance of peoples of roughly equal status without much centralized authority. Where tribes have come to assume a more integrated and central-

King Taufa'ahau Tupou IV and his wife, the Queen, tour his palace grounds in Nuku'alofa, Kingdom of Tonga, with Queen Elizabeth II of Britain. The modern kingdom was established in the second half of the nineteenth century; declared a neutral region in 1886, it became a British protectorate in 1900 and achieved independence in 1970.

ized nature, as with many North American Indian tribes and Middle Eastern pastoral nomads, this concentration is usually a result of warfare or the designs of colonial administrators. For instance, European colonialists in Africa combined many loosely organized groups and established centralized administrative structures for them, primarily to make it easier to administer them.

Kinship is often so much a part of the political organization of these societies that they sometimes are referred to as kin based. Government in acephalous societies such as the Nuer or Tallensi is structured around clan and lineage groupings. In these societies, political status is commonly based upon a person's status within the web of kin relationships. Lineage and clan elders may have authority to try to settle disputes and to punish wrongdoers. Kin groups such as lineages form the primary administrative units in these societies. Although they may be loosely allied with other kin groups, most affairs are handled within the lineage or clan. Alliances among kin groups are of primary political importance when intergroup disputes arise and members of the groups involved call upon their allies for support.

Relatively little power is available to individuals in acephalous societies. While there may be marked differences in status and authority between males and females or between adults and youths, among adult males or females the differences tend to be slight. Administration tends to be conducted by some form of council. These councils may be fairly specialized, but usually they are of a fairly general nature, handling a range of legal, religious and other administrative matters. Who may participate in a council's affairs varies. In some societies participation is quite open (although certain segments of the population will probably dominate the proceedings), while in others participation is much more restricted. For example, among the Mardudjara Aborigines only initiated males may participate in gatherings concerned with important political, economic, and religious issues.

Although power is diffused in acephalous societies, they do not lack organization. The Yakö of southeastern Nigeria illustrate how an acephalous society may be organized. The Yakö live in independent villages of as many as thirteen-thousand inhabitants, divided into wards. Young Yakö males are initiated into an age set in their village ward, and are subject to discipline imposed by fellow age mates on behalf of the senior men in the ward. As the young men mature and marry, they become eligible to join one of the ward associations that exercise various ritual and legal powers. The ward leaders are senior members of the resident lineages. They form a group known as the *Yakamban*, and advise a representative of the senior lineage who serves as ward head. Members of the *Yakamban* may also participate in associations that recruit members from the different wards within the village. Each of these associations has a distinct membership and performs distinct functions. The highest ritual and administrative body in the village, the *Yabot*, contains members of these associations.

Chiefdoms. The chiefdom differs from acephalous societies in that its administrative structure formally integrates a number of communities. Chiefdoms may be comprised of several parallel units, each headed by a chief, subchief, or council. Most chiefdoms are more stratified than acephalous societies, and the office of chief generally affords the incumbent a status noticeably above that of other members of the society. Kinship is often important politically; the position of chief may be hereditary and the chief and his kin commonly form an elite segment of the society. Chiefs normally accumulate goods, usually in the form of tribute, and redistribute some of them in the form of public feasts or doles to those in need. While there is usually a greater degree of specialization in chiefdoms than in acephalous societies, they are still a good deal less specialized than societies organized into states.

Chiefdoms were found in many parts of Polynesia before the era of European colonialism. The power and wealth of Polynesian chiefs varied, with chiefs on some of the larger islands attaining considerable power and maintaining great social distance from commoners. Marshall Sahlins (1958) has argued that the differences are to a large degree a reflection of the similar adaptational strategies employed by Polynesians in different ecological settings (e.g., high islands and atolls). Administration on Samoa, one of the larger islands in Polynesia, was characterized by a relatively high degree of stratification. Government was conducted by village councils comprised only of chiefly title holders. These titles—chiefs and talking chiefs—were inherited patrilineally. Talking chiefs served as the ceremonial attendants of chiefs, although they were not necessarily inferior in status to them. Both chiefs and talking chiefs occupied varying ranks in a hierarchy based upon presumed descent through male lines from a god or a legendary incident.

Population size and growth are key factors in the transition from acephalous to more stratified political systems such as chiefdoms. It can be argued that higher population densities require a greater degree of specialization, or at least create an environment favoring the evolution of more specialized systems, and that this in turn creates a greater potential for the accumulation of wealth and power. In a denser population there is more to be done and thus more profit that can be extracted. In Africa acephalous organization is generally associated with low population densities, whereas chiefdoms and other more stratified systems are associated with progressively higher densities. Similarly, larger and more stratified systems evolved in those places in Polynesia where there were relatively large and dense populations.

The status, and in fact the very existence, of chiefs is often influenced by colonial expansion. As the British, French, and other European colonial powers conquered large portions of the world during the eighteenth and nineteenth centuries, they commonly created chiefs where there were none and altered the status of existing chiefs to aid the task of administration or to help expand their empires. When the British conquered Australia, they appointed chiefs among the Aboriginal people, who until that time had an acephalous form of political organization. While those appointed to be chiefs (sometimes referred to as "kings") were sometimes individuals of high standing in their own society, the primary criterion was their friendliness and utility to the British. In fact, appointment as a chief or king sometimes resulted in a person's ostracism from his own society.

States

The term *state* refers to an autonomous integrated political unit, encompassing many communities within its territory, with a highly specialized central governing authority. This central authority claims a monopoly over those powers concerned with maintaining internal order and ordering external relations. States vary in degree of centralization, the extent and nature of the powers claimed by the state, the precise form of administration, how power is legitimated, and levels and manner of popular participation in the running of the state. Over the past few thousand years numerous types of state have evolved, including the city-states of ancient Greece, empire states such as the Mongol or Roman empires, theocratic states such as the Vatican or ancient Egypt, and more recently nation-states such as France or Canada. Despite many differences, these entities share enough to warrant being grouped within a single category, especially when contrasted with other, nonstate structures.

How states in general came into being has been the subject of debate among anthropologists for years. Three hypotheses dominate the discussion. First, Karl Wittfogel (1957) and others argue that *irrigation* played a significant if not primary role in the process of state formation. Irrigation supported agricultural production in such areas as central Mesoamerica, southern Iraq, and the Nile valley. According to this view, labor and management requirements of an irrigation system led to the formation of a political elite who were initially the overseers of the system. The state then grew out of the administrative needs of and the intensified production resulting from irrigation, accounting for both the formation of the political units and their hierarchical nature.

Anthropologists like Robert Carneiro (1970) feel that the primary factor was *population* pressure. Population growth in a circumscribed area led to competition and warfare, the argument runs, and larger political units evolved as particular groups proved successful in subjugating those around them. Those supporting this hypothesis draw upon examples from the northern coast of Peru as well as Mesoamerica, southern Iraq, and the Nile valley.

A third theory suggests that long-distance *trade* may have been influential in the evolution of early states (see Polanyi, et al., 1957). Careful analysis of the process of state formation in a range of settings seems to indicate that none of these theories is sufficient to account for all cases, nor does the process ever seem reduceable to a single cause. Nonetheless, factors such as irrigation, population, and trade have been considerably important in the formation of many early states.

The nature of modern nation-states and the conditions under which they have developed have been quite different than those of earlier states. The majority began as the creations of various colonial powers, and their subsequent evolution has often involved the progressive realization of a nationality that initially was little more than an ideal. The term *nation building* is often used in reference to attempts to forge nations out of disparate peoples placed together in an artificial political creation. For example, the nation of Libya was formed out of a group of Bedouin tribes (Evans-Pritchard 1949). Although the tribes had traditionally opposed one another, they shared a common Islamic culture dating from the spread of the Islamic empire in the seventh and eighth centuries. They also shared a high regard for learned and holy men. In 1843 a holy man, Sayyid Muhammad bin 'ali al Sanusi, established a religious order of preachers and teachers on a distant, isolated oasis that

King-Designate for Libya, Sayed Mohamed Idris Al Senussi, on his visit to Tripoli, 1951.

was not identified with any particular tribe. The order served a centralized unifying function for the tribes, assuming responsibility for certain aspects of local administration and conducting external affairs on behalf of the Bedouin. During the First World War and in 1923, the order led the opposition to invasion by Italians. Forced into exile in Egypt, the heads of the order were recognized as the government in exile by the British, who at the time occupied Egypt. After the war the head of the order was established as king of the newly unified state of Libya.

The degree of centralization and unity found within states is related to the extent to which those in power are able to influence or control the citizenry. Through the *bureaucracy*, the specialized administrative organization con-

The bureaucracy that supports existing power relations in a large state generates extensive paperwork, as these rows of insurance files attest.

cerned with the day-to-day running of the state, order is maintained—an order that supports existing power relations. Many of the mechanisms employed for maintainng order are subtle. Through control or influence over education and the media, the state is able to socialize people to view the world in a way deemed desirable by those in power. Public symbols and ceremonies—flags, inaugurations, parades—reinforce these views. For those who are not convinced, who represent a threat to the existing order, there are other, less subtle means of enforcing order, such as the police and imprisonment. There may be room for dissension—although in some states very little disagreement is tolerated—but the administrative arm of the state aims at keeping dissension within limits. What these limits are will vary from one state to another, in accordance with the current status of power struggles. In the next chapter we will be looking at the question of order in political systems more closely.

Summary

In all societies there is some competition for power. Political power is based on authority, ideas, symbols, and contests. Authority is the right of an individual or group in power to make certain decisions and command obedience; it may be restricted to a limited aspect of the peoples' lives or spread across many.

When ideas about appropriate political goals and behavior are organized into a systematic program, they constitute an ideology. Ideologies may be organic (stemming from the direct experiences of members of the society) or rationalistic (based on observation and introspection by intellectuals). Symbols support political ideas by associating them with strong emotions.

Competition for power takes place all the time but is keenest during political contests. Societies with hereditary access to power usually have provisions to minimize rivalries for power vacuums created by the death of a leader. Elections have been used in other societies to make moves into power more orderly, though they may not necessarily spread power democratically across the population at large.

The people behind political systems can be categorized as political communities, the political elite, and political teams. Political communities, large or small, are people with similar political norms, goals, and procedures. The political elite are those within the community who are entitled or able to compete for available power and leadership opportunities, including leaders and middlemen. Teams actively involved in politics include coalitions, political parties, and multipurpose organizations.

Entire societies have their own general form of political organization. Small-scale societies tend to be stateless, with authority limited to local realms of power, whereas in many large-scale societies power is highly centralized, with specialized administrative and judicial machinery. Stateless societies may be acephalous (headless) or chiefdoms (in which a number of hierarchically ordered communities are integrated into a formal structure with units of parallel power). There have been numerous types of states, and some are still being created through conglomerations of formerly separate groups.

Suggested Readings

General works:

Bailey, F. G. 1969. *Strategems and spoils: A social anthropology of politics.* Oxford: Blackwell.

Balandier, Georges. 1970. *Political anthropology.* New York: Random House.

Banton, Michael, ed. 1965. *Political systems and the distribution of power.* London: Tavistock Publications.

Cohen, Ronald, and Middleton, John, eds. 1967. *Comparative political systems.* Garden City, NY: Natural History Press.

Fried, Morton H. 1967. *The evolution of political society: An essay in political anthropology.* New York: Random House.

Schapera, I. 1967. *Government and politics in tribal societies.* New York: Schocken. (Africa)

Seaton, S. Lee, and Claessen, Henri M., eds. 1979. *Political anthropology.* The Hague/Paris: Mouton.

Swartz, Marc J., ed. 1968. *Local-level politics: Social and cultural perspectives.* Chicago: Aldine/Atherton.

Swartz, Marc J., Turner, Victor W., and Tuden, Arthur, eds. 1966. *Political anthropology.* Chicago: Aldine.

Works on more specialized topics:

Boissevain, Jeremy. 1974. *Friends of friends: Networks, manipulators and coalitions.* Oxford: Blackwell.

Burling, Robbins. 1974. *The passage of power: Studies in political succession.* New York: Academic Press.

Cohen, Robin, Gutkind, Peter C. W., and Brazier, Phyllis, eds. 1979. *Peasants and proletarians: The struggles of Third World workers.* London: Hutchinson.

Cohen, Ronald, and Service, Elman R., eds. 1978. *Origins of the state: The anthropology of political evolution.* Philadelphia: Institute for the Study of Human Issues.

Fogelson, Raymond D., and Adams, Richard N., eds. 1977. *The anthropology of power: Ethnographic studies from Asia, Oceania, and the New World.* New York: Academic Press.

Richards, Audrey, and Kuper, Adam, eds. 1971. *Councils in action.* Cambridge: Cambridge University Press.

Schmidt, Steffen W., Scott, James C., Lande, Carl, and Guasti, Laura, eds. 1977. *Friends, followers, and factions: A reader in political clientism.* Berkeley/Los Angeles: University of California Press.

Case studies:

Cohen, Abner. 1969. *Custom and politics in urban Africa: A study of Hausa migrants in Yoruba towns.* London: Routledge and Kegan Paul.

Dyson-Hudson, Neville. 1966. *Karimojong politics.* Oxford: Clarendon. (African pastoralists)

Epstein, A. L. 1969. *Matupit: Land, politics and change among the Tolai of New Britain.* Berkeley/Los Angeles: University of California Press.

Fagen, Richard R., and Tuoy, William S. 1972. *Politics and privilege in a Mexican city.* Stanford: Stanford University Press.

Howard, Michael C., ed. 1982. *Aboriginal power in Australian society.* Honolulu: University of Hawaii Press.

Hughes, Daniel T., and Lingenfelter, Sherwood G., eds. 1974. *Political development in Micronesia.* Columbus, OH: Ohio State University Press.

Kertzer, David I. 1980. *Comrades and Christians: Religion and political struggle in Communist Italy.* Cambridge: Cambridge University Press.

Kuper, Adam. 1970. *Kalahari village politics: An African democracy.* Cambridge: Cambridge University Press.

Paine, Robert, ed. 1971. *Patrons and brokers in the east Arctic.* St. John's: Memorial University Press.

Perlman, Janice E. 1976. *The myth of marginality: Urban poverty and politics in Rio de Janeiro.* Berkeley/Los Angeles: University of California Press.

Sklar, Richard L. 1975. *Corporate power in an African state: The political impact of multinational mining companies in Zambia.* Berkeley/Los Angeles: University of California Press.

Strickon, Arnold, and Greenfield, Sidney M., eds. 1972. *Structure and process in Latin America: Patronage, clientage, and power systems.* Albuquerque, NM: University of New Mexico Press.

Tapper, Richard. 1979. *Pasture and politics: Economics, conflict and ritual among Shahsevan Nomads of northwest Iran.* New York: Academic Press.

Chapter Thirteen

The Search for Order

Norms

Laws
Legitimacy · Evolution of Laws
Overlapping of Legal Systems

Law Enforcement and Dispute Mediation
Attitudes Toward Laws
Handling Disputes in Foraging Societies
Easing Tensions Among Small-Scale Farmers
Formal Law Enforcement in States
Maintaining World Order

The Breakdown of Order
Political Violence Within a Society
Warfare Between Societies

Summary

Suggested Readings

S O-CALLED RACE riots have been a part of American society for over a century. One was the "Zoot Suit Riot," named for the flashy tight-cuffed, wide-lapelled, padded-shouldered suits popular among Mexican-American youths during the 1940s. The riot took place in Los Angeles in early June 1943:

Marching through the streets of downtown Los Angeles, a mob of several thousand soldiers, sailors, and civilians proceeded to beat up every zoot-suiter they could find. . . . Street cars were halted while Mexicans, and some Filipinos and Negroes, were jerked out of their seats, pushed into the streets, and beaten with sadistic frenzy. If the victims wore zoot-suits, they were stripped of their clothing and left naked or half-naked on the streets, bleeding and bruised. . . . From affidavits which I helped prepare at the time, I should say that not more than half of the victims were actually wearing zoot-suits. A Negro defense worker, wearing a defense-plant identification badge on his workclothes, was taken from a street car and one of his eyes was gouged out with a knife. Huge half-page photographs showing Mexican boys stripped of their clothes, cowering on the pavements, often bleeding profusely, surrounded by jeering mobs of men and women, appeared in all the Los Angeles newspapers. [McWilliams 1961: 249–50]

Such a breakdown of social order is not a common occurrence and when it does take place people generally feel the need to try to explain it. Numerous explanations have been offered for the Zoot Suit Riot. The Los Angeles police

OVERLEAF
A rectangular brass plaque, from Benin, West Africa, depicting a chief flanked by two of his warriors. Difference in status is shown by the dress and headdresses worn, by the weapons carried, and most clearly by the size of the individuals (ca. late sixteenth–early seventeenth century A.D.; 38 × 49.2 cm, brass, lost wax casting).

felt that the riots stemmed from sailors making advances to Mexican-American girlfriends of the zoot-suiters. California state senator Jack Tenney and the members of his Committee on Un-American Activities in California blamed the Communists, relating the riot to "the current Communist Party line to stir up matters among minority groups in order to make the Communist Party appear a champion of the group" (Tenney 1943: 215). Anthropologists and other social scientists find such simplistic answers unsatisfactory. Recognizing the complexity of human actions, they search for a range of contributing factors. The zoot-suiters themselves were to a large degree a product of the Second World War: as it disrupted strong family ties, pre-draft-age youths formed into gangs. The war also heightened racial tensions; Oriental-Americans were suspected of allegiances to Japan, and blacks and Mexican-Americans moved into cities to occupy jobs previously reserved for whites. The flashy dress and undisciplined behavior of the zoot-suiters stood out in the face of such prejudice. These characteristics also seemed to be contrary to the values of patriotism and hard work being promoted to sustain the war effort. The zoot-suiters stood out and served as a focal point of competition and conflict in a city where tensions had mounted as a result of the Second World War. Once the riot began it soon turned into a general racial free-for-all.

Although such a breakdown of social order can be explained, it is often viewed as disturbing and unexpected, for all societies have mechanisms designed to prevent such disturbances of orderly living. In this chapter we will be looking at how people view social order, how it is maintained, and how it breaks down.

June 7, 1943: After a series of pitched battles with soldiers, sailors, and marines, these alleged zoot suiters are lined up in chains outside the Los Angeles jail en route for court hearings.

Norms _____

Most of us have fixed notions about how people should behave. Children should obey their parents, drivers should stop for red lights, public officials should not take bribes, bank tellers and waitresses should be courteous. Such conceptions of appropriate or expected behavior are called *norms*. Obviously, a mixed lot of conceptions falls into this grouping. While we may think of norms as part of a system, to do so pre-

sumes an order that often does not exist. Although many of our ideas about what people ought to do are closely related, not all are; people often adhere to beliefs that are actually contradictory. Norms vary from ambiguous guidelines such as "Be good to your parents" to very specific directives such as "Do not covet your neighbor's wife."

By and large norms fall into three categories:

Groups such as this motorcycle gang often possess a recognized set of norms for their members that determine their dress and behavior.

reality assumptions, ranking norms, and membership norms (Cancian 1975: 2–4). *Reality assumptions* are beliefs of a very general nature that are taken for granted regarding what actions are meaningful or possible in a particular context. For example, in our society, if a bank teller took our check and ate it before giving us the money we had requested, this would be a violation of a reality assumption—it would be seen as crazy behavior. *Ranking norms* evaluate people and their actions on the basis of how closely they conform to some standard. Such norms may be used to distinguish rank or status. A student is ranked on the basis of certain criteria—her SAT scores or grade point average, for example. *Membership norms* are standards for accepting a person within a particular group or social position. To be a king, president of a bank, or member of a Mexican-American gang, one must meet certain criteria. These may include the performance of tasks, adherence to

specific behavioral guidelines, or even the wearing of a zoot suit.

People *use* norms in social situations in accordance with particular goals. This usage is closely related to our perceptions of social identities—what a bank teller is and does and what it means to be a good one. People's support of norms commonly is related to what they think others perceive to be normative behavior, rather than to their own values. Good bank tellers wear a smile and tell the customers that they hope they have a nice day. Such behavior does not necessarily mean that they care about their customers or that they are especially happy; it shows that they are trying to live up to their image of what others expect.

Norms tend to reflect the current social environment. The obsequious behavior of such cinematic characters as Step-n-Fetchit typifies the normative expectations of many white Americans in the 1920s and 1930s regarding relations between blacks and whites. In the cinema today there is a noticeable difference in the kind of demeanor portrayed in black/white relations, reflecting changing attitudes about how members of the respective ethnic groups should behave. Norms continually change to keep pace with new social or environmental realities. This is true even in relatively stable small-scale societies, for no society is ever in perfect equilibrium.

European colonialism and the restructuring of societies based upon European ideas and economic desires had a profound effect on the normative beliefs of members of thousands of non-European societies. In Africa, for example, people had believed that wealth was primarily a group resource to be allocated by senior members of the kin group; this belief in allegiance to the extended kin group came into conflict with ideas favoring the social and economic autonomy of individuals and nuclear families. The conflict arose as a result of the shift from non-cash, subsistence production to wage labor in factories and on market-oriented farms. The result in many areas was the breakdown of extended kin groups.

Laws

Members of a society frequently systematize norms and elevate them to the status of laws. A *law* is a binding rule, created through enactment or custom, that defines right and reasonable behavior. Systems of law are not exclusive to modern large-scale societies, although such societies do exhibit unique procedures for administering and codifying laws. Traditional Australian Aborigines possessed a system of laws that dictated personal relationships with the supernatural, with physical surroundings, and with other individuals. Aboriginal law included the responsibility to perform rituals associated with mythical events and established conventions of behavior toward kin. These laws were not written down, but they were as binding and as systematic as written laws in our society.

Legitimacy

A law is a norm that states with relative precision what form of behavior is expected or appropriate in a specific situation. All legal systems are ultimately based upon more general normative concepts, such as the God-given right of a king to rule or the right of the state to maintain social order, and it is from these more general norms that laws derive their *legitimacy*. Ultimately, legitimacy refers to the traditional moral system of a society (Smith 1960: 20).

Australian Aboriginal law derives its legitimacy from Dreamtime mythology: the laws are said to have been laid down by the creative beings of the Dreamtime. Reference to the supernatural for support of a legal system is fairly common, and is found in many aspects of our own legal system ("one nation under God"). In the Guatemalan village of Chinautla custom plays a vital role, and the "law of the saints," an unwritten legal code dictating proper modes of behavior, is viewed as legitimate in large part because it is the law of the ancestors (Reina 1966). Support may also be based upon reference to a more secular idea of morality or well-being. The "custom" of legal traditions does not of necessity bear any relation to what people customarily have actually done. Rather, it is a set of norms abstracted from people's perceptions of what was done in the past. In effect, it is an idealized picture of past behavior used to sanction present-day laws.

Another source of support for many legal sys-

A Zinacanteco woman presents a complaint to the Presidente in front of the Cabildo (town hall). In this traditional court setting in Mexico, officials sit on their bench on the front porch of the Cabildo waiting for law cases; when all are present, the group listens to cases and settles the disputes.

tems is the concept of the "reasonable man": culturally acceptable ideas about what constitutes reasonable behavior in a given situation. As Max Gluckman (1973:83) notes: "The reasonable man is recognized as the central figure in all developed systems of law," and he argues that it is equally important in non-Western systems such as that of the Barotse of Zambia, upon whom his own studies focused. Significantly, he notes that the concept of the "reasonable woman" does not exist in many legal sys-

tems; the "reasonable man" is a sexist concept found in societies where women occupy a relatively low status.

Evolution of Laws

Like norms in general, laws and legal systems are constantly changing in relation to changing social or environmental conditions. For example, environmental quality and protection laws passed during the past decades resulted in part from threats to the environment and personal health related to industrial development. They were also related to a shift in political power from those profiting by environmental destruction to those affected by and concerned about this deterioration. Likewise, the more recent elimination of many of these laws has resulted from a change in the balance of power back toward industrial profiteers.

While laws do change in all societies, not all societies choose to recognize such changes. Many societies choose to emphasize the static nature of their legal codes, especially if their laws are religiously sanctioned. Australian Aboriginal law is based upon religion, the Dreaming, and even though changes do take place, Aborigines choose to ignore the changing nature of their laws, stating that the present laws have always existed (see Kolig 1978).

Especially in large-scale societies, groups often have very different perceptions of which norms should be elevated to the status of laws. We can see this in American society in the case of laws dictating the number of wives a man may have. Segments of American society that favor limiting the number of wives to one at a time have been able to have this norm established as law over the protests of others, such as Mormons, who uphold the right to have more than one wife at a time. That a group holds a norm does not necessarily mean that it will seek to establish that norm as a law for the society as a whole. Mormon polygynists simply desired to be allowed to adhere to their norm of being able to have more than one wife, not prescribe it as right behavior for all. Whether a group desires to transform a norm into law will depend in part upon that group's adaptive strategy. For instance, many Christian segments of American society view the nuclear family and monogamous marriage as an essential part of their strategy for the survival of what they consider to be the American way of life. A group's success at transforming such a norm into a law will depend upon the opposition they encounter and upon their relative power.

Overlapping of Legal Systems

The existence of two or more legal traditions within a single nation or colony is fairly common. In many of their colonies the British adhered to a policy of "indirect rule" that allowed subject peoples to retain many features of their own legal systems. British law took precedence over "native" law whenever there was a conflict, but the colonial subjects were allowed to retain that part of their legal system which promoted, or at least did not hinder, the running of the colony. The legal systems of Australian Aborigines and of the Pokomam of Chinautla are likewise encapsulated within the legal systems of the politically dominant sectors of their nations. For both groups their legal traditions have served as integral components of their ethnic identities. Since Aboriginal law and the "law of the saints" are significant markers of ethnic identity, Aborigines and Pokomam are quite resistant to attempts by outsiders to alter or do away with their laws.

How effective such peoples are in maintaining their legal systems depends upon a variety of factors. One is the extent to which they are able or forced to retain their group identity. Another is their power in relation to others. If they are not particularly powerful, maintenance of their traditional legal system depends upon the willingness of those who are in power to allow them to follow their own legal codes. Aboriginal law survived in more isolated communities with a high degree of social integration; attempts made by the government and Christian missionaries were rarely enough to cause these Aborigines to abandon their law. Adherence to the law became symbolic of Aboriginal attempts to maintain their separate identity and to avoid total subjugation. Today the Australian government is more tolerant of Aboriginal law. The Aborigines in many communities have come to recognize both laws: Blackfella (Aboriginal) law because it is theirs and legitimized by the Dreamtime powers, and Whitefella law because of its association with those who monopolize economic and political power (Maddock 1977: 14).

Law Enforcement and Dispute Mediation

It is never enough simply to establish laws. In every society, there are always some whose actions fall beyond established legal limits and some whose interpretation or acceptance of the law differs, such as parties with conflicting claims to the same property. All societies have therefore developed mechanisms, formal or informal, for enforcing their laws and handling disputes.

Attitudes Toward Laws

While all societies have ideas about what is proper and improper behavior and means of assuring a degree of conformity, precisely how order and its maintenance are viewed can vary a great deal. To begin with, there are considerable differences in the degree to which societies have transformed their ideas about correct behavior into a set of laws. The Comanches, for example, traditionally did not possess abstract rules about appropriate behavior; they had great difficulty in expressing norms about correct behavior in abstract situations (Hoebel 1940). In contrast, Australian Aborigines have a well-formulated set of rules in their law. The Comanches do not lack norms, but they have not formulated them into a roster of general laws.

Societies also vary in the extent to which compliance with laws or norms is expected. At one extreme are societies where compliance is strongly emphasized, where it is seen as the only means by which the society can survive or achieve fundamental goals such as the creation of an empire. At the other extreme are societies that are more tolerant, emphasizing manipulation and bargaining among individuals. These can be seen as representing differing adaptive strategies.

There are also differences in the kind of behavior that is tolerated. Some societies, such as the Inuit, take the theme of peace and harmony to an extreme, seeking to avoid controversy and aggressive behavior. At the other extreme, loud and aggressive behavior may be seen as desirable, with a high value placed upon individual achievement. Again, the kind of behavior a society tolerates is closely related to its overall adaptive strategy. For example, the American value placed upon individual aggression is linked to the capitalistic strategy that underlies America's adaptation.

Adherence to laws will be greater to the extent that the laws are based upon widely accepted norms. Most people in American society accept and comply with laws against murder, while fewer feel constrained by traffic laws. Murder and speeding are both related to the American emphasis upon the aggressive individual, but the incidence of murder is limited by other widely accepted norms, such as belief in the sanctity of human life. Compliance with such laws is rooted in the basic socialization patterns of a culture. The extent to which most Inuit avoid overtly aggressive behavior is to a large part a result of the fact that they are socialized from infancy not to be aggressive and are taught ways for handling and avoiding aggression in thought and deed.

Laws will affect some segments of a society differently than others. This is true even in relatively small, homogeneous societies. Many Australian Aboriginal societies have laws that favor males over females in the distribution of power and economic benefits. Such differences are even more marked in large-scale societies with greater social and economic inequality and greater cultural diversity. Thus, laws against polygyny in American society do not have much significance to the majority of people, whose cultural traditions frown upon the practice in any case, but they are of considerable importance to Mormons, whose religion allows such a practice. Often such differences are masked behind other cultural beliefs or values, ensuring that those adversely affected by the particular laws will be unaware of or willing to accept being discriminated against. Discriminatory laws against women in our own society were hidden and made more palatable until recently by an array of values concerning the "proper place" (i.e., the subservience) of women.

Despite these subtle means for getting people to go along with laws, there are always those who do not. There are those who break laws for personal reasons, those who are forced into breaking the law out of necessity, and those who break laws because they consider them to be unjust. There are individuals in every society who are misfits or trouble-makers, just as there will always be disagreements among even the strongest conformists. Because of the inevitability that laws will not automatically be adhered to, all societies have mechanisms for dealing with those who break or disagree with the laws. The need for such mechanisms is particularly pressing in large-scale societies since there are likely to be more individuals who do not adhere to or accept the laws; even entire groups within the society may disagree with the laws.

Handling Disputes in Foraging Societies

The foraging adaptation requires relatively few laws about property, since there is little personal property; the foragers' only concern is access to land, which can be handled by a few simple rules. The two areas of major tension are mating and the distribution of food. How extensive the laws are varies a great deal from people like the Inuit and Aborigines, who possess a large array of laws covering all major activities, to the Hadza and Bushmen, who have relatively few.

All foraging societies have rules for sharing food, but the actual division is often marked by suspicion and stress as people worry about getting their share. Disputes over mating or sexual jealousy are minimized in some societies by liberalizing sexual access, but in many other societies behavior such as elopement or extramarital affairs are a major source of tension and conflict.

Because of the small, close-knit nature of these societies, disputes and tensions are often handled at an interpersonal level through discussions or fights. Others may get informally involved in settling disputes, too. Shaming, gossip, and ridicule are particularly common means by which members of a foraging band seek to settle quarrels. The Mbuti of central Africa utilize public mimickry, individuals recognized as clowns mimicking the disputants in such a way as to reduce tensions. In most of these societies the primary emphasis is upon the maintenance of social order, as people try to reestablish social equilibrium through informal means.

Disputes are not always easily settled, however, and sometimes it becomes necessary to try to end tensions on a more formal basis. A common means of easing tensions among foragers is dispersal: bands split up to avoid further quarrels. The ease with which this occurs depends in part upon environmental conditions. The Hadza of East Africa live in a very hospitable terrain in which it is possible for an individual to live on his or her own; dispersal of bands is relatively common (Woodburn 1968). Where such environmental conditions as arid deserts or hostile neighbors make dispersal more difficult, the prime protagonist(s) may be ostracized. In some instances this is tantamount to a sentence of death.

Some foraging societies use more elaborate means of settling disputes. In many Australian Aboriginal societies, individuals accused of wrongdoing were able to get a public hearing at certain ceremonial gatherings and could be forgiven through the ritual of penis holding, in the case of a man, or giving herself sexually to the men involved in the hearing in the case of a woman (Berndt 1965: 187–90). Reciprocity is the focal point of such actions. This theme carries through much of the legal thought in these societies, for injured individuals or parties feel that they should be compensated in some way. Compensation tends to be negotiable. Groups may negotiate over the precise nature of goods or services they are to receive; where death is demanded, they may negotiate over who, how many, and what class of people are to be killed.

Laws in foraging societies are not concerned merely with individual quarrels. There are laws linked with less personal matters as well, such as religious practices. For example, many Australian Aboriginal societies have laws restricting access to religious paraphernalia and rites. Should an initiated man reveal sacred secrets to uninitiated persons, the elders would delegate one of their number to kill the offender. In this instance, the elders function as a court, with their delegate serving in the role of policeman/executioner.

Easing Tensions Among Small-Scale Farmers

The change from foraging to farming leads to new stresses and new legal requirements. There are more people packed into a smaller space, these people must cooperate more, and they have more material possessions at their disposal. In short, there is more to fight over and a greater likelihood that people will fight. The primary legal problems for farmers have to do with distribution of the surplus they produce, inheritance of property, and rights to land.

Farmers' ways of dealing with legal problems are similar to those employed by foragers, although in the case of farmers they tend to be more essential to the harmonious running of society because of the greater potential for stress. Many problems are handled through reciprocal obligations assigned to specific role relationships, such as role expectations of siblings and fellow lineage members. Shaming and ridicule also play a role. The Melanesians of Goodenough Island practice a form of shaming involving the exchange of food (Young 1971). A Goodenough Islander who feels he has been wronged will give the wrongdoer the finest and largest yam or other food item that he has. The intent is to shame the person by giving him something far better than he can reciprocate, since he is expected to make a return presentation of equal or higher value. In many farming societies people also practice sorcery and witchcraft and accuse one another of such practices in dealing with more mundane tensions and disputes.

As in foraging societies, there are also broad social mechanisms for dealing with disputes and tensions that cannot be handled among the disputants themselves. For farmers living in areas of relatively low population density, dispersal is a possibility. In southern Belize, for example, until recently villages would commonly fragment every few years as a result of factional disputes. Factional members would move to other villages or establish their own village in an unoccupied region. As higher population densities make such moves more difficult, other means of spacing disputants may evolve. For instance, in recent years members of opposing factions in villages of southern Belize have tended to space themselves within the village rather than leave. Ostracism is also a possible strategy for relieving tensions. After informal pressures are brought to bear, individuals sometimes choose to leave on their own, often going to nearby cities, but they may have to be forced to leave. In southern Belize, for example, the adult males in a village may gather and decide to force a troublemaker to leave. The task of eviction is given to village police, who are seen as having the right to carry out such decisions.

Another way to alleviate internal tensions in

a village is to turn attention outward. Farming societies often blame misfortunes on sorcerers or witches from elsewhere, the "elsewhere" commonly being left rather vague. Particularly where population densities run high, farmers also frequently engage in disputes and battles with their neighbors. These disputes with neighbors, often a result of disputes over land, serve as something of a safety valve within the community itself.

Formal Law Enforcement in States

Large-scale societies organized into states have different legal requirements and legal systems than small-scale societies. States' greater diversity of wealth and status and often greater cultural diversity produce a greater array of tensions that must be dealt with if social order is to be maintained. The increased scale and complexity of states make it more difficult to rely upon informal and interpersonal means of settling disputes. While gossip, shaming, and respect for role obligations remain important means of ensuring order, the state apparatus also relies upon specialized institutions for defining and upholding laws, such as a judiciary and police. These institutions derive their authority not so much from custom, as is the case with small-scale societies, as from the authority claimed by the state—the right to maintain social order. While small-scale societies can sometimes rely upon individuals functioning as police, in large-scale societies the role of police in law enforcement is much greater.

Ostracism is also practiced to encourage social order, in the form of imprisonment or deportation. Should large segments of the population pose a particular problem, they might be encouraged to leave. Guest and migrant worker schemes in many parts of the world relieve social tensions by temporarily removing poorly employed people who might otherwise seek to change the social order at home.

How laws are enforced depends in large part upon the distribution of power and wealth and the competition for them within a state. Where one segment of society is able to control the state apparatus, that segment will usually use the laws and legal institutions for its own ends. For example, Guatemala today is controlled by a small elite of wealthy landowners and capitalists who have passed laws that are unfavorable to the majority of people, and they have been able to use the police and military to attempt to control the people whenever threats to their rule arise. In other instances where political power is more diverse, as in the United States, there is greater competition over the passage of laws and often a greater judicial recognition of the rights of a larger section of the population.

Maintaining World Order

The modern nation-state is not an autonomous entity. Most share boundaries with other states and all find their affairs enmeshed with those of other states through trade, cultural affinity, and the desire for power. In this world system, it is essential to think in terms of global politics and global economics. This is most apparent in the geopolitical struggles of the United States and the Soviet Union as each seeks to control a large slice of the world. It is also apparent in the activities of multinational corporations, for the interests of a single multinational corporation may span dozens of nations. Tremendous tensions exist between those interacting at the international level, where wealth and cultural differences are far greater than anything imaginable within most individual states.

Especially during the present century, the response to the potential for chaos within the international arena has been to try to establish some ground rules that are recognized by at least a majority of the nations of the world. These include the web of treaties dealing with such things as copyright and the mail. There have also been more general attempts to create order through the establishment of international forums for disputes that transcend national boundaries, such as the United Nations and the World Court. The effectiveness of such institutions is limited, however, since they possess little coercive power. In a few instances the United Nations has succeeded in settling disputes through the use of military force or economic sanctions, but for the most part it serves as little more than an arena for airing disputes and perhaps coming to some understandings through mutual consent. Thus, while political and economic activities have moved to a world scale, so far law lags behind.

The Breakdown of Order

Interpersonal and social tensions are always present in any society; as we have seen, societies develop mechanisms for trying to deal with these tensions and the threat to order that they pose. When minor problems occur they usually can be taken care of with minimal disturbance to the social order. However, sometimes things get out of hand and gossip or the police are not able to keep a major disruption from occurring. Such major breakdowns tend to result from increasing pressures built up in a society because of underlying conflicts in the social structure.

The Zoot Suit Riot of 1943 was not merely a result of fights between sailors and Mexican-Americans. The riot and its aftermath reflected fundamental social tensions resulting from the economic and political oppression of Mexican-Americans; these were brought to the forefront by conditions generated by the Second World War. As is the case with most race riots, when order was restored the fundamental social tensions that generated the riot remained, leading to the inevitability of future threats to the existing social order. In this sense such a riot represents only a minor threat to existing political and economic relations—a ritual of rebellion. Struggles for power can, however, develop into more serious threats to the status quo. In fact, violent struggles for power are not uncommon in societies. These range from coups, rebellions, and revolutions within societies to warfare between societies.

Political Violence Within a Society

Orderly, nonviolent transferrals of power are not very common occurrences. Those with power tend to want more; they also are usually quite unwilling to give up what they have. This is true of individuals and perhaps even more so of people acting as a group. While the president of Mexico may be willing to settle for a single six-year term in office (after which he does not fall entirely from power), the small elite ruling Mexico would never consider such an easy handing over of power to another group. The presidents have little choice and most accept their constitutionally limited term in office, being satisfied with the power that they are able to accumulate without upsetting the existing order of things—for that order is responsible for their power in the first place. Individuals may curb their desire for power in the name of order or the common good, but the collective group of those who are in power are rarely so generous in regard to others. Those in power tend to identify order and the common good with their own well-being and with their staying in power.

Repetitive Rebellions. Those who wish to have power usually must seize it from those who

A tense street scene in Santiago during the September 1973 coup against Salvador Allende, President of Chile.

already have it. Major transfers of power rarely happen any other way. Eric Wolf and Edward Hansen (1972: 235) have written that "the history of Latin America from independence to the present time is a history of violent struggles of 'ins' and 'outs'." William Stokes (1952) has outlined the basic forms of violence that are present in Latin America: *machetismo, cuartelazo, golpe de estado*, and revolution. *Machetismo* (after the long knife, the machete, carried by many Latin American peasants) is a crude form of violence whereby a leader uses a mass of armed followers to seize power. This method of obtaining power often disrupts the administration and economy and may lead to a substantial loss of life. In Colombia, where *machetismo* has been common since the early nineteenth century, conflicts often take a heavy toll (between 1899 and 1903 alone more than one-hundred thousand people were killed), and affect almost every aspect of people's lives.

The *cuartelazo* involves careful planning on the part of a small group of soldiers to seize power quickly by taking over strategic locales. This transfer can be almost bloodless and the bulk of the population may not even know about it until everything is over. The most difficult part of the *cuartelazo* is making it stick. Staying in power requires, in particular, gaining recognition from other powerful elements in the society, especially other military units.

The *golpe de estado* is a coup in which the "bad" leader is replaced by a "good" one. Although the military is always involved, the *golpe* includes civilian participation. The *golpe* itself is a quick attack on those in power, generally involving the assassination or immobilization of the chief executive and the mobilization of a large number of people. As the overthrow of Salvador Allende in Chile illustrates, the successful *golpe* may involve long-term and very complex planning. Almost as soon as Allende was elected in 1970, foreign corporations with interests in Chile, United States intelligence agencies, and elements of the Chilean military and elite began planning his overthrow, which they accomplished in 1973 (see Evans 1974).

An important aspect of these forms of political violence, and of rebellions in general, is that they do not necessarily result in any structural changes in the society. After reviewing numerous rebellions in Africa, Max Gluckman found that "rebellion in most of these African states has therefore to be examined as a process of 'repetitive change,' since after it occurs there is no alteration in the structure of authoritative offices or the character of the personnel who hold them" (1965: 165). Rather than promoting change, in fact, such rebellions often act as safety valves for pressures building up in a society as a result of political or economic exploitation. The coup against Salvador Allende had profound implications for the development of Chilean society: increased repression of the people by the military, greater power for foreign corporations, and lower standards of living for many Chileans. More often, however, the structures of societies remain little changed.

Revolutions. Although political violence is fairly common within societies, true revolutions are not. Wolf and Hansen (1972: 235) define a *revolution* as a "fundamental change in the nature of the state, the functions of government, the principles of economic production and distribution, the relationship of social classes, particularly as regards the control of government—in a word, a significant breaking with the past."

The term *revolution* has been used inappropriately for a wide range of political violence, such as the wars for independence in Latin America, which resulted in relatively minor changes for the majority of people. By and large humans have demonstrated a remarkable ability to tolerate and adapt to unbelievably awful conditions without trying to create markedly different social orders. Fundamental breaks with the past that warrant the designation *revolution* are actually very rare.

There are many reasons why revolutions occur so infrequently. The majority's lack of power, inability to organize, or insufficient desire are relatively simple considerations. Gluckman, in his study of African rebellions (1965), discusses another important factor: the existence of multiple and divided loyalties that make a drastic change difficult. We are caught up in a web of social relationships that bound our actions and thoughts, and reduce our revolutionary potential. A desire for security and a fear of the unknown are common to most members of a society. People rarely risk what little they do have in the way of family, food, and shelter in the hope of obtaining something better by breaking entirely with the existing social order. Even when people do rebel because of poverty or injustice their goal is commonly not the revolutionary transformation of society, but merely the adjustment of the existing social order. Peasants' traditional response once they have overthrown the cruel tyrant is to replace him with another ruler who turns out to be not much different. Their failure to seek a truly revolutionary change may in part be related to a lack of imagination—to being unable to perceive a radically different social order—and also to a desire for predictability.

When revolutions do occur, they are the re-

A group of guerrilla fighters, members of the Farabundo Marti National Liberation Front, in southeastern El Salvador, February 1982.

sult of very exceptional circumstances. It is not enough for people to rebel; they must also create a new social order that is drastically different from what came before. It is this creative aspect that most distinguishes revolution from other forms of political violence.

Many of the complexities of the revolutionary process are perhaps best studied by specialists in disciplines other than anthropology. Economists have contributed a great deal through their analysis of such factors as inflation and deflation, and social psychologists have provided insights into the important questions of deprivation and response to authority. There are, however, a number of very important contributions that the anthropological perspective alone can make (Wolf 1971: xiv). Our detailed knowledge of peasant society resulting from research based upon participant observation is one of these; for despite the urban bias of most revolutionary leaders and revolutionary ideologies (and of those who study revolutions), peasants have played a decisive role in many revolutions. For many individuals the term *peasantry* conjures up an image of a rather conservative, homogeneous mass. This is a false image. To understand the dynamics of the revolutionary process among peasants requires that we look at the different segments of peasant society, for they are affected by and influence the process in often very different ways. In the Russian Revolution, for instance, one segment of the peasantry in particular was most important: those who were relatively affluent and who had the closest ties with the cities. This upper stratum of peasants is most likely to find its social and economic goals frustrated by existing conditions.

Understanding the mobilization of large numbers of people and the creation of a revolution does not come about simply by looking at general socioeconomic conditions or ideologies. It requires an examination of the specific social context within which people make their deci-

sions and of the actual exchanges that occur, with special attention to the role of intermediaries or middlemen. Intellectuals may be able to provide the ideological focus of a revolution, but such people are rarely easily accepted by peasants or urban laborers. Comprehending how relations actually develop between different segments of a population and how ideology is transmitted at an interpersonal level is a necessary component of any study of revolution.

Warfare Between Societies

People within a society generally try to settle their differences in a peaceful and orderly manner, although they do not always succeed. While there are numerous constraints on aggression within most societies, beyond the bounds of the society there are far fewer restraints or incentives for a peaceful resolution of differences. This is especially true when the outsiders are barely considered to be members of the same species. Fortunately, those who are perceived by the members of a society to be so different also tend to be of little social or economic relevance, and there is little reason to fight. *Warfare*, or aggression between politically autonomous communities, often occurs when relations break down between groups that usually interact on a more or less harmonious basis or when groups that generally have little to do with each other are forced into contact and competition. It is not enough to say that warfare is a natural consequence of human aggressiveness; warfare results from specific social and environmental circumstances.

Anthropologists recognize three primary categories of intergroup aggression: feuding, raiding, and large-scale warfare. The causes and patterns of each will vary from one setting to another. They will also take on very different characteristics in large-scale and small-scale societies, reflecting demographic and technological differences. In all cases the parties involved will pursue goals in a relatively ordered fashion, seeking continuously to rationalize their actions by reference to culture-specific beliefs—for example, "God is on our side."

Feuding. *Feuding* involves violence between different families or groups of kin. It may take place within a social group or between members of different groups. The feud is the most universal form of intergroup aggression, in part because of its limited requirements: All that is needed is enough people to find something to fight over.

Spencer and Gillen (1899: 489–96) describe a common pattern of feud among Australian Aborigines—the avenging party. The quarrels usually begin when a man steals a wife from some other group or when someone's death is blamed on sorcery by a member of a distant group. The aggrieved party will then form a group to attack those believed to be responsible. Although the members of the avenging party enter the enemy's camp fully armed with spears and spear throwers, boomerangs and shields, the quarrel is usually "confined to a wordy warfare, lasting perhaps an hour or two, after which things quieten down, and all is over." Physical violence is not always avoided, however. In some cases "the attacking party will steal down upon the enemy, and, lying in ambush, will await an opportunity of spearing one or two of the men without any risk to themselves." A common feature of such feuds is that acts of violence are not necessarily carried out against specific individuals, but against members of a kin group in general. Feuds do not always end with the first act of revenge; there may be counterattacks and the feud may evolve into a more general confrontation between larger social groups.

Feuding tends to be of more political significance in small-scale societies than in large-scale ones. An exception is feuds between elite families in large-scale societies in which political authority is based upon heredity, such as mon-

archies (e.g. the War of Roses between York and Lancaster in England). In such cases, and in any society in which kinship and politics are closely aligned, feuding can be of considerable significance and may easily develop into warfare.

Raiding. *Raids*—surprise predatory attacks by groups of individuals—tend to be limited to specific kinds of societies within particular settings. Small-scale farmers and foragers generally do not engage in raiding, although sometimes they are the objects of raids. Agricultural villages in West Africa were raided by slavers prior to the mid-nineteenth century, and Bushmen in southwest Africa continue to live in fear of being carried off. As population pressures increase and competition for scarce resources sets in, societies become more likely to raid their neighbors, creating in some instances a situation of almost continuous tension, as is the case throughout much of Amazonian South America. Raiding is also encouraged when neighboring peoples possess very different levels of power and have resources that are coveted, as with the Bushmen and their more powerful neighbors. Finally, some societies come to specialize in raiding because other options are closed to them or because such an adaptation has a decisive advantage over any others available to them. The Amazonian Mura evolved from aquatic agriculturists to almost full-time raiders during the eighteenth century, in response to new opportunities created by Portuguese invasion and occupation. The Mura raided both whites and other Indians all along the Amazon, living for long periods in isolated canoes. They raised few crops of their own, subsisting primarily on what they could catch in the rivers or seize from others. Some groups of Plains Indians developed a similar adaptation on the land, utilizing the horse and developing a mode of social organization suited to their need for mobility and frequent fighting.

Australian Aboriginal feuds or Mura raids involved relatively small numbers of people, as does most intergroup aggression among small-scale societies. Occasionally fighting does escalate, but because of the small population and the inability of foragers and subsistence agriculturists to afford the luxury of a prolonged period of warfare, fighting of this magnitude tends to be of short duration. Lloyd Warner (1937: 161-63) describes one form of interclan warfare among Aborigines living in northern Australia, known as the *gaingar:*

The gaingar is so deadly and results in so many casualties that it is rarely used and then only under the most extreme provocation. There are only two recorded cases in the last twenty years, one between the peoples of the Caledon Bay area and those of Buckingham Bay; the other between peoples west of the Goyder River and along the seacoast and those east of the Goyder and in the interior. . . . The writer recorded fifteen deaths in the Caledon Bay fight, and fourteen killed and one severely wounded in the Goyder River combat. Such casualty lists show clearly that the sparse population of the Murngin and the surrounding tribes cannot afford such a military luxury except at rare intervals.

The fight is held between the members of several clans and is the result of regional antagonisms. . . . It always follows a long-protracted series of killings in which each side is stimulated to an almost hysterical pitch. When one group of clans finally decides to invite its enemies for a gaingar, the people always say that this is a spear fight to end spear fights, so that from that time on there will be peace for all the clans and tribes.

Large-Scale Warfare. Larger, agriculturally based populations are able to carry out forms of warfare that are more protracted—but no more likely to result in lasting peace. As population pressures become noticeable, people begin to find more to fight about. For foragers and farmers living in sparsely populated areas, warfare is rarely initiated for the purpose of seizing territory (although territory seizure may occur as an indirect result of fighting). Rather, wars among these peoples generally begin because of interpersonal quarrels, such as fighting over women. While such quarrels occur among larger agricultural societies, the desire to conquer land also becomes significant. Mervyn Meggitt (1977: 182), in his study of Mae Enga warfare in the highlands of New Guinea, notes that "in the present and in the past, the desire of local descent groups to gain and hold arable land has been the most powerful motive impelling them to make war on each other." Mae Enga warfare usually lasts only a few days, for more prolonged periods of warfare are a severe strain on resources. There are stressful periods of inaction while waiting for possible attack; people are unable to carry out their daily tasks; and there is also the need to continue to support one's allies. The average number of warriors involved in wars among the central Enga is about 360, but the number of casualties tends not to be very great. Between 1961 and 1973, out of 46 incidents the mean number of deaths was 1.6 per incident. Clearly, Mae Enga warfare is still a far cry from the Vietnam War, although there are similarities in motives and procedures—economic motivations coupled with noneconomic rationalizations, emphasis upon male prowess and ostentation, and severe strain on the civilian economy.

Warfare on the scale we have come to know did not occur in human history until the organization of empires and states. In fact, warfare and the evolution of states are closely interrelated. In many of the early empires and states, warfare was very important, influencing many aspects of people's lives. The Aztecs of central Mexico placed great emphasis on military training. Both commoners and nobles were given formal military training as youths, and those who

A Mae Enga warrior, wearing his traditional round wig and displaying his ceremonial axe, in the highlands of New Guinea.

were most successful in battle were recruited to many posts, such as judge, constable, or steward. To remain in a state of readiness, the Aztecs engaged neighboring peoples in *xochiyaoyotl*, flowery wars, in which fighting was restrained and the nobles refrained from killing one another (the only casualties were commoners).

Within societies like that of the Aztec we see the emergence of the military specialist, a role generally lacking in small-scale societies. Warfare and the military also assume a more signifi-

cant role, as the emphasis shifts from minor boundary adjustments (as in the Mae Enga) to supporting a society based upon conquest and the extraction of tribute from conquered peoples. Even for the Aztecs, however, warfare was never rationalized solely in terms of control and plunder; it always required some other form of legitimation. As Frederic Hicks (1979: 90) has noted, "every empire has developed some high moral principle to justify its actions and for which its people would be more willing to risk

The face of modern warfare: American soldiers, on maneuvers near the East German border in 1981, flank a Lance missile.

their lives than they would be just to make their rulers rich and powerful." For the Aztecs, as for so many peoples, support for their aggression came from their religion, which "needed" sacrificial victims.

The expansion of European empires and the creation of the modern world system have had important consequences for warfare patterns. They made possible the world war, in which people who had very little direct interest in a confrontation could be drawn into it through sometimes subtle forms of manipulation. They also meant that localized wars frequently assumed international importance. The effects on small-scale indigenous societies were often profound. In the Amazon, societies that had in many instances not been particularly warlike were pushed together, forced to contend with the Portuguese invaders and to compete with each other for dwindling resources. For example, the warfare that has become endemic to the Yanomamo of southern Venezuela (Chagnon 1977) is largely a consequence of their being pushed into a refuge area with a relatively poor resource base. Yanomamo adaptation is significantly influenced by the fact that their neighbors, the Makiritare, acquired guns and were able to establish a relationship of dominance over them. In many parts of the world, differential access to European military technology allowed some groups to establish hegemony over their neighbors. In Africa, those states which supplied the slave trade were able to create far-flung empires with the support of such technology. In Polynesia petty chiefs were able to defeat their neighbors and establish island-wide kingdoms. In most of these instances, the success of the conquerors was short-lived as the Europeans who made their success possible assumed control.

Despite the frequent eruptions of wars, people have always longed for peace. Perhaps one of the most important ideas to come out of anthropological studies of warfare is that wars are clearly "cultural artifacts" (Mead 1967: 219), that they are created by specific, nonbiological conditions. By altering these conditions it should be possible to eliminate warfare. The problem is first gaining a thorough understanding of the conditions that generate warfare and then implementing changes that will eliminate these conditions.

Summary

From local race riots to world wars, political violence has always been with us. Its incidence is limited, however, by norms, laws, and provisions for law enforcement and dispute mediation.

Norms are conceptions of how people should behave. These change with changes in the social environment. The spread of European ideas has had a particularly strong impact on the norms of other peoples.

Often norms are elevated to the systematized status of laws, binding rules about behavior. Laws may be written or unwritten, formally enacted or followed by custom. All are legitimized by reference to some general normative idea and perhaps by concepts of how a "reasonable man" would behave in a given situation. Like the norms on which they are based, laws change with the social environment. However, sometimes the legal systems of differing cultures are allowed to coexist.

Attitudes toward laws and the necessity for their enforcement vary from one society to another. Those laws based on widely accepted norms usually meet with the most compliance. In every society, however, there are those who break laws or disagree with others or with the laws themselves. Ways of handling such situations are related to the society's adaptive strategy. Foraging societies, in which disputes sometimes arise over food sharing or sexual jealousy, handle these disputes either by informal, interpersonal means or by somewhat more formal methods, such as dispersal, group negotiation, or decisions by the elders of the community.

Small-scale farmers add to the list of potential quarrels arguments over distribution of surplus food, property inheritance, and land rights. Like foragers, they may use informal interpersonal methods or more formal dispersal or decision-making methods to deal with disputes.

Tensions are also often blamed on outsiders, and disputes with neighboring communities over land are common.

In large-scale societies people have so much to fight over that law enforcement and dispute mediation are institutionalized. Attempts have been made to institutionalize settlement of disputes between states in the world system, but the effectiveness of the institutions set up has been limited.

Despite attempts to deal with threats to social order, tensions sometimes lead to violent struggles for power. Within a society, there may be repeated rebellions that change the personnel in power but leave the social structure intact, or (rarely) revolutions, in which the entire order of the society is radically changed. Warfare between politically autonomous communities may be on as small a scale as an interfamily feud or as large a scale as a world war involving many nations.

Each kind of warfare tends to be linked to specific adaptations and environments. Feuding is most common in small-scale societies, raids become more frequent as population pressures and competition for resources increase, and large-scale warfare was unknown until empires and states developed. The expansion of European empires and the modern world system have created warring patterns in some small-scale indigenous populations. An anthropological understanding of the specific settings in which political violence develops could provide a basis for alterations in those settings and perhaps reduction in the incidence of violence.

Suggested Readings

General studies on law:

Bohannon, Paul, ed. 1967. *Law and Warfare.* New York: Natural History Press.

Burman, Sandra B. and Harrell-Bond, Barbara E., eds. 1979. *The imposition of law.* New York: Academic Press.

Gulliver, P. H. 1979. *Disputes and negotiations.* New York: Academic Press.

Hamnett, Ian, ed. 1977. *Social anthropology and law.* New York: Academic Press.

Hoebel, E. A. 1954. *The law of primitive man.* Cambridge, MA: Harvard University Press.

Malinowski, Bronislaw. 1926. *Crime and custom in savage society.* London: Kegan Paul, Trench, Trubner.

Moore, Sally Falk. 1978. *Law as process: An anthropological approach.* London: Routledge and Kegan Paul.

Nader, Laura, ed. 1969. *Law in culture and society.* Chicago: Aldine.

Pospisil, Leopold. 1971. *Anthropology of law.* New York: Harper & Row.

Roberts, Simon. 1979. *Order and dispute: An introduction to legal anthropology.* Harmondsworth: Penguin.

Case studies on law:

Barton, R. F. 1919. *Ifugao law.* Berkeley: University of California Press. (Philippines)

Bohannon, Paul J. 1957. *Justice and judgement among the Tiv.* Oxford: Oxford University Press.

Collier, Jane F. 1973. *Law and social change in Zinacantan.* Stanford: Stanford University Press.

Eggleston, Elizabeth. 1976. *Fear, favour or affection: Aborigines and the criminal law in Victoria, South Australia and Western Australia.* Canberra: Australian National University Press.

Fallers, Lloyd A. 1969. *Law without precedent: Legal ideas in action in the courts of colonial Busoga.* Chicago: University of Chicago Press.

Gluckman, Max. 1973. *The judicial process among the Barotse of Northern Rhodesia (Zambia).* Manchester: Manchester University Press.

Gulliver, P. H. 1963. *Social control in an African society.* London: Routledge and Kegan Paul. (Tanzania)

Studies on rebellion, revolution, and warfare:

Fried, Morton, Harris, Marvin, and Murphy, Robert, eds. 1967. *War: The anthropology of armed conflict and aggression.* Garden City, NY: Natural History Press.

Friedrich, Paul. 1970. *Agrarian revolt in a Mexican village.* Englewood Cliffs, NJ: Prentice-Hall.

Gardner, Robert, and Heider, Karl G. 1968. *Gardens of war: Life and death in the New Guinea Stone Age.* New York: Random House.

Hobsbawm, E. J. 1959. *Primitive rebels.* Manchester: Manchester University Press.

Huizer, Gerritt. 1973. *Peasant rebellion in Latin America.* Harmondsworth: Penguin.

Lloyd, Peter C. 1973. *Classes, crises and coups: Themes in the sociology of developing countries.* London: Paladin.

Meggitt, Mervyn. 1977. *Blood is their argument: Warfare among the Mae Enga tribesmen of the New Guinea highlands.* Palo Alto, CA: Mayfield.

Migdal, Joel S. 1974. *Peasants, politics and revolution.* Princeton: Princeton University Press.

Post, Ken. 1978. *Arise ye starvlings: The Jamaican labour rebellion of 1938 and its aftermath.* The Hague: Martinus Nijhoff.

Rudé, George. 1980. *Ideology and popular protest.* New York: Pantheon.

Vayda, Andrew P. 1960. *Maori warfare.* Auckland: Polynesian Society.

Wolf, Eric R. 1971. *Peasant wars of the twentieth century.* London: Faber and Faber.

Religion

ONE THEME HAS turned up repeatedly in the preceding chapters: fearing chaos, we have striven to create order in ideology and behavior. The social and mental order that we find among humans is not so much an innate quality of our species as it is a reflection of our dread of anarchy, of a universe without order and meaning. Our social institutions, our norms, and our experiences are not always sufficient to maintain the delicate balance between order and anarchy, however. Despite all the precautions we have taken, our ability to interpret life as orderly and meaningful breaks down when we seek answers to the ultimate questions of our existence: Where did we come from? Why are we as we are? Why must we die? In response to such questions humans often turn to *religion*, the assumption that there are supernatural forces or beings that provide shape and meaning to the universe.

Elements of Religion

The term *supernatural* in the religious sense refers to a shift away from the secular order of reality into the *sacred*, the realm of symbolic meanings and actions through which we interpret the forces that ultimately control and give shape to the universe. Religion, then, involves the use of sacred symbols through beliefs and actions. In studying religious beliefs, anthropologists are concerned with how people construct a religious view of the world. We refer to this view as *cosmology*. We are also concerned with the symbols that people employ to express these beliefs. Anthropologists argue that cosmologies and the meanings attached to religious symbols (as well as the symbols themselves) are grounded in the environment within which a people live and in their particular mode of adaptation and social structure. In this sense, religion is an aspect of a people's adaptation to their environment. The religious beliefs of Australian Aborigines are grounded in their foraging way of life and in the physical environment surrounding them. Their beliefs also relate to the structure of their society and to their relationship with neighboring societies. The same point can be made of religious beliefs in our own society, whether those of impoverished miners or farmers in Kentucky who belong to snake-handling Pentecostal sects or those of middle-class suburbanites in Los Angeles who are members of more sedate status quo-oriented churches.

Religion is not merely a matter of belief. It also involves institutionalized patterns of behavior—rituals, ceremonies, and the like—that express and reinforce religious beliefs. Through ceremonies, whether a high mass in Notre Dame or performance of the Gunabibi fertility rite by Australian Aborigines, members of a society are brought into the realm of the sacred. They are made to feel as if they are a part of the supernatural. When Aborigines perform the ceremonies associated with their Dreamtime creation mythology they are not simply reenacting events from the Dreamtime; they are becoming a part of it. Such a transition often results in a change in consciousness as their thoughts are transformed to a "higher" plane

OVERLEAF

This mask comes from the Indian peoples in the Lower Kuskokwim River or Bristol Bay region of Alaska. Whether worn for ritual, disguise, as a symbol of authority or prestige, or to effect cures, masks hold a deep power. Made of wood, with white, black, and red pigment, willow bands, brown feathers, baleen and fiber lashings, this mask (70.5 cm high) once belonged to Claude Levi-Strauss.

Though a religious leader primarily, the Catholic Pope wields considerable secular power.

that transcends everyday experience. Such transcendental states are not a necessary part of religion, as witnessed by the millions of church-goers who sit passively through the performance going on before them, but achieving such a condition does often accompany or may even be a goal of religious activities. At the very least, there is a feeling of belonging to a community of believers and an accompanying sense of security.

Religion is also concerned with power, both sacred and secular. Religious belief entails acceptance of the existence of power that is neither a part of "nature" in its physical manifestations nor a creation of human society. An important part of religion is the attempt to use or to come to grips with this power. Precisely

how the relationship between humankind and these supernatural powers is defined can vary a great deal from one society to the next, as may the recognized modes for dealing with such power. In some societies, power may be viewed as something that simply exists, and over which humans have little influence. In others (with, for example, a Judeo-Christian tradition) we at least may be able to make requests, hoping that they will be granted. Still others have a more egalitarian view. The Australian Aboriginal view of their relation with the Dreamtime beings is essentially an interdependent one (Kolig 1978), based upon the notion that continuance of the world order created by these beings requires the performance of rituals by humans. Mesoamerican Indians may reward statues of their saints with candles and other presents for granting them favors, or punish them by removing their clothes (*vestimenta*) or turning them to face the wall should they fail to answer requests.

Religion is also closely linked with more mundane dimensions of power in most societies. Even in relatively egalitarian societies, religious specialists have an edge in the competition for power because of their association with the forces controlling the universe. The Inuit shaman whose soul is said to be able to leave his body to commune with the gods, Australian Aboriginal elders who monopolize the fundamental elements of their religion, and the Pope all wield secular power because of their ties to the sacred. At the same time, the dominant religious dogma in a society—that is, a formal system of beliefs—commonly reflects and supports the interests of those in power; widespread acceptance of this dogma helps to maintain existing power relations. In the religious traditions of Western Desert Aborigines like the Mardudjara, for example, the ideology supports the established inequality between males and females and between initiated and uninitiated males. When such beliefs are challenged, as with the numerous schisms within the Christian tradition, the challenge is often related to secular competition for power within the religious institutions or between segments of the society at large. These examples, though something of an oversimplification, do point to the close interrelationship between religion and social process.

Understanding Religious Belief

Although religious beliefs are built upon and reflect everyday experience, they go beyond our more mundane thoughts of life. They represent what we perceive through faith to be the ultimate truths of existence. Because of religion's transcendental quality—the idea that it is related to a truth that is beyond human comprehension—religious belief is not subject to the same proofs of truth or falsehood, the same pragmatic constraints, or the same logic as nonreligious thought. It is this detachment from temporal rationality, as well as the claim to being the key to the secrets of the universe, that give religious belief its power. The existence of gods or the truth of myths cannot be proven or disproven; we can only believe or disbelieve.

What concerns anthropologists more than the ultimate reality of a religious assertion is the question of why people have come to hold a given belief. Why, for instance, have some people selected the idea of reincarnation out of a range of possible means of dealing with the question of death? Answers to such questions, to the extent that they can be found, are both complex and difficult to arrive at. In searching for answers we must look at the particular religious beliefs, their relationship to social processes, and their relationship to historical and ecological factors.

Belief Systems in Context

Religious beliefs tend to be systematically centered on a core of precepts about the nature of things, presented in symbolic form. It is this core that gives direction and shape to a belief system as people work out the implications of these primary premises. We can see how a belief system is shaped by looking at the Rastafarians, members of a religious cult founded in Jamaica.

The Rastafarians believe that they are eternal and shall never die. They declare, "We who are Rastafarians are the disciples who have walked with God from the time when the foundation of creation was laid, through 71 bodies, to behold the 72nd house of power which shall reign forever" (Barrett 1977: 112). Other core elements of their beliefs include deification of the Ethiopian emperor Haile Selassie; the assertion that the black person is the reincarnation of ancient Israel, living in exile because of the "Whiteman"; belief that Jamaica is the modern-day Babylon, in contrast to Ethiopia, which is heaven; and belief that whites are inferior to blacks (Barrett 1977: 104).

We can trace the historic origins of Rastafarian beliefs to such sources as Christianity and the early twentieth-century teachings of Marcus Garvey. The Rastafarians see the Bible as a

source for many of their beliefs. They argue, however, that it has been subject to distortion by the Whiteman, and that they alone are able to interpret the meaning of its contents correctly.

The Rastafarians' interpretation of the Bible is linked to their own circumstances. For instance, they base their belief in their own immortality and reincarnation on a passage from the Bible in the Book of Romans: "The wages of sin is death, but the gift of God is eternal life." This passage guaranteeing eternal life has been interpreted in a multitude of ways, the Rastafarians' version being derived from the peculiarities of their situation in Jamaica—their poverty, the discrimination that they have faced, and the near hopelessness that they feel for changing things by "rational" means. The

Now-deceased Ethiopian Emperor Haile Selassie, proclaimed by Rastafarians to be not only their spiritual leader, but also a deity.

Rastafarian variant of Christianity is an example of what can be termed a "religion of the oppressed" (see Lanternari 1963). It is an attempt by oppressed peoples to deal with their situation through the medium of religion. Such religions represent a form of rebellion, and it is from the impoverished population of Jamaica that followers of the Rastafarian movement are recruited. They may be seen as seeking to escape from their condition through faith and the promise of a reversal of the world order by supernatural forces.

Choices Available

A person's decision to become a Rastafarian is often a matter of conscious choice, but given the life of most poor Jamaicans, it represents one of only a few choices seen as available to them. In seeking the answer to why a person chooses to become a Rastafarian, or to adhere to any other religious belief, we can look at psychological and social pressures and constraints. The Rastafarian faith represents security and hope in an otherwise insecure and often rather miserable world. The potential Rastafarian is raised in an environment of poverty and illiteracy in which individual attempts at upward mobility rarely succeed and rebellions have continually failed. That persons living under such conditions will turn to such religions as the Rastafarian is almost to be expected. To figure out why a choice is made, we can look at what one religion offers that others do not, and how each recruits its members. Some actively seek new members; others emphasize socialization of children of existing members.

How much choice a person has in choosing a religion can vary a great deal from one society or situation to the next. In small-scale societies individuals rarely have much choice in their beliefs. For example, Australian Aborigines traditionally were provided with only one possible view of the world. There was little basis for questioning any of the basic tenets of this belief system. Their very personalities were too intertwined with these beliefs to allow fundamental questioning or change. Even small alterations were left largely in the hands of a small religious elite who knew the more esoteric meanings of the rites and myths. Similar situations exist in many small communities in our own society, where the choice is between two or three very similar religious sects.

Increasing social scale presents a potential challenge to this monopolization of religious belief, although when state religions are promoted choices may still be severely limited, as they were in Spain during the Inquisition. European contact brought Aborigines a choice between their own faith and that of their conquerors. In some areas they chose to keep their own, seeing no reason why they should adopt the Whiteman's religion. But attempts were made to undermine the Aboriginal religion, and in many areas Aboriginal children were taken away from their parents to be instructed as Christians. Such high-handed tactics encouraged some Aborigines to cling even more tenaciously to their own faith. For many their religion became a symbol of their remaining autonomy, one of the few realms in which Aborigines could exercise some freedom. In some areas, missionary activity led not to the conversion of Aborigines to Christianity, but to their·rejection of both white and Aboriginal religion (Sackett 1978).

Conversions to Christianity have occurred among the Australian Aborigines, however. In relatively small homogenous communities, those converting to Christianity often have been individuals who had not done well under the traditional system and/or who stood to gain materially or otherwise by converting. Where Aborigines have moved into larger, more heterogenous communities Christianity has commonly remained important, for church personnel offer welfare services that many Aborigines are highly dependent upon.

Even in large-scale societes individual choice about religious belief may be limited. As in smaller-scale societies, early socialization is usually an important factor, for people are conditioned to view the world from a particular perspective and to feel that their religious affiliation is a vital part of their social identity. This religious socialization may influence their choice of friends and spouse, interaction with whom will further encourage them to retain their initial allegiance. Contact with people who do not share one's beliefs may lead to a change, although it may on the other hand reinforce one's own beliefs. A drastic change of status (such as sudden impoverishment) or changing peer pressures (such as becoming caught up in new religious movements) may also affect one's religious beliefs. There is never any single answer as to why a person comes to believe one way or another, but the choice is never entirely random. At least in general terms, patterns of religious belief can be explained by certain social and psychological variables.

Religious Belief and Adaptational Strategy

As a final consideration in understanding religious belief, it is important to note that certain forms tend to be associated with particular modes of economic adaptation. Among foragers, such as traditional Australian Aborigines, religious beliefs are closely related to the things most important to them: the land over which they range and the plants and animals they procure. Aboriginal religion therefore places a heavy emphasis on the procreation of important animal species. The Gunabibi fertility ritual contains a great deal of procreative imagery. The sacred ground on which the rite is performed includes a large crescent-shaped pit representing the uterus of the mythical rock python, which is the central image upon which the ritual is based. As part of the ritual, young boys are led into the pit and symbolically swallowed by the rock python; they later emerge as if reborn. Many of the objects used in the ritual are phallic. Ritual activities include imitations of the matings of various species; in one of the final acts of the Gunabibi, the men place two large *jelmalandji* (twelve-to-twenty-foot-long poles with pads of grass and paper bark tied to them) across the uteral pit. The rite represents a way to ensure the growth and perpetuation of the animals most important in the Aboriginal diet.

A shift to agriculture results in a shift of emphasis in a people's religion. The gods, prayers, rites, and so forth are concerned primarily with the things that influence agriculture: pestilence, natural disaster, rain, time. Among the most important deities among various groups of Maya are those associated with the weather, especially with rain. Maya religious specialists in many areas devote much of their effort to divining knowledge useful in planting and harvesting.

Changes from foraging to agricultural forms of religion are not always complete. Those Amazonian Indians who continue to value foraging even though agriculture dominates their productive activities tend to have religious beliefs and practices that reflect their dual interests. People may also simply retain religious beliefs that were part of their hunting and gathering past. The Huicholes of northwestern Mexico were foragers until a few centuries ago, when they adopted agriculture because of Spanish influence. Their religion, which centers on what Barbara Myerhoff (1970) refers to as the Deer-Maize-Peyote complex, represents an "incomplete transition." They have retained many social and cultural elements from their foraging past, and these continue to be reflected in their religion, especially in the deer symbolism. Agriculture in turn is associated symbolically with maize. Through such religious practices as the ceremonial annointing of maize with deer blood these two elements of their life are united.

Religious Symbols

Symbols like the deer and maize of the Huichol draw together or focus significant elements of a people's existence, unifying the everyday with the supernatural. They objectify experience in a concrete fashion, and in so doing are able to get at our most fundamental feelings. It is because of their ability to unify and express the core elements of our lives that symbols play such an important role in religion.

Culture-Specific Symbols

Certain religious symbols are universal, but most are culturally specific, and individuals must be conditioned to understand and appreciate them. Conditioning occurs in formal or informal instruction, as when Aboriginal youths are taught the meanings of the marks on the sacred boards that serve as physical representations of the actions of the Dreamtime beings.

Such learning is enhanced by creating an environment designed to stir emotions when confronted with the symbols. Such an environment may include a particularly impressive church or physical setting, a stirring ritual or ceremonial gathering, or a combination of the two. Aboriginal youths are also prepared psychologically through ritual and other means to greet the sacred revelations of the elders with great respect, fear, and perhaps even awe. Pintubi youths are already in an otherworldly state when the elders bring forth the sacred paraphernalia and tell them: "Dead men held this" (Myers, 1982).

The power of culture-specific religious symbolism is exemplified in what is perhaps the best-known Rastafarian symbol: their long and unkempt hair, their "dreadlocks." The wearing of their hair in this fashion is justified by reference to the Bible: "They shall not make baldness upon their head, neither shall they shave

People of Jigalong, Western Australia, prepare for a ceremonial gathering by decorating themselves with rain-making motifs.

off the corner of their beard, nor make any cuttings in the flesh" (Leviticus 21:5). The dreadlock serves as a powerful public symbol of what the Rastafarian religion is about. It sets the Rastaman off as "the natural man, who typifies in his appearance the unencumbered life" (Barrett 1977: 137). But beyond this there is the association with rebellion, with a refusal to accept the world as defined by the Whiteman. As Barrett has noted, hair is used by many Jamaicans as an index of social differences. By wearing long, unkempt hair the Rastafarian is considered wild, dangerous, effeminate, and dreadful. He underscores contradictions within Jamaican society and represents a threat to the social order: "The hair-symbol of the Rastas announces that they are outside Jamaican society and do not care to enter under any circumstances other than one of radical change in the society's attitude to the poor" (1977: 138). The response of those concerned with maintaining the status quo has been to cut off the Rastafarians' hair.

Within our own cultural tradition hair takes on some of the same images, but this is certainly not a universal interpretation. In many societies long hair is associated with holiness; in others it is a common occurrence. Before the arrival of the Spanish, lowland Maya, especially those of high status, commonly wore their hair long. Under Spanish influence and pressure they began cutting their hair, and today most Maya view unkempt hair unfavorably. It is only among the non-Christian Lacandon that long hair continues to be worn, and this has helped to enforce other Mayas' aversion to long hair because of its association with paganism. While hair is assigned some social significance in virtually all societies, its specific symbolic significance can vary a great deal.

Food Symbolism

The food people eat or do not eat is also often closely associated with religious beliefs. In many religious traditions particular animals or plants are assigned a symbolic role; in religions with food taboos, people are permitted to eat certain foods only in sacred contexts or not at all.

Rastafarians have relatively strict ideas about their diet that are tied to their religion. They are for the most part vegetarians, although they may eat small fish. Pork and beef are considered pollutants. Basically they favor a diet that is natural and derived directly from the earth.

The cow has symbolic significance in many societies beyond that of being a supply of meat and milk. It is a relatively poor source of protein, and in many areas of the world the grazing of cattle severely reduces the potential for food production. Despite these drawbacks, the cow is important to many Americans as a symbol of wealth and well-being. This and other factors have led American development experts to promote the spread of cattle raising in many parts of the world, often through rather suspect economic rationales. We are not alone in our reverence of the cow. Pastoralists in the southern Sudan and western Ethiopia like the Nuer and Dinka see their lives and those of their cattle as inextricably intertwined. The Dinkas' perceptions of color, light, and shade are connected with the color configurations in their cattle. The centrality of the cow to Dinka culture has resulted in its serving as the most important element in their religious beliefs and practices. Animal sacrifice is the central religious act, and the sacrificial animal symbolizes Dinka society as the meat is divided to reflect social relations on the basis of sex, age, and clanship (Lienhardt 1961).

While most Hindus do not depend as heavily upon cattle for their survival as the Dinka, the cow has assumed an important place in their religion as well. To Hindus the cow is "worshipped as a symbol of warmth and moisture, as earth mother, and as a producer of milk and indirectly ghi [clarified butter], so essential in sacrifices" (Heston 1971: 192). In India, this belief and the Indian tradition of nonviolence eventually led to a constitutional ban on the slaughter of cattle (see Simoons 1973). Many observers who have seen cattle wandering about amidst starving and malnourished people have viewed this ban as dysfunctional. Marvin Harris (1974), however, argues that the Indian sacred cow situation represents a reasonable adjustment to the environment. According to Harris, cows prove useful as sources of manure for fertilizer, of stock-breeding draft animals, and of investment for poor farmers because the cows can survive very lean periods. Several critics disagree with his views, however. Alan Heston (1971), for example, argues that the Hindu treatment of cattle has led to patterns of poor herd management resulting in far from optimal use of cattle, and furthermore that in many areas cattle use land and feed that could be put to much better use in feeding people. To Heston and others the ban is based solely on ideological grounds and represents a very poor use of resources.

Totems

In many religious traditions animals are much more closely linked to humans. Australian Aborigines, like many people, "conceptualize a single, unified cosmic order in which man and the natural species, ancestral beings, spirits, and other conceived entities are on equal terms. All are interrelated in a genealogical and pseudo-genealogical manner" (Tonkinson 1974: 74). This view of the cosmos is referred to as *totemic*. The links between individuals and groups and particular plants, animals, and other natural phenomena are represented symbolically in the form of totemic emblems, and this relationship forms the basis for ceremonial and ritual activities.

Australian Aborigines recognize several varieties of totemism. Two primary types are conception totemism and ancestral totemism. *Conception totems* are associated with aspects of a person's birth—plants, animals, insects, secretions, or minerals of the locale where they are believed to have been conceived. In many parts of Australia there is a strong emotional bond with this totem. Since the totem and the individual are said to be of the same flesh, individuals may refrain from eating or otherwise harming them. This caring bond is not universal. The Mardudjara of Jigalong in Western Australia tend to feel no special attachment to their conception totem and there are no dietary restrictions. Even within a similar environment practices can vary. While the Aranda of central Australia place restrictions on eating their conception totems, the nearby Warramunga will eat certain conception totems if they are killed by someone else, and the neighboring Walbiri consider "that men would be stupid not to eat such foods when available" (Meggitt 1962: 208).

Ancestral totems link individuals with the historical or mythical past. For the Australian Aborigines, ancestral totems are associated with the activities of the Dreamtime beings. During their travels, as recorded in myth, they left objects behind; these became animated with a life force from which came spirit children waiting in plant or animal form to be born as humans. These totems place individuals within their physical environment and create a spiritual map of the terrain. It is often through them that individuals gain access to land, in return for which they perform ceremonies at sites associated with these ancestral totems. The rites, known as increase rites, usually involve activities aimed at procreating species of animals (see Berndt 1965: 227-31). Attitudes toward the treatment of plants or animals acknowledged as ancestral totems tend to be similar to those regarding conception totems. The Walbiri have no rules against eating their ancestral totems, Meggitt says, although "occasionally a man would express sorrow, in a half-joking fashion, when he ate a bird or animal he called 'father.' . . . The usual comment, accompanied by winks and smiles, was: 'What a pity—I am eating my poor father! I am so sorry for him!'" (1962: 209). Some anthropologists claim that restrictions on the eating of totemic animals play an important role in preserving species in a given area, but the evidence is far from conclusive.

Myth

Since the nineteenth century it has been common to use the term *myth* to refer to something that is untrue: the myth of equality, the myth of democracy, and so forth. This use of the word *myth* reflects the secularization of our beliefs, for myth in its true sense, a sacred tale, is certainly not seen as a falsehood by members of the society in which it is current. For members of a particular religion, *their* myths represent received truth. Other peoples' myths may be false, but not their own. (Our use of *myth* to mean falsehood therefore also reflects our own ethnocentrism.)

Although anthropologists use the word *myth* to describe a type of sacred narrative, it is more than just a tale. Myths express the unobservable realities of religious belief in terms of observable phenomena. Like symbols, they link the supernatural and sacred with the mundane and concrete. If religious beliefs are based upon social realities and contradictions, but transformed into realities that are thought to transcend these more mundane conditions, it is through myth that we bring religion back to earth.

Functions of Myths

Myths in fact serve a variety of functions. They may serve as cultural histories, alluding to actual events and practices from the past such as migrations, earlier forms of social organization, and natural occurrences like meteor showers, eclipses, or floods. This is not always the case, however; the events described in myths may be apocryphal. Even when the events depicted in a myth do have historical validity, they do not simply represent records of the past, for myths use history for social and religious purposes.

Sacred history myths may serve as charters for social interests and as warrants for particular institutions (Malinowski 1926). They link the present social order with a sacred past and condition behavior toward desired ends. Instructing Aboriginal youths in their mythic traditions is not simply a matter of entertaining them. The myths strive to produce in them a prescribed view of the world and an attitude toward social institutions and those responsible for maintaining the status quo that will ensure reproduction of the existing social order. In this regard myths often "constitute a conservative, socializing force whose function is to sanctify existing institutions and foster the values of sociality" (Hiatt 1975: 5).

The events depicted in a myth deal with fundamental questions concerning the human condition from a particular society's point of view. They represent attempts to analyze the world around us and its contradictions or paradoxes. The themes that occur over and over again in myths are those associated with fundamental philosophical questions: the relationship between life and death, the origins of life and human society, and the strains with which people in all societies must come to terms, such as tensions between parents and children or siblings.

Analyzing Myths

To explain why a particular myth exists in a particular society, we can consider how its elements serve some of these functions. Consider the following myth, which comes from the Mundurucu of the Amazonian region of Brazil (Murphy and Murphy 1974: 88–89):

The sacred trumpets of the Mundurucú, called the karökö, are taboo to the sight of women, but the women once owned them. In fact it was the women who first discovered the trumpets.

There were once three women named Yanyonböri, Tuembirú, and Parawarö. When these women went to collect firewood, they frequently heard music from some unknown source. One day they became thirsty and went off in search of water. Deep in the forest they found a beautiful, shallow, and clear lake, of which they had no previous knowledge. This lake came to be named Karököboaptí, or "the place from which they took the karökö." The next time the women heard the music in the forest, they noted that it came from the direction of the lake and went off to investigate. But they found only jiju fish in the water, which they were unable to catch.

Back in the village, one of the women hit upon the idea of catching the fish with hand nets. They rubbed the mouths of the nets with a nut which had the effect of making fish sleepy, and returned to the lake properly equipped. Each woman caught one fish, and these fish turned into hollow cylindrical trumpets. The other fish fled. This is why each men's house now has a set of only three instruments. The women hid the trumpets in the forest where no one could discover them and went secretly every day to play them.

The women devoted their lives to the instruments and abandoned their husbands and housework to play them. The men grew suspicious, and Marimarebö, the brother of Yanyonböri, followed them and discovered their secret. He did not, however, actually see the instruments. Marimarebö went back to the village and told the other men. When the women returned, he asked if it was true that they had

musical instruments in the forest. The women admitted this and were told, "You can play the instruments, but you have to play them in the house and not in the forest." The women agreed to this.

The women, as possessors of the trumpets, had thereby gained ascendancy over the men. The men had to carry firewood and fetch water, and they also had to make the beijú [manioc cakes]. To this day their hands are still flat from patting the beiju into shape. But the men still hunted, and this angered Marimarebö, for it was necessary to offer meat to the trumpets, and the women were able to offer them only a drink made from sweet manioc. For this reason, Marimarbö favored taking the trumpets from the women, but the other men hesitated from fear of them.

On the day on which the women were to bring the trumpets to the village, they ordered the men out to the forest to hunt while they made the sweet manioc drink. When the men returned from the hunt, the three discoverers of the trumpets led the other women out to get the instruments. The leader of the women, Yanyonböri, sent one of the women back to tell the men that they should all shut themselves securely inside the dwelling houses. The men refused to do this and insisted upon remaining in the men's house. Finally, Yanyonböri herself went back to order the men inside the dwelling houses. Her brother, Marimarebö, replied, "We will go into the house for one night only, but no more. We want the trumpets and will take them tomorrow. If you do not give them to us, then we will not go hunting, and there will be no meat to offer them." Yanyonböri agreed, for she knew that she could not hunt the food for the trumpets or for the guests at the ceremonies.

The men entered the dwelling houses, and the women marched around and around the village playing the trumpets. They then entered the men's house for the night and installed the

Xingu River Indians in the Amazon region of Brazil play ancient flutes. Like the sacred trumpets of the Mundurucu, these instruments play an important role in local myth.

instruments there. Then, one by one the women went to the dwelling houses and forced the men to have coitus with them. The men could not refuse, just as the women today cannot refuse the desires of the men. This went on all night, and the women returned to the men's house all slippery inside.

The next day the men took the trumpets from the women and forced them to go back to the dwelling house. The women wept at their loss. When the men took the trumpets from the women they sang this song:

It was I who went and hid
I entered the house and hid
I entered the house and almost hid
Because I did not know I was ashamed
Because I did not know I was ashamed
Because I did not know
I entered the house and hid
I entered the house and almost hid.

Does this myth function as true cultural history, or does it teach something else about Mundurucu culture? The myth suggests that at one time there was almost a complete reversal of the present social order. Women were the dominant sex, controlling the karökö and the men's house. Men carried out those activities which today they identify as women's, and therefore inferior: they carried firewood and water and made manioc cakes. The inversion was carried over into sexual relations. The women initiated sex and the men could not refuse, and female rather than male gratification was emphasized. The men were also deprived of their status as public figures. As Mundurucu women do today, the men in the myth "entered the house and hid" when the women occupied the men's house and paraded about with the trumpets. Finally, the men were "ashamed," although they were not aware of their shame until they had taken control of the karökö.

The dominant status of women presented in the myth may have some basis in fact, for there is evidence that female status in the Amazonian region deteriorated as a result of increasing warfare under the pressure of European expansion. Perhaps more important, however, the myth points to a fundamental contradiction in Mundurucu society in regard to male domination, and to the tensions this engenders. Mundurucu males do not feel that women are inherently inferior. Unlike many of their North American and European counterparts, they recognize the social basis of their domination. The myth's statement that women were once superior and had to be overthrown implies that they could once again assume the dominant role in Mundurucu society—that the elevated status of the male is inherently insecure and must be continually reinforced. The myth also points to the basis of male superiority—the division of labor.

It is only as hunters that men can maintain their domination. Hunting is therefore given exaggerated emphasis in contrast to agriculture, which despite its more significant role in subsistence is denigrated in many ways. The myth thus serves to sanctify the existing social order, while at the same time highlighting its weakness. It points to some of the fundamental problems to be found in any society with marked inequality of the sexes in certain areas, especially when there is also an espousal of relative equality in other social contexts.

Supernatural Forces and Beings

All religious beliefs include recognition of some named force or entity. The variety of forms these take is extensive and even within a single tradition there can be many different forces or supernatural beings populating the cosmos. Following Annemarie de Waal Malefijt (1968: 146–62), we will review briefly the major varieties.

Unseen Power

Many religious traditions posit the existence of some *impersonal supernatural force*, of a power that although unseen is believed to be present everywhere. R. R. Marett (1909, 1912) referred to belief in such a force as *animatism*. This force is conceived of as a massive reservoir of power that may infuse or possess, and perhaps be used by, individuals, gods, the forces of nature, and even natural objects. The concept of *mana*, which is found in many religious traditions throughout the Pacific area, the Sioux *wakan*, the Algonquian *manitou*, the Ekoi *njomm* and the Nkundu *elima* in Africa, and the West Indian *zemi* are examples of such a force. It exists in many literate traditions as well; Hutton Webster (1948) has pointed to the similarity be-

tween mana and the Hebrew *el*, the Latin *numen*, the Greek *dynamis*, and the Indian *brahma*. The concept also has parallels in our own culture, as exemplified in George Bernard Shaw's "life force" and Henri Bergson's *élan vital*. People almost never seem to be satisfied with leaving things up to such an ambiguous entity, however. The concept of an impersonal supernatural force is almost universally accompanied by beliefs in more precisely conceived supernatural beings.

Spirits

People in many societies believe in the existence of an almost endless number of *spirits* that dwell in animals and places or simply wander about the earth. We refer to this belief as *animism*. Because of their great number, spirits usually are viewed collectively and not given individual identities.

The number of categories of spirits recognized can vary a good deal. The Gururumba of New Guinea (Newman 1965: 62–63) recognize only two types of spirit: those who live in the highland forest area and those who inhabit the lowlands along riverbanks. In contrast, the Javanese (Geertz 1960: 16–29) have a large number of categories, including frightening spirits, possessing spirits, familiar spirits, place spirits, and guardian spirits. Certain spirits may be given individual names, but even then they are recognized as members of a broader category of similar beings, failing to achieve the degree of individualization reserved for gods.

Spirits are sometimes of human origin. The spirit children that form the pool from which new Aborigines are born are closely tied to the human population. And many peoples recognize a category sometimes referred to as *souls of the dead*. These are supernatural beings of human origin which may for a time be individually remembered as *ghosts*; later they merge into an unnamed collectivity. The Walbiri of central Australia (Meggitt 1962: 192) believe that upon death a person's spirit becomes a *manbaraba*, "an ethereal, pale ghost, whose features resemble those of its previous owner." The ghost remains near the tree platform where the corpse has been placed until the death is avenged (death is never considered to have occurred naturally). The ghost then dissipates, with its spirit joining the collective pool of matrispirits and patrispirits associated with particular kin groups.

The dead may retain their individual identity and continue to play an active role in society. These entities are called *ancestor souls* or *ancestor spirits*. In many societies ancestor worship is central to religious beliefs and practices, but this is not always the case with ancestors. The Swazi of South Africa consider their ancestors to be important only on special occasions. Each family pacifies its dead only at births, marriages, deaths, the building of new huts, and when calamities befall the family (Kuper 1963: 60). In parts of rural Japan and China contact between the living and the dead was often much more regular, at least in the past. The ancestral shrine was prominent in every home, serving as a center for much of family life. There would be daily offerings of food to the ancestors in conjunction with other daily rites performed on their behalf. These rites often included a reading or reciting of recent events to ensure that the ancestors were able to keep up with what was happening. The importance of ancestors is sometimes related to how important they were when alive. Those who served as lineage or clan leaders might be worshiped by all members of their kin group, while those of lower status might be worshiped by fewer kin.

Gods

Ancestors sometimes make it a bit further up the religious hierarchy, being elevated to the status of a god. The term *god* (or deity) refers to a supernatural being with an individual identity and recognizable attributes who is worshiped as having power over nature and human fortunes. By and large gods are of nonhuman origin, but this is not always the case. In fact, there are many living humans who either proclaim themselves to be gods or are considered gods by a large number of followers. The Rastafarians believe the Ethiopian emperor Haile Selassie is a deity, for example. Such concepts are often related to extreme systems of social stratification, for it is not uncommon for monarchs to become gods. Like the Roman emperor Nero, they may simply proclaim themselves gods, but usually deification is a more complex process. Sometimes the divinity of rulers is based upon a claim of descent from gods. Until 1947 the Japanese emperor was considered divine, based upon a claim of descent from the sun goddess, Amaterasu Omikami (Sakamaki 1967: 25–26).

The number, roles, and attributes of gods in any religious system can vary a great deal. As in the Christian tradition, there can be only one god. We refer to this as *monotheism*. In *polytheism* there can be an almost limitless number of gods, or perhaps a finite number arranged in some sort of hierarchy. Monotheism tends to be related to the development of social stratification and the rise of large-scale societies. Thompson (1970), for example, discusses how the lowland Maya god Itzam Na assumed an ever greater role during the classic period, other gods being placed under Itzam Na or being incorporated into the god as one of its many manifestations. This process was closely related to the rise of the Maya aristocracy. When the aristocrats' power appears to have collapsed, so too did Itzam Na, as a more diverse and egalitarian polytheism reasserted itself.

An important role for a god or the gods in most religious traditions is creation—the creation of the universe, of life, and of the prevailing order within the universe. For the Australian Aborigines, the creative acts of the mythical Dreamtime beings remain in the forefront of their religious practices and beliefs. Other traditions take creation more for granted, placing a heavier emphasis upon the postcreative activities of the gods. Some religions also posit the existence of an omnipotent and omniscient god who created the universe and then more or less withdrew, often leaving the subsequent direction of the world in the hands of lesser deities. Such a god is called *otiose*, which literally means sterile, serving no practical purpose. Otiose deities tend not to have an important place in worship or ritual. The Igbo of Nigeria believe in such a god, and since it is so withdrawn there are neither priests nor shrines dedicated to its service. They call upon this god only in cases of great distress, but even then feel that this will do little good.

Religions that allow for a number of gods frequently recognize the existence of relatively specialized gods, sometimes called *attribute gods*. Pre-Columbian lowland Maya, for example, had merchant gods, gods of hunting and fishing, gods of cacao growers, gods of beekeepers, a god of *balche* (a fermented ritual drink made of honey and the bark of the *balche* tree), gods of medicine and curers, gods of war, gods of poetry and music, a god of tattooing, a god of ballgame players, a god of fire, and a god of birth, to name just a few. Such supernatural departmentalization is largely a function of secular specialization in a society. Particularly important activities may have several highly specialized gods: the ancient Romans had three separate gods of the plow, since the fields were plowed three times. Areas of less interest might share a god or be lumped with some generalized deity, or do without altogether.

Minor Beings

Finally, many religions also possess a range of divine or semidivine beings of minor theological significance. In western Europe there are dwarfs, elves, pixies, and the like. The traditions of the Kekchi of southern Belize populate the forests with a number of semidivine denizens. These include the *cheil*, who live in large caves and in pre-Columbian ruins. They are said to live much like people, and on occasion they visit human settlements. There is also Xtabai, who shakes her breasts at young men to lure them into the forest, only to cause them to go insane. She has a male counterpart. A common character in many religions is the *trickster*. These are semidivine beings who may accidentally establish cultural practices for a group, but who basically are not concerned with human welfare. Among Native Americans one of the best-known tricksters is Coyote:

He stole the sun, the moon, and the stars from the spirits who had them before, but he did not know what to do with them, so he placed them in the sky. He carried out his theft for his own pleasure, and not, like Prometheus, because he pitied mankind. Similarly, Coyote stole fresh water from the spirits because he was thirsty, and clumsily spilled it all over the world when he tried to escape, thus creating lakes and rivers. [Malefijt 1968: 161]

Religious Behavior and Consciousness

Religious beliefs are not simply stated; they are presented in such a way as to drive them into the innermost recesses of one's being. Often through the agency of religious specialists (examined in the next section), attempts are made to ensure that a complex, multidimensional message concerning the nature of the cosmos and one's place in it becomes a fundamental part of an individual's personality. When beliefs are presented, they are therefore accompanied by actions that create or cause the beliefs to be identified with very basic emotions, such as respect, awe, and security. While the precise aims and methods of religious practices may vary a little from one setting to the next, there are features that are common to most religious traditions.

Separation

One important aspect of religious behavior is separation. It involves the recognition of two relatively distinct realms, the secular and the sacred, and the association of these realms with particular actions and objects. Western Desert Aborigines in Australia categorize as "secret-sacred" certain acts, beliefs, and related objects; they are reserved exclusively for fully initiated men or women because of the danger resulting from their close association with the Dreamtime. Punishment for transgressions traditionally was severe, in some cases entailing death. The ideological and emotional boundary between the sacred and the secular is far less extreme in most present-day Christian religions, but there is a boundary nevertheless.

Separation of the sacred is often related to an idea of exclusiveness: entry into this realm is special and not for everyone. To be able to enter one may have to meet special preconditions. Birth may be a factor, in which case only the

chosen few are allowed entrance—or some sort of initiation may be required, as in the Christian practice of baptism. Special knowledge of esoteric language, rites, or symbols may also be important, and can be learned only from those who are already initiated.

The specialness of the sacred is further emphasized by how the transition from the realm of the secular to that of the sacred is marked. Some form of purification is frequently involved, ranging from abstaining from sex, to becoming thoroughly drunk, to bathing and putting on one's Sunday best. There may be other transitional rites actually marking entry into the realm of the sacred as well, such as kneeling and praying, and crossing oneself.

Ritual

Another common feature of religious behavior is its routinization and repetitiveness. Religious performances in any tradition tend to be highly routinized. While there may be variations in a Catholic mass or an Aboriginal Gunabibi, the basic format remains much the same from one performance to the next. Within this framework we find even more precise routinization in the acting out of *rituals,* highly stereotyped, stylized, and repetitive behaviors that take place at a set time and place. This orderliness serves to create a sense of security, ensuring that participants feel that they know what is going on. It supports the basic religious tenet of an ordered universe. Repetitive chants and the use of repetitive themes in music and discourse also reinforce the primary messages of a religion.

Altered Consciousness

Religions may go beyond simply trying to make people feel a little different. The aim may be to create an extreme emotional state, sometimes in the form of a trance. The idea here is to produce experiences or visions of so overwhelming a nature as to reinforce the individual's belief in the reality of the supernatural. There are numerous means of achieving such states of consciousness, including fasting, flagellation, self-torture, sensory deprivation, breathing exercises, yogi meditation, and ritual dancing and drumming. Certain yogi practices originating in Tibet, for example, include the recitation of *mantras*, words or sounds of power, in almost hypnotic fashion. By uttering the sound of a *mantra* associated with a deity, the person tries to transcend human thought and make contact with the deity (Evans-Wentz 1960: 220–22). A trancelike state is achieved by voodoo practitioners during special gatherings where excitement is generated by drumming and dancing. The trance, like the one described below, involves possession by a spirit (in this case, Ogu):

The hunsi *(initiates), with red cloths round the heads and coloured dresses, dance in honour of Ogu. At the very first dance* mambo *(priestess) Lorgina is possessed by this god. In spite of her age, her infirmities and her weight, she dances nimbly in front of the drums, hands on hips, shaking her shoulders in time to the music. She then fetches a sabre and jams the hilt of it against the* poteau-mitan *(a post regarded as the thoroughfare of the spirits) and the point against her stomach. Now, by pushing with all her strength, she bends the blade. She repeats this dangerous practice, this time basing the hilt on the post's concrete plinth. A* hungan *(priest) sprays rum from his mouth on to her stomach and rubs her legs. Lorgina in a sudden frenzy fences with the* la-place *(master of ceremonies); he, too, being armed with a sabre. The ceremonial duel degenerates into a real fight, so that spectators, fearing an accident, have to intervene. Lorgina is then seized by another wave of bellicose frenzy. She hacks the* poteau-mitan *with her sabre and chases the* hunsi *who flee in terror. She is on the point of catching them when prevented by the shafts of the sacred flags which two women cross in her path. At once she becomes calm. . . . A priest comes up to talk to her, keeping prudently in the safety-zone of the banners. The* mambo *winds up by going back to the* hunsi *whom she beats violently with the flat of her sabre; and this outlet has a soothing effect on her. Suddenly all smiles, she salutes everyone present and overflows with politeness in every direction. She has a cigar brought to her which she smokes in a nonchalant way. Then she gives orders that the meat-safe hanging on the* poteau-mitan *should be placed before her. She eats heartily and distributes what is left among the* hunsi. *She calls up a trembling and excited little girl whom she has already spanked hard with the flat of her sword: she gives her a long lecture on her future behaviour and foretells a terrible fate for her unless she takes the warning to heart. Having forced the little girl to prostrate herself before her, Lorgina—still in the tones of Ogu—lectures her* hunsi, *giving them detailed advice on dress. Then, speaking of herself in the third person, she boasts of her own labours, and tells how she managed to save up to build the sanctuary. The* hunsi *listen with respect. Shortly afterwards the god leaves the* mambo, *who then returns to herself.* [Métraux 1972: 126–27]

Trances like this tend to be culture specific, following the rules or guidelines of the particular tradition and adhering to the behavioral norms of the culture. Furthermore, they are not random affairs: the people have a fairly good idea of what to expect.

A very ancient and widespread means of achieving trancelike states is the use of narcotics (see Furst 1972, Harner 1973, Wasson 1973). Relatively mild narcotics such as alcohol, tobacco, and marijuana are employed by many religions to assist in achieving a proper frame of mind. Rastafarians use marijuana for symbolic purposes and because of its mind-altering properties, as "the smoother of mental imbalances and as a meditatory influence" (Barrett 1977: 130). Because of its psychological effects in religious contexts and its symbolic meaning of freedom from the laws of "Babylon," marijuana has assumed an important place in the Rastafarians' religion. They turn to the Bible in support of its use (Barrett 1977: 129):

And the earth brought forth grass, and herb yielding seed after his kind, and the tree yielding fruit, whose seed was in itself, after his kind: and God saw that it was good. [Genesis 1:12]

and

Thou shalt eat the herb of the field. [Genesis 3:18]

Eat every herb of the land. [Exodus 10:12]

Better is a dinner of herb where love is, than a stalled ox and hatred therewith. [Proverbs 15:17]

He causeth the grass to grow for the cattle, and herb for the service of man. [Psalms 104:14]

Other religions employ much more powerful hallucinogens in an effort to bring the individual face to face with the supernatural. In a rather controversial study, John Allegro (1970) has argued that the hallucinogenic mushroom *Amanita mascaria* played a central and formative role in early Hebraic-Christian religion. The same mushroom is used by Siberian shamans to communicate with the supernatural, by allowing them to go into a trance in which they feel that their soul leaves the body. Some scholars maintain that narcotic-induced soul flights may have led to the initial belief in souls and ghosts. Other mushrooms, such as *Psilocybe mexicana*, are used for divination and other magical and

Rasta with Ganja (marijuana). Marijuana is smoked in a religious context and for its symbolic meaning of freedom from the laws of "Babylon."

religious purposes by Mexican Indians such as the Mazatec of northeastern Oaxaca. Another hallucinogen, peyote, has assumed a major role in the religions of many indigenous peoples in northern Mexico and the southwestern United States (see Myerhoff 1974). Other vision-producing plants used in a religious context in the New World include the morning glory, various members of the nightshade family, the South American vine *Banisteriopsis caapi*, known as *Yajé* or *Ayahuasca* (the liana of death or souls), and several types of Leguminosae, from which the Indians of northern South America make a potent snuff.

The use of narcotics in religion is related to a number of environmental and social factors. An obvious one is the availability of plants. The widespread use of hallucinogenic plants in the New World is no doubt facilitated by the unusual number available (Schultes 1963: 147). Where plants are not locally available, trade lines may be developed. Thus, one finds traders supplying hallucinogenic mushrooms to Kekchi curers in lowland areas where they are not to be found readily. In some instances, the use of hal-lucinogenic plants in religions may be related to the diffusion of practices as well as trade in the plants themselves. Gordon Wasson (1972) argues that the religious complexes in Eurasia and the New World have many roots in the Amanita-using shamanistic traditions of Siberia.

It may also be possible to link the use of narcotic plants in religions to types of social structure. They are widely used in egalitarian societies with shamanistic traditions (there are some notable exceptions, such as the Australian Aborigines, who do not use narcotics for religious purposes). With increasing social stratification, their use tends to become much more restricted. In contrast to less stratified Mexican Indian societies, where the use of hallucinogens is widespread, narcotic use among the highly stratified Aztec in pre-Columbian times was restricted to a small elite. In general, the use of narcotics for religious purposes has survived only where there has been little or no competition from state religions. The unrestricted use of narcotics for religious purposes threatens the monopolization of sacred truth that serves as a fundamental support for these institutions.

Religious Specialists

People who are more skilled in the performance of certain religious tasks and who have a greater knowledge of religious traditions than other members of a community exist in most societies. In small-scale societies, where there is minimal division of labor, such individuals tend not to be full-time specialists. They are people who must perform many of the same tasks as other members of their society, but who also do a little extra. For this, they are afforded a status somewhat above the others. As social scale increases and the division of labor becomes more developed, we find the emergence of full-time specialists—individuals who support themselves exclusively by carrying out religious tasks.

Shamans

A type of specialist particularly common in foraging societies is the *shaman*. Michael Harner (1973: xi) has defined a shaman "as a man or woman who is in direct contact with the spirit world through a trance state and has one or more spirits at his command to carry out his bidding for good or evil." Perhaps the most definitive characteristic of shamans is their claim

Initiation of a sixteen-year-old Mapuche woman as a shaman in Chile after an apprenticeship of several months.

to have established direct contact with the supernatural through trance. The shaman's status is highly personalistic, for it depends upon ability to contact and influence the spirit world, rather than knowledge of sacred lore or ritual. Furthermore, while the shaman's ritual activities may adhere to a general culturally prescribed pattern, there is great leeway in how the shaman may carry out the task of communicating with the supernatural.

The Inuit provide a good example of shamanistic practices and beliefs (Holtved 1967). The primary role of the Inuit shaman is to take charge of relations with supernatural beings who interfere with human life. This includes intervening to ensure a supply of game, driving away evil spirits, procuring good weather, divining the future, and curing the sick. For instance, if game were scarce, it would be assumed that the Moon-Man or Sea-Woman who controls the animals was angry because someone had committed an offense such as eating a prohibited part of an animal. To the Inuit of Greenland and Labrador these offenses become dirt in the hair of the Sea-Woman, and the shaman must struggle to be allowed to cleanse and

comb her hair before she will promise to free the animals so that they may be hunted again. The shaman communicates with the Sea-Woman, or any other deity, by working himself into a trance with the assistance of a drum. The shaman is assisted by helping spirits, who take on a variety of forms and who are communicated with in a special spirit language.

An Inuit usually decides to become a shaman after a dream or some extraordinary experience. The individual may try to resist the call, giving in to his or her destiny only after great mental anguish. The next step is to consult with older shamans, providing them with a gift, and then undergoing a period of instruction that might last anywhere from a couple of days to a few years. During this apprenticeship the novice spends long periods alone in desolate places, undergoing severe suffering from cold and hunger. During these periods the novice meets the various supernatural beings who will later serve as helping spirits. Another element of the shaman's preparation is experiencing the mystery of life and death. How this is done varies. Among the Caribou Eskimo, reported practices entail hanging, drowning, and shooting. In

Greenland there was a custom of hypnotizing the novice, who while under hypnosis is attacked and eaten by a bear-spirit. Upon awakening the novice finds himself naked on the shore of a lake. An Iglulik shaman must be able "to see himself as a skeleton" and be able to name all the parts of his body in a special shaman's language.

Keepers of the Law

Societies with shamans often possess other types of religious specialist as well. Personalistic specialists who communicate with the spirit world and who may be termed shamans are common to Australian Aboriginal societies (see Elkin 1944), but there are other kinds of religious functionaries who act in very different ways and perform very different functions. These are *keepers of the law*—individuals whose primary roles are the performance of ritual and the maintenance of tradition.

In small-scale societies, keepers of the law are not usually full-time religious specialists. In Aboriginal society all adults are involved to differing degrees in religious activities. On the basis of kinship, individuals are responsible for certain rituals associated with the Dreamtime and for maintaining particular mythic traditions. There is not, however, an equal distribution of responsibility or authority. On the basis of age, inclination, experience, and ability some persons assume more important roles in religious affairs than others. While these individuals may devote much time to ceremony and to discussions of religious matters, they are never full-time specialists, except sometimes in old age. Although they may receive something for their efforts, they are almost never able to support themselves as religious functionaries—they must hunt or work for wages along with others, or depend upon what is their due because of their age.

Similar situations prevail in many small-scale

agricultural societies. The Tzotzil-speaking Maya of Zinacantan in southern Mexico include a large number of shamans who are ranked hierarchically on the basis of kin groupings and residential units (Vogt 1970: 26–27). Perhaps the most important tasks of these shamans involve curing. In addition, these Maya have office holders responsible for the performance of ceremonies associated with particular Catholic saints. These offices form part of the civil-religious hierarchy or cargo system, with sixty-one religious positions at four levels of the ceremonial hierarchy. To assume his burden (*cargo*), the cargo holder moves from his residential hamlet to the ceremonial center for one year. There he and his wife engage in a series of costly ceremonies, spending money on food, liquor, and ritual paraphernalia such as candles, incense, and fireworks (Vogt 1970: 19). Performance of these tasks entails withdrawal from farming and other economically rewarding pursuits, and the cargo holder is forced to live off savings and loans for the year. Such specialists therefore are only able to function on a full-time basis periodically, at the expense of their normal economic activities. Their reward is the prestige that comes with community service. Zinacantan is also visited on occasion by a Catholic priest and one of the responsibilities of some of the cargo holders is to collect money to pay the priest for saying mass.

A full-time, permanent religious functionary is a luxury that small, relatively poor communities or societies can rarely support. Occasionally, older members of a small-scale society are able to devote themselves on a full-time basis to religious activities, reflecting their limited abilities as foragers or farmers, but for the most part full-time ritual specialists, or *priests*, are found only in large-scale societies. Only societies that can support an extensive division of labor and a large nonproductive class can accommodate religious specialists on such a permanent basis. Even priests are not always full-time functionaries, and many small religious sects in our own society are unable to support full-time personnel.

Priests and keepers of the law are primarily concerned with maintaining a particular social order. They tend to represent the interests of the establishment in a society, or within some segment of a society. The order that they represent may come into conflict with other orders, as with the church-state conflicts in the Philippines and Brazil in recent years, but they nonetheless seek to maintain or assert an existing social order as represented in existing religious institutions.

Prophets

Not all religious specialists represent such conservative forces in society. Perhaps the most noteworthy exceptions are prophets. *Prophets* are individuals who receive divine revelation, usually by visions or dreams, concerning a restructuring or a redirecting of some aspect of society or of a people's beliefs. On the basis of revealed rather than taught truth, prophets seek to alter the existing social order through teaching or example. They do not represent a complete break with the sociocultural order around them. Like Christ, they are to some extent a product of their environment and of the religious traditions of the society within which they live. They do, however, represent a threat to those holding religious power (and sometimes to those holding secular power as well). Because of their reliance on their ability to arouse loyalty and enthusiasm and their claim of direct communication with the supernatural, prophets have much in common with shamans, although their aims are quite different. The goal of the prophet is the creation of a new order. Success as a prophet usually leads to the foundation of a new religious institution, transforming the seer from a renegade to a person who is at least quasi-respectable, and at most may become a deity and leader of millions.

Religion and Social Change

Australian Aboriginal religious dogma proclaims a perfectly ordered world in which change is unnecessary. Such a claim of permanency is common to many religious traditions, as a fundamental source of their strength. The ideal of permanency does not reflect actual practice in which nothing changes, however. In fact, Aboriginal religious practices, their relationship to the world around them, and their society have been continually changing for thousands of years. Their claim of an unchanging universe is an ideological statement that is seen to reflect sacred and not secular order. Like the societies of which they are a part, the religious beliefs and practices of any people are never entirely static. The extent to which they change and the ways in which they change are influenced by social processes in their surroundings.

Change with Cultural Transformations

So long as Australian Aboriginal society continued to depend upon foraging and remained relatively isolated, changes in religious beliefs and practices tended to be minor. New cults or practices might arise and diffuse to other parts of Australia, but the basic religious precepts remained unaltered. Similar processes occur in many other societies, as in the case of the minor schisms that occur with great frequency in the various Christian denominations.

More fundamental sociocultural transformations lead to much greater changes in people's religions. For instance, the shift from foraging to agriculture among the Huicholes of Mexico also led to changes in their religious beliefs and practices. Oversimplifying somewhat, Anthony Wallace (1966) has proposed four basic categories of religion that he associates with particular modes of adaptation and social formation:

1. *Shamanistic*, characterized by individualistic and shamanic cult institutions and part-time practitioners, and usually found in conjunction with relatively independent foraging bands such as those of the Inuit or native Siberians.

2. *Communal*, in which communal religious institutions are added to individualistic and shamanic religious practices. Communal cults are characterized by periodic gatherings of members of a society for ceremonial purposes, often in association with the seasons, harvests, or rites of passage. This type is associated with relatively well integrated foraging societies, such as those of the Australian Aborigines, and with small-scale agricultural societies.

3. *Olympian*, which add to the above a hierarchically and bureaucratically organized professional priesthood that manages rituals and beliefs. This type of religion is characterized by a hierarchy of deities that usually includes a number of powerful high gods. It is associated with chiefdoms and nonindustrial states such as those of the Aztec and the Inca.

4. *Monotheistic*, which includes all of the various cult forms, but is unique in that it concentrates supernatural beings or forces under the control or in the identity of a single supreme being. This type of religion is closely associated with the growth and expansion of state organization and the centralization of power in the hands of the state.

Change Through Contact or Conquest

Changes in religious belief and practice can be associated with the gradual evolution of a society from one social form to another. Over the past few centuries, however, the primary impetus to change has been contact between differing societies, and in particular contact between expansive state organizations with monotheistic religions and small-scale societies. European expansion throughout the world was not merely a political and economic conquest; it included an attempt to conquer the minds of the conquered peoples, largely through religion. The resultant war of the gods has taken on a variety of manifestations, depending upon the nature of contact, the resultant changes, and the subsequent ways indigenous peoples have been incorporated into the newly formed colonies or states.

In many settings conquest has destroyed all or part of the existing religion of a people. This loss sometimes leads to their adopting the beliefs and practices of the conquerors, especially when the conquerors' success is associated with the superior strength of their gods. The religion that results from this process is often neither precisely that of the conqueror nor the traditional one of the conquered. It is a new one using elements of both, created through a process known as *syncretism*, or the conscious adaptation of an alien idea or practice in terms of some indigenous counterpart (Barnett 1953: 49,54). The process can be exemplified by looking at the changes in religious beliefs and practices of indigenous peoples in Middle America resulting from the Spanish conquest (Madsen 1967).

Spanish conquest of central Mexico put an end to public worship of the primary gods, destroyed the priesthood, and undermined faith in the power of the gods and the truth of religious teachings, thus shattering the focal values of Aztec religion and culture. This did not lead the Aztec to accept Christianity, though, for their attitude toward the religion of the Catholic priests was too closely related to hatred of their conquerors. There were also tremendous differences in the religious traditions to overcome. Slowly things began to change, however, especially once the priests instituted compulsory education of Indian children. In these schools children were punished for noncompliance and rewarded for at least outward adherence to the new faith. Older people who worshiped their old idols in secret began to add images of the crucified Christ and the Virgin Mary to their collection. They also found a few similarities. Catholic baptism had a counterpart in an Aztec rite in which consecrated water was used to remove impurity from a newborn baby's heart. For their part, the Catholics searched for common ground to convert the pagan Aztecs, including the modification of traditional Aztec songs and dances to fit with Catholic teachings. A crucial change leading to widespread acceptance of Catholicism followed the miraculous appearance of the Indian Virgin of Guadalupe on the site of a shrine dedicated to one of the Aztec earth goddesses. The dark-skinned virgin became a symbol of a new Indian Catholicism that could be distinguished from the Catholicism of the Spanish conquerors. Away from the direct influence of the Spanish priests, the Indians began to develop their own version of Catholicism. Patron saints took on the characteristics of old pagan gods, Catholic rites were interpreted in ways quite different from those of the Spanish, and Catholic ceremony and ritual were incorporated into the political and economic fabric of the village.

Traditional indigenous religions do not always collapse or suffer major restructuring as a result of conquest. Despite drastic changes people are sometimes able to retain something of their religion. In fact, clinging to their religious heritage can serve as a source of strength. In many parts of Australia the Aboriginal religion was utterly destroyed by the European conquest and the subsequent Aboriginal integration into Australian society, but the destruction was not always immediate. In parts of the southwest, despite very early contact with whites, Aborigines were able to cling to a few of their beliefs and practices into the twentieth century. Occasional ceremonies were held on the outskirts of Perth as late as the 1920s. By the Second World War, however, all was gone, and what remained was either a lack of religious belief or acceptance of the Whiteman's religion.

In more isolated areas, especially in the desert interior, Aborigines were sometimes more successful in resisting the efforts of missionaries and others to destroy their religion. At Jigalong (Tonkinson 1974), despite relocation and destruction of much of their traditional economy and their nomadic way of life, the Aborigines have been able to retain certain key elements of their culture—in particular, their religion and their system of kinship relationships. In fact, by congregating them in one place and providing them a great deal of idle time, the whites have actually promoted religious activities. The success of the Aboriginal inhabitants of Jigalong in retaining their religion is also related to the inadequate efforts of the local Apostolic missionaries to convert them to Christianity. The Apostolic missionaries view the Aborigines at Jigalong as unintelligent children of the devil who are steeped in sin, and all Aboriginal culture and religion as the work of the devil. Such a view effectively rules out any syncretic joining of the two religions. The missionaries' failure to gain converts is also related to their life-style, which the Aborigines find very unappealing: no smoking, drinking, swearing, blaspheming, or sexual joking.

The missionaries at Jigalong were reluctant to interact with adult Aborigines on any more than a very superficial basis, for they were already lost souls. Social distance was increased by the fact that the missionaries were unable to speak more than a few Aboriginal words and most adult Aborigines spoke little English or English that was difficult for the missionaries to understand. In communicating with adult Aborigines the missionaries would often maintain considerable physical separation, talking to them across a space of several yards. The adults were thus allowed to continue in their pagan ways virtually unimpeded: they had their religion and the Whitefellas had theirs and they perceived little that the two had in common.

As in the case of nearby Wiluna (Sackett 1978), the missionaries at Jigalong preferred to rest their hopes on converting the children, whom they herded into dormitories at an early age. It was not early enough, however; by the time they got them the children had already experienced five or six years of life in the Aboriginal camp and were speaking an Aboriginal dialect as their first language. This early socialization might have been undermined except for the harsh treatment of the children in the dormitories (they were forced to obey strict rules of conduct, to carry out numerous daily chores, and to suffer physical punishment for wrongdoing), which compared so unfavorably to life back in the Aboriginal camp as to prevent the children from any positive feelings about their stay with the missionaries. In 1969 the missionaries left and that threat to the Aboriginal religion disappeared.

Millenarian Movements

A weakening or disruption of the old social order, periods of social unrest, or subjugation and a loss of power frequently result in religious movements that may be categorized as *millenarian*. These are religions born of frustration and despair that seek to cut through a seemingly hopeless situation with a promise of the millennium—a period of good government, great happiness, and prosperity. Millenarianists call for a complete change, although their actual visions are of course derived from their own sociocultural milieu. As Kenelm Burridge (1969: 141) has pointed out, their main theme is moral regeneration and the creation of a new kind of person. Such aspirations are often articulated or symbolized in a hero or prophet. The Rastaman, the prophet Jesus, or Buddha serve as focal points for the call for a new life.

The precise nature of millenarian movements (sometimes referred to as natavistic or revitalization movements) varies somewhat according to circumstances and cultural traditions. The Rastafarian movement, with its promise of return to Africa and black rule with the coming of the millenium and the Blackman's escape from Babylon (Jamaica), is an example of such movements in Afro-American culture. Among Native Americans, perhaps the best-known millenarian movements are those associated with the Ghost Dance (Mooney 1965). These are movements which emerged among the Plains Indians following the failure of their military attempts to stop American expansion. The central theme of these movements is a belief that the dead will return to announce the dawn of a new day. The Ghost Dance first appeared among the Paviotsos who lived between Nevada and California in 1870, following a revelation received on a mountaintop by the prophet Wodziwob in 1869. The Great Spirit announced to Wodziwob that a major cataclysm was soon to shake the world. The earth would open up and swallow all the whites, leaving all their material goods for the Indians. The Indians too would be engulfed in the great chasm, but the followers of the new cult would return to live in the heavenly era brought about by the Great Spirit. The movement was slow to start, but within a few years it had reached all of the Indian tribes in the western United States.

In Melanesia, millenarianism took the form of *cargo cults*. As we saw in chapter 12, Melanesian "Big-Men" gained and maintained their

Millenarianism in Melanesia (the New Hebrides Islands): "Cargo cult" members from Vanuatu worship a red cross in the belief that this will bring a return of the Americans who brought many goods there during World War II.

high status by holding feasts and distributing their wealth. European colonists deprived Melanesians of power and autonomy, thus laying the seeds for millenarian activity, and they also failed to behave in a way considered proper for those with such wealth and power—they had unbelievable wealth and yet they refused to meet their obligations to share it. The resultant cults blended Christian missionary teachings concerning the eventual millenarian resurrection of Christ with the Melanesians' own myths in which mythical ancestors would become transformed into powerful beings and the dead would return to life. The millenium would occur when the ancestors would return in steamships or airplanes bringing European goods (the cargo) and initiating a reversal of the social order. Those on top would be relegated to the bottom and those on the bottom would gain preeminence, and brown would become white and white would become brown.

When the millenium fails to arrive, people may simply return to their normal life, sometimes to await a new prophet, or they may redirect their efforts along more secular political lines. Peter Worsley (1957) has referred to Melanesian cargo cults as prerevolutionary attempts by oppressed peoples to deal with their situation. It is through religion that they first try to deal with the new order; subsequent experience later leads them to search for other, more secular routes to the millenium. Many Rastafarians have moved from passively awaiting the millenium to political action, by trying to create a new and more just social order in Jamaica. Such developments should not lead one to assume that millenarian movements will disappear. As long as the conditions that have generated them in the past persist (and there is little to indicate that they will disappear), we can expect people to turn to religion as a route to escape the seeming hopelessness of their circumstances.

Summary

Although religions are based on mystical understandings of the cosmos, their features can be analyzed on a down-to-earth anthropological level. Religious systems commonly comprise a set of prescribed beliefs and behaviors and an understanding about the distribution of sacred and secular power. Though belief systems vary widely, their particular religious understandings can be partially explained by local social processes, history, and environmental factors. An individual's choice of a particular system may also be explained by factors that circumscribe personal choice. For the society as a whole, the form of religion is often related to adaptational strategy; religious behaviors and beliefs may change as the adaptational strategy shifts.

Symbols are often used to express concretely the core elements of a religion. How people wear their hair, for instance, is often given symbolic religious significance. Foods may assume symbolic meanings, too. And in many religious traditions, natural phenomena are seen as closely linked to humans within a totemic view of the cosmos.

Myths, or sacred tales, are another way of linking the supernatural with the mundane. They may function as culture histories, as justification for the existing social order and institutions, or as attempts to deal with basic questions of the human condition from the particular society's point of view. In analyzing myths, we may gain insights into how a social order works and how its contradictions are handled.

In addition to symbols and myths, religious traditions always posit the existence of certain supernatural beings. Many peoples believe in an unseen supernatural force infusing everything. Often there are also spirits, gods, and minor beings populating the cosmos.

Religious beliefs are typically presented in ways that have great emotional impact: practices enhancing a feeling of separation of the sacred from the secular and rituals that repeat the basic messages of a belief system. Sometimes people also strive for transcendent experiences of the supernatural by altering their state of consciousness. Hallucinogens, which offer one way of inducing the desired trance state, are most often employed in egalitarian societies that do not restrict access to sacred truths to a small elite.

Men and women who specialize in communications with the spirit world through trance states are called shamans. Others who specialize in keeping religious laws and performing rituals usually do so on a part-time basis. Only large-scale societies with an extensive division of labor can afford full-time priests. Whether full- or part-time, keepers of the law tend to be conservative upholders of a religious tradition. Radical change is more likely to be encouraged by prophets who have visions of a new way; such transformations are nevertheless shaped by the existing social order.

A religion may change as the culture itself does, since religion is closely linked to a society's history, adaptational strategy, and social processes. Sometimes cultures slowly evolve from within; sometimes contact with or conquest by another culture brings the possibility of more rapid change in religious beliefs. A conquered people may accept the conqueror's religion, assert their own, or join the two in a process known as syncretism. When things seem particularly bleak for an oppressed people, a millenarian movement may bring hopes of a complete change.

Suggested Readings

General works:

Banton, Michael, ed. 1966. *Anthropological approaches to the study of religion.* London: Tavistock Publications.

Evans-Pritchard, E. E. 1965. *Theories of primitive religion.* Oxford: Clarendon Press.

Lessa, William A., and Vogt, Evon Z., eds. 1979. *Reader in comparative religion* 2d ed. New York: Harper & Row.

Lowie, Robert H. 1948. *Primitive religion.* New York: Liveright.

Malefijt, Annemarie de Waal. 1968. *Religion and culture: An introduction to anthropology of religion.* New York: Macmillan.

Middleton, John, ed. 1967. *Gods and rituals: Readings in religious beliefs and practices.* Garden City, NY: Natural History Press.

Wallace, Anthony. 1966. *Religion: An anthropological view.* New York: Random House.

Specialized studies:

Edsman, Carl-Martin, ed. 1967. *Studies in shamanism.* Stockholm: Almquist and Wiksell.

Eliade, Mircea. 1964. *Shamanism: Archaic techniques of ecstasy.* Princeton: Princeton University Press.

Furst, Peter T., ed. 1972. *Flesh of the gods: The ritual use of hallucinogens.* London: Allen & Unwin.

Georges, Robert A., ed. 1968. *Studies in mythology.* Homewood, IL: Dorsey.

Harner, Michael J., ed. 1973. *Hallucinogens and shamanism.* New York: Oxford University Press.

Lévi-Strauss, Claude. 1973. *Totemism.* Harmondsworth: Penguin.

Lewis, I. M. 1971. *Ecstatic religion: An anthropological study of spirit possession and shamanism.* Harmondsworth: Penguin.

Newell, William H., ed. 1976. *Ancestors.* The Hague/Paris: Mouton. (Ancestor worship)

Religious movements, religion of the oppressed:

Barrett, Leonard E. 1977. *The Rastafarians: The dreadlocks of Jamaica.* Kingston: Sangster's/Heinemann.

Berndt, Ronald M. 1962. *An adjustment movement in Arnhem Land: Northern territory of Australia.* Paris/The Hague: Mouton.

Burridge, Kenelm. 1960. *Mambu: A study of Melanesian cargo movements and their social and ideological background.* New York: Harper & Row.

——. 1969. *New heaven new earth: A study of millenarian movements.* Oxford: Blackwell.

Cohn, Norman. 1957. *The pursuit of the millenium: Revolutionary millenarians and mystical anarchists of the Middle Ages.* London: Secker & Warburg.

La Barre, Weston. 1969. *The peyote cult.* New York: Schocken.

Lanternari, Vittorio. 1963. *The religions of the oppressed: A study of modern messianic cults.* New York: Knopf.

Mooney, James. 1965. *The ghost-dance religion and the Sioux outbreak of 1890.* Chicago: University of Chicago Press.

Wallace, Anthony F. C. 1972. *The death and rebirth of the Seneca nation.* New York: Vintage. (Seneca revitalization movement)

Worsley, Peter. 1957. *The trumpet shall sound: A study of "cargo" cults in Melanesia.* London: MacGibbon & Kee.

Case studies:

Belo, Jane. 1949. *Bali: Rangda and Barong.* Seattle: University of Washington Press.

Bond, George, Johnson, Walton, and Walker, Sheila, eds. 1979. *African Christianity.* New York: Academic Press.

Bunnag, Jane. 1973. *Buddhist monk, Buddhist layman: A study of urban monastic organization in central Thailand.* Cambridge: Cambridge University Press.

Geertz, Clifford. 1960. *The religion of Java.* Glencoe, IL: Free Press.

Hugh-Jones, Stephen. 1979. *The palm and the pleiades: Initiation and cosmology in northwest Amazonia.* Cambridge: Cambridge University Press.

Hunt, Eva. 1977. *The transformation of the hummingbird: Cultural roots of a Zinacantan mythical poem.* Ithaca, NY: Cornell University Press. (Southern Mexico)

Lamb, F. Bruce. 1975. *Wizard of the upper Amazon: The story of Manuel Cŏrdova-Rios.* Boston: Houghton Mifflin.

Lienhardt, Godfrey. 1961. *Divinity and experience: The religion of the Dinka.* Oxford: Clarendon Press. (Northern Africa)

Lincoln, Bruce. 1980. *Priests, warriors and cattle: Study in the ecology of religion.* Berkeley/Los Angeles: University of California Press. (Africa)

Métraux, Alfred. 1972. *Voodoo in Haiti.* New York: Schocken.

Munn, Nancy D. 1973. *Walbiri iconography: Graphic representation and cultural symbolism in a central Australian society.* Ithaca, NY: Cornell University Press.

Myerhoff, Barbara G. 1974. *Peyote hunt: The sacred journey of the Huichol Indians.* Ithaca, NY: Cornell University Press.

Neihardt, John G. 1979. *Black Elk speaks: Being the life story of a holy man of the Ogalala Sioux* 2d ed. Lincoln, NE: University of Nebraska Press.

Spiro, Melford E. 1978. *Burmese supernaturalism.* Philadelphia: Institute for the Study of Human Issues.

Tanner, Adrian. 1979. *Bringing home animals: Religious ideology and mode of production of the Mistassini Cree hunters.* London: Hurst.

Focus on People

The Captain Cook Myth

Deborah Bird Rose

Deborah Bird Rose has lived in Yarralin in the Northern Territory of Australia since September of 1980. As part of her study of cultural identity among Aborigines, Rose has had to learn a great deal about economic and political systems (both Aboriginal and Australian). She has logged thousands of miles learning about geography, territories, dreaming sites, food resources, linguistic boundaries, ceremonies, and so on. In her travels, Rose discovered that the single most important issue to Aboriginal people is their right to land; Rose is currently working for the Northern Land Council, the Aboriginal representative body for land rights.

IN 1768, CAPTAIN James Cook, an English explorer, sailed for the South Pacific in the *Endeavour*, and before he returned to England three years later, he had charted the coasts of New Zealand, eastern Australia, and New Guinea. For the British, this expedition yielded invaluable navigational charts; for the people on these islands, the expedition yielded their first view of the white man.

White people did not arrive in the northwestern part of Australia until the 1880s, and with them arrived a new and different "law"—a new set of relationships between white people and black. Over the past hundred years, the Aboriginal people have gone from being healthy, strong, and independent to being the virtual slaves of a system that denied them resources, health, dignity, and autonomy. The Captain Cook myth explains this change as Aborigines of the Northern Territory see it. The story is an important, but not secret, part of Aboriginal knowledge that has been handed down from generation to generation.

Though there are many variations of the Captain Cook myth, there is a basic pattern that serves as the foundation of the story. Captain Cook lands at Sydney, Australia, explores the region, shooting people and stealing land, and lays down his "law"—that black people must work for white people for no pay and get none of the schooling, medical care, and other services that white people have. White people get rich, by stealing land and labor, while the Aboriginal people remain poor.

Part of the Captain Cook myth is the belief that white Australians owe the Aborigines a lot—in terms of money, land, and in retribution for the many lives lost. The following words, spoken by Daniari, a sixty-five-year-old Australian Aborigine, clearly express that belief. Daniari, a highly respected elder among Aborigines in the northwest part of the Northern Territory, whose reputation rests on his traditional knowledge and his political savvy, agreed to have his words recorded in this text so that people far away from the Territory can know something about Aboriginal people.

Daniari, a sixty-five-year-old elder
among Aborigines in the Northern
Territory of Australia.

We have been shot. Captain Cook came
knocking [killing] people for gold. Captain
Cook been starting to talk about his law, that's
the beginning time of white men; our fathers
and fathers' fathers been telling us. They were
working for old Australia people and Captain
Cook the one that brought the law; we don't
give any clothes to any boy, and the women, we
don't give them a dress. They can work naked,
no clothes. They can work. And if they got a
crippled foot or knee, well no medicine for
them. If a horse kick him, they take him in a
gully along a creek and knock him or shoot him.

No school for him. The children got no school.
When a baby is born, no food for the mother;
when a baby is sick, no medicine. This is the
way Captain Cook put it over and put a lot
trouble on Aboriginal people. But you not the
boss for this land now. This land belongs to
Aboriginal people. That law belong you is fin-
ished from Captain Cook's time. You know
Captain Cook is passed away now. And people
here got no bit of money, got no better clothes.
We been taking that job for you and we been
making that money for you and there been
nothing for Aboriginal people. Just give them

tea, sugar, flour, bar of soap. That's Aboriginal people making big money for Australian men and that's how those Australian men got up and made a government, made this Australia. We not trying to push you back to Big England, but you the blokes, Australian people, you been making a mistake making a lot of mistakes. You got to give us back land, money, buildings, you got to work for us now, make things right for us.

I'm speaking about now. We can have a friend, be friends together. Because we own Australia, every one, no matter who, white and black. We can come together, join in. Because this country now getting filled up. And if he go to make a war, every one of us going to get killed, even dogs and trees. We should come together now, join in, and make it all right, make it more better out of that big problem, before. Captain Cook making a lot of cruel. But now these days we'll be friendly, we'll be mates. But

what we think, Aboriginal people up in the Northern Territory, we look out for minerals. We own that mineral, and when a bloke come look around for minerals he should ask the Aboriginal people first. You just can't put in your big machine. No, you got to ask Aboriginal people. We'll give you a fair go. We own the land, we own the minerals, we own the oil. All that thing. You got to ask Aboriginal people. You know, we people very sad, Aboriginal people. Because this land for we people, not for white people. We know that Captain Cook been catching people; caught them all over Australia. But this time now, any man who's wanting for minerals, wanting for oil, he can come and see the Aboriginal people. That's his oil, Aboriginal people's, and that's his mineral. Because he owns the land. He's got the secret, he's got the ceremony, he's the one sitting on that land.

Chapter Fifteen

Illness and Curing

ILLNESS AND THE desire to treat those who are ill are common features of all human societies. The types of diseases found, how illness is viewed, and how people treat illness, however, vary considerably from society to society. In the industrial nations of Western Europe and North America cancers and cardiovascular diseases are of major concern. In many tropical and subtropical regions they are of relatively little significance, but such diseases as malaria, cholera, and dysentery are more important. Treatment of illness in Western industrial societies tends to focus on curing specific diseased organs or controlling a specific virus. In many non-Western societies greater emphasis is placed on the social and psychological dimensions of illness.

Anthropologists emphasize that patterns of disease or illness and methods of curing exist within particular physical and sociocultural settings. The medical systems of Canada and the United States are as much a product of their respective environments as the systems of Australian Aborigines and Amazonian Indians. By *medical system* we mean "the culturally based behavior and belief forms that arise in response to the threats posed by disease" (Foster and Anderson 1978: 33). Anthropologists study the medical systems of small-scale non-Western societies as well as of large-scale industrial societies. Such systems are not isolated. Western medical beliefs, technology, and practices have had a profound influence on medical systems throughout the world. Likewise, after overcoming their initial prejudices (in part because of the work of anthropologists), Western physicians and medical researchers have been influenced by their "primitive" counterparts.

In this chapter we will look at the cultural context of disease and illness—at how they are locally understood and treated and how their occurrence seems to be related to specific environmental factors. Note that the terms *disease* and *illness* do not refer to the same thing. *Disease* is a concept referring to a pathological condition of the body, or of some part of it, in which its functioning is disturbed or deranged. *Illness* is a cultural concept: a condition marked by pronounced deviation from what is considered a normal healthy state. Even though beliefs about disease and patterns of incidence may be viewed as sociocultural phenomena, diseases themselves are strictly physiological processes. Illness, on the other hand, is a broad concept referring to how people conceive of deviant mental and physical states.

OVERLEAF
Sand paintings are among the most potent symbols in Navaho healing rituals. The patient sits on top of the stylized images of mythic heroes and gods while the medicine man transfers the power of the painting by pressing colored sand onto the patient. This painting from the Blessing Way chant is used to correct mistakes in rituals, to protect herds of animals, to promote mental health, and to dispel fears from bad dreams and omens. After the ceremony, the healer disperses the sand in the wind.

The Epidemiology of Disease

Epidemiology is the study of the relationships of the various factors that determine the frequency and distribution of diseases in societies. Medical sociologists interested in epidemiology in complex societies study the effects of age, sex, marital status, occupation, social class, and natural environment on disease patterns. By analyzing statistical correlations they seek to discover the causes of the occurrence of diseases. Anthropologists have tended to focus on epidemiological characteristics of diseases among non-Western peoples living in small-scale societies. Unlike medical sociologists, anthropologists studying epidemiology have relied heavily upon direct observation and attention to particular cultural patterns in drawing their conclusions, rather than on statistical correlation.

One of the best-known examples of the contribution of anthropology to epidemiological research is the case of *kuru*, a disease of the central nervous system that was discovered in the

Kuru victim is treated by "bleeding" by a medicine man (New Guinea, 1962).

1950s among the South Fore of the eastern highlands of New Guinea. No known treatment will cure or arrest kuru, which usually leads to death within six to twelve months. The disease was found to be unique to the South Fore, and among them it was limited to women, children, and occasionally young men.

Initial investigation revealed that the disease tended to follow family lines. Numerous hypotheses—genetic, infectious, sociological, and nutritional—were offered to explain the disease, but all proved unsatisfactory (Hunt 1978). The first breakthrough came from laboratory studies with sheep and chimpanzees that led to the discovery of "slow virus infections," in which a disease appeared only after a long period of incubation for the virus in its host. Kuru proved to be the first known human disease caused by a slow-acting virus.

The discovery of the slow-acting virus failed to explain the epidemiological characteristics of kuru, however. Why was the disease limited to the South Fore, and why to only a limited segment of the population? And why had its incidence changed over time? The disease had first appeared during the early part of the twentieth century, with its incidence increasing up to the 1950s and declining thereafter. A partial answer to these questions was arrived at by anthropologists Robert and Shirley Glasse (see Lindenbaum 1979). They found that cannibalism among South Fore women was introduced around 1910, roughly the same time that the disease first appeared. In particular, eating the brains of deceased kinswomen became part of their mourning ceremonies. The brains were prepared and eaten primarily by women, with small portions occasionally being given to children of either sex. It was found that the virus was transmitted in the preparation; the women who touched the mucous membranes of the brains contracted the disease. The decline of kuru was linked to the cessation in the 1960s of this ritual cannibalism.

Endemic Diseases

A society's characteristic diseases are closely related to its physical environment, as well as its cultural practices. Part of a population's adaptation to a particular environment entails biocultural adjustment to the local disease-causing features. Especially when the population and its adaptation are rather stable, relatively constant epidemiological patterns will emerge. One result is the development of *endemic diseases*: diseases that have a relatively low incidence but are constantly present in a given community. In our own society such diseases include the "common cold," flu, and chickenpox.

Evidence indicates that during the thousands of years of our existence as foragers disease patterns were fairly constant, depending upon the local environment (Dunn 1968). The original immigrants to the New World who crossed the Bering land bridge carried few diseases with them and in their isolation developed tolerances for the limited selection of disease-causing agents in the New World. One of the endemic diseases to develop in the New World was syphilis. A syndrome of the worldwide disease treponematosis, syphilis evolved as a disease that was unique to the New World. Among New World inhabitants syphilis appears not to have been a particularly serious problem. It was only once it spread to Europe and Asia after 1492 (the first epidemic in Europe occurring in Italy in 1494 or 1495) that it took on the more severe characteristics for which it has subsequently been known (Crosby 1972: 122–64).

The fact that human populations, their environments, and viruses as well are constantly changing contributes to the dynamism of disease patterns. Entirely new diseases may emerge (and subsequently disappear). Treponematosis has taken on a variety of different characteristics, according to the environment of the host population. E. H. Hudson (1965) asserts that the disease originally appeared as a surface disease, yaws, in tropical Africa. In drier areas the virus became internal, evolving into a kind of nonvenereal syphilis, a childhood disease known as *bejel* in the Middle East, which is transmitted by close contact under very unhygienic conditions. With improved hygiene the virus moved deeper into the human body, reappearing as venereal syphilis.

Epidemic Diseases

Migration and contact between previously isolated human populations are the prime causes of epidemics. An *epidemic disease* is one that is not commonly present in a community, characterized by high incidence and rapid and extensive diffusion. Perhaps the most devastating series of epidemics in world history were those brought by the opening of regular contact between the New World and the old after 1492. The long isolation of the New World population made it especially vulnerable to diseases brought from Europe and Africa. Smallpox was one of the leading killers. Endemic to the Old World, it was a steady, predictable killer, responsible for less than 10 percent of the yearly deaths. But among people with no previous contact, smallpox will infect nearly every individual. Within two years after smallpox first appeared in Iceland in 1707, 18,000 of the island's 50,000 inhabitants had died of it. In Mexico, Toribio Motolinia noted that the indigenous inhabitants "died in heaps, like bedbugs" from such epidemics. In many areas the Spanish *conquistadores* gathered the scattered inhabitants into larger and more centralized communities for greater ease of administration. This practice accelerated the spread of diseases. Within ten years of contact with Europeans the population of central Mexico declined from 25 to 16.8 million, primarily because of the direct and indirect effects of the epidemics.

Anthropologists and other social scientists are not interested simply in the effects of socio-cultural factors on disease; they are also concerned with its social consequences. Severe epidemics generally have highly noticeable effects on societies. Many authors have argued that the sixteenth-century collapse of the various Indian empires in the New World, such as the Inca and Aztec empires, was caused primarily by the ravages of newly introduced epidemic diseases. The more subtle effects of diseases are also significant. Endemic malaria in a region may kill only a small percentage of the population, but it may debilitate a much larger proportion, contributing to a general malaise that adversely affects economic and cultural life.

Diseases of Development

Charles Hughes and John Hunter (1972: 93) coined the term "diseases of development" to refer to "those pathological conditions which are based on the usually unanticipated consequences of the implementation of development schemes." Such diseases can be divided into three general categories. First, there are those diseases that result from integrating people into large-scale industrial societies: diabetes, obesity, hypertension, and so on. In a study of the Polynesian island of Rarotonga, Prior (1971: 2) found that the introduction of town life, imported foods, and especially increased intake of sugar and salt had resulted in a ninefold increase in the incidence of high blood pressure among the islanders, a doubling or tripling of the incidence of diabetes, a doubling for men and a quadrupling for women of the rate of heart disease, and a tenfold increase in serious obesity among women.

The second category includes instances where development programs have upset existing environmental conditions and introduced or increased bacterial and parasitic diseases. For example, onchocerciasis (African river blindness) is a disease that has traditionally affected the population living in the Volta River basin of West

Africa. It is carried by a tiny blackfly and results in reduced or total loss of vision. In 1974 and 1975 the disease, which had been present in Mexico since the 1940s, was reported to be spreading throughout the northwestern part of the Amazonian Basin in South America (Davis 1977: 101–3). The indigenous population of the region proved particularly susceptible. Among some groups of Yanomamo up to 100 percent of the population became infected. Two American scientists, Robert Goodland and Howard Irwin (1975), found that the blackfly population was thriving in the cleared areas along the newly constructed Northern Perimeter Highway, which was penetrating areas occupied by indigenous groups.

The slowly debilitating disease bilharziasis, caused by a parasitic blood fluke found in certain water snails, is another that has spread as a result of development projects. The number of persons suffering from bilharziasis has grown to perhaps 200 million, and the disease continues to spread at a rapid rate. This spread is almost entirely the result of the expansion of irrigated lands made possible by the construction of high dams. Within three years of completion of the Nasser High Dam in Egypt, the incidence of bilharziasis among children in the areas affected rose from 5–25 percent to 55–85 percent (Miller 1973: 15). With the completion of dams elsewhere, the disease has spread throughout the world. Today it is found in Africa, the Near East, the Orient, and South America. Greater use of irrigation has also been responsible for increasing the incidence of malaria, since the mosquito that transmits malaria finds the waters of rice paddies and irrigation ditches ideal places to breed.

Finally, there are the innumerable diseases associated with poverty, undernourishment, and unsanitary living conditions that result from the failure of development programs: the underdevelopment that results from unsatisfactory integration of people into large-scale societies.

Solutions to these problems are difficult. An understanding of the causes of these diseases helps, and anthropology plays an important role in this thorough analysis of very complex social, cultural, and natural factors which influence disease. Diseases like malaria and bilharziasis will not be cured simply through the development of wonder drugs or spraying with pesticides. Finding cures can result only from a willingness to look beyond the disease to its total context.

Malnutrition

Closely related to the study of disease is the study of nutrition among human populations. Hundreds of millions of people are undernourished, and trying to understand the causes and find solutions to malnutrition are among the most important problems in the world today. Minor cases of malnutrition may impair people's ability to perform daily tasks. Malnutrition also reduces resistance to disease. In extreme form malnutrition may lead to permanent brain damage or to starvation and death.

An initial difficulty in studying nutritional problems is determining human nutritional standards. Traditionally, criteria have been based almost exclusively on the perceived needs of "white" Europeans and North Americans. To apply this standard to all peoples may be a mistake, however. For example, recent analyses of diets and physical work capacities in Ethiopia and New Guinea have led to serious reconsideration of existing standards of protein requirements (Weiner 1978: 11). We are also learning more about the adaptability of humans to varying diets. In New Guinea, while the diet of coastal peoples includes protein derived from fish, many highland people subsist largely on sweet potatoes, a diet of almost pure carbohydrates. Yet these people are well muscled and able to carry very heavy loads over long distances. They do not suffer from protein-related malnutrition. Such studies demonstrate the need for flexible, community-specific nutritional standards.

When the results of malnutrition, however the nutritional lacks are defined, are evident, the causes are often both cultural and social. That is, they are related to people's ideas about what they eat (what they consider to be "food") and to social factors (such as economic impoverishment) influencing what they can eat and how much.

Malnutrition and Subsistence Patterns

Malnutrition is to a large extent a reflection of increasing social scale. It tends to be more a feature of large-scale agricultural and industrial societies than of small-scale societies. Dunn (1968: 233) cites numerous studies that indicate the relatively good nutritional status of the members of foraging societies in comparison with neighboring agriculturists and urban dwellers. Hunger was rare among traditional foragers and their diets were usually sufficient to meet their nutritional needs. The extent to which malnutrition exists today among contemporary foraging societies is primarily a function of their integration into a world system that has destroyed their customary subsistence bases while failing to replace them with new ones that are adequate.

In a study of nutrition among Australian Aborigines living at the Edward River settlement of the Cape York Peninsula, John C. Taylor (1977) notes that since the Aborigines gave up their traditional nomadic existence in the 1950s their diet has been characterized by shortcomings in most important nutrients. The post-

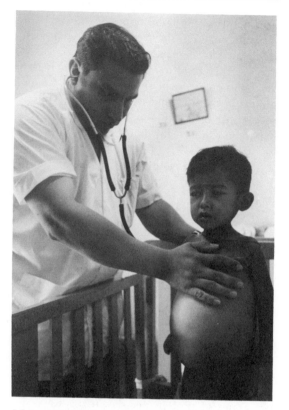

Malnutrition is a major problem throughout the Third World. Ignorant of the symptoms of malnutrition, many parents assume that a big stomach is the sign of a child's good health.

settlement diet of most Australian Aborigines consists of damper (flour and water), sweet black tea, and occasionally meat. Such a diet is particularly lacking in protein, calcium, vitamin A, and vitamin C. It provides especially poor nourishment during pregnancy, resulting in the birth of babies of less than optimal weight and impaired resistance to disease. Problems continue after birth, and Australian Aboriginal societies today are noted for high disease and death rates. Perhaps the most significant finding of Taylor's study, however, is that improvement in economic conditions for the Edward River Aborigines has not resulted in dietary improvements. In fact, just the opposite has occurred. Increases in wages have been diverted toward satisfaction of demands for nonfood consumer items, rather than foods. One problem is that the Aborigines do not think of their diet as inadequate: the flour and tea are, after all, filling. As a result of their dietary outlook and these economic changes, the nutrition of the people has deteriorated to the point where some people are unconsciously starving themselves as they divert more of their income to material goods.

By employing a complex mixed foraging and agricultural adaptation, small-scale farming societies are also generally able to meet the subsistence needs of their members, as long as population pressure or external threats to their subsistence base do not become too great. The Achuara Jivaro of Amazonian South America, for example, have one of the highest population densities in the area, and yet are able to maintain a diet that exceeds their nutritional requirements. Each member of this group consumes on the average 3,257 calories of food and 107 grams of protein per day (Ross 1978: 4). Both of these figures exceed the daily averages of those living in the more "developed" regions of the world.

For many small-scale farming societies, nutritional problems begin to emerge as they are integrated into large-scale market economies. As peasant agriculturists, they find a large percentage of what they produce usurped by nonagriculturists, and what they receive in return for their products is rarely sufficient to meet their requirements, nutritionally or in any other sense. Their diet begins to suffer in both quantity and variety. Protein intake, in particular, tends to be greatly reduced. The protein intake of most rural peasants in Africa, Asia, and Latin America is less than half of that of the Achuara Jivaro, and their nutritional deficiencies in other categories are often even greater. The average daily intake in Latin America is around

1,200 kilocalories—only half of normal subsistency. In poorer areas of such countries as Haiti, Peru, and Chile people commonly are not able to eat every day, and daily intakes may average as low as 500 kilocalories.

Large-scale societies produce a tremendous amount of food, but they also have a lot of people to feed. In some countries, such as India, production simply does not keep up with population growth. In many other cases, however, and even to some extent in countries like India, the problem is not so much the total amount of food produced or marketed, as it is the distribution of what is available. In these instances nutritional problems become a reflection of relative socioeconomic inequality. The most obvious example is the United States, a nation with an abundant supply of food, an overfed and overweight middle and upper class, and millions of undernourished people occupying the lower socioeconomic rungs of society.

Cultural Perceptions of Food

Malnutrition can also develop in the midst of plenty, because what people consider to be food is largely a matter of cultural definition, especially in large-scale societies. It is not only relatively poor and uneducated people like the Aboriginal inhabitants of Edward River who are unaware that their diet is lacking in vital nutrients; the same can be said of many affluent North Americans.

In every society people select from a range of edible substances things to be designated as food, and many nutritious items are usually excluded. People of different cultures eat many "disgusting" things that we would never consider eating, such as dogs—commonly eaten in many parts of the Orient and Pacific (Ishige 1977 provides a Ponapean recipe for roasting dogs in an earth oven). Even less obvious are the numerous nutritious insects and "weeds" found in cities and around our homes. Often such things are quite plentiful, yet because they are not considered food people will go hungry or even starve while living in what members of many traditional foraging societies would consider a veritable supermarket.

Trying to change people's perceptions of food is a very difficult task; improving their dietary habits is rarely as simple as providing alternative types of food. We all know how little good it does to tell a child (or an adult, for that matter), "Here, eat this, it's good for you." Cross-cultural innovations may be even more difficult, especially where there are already existing prejudices against the food ("We feed that to pigs"). Furthermore, often what is perceived to be nutritious, even by "experts," may not be. For example, programs aimed at promoting the use of dietary formulas for infants were popular in many poorer nations until recently due largely to the promotional activities of companies such as Nestlé. Wholesale support of this innovation has waned as people have looked at the relative cost of such products and begun to question their superiority to mothers' milk.

Mental Illness

All peoples recognize illnesses associated with mental states perceived as abnormal. *Mental illness*, includes disorders caused by physiological conditions such as certain "birth defects," as well as those caused by individual adaptations to sociocultural conditions. In the latter, mental illness is seen as resulting from *stress* produced by individuals' attempts to deal with perceived inadequacies in their environment.

Stress is a feature of life in all societies. It may result from natural causes, as in damage resulting from storms or volcanic eruptions, or it may be intentional, as in torture. It may also simply be a "normal" part of the life cycle. In our own society driving to and from work is a common point of stress for many people. The trauma for a young Australian Aboriginal male preparing to undergo subincision can be as great as anything we could imagine in a large-scale society.

Patterns of Stress Disorders

After decades of careful research on mental illness in different cultures, it now appears that the major patterns of mental illness known to Western psychiatrists are universal (Kennedy 1973). However, since patterns of stress-producing situations will vary from one setting to another and because cultural methods of dealing with stress differ, the distribution of forms of mental illness varies between societies. Physical surroundings, economic conditions, child-rearing practices, religious traditions, and so forth all combine to produce an environment with which the individual must come to terms. It is therefore possible—albeit difficult—to study mental illness from an "epidemiological" perspective, noting distributional patterns and searching for variables in the environment that appear to influence such patterns.

In addition to universal forms of mental illness that vary in frequency from one society to another, particular environments and cultural traditions occasionally lead to unique manifestations. These are commonly referred to as *culture-specific disorders*. Among these disorders are "Arctic hysteria," found among a variety of circumpolar peoples; "running amok," a frenzied killing spree by males in Malaysian society; and "koro," a fear among Chinese males that the penis will withdraw into the body. While most of these disorders are based upon universal forms of mental illness, they have taken on certain unique characteristics as well.

Another culture-specific disorder is *Windigo*

psychosis, a cannibalistic obsession of Algonquan-speaking Indians in northeastern North America (Parker 1960). The disorder is said to begin when a sorcerer or spirit-helper *(windigo)* appears in a man's dream, transforming him into a windigo with a compulsive desire to eat flesh. The windigo's guilt over his compulsion results in a desire to be killed. Transcultural psychiatrist Ari Kiev (1972: 99) describes the syndrome as a "classical depressive disorder, showing a specifically prominent secondary symptom of self-deprecation and need for punishment, with a culturally available explanation." A partial explanation: Algonquan-speaking societies occasionally suffer from food shortages and cannibalism is not unknown under extreme circumstances. Much of their mythology concerns hunger and cannibalistic monsters. Parker further

Life in the slums of Lima, Peru, is difficult, especially for migrants from the highlands, and often leads to both physical and mental health problems.

argues that the windigo psychosis is a result of stress in the male role. The male fears failure to live up to the narrow and rigidly defined masculine role, while also being afraid of success, since it may lead to envy and social rejection. Failure as a hunter would bring shame, but success may also lead to problems because of the envy of less successful hunters. When his feelings of depression resulting from either success or failure or from his sheer inability to resolve the contradiction become too great, the person becomes a windigo, a "pathological adjustment" to the contradictory pressures of being an Algonquan male.

Social Change and Stress

Rapid social change is a primary source of stress for many people. Often the strains may be temporary, but the stress may be sufficient to cause severe mental disorders nevertheless. Migration

commonly results in considerable stress. Margaret Mead (1947) pointed out that the migrant is frequently culturally disoriented and subject to special strains, while at the same time being without the accustomed means of reducing tensions. Many Okinawans who migrated to Hawaii during the immediate postwar period found life there very stressful; they developed rates of psychoses that were significantly higher than for other groups on the islands. By contrast, in Okinawa there was a relatively low incidence of mental illness (Moloney 1945; Wedge 1952). The problem may be even worse if the migrant must make difficult physical adjustments. Peruvian Indians moving to Lima from the mountains are not only faced with social and cultural problems of adjustment, but also have difficulty adjusting to the higher oxygen content in the coastal air. The combination of factors results in a syndrome characterized not only by depression and anxiety, but also by a number of circulatory, respiratory, neurological, and gastrointestinal symptoms during their first year in Lima (Seguin 1956; Fried 1959).

Migration and other forms of rapid social change may result in a state of *anomie*: disorganization of personality and a feeling of alienation. In his famous study of suicide (1951), Durkheim described anomie as a result of the abandonment of community goals and of the social rules for reaching them. In small, closely knit rural communities people's lives tend to be highly organized and closely regulated. There are constraints, but also a sense of security. Movement to the city often results in liberation from many of the constraints of rural small-town life, but the individual suddenly has to live in a very unfamiliar environment, with no sure way for finding happiness in this new setting.

For many indigenous peoples around the world, rapid social change has meant the destruction of the existing social order, and, all too often, its replacement with a social order based upon impoverishment and exploitation. The psychological consequences are often severe, suicide or loss of a will to live being a familiar result. In such cases, the individual has not made an adaptation to the environment, but rather has decided not to make the required adjustments. For those who make the attempt, the result may well be a variety of mental illnesses.

Concepts of Illness Causality

A people's own understanding of and methods of curing a perceived illness are based on their notions of what caused it. Such ideas vary widely.

Mind-Body Dualism

Western medical traditions have posited a distinction between illnesses originating in the mind and those originating in the body, between "psychological" and "physiological" illnesses. Other traditions have taken a more holistic approach, viewing health and illness as manifestations of the totality of a person's life. For instance, most non-Western medical systems do not have a separate category for "mental illness." Mental illness and physiological illness in such systems are placed in the same general category. To the Azande of the southern Sudan, mental illnesses are viewed as illnesses not unlike such diseases as malaria, smallpox, and dysentery, and all are seen as ultimately caused by sorcery. Categorical distinctions between mental and physiological illness tend to be a feature of Western medical traditions, and are in part a reflection of greater specialization (occupational and otherwise) in Western societies.

Despite the traditional mind-body split in the West, it is now widely recognized by Western medical practitioners that psychological factors often play a significant role in causing illnesses of a physiological nature, and that many of these psychological factors are related to specific sociocultural conditions. Malgri, for example, an illness found among the Aboriginal inhabitants of Wellesley Island in northern Australia (Cawte 1974: 106–19), is now understood as a physiological manifestation of a culture-specific psychological condition. It is characterized by drowsiness and abdominal pain, and appears to be brought on as a result of concern over violation of food taboos. Each primary social group on Wellesley Island occupies a specific territory over which it possesses rights of forage. Malgri is said to strike only those persons who have secured food from outside of their home range. Such a belief serves as a defense mechanism against poaching.

Personalistic vs. Naturalistic Explanations

So-called "modern" or "scientific" concepts of disease causality have developed only since the sixteenth century, and in many parts of the world people continue to adhere to alternative beliefs that vary considerably from each other, as well as from "scientific" beliefs. Nevertheless, there appear to be basic principles common to many of these belief systems. Foster and Anderson (1978: 53) have distinguished two major systems of disease causality beliefs—*personalistic* and *naturalistic*—although this division oversimplifies matters somewhat.

In a *personalistic system,* illness is thought to be purposely caused by a supernatural being (such as a ghost or evil spirit), or a human being (such as a witch or sorcerer). According to Foster and Anderson (1978), "The sick person literally is a victim, the object of aggression or pun-

ishment directed specifically against him, for reasons that concern him alone."

Personalistic belief systems predominate among non-Western peoples living in small-scale societies throughout much of Africa south of the Sahara, in the Pacific region, and among tribal peoples in Asia. One important aspect of such belief systems is that they tend to lack a concept of accident. If a man falls from a tree and dies it is assumed that someone or some being caused his death. This is not to say that people subscribing to such beliefs do not recognize more immediate causes of illness or injury, but they believe that there are other forces at work beyond the more apparent ones. It is not enough to say that a person fell out of a tree or caught a disease. One must then ask who or what was responsible for what happened, and the answer is to be found in some malicious person or noncorporeal being.

Evans-Pritchard (1937: 479) discusses such beliefs among the Azande:

Azande attribute sickness, whatever its nature, to witchcraft or sorcery. This does not mean that they entirely disregard secondary causes but, in so far as they recognize these, they generally think of them as associated with witchcraft and magic. Nor does their reference of sickness to supernatural causes lead them to neglect treatment of symptoms any more than their reference to death on the horns of a buffalo to witchcraft causes them to await its onslaught. On the contrary, they possess an enormous pharmacopoeia ... and in ordinary circumstances they trust to drugs to cure their ailments and only take steps to remove the primary and supernatural causes when the disease is of a serious nature or takes an alarming turn. Nevertheless, we must remember in describing the Zande classification of diseases and their treatment that the notion of witchcraft as a participant in their origin may always be expressed, and that if Azande do not always and immediately consult their oracles to find out the witch that is responsible it is because they consider the sickness to be of a minor character and not worth the trouble and expense of oracle consultations.

By contrast, belief systems based upon *naturalistic causes* explain illness in impersonal, systematic terms. Such systems commonly posit that good health depends upon maintaining an equilibrium within the body. When this balance is upset by natural external forces such as heat or cold or internal forces such as strong emotions, illness results.

Most contemporary naturalistic systems have been derived largely from the medical traditions of ancient classical civilizations, particularly Greece, India, and China. These include those naturalistic systems which are based upon the concept of bodily *humors*, a belief which originated in ancient Greece. There were thought to be four humors, or fluids, in the body: blood, phlegm, black bile (or melancholy), and yellow bile (or choler). Each was associated with certain qualities: blood with heat and moisture, phlegm with cold and moisture, black bile with cold and dryness, and yellow bile with heat and dryness. For the ancient Greeks illness or suffering resulted when one of these humors was either deficient or excessive, or if they should fail to mix properly. Curing was largely a matter of balancing such imbalances.

Moslem scholars maintained this medical tradition, called *humoral pathology*, after the collapse of classical Greek civilization, and from them it was reincorporated into European medicine, beginning in the eleventh century. From Europe humoral pathology spread to the New World with the English, Spanish, and Portuguese. The eastward expansion of the Moslems led to its diffusion as far as Java, Malaysia, and the Philippines (where Spanish and Moslem humoral traditions met). Today humoral pathology remains an important medical concept in many parts of the world, especially in Latin America.

In the contemporary Latin American variant of humoral pathology, illness is ascribed to excesses of "heat" or "cold." These may be related to the actual temperatures of things one comes into contact with (such as water, the air, and food), but more often the terms are used metaphorically. Foods are particularly important in maintaining a balance between hot and cold, so people adhering to such a concept of humoral pathology generally classify foods according to their "temperature." In one Mexican-American community (Clark 1970: 166) white beans, garlic, and chile peppers are considered to be "very hot"; salt, pork, and onion to be "hot"; corn tortillas, lamb, and radishes to be "cold"; and cucumbers and tomatoes to be "very cold." Illness is commonly attributed to eating an excess of hot or cold foods, and curing often entails eating things that will restore a balance.

Systems of causation belief are rarely so rigid as to ascribe *all* illness or misfortune to a single cause. Even the Azande recognize that not all illness is caused by witchcraft. For example, they do not ascribe certain diseases that afflict infants exclusively to witchcraft or magic. In fact their ideas about the causes of these diseases are fairly vague. This is in part a reflection of the status of infants in Azande society. There is a very high infant mortality rate and small children are barely considered social beings, their "sojourn in the world" at this stage being very tenuous. Much the same point can be made concerning our own medical system, which recognizes that not all illness results from physiological causes and that social and psychological factors play an important role in causing many diseases. A "cold" is not simply caught from "germs"; such factors as anxiety, exhaustion, exposure to cold air, or living in damp or crowded conditions may also be part of the cause.

Curing

How people attempt to cure illness is primarily a product of social and cultural factors rather than of any inherent properties of the illness itself. It is not particularly surprising to find that cultural beliefs about causality influence how people decide to treat illness. If an imbalance of humors is seen as the cause, then the cure will rest in trying to effect a balance. The Aztecs believed that headaches were caused by excessive blood in the head. Curing therefore involved the use of medicines that produced violent sneezing and nasal bleeding to remove the excess blood. If this approach failed, they would remove excess blood by making an incision with an obsidian point (Ortiz de Montellano 1977: 25). If one views the cause of an illness as being bacteria or other micro-organisms, the cure will probably include use of antibiotics. If sorcery is to blame, something may have to be done about the sorcerer. However, before searching for the ultimate cause a person is likely to try simpler, less expensive methods of alleviating the pain. According to the canons of our own medical system, mild heart problems do not immediately lead to heart surgery. Less drastic methods are usually tried first.

The Effectiveness of Cures

All healing systems seem to work at least part of the time. Methods and rationales used vary considerably, however, and it is hard to prove just what creates the cure. When a person comes down with malgri, the Aboriginal curer kneels and begins massaging sweat from his armpit into the victim's body. A belt of grass or hair is then unraveled and tied to the person's foot. The cord is run down to the water to point the way home for the intruding spirit. The curer begins to sing, continuing into the night until a shooting star (the incarnation of malgri's eye) is seen, indicating the dispossession and banishment of the spirit. The string is then snapped and the victim recovers (Cawte 1974: 110). The basis for this cure is hard to explain in Western terms, though it can be argued that because the illness was of a psychological nature, all that was required was a performance that would alter the victim's state of mind. Such an explanation can be applied to certain Western "cures," too, such as the ability of a placebo, or sugar pill, to cure a headache. It is rarely a simple matter to "prove" that something specific has cured an illness. Most of our medical beliefs about cures are based upon statistical averages. If something works often enough we assume that it is effective. Sometimes, however, more clearly demonstrable physiological processes are at work, as in the case of antibiotics.

The ambiguity that exists in all curing systems creates both difficulties and opportunities for healer and patient. For someone earnestly trying to cure a patient, diagnosis and an appropriate cure are rarely automatic, and there is always the possibility of error. Failure to arrive at a successful cure may be attributed to the nature of the affliction or to a lack of skill on the part of the curer, or more rarely to a general questioning of the effectiveness of the curing system. As more than one curing system may be in operation in a single setting (for instance, an indigenous system and a Western system) the patient may resort to an alternative system if the first fails. In trying to find a remedy for their afflictions people are often willing to try anything, even things that they might scoff at under other circumstances. Such a situation creates opportunities for diverse systems, and for "quacks." Most medical systems recognize the possibility of charlatanism, although this recog-

Two curers attend an old man who is complaining of a headache (Jigalong, Western Australia).

nition tends to be more common in large-scale societies. Along more legitimate lines, it is not uncommon for people to utilize a variety of systems. For some illnesses the Aboriginal inhabitants of Wellesley Island might go to a Western-trained curer, but for a case of malgri they would prefer to consult an Aboriginal curer.

Health Care Delivery Systems

The social components of curing include aspects of the overall social structure that influence the curing process and, more specifically, what may be referred to as the *health care delivery system* (Colson and Selby 1974:

254–57). A health care system mobilizes resources to care for those who are ill. Patient, curer, and auxiliary personnel all have role expectations. The system also includes available or appropriate technology and the physical setting within which the curing process takes place.

Health care systems may prescribe different settings for treating the ill, and within the same system settings may vary. There are two dimensions to the question of setting: privacy and specialization. Among the Azande diagnosis takes place in public. Heralded and accompanied by drums, diagnoses of patients are considered "local events of some importance," drawing spectators from throughout the neighborhood (Evans-Pritchard 1937: 154). Hausa barber-surgeons in Ibadan, Nigeria, place their operating tables under a tree in public view and there "ply their an-

In large-scale societies, health care often takes place in a specialized setting like this large, modern hospital complex in Houston, Texas.

cient trade" (Maclean 1971: 65). In contrast, in Western medical systems a premium is placed upon privacy for both diagnosis and treatment.

In many non-Western settings curing takes place in a nonspecialized locale, such as the village center or the patient's or curer's own home. Among the Maya of southern Belize patients often move into the home of the curer for the duration of their treatment, sometimes bringing their entire family with them. In several instances the male patient died and his wife subsequently remained with the curer. Such events become the subject of gossip, but rarely do they influence the professional reputation of the curer.

In large-scale societies health care often takes place in a specialized setting, such as a hospital.

Hospitals have evolved into very complex institutions, functioning as small societies with many of their own cultural attributes. While it is essential to analyze hospitals within the context of their external environment (i.e., "the world beyond"; see Freidson 1970: 173–74), a good deal can be learned by studying a hospital in much the same way as we would a Mayan village or a South Sea island.

In addition to prescribing the appropriate setting for curing, every society recognizes only a limited number of people who are able to treat illnesses. Contrary to popular belief, the practice of medicine is probably the oldest profession, as well as the most universal. The role of the curer, however, varies a good deal from society to society. In societies with personalistic views of disease causality, there is a need for someone who is able to determine who caused an affliction and why—usually someone with ties to the supernatural. In such societies the curer is usually a "shaman," "sorcerer," or "witch doctor." On the other hand, societies with naturalistic beliefs require "doctors" who have learned curing skills through practice and observation of illnesses and the properties of medicines.

In many small-scale societies curing is not a full-time vocation. There simply is not enough work, and the curer will generally engage in the same primary economic activities as other members of the society—hunting or farming. In large-scale societies curing is more often a full-time occupation, but not always. Physicians in our own society are accused, often unjustly, of devoting more time to playing golf or looking after their investments than to their profession. The reasons for such extracurricular activities are different than in the case of small-scale societies, and they reflect the income physicians receive.

Most societies also recognize specialization within the medical profession. Although by far the greatest degree of specialization occurs in Western medical systems, even very small non-Western societies tend to have different sorts of curers. Peasants in the Philippines recognize midwives, bonesetters, and general practitioners (Lieban 1962: 512). The Maya of southern Belize divide medical roles according to level of skill and specialty. At the lower level of skill are midwives and snakebite doctors. At higher levels there are several grades of general practitioner.

Analysis of curers requires attention not only to their role(s), but also to other career-related factors such as recruitment, training, and reputation. In personalistic systems recruitment may be by personal dream or physical affliction, such as epilepsy. Recruitment in other instances may be linked to the would-be curer's personal inclination, ability, or social status. In some cases only the children of curers can become curers; sometimes recruitment is limited to members of certain socioeconomic classes. Often all of these factors are necessary.

For shamans or sorcerers training may be transmitted via dreams from supernatural beings. In many systems a period of apprenticeship is involved, sometimes lasting for a number of years. At the end of the training period, there is usually some rite of passage, and often a form of certification. Eric Thompson (1930: 68–69) describes the initiation of a Mayan curer in southern Belize:

The instructor and the initiate retire to a hut in the bush for a month so that there may be no eavesdropping. During this period the initiate is taught by his master all the different prayers and practices used in causing and curing sickness. At the end of that period the initiate is sent to meet Kisin (a diety). Kisin takes the form of a large snake called Ochcan (otskan), which is described as being very big, not poisonous and having a large shiny eye. When the initiate and the ochcan meet face to face, the latter rears up on his tail, and approaching the initiate till their faces are almost touching, puts his tongue in the initiate's mouth. In this manner he communicates the final mysteries of sorcery.

To the north, in Belize, the snake is said to swallow the initiate whole as the finale of the initiation, passing him out of his body with excrement. Although his sequence may be somewhat more dramatic than that for graduating medical students in Western medical systems, the result is much the same: legitimation as a recognized curer is sanctioned by those who dominate the profession.

The ability of a curer to continue working is in large part a matter of reputation. Curers generally must have a relatively good record of success, although within any system a good public relations effort can make up for lack of success in curing patients. All systems have norms regarding appropriate "bedside manners," which play an important role in assessment of the curer. Success as a physician has its pitfalls, however. Inuit shamans and American brain surgeons alike run the risk of negative sanctions resulting from the envy of others or feelings that they have too much wealth or power.

In addition to powerful chief curers, health care systems also often include a number of auxiliary persons who assist in the treatment process. In Western systems these include nurses, orderlies, and assorted administrators. In nonwestern systems assistance may be left to an apprentice or to readily available nonspecialists. Among peoples like the Azande, assistants may include musicians or chanters who provide an accompaniment to the curer's activities.

The other essential participant in any health care system is the patient. Patients too have role expectations, ways in which they are expected to behave. Perhaps the most important part of any health care system is the interaction between the patient and those responsible for his or her treatment, based on the patient's belief in the healers' power to diagnose and cure, and on their mutual understanding of what should take place. The significance of such interaction becomes especially clear when patient and physician come from different sociocultural backgrounds and communication is impaired. Among the Bomvana Xhosa of southern Africa, the diviner starts the consultation by intuitively "guessing" what the illness is:

He is not supposed to take "the medical history" by interviewing the patient and/or his relatives. On the contrary, he is the one who has to give answers to all the questions about the patient and the causes of his disease. [Jansen 1973: 43]

As a result of this practice, when a Xhosa patient is confronted with a Western-trained doctor's "What is wrong with you?" he is usually puzzled, since it is the doctor and not the patient who is supposed to answer that question.

The Costs of Health Care

Twenty or thirty years ago attention in Western medicine tended to focus upon discoveries of miraculous cures. More recently questions of cost have been dominant. Medical care costs something in all societies; what the costs are, who pays them, and how the payment is distributed vary. Whether they are Western-trained physicians or African witch doctors, curers expect some compensation for their services. Even in societies that are relatively poor in material goods, treatments can be quite expensive. Among the Inuit of North Alaska payment traditionally might involve the offering of a wife or daughter as a sexual partner or a gift of an *umiak* (women's boat), a substantial fee (Spencer 1959: 308).

Curers are not always wealthy, however. Part-time curers in the Mayan village of Zinacantan in southern Mexico receive relatively little for their work—a bottle or two of rum, a few tortillas or a loaf of bread, and a chicken or two. Fabrega and Silver (1973: 54) found that the incomes of Zinacantan curers were roughly the same as other villagers', the primary difference being that their payments were not in the form of liquid assets. That is, they were not things that could be readily exchanged or used for commercial purposes. By and large, curers in Zinacantan are not well off; many of them are among the poorest villagers. Generally only very poor people become full-time practitioners, since most can earn a better living in other ways. Those who do become full-time practitioners are characterized by a hand-to-mouth existence, usually possessing no house of their own or having no land under cultivation. This common situation among those of the healing profession is a far cry from that of the average physician in the United States.

Summary

Illness and disease cannot be understood outside of their cultural context. Epidemiologists working from an anthropological perspective have helped to uncover reasons for the occurrence of mysterious diseases such as kuru, and have found environmental factors explaining the incidence of both endemic and epidemic diseases. The environmental context is also critical to an understanding of "diseases of development."

Malnutrition, while not a disease in itself, may have debilitating or fatal effects. Its occurrence is linked to subsistence patterns: it is more common in large-scale agricultural and industrial societies than in small-scale societies. Foragers and small-scale farmers are usually malnourished only when their traditional subsistence pattern has been disrupted and then not adequately replaced by a new pattern. Even in societies like our own that produce plenty of food, inequalities in food distribution reflect socioeconomic inequalities and leave many people hungry. Hunger is also linked to people's perceptions of food: potentially nutritious resources are often defined as "nonfood," and nutrition is not clearly understood, even by "experts."

In addition to physiological diseases and malnutrition, mental illness is recognized in all cultures. Often it is caused by the stress of trying to deal with a particular environment. Certain patterns of mental illness are universal; others are culture specific, linked to particular physical environments and cultural traditions. Sometimes rapid social change can be so stressful that individuals become seriously disoriented or lose the will to live.

Notions of the origins of illness vary considerably. Western medical specialists have traditionally viewed mind and body as two separate systems involved in separate kinds of illness; other traditions have taken a more holistic approach. Another distinction can be made between personalistic systems, in which illness is thought to be intentionally caused by some malicious being, and naturalistic systems, in which impersonal factors are recognized as the cause of illness.

Attempts to cure illness vary greatly, but all traditions can claim some degree of success. Precisely how and why they work is hard to prove, however. In social terms, the health care delivery system consists of a culturally defined setting for curing, curing specialists and helpers, and the patient. Treatment always costs something, although curers may be poorly paid.

Suggested Readings

General:

Foster, George M., and Anderson, Barbara G. 1978. *Medical anthropology*. New York: Wiley.

Grollig, Francis X., and Haley, Harold B., eds. 1976. *Medical anthropology*. The Hague/Paris: Mouton.

Kiev, Ari. 1972. *Transcultural psychiatry*. New York: Free Press.

Kleinman, Arthur. 1979. *Patients and healers in the context of culture*. Berkeley/Los Angeles: University of California Press.

Logan, Michael H., and Hunt, Edward E., Jr., eds. 1980. *Health and the human condition: Perspective on medical anthropology*. North Scituate, MA: Duxbury.

Loudon, J. B., ed. 1976. *Social anthropology and medicine*. New York: Academic Press.

McElroy, Ann, and Townsend, Patrick K. 1979. *Medical anthropology in ecological perspective*. North Scituate, MA: Duxbury.

Morley, Peter, and Wallis, Roy, eds. 1978. *Culture and curing: Anthropological perspectives on traditional medical beliefs and practices*. Pittsburgh: University of Pittsburgh Press.

Nader, Laura, and Maretzki, Thomas W., eds. 1973. *Culture, illness and health: Essays in human adaptation*. Washington, DC: American Anthropological Association.

Weaver, Thomas, ed. 1968. *Essays on medical anthropology*. Athens, GA: University of Georgia Press.

Case studies:

Beck, Jane C. 1979. *To windward of the land*. Bloomington, IN: University of Indiana Press.

Becker, Howard S., et al. 1961. *Boys in white: Student culture in medical school*. Chicago: University of Chicago Press.

Clark, Margaret. 1959. *Health in the Mexican-American culture: A community study*. Berkeley/Los Angeles: University of California Press.

Crapanzano, Vincent. 1973. *The Hamadsha: A study in Moroccan ethno-psychiatry*. Berkeley/Los Angeles: University of California Press.

Fabrega, Horacio, Jr., and Silver, Daniel B. 1973. *Illness and Shamanistic curing in Zinacantan: An ethnomedical analysis*. Stanford: Stanford University Press.

Jansen, G. 1973. *The doctor-patient relationship in an African tribal society*. Assen, The Netherlands: Van Gorcum. (southern Africa)

Leslie, Charles, ed. 1976. *Asian medical systems*. Berkeley/Los Angeles: University of California Press.

Maclean, Una. 1971. *Magical medicine: A Nigerian case-study*. Harmondsworth: Penguin.

Ohnuki-Tierney, Emiko. 1981. *Illness and healing among the Sakhalin Ainu*. Cambridge: Cambridge University Press.

Spicer, Edward, ed. 1977. *Ethnic medicine in the Southwest*. Tucson, AZ: University of Arizona Press.

Velimirovic, B., ed. 1978. *Modern medicine and medical anthropology in the U.S.-Mexico border populations*. Washington, DC: Pan American Health Organization.

Woods, Clyde M., and Graves, Theodore D. 1973. *The process of medical change in a highland Guatemalan town*. Los Angeles: Latin American Center, University of California.

Young, James C. 1980. *Medical choice in a Mexican village*. New Brunswick, NJ: Rutgers University Press.

Focus on People

A View of Health and Sickness from Aboriginal Australia

Janice Reid

Dr. Janice Reid is a medical anthropologist at the Commonwealth Institute of Health, Sydney University, Australia. In 1974 and 1975, she lived for twelve months with the Yolngu people of Yirrkala; she made subsequent visits in 1978, 1979, and 1981 to study the effect of social change on the indigenous medical system.

THE YOLNGU OF Australia live in the far northeast of the Northern Territory, one of the remotest parts of the continent. Until just before World War II most of the Yolngu had never seen any of the white Australians whose ancestors had settled their land one hundred fifty years before. Arnhem Land, the rectangular peninsula that is home to the Yolngu and other Aboriginal groups, was an afterthought in colonial exploration. When it finally attracted the attention of governments and missions it was declared an Aboriginal reserve. To this day there are no all-weather roads into Arnhem Land from either the north or the south. The annual tropical monsoons regularly isolate its scattered communities, which have come to depend on seagoing barges for food and goods and air services for travel.

Although this impressive region is geographically remote from the urban centers of Australia, it is no longer socially or politically isolated. In the late 1960s one of the largest bauxite mining operations in Australia was established at Nhulunbuy, and with it was built a town to house four thousand white workers and their families. Aboriginal resistance to this development and an increasing concern all over Australia with rights of Aborigines led to the declaration of the Aboriginal Land Rights Act in the Northern Territory in 1976 and the transfer of reserves to Aboriginal hands—a few societies now legally own the land they have occupied for forty thousand years. Family and clan groups who had been living in crowded mission settlements decided to "go home" and reestablish small communities on their own lands.

The "outstation movement," as this development was called, was motivated by the Aborigines' complex set of needs and fears—the specter of further allocation of land for mining and development, the social conflicts, inflamed by alcoholism, in the mission settlements, their desire for autonomy, and their love of the land and the livelihood, religious inspiration, and identity it gives. Another factor that motivated the movement was the severe breakdown in physical and emotional health on settlements. The high incidence of infectious and degenerative diseases, low life expectancy, and high infant mortality rates in contemporary Aboriginal society have caused it to be described as "a developing country within a developed country."

Yolngu clearly perceive the breakdown in health that has followed colonization. Much of it they attribute to a lack of public amenities, poor living conditions, and the processed store food most settlement dwellers eat. Critical illnesses and deaths, however, are often attributed to sorcery.

Sorcerers, they believe, are either people from hostile clans to the west and south of Yolngu territory or other Yolngu seeking revenge for past wrongs and conflicts (murder, adultery, theft, trespassing, jealousy, and gossip, for example). Many Yolngu claim that frictions and fights among them are on the increase because of the conditions of settlement living, alcohol, the waning of Yolngu social controls, and the imposition of Australian laws and values. They fear, accordingly, that serious illness and pre-

mature deaths will continue to increase; changes for the better will come only when the Australian government permits them the resources and freedom to reassert their own authority, laws, and values.

When Yolngu speak about health and illness, two themes emerge: the contrast in the quality of life on the settlement and on outstations; and the risks to health and peace of mind posed by sorcery. The first model of health is what Foster calls "naturalistic," and accords in some aspects with Western ideas of illness causation. The second model Foster calls "personalistic" and is essentially a social model that attributes health (or illness) to the quality of relationships between groups and individuals (Foster 1976). Conflict causes sickness. Harmony brings health. In Yolngu thinking, both sets of ideas coexist and are invoked according to the attendant circumstances and severity of an illness.

One clan leader spoke of the value of out-

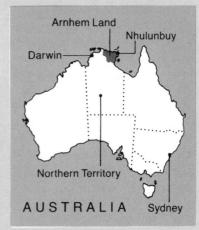

Janice Reid with the Yolngu people of Northern Territory, Australia.

station living in the following terms:

When the old men living at the outstations come to [the settlement] they get sickness every time. When they go back to their homeland and taste many different foods they die at the right time [that is, not prematurely]. The young people always change when they go to the outstations and become strong. But even when people go to the outstations, tobacco, sugar, and tea will follow the people and make them sick in their land. But we get hunted food, bush honey, wild meat and many other foods. When I go there I have oysters, crabs, fish, turtle eggs, and stingray and it makes me happy and strong and opens my life.

Describing the establishment of his clan's outstation, another senior man affirmed the health benefits of their move. His statement illustrates the nature of life on outstations where the resources of both the Western and Aboriginal cultures are used:

We've had no diarrhea or other illnesses since being here—no flu or bad colds. I think the fresh spring water may contribute to this. Our food consists of fish, waterlily, wild honey, wild yams, kangaroo, emu, goanna, blue-tongued lizard, blanket lizard, freshwater turtles, flour, Uncle Toby's Oats, Cornflakes, Weetabix, rice, sugar, tea, syrup, jam, and tobacco.

But when life-threatening illness or death occurs, according to one of the most respected and prominent community leaders, "people talk and worry." This man undertook to teach the author about the various modes of sorcery and its causes (Reid and Munuggurr 1977) because:

These are things we'd like to teach to help Europeans and Aboriginal people. Nobody, no doctors and nurses, have been taught this way before. This is something in our lives we fear— that sorcerers will come and destroy our people. This is for people who are interested in these things. Now that Europeans are living in Arnhem Land, Yolngu are afraid to fight with spears because they'll go to jail. So they now fight secretly [with sorcery]. So many people have died suddenly from this over the years.

The modes of sorcery believed to be used are numerous, but the most feared and often mentioned is *galka:*

Galka hunt for people at night. They are real people. First the galka spears his victim or cuts him open [after hypnotizing him magically] and damages his liver, or pierces his heart so the blood flows out. Then he'll heat his spear in the fire and put it on the wound to seal it so no one can see it. After this there are several things he might say to the victim. For instance, "When you go back to camp you'll only be alive for two days and a crocodile [or snake, or shark] will kill you." Or, "When you go back to camp you'll get in a fight with your wife or relatives, someone will hit you with a spear and you'll die straight away." Or the victim might just go home, forgetting what has happened to him, and drop dead. Even if the person goes to the hospital he'll still die, because the galka has spoiled his lungs, his liver, or his heart.

For the Yolngu most of the short-term, readily treated sicknesses of daily life either are not given much thought or are attributed to natural causes. But, as in many societies in other parts of the world, Yolngu explanations of tragedy and suffering reflect the Yolngu experience of the order of things, which gives prominence to human relations and orders (perhaps masters) the threats to life which are found in all societies.

Chapter Sixteen

Anthropology and Human Problems

Contemporary Adaptation Problems
Development and Underdevelopment
The Plight of Indigenous Peoples

Toward Solving the Problems
Improving Dialogue and Understanding
The Role of Applied Anthropology
Anthropology in the Contemporary World

Summary

Suggested Readings

Focus on People
The International Campaign on Behalf of Brazilian Indians

ALTERING OUR ADAPTIVE patterns to meet new demands is not easy, and humans are not always entirely successful at finding solutions to new problems. Certainly our early attempts to improve transportation through flight were far from successful. It took centuries of unsuccessful attempts before we came up with a flying machine that could actually fly. Even when we do find "successful" solutions to problems, we seldom perceive many of the implications of our actions; our solutions therefore inevitably create new problems. After the Second World War DDT spraying programs seemed the ideal way to deal with the problem of malaria. While such programs have been temporarily successful in controlling malaria, they have also led to some serious problems. There are severe health risks for humans handling the DDT and living in areas where it is sprayed, as well as for many other animals. At the same time, malarial mosquitoes have proven adept at evolving DDT-resistant strains. But if the programs are discontinued there is often a rebound effect that increases the incidence of malaria. And even when spraying programs have temporarily limited the incidence of malaria, the resulting dramatic local population increases have led to myriad other problems.

It may be easy to see a problem—thousands of people may be on the verge of starvation in a drought-stricken area, for instance—but it is more difficult to make people aware of the complex web of social and ecological factors that have created the situation. If we want to know why Haitians are starving it is not enough to look only at their soil, or their marketing techniques, or the amount of capital available to them, or their eating habits. We must look at all of these things and a number of other factors as well, such as political decisions by Haitian elites and foreign capitalists. And most problems are not so easily detectable as near starvation—they tend to remain hidden until conditions force them upon the scene unexpectedly.

Anthropology, and the social sciences in general, attempt to influence people's awareness of the social forces around them and their relationship to their surroundings. Whether he or she ignores or glosses over social problems or seeks to highlight them, merely by describing human existence in a certain setting an author can influence perceptions of problems faced by the members of the society.

Anthropologists frequently are not content simply to describe problems and point out their causes. They often take a more active role in pointing out and seeking solutions to problems, assuming roles as applied anthropologists, stepping outside of the "ivory tower" to work toward positive changes in their own society or in other societies with which they are familiar.

Peasants are dusted with DDT as part of a massive campaign against insect-borne diseases in Central America, 1953.

Contemporary Adaptation Problems

Many of today's problems center on adaptation to the modern world system. Over the past century we have created an ever-more-integrated world system based in part upon technological innovations that have given us a productive capacity far in excess of anything previously imagined. The benefits that humankind has derived from this system are considerable. Our knowledge of the universe has increased dramatically; so has our ability to find solutions to many of the problems that confront us. It is possible to fly to any part of the world in a matter of hours. Satellite communication allows incredibly rapid communication. We can cure a majority of the diseases that afflict us. Such innovations allow us to learn of and begin dealing with natural disasters or major outbreaks of disease immediately, anywhere in the world.

These advances have not been without their price, however. The creation of the world system has left great destruction in its wake. Millions of humans have been killed and millions more left impoverished and on the verge of starvation. The destruction of the environment and of other animal species has been considerable as well. Furthermore, despite the advances that we have witnessed over the past century, the fact remains that the majority of people today are unable to benefit from them. Jet flight, the miracles of modern medicine, and most of the

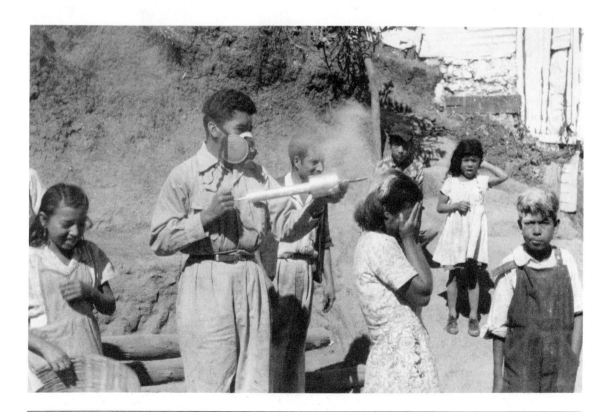

things that our modern technology can produce are available to only a small percentage. The modern world system has in fact resulted in a deterioration of the quality of life for hundreds of millions of people—people whose ways of life have been destroyed, to be replaced by a life that is qualitatively and quantitatively worse.

Development and Underdevelopment

In its most basic sense *development* means improvement in the quality of human lives. In material terms this entails achieving an adequate level of consumption and assuring suitable physical surroundings. Development means more than just meeting material goals, however. It is also important that there be social, political, and economic systems that allow self-esteem and realization of individual potentiality. Virtually all societies in the world today fall short of achieving such goals. Those countries which come closest to achieving them (such as the United States, France, and Australia) are referred to as *developed* countries. Those that are further from achieving these goals, especially the material ones, are called *underdeveloped*.

As noted in chapter 6, the differences between developed and underdeveloped countries are considerable. While many people in countries like the United States are able to meet minimal requirements in nutrition and health, in underdeveloped countries even the barest necessities are out of the reach of most people. In Guatemala, one of the more affluent underdeveloped countries, in 1980 over 80 percent of the population consumed less than the minimum daily number of calories; 82 percent of the children under 5 years of age had nutritional problems.

One of the fundamental problems in most underdeveloped countries is the extremely unequal distribution of wealth. In Guatemala in 1978 the richest 5 percent of the people received 59 percent of the country's earnings,

Peasant children in Guatemala, 1976. In 1980, 82 percent of Guatemalan children under five years of age had nutritional problems.

while 50 percent received only 7 percent. One of the reasons for this striking inequality is the distribution of land. A mere 1.4 percent of the farms occupy 52 percent of the arable land, while 90 percent of the farms occupy only 20 percent of the arable land. The land occupied by these smaller farms also tends to be the worst and least accessible. This unequal distribution of wealth is related to many of the other political and social problems faced by underdeveloped countries because of the exploitative, oppressive means by which the elite gains its wealth and maintains its position. Wages of one dollar a day and less are common in Guatemala, and the military and police have a long history

Only foreign tourists and the wealthy elite could afford the comfort of this country hotel on the shores of Lake Atitlán in Guatemala.

of repression against all opposition to the ruling elite. While wealth is unequally distributed in all countries—in the United States, for example, 30 percent of the population receives 70 percent of the income—the differences tend to be more extreme in underdeveloped countries.

In many underdeveloped countries, an already bad situation is getting worse. The richest 5 percent of the population in Guatemala has increased the percentage of the country's earnings it receives by 10 percent since 1950, while the share of the poorest 50 percent has dropped by 2 percent. In 1965, 42 percent of the population consumed less than the necessary calories; today that figure is 80 percent. The literacy rate has decreased and health care has become poorer. The inflation rate in Guatemala is currently over 15 percent and rapidly increasing, posing increasingly serious problems for the 80 percent of the population that earns three hundred dollars a year or less. Many other underdeveloped countries have inflation rates of 50 to 100 percent.

The Evolution of Underdevelopment. Underdevelopment is a relatively new phenomenon that differs considerably from the lack of material wealth traditionally found in many small-scale societies. People living in a traditional Aboriginal society had far less than many people living in modern societies. Many of their descendants living in industrial societies are also poor, but the nature and causes of the poverty of these traditional and contemporary groups

Guatemalan refugees, having fled government-sponsored terrorism, pose at a camp in Mexico, 1982.

are very different. Small-scale foraging societies were materially poor because they had not developed technological complexity. They were *undeveloped*. By contrast, most of the poor people in the world today are poor largely because they have been denied access to resources and material wealth available in the modern world system. They are poor as a result of the progressive *underdevelopment* that has accompanied the spread of the present world system.

Members of traditional small-scale societies were able to work out adaptive strategies that ensured that there were no great differences in wealth and provided individuals with a sense of self-esteem within their cultural context. Their modern counterparts find themselves exploited

by or excluded from the economic system of the society within which they live. While many poor people have sought to make the best of a bad situation, developing goals and means of attaining a sense of worth within the confines of their impoverished condition, none can escape entirely from the adverse effects of their poverty. Poverty has left its mark in the world today, encouraging brutality or hopelessness in extreme cases, and in one way or another damaging the spirit and will of all who are poor.

Underdevelopment is a reflection of how people are integrated into the modern world system. The underdeveloped parts of the world are those which occupy disadvantageous positions within the international division of labor. They are the areas whose resources are drained to support the wealthier portions of the world and whose people are most poorly rewarded for their labor in extracting the resources and producing the goods consumed by the world economic order.

Underdevelopment is an historical process related to a society's place within the international division of labor. Guatemala again provides a good example. When the Spaniards conquered Guatemala in the sixteenth century they transformed it from a relatively self-sufficient region into one that produced primarily for an international market. Production was also reoriented to support the Spanish conquerers who formed the local elite. To support both Spaniards and the demands of international markets, the indigenous population was deprived of its land and forced to work on farms and in mines under very adverse conditions. By providing the Indians with minimal rewards for their work, the Spaniards were able to export goods at a favorable rate on the world market and at the same time extract a considerable profit. Production not intended for export was siphoned off by the local elite, leaving the Indians barely able to meet subsistence needs.

Little changed for the majority of Guatemalans with independence in the early nineteenth century. By the mid-century, however, their condition took a definite turn for the worse as the Guatemalan elite sought to increase the production of export crops, particularly coffee, to increase its own wealth. Coffee provided wealth for a few, but pushed the majority even further into poverty. More land was seized from the Indians and given to wealthy coffee growers, and laws were passed to force the Indians to work on the coffee plantations for incredibly little pay. Guatemala's land and its people's labor produced wealth not only for the local elite, but for foreigners as well, as companies like United Fruit and W. R. Grace purchased large pieces of land to grow such export crops as bananas. These companies extracted large profits

from Guatemala, spending relatively little within the country and paying almost nothing in taxes.

Guatemala today remains a source of inexpensive labor and goods, which is now diversified to include textiles, beef, cotton, and other agricultural products. It is also a source of nonrenewable natural resources such as oil and nickel, the profits from which are divided between foreign corporations and the local elite. This situation has evolved at the expense of the majority of the people, as food crops have been taken out of production to make way for export crops and cow pastures and as people have been pressured to work on plantations and in factories at low wages and under unsafe conditions. Guatemala also serves as a market, albeit a small one, for foreign companies. Luxury goods produced in the United States and Western Europe are sold to the Guatemalan elite. Pharmaceutical, chemical, and other companies are able to sell a range of goods, often under more favorable conditions than at home. In addition, countries like Guatemala serve as a dumping ground for drugs, pesticides, and other items that cannot be sold in more developed countries because of restrictive laws.

Dependency. Underdevelopment is commonly linked with dependency on outside powers. For instance, the majority of people in Guatemala have little control over the direction its economy takes. In many countries this lack of control is in part a reflection of the concentration of power in the hands of a small elite. Even in relatively democratic underdeveloped countries, however, people have little control over their economy. They find that they are highly dependent upon external markets as places to sell what they produce and as sources of the things they need to survive. This dependency contributes to their underdeveloped status, since they generally receive much less for what they sell than they pay for what they buy. Their lack of power creates inability to ensure that they receive more favorable prices for their resources and products.

The effects of dependency upon external markets over which a society or group has little power is apparent in many peasant communities. Here, because of coercion or a lack of alternatives, people are forced to sell their products or their labor for relatively little. In return they must purchase many of the things they need from industrial centers at relatively high prices. The situation becomes worse as these communities are able to produce fewer and fewer items locally. Once they begin to sell themselves and their goods, less time can be devoted to making the range of goods formerly produced for local consumption, as pressure mounts to sell more and work harder just to keep up.

In such dependent underdeveloped areas, increased productivity frequently does not benefit the majority of people; often it only means greater profits for the wealthy. The so-called Brazilian economic "miracle" of the 1970s served primarily to benefit wealthy Brazilians and foreign corporations. The expansion of the Brazilian economy failed to benefit the Indians, peasants, and small farmers, who lost their land to large commercial enterprises, or industrial workers, whose wages failed to keep pace with inflation and who work in factories with one of the highest rates of industrial accidents in the world. The "Brazilian miracle" meant great wealth for some, greater exploitation of others, and pushed millions into an impoverished existence on the margins of the economy. Such growth has also increased Brazil's dependent status as more money has been borrowed from abroad to fuel economic growth (currently 107 percent of Brazil's export earnings go to pay for oil imports and interest on foreign debts), as more of its productive activity has gone into producing for export and meeting the needs of the Brazilian elite, and as those who are relatively well off have developed an ever greater interest in maintaining the existing system of dependent productivity.

In the past, when countries or communities tried to break away from their dependent status those who profited from it usually resorted to force to stop them. Today it is more common for outside powers to ensure maintenance of the status quo by relying upon economic pressures and the local elite who themselves have profited from the dependent relationships. Instead of "sending the marines," foreign powers are more likely simply to provide military assistance to the local elite or to offer economic incentives to those who will resist when threats to the system of exchange arise.

One solution to this dependency is a complete break with the external economic order, but this is not the only way to improve a country's or community's economic status. As in the case of the OPEC cartel, a few primary producers can act together to take advantage of the industrial world's dependency on natural resources in order to acquire a greater share of the profits, although this can have disastrous results for other underdeveloped countries. Likewise, peasant groups can organize cooperatively to try to get a better deal. It is difficult for such moves to succeed, however, largely because of the international character of the existing economic order. If peasants increase the prices of their goods and services those buying them are likely to go somewhere else, where labor, often for political reasons, is cheaper. In addition, there are few resources that lend themselves as easily as oil to control by producer cartels. Most resources are either available in too large a quantity, are not sufficiently strategic, or are produced by too diverse a group of political entities.

Multinational Corporations. The relative development or underdevelopment of countries is closely related to the activities of *multinational corporations*—corporations with headquarters in one country and divisions in a number of others. They are one of the prime ingredients of Western industrial societies' adaptive strategies in the latter half of the twentieth century. The adaptive advantage of the multinational corporation lies in the efficient manner in which it can reallocate resources to maximize profit on a global scale. If taxes and the cost of labor increase for companies engaged in bauxite mining in Jamaica, capital is simply shifted elsewhere, either permanently or until costs in Jamaica are forced down. For the major industrial societies multinational corporations can be seen as helping to provide a degree of stability, minimizing external threats to their control and production of wealth.

Although multinational corporations have succeeded in providing a great deal of wealth for a number of people, these successes have their price. While the extent to which multinational corporations are responsible for many of the problems of underdevelopment is subject to debate, there are many instances where their activities have clearly contributed to political, economic, and social problems.

One of the arguments advanced in favor of multinationals is that they bring the benefits of modernization to many parts of the world. Yet often such modernization has worsened the problems of underdevelopment. Employment is a key area where the benefits of multinationals have come into question. Multinationals have invested over $100 billion in the Third World, but have created fewer than four million jobs. In fact, in many areas they have eliminated more jobs than they have created, through the introduction of new technologies and production priorities. In many cases they have also increased disparities in wealth, increasing the wealth of locally influential individuals but depressing wages for most of those they employ and putting more people out of work entirely.

Indonesia exemplifies some of the problems created by multinationals and their local allies. In the late 1960s the military government in

The twin towers of Pennzoil Place, Houston, Texas. Multinational corporations, like Pennzoil, have come to control much of the world's wealth and today exercise tremendous political, economic, and cultural influence over the world's peoples.

Indonesia decided to promote economic development by opening its door to investment by foreign companies. The result was an influx of billions of dollars in foreign investment and aid from industrial nations. Japanese and American firms were the heaviest investors, with oil companies being the most active. So as not to rely solely on revenues from oil, the main source of foreign exchange, Indonesia has also sought to develop other sources of export earning by attracting foreign companies with the country's huge labor force. Laborers in Indonesia presently work for some of the world's lowest wages.

As *Wall Street Journal* reporter Barry Newman has pointed out:

> All of this has brought benefits. A few Indonesians have gotten very rich. Multinationals got a 56 percent return on investment in 1977. The World Bank foresees manufactured exports from Indonesia leaping by as much as 20 percent in each of the next five years. But the poorest Indonesians aren't any better off than they were a decade ago. Some are worse off. [1979: 1]

Despite economic growth in Indonesia, the number of jobs available has decreased. Foreign investment in the textile industry and the introduction of Japanese spinning and weaving equipment has done away with handloom production that once kept two hundred thousand women employed. Mechanization in agriculture has cost tens of thousands of people jobs. Investment in capital-intensive forms of production has resulted in the destruction of far more jobs than it has created.

One of the other problems for underdeveloped countries is the multinationals' political power. While the smaller corporations have relatively little direct political influence, many of the larger ones have consistently sought to influence the internal politics of countries where they have investments. Such political involvement has rarely been of much obvious benefit to most of the people in the countries concerned. During the early part of this century United Fruit Company was able to gain control of huge parcels of land in Guatemala and to extract large profits, primarily from the sale of bananas. When Guatemalan president Jacobo Arbenz proposed nationalizing the company in

Banana workers, United Fruit Company. Low-paid workers in underdeveloped countries help to create wealth for corporations based in the developed world.

1954—proposing to pay either what United Fruit claimed the company was worth for tax purposes or the actual value minus what it would then owe in back taxes—the company responded by helping to organize a coup that overthrew Arbenz and returned Guatemala to military rule. That multinationals are able to wield such power in countries like Guatemala should not be surprising—dozens of the largest companies have much greater annual gross sales than the entire gross national products of most underdeveloped countries.

In recent years questions have arisen concerning the benefit of multinationals to wealthier industrial nations themselves. In many parts of the United States, for example, companies have pulled out and moved overseas where they can produce goods for less, leaving thousands of people unemployed and destroying the economies of many small communities. Multinationals are also seen to have played a major role in drawing governments into costly wars that have served corporate, but not necessarily national, interests. In short, it is not just the people of underdeveloped countries who have found themselves adversely affected by multinationals and apparently powerless to do anything about it. The boon to some has proven to be a Frankenstein's monster to many.

The Plight of Indigenous Peoples

Those who have probably suffered most from the spread of Western industrial society and the resultant underdevelopment are the indigenous peoples of the newly colonized or incorporated lands: Native Americans, Australian Aborigines, Amazonian Indians, and others. As these peoples have been conquered and forced into the world system they have lost their land, their autonomy, and often their lives. Many have fought back, and sometimes they have been briefly successful in postponing their fate: rounded up on reservations to become wards of the state, left to roam, broken and improverished, on the margins of society in a land that had once been theirs, or death.

The progressive destruction of such peoples is exemplified by the history of the Kaingang, an indigenous Indian group in Brazil. At the turn of the century, the Kaingang lived a semi-nomadic existence inland from the growing city of São Paulo. As railroad construction began through Kaingang territory and as settlers began moving onto their land, clearing the forests and planting coffee trees, the Kaingang found themselves forced into a war for survival. They had tried to accommodate the settlers and to make peace with them, but to no avail. Their subsequent attacks on railway workers and settlers spread terror among local Brazilians; in São Paulo preparations were made to destroy these Indians, who were seen as impeding the march of civilization. Their destruction was avoided by the Indian Protection Service (SPI), which pacified them between 1912 and 1915. Newly introduced diseases made the pacification campaign easier: between 1912 and 1916 the Kaingang population decreased from seven hundred to two hundred, primarily because of deaths related to influenza and measles (Ribeiro 1970).

The pacified Kaingang were placed on a small reserve and the man who owned the land that they had previously occupied became wealthy. In 1949 the state governor took away half of their reserve, giving the land to three business enterprises, and profiting greatly himself in the process. The remaining land has since been used by private companies and the government Indian agency for logging. Most of the profits have gone to the companies and employees of the Indian agency; only a small fraction has been returned to the Indian communities.

In response to the destruction of the forests and land grabbing by settlers, the Kaingang and other local Indians organized a resistance movement. In 1977 they expelled twenty-two hundred non-Indian families from their lands. The government response was to establish schools with the assistance of foreign missionaries to train Indian leaders who would be more receptive to government control. A young Kaingang chief who had been a leader in the resistance movement was killed in 1980 after receiving several death threats. Other leaders have also been the objects of attack. With Indian resistance weakening once again the government is proceeding with the construction of hydroelectric dams that will flood much of the remaining reserve (Anthropology Resource Center 1981a).

The fate of the Kaingang is a common one for indigenous peoples around the world. Having survived outright attacks and introduced diseases, they have seen what little they have left gradually taken away by others seeking to profit at their expense. Their attempts at resistance are met with subtle overpowering maneuvers, and if these are not fully successful, with a return to violence.

Genocide. Many indigenous peoples have been the object of campaigns of *genocide*, the deliberate and systematic destruction of a political or cultural group. From the seventeenth to the early nineteenth centuries, the settlers of Newfoundland hunted and killed the local indigenous people, the Beothucks, at "first because they were considered a nuisance, and later for the sport of pursuing such elusive game" (Horwood 1969: 72). The Beothucks' peaceful overtures were constantly met with violence, and settlers would frequently organize hunting parties to hunt them, much as they hunted other game. Genocide did not end with the early colonial era. Australian Aborigines continued to be the object of attacks into the 1920s, with organized groups of whites attacking the Aborigines' camps and ranchers going so far as to leave out poisoned flour for them to eat. Raids on peaceful groups of Indians by organized groups of non-Indians continue to occur in parts of South America today.

Indigenous minorities are commonly denied access to or are treated unfairly by legal institutions. When out of desperation they try to fight back, peaceful means having been denied them, their belligerence is used as an excuse to slaughter them. When the Embera Indians of Colombia sought to retain control of a gold mine one of their people had discovered in the late 1970s, they were subjected to constant attacks by local landowners and prospectors. As a result of pressures from the landowners and rumors that the Indians were subversives, in early 1981 the government sent in armed police. In the ensuing armed battle, several Indians were killed and others captured (IWGIA 1981: 43–44). Similarly, gunmen hired by large landowners in Colombia have killed dozens of Indian leaders without a single case of murder ever being brought to trial.

Ethnocide. Even when ethnic minorities are not wiped out, their cultural traditions may be. Maintenance of a distinct cultural identity by indigenous peoples is difficult in the face of expanding industrial society. As their resources are seized and as they are overwhelmed by the new technology, such peoples find the very bases of their societies undermined.

For at least nine hundred years the Lacandon lived as subsistence farmers in the jungles of southern Mexico. Until recently they were able to remain relatively isolated from the outside world. Today, however, they must share their forest homeland with more than one hundred thousand peasants who have moved there from other densely populated areas, with loggers who have already cleared half of the land, with Christian missionaries, tourists, and a host of government officials. As they have been incorporated into the Mexican national economy their culture has changed, until today a strong possibility exists that within a decade or two there will no longer be a distinct group known as the Lacandon. Some of the new gods represent attempts to bridge the gap between the old religious traditions and the new ones introduced by foreigners, but the gods prayed to by some of the younger Lacandon represent a more fundamental break with the past. Hunting, which played a vital role in Lacandon culture, is rapidly becoming impossible as the game disappears. The remains of ancient Maya buildings, once isolated sacred sites, have been transformed into tourist attractions. Many Lacandon speak Spanish, and many have become desirous of consumer goods, such as watches and jeans.

It can be argued that such changes are benefiting the Lacandon by bringing them into the twentieth century, but evidence from elsewhere indicates that this is a dubious supposition. What is likely to await them is the fate of millions of indigenous peoples around the world—the life of struggling fringe dwellers, their old culture destroyed and unable to fulfill the material cravings central to the new culture. Those who benefit most from such cultural changes are the handful of entrepreneurs who stand to profit by gaining access to these people's land, their minds, and what money they possess—those who want to cut their trees to raise cattle, to sell them Coca-Cola, to give them Bibles. It is probable that the Lacandon will soon be reduced to the poverty of the thousands of peasants presently being driven onto their lands—from undeveloped they will join the ranks of the underdeveloped.

The destruction of a people's culture carried out on a systematic basis is referred to as *ethnocide*. Ethnocide is the intended result of policies aimed at incorporating minorities into the dominant culture through coercion or incentive. It tends to be based upon a belief that the indigenous culture is inferior, and that to replace it by the culture of those who consider themselves superior is desirable, or inevitable. Ethnocide is ethnocentrism put into extreme practice. A common means of promoting ethnocide is to force parents to send their children to distant schools, where they will learn to accept the values of the new culture. Another tactic is to provide the first converts to the new ways with material rewards in the hope that this will encourage others to follow. Traditional practices—dances, clothing, speech—can also simply be banned. Such actions are almost always defended in terms of the benefits they bring to the indigenous peoples—"bringing them from the stone age into the space age." More significant, however, are the benefits accruing to the civilized. It was probably not in the Native Americans' best interest to accept the white man's civilization—what little they have gained is small compensation for their cultural and economic losses.

While some indigenous peoples readily accept their cultural loss, hoping for greater rewards in the new order, and others accept the change with fatalism, others choose to resist. To the chagrin of those most convinced of the superiority of Western industrial culture, not everyone has welcomed it wholeheartedly. Many have given their lives rather than accept the blessings of civilization. One of the major struggles confronting the world today concerns the right of native peoples to retain their own identities and to continue their cultural practices, and to utilize resources in ways that they view as most appropriate. In countries like Canada, the United States, Brazil, and Australia, the struggle focuses upon *land rights:* the right of native peoples to control what happens on the lands where they live and to be compensated for lands that they have lost.

While struggles for land rights and other aspects of cultural autonomy take place mainly in the courts in countries like Australia and the United States, armed resistance has been the response in many parts of the world where legal actions have not been possible. The Karens, Kachin, and other indigenous peoples in Burma have been fighting the Burmese government since independence in 1948 to keep from being forced into the status of a powerless minority within the state, subject to political and economic exploitation by those in power. Likewise, although the Indonesian military has succeeded in killing almost 10 percent of the population of East Timor since invading the former Portuguese colony in 1976, the Timorese have continued to fight to retain their independence. Similar examples of resistance to oppression can be found throughout the world. Why do these people resist? One reason is their desire to have the right to their own culture. There is also an economic motive. For many of these people, giving in does not simply mean being unable to dance in a certain way or dress after a certain fashion; it means being pushed to the bottom of the heap in the world system, following the path of the Kaingang into ever deeper poverty.

Land rights have become a major issue in Australian Aboriginal affairs. In a precedent-setting move, the Pitjantjatjara Aborigines of South Australia were given title to their traditional land in 1981. Here the Premier of South Australia hands the title deed to 39,615 square miles to a member of the National Aboriginal Council.

Wounded Knee, South Dakota, 1973: Sioux protest the application of treaties passed between their ancestors and the federal government in a tense confrontation that involved gunfire, hostages, the FBI, troops, and Senator George McGovern.

Toward Solving the Problems

Given the immensity of the problems facing people around the world today, finding solutions to even small problems might seem impossible. It is little wonder that many people seek to ignore problems, give up in despair, or retreat into cynicism. Yet thousands of organizations, agencies, and individuals are working to try to find solutions. That so many problems continue to exist attests not so much to the failures of those seeking solutions as to the scale and complexity of the difficulties we face in searching for an adaptational strategy that provides a more equitable standard of living on a worldwide basis.

Improving Dialogue and Understanding

Successful solutions will require, among other things, improvement in dialogue and understanding between helpful experts and those they seek to help. Many international and national agencies, politicians and planners are trying to devise policies to improve people's lives. Such attempts can be referred to as *development from above*, for they are actions devised by those who are relatively well off to improve the lot of those who are not, or devised by those who do not suffer from a particular problem to eliminate it for those who do. Development from above can be contrasted with *development from below*, attempts by the sufferers to find a solution themselves. Poor people are viewed by many as apathetic and ignorant, unwilling and unable to solve their own problems. This view is disputed by many studies that point to constant attempts by the poor to find their own solutions to their problems, and even more dramatically, to the long history of rebellions by the poor against unfair conditions.

Each of these approaches to development by

itself has severe limitations. Without an understanding of the poor and communication with them, the experts are unlikely to arrive at workable plans or be able to implement them. Also, the goals and plans of such experts are influenced by their own biases, those of the agencies worked for, and often by the desires of those in power. Such biases may or may not be to the advantage of the poor. Also, being from "the government," the expert is likely to find the poor suspicious of his or her motives and less than anxious to accept the schemes of such an outsider. On the other hand, while the poor or others with problems may know a lot about their problems, their knowledge of the causes are likely to be limited. They are also unlikely to be aware of all the ramifications of the solutions that they propose. They need expert advice.

It is difficult to get those on the bottom together with the experts in a productive way, with each willing to listen to the other, to offer suggestions and to be open to criticism. Experience has taught indigenous peoples and peasants that the experts are rarely willing to listen to what they have to say. The planners for their part all too often have an inflated view of their own understanding of how the world works and how to improve things. It is difficult to get the two parties to recognize that they may have very different goals; understanding and discussing this disparity is an essential preliminary step before any solution can evolve. When a group of housing experts in Australia found that a particular Aboriginal community was not the least bit interested in the special "Aboriginal" houses the experts had designed for them, they were upset. The experts had designed houses that they had decided would best reflect the unique flavor of Aboriginal life without asking these people if they wanted such houses and without a thorough knowledge of conditions in the particular community. For their part, the Aborigines were anxious to have houses that looked just like those of whites, so that they would not stand out. While the "Aboriginal" houses were appropriate in some isolated communities, they were not appropriate in this instance where people living in close proximity to whites were anxious to minimize antagonisms. Of course, experts often do have ideas that will benefit people, even though the people themselves may not recognize the benefits at that time. In such cases success depends upon the planner's being able to convince the people that he or she is right. Using force or simply expecting people to accept something on its own merits without explanation rarely succeeds.

Related to the problem of creating a meaningful dialogue is achieving an understanding of the complexity of a situation. People like to believe that there are simple solutions. Poverty is caused by _____. To solve it all we need to do is _____. While such ideas may be fine for political campaigning or dinner table small talk, they do not reflect a sound understanding of the causes of problems or their solutions. The world is complicated, and understanding human problems requires a thorough and intimate knowledge of both the big picture and the grass roots and an understanding of how they are related. Such an understanding is difficult to achieve and it is only even remotely possible with open and critical discussion between those planning and those being planned for.

Because of their emphasis upon context, integration, and dynamism and their methodology of participant observation, antropologists are in an excellent position to promote an understanding of the complexity of human problems. The anthropologist's background, training, and research methodology also make him or her useful in promoting dialogue among those who need to communicate and in getting people to understand the view and situations of others. The anthropologist has a foot in both camps, though usually with a bias toward those with problems rather than toward those on top, allowing him to function as a middleman or broker in the search for solutions.

The Role of Applied Anthropology

Although the role of many anthropologists in seeking solutions to human problems is indirect, through teaching and writing, others have determined to take a more active role in producing changes. Those who engage in such activities are called applied anthropologists. The term *applied anthropology* refers to goal-oriented research and instrumental activities which, through the provision of information, the formulation of policy recommendations, or the initiation of direct action, are intended to produce a desired sociocultural condition. Often the condition thought to be desirable represents a shift from underdevelopment to a degree of development that prevents a people from being exterminated by conditions generated within the modern world system.

Applied anthropology originated as "a kind of social work and community development effort for non-white peoples" (James 1973: 41) under the sponsorship of European and American colonial authorities. Anthropologists in British universities helped to train colonial officers, while other anthropologists carried out research on behalf of the colonial establishment. In Africa, for instance, anthropologists conducted research on topics of interest to policy makers, such as indigenous legal systems, land tenure, religious movements, diet and nutrition, and migration. Anthropologists were also commissioned by the colonial authorities to carry out ethnographic research, especially in crisis-ridden areas, and to facilitate the smooth functioning of colonial rule. In the United States in the 1930s anthropologists were hired by the Bureau of Indian Affairs and the Soil Conservation Service to work on problems concerning reserve-dwelling Native Americans. During the Second World War anthropologists were employed to study and make recommendations about problems associated with the forced removal of Japanese from the West Coast; after the war, a large number of anthropologists worked with the American administration in its new, sometimes unruly Micronesian colonies.

The destruction of the colonial order following the Second World War left anthropology, particularly applied anthropology, especially vulnerable. In many parts of the world, nationalist elites who had replaced colonial administrators identified anthropologists with the colonial regimes, viewing anthropologists as agents of colonial repression. Though this attitude was in some instances quite justifiable, it was a distorted oversimplification. There were anthropologists who were active proponents of colonialism, but they were few in number. Rather, most avoided the bigger issues and sought in limited ways to try to improve conditions for those living under colonial rule. For example, American anthropologists did succeed in making things a little better for Native Americans through educational and health-related projects.

Nevertheless, the immediate postcolonial period left applied anthropology in ill repute in many circles. Anthropologists tended to shy away from such involvement and retreat into the "ivory tower" of university teaching. Some continued to work for international development agencies, for government departments, and for industry, but such work remained far from the mainstream of anthropological research and writing. Applied anthropology survived the demise of traditional colonialism best in the United States, partly because the United States continued to have a large indigenous population and partly because of its neocolonial expansion into the rest of the world. The kind of work done by applied anthropologists during this period and their orientation toward ignoring larger issues in favor of solving smaller problems differed little from those of the colonial era.

For applied anthropology as it now stands in the United States the late 1960s and early 1970s was a critical period. In the wake of racial violence and conflict over the Vietnam War, and as a result of a narrowing academic job market, there was a tremendous increase of interest in applying anthropology to solving practical problems. There was also a significant questioning of many assumptions left from the colonial past that had continued to dominate the field of applied anthropology. Of particular concern were ethical problems associated with employment by business and government—the risk of serving the rich and powerful instead of those supposedly being helped. Debate was especially intense over the role of anthropologists in Southeast Asia in the Vietnam War and in counterinsurgency activities in neighboring countries.

While debate continues concerning the ethics of some applied work, the number of full-time applied anthropologists and academics doing part-time applied work has expanded markedly in recent years. Activities ranging from the preservation of material culture to helping to implement bilingual education programs, from studying the social impact of highways and oil pipelines to helping indigenous peoples with the land claims, have moved into the mainstream of anthropology. Such activities fall largely within two categories: planning and working as an advocate.

Development Planning. Promoting development in an area involves anthropologists in formulating and implementing plans. But in development planning anthropologists rarely work on their own. Rather, they serve as part of multidisciplinary teams including other experts such as agronomists, engineers, physicians, economists, and geographers. The anthropologist brings to such a team detailed knowledge of the people in an area and the holistic, integrated anthropological perspective that is essential to successful planning. In reviewing her role in an AID program in Nepal Laurie Mailloux (1980–81: 18) notes that she is involved in

analyzing the social feasibility of current and proposed projects, preparing social soundness analyses for project papers, and advising project designers on how they might best overcome social constraints that might arise during any part of the project cycle. . . . I am also assigned to assist project officers with social monitoring during project implementation . . . a field activity which requires an investigation into the socioeconomic ramifications that a project is having on the villagers.

The specific kinds of projects she has been involved in include "an agriculture resource inventory project, a resource conservation project, a rural health and family planning project, a landslide stabilization project, and a rural area development project" (1980–81: 61).

One of the most valuable roles played by anthropologists in development projects is in bringing about discussion between planners and those being planned for, so that the latter are allowed input into the planning. This is a difficult and complex task, because the people typically distrust planners, while the planners often lack knowledge of the local culture and the peoples' specific needs and goals. Peter Weil (1980: 315) notes that to bridge the gap between the people and the planners, the anthropologist must (1) identify and explain the local decision-making processes and (2) help both the people and the planners adapt local structures to better meet development needs expressed by the people. The first component allows the plan-

ners to know who to talk with and how to go about doing it; the second helps to ensure that plans do not do unnecessary damage to local customs and that they reflect local needs as much as possible.

In making and implementing development plans, anthropologists do not just work with national and international agencies. They may also work with community-based or private local-level groups. Some indigenous peoples in Canada, Australia, and the United States employ anthropologists as community advisors to assist the people with local problems and help them in their dealings with government agencies. And in some Third World countries impoverished by the stranglehold that multinational corporations have on production and marketing, people have begun to ask anthropologists to help them search for ways around this problem. Pueblo to People, for example, a nonprofit organization based in Honduras, seeks alternative ways of marketing the products of peasant groups. Such items as hats from the Quiche Indians of Guatemala and cashews from peasants in Honduras are marketed through flea markets and cooperatives in the United States. The peasants receive more for their goods and take a more active role in their distribution than when they sell to large corporations. Anthropologists have been involved with such cooperatives all over the world, using their knowledge of both local conditions and the outside world to help meet the developmental goals of the primary producers and to educate those who purchase the goods about the people who make them and their problems.

In addition to work on specific projects, anthropologists also contribute to the development process through studies aimed to increase understanding of planned change in general (see Bastide 1973). This means studying the culture of development, examining the planning process in the same way as anthropologists approach any other sociocultural phenomenon. An important component of such studies is looking at the culture and social organization of the planners themselves. Instead of being viewed as neutral agents of scientific principles, planners are seen as social beings with their own goals whose actions are influenced by the environment within which they live. An example of an early study of this sort is John Wilson's analysis of the social organization of the Department of Native Welfare in Perth, Western Australia (1958) and how things like internal power struggles and career considerations influenced policy making in Aboriginal affairs. All too often the goals that planners perceive to be those of the people for whom they are planning are in fact merely reflections of their own goals, based upon their own particular environments; these may not be shared by others in different environments.

Studies of the development process may also include analysis of social networks. This is particularly important for understanding how decisions are actually reached. There are always competing ideas within development planning, and resources are always scarce enough to require the establishment of priorities. The question then is how is a particular plan decided upon. In trying to understand a school-building program in southern Mexico, for example, it is important to know why education is a developmental priority and why schools are placed where they are and structured in particular ways. One factor in the priority given to education may be recruitment procedures within the agency responsible that favor those who believe in the efficacy of education in solving developmental problems. Placement of schools is often a matter of politics, or perhaps of the prior experiences of those making decisions. Without such an understanding of the ethnography of planning itself, it is not possible to make reasonable plans that have a chance of success and that reflect people's goals and needs.

Advocacy. Anyone engaged in planning or implementing change is in a sense advocating particular goals and a particular way of life. In most applied work this advocacy role is not made explicit. The applied anthropologist is viewed more or less as a technician utilizing his or her particular skill in pursuit of some neutral goal. But applied anthropologists do not always claim to be neutral, or even try. Many feel compelled by the poverty and exploitation of people with whom they work to serve as lobbyists on their behalf, as suggested in Thomas Melville's plea for the embattled Indians of Guatemala:

Anthropologists have sat at the tables of Guatemalan Indians, eaten their meager food, laughed, smoked, and drunk with them, and made livings writing about their culture. It will be a shame if we leave the stage in silence. [1981: 1]

This advocacy approach does not represent a paternalistic attitude that these people are incapable of speaking on their own behalf. Rather, it is recognition that the anthropologist is often in a better position to be heard, and that because of his or her training and education the anthropologist is likely to express problems in a manner more understandable by members of another culture.

An example of anthropologists' efforts at advocacy appeared at a 1981 conference on hunters and gatherers. Richard Lee, who has worked among the !Kung Bushmen for years, circulated a petition condemning military recruitment of 40 percent of the !Kung by the South African army in its campaign against Namibian independence and confinement of their families in densely packed military settlements. Lee's action was designed to bring world attention to the problem of the !Kung and pressure the South African government to alter its policies. Upset about the South Africans' ethics and methods of bringing the !Kung into the modern world system, sixty-three of the seventy-five delegates signed the petition. Lee's views are disputed by the South Africans and some anthropologists, however. He maintains that packing the !Kung, traditional nomadic foragers, into crowded camps has resulted in widespread alcoholism and a high homicide rate. The South Africans counter that health measures in the camp have resulted in a decline in the !Kung infant mortality rate. Lee argues that enforced dependency in the camps has led to a destruction of the people's identity, pride, and way of life. The South Africans point out that the !Kung now earn what for them is a great deal of money, $120 a month; Lee counters that much of their newfound wealth is spent on things like hair straighteners and skin lighteners. To such complaints another anthropologist has responded that Lee is being paternalistic, that he has a myopic and romantic view of things, and that what is happening is simply the !Kung's inevitable assimilation into the modern world. Few anthropologists agree with such criticisms. In support of Lee's argument, Michael Asch has pointed out that the destruction of foraging is not a necessary part of entry into the modern world system. Asch's own experience with foraging groups in Canada has convinced him that foragers can find a place in the modern world. In short, Lee and Asch are not arguing that the !Kung should be preserved in a pristine state like animals in a cultural zoo, but that they should be allowed to enter the modern world system on a better footing (Poulton 1981).

In addition to criticizing the treatment of indigenous peoples, anthropologists also actively push for the implementation of particular plans. For example, anthropologists have been at the forefront of an international movement to pressure the Brazilian government to create a reserve for the Yanomamo Indians in northern Brazil. The eighty-four hundred Yanomamo have been threatened with extinction as mines have been opened in their homeland and as roads have opened the land to outsiders. Anthropologists have helped to determine the size of reserve the Yanomamo would need to maintain an adequate standard of living without destroying the environment. They have also attempted to educate people about the problems faced by the Yanomamo, and have joined with international voluntary agencies, church groups, numerous organizations in Brazil, and organizations of indigenous peoples in pressuring the Brazilian government and corporations active in the Amazon to set aside the necessary land.

In those areas where their expertise has provided important insights, anthropologists have also become involved in major political issues concerning domestic and foreign policy in their own countries. Anthropologists who have worked among drug addicts and users, alcoholics, retired people, and the terminally ill have sought both to educate people about the cultures of these particular groups and to promote policies designed to deal more accurately with the cultural requirements of such groups of people, who often are poorly understood by others. In terms of foreign policy, perhaps the most controversial actions by anthropologists have been associated with recent wars. In the United States, anthropologists were among those who helped to organize teach-ins during the Vietnam War. More recently there have been anthropologists involved in trying to stop United States military assistance to military regimes in Central America (see Davis and Howard 1981). Like Richard Lee's actions on behalf of the !Kung, such activities in the field of foreign affairs have been controversial, generating debate among anthropologists themselves over their roles as scholars and citizens. The debate is far from resolution, but it points to the fact that anthropologists themselves are active participants in the modern world system.

Anthropology in the Contemporary World

Anthropology has changed a great deal since the nineteenth century. It is no longer a collection of amateurs interested in the exotic with rather naïve notions about how the world works. Anthropology has grown in its professionalism, in its understanding of how humans live and interact, and in its methodology. It has not grown in a vacuum, however. Like any other group, anthropologists are influenced by their environment. The state of the discipline today is very much a reflection of the nature of the contemporary world system. Greater world integration, for example, has made possible a discipline that consists of persons in every part of the globe—it is no longer the domain of a few Europeans and North Americans. The 1978 International Congress of Anthropological and Ethnological Sciences, held in India, was attended by anthropologists from every continent.

The small-scale societies that were the focus of anthropological attention for decades remain an important part of our study. Because ways of life associated with these societies are disappearing more rapidly every year, contemporary anthropologists share the concern of earlier anthropologists in recording these significant aspects of the human enterprise. They feel a humanistic concern for those whose life-style is disappearing and a scientific desire to ensure that we are aware of mankind's potentialities. There remain many important lessons to be learned from studying people living in smaller, non-industrial societies. There is still much that they can tell us about ourselves and about how we as humans relate to the physical environment. Perhaps most important, they reinforce the notion that humans are highly adaptive. Furthermore, they teach us that many of the characteristics that we often assume to be instinctive, biologically based, such as aggression, are not—that they are largely based on cultural shaping.

Anthropologists' continuing interest in small-scale societies involves a different theoretical approach than in the past, however. They have shifted from looking at smaller societies as isolated entities to examining how they fit into the broader environmental context. And no longer do anthropologists merely study these societies. As noted in the previous section, many anthropologists have worked as planners and advocates to help stop the genocide and ethnocide that have often characterized integration of small-scale societies into the world system.

Anthropologists, of course, do not study only these remaining small-scale societies. The majority of anthropologists today study people who are fully integrated into large-scale industrial societies. Many anthropological studies focus upon aspects of urban life. Urbanism is one of the major features of modern life: the World Bank (1979: 72) projects that "by the year 2000 over half of the world's population is likely to be living in urban areas." Anthropologists have long looked at urban life in Western nations, where urbanism has been a significant feature of social organization for centuries. And as people in underdeveloped countries have moved into cities in tremendous numbers, anthropologists have devoted considerable effort to understanding these newly emerging forms of social organization and the problems associated with rapid urbanization.

An important role for anthropology continues to be the recording of human diversity. It has become commonplace to talk about how everything and everyone is becoming homogenized—wearing polyester and eating fast food at McDonald's. But while many aspects of Western industrial society have spread across the globe, considerable diversity remains. Many Africans now wear polyester, but their fashions remain different from Americans' in many ways. Within the highly integrated world system there remains great room for difference. This is a reflection of the tenacity of many aspects of culture, environmental differences that remain, and different statuses within the world system. Many of the distinctive old "tribes" are gone, but they have been replaced by such new ones as those associated with suburban-dwelling computer technicians or long-distance truck drivers.

As it has always been, anthropology's role is not only to look at human diversity, but also to put it all together in a holistic fashion. In an age subject to specialization and simplistic glosses passing for generalized understanding, the role of anthropology is perhaps more important than at any time in the past. A view that provides an understanding of both the diversity and the integration of the totality of human existence is essential if we are to begin to understand the modern world system.

Summary

In studying specific cultures, anthropologists inevitably run into situations that can be seen as problems. Today many of these involve the ways in which small-scale societies have been rapidly integrated into the modern world system. *Development*—true improvement in the quality of life—has not been achieved anywhere. The so-called "developed" countries have advanced toward material goals, but many other cultures are worse off than in the past.

In contrast to the *undeveloped* life-style of traditional small-scale societies, those who have been denied access to resources and material wealth in the modern world system know a new kind of poverty called *underdevelopment*. They serve as inexpensive sources of labor and goods for more developed peoples, while their own economy shifts from traditional self-sufficient subsistence to ever greater dependence on these outside powers. Multinational corporations are often instrumental in this loss of local power.

Those who have suffered most from underdevelopment are the indigenous peoples of lands taken over by outside powers. In some cases whole groups have been wiped out, in deliberate *genocide*. Others have been subjected to *ethnocide*, destruction of their traditional cultural patterns.

Some indigenous peoples have fought to maintain their identity or to develop better ways of subsisting within the world system; others have been the subjects of outside planners' attempts to accomplish the same thing from above. However, the most successful solutions to the problems of underdevelopment and ethnocide grow out of communication between the planners and the people.

Anthropologists are well suited by training and knowledge to promote such communication. Those who thus take an active role in promoting change are called *applied anthropologists*. Sometimes they are part of planning teams working to help indigenous peoples develop along lines they consider desirable. Sometimes they act as political advocates for these peoples, trying to pressure more powerful peoples into recognizing their plight and making adjustments that will allow them to enter the modern world system on a better footing.

Anthropologists' political activities have been controversial, particularly when they have touched on matters of foreign policy in their own countries. But anthropologists are clearly part of the world system itself. Although they continue to study small-scale societies, as in the past, they also look at the cultures of small groups within large-scale societies. And no longer do they study human groups as isolated entities; all are seen as integrated, for better or for worse, into the world system. At the same time, anthropologists continue to reveal the great diversity of human cultures that coexist within this integrated modern world.

Suggested Readings

Development and underdevelopment (the amount of literature available on the subject of underdevelopment and development is overwhelming and the following represent only a select portion of what there is):

Beckford, George L. 1972. *Persistent poverty: Underdevelopment in plantation economies of the Third World.* New York: Oxford University Press.

Bernstein, Henry, ed. 1973. *Underdevelopment and development: The Third World Today.* Harmondsworth: Penguin.

Cardoso, Fernando H., and Faletto, Enzo. 1979. *Dependency and development in Latin America.* Berkeley/Los Angeles: University of California Press.

Cockcroft, James D., Frank, André Gunder, and Johnson, Dale L. 1972. *Dependence and underdevelopment: Latin America's political economy.* Garden City, NY: Anchor.

de Kadt, Emanuel, and Williams, Gavin, eds. 1974. *Sociology and development.* London: Tavistock Publications.

Frank, André Gunder. 1980. *Crisis: In the Third World.* New York: Holmes and Meier.

Oxaal, Ivar, Barnett, Tony, and Booth, David, eds. 1975. *Beyond the sociology of development: Economy and society in Latin America and Africa.* London: Routledge and Kegan Paul.

Vogeler, Ingolf, and de Souza, Anthony, eds. 1980. *Dialectics of Third World development.* Montclair, NJ: Allenheld, Osmun.

Wallerstein, Immanuel. 1979. *The capitalist world-economy.* Cambridge: Cambridge University Press.

Wallman, Sandra, ed. 1977. *Perceptions of development.* Cambridge: Cambridge University Press.

Wilbur, Charles K., ed. 1973. *The political economy of development and underdevelopment.* New York: Random House.

Multinational corporations:

Barnett, Richard J., Jr., and Muller, Ronald E. 1974. *Global reach: The power of multinational corporations.* New York: Simon and Schuster.

Burbach, Roger, and Flynn, Patricia. 1980. *Agribusiness in the Americas.* New York: NACLA/Monthly Review Press.

Cohen, Robert B., et al., eds. 1979. *The multinational corporation.* New York: Cambridge University Press.

Herman, Edward S., ed. 1981. *Corporate control, corporate power.* New York: Cambridge University Press.

Idris-Soven, Ahmed, and Idris-Soven, Elizabeth, eds. 1978. *The world as a company town.* The Hague/Paris: Mouton.

Kumar, Krishna, ed. 1980. *Transnational enterprises: Their impact on Third World societies and cultures.* Boulder, CO: Westview Press.

Perelman, Michael. 1979. *Farming for profit in a hungry world.* Montclair, NJ: Allenheld, Osmun.

Indigenous peoples (publications):

Bodley, John H. 1975. *Victims of progress.* Menlo Park, CA: Cummings.

Brain, Robert. 1972. *Into the primitive environment.* Englewood Cliffs, NJ: Prentice-Hall.

Davis, Shelton H. 1977. *Victims of the miracle: Development and the Indians of Brazil.* Cambridge: Cambridge University Press.

Dostal, W., ed. 1972. *The situation of the*

Indian in South America. Geneva: World Council of Churches.

Kiste, Robert. 1974. *The Bikinians*. Menlo Park, CA: Cummings.

Maybury-Lewis, David, and Howe, James. 1980. *The Indian peoples of Paraguay: Their plight and prospects*. Cambridge, MA: Cultural Survival.

Ramos, A. R., and Taylor, K. I. 1979. *The Yanoama in Brazil: 1979*. Boston: Anthropology Resource Center.

Roberts, Janine. 1978. *From massacres to mining: The colonization of Aboriginal Australia*. London: CIMRA/ and War on Want.

Simon, Brigitte, et al. 1980. *I sold myself; I was bought—A socio-economic analysis based on interviews with sugarcane harvesters in Santa Cruz de la Sierra, Bolivia*. Copenhagen: International Work Group for Indigenous Affairs.

Indigenous peoples (organizations publishing newsletters):

Anthropology Resource Center, 59 Temple Place, Suite 444, Boston, MA 02111

Cultural Survival Inc., 11 Divinity Avenue, Cambridge, MA 02138

International Work Group for Indigenous Affairs, Fiolstraede 10, DK-1171, Copenhagen K, Denmark.

Minority Rights Group, 36 Craven Street, London WC2N 5NG, England.

Survival International (U.S.A.), Suite 2305, 245 Fifth Avenue, New York, NY 10016

Applied anthropology:

Angrosino, Michael V., ed. 1976. *Do applied anthropologists apply anthropology?* Athens, GA: University of Georgia Press.

Asad, Talal, ed. 1973. *Anthropology and the colonial encounter*. London: Ithaca Press.

Bastide, Roger. 1973. *Applied anthropology*. London: Croom Helm.

Belshaw, Cyril S. 1976. *The sorcerer's apprentice: An anthropology of public policy*. New York: Pergamon.

Clifton, James A., ed. 1970. *Applied anthropology: Readings in the uses of the science of man*. Boston: Houghton Mifflin.

Cochrane, Glynn. 1971. *Development anthropology*. New York: Oxford University Press.

Eddy, Elizabeth M., and Partridge, William L., eds. 1978. *Applied anthropology in America*. New York: Columbia University Press.

Foster, George M. 1969. *Applied anthropology*. Boston: Little, Brown.

———. 1973. *Traditional societies and technological change* 2d ed. New York: Harper & Row.

Franke, Richard W., and Chasin, Barbara H. 1980. *Seeds of famine: Ecological destruction and the development dilemma in the West African Sahel*. Montclair, NJ: Allenheld, Osmun.

Hegeman, Elizabeth, and Kooperman, Leonard, eds. 1974. *Anthropology and Community action*. Garden City, NY: Anchor.

McPherson, Laura, ed. 1978. *The role of anthropology in the agency for International Development*. Binghamton, NY: Institute for Development Anthropology.

Nuñez del Prado, Oscar. 1973. *Kuyo Chico: Applied anthropology in an Indian community*. Chicago: University of Chicago Press.

Pitt, David C., ed. 1976. *Development from below: Anthropologists and development situations*. The Hague/Paris: Mouton.

Sanday, Peggy R., ed. 1976. *Anthropology and the public interest*. New York: Academic Press.

Young, John, and Newton, Jan. 1980. *Capitalism and human obsolescence: Corporate control versus individual survival*. Montclair, NJ: Allenheld, Osmun.

The International Campaign on
Behalf of Brazilian Indians

Shelton H. Davis

Shelton H. Davis has done field research in Guatemala, Brazil, and the United States. For the past ten years, he has been actively involved in the international campaign on behalf of the rights of indigenous peoples. Davis has published several articles on Brazilian Indian policy, economic development in the Amazon region, and foreign policies of the United States, and he is the author of Victims of the Miracle: Development and the Indians of Brazil *(Cambridge University Press, 1977). Currently, he is the director of the Anthropology Resource Center in Boston, Massachusetts, where he has been active in developing the new field of public-interest anthropology.*

ANTHROPOLOGISTS, WHO PRIDE themselves on their objective view of humanity, are increasingly becoming advocates of the human and cultural rights of the peoples whom they study. Anthropology is by nature an extremely personal enterprise, and it is not surprising that many anthropologists have taken sides with the people they studied, rather than merely observed them as disengaged outsiders. What is new, however, is the growth of several organizations, staffed by anthropologists, whose main purpose is to advocate the rights of indigenous peoples. Among these organizations are the In-ternational Work Group for Indigenous Affairs (IWGIA) in Denmark, Survival International in England, and Cultural Survival and the Anthropology Resource Center (ARC) in the United States. The anthropologists who are members of these organizations are not content with merely studying the exotic lifeways and customs of tribal peoples; they want to ensure that the voices of these peoples will be heard in government policies and modern programs of economic development.

For the past decade, I have been an active participant in the international campaign on behalf of the rights of the more than 250,000 Indian people of Brazil. When I first visited Brazil in 1969, it was going through a period of phenomenal economic growth. As a North American familiar with less developed countries in Latin America, I could easily understand the economic euphoria that was gripping Brazil. New automobile factories were being opened in the booming industrial suburbs of São Paulo; high-rise apartments were going up along the beautiful beaches of Rio de Janeiro; television sets were being displayed in the windows of department stores; and highways were being built through the most isolated rural villages. Rapid economic development, at least according to the military government that had controlled

The Northern Perimeter Highway, Roraima Territory, northwestern Brazil. Uncontrolled contacts such as this highway have had devastating effects on the health and culture of the Yanomami.

Brazil since 1964, promised to make the country one of the world's major industrial and political powers.

Not everyone, however, was pleased with the results of the Brazilian "economic miracle." Many observers noted that Brazilian economic growth was causing increased income disparities between the rich and the poor, urban sprawl and environmental pollution, and the suppression of basic political rights. The government's own statistics showed that for every increase in the gross national product, there was a corresponding rise in the country's infant mortality rate. Brazil was growing, but at the expense and welfare of more than two-thirds of its population (Hewlitt 1980).

Perhaps the most tragic victims of the Brazilian "economic miracle" were the country's Indian tribes. In 1970, the Brazilian government announced that it was going to build a transcontinental highway network across the largely undeveloped and unexplored Amazon region. The government did not conduct an assessment of the potential social and environmental impact of the development program before building this highway network. The first reports that came back from the region after the roadwork had begun concerned the decimation of Indian tribes and the destruction of the delicate ecology of the Amazon rain forest (Davis 1977).

Many Brazilian anthropologists were outraged that the government had neither demarcated native lands nor vaccinated Indians against diseases before the building of the new roads. There is a long history of protectionist Indian legislation in Brazil, and one article in the Brazilian Constitution specifically recognizes Indian land rights. Because of the repressive political situation that existed in Brazil during the early 1970s, however, it was impossible to protest the government's failure to fulfill its legal responsibilities to Indians. If anthropologists spoke out, they faced the prospect of imprisonment and torture at the hands of the military government's police and security forces.

The political situation posed special ethical responsibilities for foreign anthropologists who were doing research in Brazil. Increasingly, we found that our Brazilian colleagues were asking us to carry information back to the United States and Europe to alert the world about what was happening to Brazilian Indians. A number of our Brazilian colleagues felt that the government might respond to international pressure and publicity (Davis 1978).

Because much of the technical and financial support for the Amazon development program came from institutions outside of Brazil, it was essential to place the Brazilian Indian situation in an international context. The World Bank and the Inter-American Development Bank, for example, had provided the Brazilian government with loans for highway, port, and hydroelectric plant construction. Companies such as U.S. Steel, Bethlehem Steel, Alcoa Aluminum, King Ranch, and Georgia-Pacific had large investments in the Amazon. Without this foreign aid and investment, the regional development program in the Amazon could not move ahead.

In 1976, my colleagues and I at the Anthropology Resource Center conducted a study of multinational mining and petroleum companies in the Amazon and the effects of their activities on Indian tribes. In contrast to conventional anthropological research, which is based on fieldwork among a specific group of people, we gathered our information from trade journals, interviews with international development agency officials, and site reports that other anthropologists had sent from Brazil, Ecuador, and Peru. To obtain maximum public exposure for our findings, we released a report on our study at a press conference during the annual meetings of the American Anthropological Association in Washington, D.C. (Davis and Mathews 1976).

In January of 1977, just when President Carter was unveiling his human rights policy, we established an office in Washington to bring the situation of Brazilian Indians to the attention of policy makers, members of Congress, and human rights activists. As a result of this effort, ARC was invited to participate in a special United Nations nongovernmental organizations conference on the topic of "Discrimination Against Indigenous Populations in the Americas" held in Geneva in 1977. A year later, ARC testified before a briefing of the House Subcommittee on International Development on the subject of "The Impact of Brazil's 'Economic Miracle' on the Amazonian Indians" (United States, House of Representatives 1978).

Since then, the center has helped to coordinate the international campaign in support of the land rights of the Yanomami Indians of Brazil. Until recently, the Yanomami were considered to be one of the last and largest unacculturated Indian groups in South America. In 1974, the Brazilian government began constructing the Northern Perimeter Highway along the southern part of Yanomami territory. At the same time, mineral companies discovered large deposits of uranium and cassiterite (an ore used in the production of tin) in an area occupied by more than four thousand Indians. Along the southern and eastern border of the Yanomami homeland, the government established settlements of colonists and cattle ranchers. These abrupt and uncontrolled contacts have had devastating effects on the health and culture of the Yanomami. Kenneth Taylor and Alcida Ramos, who have done fieldwork among the Yanomami, report that several hundred Indians have already died from diseases as a result of contacts with highway workers, prospectors, and settlers (Taylor and Ramos 1979).

In June of 1979, a group of Brazilian anthropologists, clerics, and citizens submitted a proposal to the Brazilian government calling for the creation of a sixteen-million-acre Yanomami Indian park. Despite numerous promises, the Brazilian government has yet to create a land area for the Yanomami. Throughout 1980 and 1981, gold and diamond prospectors invaded the Yanomami territory, and the government did nothing to stop them. Recent reports indicate that measles and whooping-cough epidemics are now spreading throughout the Yanomami homeland. In July of 1981, missionaries reported that twenty-one Indians had died from measles in one village and that other villages were in jeopardy.

In response to this situation, ARC, the American Anthropological Association, the Indian Law Resource Center, and Survival International of England and the United States submitted a formal complaint on behalf of the Yanomami to the Inter-American Commission on Human Rights of the Organization of American States (OAS). This complaint, the first of its kind ever presented to the OAS, called for international intervention to alleviate the conditions faced by the Yanomami tribe (Anthropology Resource Center 1981b).

The Yanomami have brought to world attention the serious human-rights violations being committed against indigenous peoples. In November of 1980, the IV Russell Tribunal met in Holland to discuss the current genocide and ethnocide faced by several Indian nations throughout the Americas. In September of 1981, another international conference was held under UN auspices in Geneva to discuss the land rights of indigenous peoples. Currently, ARC is planning an international conference on the subject of "Transnational Corporations and Indigenous Peoples." This conference will bring together indigenous leaders and non-Indian experts to discuss international strategies for dealing with transnational companies who are exploiting mineral and energy resources on Indian lands.

In the future, Indian organizations themselves will bring their grievances before such official agencies as the United Nations and the Organization of American States. Anthropologists can play a role in these efforts by providing indigenous organizations with information and by showing the relationships between their struggles and the wider problems of human and planetary survival. As many people have noted, the world today is a "global village." Working together with indigenous peoples, rather than just studying them as objects of curiosity, anthropologists can make that village a better place to live.

Glossary

acephalous society Literally a "headless" society. Refers to a highly decentralized and relatively egalitarian form of political organization.

adaptation The process by which a population or an individual adjusts to environmental conditions in order to maintain itself and survive, if not prosper.

adaptive strategy The conscious or unconscious plans of action carried out by a population in response to its environment.

affinity Relationships brought about by marriage.

age grades A series of recognized age-based categories.

age set A group of individuals of similar age and of the same sex who share a common identity, maintain close ties throughout their lives, and together pass through a series of age-related statuses.

allomorph A variant of a single morpheme.

allophone A variant of a single phoneme that does not affect meaning.

ambilineal descent A situation in which descent is recognized through male and female lines, but in which the individual must choose one through which to trace descent.

ambilocal residence The pattern or prescription that residence after marriage is with or near the parents or kin of either the bride or groom.

animatism Belief in an impersonal supernatural force or power, which although unseen is believed to be present everywhere.

animism Belief in the existence of almost numberless spirits that dwell in animals and places or simply wander about the earth.

anomie Disorganization of personality and a feeling of alienation.

anthropology The scientific study of humanity.

applied anthropology Goal-oriented research and instrumental activities which, through the provision of information, the formulation of policy recommendations, or the initiation of direct action, are intended to produce a desired sociocultural condition.

archaeology The anthropological study of past cultures through their material remains.

assimilation The process by which distinctions between ethnic groups are eliminated.

authority The right to make a particular decision and to command obedience.

avunculocal residence The pattern or prescription of residence after marriage near the husband's mother's brother or father's brother.

bilineal descent Tracing descent patrilineally for some purposes while at the same time tracing descent matrilineally for others.

bilocal residence The pattern or prescription that a married couple live for a period with or near the bride's parents and for another period with or near the groom's.

bride service Service performed by a future husband for his bride-to-be's parents.

bridewealth (brideprice) The passage of wealth of some sort as a result of marriage from the husband's group to the wife's.

bureaucracy The specialized administrative organization concerned with the day-to-day running of the state.

capitalists Those who own the means of production, are concerned with the appropriation of what is produced, and control the circulation of what is appropriated, in a modern class-based industrial society.

cargo cult A millinarian movement found in the southwest Pacific, characterized by the expectation that Western material goods will be received by supernatural means.

caste Occupationally specific, hierarchically ordered statuses to which a member of a society is assigned at birth.

chiefdom A stateless political structure integrating a number of communities comprised of several parallel units, each headed by a chief, subchief, or council.

clan A group of kin who believe themselves to be descended from a common ancestor, but who cannot specify the actual links back to that ancestor.

class *See social class.*

class consciousness The awareness of class membership and of the structure of class relations.

coalition A temporary alliance for a limited political purpose.

cognates Words that have evolved from a common ancestral word.

cognatic descent Tracing descent through all ancestors, male and female.

commerce The exchange of goods among different countries or regions.

communication The exchange of information between senders and receivers.

compadrazgo A term used in many hispanic cultures to denote social links created by sponsorship of children in rites of passage like baptism or confirmation.

consanguinity Relationships based on presumed biological links.

core values The fundamental values that provide the basis for social behavior and the goals pursued by the members of a society.

corporate group A group that is theoretically permanent, its members being recruited on the basis of recognized principles, and having common interests or property, as well as norms or rules fixing their rights and duties in relation to one another and to their property or interests.

cosmology Philosophy concerned with the fundamental causes and processes in things.

creole A *pidgin* that has become the mother tongue of a people.

cross-cousins The children of a parent's sibling of the opposite sex; e.g., children of the father's sister.

cultural ecology The study of how human culture influences the relationships of humans to their environment.

cultural relativism Judging and interpreting the behavior and beliefs of others in terms of their traditions and experiences.

culture The customary manner in which human groups learn to organize their behavior in relation to their environment.

culture shock The psychic distress caused by the strains of adjusting to a different culture.

demography The statistical study of population composition, distribution and trends.

dependency A situation in which the economy of underdeveloped countries and its direction is dependent upon inputs from developed countries.

descent Socially recognized links between a person and his or her ancestors.

development Improvement in the quality of human life by achieving an adequate level of consumption and assuring suitable physical surroundings as well as developing social, political, and economic systems which allow a realization of individual potentiality and a feeling of self-esteem.

deviants Persons identified by the majority or influential and powerful members of a society as thinking or acting in ways considered too far from what is normal or acceptable.

dialect A patterned language variant that is associated with a geographically or socially distinct speech community or speech context.

diffusionism The view that the main process by which cultures grow, change, and develop is cultural borrowing.

diglossia A situation where two varieties of one language ("standard" forms, *dialects*, *pidgins*, or *creoles*) are spoken by persons in a speech community under different conditions.

disease A pathological condition of the body, or some part of it, in which its functioning is disturbed or deranged.

division of labor The technical and social manner in which work is organized in a society.

dowry The woman's share of her inheritance from the group of her birth, which is taken with her upon marriage.

ecology The study of the relationship between organisms and their physical, biotic, and social environments.

economic system The organizational and institutional structure or system people have developed to supply themselves with the necessities and niceties of life.

education Systematic instruction or training.

egalitarian society A society characterized by few individual or group differences in wealth and power.

enculturation The process of learning and absorbing cultural rules and values.

endemic disease A disease that has a relatively low incidence but is constantly present in a given community.

endogamy Pattern or rule of marriage within a group, class, or category.

environment Physical, biological, and social surroundings.:

epidemic disease A disease that is not commonly present in a community, and that is characterized by high incidence and rapid and extensive diffusion.

epidemiology The study of the relationships of the various factors that determine the frequency and distribution of diseases in societies.

ethnicity The lumping of people into groups on the basis of selected cultural or physical characteristics.

ethnocentrism The interpretation of the behavior of others in terms of one's own cultural values and traditions.

ethnocide The destruction of a people's culture carried out on a systematic basis.

ethnography The process of describing cultures, largely through fieldwork.

ethnology The process of understanding how and why cultures work.

exchange The pattern of trade that exists in resources, goods, ideas, and services.

exogamy Pattern, preference, or requirement of marriage outside of a social group or category.

extended family group Residential group consisting of two or more families of at least two generations.

faction A political group which acts together within and in opposition to some element of a larger unit.

family An intimate kin-based group, consisting of at least a woman and her children, that forms the minimal social unit that cooperates economically and is responsible for the rearing of children.

feud Prolonged violence between different families or groups of kin.

feudalism A social and economic system whereby land is held by conferred right by members of a privileged class, who can command the labor of a lower class that works the land.

First World Western industrial capitalist nations.

foraging Collecting wild plants and animals for subsistence.

functionalism A theoretical perspective that seeks to discover the interconnections between social phenomena.

functions The purpose and effects, the intended and actual consequences of particular beliefs and actions.

general purpose money A medium of exchange that can be used to buy or pay for a wide range of material things and services.

genocide The deliberate and systematic destruction of a political or cultural group.

ghost marriage Practice in which a woman is married to or may simply bear children in the name of a dead man.

glottochronology Estimating the dates at which two languages diverged from one another through comparison of core vocabularies.

god A supernatural being with an individual identity and recognizable attributes who is worshiped as having power over nature and human fortunes.

historical archaeology The branch of archaeology devoted to the study of the material remains of societies possessing historical records.

horticulture Garden cultivation.

hypothesis A statement that something observed is associated with and/or caused by a particular set of factors.

ideology Values and beliefs about how the world is or should be ordered that are consciously and systematically organized into some form of program.

illness Pronounced deviation from what is considered to be a normal healthy state.

incest taboo A rule prohibiting sexual intercourse between specific categories of kin.

instincts Inheritable and unalterable behavioral tendencies to make complex and specific responses to environmental stimuli.

institutionalization The standardization of modes of joint activity.

institutions Practices based upon similar principles that display some degree of regularity.

interference Deviation from speech norms as a result of a speaker's familiarity with multiple languages or dialects.

jajmani relationships Patron-client relationships between families of different castes.

joint family group Residential group consisting of two or more relatives and their spouses and children.

judgment sample Collecting data from a limited number of key informants who have been selected on the basis of criteria deemed critical to research.

kinesics The study of gestural communication.

kinship Social relations based on culturally recognized ties by descent and marriage.

land rights The right of native peoples to control what happens on the lands where they live and to be compensated for the lands that they have lost.

language A set of rules for generating speech.

large-scale societies Societies characterized by a high degree of social complexity and dependence on extensive and highly specialized interchange of goods, ideas, and people.

latent functions Effects that are not overly apparent, often emerging only after careful study.

law A binding rule, created through enactment or custom, that defines right and reasonable behavior.

leader An individual who has the power to make decisions within and for a group.

learning Modifying behavior in response to experience within an environment.

legitimacy General normative concepts based ultimately on the traditional moral system of a society.

levirate The custom of a man's brother, or some other member of his kin group, marrying his widow.

life cycle The life process through birth, maturation, old age, death, and in some traditions beyond.

lineage Descent in a line from common ancestors through known links.

linguistic anthropology The branch of anthropology that concentrates on the study of language.

linguistic community Any group within which communication occurs and which has a recognizable boundary.

manifest function The results or purposes that are most obvious and that are explicitly stated.

marriage A socially sanctioned sexual and economic union between two (or more) members of opposite sexes (occasionally between members of the same sex).

matrilineage A lineage formed on the basis of *matrilineal descent.*

matrilineal descent Descent through female lines.

matrilocal residence Residence after marriage with the wife's kin.

medical system "The culturally based behavior and belief forms that arise in response to the threats posed by disease" (Foster and Anderson 1978: 33).

mental illness An illness associated with a mental state perceived as abnormal.

middleman (or broker) An individual who strives to benefit from the sociocultural gaps between groups by providing service as an intermediary.

millenarian movement A social movement espousing a belief in the coming of a new world (a millenium), in part through supernatural action.

modal personality The central tendencies of the personality characteristics found within a population.

moiety A division of a society into two social categories or groups.

money An object characterized by durability, transferability, and acceptability over a wide range of functions used for the purpose of exchange.

monogamy Marriage of one man to one woman at the same time.

monotheism Belief that there is only one god.

morpheme The smallest unit of sound that conveys meaning.

morphology The study of how simple sounds are organized to form units of meaning.

multinational corporation A corporation having divisions in a number of countries.

myth A sacred tale expressing the unobservable realities of religious belief in terms of observable phenomena.

neolocal residence Residence of a couple after marriage in a new household, not linked to the households of either of their families.

norms Conceptions of appropriate or expected behavior.

nuclear family group A group composed of a man, a woman, and their children.

organic evolution The continuous process by which populations adapt to the opportunities and limitations of ever-changing environments.

ownership Acknowledged supremacy, authority, or power over a physical object or process.

parallel cousins Children of a parent's siblings of the same sex; e.g., children of the father's brother.

parallel descent Women tracing descent through female lines only and men tracing descent through male lines only.

participant observation A research method in which a researcher lives with a group of people and observes their daily activities, learning how the group views the world and witnessing firsthand how they behave.

pastoral nomadism An economic adaptation and life-style characterized by a lack of permanent habitation and primary dependence upon the herding of animals for subsistence.

patrilineage A lineage formed on the basis of *patrilineal descent.*

patrilineal descent Tracing descent through male lines.

patrilocal residence Residence after marriage with the husband's kin.

personality "An inner system of beliefs, expectations, desires, and values" (Stagner 1961: 8).

phoneme The smallest linguistically significant unit of sound, which does not alter the meaning of the words in which it occurs.

phonology The study of a language's sounds.

phratry A descent group comprised of a number of supposedly related clans, the actual links usually being unrecognized.

physical anthropology The branch of anthropology that concentrates on the biological basis of the human condition.

pidgin A simplified hybrid language developed to fulfill the communication needs of peoples who have no common language.

plural marriage Marriage to more than one person at the same time.

political norms Ideas about appropriate political goals and behavior.

politics Competition for power.

polyandrous family group A group resulting from a polyandrous marriage, consisting of a wife and her husbands and children, the men living under a single roof with their wife or jointly occupying a separate men's hut.

polyandry Marriage of a woman to two or more men at the same time.

polygamy Marriage to more than one person at the same time.

polygynous family group A group resulting from a polygynous marriage, consisting of a man, his wives, and his or their children, all living in a single household (or sometimes the wives having separate dwellings).

polygyny Marriage between one man and two or more women at the same time.

polytheism Belief that there can be an almost limitless number of gods, or a finite number arranged in some sort of hierarchy.

population The people a researcher decides to include in a study.

potlatch An elaborate, and at times quite dramatic, feast and gift-giving ceremony performed among northwest coast Indians.

power The ability to act effectively over people or things.

prehistory The branch of archaeology devoted to the study of ancient pre-literate cultures.

priest A person who is authorized to perform religious functions.

primatology The study of primates (apes, monkeys, and prosimians).

primitive A term, often with derogatory connotations, used for members of small-scale, nonindustrial societies. Also used in reference to simple forms of technology.

primogeniture Practice of the oldest child inheriting most or all of the parent's property.

probability sampling Selection of a segment of the population whose responses will be taken as a miniature, relatively unbiased replica of the larger population.

production Significant transformation of an object for cultural purposes.

proletariat Members of a class society who are engaged in the production of agricultural and industrial goods and sell their labor for a wage.

prophet An individual who receives divine revelation, usually by visions or dreams, concerning a restructuring of some aspect of society or of a people's beliefs.

proxemics The study of the cultural use of space.

race A category based upon physical traits.

random sample A significant number of persons selected for questioning from a population on a random basis.

rank society A society in which people differ in prestige according to a series of recognized graded ranks, associated historically with relatively productive foraging and farming societies that are organized on a multi-community basis.

reciprocity The mutual exchange of goods and services.

redundancy The repetition or reinforcement of a signal or message.

religion The worship of supernatural forces or beings that provide shape and meaning to the universe.

revolution A "fundamental change in the nature of the state, the functions of government, the principles of economic production and distribution, the relation of social classes, particularly as regards the control of government" (Wolf and Hansen 1972: 235).

rite of passage A ritual associated with a transition period in a person's life cycle.

ritual Highly stereotyped, stylized, and repetitive behavior that takes place at a set time and place.

role The part a society expects an individual to play in a given relationship.

role models Fictional or actual persons whose activities provide an ideal for role performances.

sampling See *probability sampling*.

Second World Industrialized socialist countries.

shaman "A man or woman who is in direct contact with the spirit world through a trance state and has one or more spirits at his command to carry out his bidding for good or evil" (Harner 1973: xi).

shifting cultivation Use of the slash-and-burn method of field preparation in farming, resulting in the need to leave plots fallow for a period of a few years to several decades.

sign Anything that can convey information, including physical objects, colors, sounds, movements, and even silence.

small-scale societies Societies characterized by highly localized social interaction and the exploitation of local resources.

social class A division of society, defined in terms of its relationship to the means of production, with a collective identity and interests.

social networks The social bonds and links that form the social web within which members of a society act.

social relationship Regularized pattern of action between individuals within a particular social context.

social stratification The division of members of a society into strata (or levels) with unequal wealth, prestige, and power.

socialization The process of acquiring views and values from others through social interaction.

society An abstraction of the ways in which interaction among humans is patterned.

sociocultural anthropology The study of the social, symbolic and material lives of humans.

sororate Practice of a man marrying the sister of his deceased wife.

special purpose money Objects that serve as a medium of exchange in only limited contexts and that are interchangeable for only a particular range of goods and services.

speech Patterned verbal behavior.

speech community A "community sharing rules for the conduct and interpretation of at least one linguistic variety" (Hymes 1972: 54–55).

state An autonomous integrated political unit, encompassing many communities within its territory, with a highly specialized central governing authority.

status Relative social position assigned on the basis of birth or attained through individual efforts.

stratified sample A significant number of persons selected for questioning from distinct subgroups within a population.

structural functionalism Theory that emphasizes how various elements of social structure are integrated and function to maintain social order and equilibrium.

symbol A sign whose meaning is arbitrary, being determined by social convention and learning.

syncretism The conscious adaptation of an alien idea or practice in terms of some indigenous counterpart.

syntax Standardized conventions for combining words to form statements that make sense to other speakers of the same language.

technology The skills and knowledge by which people make things and extract resources.

Third World A loose category of about 120 countries characterized by low standards of living, high rates of population growth, and general economic and technological dependence upon wealthier industrial nations.

totem Symbolic representation linking individuals or groups with human ancestors, plants, animals, or other natural phenomena.

transhumance An economic adaptation and life-style characterized by residence in a permanent village and subsistence based on limited crop production and migratory herding of animals.

tribe A group of people who share patterns of speech, some cultural characteristics, and a common territory, and who in general feel that they have more in common with one another than with those around them.

ultimogeniture Practice of the youngest of a couple's children remaining in their household and eventually inheriting their property.

underdeveloped society or country A society or country with persistent low levels of living that can be linked historically and structurally with the manner of its integration into the world system.

undeveloped society A society that is materially poor because it has not developed a complex technology.

unilineal descent Tracing descent through a single line, male or female.

unilineal evolutionism Belief that all cultures pass through essentially the same stages along a single line of development, moving from the "savage" to the "civilized."

values Emotionally charged beliefs about what is desirable or offensive, right or wrong, appropriate or inappropriate.

varna The four primary caste divisions, ranked according to their relative ritual purity: Brahmin, Kshatriya, Vaisha, and Shudra.

voluntary association A special-purpose group whose members are recruited on a nonascriptive basis.

warfare Formalized armed combat by groups representing rival political communities.

wealth Objects or resources that are useful or that have exchange value.

wife inheritance Practice of a man's heir marrying his widow.

world system A social system encompassing the entire world and entailing a single division of labor.

world view The basic cultural orientation of the members of a society.

Bibliography

Aberle, David F.
  1961 Matrilineal descent in cross-cultural perspective. *In* David M. Schneider and Kathleen Gough (editors) *Matrilineal kinship:* 655–727. Berkeley: University of California Press.
  1966 *The peyote religion among the Navaho.* Chicago: Aldine.

Achebe, Chinua
  1960 *No longer at ease.* New York: Obolensky.
  1967 *Things fall apart.* London: Heinemann Educational Books.

Acheson, James M.
  1972 Limited good or limited goods? Response to economic opportunity in a Tarascan pueblo. *American Anthropologist* 74:1152–69.

Allan, W.
  1965 *The African husbandman.* New York: Barnes & Noble.

Allegro, John M.
  1970 *The sacred mushroom and the cross.* Garden City, NY: Doubleday.

Andreas, Joel
  1974 *The incredible Rocky.* New York: North American Congress on Latin America.

Anthropology Resource Center
  1981a The case of the Kaingang and Guarani of Mangueitinha. *ARC Bulletin* 4:12–13.
  1981b *The Yanomami Indian park: A call for action.* Boston: Anthropology Resource Center.

Asad, Talal
  1970 *The Kababish Arabs: Power, authority and consent in a nomadic tribe.* London: Hurst.

Bailey, Frederick G.
  1969 *Stratagems and spoils: A social anthropology of politics.* Oxford: Blackwell.

Banton, Michael
  1957 *West African city: A study of tribal life in Freetown.* London: Oxford Univ. Press.

Barnett, Homer G.
  1953 *Innovation: The basis of cultural change.* New York: McGraw-Hill.

Barrett, Leonard E.
  1977 *The Rastafarians: The Dreadlocks of Jamaica.* Kingston: Sangster's/Heinemann.

Barth, Frederick
  1969 Introduction. *In* Frederick Barth (editor) *Ethnic groups and boundaries:* 9–38. Bergen/Oslo: Universtetsforlaget.

Bastide, Roger
  1973 *Applied anthropology.* London: Croom Helm.

Beattie, John
  1964 *Other cultures: Aims, methods and achievements in social anthropology.* New York: Free Press.

Belshaw, Cyril S.
  1965 *Traditional exchange and modern markets.* Englewood Cliffs, NJ: Prentice-Hall.

Benedict, Ruth
  1934 *Patterns of culture.* Boston: Houghton Mifflin.

Bennett, John W.
  1969 *Northern plainsmen: Adaptive strategy and agrarian life.* Chicago: Aldine.

Berlin, Brent, and Paul Kay
  1969 *Basic color terms: Their universality and evolution.* Berkeley: University of California Press.

Berndt, Ronald M.
1951 *Kunapipi.* Melbourne: Chesire.
1965 Law and order in Aboriginal Australia. *In* R. M. Berndt and C. H. Berndt (editors) *Aboriginal man in Australia:* 167–206. Sydney: Angus & Robertson.
1978 *Love songs of Arnhem Land.* Chicago: University of Chicago Press.

Berreman, Gerald
1962 Pahari polyandry: A comparison. *American Anthropologist* 64:60–75.
1972 *Hindus of the Himalayas: Ethnography and change,* 2nd ed. Berkeley: University of California Press.
1975 Himalayan polyandry and the domestic cycle. *American Ethnologist* 2:127–38.

Bicchieri, Marco G., ed.
1972 *Hunters and gatherers today.* New York: Holt, Rinehart & Winston.

Birdwhistell, Ray L.
1960 Kinesics and communication. *In* E. Carpenter and M. McLuhan (editors) *Explorations in communications:* 54–64. Boston: Beacon.

Bohannon, Laura
1966 Shakespeare in the bush. *Natural History* 75 (Aug.–Sept.):28–33.

Bohannon, Laura, and Bohannon, Paul
1953 *The Tiv of Central Nigeria.* London: International African Institute.

Bohannon, Paul
1959 The impact of money on an African subsistence economy. *The Journal of Economic History* 19:491–503.

Boissevain, Jeremy
1973 Preface. *In* J. Boissevain and J. C. Mitchell (editors) *Network analysis: Studies in human interaction:* vii–xiii. The Hague/Paris: Mouton.
1974 *Friends of friends: Networks, manipulators and coalitions.* Oxford: Blackwell.

Bolinger, Dwight
1968 *Aspects of language.* New York: Harcourt, Brace & World.

Bott, Elizabeth
1957 *Family and social network.* London: Tavistock.

Briggs, Jean L.
1970 *Never in anger: Portrait of an Eskimo family.* Cambridge, MA: Harvard Univ. Press.

Broehl, Wayne G., Jr.
1978 *The village entrepreneur: Change agents in India's rural development.* Cambridge, MA: Harvard Univ. Press.

Bruner, Edward
1973 Kin and non-kin. *In* A. Southall (editor) *Urban anthropology:* 373–92. New York: Oxford Univ. Press.

Buchbinder, Georgeda, and Roy A. Rappaport
1976 Fertility and death among the Maring. *In* P. Brown and G. Buchbinder (editors) *Man and woman in the New Guinea Highlands:* 13–35. Washington, DC: American Anthropological Association.

Burridge, Kenelm
1969 *New heaven new earth: A study of millenarian activities.* Oxford: Blackwell.

Campbell, J. K.
1974 *Honour, family, and patronage: A study of institutions and moral values in a Greek mountain community.* Oxford: Oxford Univ. Press.

Cancian, Francesca
1975 *What are norms? A study of beliefs and action in a Maya community.* New York: Cambridge University Press.

Carneiro, Robert
1970 A theory of the origin of the state. *Science* 169:733–38.

Carroll, Vern
  1970 Adoption on Nukuoro. *In* V. Carroll (editor) *Adoption in eastern Oceania:* 121–57. Honolulu: University Press of Hawaii.
Carter, William E.
  1969 *New lands and old traditions: Kekchi cultivators in the Guatemalan lowlands.* Gainesville, FL: University of Florida Press.
Cawte, John
  1974 *Medicine is the law: Studies in psychiatric anthropology of Australian tribal societies.* Honolulu: University Press of Hawaii.
Chagnon, Napoleon A.
  1977 *Yanomamo: The fierce people* (second edition). New York: Holt, Rinehart and Winston.
Chenery, Hollis, et al.
  1974 *Redistribution without growth: An approach to policy.* London: Oxford University Press.
Chodorow, Nancy
  1974 Family structure and feminine personality. *In* M. Rosaldo and L. Lamphere (editors) *Women in culture and society:* 45–56. Stanford: Stanford University Press.
Clark, Margaret
  1970 *Health in the Mexican-American culture: A community study.* Berkeley: University of California Press.
Codere, Helen
  1950 *Fighting with property.* Seattle: University of Washington Press.
Cohen, Abner
  1969 *Custom and politics in urban Africa.* Berkeley: University of California Press.
  1971 The politics of ritual secrecy. *Man* 6:427–48.
  1974 *Two-dimensional man.* Berkeley: University of California Press.

Cohen, Albert
  1955 *Delinquent boys: The culture of the gang.* Glencoe, IL: Free Press.
Collier, P., and Horowitz, D.
  1976 *The Rockefellers.* New York: Holt, Rinehart & Winston.
Colson, Anthony C., and Selby, Karen F.
  1974 Survey article on medical anthropology. *Annual Review of Anthropology* 3:245–262.
Colson, E.
  1971 *Social consequences of resettlement.* New York: Humanities Press.
Conklin, H. C.
  1955 Hanunoo color categories. *Southwestern Journal of Anthropology* 11:339–44.
Coon, C.
  1958 *Caravan: The story of the Middle East.* New York: Holt.
Crane, Julia, and Angrosino, Michael
  1974 *Field projects in anthropology: A student handbook.* Scott Foresman.
Crosby, Alfred W., Jr.
  1972 *The Columbian exchange: Biological and cultural consequences of 1492.* Westport, CT: Greenwood.
Curr, E. M.
  1886–87 *The Australian race.* 4 volumes. Melbourne: Government Printer.
Dagmar, Hans
  1978 *Aborigines and poverty: A study of interethnic relations and culture conflict in a Western Australian town.* Nijmegen, The Netherlands: Katholieke Universiteit.
Damas, David
  1972 The Copper Eskimo. *In* M. G. Bicchieri (editor) *Hunters and gatherers today:* 3–50. New York: Holt, Rinehart & Winston.
Darwin, Charles
  1968 *The voyage of the "Beagle."* Distributed by Heron Books.

Davis, Shelton H.
  1977   *Victims of the miracle: Development and the Indians of Brazil.* Cambridge: Cambridge University Press.
  1978   The social responsibility of anthropological science in the context of contemporary Brazil. *In* Ahamed Idris-Soven, Elizabeth Idris-Soven, and Mary K. Vaughan (editors) *The world as a company town: Multinational corporations and social change.* Elmsford, NY: Mouton Publishers.

Davis, Shelton H., and Michael C. Howard
  1981   US military aid: Turning sardines into sharks. *ARC Newsletter* 5(2):7.

Davis, Shelton H., and Robert O. Mathews
  1976   *The geological imperative: Anthropology and development in the Amazon Basin of South America.* Boston: Anthropology Resource Center.

DeCamp, David
  1971   Toward a generative analysis of a post-creole speech continuum. *In* D. Hymes (editor) *Pidginization and creolization of languages:* 349–70. Cambridge: Cambridge University Press.

Dentan, Robert
  1968   *The Semai: A nonviolent people of Malaya.* New York: Holt, Rinehart and Winston.

Despres, Leo A.
  1967   *Cultural pluralism and nationalist politics in British Guiana.* Chicago: Rand McNally.

Diamond, S., ed.
  1981   *Toward a Marxist anthropology.* New York: Mouton.

Dix, Warwick
  1978   The Aboriginal Heritage Act of 1972. *In* M.C. Howard (editor) *"Whitefella business":* 81–92. Philadelphia: Institute for the Study of Human Issues.

Douglas, Mary
  1958   Raffia distribution in the Lele economy. *Africa* 21:1–12.

DuBois, Cora
  1960   *The people of Alor: A social-psychological study of an East Indian Island.* 2 volumes. New York: Harper & Row.

Dumont, Louis
  1970   *Homo hierarchicus: The caste system and its implications.* London: Weidenfeld & Nicolson.

Dunn, Frederick L.
  1968   Epidemiological factors: Health and disease in hunter-gatherers. *In* R. B. Lee and I. deVore (editors) *Man the hunter:* 221–28. Chicago: Aldine-Atherton.

Durkheim, Emile
  1933   *The division of labor in society.* New York: Macmillan.
  1951   *Suicide: A study in society.* Glencoe, IL: Free Press.

Dusenberry, William H.
  1963   *The Mexican mesta: The administration of ranching in colonial Mexico.* Urbana, IL: University of Illinois Press.

Duvignaud, Jean
  1970   *Change at Shebika: Report from a North African village.* New York: Random House.

Dyson-Hudson, V. Rada and Neville
  1969   Subsistence herding in Uganda. *Scientific American* 220:76–89.

Eidheim, Harald
  1971   *Aspects of the Lappish minority situation.* Oslo/Bergen: Universtetsforlaget.

Elkin, A. P.
  1944   *Aboriginal men of high degree.* Sydney: Australasian Publishing Company.

Epstein, A. L.
  1958   *Politics in an urban African community.* Manchester: Manchester University Press.

1969 *Matupit: Land, politics, and change among the Tolai of New Britain.* Berkeley: University of California Press.

Evans, Les (editor)

1974 *Disaster in Chile: Allende's strategy and why it failed.* New York: Pathfinder Press.

Evans-Pritchard, E. E.

1937 *Witchcraft, oracles and magic among the Azande.* Oxford: Clarendon Press.

1940 *The Nuer: A description of the modes of livelihood and political institutions of a Nilotic people.* Oxford: The Clarendon Press.

1949 *The Sanusi of Cyrenaica.* Oxford: Clarendon Press.

Evans-Wentz, W. Y.

1960 *The Tibetan book of the dead.* London: Oxford University Press.

Fabrega, Horacio, Jr., and Daniel B. Silver

1973 *Illness and shamanistic curing in Zinacantan: An ethnomedical analysis.* Stanford: Stanford University Press.

Ferguson, Charles A.

1959 Diglossia. *Word* 15:325-40.

Forde, C. Daryll

1964 *Yako studies.* London: Oxford University Press.

Fortes, Meyer

1949 *The web of kinship among the Tallensi.* London: Oxford University Press.

1958 Introduction. *In* J. Goody (editor) *The developmental cycle in domestic groups:* 1-14. Cambridge: Cambridge University Press.

Foster, G. M.

1976 Disease etiologies in non-western medical systems. *American Anthropologist* 78:773-82.

Foster, George M.

1965 Peasant society and the image in limited good. *American Anthropologist* 67:293-315.

Fox, Robin

1967 *Kinship and marriage.* Baltimore, MD: Penguin.

Fraenkel, M.

1964 *Tribe and caste in Monrovia.* London: Oxford University Press.

Frank, André Gunder

1972 The development of underdevelopment. *In* J. C. Cockcroft, A. G. Frank, D. L. Johnson, *Dependence and underdevelopment:* 3-18. Garden City, NY: Anchor Books.

Freeman, J. D.

1958 The family system of the Iban of Borneo. *In* J. Goody (editor) *The developmental cycle in domestic groups:* 15-52. Cambridge: Cambridge University Press.

Freidson, Eliot

1970 *Professional dominance: The social structure of medical care.* New York: Atherton Press.

Fried, Jacob

1959 Acculturation and mental health among Indian migrants in Peru. *In* M. K. Opler (editor) *Culture and mental health:* 119-37. New York: Macmillan.

Furst, Peter T. (editor)

1972 *Flesh of the gods: The ritual use of hallucinogens.* London: Allen & Unwin.

Galbraith, John K.

1977 *The age of uncertainty.* Boston: Houghton Mifflin.

Geertz, Clifford

1960 *The religion of Java.* Glencoe, IL: Free Press.

1973 *The interpretation of cultures: selected essays.* New York: Basic Books.

Gillen, John

1951   *The culture of security in San Carlos: A study of a Guatemalan community of Indians and Ladinos.* New Orleans: Middle American Research Institute, Tulane University.

Giuliano, Bruce B.

1976   *Sacro o profano?: A consideration of four Italian-Canadian religious festivals.* Ottawa: National Museums of Canada.

Glasse, R. M.

1969   Marriage in South Fore. *In* R. M. Glasse and M. J. Meggitt (editors) *Pigs, pearlshells and women:* 16–37. Englewood Cliffs, NJ: Prentice-Hall.

Gluckman, Max

1949   *Malinowski's sociological theories.* The Rhodes-Livingstone Papers, no. 16. Oxford.

1950   Kinship and marriage among the Lozi of Northern Rhodesia and the Zulu of Natal. *In* A. R. Radcliffe-Brown and C. D. Forde (editors) *African systems of kinship and marriage:* 166–206. London: Oxford University Press.

1955   *The judicial process among the Barotse of Northern Rhodesia.* Manchester: Manchester University Press.

1956   *Custom and conflict in Africa.* Oxford: Blackwell.

1965   *Politics, law and ritual in tribal society.* Chicago: Aldine.

1973   *The judicial process among the Barotse of Northern Rhodesia (Zambia)* (second edition). Manchester: Manchester University Press.

Godelier, M.

1977   *Perspectives in Marxist anthropology.* Cambridge: Cambridge Univ. Press.

Goldkind, Victor

1966   Class conflict and cacique in Chan Kom. *Southwestern Journal of Anthropology* 22:325–44.

Goodale, Jane C.

1971   *Tiwi wives: A study of the women of Melville Island, North Australia.* Seattle: University of Washington Press.

Goodenough, Ward H.

1949   Premarital freedom on Truk: Theory and practice. *American Anthropologist* 54:615–20.

Goodland, Robert, and Howard Irwin

1975   *Amazon jungle: green hell to red desert?* New York: Elsevier.

Goody, Jack R.

1959   The mother's brother and sister's son in West Africa. *Journal of the Royal Anthropological Institute* 89:61–88.

1970   Cousin terms. *Southwestern Journal of Anthropology* 26:125–42.

Graves, Nancy B. and Theodore D.

1978   The impact of modernization on the personality of a Polynesian people. *Human Organization* 37:115–35.

Greenberg, Joseph H.

1968   *Anthropological linguistics: An introduction.* New York: Random House.

Grigg, D. B.

1974   *The agricultural systems of the world.* Cambridge: Cambridge University Press.

Gruen, F. H.

1965   Rural Australia. *In* A. F. Davies and S. Encel (editors) *Australian society:* 253–73. London: Pall Mall.

Gumperz, John

1962   Types of linguistic communities. *Anthropological Linguistics* 4:28–40.

Hall, Edward T.

1966   *The hidden dimension.* Garden City, NY: Doubleday.

Hancock, Ian F.

    1971 A survey of the pidgins and creoles of the world. *In* D. Hymes (editor) *Pidginization and creolization of languages:* 509–23. Cambridge: Cambridge University Press.

Harner, Michael J. (editor)

    1973 *Hallucinogens and shamanism.* New York: Oxford University Press.

Harris, Marvin

    1974 *Cows, pigs, wars and witches: The riddles of culture.* New York: Vintage Books.

Hart, C. W. M., and A. R. Pilling

    1979 *The Tiwi of North Australia* (Fieldwork edition). New York: Holt, Rinehart and Winston.

Helms, Mary W.

    1976 Competition, power and succession to office in pre-Columbian Panama. *In* M. W. Helms and F. O. Loveland (editors) *Frontier adaptations in lower Central America:* 25–36. Philadelphia: Institute for the Study of Human Issues.

Henry, Jules

    1963 *Culture against man.* New York: Random House.

Heston, Alan

    1971 An approach to the sacred cow of India. *Current Anthropology* 12:191–209.

Hewlitt, Sylvia Ann

    1980 *The cruel dilemmas of development: Twentieth-century Brazil.* New York: Basic Books.

Hiatt, Les R. (editor)

    1975 *Australian Aboriginal mythology.* Canberra: Australian Institute of Aboriginal Studies.

Hicks, Frederick

    1979 "Flowery war" in Aztec history. *American Ethnologist* 6:87–92.

Hoare, Q., and G. N. Smith (editors)

    1971 *Selections from the Prison notebooks of Antonio Gramsci.* London: Lawrence & Wishart.

Hoebel, E. Adamson

    1940 *The political organization and lawways of the Commanche Indians.* American Anthropological Association, Memoir 54.

    1960 *The Cheyennes: Indians of the Great Plains.* New York: Holt, Rinehart and Winston.

Hogbin, Ian

    1970 *The island of menstruating men: Religion in Wogeo, New Guinea.* Scranton, PA: Chandler.

Holtved, Erik

    1967 Eskimo shamanism. *In* C-M Edsman (editor) *Studies in shamanism:* 23–31. Stockholm, Sweden: Almquist & Wiksell.

Honigmann, John J.

    1970 Sampling in ethnographic fieldwork. *In* R. Naroll and R. Cohen (editors) *A handbook of method in cultural anthropology:* 266–81. New York: Columbia University Press.

Horwood, Harold

    1969 *Newfoundland.* Toronto: Macmillan of Canada.

Hough, Richard A.

    1972 *Captain Bligh and Mr. Christian: The men and the mutiny.* London: Hutchinson.

Howard, Michael C.

    1977 *Political change in a Maya village in southern Belize.* Greeley, CO: Katunob, University of Northern Colorado.

    1978 Aboriginal "leadership" in the southwest of Western Australia. *In* M. C. Howard (editor) *"Whitefella business":* 13–36. Philadelphia: Institute for the Study of Human Issues.

1980 Ethnicity and economic integration in southern Belize. *Ethnicity* 7:119-36.

1981 *Aboriginal politics in southwestern Australia.* Nedlands: University of Western Australia Press.

Hudson, A. B.

1972 *Padju Epat: The Ma'anyan of Indonesian Borneo.* New York: Holt, Rinehart and Winston.

Hudson, E. H.

1965 Treponematosis and man's social evolution. *American Anthropologist* 67:885-901.

Hugh-Jones, Stephen

1979 *The palm and the pleiades: Initiation and cosmology in northwest Amazonia.* Cambridge: Cambridge University Press.

Hughes, Charles C., and John M. Hunter

1972 Diseases and "development" in Africa. *Social Science and Medicine* 3:443-93.

Hughes, Daniel T.

1982 Continuity of indigenous Ponapean social structure and stratification. *Oceania* 53(1):5-18.

Hume, David

1748 Of national characters. *In Essays moral, political, and literary,* Essay 21 (third edition). London: A. Millar.

Hunt, Edward E., Jr.

1978 Ecological frameworks and hypothesis testing in medical anthropology. *In* M. H. Logan and E. H. Hunt, Jr. (editors) *Health and the human condition:* 84-99. North Scituate, MA: Duxbury Press.

Hymes, Dell

1972 Models of the interaction of language and social life. *In* J. J. Gumperz and D. Hymes (editors) *Directions in sociolinguistics:* 35-71. New York: Holt, Rinehart and Winston.

International Work-Group on Indigenous Affairs

1981 Colombia: Embera Indians killed by police. *IWGIA Newsletter* 25/26: 43-44.

Ishige, Naomichi

1977 Roasting dog in an earth oven (Ponape). *In* J. Kuper (editor) *The anthropologists' cookbook:* 203-5. New York: Universe Books.

James, Wendy

1973 The anthropologist as reluctant imperialist. *In* T. Asad (editor) *Anthropology and the colonial encounter:* 41-70. London: Ithaca Press.

Jansen, G.

1973 *The doctor-patient relationship in an African tribal society.* Assen, The Netherlands: Van Gorcum.

Jones, Delmos

1971 Social responsibility and the belief in basic research: An example from Thailand. *Current Anthropology* 12:347-50.

Kahn, Joel S.

1980 *Minangkabau social formations: Indonesian peasants and the world-economy.* Cambridge: Cambridge University Press.

Kapferer, Bruce

1972 *Strategy and transaction in an African factory.* Manchester: Manchester University Press.

1973 Social network and conjugal role in urban Zambia: Towards a reformulation of the Bott hypothesis. *In* J. Boissevain and J. C. Mitchell (editors) *Network analysis:* 83-110. The Hague/Paris: Mouton.

Kaut, C. R

1957 *The Western Apache clan system: Its origins and development.* Albuquerque, NM: University of New Mexico Press.

Kay, Paul, and Chad K. McDaniel
1978 The linguistic significance of the meanings of basic color terms. *Language* 54:610–646.

Kennedy, John G.
1973 Cultural psychiatry. *In* J. J. Honigmann (editor) *Handbook of social and cultural anthropology:* 1119–98. Chicago: Rand McNally.

Kiev, Ari
1972 *Transcultural psychiatry.* New York: Free Press.

Kolenda, Pauline
1978 *Caste in contemporary India: Beyond organic solidarity.* Menlo Park, CA: Cummings.

Kolig, Erich
1978 Dialectics of Aboriginal life-space. *In* M. C. Howard (editor) *"Whitefella business":* 49–80. Philadelphia: Institute for the Study of Human Issues.

Kottak, Conrad P.
1979 *Cultural anthropology.* New York: Random House.

Kracke, Waud H.
1978 *Force and persuasion: Leadership in an Amazonian society.* Chicago: University of Chicago Press.

Kuper, Adam
1971 Council structure and decision-making. *In* A. Richards and A. Kuper (editors) *Councils in action:* 13–28. Cambridge: Cambridge University Press.

Kuper, Hilda
1963 *The Swazi: A South African kingdom.* New York: Holt, Rinehart and Winston.

Lambert, Wallace E., et al.
1960 Evaluational reactions to spoken languages. *Journal of Abnormal and Social Psychology* 66:44–51.

Lang, Norris G.
1977 Transplanted technicians: Americans on an Ecuadorian sugar plantation. *In* G. Hicks and P. Leis (editors) *Ethnic encounters:* 103–17. North Scituate, MA: Duxbury Press.

Langness, L. L.
1969 Marriage in Bena Bena. *In* R. M. Glasse and M. J. Meggitt (editors) *Pigs, pearlshells and women:* 38–55. Englewood Cliffs, NJ: Prentice-Hall.

Lanternari, Vittorio
1963 *The religions of the oppressed: A study of modern messianic cults.* New York: Knopf.

Leach, Edmund R.
1954 *Political systems of highland Burma.* London: Athlone Press.

Lee, Richard
1969 Eating Christmas in the Kalahari. *Natural History* 78 (Dec.): 14–22, 60–63.

Lévi-Strauss, Claude
1969 *The elementary structures of kinship.* Boston: Beacon Press.

Lewis, Oscar
1966 The culture of poverty. *Scientific American* 215:19–25.

Lieban, Richard W.
1962 Qualifications for folk medical practice in Sibulan, Negros Oriental, Philippines. *The Philippine Journal of Science* 91:511–21.

Lienhardt, Godfrey
1961 *Divinity and experience: The religion of the Dinka.* Oxford: Clarendon Press.

Lindenbaum, Shirley
1979 *Kuru sorcery: Disease and danger in the New Guinea Highlands.* Palo Alto, CA: Mayfield.

Linné, Karl von
1758-59 *Systema naturae per regna tria naturae, secundum classes, ordenes, genera, species, cum characteribuus differentiis, locis . . .* (tenth edition). Holmiae, impensi: L. Salvii.

Linton, Ralph
1936 *The study of man.* New York: Appleton-Century.

Little, Kenneth
1965 *West African urbanization: A study of voluntary associations in social change.* Cambridge: Cambridge University Press.
1965/66 The political functions of the Poro. *Africa* 35:349-65; 36:62-72.

Lloyd, Peter C.
1974 *Power and independence: Urban Africans' perception of social inequality.* London: Routledge and Kegan Paul.

Long, Norman
1975 Structural dependency, modes of production and economic brokerage in rural Peru. *In* I. Oxaal, T. Barnett, D. Booth (editors) *Beyond the sociology of development.* London: Routledge and Kegan Paul.

Maclean, Una
1971 *Magical medicine: A Nigerian case-study.* Harmonsworth: Penguin.

Maddock, Kenneth
1972 *The Australian Aborigines: A portrait of their society.* London: Allen Lane.
1977 Two laws in one community. *In* R. M. Berndt (editor) *Aborigines and change:* 13-32. Canberra: Australian Institute of Aboriginal Studies.

Madsen, William
1967 Religious syncretism. *In* R. Wauchope (editor) *Handbook of Middle American Indians,* vol. 6: 369-91. Austin: University of Texas Press.

Mailloux, Laurie
1980/81 Anthropology in AID: Case study of the Nepal mission. *Practicing Anthropology* 3(2):17-18, 61-62.

Malefijt, Annemarie deWaal
1968 *Religion and culture: An introduction to anthropology of religion.* New York: Macmillan.

Malinowski, Bronislaw
1926 *Crime and custom in savage society.* London: Kegan Paul, Trench, Trubner.
1929 *The sexual life of savages in north-western Melanesia.* London: Routledge and Kegan Paul.

Mangin, William
1959 The role of regional associations in the adaptation of rural populations in Peru. *Sociologus* 9:23-36.

Marett, Robert R.
1909 *The threshold of religion.* London: Methuen.
1912 *Anthropology.* New York: Holt, Rinehart and Winston.

Marshall, Ingeborg
1981 Disease as a factor in the demise of the Beothuck Indians. *Culture* 1(1):71-77.

Marshall, Lorna
1961 Sharing, talking, and giving: Relief of social tensions among !Kung Bushmen. *Africa* 31:231-49.

Martin, M. K.
1974 *The foraging adaptation—uniformity or diversity?* Reading, MA: Addison-Wesley.

Martin, M. Kay, and Barbara Voorhies
1975 *Female of the species.* New York: Columbia University Press.

Martinez-Alier, Verena
1974 *Marriage, class and colour in nineteenth-century Cuba.* Cambridge: Cambridge University Press.

Maybury-Lewis, David
1968 *The savage and the innocent.* Boston: Beacon Press.

Mayer, A. C.
1963 Municipal elections: A central Indian case study. *In* C. H. Philips (editor) *Studies in modern Asia and Africa*, no. 1: 115-32. London: George Allen & Unwin.
1966 Quasi-groups in the study of complex societies. *In* M. Banton (editor) *The social anthropology of complex societies:* 97-123. London: Tavistock Publications.

McWilliams, Cary
1961 *North from Mexico.* Philadelphia: J. B. Lippincott.

Mead, Margaret
1947 The concept of culture and the psychosomatic approach. *Psychiatry* 10:57-76.
1967 Alternatives to war. *In* M. Fried, M. Harris, R. Murphy (editors) *War:* 215-28. Garden City, NY: Natural History Press.

Meggitt, Mervyn J.
1962 *Desert people: A study of the Walbiri Aborigines of Central Australia.* Sydney: Angus & Robertson.
1977 *Blood is their argument: Warfare among the Mae Enga tribesmen of the New Guinea Highlands.* Palo Alto, CA: Mayfield.

Meillassoux, C.
1981 *Maidens, meal and money.* Cambridge: Cambridge Univ. Press.

Meillassoux, Claude
1968 *Urbanization of an African community: Voluntary associations in Bamako.* Seattle: University of Washington Press.

Melville, Thomas
1981 Guatemala: the Indian awakening. *ARC Newsletter* 5(2):1.

Merton, Robert
1968 *Social theory and social structure.* New York: Free Press.

Métraux, Alfred
1972 *Voodoo in Haiti.* New York: Schocken.

Miller, Max J.
1973 Industrialization, ecology and health in the tropics. *Canadian Journal of Public Health* 64 (Monograph Supplement):11-16.

Mitchell, J. Clyde
1956 *The Kalela dance: Aspects of social relationships among urban Africans in Northern Rhodesia.* Rhodes-Livingstone Paper No. 27.
1969 The concept and use of social networks. *In* J. C. Mitchell (editor) *Social networks in urban situations:* 1-50. Manchester: Manchester University Press.

Moloney, James C.
1945 Psychiatric observations on Okinawan Shima. *Psychiatry* 8:391-99.

Mooney, James
1965 *The ghost-dance religion and the Sioux outbreak of 1890.* Chicago: University of Chicago Press.

Moorehead, Alan
1960 *The White Nile.* New York: Harper & Brothers.

Moran, Emilio F.
1979 *Human adaptability: An introduction to ecological anthropology.* North Scituate, MA: Duxbury.

Morgan, Lewis H.
1877 *Ancient society.* New York: H. Holt.

Mörner, Magnus
1967 *Race mixture in the history of Latin America.* Boston: Little, Brown.

Morris, Desmond, Peter Collett, Porter Marsh, and Marie O'Shaughnessy
1979 *Gestures, their origins and distribution.* New York: Stein and Day.

Murphy, Yolanda and Robert F.
1974 *Women of the forest.* New York: Columbia University Press.

Myerhoff, Barbara
  1970 The deer-maize-peyote symbol com-
       plex among the Huichol Indians of
       Mexico. *Anthropological Quarterly*
       39(2):60–72.
  1974 *Peyote hunt: The sacred journey of the
       Huichol Indians.* Ithaca, NY: Cornell
       University Press.
Myers, Fred R.
  1982 Ideology and experience: The cultural
       basis of politics in Pintupi life. *In* M.
       C. Howard (editor) *Aboriginal power
       in Australian society:* 79–114. St. Lucia:
       University of Queensland Press.
Nemec, Thomas F.
  1972 I fish with my brother: The structure
       and behavior of agnatic-based fishery in
       a Newfoundland Irish outport. *In* R.
       Anderson and C. Wadel (editors)
       North Atlantic fishermen. St. John's,
       Newfoundland: Memorial University
       of Newfoundland (Institute of Social
       and Economic Research).
Newman, Barry
  1979 Mixed blessing: Do multinationals
       really create jobs in the Third World?
       Wall Street Journal 64 (Sept. 25):1, 18.
Newman, Philip L.
  1965 *Knowing the Gururumba.* New York:
       Holt, Rinehart and Winston.
Nicholas, Ralph W.
  1968 Factions: A comparative analysis. *In* M.
       Banton (editor) *Political systems and
       the distribution of power:* 21–61. Lon-
       don: Tavistock Publications.
Nind, Scott
  1831 Description of the natives of King
       George's Sound (Swan River Colony)
       and adjoining country. *Royal Geo-
       graphical Society,* Journal 1:21–51.
Norton, Robert
  1973/74 The management of racial confict
       in Fijian politics. *Anthropological
       Forum* 3(3–4):312–24.

Onwuejeogwu, M. Angulu
  1975 *The social anthropology of Africa: An
       introduction.* London: Heinemann
Ortiz de Montellano, Bernard
  1977 The rational causes of illness among
       the Aztecs. *Katunob* 10(2):23–43.
Paine, Robert
  n.d. In search of friendship: A frame of ref-
       erence and a methodology. Unpub-
       lished paper (mimeograph). St. John's,
       Newfoundland: Memorial University
       of Newfoundland (Institute of Social
       and Economic Research).
Parker, S.
  1960 The windigo psychosis in the context
       of Ojibwa personality and culture.
       American Anthropologist 62:603–23.
Parkin, David
  1969 *Neighbours and nationals in an Afri-
       can city ward.* London: Routledge and
       Kegan Paul.
  1974 Congregational and interpersonal ide-
       ologies in political ethnicity. *In* A. Co-
       hen (editor) *Urban ethnicity:* 119–58.
       London: Tavistock Publications.
Patterson, Horace Orlando
  1971 *Children of Sisyphus.* Kingston,
       Jamaica: Bolivar Press.
Pimentel, David, William Dritschilom,
John Krummel, and John Kutzman
  1975 Energy and land constraints in food
       protein production. *Science* 190:
       754–61.
Piven, Frances F., and Richard A. Cloward
  1971 *Regulating the poor: The functions of
       public welfare.* New York: Vintage.
Polanyi, Karl, Conrad M. Arensberg, and H. P.
Pearson (editors)
  1957 *Trade and market in the early empires.*
       Glencoe, IL: Free Press.

Poulton, Terry

1981 A race against time and assimilation: Canadian anthropologists are concerned about the fate of the African Bushman. *Macleans* (April) 13:49–50.

Powdermaker, Hortense

1962 *Copper town: Changing Africa.* New York: Harper & Row.

Prior, Ian A. M.

1971 The price of civilization. *Nutrition Today* 6(4):2–11.

Radcliffe-Brown, A. R.

1950 Introduction. *In* A. R. Radcliffe-Brown and D. Forde (editors) *African systems of kinship and marriage:* 1–85. London: Oxford University Press.

Randall, Robert A.

n.d. Steps toward an ethnosemantics of verbs: Complex fishing technique scripts and the problem of listener identification. *In* J. D. W. Dougherty (editor) *New directions in cognitive anthropology:* (unpublished).

Rappaport, Roy A.

1967 Ritual regulation of environmental relations among New Guinea people. *Ethnology* 6:17–30.

Reaves, Dick

1978 Never love a Bandido. *Texas Monthly* (May): 100–107, 208–19.

Redfield, Robert

1952 The primitive world view. *Proceedings of the American Philosophical Society* 96: 30–36.

Redfield, Robert, and Alfonso Villa Rojas

1962 *Chan Kom: A Maya village.* Chicago: University of Chicago Press.

Reichel-Dolmatoff, Gerardo

1971 *Amazonian cosmos: The sexual and religious symbolism of the Tukano Indians.* Chicago: University of Chicago Press.

Reid, J., and Munuggurr, D.

1977 "We are losing our brothers": Sorcery and alcohol in an Aboriginal community. *Med. J. Aust. Spec. Supp.* 2:1–5.

Reina, Ruben E.

1966 *The law of the saints: A Pokomam pueblo and its community culture.* New York: Bobbs-Merrill.

Ribeiro, Darcy

1970 *Os Índios e a civilização.* Rio de Janeiro: Editora Civilização Brasileira.

Riesman, David

1953 *The lonely crowd: A study of the American character.* Garden City, NY: Doubleday.

Roberts, Janine

1978 *From massacres to mining: The colonization of Aboriginal Australia.* London: CIMRA and War on Want.

Robertson, W.

1822 *The history of America.* 2 vol. Philadelphia: Robert Thomas Desilver.

Rudé, George

1980 *Ideology and popular protest.* New York: Pantheon.

Ruhlen, Merritt

1976 *A guide to the languages of the world.* Stanford: Stanford University Press.

Sackett, Lee

1978 Clinging to the law: Leadership at Wiluna. *In* M. C. Howard (editor) *"Whitefella business":* 37–48. Philadelphia: Institute for the Study of Human Issues.

Sahlins, Marshall

1958 *Social stratification in Polynesia.* Seattle: University of Washington Press.

1965 On the sociology of primitive exchange. *In* M. Banton (editor) *The relevance of models for social anthropology:* 139–236. London: Tavistock Publications.

1972 *Stone age economics.* Chicago: Aldine/ Atherton.

Sakamaki, Shunzō
1967 Shinto: Japanese ethnocentrism. *In* C. Moore (editor) *The Japanese mind:* 24–32. Honolulu: East-West Center Press.

Salzman, Philip C.
1971 Movement and resource extraction among pastoral nomads: The case of the Shah Nawazi Baluch. *Anthropological Quarterly* 44(3):185–97.

Sapir, Edward
1915 The social organization of the west coast tribes. *Proceedings and Transactions of the Royal Society of Canada,* section 2, series 3, vol. 9. Ottawa.

1929 The status of linguistics as a science. *Language* 5:207–14.

Schapera, I.
1940 *Married life in an African tribe.* London: Faber and Faber.

Schultes, Richard E.
1963 Botanical sources of the New World narcotics. *Psychedelic Review* 1: 145–66.

Seguin, C. Alberto
1956 Migration and psychosomatic disadaptation. *Psychosomatic Medicine* 18(5):404–9.

Shanin, Teodor
1972 *The awkward class.* Oxford: Clarendon Press.

Shapiro, Judith
1968 Tapirapé kinship. *Boletim do Museu Paraense Emílio Goeldi, Antropolgia,* no. 37.

Siegel, Lenny
1980 Delicate bonds: The global semiconductor industry. *Pacific Research* 11(1): Special Issue.

Simoons, Frederick J.
1973 The sacred cow and the constitution of India. *Ecology of Food and Nutrition* 2:281–95.

Sinha, D. P.
1972 The Birhors. *In* M. G. Bicchieri (editor) *Hunters and gatherers today:* 371–403. New York: Holt, Rinehart and Winston.

Siverts, Hennig
1971 On politics and leadership in highland Chiapas. *In* E. Z. Vogt and A. Ruz L. (editors) *Desarrollo cultural de los Mayas:* 387–408. Mexico: UNAM.

Smith, M. G.
1960 *Government in Zazzau, 1881–1950.* London: Oxford University Press.

1974 *Corporations and society.* London: Duckworth.

Smith, Waldemar R.
1977 *The fiesta system and economic change.* New York: Columbia University Press.

Sorensen, Arthur P.
1973 South American Indian linguistics at the turn of the seventies. *In* D. R. Gross (editor) *Peoples and cultures of native South America:* 312–41. Garden City, NY: Doubleday/Natural History Press.

Southall, A. W.
1961 Introductory summary. *In* A. Southall (editor) *Social change in modern Africa:* 217–30. London: Oxford University Press.

Spencer, Baldwin, and F. J. Gillen
1899 *The native tribes of central Australia.* London: Macmillan.

Spencer, Robert F.
1959 *The north Alaskan Eskimo: A study in ecology and society.* Washington, DC: Bureau of American Ethnology, Bull. 171.

Stagner, Ross
    1961 *Psychology of personality* (third edition). New York: McGraw-Hill.

Steward, Julian H.
    1947 American culture history in the light of South America. *Southwestern Journal of Anthropology* 3: 85–107.

Steward, Julian H., et al.
    1956 *The people of Puerto Rico.* Urbana: University of Illinois Press.

Stokes, William
    1952 Violence as a power factor in Latin American politics. *Western Political Quarterly* 5(3):445–68.

Swadesh, Morris
    1971 *The origin and diversification of language.* Chicago: Aldine/Atherton.

Swanton, John R.
    1902 Social organization of the Haida. *Proceedings of the International Congress of Americanists,* 13th session: 327–34. Easton, PA: Eschenbach Printing Company.

Taira, Koji
    1969 Urban poverty, ragpickers, and the "Ants' Villa" in Tokyo. *Economic Development and Culture Change* 17:155–77.

Tanner, Adrian
    1979 *Bringing home animals: Religious ideology and mode of production of the Mistassini Cree hunters.* London: Hurst.

Taylor, John C.
    1977 Diet, health and economy: Some consequences of planned social change in an Aboriginal community. *In* R. M. Berndt (editor) *Aborigines and change:* 147–58. Canberra: Australian Institute of Aboriginal Studies.

Taylor, Kenneth, and Alicida Ramos
    1979 *The Yanomama in Brazil,* 1979. International Work Group for Indigenous Affairs, Document 37.

Tenney, Jack B. (chairman)
    1943 *Report: Joint fact-finding committee on un-American activities in California.* California Legislature, Senate, 55th session. Sacramento: California State Printing Office.

Terrace, Herb S., L. A. Petitto, R. U. Sanders, and T. G. Bever
    1979 Can an ape create a sentence? *Science* 206:891–902.

Thompson, J. E. S.
    1930 *Ethnology of the Mayas of southern and central British Honduras.* Field Museum of Natural History, publication 274. Chicago.
    1970 *Maya history and religion.* Norman, OK: University of Oklahoma Press.

Todaro, Michael P.
    1977 *Economics for a developing world.* London: Longman.

Todd, Loreto
    1974 *Pidgins and creoles.* London: Routledge and Kegan Paul.

Tonkinson, Robert
    1974 *The Jigalong mob: Aboriginal victors of the desert crusade.* Menlo Park, CA: Cummings.
    1978 *The Mardudjara Aborigines: Living the dream in Australia's desert.* New York: Holt, Rinehart and Winston.

Tozzer, Alfred M.
    1907 *A comparative study of the Mayas and Lacandones.* New York: Macmillan.

Turnbull, Colin
    1976 *Man in Africa.* Garden City, NY: Anchor Press/Doubleday.

Turner, Victor W.
    1957 *Schism and continuity in an African society: A study of Ndembu village life.* Manchester: Manchester University Press.

Tylor, Edward B.
    1891 *Primitive culture.* 2 vol. London: John Murray.

U.S. House of Representatives
  1978 Briefing on impact of Brazil's "Economic Miracle" on the Amazonian Indians. Subcommittee on International Development, Committee on International Relations, 6 September.
Valdman, Albert
  1975 The language situation in Haiti. *In* V. Rubin and R. P. Schaedel (editors) *The Haitian potential*: 61–82. New York: Teachers College Press.
van Baal, J.
  1966 *Dema: Description and analysis of Marind-anim culture (south New Guinea)*. The Hague: M. Nijhoff.
van Gennep, Arnold
  1960 *The rites of passage*. Chicago: University of Chicago Press.
Vivelo, Frank R.
  1978 *Cultural anthropology handbook*. New York: McGraw-Hill.
Voegelin, Charles F. and F. M.
  1977 *Classification and index of the world's language*. New York: Elsevier.
Vogt, Evon Z.
  1970 *The Zinacantecos of Mexico: A modern Maya way of life*. New York: Holt, Rinehart and Winston.
Wagley, Charles
  1977 *Welcome of tears: The Tapirape Indians of Central Brazil*. New York: Oxford University Press.
Wallace, Anthony F. C.
  1966 *Religion: An anthropological view*. New York: Random House.
  1970 *Culture and personality* (second edition). New York: Random House.
Wallerstein, Immanuel
  1979 *The capitalist world-economy*. Cambridge: Cambridge University Press.
Warner, W. L.
  1937 *A black civilization*. New York: Harper & Row.

Wasson, R. Gordon
  1972 The divine mushroom of immortality. *In* P. T. Furst (editor) *Flesh of the gods*: 185–200. London: George Allen & Unwin.
  1973 *Soma: Divine mushroom of immortality*. New York: Harcourt Brace Jovanovich.
Wedge, B. M.
  1952 Occurrence of psychosis among Okinawans in Hawaii. *American Journal of Psychiatry* 109:225–58.
Weil, Peter
  1980 Mandinko adaptation to colonial rule in the Gambia. *Cultures et développement* 12(2):295–318.
Weiner, J. S.
  1978 Progress in human biology. *Royal Anthropological Institute News* no. 24: 9–11.
White, Leslie
  1949 *The science of culture*. New York: Grove Press.
  1959 *Evolution of culture*. New York: McGraw-Hill.
Williams, Glyn
  1979 Welsh settlers and native Americans in Patagonia. *Journal of Latin American Studies* 11:41–66.
Wilson, John
  1958 Cooraradale. Unpublished B.A. (Hons) thesis. Nedlands, University of Western Australia.
  1965 Assimilation to what? Comments on the white society. *In* M. Reay (editor) *Aborigines now*: 151–66. Sydney: Angus & Robertson.
Wilson, Monica
  1963 *Good company: A study of Nyakyusa age-villages*. Boston: Beacon Press.
Wirth, Louis
  1938 Urbanism as a way of life. *American Journal of Sociology* 44:1–24.

Wittfogel, Karl A.

1957 *Oriental despotism: A comparative study of total power.* New Haven, CN: Yale University Press.

Wolf, Eric R.

1971 *Peasant wars of the twentieth century.* London: Faber and Faber.

Wolf, Eric R., and Edward C. Hansen

1972 *The human condition in Latin America.* New York: Oxford University Press.

Woodburn, James

1972 Ecology, nomadic movement and the composition of the local group among hunters and gatherers: An East African example and its implications. *In* Peter J. Ucko, R. Tringham, and G. W. Dimbleby (editors) *Man, settlement and urbanism.* Cambridge, MA: Schenkman.

The World Bank

1979 *World development report, 1979.* New York: Oxford University Press.

Worsley, Peter

1957 *The trumpet shall sound: A study of "cargo" cults in Melanesia.* London: MacGibbon & Kee.

Young, M. W.

1971 *Fighting with food: Leadership, values and social control in a Massim society.* Cambridge: Cambridge University Press.

Zaldívar, Ramon

1974 Agrarian reform and military reformism in Peru, *In* D. Lehman (editor) *Agrarian reform and agrarian reformism:* 25-70. London: Faber and Faber.

Acknowledgments (continued)

Page 146: From Eugene N. Cohen and Edwin Eames, *Cultural Anthropology.* Copyright © 1982 by Eugene N. Cohen and Edwin Eames. Reprinted by permission of the publisher, Little, Brown and Company.

Page 291: Henning Siverts, "On Politics and Leadership in Highland Chiapas," in *Desarrollo Cultural de los Mayas,* ed E. Z. Vogt and A. Ruz L. (Mexico: UNAM, 1971), pp. 390-393.

Pages 338-339: Yolanda and Robert F. Murphy, *Women of the Forest* (New York: Columbia University Press, 1974), pp. 88-89.

Page 344: Reprinted by permission of Schocken Books Inc. from *Voodoo in Haiti* by Alfred Métraux. Copyright © 1959 by Alfred Métraux. Introduction copyright © 1972 by Schocken Books Inc. © Editions Gallimard 1959.

Page 395: Reprinted by permission of *The Wall Street Journal,* © Dow Jones & Company, Inc. 1979. All rights reserved.

Photo Credits

Chapter 1: Page 2, © Jean Arlaud/Documentary Educational Research; page 6, Marjorie Shostak/Anthro-Photo; page 7, Peter Vandermark/Stock, Boston; page 9, Steve McCutcheon; page 10, courtesy of The Essex Inst., Salem Ma.; pages 12-13, Historical Pictures Service, Inc.; page 14, Bobbie Brown; page 15, Michael Moseley/Anthro-Photo; page 19, © Bruno Barbey/Magnum.

Chapter 2: Pages 22-23, Babangi mask, French Congo. The Museum of Modern Art, New York; Pablo Picasso, *Demoiselles d'Avignon* (1907), The Museum of Modern Art, New York; acquired through the Lillie P. Bliss Bequest; page 25, from *Master Mariner, Captain James Cook, People of the Pacific;* page 27, Lester V. Bergman, N.Y.; page 30, National Anthropological Archives, Smithsonian Institution; page 32, courtesy of Helena Malinowski Wayne; page 34, Martin Etter/Anthro-Photo; page 38, © Margaret Thompson/Anthro-Photo; page 39, E. Aubert De La Rue.

Chapter 3: Page 44, Saba UXIU, courtesy Anthropology Resource Center; page 47, Irven DeVore/Anthro-Photo; page 49 top, J. F. E. Bloss/Anthro-Photo; page 49 bottom, Peter Menzel/Stock, Boston; page 54, Y. Kahana/Peter Arnold, Inc.; page 58, Irven DeVore, Anthro-Photo; page 60, National Anthropological Archives, Smithsonian Institution; page 67, Eugene Ogan.

Chapter 4: Page 68, Yuze Vort; page 71, Ted Spiegel/Black Star; page 72, Richard Wrangham/Anthro-Photo; page 74 top, Arthur Tress; page 74 bottom, Wide World Photos; page 76, Herbert Terrace/Anthro-Photo; page

78, Smolan/Stock, Boston; page 84, Photo Museum of Modern Art, courtesy Warner Bros.; page 87, Huffman/Monkmeyer Press Photo Service; page 90, courtesy The Peace Corps; page 95, Robert Randall.

Chapter 5: Pages 98–99, Hiroji Kubota/Magnum; page 102, from *At Home with the Patagonians* by George C. Musters, 1897; page 105, from Robert Bruce, *Lacandon Dream Symbolism* (1975); page 108, Barrie Machin, University of Western Australia; page 113, Francke/Peter Arnold, Inc.; page 114, Ruben E. Reina, University of Pennsylvania; page 116, Thomas Nemec, Memorial University, Newfoundland; page 118, Norris G. Lang, University of Houston; page 121, J. C. Allen and Son; page 122, Roy Kriegler/Flinders University.

Chapter 6: Page 128, Lee Boltin; page 131, Robert Tonkinson, Australian National University; page 133, John Dominis, Life © Time Inc.; page 135, Audio-Visual; page 137, Australian Consolidated Press Ltd.; page 142, Courtesy of the British Columbia Provincial Museum, Victoria, British Columbia; page 143, Stuart Colun; page 148, Louis Goldman, Freelance Photographers Guild; page 150, Claude Dumenil/Anthropology Resource Center; page 154, Peter M. Weil.

Chapter 7: Pages 156–157, Brian Seed: CLICK/Chicago and William S. Nawrocki; page 159 top, Richard Katz/Anthro-Photo; page 159 bottom, Cary Wolinsky/Stock, Boston; page 160, Lee Sackett, University of Adelaide, Australia; page 162, Mary Frey/The Picture Cube; page 165, Photoworld, Div. of Freelance Photographers Guild; page 167, © 1979 Lisa Kroeber/Black Star; page 170, David Maybury-Lewis/Anthro-Photo; page 173, Cunningham, Prettyman Collection, The Univ. of Oklahoma.

Chapter 8: Page 176, courtesy New England Historic Genealogical Society; page 189, J. F. E. Bloss/Anthro-Photo; page 190, The Peabody Museum, Harvard University; page 195, United Press International.

Chapter 9: Page 198, Henry Moore, *Family Group*, Collection, The Museum of Modern Art, New York. A. Conger Goodyear Fund; page 201, Werner Stoy/Camera Hawaii; page 202, Barrie Machin, University of Western Australia; page 207, Mac Marshall from *Weekend Warriors: Alcohol in a Micronesian Culture*; page 211, BBC Hulton Picture Library; page 214, Arthur Tress; page 216, Mike Howard; page 217, Irven DeVore/Anthro-Photo; page 226, Margarita Melville.

Chapter 10: Page 228, Norman Rockwell, reprinted from *The Saturday Evening Post* © 1957 The Curtis Publishing Company; page 231, Michael Leunig from 1974 *The Penguin Leunig*; page 234, Cary Wolinsky/Stock, Boston; page 238, Stan Washburn/Anthro-Photo; page 240, Robert Tonkinson, Australian National University; page 245, Peter Olwyler/Freelance Photographers

Guild; page 246, courtesy Fabragé, Inc.; page 249, Ed Hof/The Picture Cube; page 253, Monte Tidwell.

Chapter 11: Pages 256–257, Peter Vandermark/Stock, Boston; page 260, Wayne Stayskal, copyrighted, Chicago Tribune. Used with permission; page 261, Randy Taylor-SIPA Press/Editorial Photocolor Archives; page 267, Arthur Tress; page 270, The Peabody Museum of Salem, Mass.; page 271, Werner Bischof/Magnum; page 273, The Bettmann Archive; page 275, Alex Webb © Magnum Photos, Inc.

Chapter 12: Page 280, Ben Shahn, *CIO PAC, Register-Vote: For all these rights we've just begun to fight.* 1946. Poster. 29 × 38⅛". Collection, The Museum of Modern Art, New York. Gift of S. S. Spivack; page 283, Mark Godfrey/Archive Pictures, Inc.; page 285, Lee Sackett, University of Adelaide; page 286, Bradley Smith, N.Y., from the Museo Nacional de Historia, Mexico City; page 288, Michael Serino/The Picture Cube; page 294, Carolyn Redenius/Monkmeyer Press Photo Service; page 298, United Nations; page 299, Ellis Herwig/Stock, Boston.

Chapter 13: Page 302, The Peabody Museum, Harvard University; page 305, United Press International; page 306, Barbara Klutinis © Jeroboam; page 308, Frank Cancian, University of California, Irvine; page 315, Chas Gerretsen/Gamma; page 317, Alain Keler/Sygma; page 321, Robert Glasse, CUNY; page 322, Chip Hires/Gamma.

Chapter 14: Page 326, Metropolitan Museum of Fine Arts. Formerly in the collections of the Museum of the American Indian, Heye Foundation and Claude Lévi-Strauss; page 329, Giansanti/Sygma; page 331, Freelance Photographers Guild; page 334, Robert Tonkinson, Australian National University; page 339, Robert Harding Associate; page 345, Peter Simon; page 347, Margarita Melville, University of Houston; page 353, © Kal Muller 1982/Woodfin Camp & Associates; page 358, Deborah Bird Rose.

Chapter 15: Pages 360 and 361, Michal Heron; page 363, Robert Glasse, CUNY; page 367, © Cornell Capa/Magnum; page 370, Fernando Yovera/Black Star © 1981; page 375, Robert Tonkinson, Australian National University; page 376, courtesy Texas Medical Center, Galveston; page 382, Janice Reid.

Chapter 16: Page 384, Charlotte Fardelman; page 387, United Nations; page 388, Jean-Pierre Laffont/Sygma; page 389, Charles Marden Fitch/Freelance Photographers Guild; page 390, D. Donne Bryant/Freelance Photographers Guild; page 393, Wide World Photos; page 394, Richard Bellak/Black Star; page 398, Australian Information Service; page 399 bottom, Malcolm Hancock; page 399 top, Sam Griffith/Sygma; page 411, Claudia Andujar/Anthropology Resource Center.

Index